THE
PRO FOOTBALL
HISTORICAL ABSTRACT

THE
PRO FOOTBALL
HISTORICAL ABSTRACT

A Hardcore Fan's Guide to All-Time Player Rankings

SEAN LAHMAN

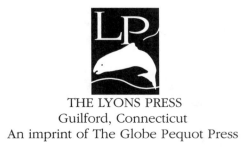

THE LYONS PRESS
Guilford, Connecticut
An imprint of The Globe Pequot Press

Copyright © 2008 by Sean Lahman

The Lyons Press is an imprint of The Globe Pequot Press.

Text design by Lesley Weissman-Cook

Library of Congress Cataloging-in-Publication Data

Lahman, Sean.
   The pro football historical abstract: a hardcore fan's guide to all-time player rankings/Sean Lahman.
      p. cm.
   Includes bibliographical references and index.
   ISBN 978-1-59228-940-0 (alk. paper)
  1. Football players--United States--Rating of. 2. Football players--United States--Statistics. 3. Football--Record--United States. 4. National Football League. I. Title.
   GV939.A1L34 2008
   796.33092--dc22

                                        2008024509

Printed in the United States of America

10 9 8 7 6 5 4 3 2 1

CONTENTS

PART 3

THE COACHES

PART 4

THE RECORDS

INTRODUCTION

THE TITLE AND THE BASIC PREMISE of this book are borrowed from one that Bill James wrote in 1985 called *The Historical Baseball Abstract*. In the late 1970s, James began writing an annual book he called *The Baseball Abstract,* reflecting on the previous season and offering analysis, not just of the teams and players but also of more fundamental issues. In each edition, he examined subjects such as the impact a player's ballpark had on his performance and the usefulness of minor league statistics as a predictor of major league success.

James self-published the first five editions, and after a favorable mention by Daniel Okrent in *Sports Illustrated,* he signed a deal with Ballantine Books for future editions. By 1984, the book was selling 150,000 copies a year, pushing as high as number four on the *New York Times* Best Seller List. Although James is not a household name out-side of the sports world, his work has shaped an entire generation of sportswriters. In 2006, *Time* named him to their list of the 100 most influential people in the world.

At one point, James decided to take the tools and methods he had developed for analyzing current players and applied them to players from earlier eras, and that's essentially the same path that I'm following. I've been writing about the NFL since 1992, always focusing on the present, but I think it's only natural that a curious observer would eventually set his sights on the past.

With the proliferation of statistics and the impact of the Internet, sports fans have more raw data available now than ever before. The avalanche of numbers too often obscures the fundamental truths that lie beneath, and the lust for number crunching makes it more difficult to see the bigger

picture. In many cases, we've stopped asking the basic questions altogether.

When I created the *Pro Football Prospectus* series in 2002, I didn't want to include projected stats, predicting the numbers that each individual player would compile. There just aren't any good predictive models for football, and there are too many variables that can't be accounted for (injuries, playing time, impact of teammates, coaching style, and so on). No matter how good a method you come up with, it's never going to be much better than simply picking numbers out of a hat. I told the publishers that I thought including them would detract from the quality of the book. My editor laughed and said, "I know that projected stats are just junk science, but that's what sells books."

While James offered me the model for this book, the inspiration really came from somewhere else. Over the years I've been a voracious student of pro football history, and it gradually became clear to me that there were some massive gaps in the body of literature. Countless volumes proclaimed the virtues of specific players—often going so far as to list them in rank order—but nobody had taken the time to answer the most basic questions. It's easy to say that Jim Thorpe was a great player . . . but tell me why. Explain to me what he did that set him apart. If you really know what you are talking about, it shouldn't be that difficult.

What bothered me most was a flood of recent books that ranked the greatest players of all time with no discussion of any methodology. I mean, you don't have to base your ratings on statistical formulas, but you have to establish some set of criteria. How can you tell me who the top-ten linebackers were if you haven't taken the time to consider what it is that linebackers do, and what makes the great ones stand out? If you can't say one meaningful thing about Ray Nitschke that distinguishes him from his peers, then how can I trust you to tell me he was the greatest linebacker of all time?

The reality is that the authors of all these books start by building their lists, and then look for "evidence" to justify the selections. One of the most obvious problems with this approach is that it's inconsistent. One player will get credit for something that others won't. They'll overlook a quarterback's poor numbers because his team won, but in another case, they'll say a guy was just a mediocre player surrounded by a great team. They'll credit one guy for longevity but ignore the fact that someone else had a remarkably short career.

What particularly irked me was how little these books actually had to say about the players—in most cases, there was no attempt to describe their playing style or their particular strengths and weaknesses on the field. There were countless examples of players who the authors claimed had "redefined their position" or had "changed the game," with no effort to explain how, even in the most rudimentary terms.

What I have done with this book is to start by asking some basic questions about player performance and lay out a method for rating player performance. After doing that, I ran the numbers for every man who ever played in the National Football League or the two leagues that merged with it—more than 20,000 in all. For each man, I compared his performance in each individual season to all of the players he competed against, and I came up with a measure for how they fared. The end result is my ranking of the top players at each position from 1920 to the present.

One of the greatest challenges of this sort of undertaking is to understand the way that the game has changed over time. Differences in playing styles and rules have to be accounted for, and in part 1 of this book I look at these issues decade by decade.

In part 2 I present those rankings, along with comments on the top players in each position. I include players from offense, defense, and special teams, as well as head coaches. Players from the two-way era are considered in a separate grouping.

In part 3 I take a look at the coaches.

Part 4 contains the raw numbers for the ranked players, as well as a list of resources for those who are interested in further exploration.

PART 1
THE DECADES

The 1920s

DECADE IN A BOX

Best Team Season
1929 Green Bay Packers, 12-0-1; 1923 Canton Bull-dogs, 11-0-1; 1922 Canton Bulldogs, 10-0-2

Best Team of the Decade
The Canton Bulldogs had been the premier pro team in the 1910s, and they were the league's dominant team in the early twenties. They won back-to-back championships in 1922 and 1923, going 21-0-3 over the two-year span. In 1923 they scored 246 points in twelve games while only allowing 19.

Winners of Multiple Championships
Canton Bulldogs (1922 and 1923). Some historians consider the 1924 Cleveland Bulldogs a continuation of this franchise. That team also won the NFL championship.

Worst Team Season
1925 Columbus Panhandles, 0-9

Worst Team of the Decade
This decade is full of examples of teams who didn't belong in the league, teams that just couldn't compete on the same level. The Columbus Panhandles were 1-21-0 in three seasons. The Hammond Pros were 5-28-4 and went the entire 1922 season with-out scoring a single point. Among the teams that survived the decade, the Dayton Triangles were undoubtedly the worst. They went 17-51-8 in the twenties, and after scoring 19 points in their 1924 season opener, the Triangles went the rest of the decade without scoring more than 7 points in a single game.

New Teams
All of them. Fourteen teams banded together in 1920 to form what would come to be known as the National Football League. They all had been competing independently before that, so perhaps calling them new isn't entirely accurate.

Twelve of those original 14 teams folded or left the league by the end of the twenties. Only two of the league's original teams from 1920 have survived to this day: the Bears and the Cardinals. Among existing NFL teams, only two others joined during the decade: the Green Bay Packers (1921) and New York Giants (1925).

Defunct Teams
Most of them. Fifty-two different teams joined the league during the twenties, but most of them didn't survive. Only the four teams mentioned above were still in the league in 1933.

Significant Moves

Franchises were bought, sold, and merged at a rapid pace. Teams drifted in and out of the league in the early years, and some even jumped to rival leagues. The most significant move came in 1921, when George Halas assumed ownership of the Decatur Staleys. Food starch magnate A. E. Staley wasn't terribly interested in running a football team. He simply saw it as an opportunity to promote his business. Halas acquired the team from Staley in exchange for an ad in the game day program and an agreement to keep the name "Staleys" for the 1921 season. Halas moved the team to Chicago and changed their name to the Bears in 1922.

Most Passing Touchdowns

Season: 21, Benny Friedman, Giants, 1929
Decade: 42, Benny Friedman, Cleveland Bulldogs, Detroit Wolverines, and New York Giants

Most Rushing Touchdowns

Season: 12, Ernie Nevers, Cardinals, 1929
Decade: 24, Ernie Nevers, Duluth Eskimos and Chicago Cardinals

Most Receiving Touchdowns

Season: 8, Ray Flaherty, Giants, 1929
Decade: 13, Ray Flaherty, Yankees and Giants

Best Coaching Record

.738, Guy Chamberlin, 57-18-7, Canton Bulldogs, Cleveland Bulldogs, Frankford Yellow Jackets, and Chicago Cardinals. Chamberlin won four NFL championships in a five-year stretch, and he did it with three different teams: Canton in 1922 and 1923, Cleveland in 1924, and Frankford in 1926.

Biggest Player

Eddie Keenan (6-foot-4, 320 pounds) played one season for the Hartford Blues. Howard "Cub" Buck was the heaviest regular at 260 pounds.

Smallest Player

Jack Shapiro was a fullback listed at 5-foot-2, 126 pounds. He played in just one NFL game, appearing for the Staten Island Stapletons in 1929. Henry "Two Bits" Homan was a star runner for the Frankford Yellow Jackets who stood 5-foot-5 and weighed 145 pounds

All-Decade Team

B	Paddy Driscoll
B	Verne Lewellen
B	Benny Friedman
B	Ernie Nevers
E	Lavvie Dilweg
E	Ray Flaherty
C	George Trafton
G	Ed Healey
G	Jim McMillen
T	Pete Henry
T	Bull Behman
K	Joey Sternaman

Where They Played

With the exception of two entrants from western New York, the NFL's original teams came from two clusters. One was in and around Chicago, and the other was in northern Ohio.

While there was clearly some great football being played in both regions, the fourteen teams who chose to band together were not the only professional teams playing in 1920, nor were they necessarily the best. The fact that they came largely from these two geographic clusters suggests that familiarity was their primary reason for joining together.

Financial considerations caused many teams to play primarily road games. The Los Angeles Buccaneers were one example, a barnstorming team of west coast college stars that was actually based in Chicago. They never played a game in Los Angeles. The Hammond Pros (from Hammond, Indiana)

scheduled just three home games in seven NFL seasons, and one of them was cancelled due to poor field conditions.

Finding a home field was sometimes difficult. Halas moved the Bears from Decatur, Illinois, to Chicago so the team could play in a larger stadium: first Cubs Park, then Wrigley Field. A few other teams also signed leases to play in baseball parks, such as New York's Polo Grounds or Sportsman's Park in St. Louis.

Most other teams played at sites that couldn't rightly be called stadiums. They were high school fields, fairgrounds, public parks, or in the case of the Hammond Pros, a country club. Playing conditions at these places were inconsistent, and those small venues weren't conducive to drawing large crowds.

Who Played the Game

Pro football was an avocation for those who had finished their college eligibility and either had a great love for the game or couldn't find a regular job. There wasn't much money to be made and even less glory. The pro game was often referred to derisively as "post-graduate football."

Most teams tried to find one star player and build everything around that one man. Having a guy who was a box-office draw was often more important than actually winning games.

There were a substantial number of Native Americans playing the game in the twenties, due largely to the presence of Jim Thorpe, a legendary athlete who was the best known Native American of his era.

For two seasons, Thorpe led a team made up entirely of Native Americans that played its home games in LaRue, Ohio, sixty miles north of Columbus. Owner Walter Lingo was a dog breeder who wanted to promote his business, which was called Oorang Kennels. The team was called the Oorang Indians, and though both Thorpe and fellow Hall of Famer Joe Guyon played for them, they didn't win very many games.

African Americans played in the league, although they were excluded from Major League Baseball, most major colleges, and many other institutions of American culture. It would be misleading, however, to say that pro football was truly integrated in the twenties. Roughly 1800 players participated in NFL games during the decade, and only eleven of them were African Americans. Five of them played for one team, the Hammond Pros.

African Americans in the NFL, 1920–1932

Player	Yrs	NFL Teams
Duke Slater	10	Milwaukee, Rhode Island, Chicago Cardinals
Fritz Pollard	6	Akron, Milwaukee, Hammond, Providence
Jay Williams	6	Canton, Hammond, Dayton, Cleveland
Sol Butler	3	Rhode Island, Hammond, Akron, Canton
Dick Hudson	3	Minneapolis, Hammond
Rube Marshall	3	Rhode Island, Duluth
Joe Lillard	2	Chicago Cardinals
David Myers	2	Staten Island, Brooklyn
Paul Robeson	2	Akron, Milwaukee
Harold Bradley	1	Chicago Cardinals
Ray Kemp	1	Pittsburgh
John Shelbourne	1	Hammond
James Turner	1	Milwaukee

Total African Americans by Season

Year	Players
1920	2
1921	4
1922	5
1923	6
1924	3
1925	5
1926	5
1927	1

1928	2
1929	1
1930	2
1931	2
1932	1
1933	2

The league never "officially" barred African Americans from playing, but none appeared on a roster between 1934 and 1945.

How the Game Was Played

Everybody was a two-way player, with responsibilities on both offense and defense. The rules said that if a player came off the field, he couldn't return until the following quarter. This discouraged substitution and specialization, and put an emphasis on versatility and durability. While the positions of quarterback, fullback, and end were defined, everybody in the backfield would run, throw, and catch passes.

Most teams played the same basic formation on offense and defense, and strategies were focused more on overpowering opponents than trying to deceive them. The running game was the foundation of the offensive game plan for nearly everyone.

Teams had one coach, and he was often but not always one of the players. Because most players had other jobs during the week the teams did not practice.

A Brief History of Football Before 1920

The earliest known reference to the game of baseball comes from Pittsfield, Massachusetts, in 1791. The town bylaws prohibited playing baseball within 80 yards of the new meeting house (presumably in response to some broken windows!). A hundred years later and some fifty miles to the south, the game of basketball was invented in Springfield, Massachusetts. James Naismith, a physical educa-

tion teacher, was looking for an indoor activity to keep his students occupied during the winter months.

It probably won't surprise you to learn that the game of football was also born in Massachusetts. While many colleges were fielding teams to play soccer or rugby in the 1860s and 1870s, students at Harvard were playing their own hybrid called "the Boston Game." Their 1874 match with a team from Montreal's McGill University is recognized by most historians as the first intercollegiate football game. Two years later, representatives from Rutgers, Yale, Columbia, and Harvard met in Springfield, Massachusetts, to hammer out a set of common rules, and college football was born.

Those rules would be refined throughout the 1880s. Yale coach Walter Camp helped introduce some key concepts that made the game look less like rugby and more like what we would recognize as football today—things like the line of scrimmage and the idea of requiring a team to gain a certain amount of yardage within a fixed number of plays.

Like other sports, football was popular with the athletic clubs that proliferated in the late nineteenth century. These clubs formed teams to compete against one another, and it didn't take long for professionalism to enter the world of club football. The first professional player that we know about was Pudge Heffelfinger, who received $500 to play one game for the Allegheny Athletic Association on November 12, 1892. Undoubtedly, there were others before him who managed to keep their earnings secret. The next year, the Pittsburgh Athletic Club signed one of its players to a contract to play for the entire season, and by 1896, several of the clubs from the Pittsburgh area were openly professional.

The first attempt at a professional football league came in 1902. John Rogers, owner of baseball's Philadelphia Phillies, founded a football team with the same name in 1901. Not to be outdone, Ben Shibe, owner of Philadelphia's other baseball team formed a football team in 1902. The baseball rivals tried to get other teams to join with them to compete for a self-proclaimed "world championship."

They found only one taker, a promoter in Pittsburgh, but the three teams christened themselves the National Football League and played each other in a round-robin tournament. Each team finished with a 2-2 record, and all three teams claimed the championship. Many of the best football players of the day participated in this league, as did three baseball Hall of Famers. Christy Mathewson, ace pitcher for the New York Giants, played halfback and punter for the Pittsburgh Stars. Connie Mack, manager of the Athletics baseball team, also managed the Athletics football team, and Rube Waddell, one of the best left-handed pitchers in history, was a reserve lineman for Mack's squad.

A yearly football tournament was played in New York in 1902 and 1903, dubbed the "World Series of Football." With less than 2000 tickets sold for each game, there wasn't much evidence that there was money to be made by running a football team. Baseball teams played games every day for six months, and that produced enough revenues that teams could afford to travel from New York to Chicago, Boston to Cincinnati, or St. Louis to Philadelphia. The pageantry of college football drew fans in droves, and it wasn't unusual for crowds of 60000 to see a matchup between rival schools, and that enabled colleges to build their own stadiums and pay coaches handsomely.

The pro game drew only passing interest, so teams were forced to minimizes their costs. The best way they could do that was to limit their travel. Thus, there wasn't great incentive for a nationwide league of professional football teams in the 1910s. It made more sense to stay closer to home, with teams sponsored by local businessmen whose chief interest was promoting their company.

Over the next few years, the center of pro football shifted from western Pennsylvania to Ohio. By 1905 there were at least seven pro teams playing in Ohio, most notably the Massillon Tigers and the Canton Bulldogs. These independent teams had to fend for themselves, and while some were more successful than others, they all faced the same challenges.

Fans were clamoring for entertainment after the end of World War I, but it was difficult for teams to generate revenues without good players, and good players cost money. Rising salaries were making it difficult for many teams to continue operating.

Finding and signing players was tough enough, but keeping them was even tougher. Rival teams would snatch players from each other by offering bigger paydays, and this often left teams in the lurch.

Another issue was the controversial use of college players who were still enrolled in school. It was easy for one pro team to take a unilateral stand against encroaching on the amateurs. However, if your opponents were stockpiling college stars and you weren't, the talent levels left you at a disadvantage.

Cooperation could resolve most of these issues. During the summer of 1920, representatives from four pro teams met in Canton, Ohio, to discuss the idea of forming a league. They met again in September, with six additional teams attending and four others sending letters of interest. Originally these representatives called their league the American Professional Football Association, but two years later they changed the name to the National Football League.

Problems of the 1920s

There are several challenges that make it difficult to have a good grasp on the early history of the National Football League. First is the rapid turnover of teams. Fifty-two teams joined the league during the 1920s, and forty-eight of those teams folded or dropped out by 1932. I call these the "twenties teams." While they accounted for six of the first eight league championships and produced some of the game's first stars, the history of those teams has not been well preserved.

Second, the lack of a formal championship game and irregular schedules makes it difficult to weigh the relative strengths of each team. Teams set their own schedules, often including games against nonleague opponents. And while the owners set aside money in their budget for a championship trophy, they didn't agree on how the champion would be determined. This led to several controversies in the league's early years when yearly champions were not decided on the playing field but rather by an owners' vote.

The biggest challenge, however, is the lack of any official playing statistics from the era. Nothing was kept before 1932, and even the limited information that is available is subject to some interpretation. Historian David Neft spent years meticulously reconstructing the historical record from newspaper accounts, and his work has been monumental in advancing our understanding of the game in the 1920s. Some newspapers of the era carried full play-by-play accounts. Others carried box scores and detailed stories of their local team's exploits. Sadly, there are many games for which we have no details other than the final scores.

To best understand the NFL in the 1920s, you should draw a line through the middle of the decade, and consider everything before 1926 and everything after in separate contexts.

From 1920 to 1925, most teams were struggling to keep afloat. Financial margins were slim, and a disappointing turnout for a single game could force a team out of business. One story about the Rochester Jeffersons offers a perfect illustration of just how precarious it could be. In 1921, owner Leo Lyons had taken his team from upstate New York to Washington, D.C., by train for a game against the Washington Senators. The Jeffs were supposed to be paid $800 plus a share of the gate, but a snowstorm kept most of the fans away.

Tim Jordan, manager of the Washington team, didn't have the $800 to pay Lyons. That money was intended to come from ticket sales, and the poor turnout made that impossible. Jordan offered to pay just $200, or else he'd have to cancel the game altogether.

Lyons was in a bind, because the $200 wouldn't cover the player salaries for the game, let alone the train fare back to Rochester. Unable to compromise, the two teams cancelled their contest, and the Rochester players had to reach into their own pockets to get home.

Lyons filed a grievance with the league over the $800, but the Senators decided to drop out of the league rather than pay.

These sorts of struggles afflicted most of the teams in the NFL's first few years. From 1921 to 1926, the size of the league ranged from eighteen to twenty-two teams, but at least half were losing money and unable to field competitive teams.

NFL Teams Per Season

Year	Teams
1920	14
1921	22
1922	18
1923	20
1924	18
1925	20
1926	22
1927	12
1928	10
1929	12

Things came to a head in 1926, when Red Grange formed his rival league, the American Football League. After signing with the Bears late in the 1925 season and barnstorming through the off-season, Grange felt that he should get the lion's share of the profits from the fans who paid to see him play. He signed a lease for Yankee Stadium and petitioned the NFL for a franchise, but they refused. The league already had a team in New York, and Giants owner Tim Mara balked at the idea of having to compete with another team, especially one with a huge drawing card like Grange.

So Grange formed his own league, put three teams in New York City, and used his fame to help convince both new owners and top players to join him. Nine AFL teams and twenty-two NFL teams competed that season, and everybody lost money. There simply wasn't enough talent to field thirty-one competitive teams, and there wasn't enough interest in pro football to keep thirty-one teams financially solvent. Grange's league folded at the end of one season, and several NFL teams were struggling to stay afloat.

Those that did survive learned a number of valuable lessons. If the league was going to prosper, they needed to be more discriminating about which teams were allowed to remain as members. They needed owners who could run a viable business, and they wouldn't likely be in small towns like Rochester, Muncie, or Akron. They also needed to avoid the talent dilution that had caused many fans to lose interest in pro football during the 1926 season.

What remained in 1927 was a much slimmer but much healthier National Football League. The owners raised the annual membership fees as a way to discourage weaker teams from remaining. The strategy was overwhelmingly successful. The total number of teams dropped from twenty-two to twelve, but each team was stronger, both on and off the field.

The Joe Carr Influence

Grange helped bring attention to the game just by his presence. Crowds turned out in record numbers, and other college stars followed in his footsteps. More significant, by starting his rival league, Grange unwittingly forced the owners to reevaluate the way they did business.

The architect of this change was Joe Carr, who served as president of the NFL from 1921 to 1939. More than anything, he asserted the importance of the teams working together off the field to make the league stronger. He cracked down on the practice of signing college players under assumed names. This helped to alleviate the growing animosity between the league and the college football system. He believed that in order to attract a larger following, the league had to demonstrate that it was being run with honesty and integrity. Carr furthered this aim by introducing a standard player's contract, and fighting vigorously against both players who jumped from one team to another and the teams who encouraged it.

Carr also knew that the league could never reach the national stage with teams in small towns like Akron, Muncie, and Rochester. He worked tirelessly to attract owners in large cities. During his tenure he helped to put teams in New York, Boston, Philadelphia, Washington, and Detroit, in each case finding owners with enough financial clout to endure the inevitable early losses. The big cities also had existing stadiums and larger populations that could drive bigger revenues.

The National Football League would not have survived if Carr had not been successful in these efforts. The Great Depression killed off most of the weaker teams, and World War II presented challenges that nearly destroyed some of the stronger teams.

Pottsville's Claim

Who won the NFL championship in 1925? The record books all say that it was the Chicago Cardinals. For some folks in northeastern Pennsylvania that fact is still very much in dispute.

This area of the country was a hotbed for football during the twenties. It was home to the Eastern League and the Anthracite League, and while these were considered semi-pro or minor leagues, the quality of play was pretty strong. Some of the teams also paid well, which helped them steal away some players from the NFL.

One of the strongest teams in the area was the Pottsville Maroons, whose roster of NFL defectors included future Hall of Fame tackle Wilbur Henry. Pottsville is a coal-mining town about 100 miles north of Philadelphia. Thanks to strong ownership and rabid fan support, they had become the strongest team on the east coast.

As the saying goes, if you can't fight 'em, join 'em, or in this case, invite them to join you. League president Joe Carr asked the Pottsville Maroons to become league members in 1925 and they were more than happy to comply. Pottsville's players and fans were anxious to prove that the Maroons were the best pro team in the country.

It didn't take long for them to do just that. The Maroons started the season 5-1, with all of their wins coming by shutout. They beat the defending champion Cleveland Bulldogs 24–6 in November, and then dispatched their next two opponents to set up a season-ending match with the only other challenger, the Chicago Cardinals. The game took place on December 6 at Comiskey Park, and after the Maroons won convincingly, they declared themselves league champions.

Prior to 1933, the annual champion was the team with the best winning percentage at the end of the regular season. Pottsville posted a 10-2-0 record compared to Chicago's 9-2-1, and beating the Cards head-to-head seemed to cement Pottsville's case.

Not so fast. Over the next two weeks, an odd series of events would transpire that would take the title away from the Maroons and send it back to Chicago.

First, the Cardinals took advantage of a decision by the owners the previous year that set the official end date of the season at December 20. After losing to the Maroons on the sixth, Cards' owner Chris O'Brien hastily arranged two additional games against weaker teams on December 10 and 12. The Milwaukee Badgers had trouble finding eleven players, and had to recruit some local high school players in order to play the game. Neither they nor the Hammond Pros offered much resistance to the clearly superior Cardinals. O'Brien's team added two late wins to their record, improving to 11-2-1 and hopscotching the Maroons in the standings.

Meanwhile, the jubilant Maroons hoped to cash in on their success with a postseason exhibition game. They scheduled an exhibition game at Philadelphia's Shibe Park on December 13, against a team of former college stars, led by Notre Dame's famed "Four Horsemen." They expected to draw a big crowd, much to the consternation of the Frankford Yellow Jackets, who had a game against Cleveland across town on the same day. Frankford and Pottsville were bitter rivals, and the Yellow Jackets protested that the Maroons had infringed on their territory and hurt their gate receipts. Since the Maroons had ignored warnings from league president Joe Carr not to play the game, he was

obliged to take immediate action when they did. He fined the Pottsville team, ruled them ineligible for the league championship, and kicked them out of the league.

While the latter decision was later reversed, the Maroons' attempts to preserve their championship have never been successful, in a controversy that still rages to this day. On the first matter, O'Brien's decision to schedule more games was certainly within the letter of the rules, although clearly not within their spirit. Some critics complained that the hastily assembled Milwaukee squad wasn't a legitimate NFL opponent, and that contest shouldn't be considered a league game.

When the owners met in February, they decided that since the Pottsville franchise had been suspended before the end of the regular season, they weren't eligible for the league title. Even if the Milwaukee game were stripped from the standings, the Cards would have the best record of any eligible team. The owners voted to name the Cardinals league champions. O'Brien refused to accept the trophy, wary of the controversy that was swirling, but the ruling stood.

When the dust settled, Pottsville decided to return to the NFL. They competed for the title again in 1926, finishing in third place with a 10-2-2 record. Although they added stars such as Johnny "Blood" McNally and Walt Kiesling, the team struggled both on and off the field over the next two seasons. The club was sold after the 1928 season, relocating to Boston where they were renamed the Bulldogs. They folded after a 4-4 performance in 1929.

A reunion of former Pottsville players in 1960 prompted renewed interest in the disputed championship, and they petitioned the league to reexamine the team's claim to the 1925 title. NFL Commissioner Pete Rozelle appointed a special committee to investigate the facts, but the owners eventually voted 12–2 against making any change. The league addressed the issue again during their annual meeting in 2003, with the owners voting 30–2 against reopening the case.

The 1930s

Best Team Season
1934, Chicago Bears, 13-0

Best Teams of the Decade
Green Bay Packers (86-35-4); Chicago Bears (85-28-11)

Winners of Multiple Championships
Green Bay Packers (1930, 1931, 1936, and 1939). The Packers won three in a row, from 1929 to 1931; Chicago Bears (1932 and 1933); New York Giants (1934 and 1938).

Worst Team Season
1936 Philadelphia Eagles, 1-11

Worst Teams of the Decade
Chicago Cardinals (35-67-9); Brooklyn Dodgers (40-67-9)

New Teams
Nine teams joined the NFL during the 1930s. Five would stick: the Portsmouth Spartans (who would move to Michigan and become the Detroit Lions), the Boston Braves (who would become the Washington Redskins), the Cleveland Rams (later of Los Angeles and then St. Louis), the Pittsburgh Steelers, and the Philadelphia Eagles. The Brooklyn Dodgers survived until 1944, making them the longest-lasting NFL franchise to fold. Three other new entrants lasted just a single season.

Defunct Teams
Eight teams folded during the 1930s. Notable among them are the Providence Steam Roller, NFL champions in 1928, and the Frankford Yellow Jackets, NFL champions in 1926. With the exception of the Green Bay Packers, all of the teams in smaller towns were crushed by the financial problems brought on by the Great Depression.

Significant Moves
The Portsmouth Spartans moved to Detroit in 1934 and became the Lions. The league had tried three times to get a healthy franchise in Detroit, but each time had failed. The Lions, of course, survive to this day. The league was also trying to put a team in Boston without much success. The Boston Braves changed their name to the Redskins in 1933 and moved to Washington, D.C., in 1937.

Most Passing Touchdowns
Season: 13, Benny Friedman, Giants, 1930
Decade: 62, Arnie Herber, Packers

Most Rushing Yards
Season: 1004, Beattie Feathers, Bears, 1934
Decade: 3511, Cliff Battles, Boston Braves/
Redskins and Washington Redskins

Most Receptions
Season: 41, Don Hutson, Packers, 1937; 41,
Gaynell Tinsley, Cardinals, 1938
Decade: 159, Don Hutson, Packers

Best Coaching Record
.704, Curly Lambeau, 86-35-4, Packers

Biggest Player
Jack Torrance of the Bears (6-foot-3, 285 pounds)
or Ted Isaacson of the Cardinals (6-foot-4, 272
pounds)

Smallest Player
Herb Meeker, a 5-foot-3, 145-pound tailback with
the Providence Steam Roller

All-Decade Team

B	Dutch Clark
B	Cliff Battles
B	Clarke Hinkle
B	Tuffy Leemans
E	Don Hutson
E	Bill Hewitt
C	Mel Hein
G	George Musso
G	Dan Fortmann
T	Turk Edwards
T	George Christensen
K	Armand Niccolai
P	Parker Hall
Ret	Cliff Battles

Where They Played

During the thirties, most NFL teams were playing their games at ballparks built by and for Major League Baseball teams.

NFL Team	Stadium
Bears	Wrigley Field
Cardinals	Wrigley Field, Comiskey Park
Dodgers	Ebbets Field
Eagles	Baker Bowl, Municipal Stadium (aka RFK Stadium)
Giants	Polo Grounds
Rams	Cleveland Municipal Stadium
Redskins	Fenway Park, Griffith Stadium
Steelers	Forbes Field
Yellow Jackets	Baker Bowl

Among the few exceptions were the Packers, who played in City Stadium, a 6000-seat venue located behind East High School. The Packers used the school's locker room, but there were no facilities for visiting teams. Because their home stadium was so small, the Packers began playing some of their home games in nearby Milwaukee in 1935. That tradition lasted for sixty years.

The Staten Island Stapletons played at Thompson's Stadium, which was a minor league baseball park. The Providence Steam Roller, who folded after the 1931 season, played their home games at the Providence Cycledrome. As you might guess from the name, it was a facility built primarily for bicycle racing.

The only NFL team playing its games in a stadium designed for football was the Lions, whose home field was Titan Stadium on the campus of the University of Detroit.

Who Played the Game

College football stars began to enter the league in larger numbers, especially after the adoption of the player draft in 1936. Among them were well-known players like halfbacks Byron "Whizzer" White and Marshall Goldberg, and quarterback Davey O'Brien.

Player salaries weren't high enough to keep most of them around for very long. O'Brien, the 1938 Heisman Trophy winner, spent just two seasons in the NFL before leaving to serve as an FBI agent. White left after one season with Pittsburgh to study at Oxford University as a Rhodes scholar. He would return for two more seasons with the Lions, but would leave again for military service and then law school. In 1962 White was appointed as a Supreme Court Justice by President Kennedy.

Others who became household names as pro football players capitalized on their fame for big paydays off the field. Cliff Battles, the best running back of the early thirties, left the Redskins for a better-paying job coaching at Columbia University. Gus Sonnenberg and Bronko Nagurski abandoned football for professional wrestling. All-Pro end Red Badgro left the NFL to play baseball with the St. Louis Browns. Cal Hubbard went on to become a baseball Hall of Famer as an umpire. (He's also in the Pro Football Hall of Fame—the only man inducted in both places.)

African Americans disappeared from the NFL landscape in 1934 and didn't return until 1946. In his book *Outside the Lines,* professor Charles Ross wrote: "George Preston Marshall was likely the driving force behind the color ban." The Washington Redskins owner had declared that his team was "the team of the South," and Marshall vowed that he would never employ minority athletes.

Other owners were accused of bowing to Marshall's segregationist desires, but the fact is that most of the NFL teams had been segregated all along. A handful of African Americans played between 1920 and 1932. However, seven of the league's ten teams in 1934 had never had an African-American player on the roster.

While minority players banned from Major League Baseball had the consolation of playing in the Negro Leagues, no such opportunity existed for football players. There were a handful of African-American players on semi pro teams, and a few all black teams, most notably the Harlem-based Brown Bombers. But there was no large-scale alternative for African-American football players.

How the Game Was Played

Throughout the decade, most teams played some variation of the single-wing offense. It typically featured two ends and four backs. The fullback and halfback had largely the same roles then as they do now. The wingback was more analogous to the modern tight end, used almost exclusively for blocking. The tailback was the one who received the snap. He was the team's primary runner, and usually also responsible for passing and kicking.

The Bears stayed with the T-formation, an offense that most pro and college teams had abandoned and considered outdated. Coaches Ralph Jones and Clark Shaughnessy added some new wrinkles. Their innovations not only turned the Bears into a powerhouse, they launched an offensive revolution.

Jones and Shaughnessy put the quarterback directly under center, with two ends lined up next to the tackles and three backs in the backfield. This lineup made it more difficult for the defense to predict where the ball was going because the play developed much more quickly. Ball carriers would get a handoff while they were running toward the line of scrimmage, rather than getting a toss while they stood stationary in the backfield. The Bears also made liberal use of motion before the snap, forcing the defense to make last-second adjustments.

A number of rule changes also helped to open up the game. Hashmarks were added in 1933, so that when the ball was run out of bounds, it was placed ten yards from the sideline. Prior to this change, the ball would be spotted right on the sideline, and teams were often forced to waste a down to get the ball back towards the middle of the field.

The goal posts were also moved in to encourage field goal attempts. Prior to 1933, they were located at the back of the end zone. The NFL moved them ten yards forward to the goal line.

Two rules that limited the passing game were eliminated. The first required that a forward pass had to be thrown from at least five yards behind the scrimmage. The second was a rule that said an incomplete pass in the end zone was a touchback.

A new ball with a different shape was adopted. It was more oblong—less round—which made it easier to throw. One downside was that it was tougher to kick. While players would eventually find effective kicking techniques, the new ball essentially forced them to abandon the popular drop-kick.

These changes marked the NFL's first attempt to create its own rulebook rather than just use the same one as college football.

The 1932 Playoff Game

The 1932 season nearly ended in disaster, but a series of events helped turn it into a triumph. In one moment, the league was forced to confront most of the issues that were holding them back, that were keeping fans from maintaining strong interest in the pro game. And when it was over, the NFL had re-invented itself, setting pro football on a path toward national prominence.

It began when two teams ended the regular season with identical records. The Portsmouth Spartans and Chicago Bears had played each other twice during the regular season, with each game ending in a tie. At the time, ties did not count in the standings, leaving each team with a 6-1 record.

In the league's first twelve seasons, the annual champion was crowned based on the team that finished with the best winning percentage. This method had led to conflicts on at least two occasions, and the NFL owners recognized that there could be no satisfactory solution other than having the two teams meet for a postseason playoff game.

In retrospect, bringing the league's top two teams together for a championship game seems like an obvious step. Most of the owners recognized this too, but the mechanics of making that

happen were something they couldn't agree on. They had discussed various systems for splitting the league into two divisions and the methods for setting up a title game, but they could never agree on the details.

Fans' interest in the 1932 season could not be ignored, and for once that trumped the owner's infighting. Although it was not officially a playoff game, league president Joe Carr approved adding one more game to the schedule to determine a champion. The folks from Portsmouth proposed playing the game in nearby Cincinnati, but Bears owner George Halas insisted on playing the game in Chicago. In their season finale, the Bears had played through a snowstorm that dumped three inches on the field. Halas promised to have a crew work overtime to get the field ready, and he convinced the Spartans that a capacity crowd at Wrigley Field would give them both a handsome payday.

Unfortunately, the blizzard continued, and by midweek it was clear that the rising snow drifts and subzero temperatures would make playing at Wrigley impossible. Halas quickly arranged to move the game indoors, to Chicago Stadium. This presented several challenges. First, the arena's concrete floor had been covered with dirt for the circus that had performed there the previous week. Copious amounts of elephant dung were mixed in with the dirt, and there was no time to change it.

More significantly, the arena was simply not big enough for a regulation field. The result was a field just 60 yards long, and 30 yards narrower than usual. The goal posts had to be moved in from the back of the end zone to the goal line, and the sidelines butted right up against the stands.

Just reading this, you would think the league was headed for a huge embarrassment. Actually, it came off pretty well. Although only 12000 fans attended, the game attracted nationwide attention. And while the play was pretty sloppy, the special rules adopted for the small field helped to make the game more energetic.

More than anything, the owners saw that if pro football was going to compete on the same stage as baseball for national attention, they needed the drama of a playoff race and the climax of a title game. In 1933, they split the league into two divisions with the winners to meet for a championship game a week after the regular season ended.

Keeping the Books

While a championship game seems like an obvious choice the owners overlooked, so does the decision to not keep official statistics. From 1920 to 1932, the only thing that the league tracked was wins and losses, which they needed to maintain the standings.

Why weren't they doing this before 1933? Well, the simple answer is that the owners had to focus all of their efforts just to keep their teams—and the league—financially solvent. There also wasn't a strong central office, no league staff that could oversee the process. The NFL started recording playing statistics in 1933, but their initial efforts were spotty at best.

The NFL did not hire an official statistician until 1960. The Elias Sports Bureau had been compiling statistics for Major League Baseball since the mid-twenties, making them a natural choice for the job.

It wasn't until the late seventies that there was an organized effort to reconstruct the statistical record from the 1920s and to clean up the problems from the 1930s. This work began with researchers David Neft and Bob Carroll, and eventually helped lead to the formation of the Professional Football Researcher's Association.

Bert Bell's Legacy

After three seasons in the National Football League and very little measurable success, Philadelphia Eagles' owner Bert Bell was growing tired of being outbid for talent by wealthier owners like Chicago's George Halas and New York's Tim Mara. Bell was particularly frustrated by his inability to lure young college stars to his team, and he knew he wasn't alone. He proposed a draft of college players, with the teams who finished worst in the standings getting the first pick. Bell made a passionate argument that this would help restore competitive balance, and the other owners agreed.

Bell's Eagles owned the top pick by virtue of their 2-9 record the previous season, and they used it to select Jay Berwanger. The University of Chicago halfback had won the Heisman Trophy, but he didn't have any interest in playing pro football. He went into private business and the Eagles stayed in the cellar.

Berwanger wasn't the only college prospect to spurn the NFL. Only twenty-four of the eighty-one players selected in that first draft signed NFL contracts. Some opted to play in a rival pro league—the short-lived American Football League—but most simply followed Berwanger's path and opted not to play professional football at all.

Ironically, the biggest beneficiaries of the NFL's first draft seemed to be the two wealthiest teams. The Giants signed three of their picks, most notably workhorse fullback Tuffy Leemans. The Bears found a pair of future Hall of Famers to bolster their offensive line—tackle Joe Stydahar and guard Dan Fortmann.

Although the draft did not have the immediate impact that Bell had hoped it would have for the Eagles, it did fulfill his larger goals. It served as a method for funneling college players into the NFL, helping to distribute the talent somewhat evenly throughout the league. Sure, it helped to attract the star college players, but more important, it helped the teams raise their overall quality of play by raising the skill level for nonstars as well.

Bell was a firm believer in the philosophy that teams should compete on the field but cooperate everywhere else. He recognized that the league would only be as strong as its weakest franchise, and that raising the level of competition would help everybody. Even though he was a relative newcomer, the owners quickly recognized that Bell had some great ideas for improving the league.

The 1940s

Best Team Seasons
NFL: 1942 Chicago Bears, 11-0
AAFC: 1948 Cleveland Browns, 14-0

Best Teams of the Decade
NFL: Chicago Bears (81-26-3)
AAFC: Cleveland Browns (47-4-3); San Francisco
49ers (38-14-2)

Winners of Multiple Championships
Chicago Bears (1940, 1941, 1943, and 1946);
Philadelphia Eagles (1948 and 1949). The Cleveland Browns won the AAFC's championship game
in every season of the league's existence (1946
to 1949).

Worst Team Seasons
NFL: 1943 and 1944 Chicago Cardinals, 0-10; 1944
Brooklyn Dodgers; Postwar: 1946 Detroit Lions, 1-10
AAFC: 1948 Chicago Hornets, 1-13

Worst Team of the Decade
NFL: Detroit Lions (35-71-4)
AAFC: Chicago Rockets/Hornets (11-40-3); Brook-
lyn Dodgers (8-32-2)

New Teams
The rival All America Football Conference (AAFC)
began play in 1946 with eight teams. They went
head-to-head with the NFL in Chicago and New
York, replaced the Rams in Cleveland, and put new
teams in Los Angeles, San Francisco, Buffalo, and
Miami.

Despite the harsh economic environment created by World War II, the NFL expanded in 1944
with a team in Boston. Owner Ted Collins wanted
to play at New York's Yankee Stadium and call his
team the New York Yankees. Tim Mara of the Giants
insisted that he still had exclusive rights to playing
in New York, however, so Collins was forced to relocate to Boston. He still called his team the "Yanks."

Collins eventually moved his team to New York
in 1949, changing their name to the Bulldogs. He
shared the Polo Grounds with the Giants, a situation
that left all parties unhappy.

Defunct Teams
The Brooklyn Dodgers folded in 1944 after fifteen
seasons in the NFL. One of the original AAFC
teams adopted that name two years later, and the

15

new Brooklyn Dodgers played three seasons before merging with the New York Yankees in 1949.

Three of the seven surviving AAFC teams folded when the league merged with the NFL at the end of the 1949 season—the Buffalo Bills, Chicago Hornets, and Los Angeles Dons.

Significant Moves

Pittsburgh owner Art Rooney changed his team's name from the Pirates to the Steelers in 1940. During the war, financial pressures and the loss of players to military service nearly forced his team to fold. In order to keep the franchise alive, Rooney temporarily merged his club with the Philadelphia Eagles in 1943. Officially, the combined team played as the Philadelphia Eagles, but fans called them the "Steagles"—a combination of "Steelers" and "Eagles." They played four home games in Philadelphia and two in Pittsburgh.

The following season, Rooney joined forces with the Chicago Cardinals, a team appropriately nicknamed the Carpets because opponents walked all over them. The merged squad finished 0-10, making them the last non-expansion team to go winless in a full NFL season.

The Rams moved from Cleveland to Los Angeles in 1946, making them the first major league sports team on the west coast.

As mentioned above, the Boston Yanks moved to New York in 1949 and changed their name to the New York Bulldogs. This was to avoid confusion with an AAFC team already playing under the name New York Yankees.

The AAFC's Miami Seahawks struggled to develop fan interest, in large part due to the unusual schedule they played. They opened with three road games, returning home to get trounced 34–7 by the San Francisco 49ers. They followed that debacle with four more road games before returning to play their last six at home. By that point, nobody cared. The club moved to Baltimore for the 1947 season, adopting the "Colts" nickname in a fan contest. This version of the Colts would fold in 1950, and although the name was adopted by another team in Baltimore a few years later, the two franchises have no other connection.

Most Passing Touchdowns

NFL Season: 28, Sid Luckman, Bears, 1943
AAFC Season: 29, Frankie Albert, 49ers, 1948

NFL Decade: 149, Sammy Baugh, Redskins
AAFC Decade: 88, Frankie Albert, 49ers

Most Rushing Yards

NFL Season: 1146, Steve Van Buren, Eagles, 1949
AAFC Season: 1432, Spec Sanders, Yankees, 1947

NFL Decade: 4904, Steve Van Buren, Eagles
AAFC Decade: 3024, Marion Motley, Browns

Most Receptions

NFL Season: 77, Tom Fears, Rams, 1949
AAFC Season: 67, Mac Speedie, Browns, 1947

NFL Decade: 329, Don Hutson, Packers
AAFC Decade: 211, Mac Speedie, Browns

Best Coaching Record

NFL: .791, George Halas, 58-15-1, Bears
AAFC: .898, Paul Brown, 47-4-3, Browns

Biggest Player

Forrest "Chubby" Grigg is listed in the record books at 294 pounds, but newspaper accounts talk about him reporting to training camp at more than 300. John Adams of the Redskins was 6-foot-7, making him the tallest player of his era.

Smallest Player

Quarterback Frankie Albert was listed generously as 5-foot-10 and 160 pounds. There were some short-timers during the decade who were a bit smaller, like quarterback Davey O'Brien (5-foot-7, 150).

NFL All-Decade Team

QB	Sammy Baugh
RB	Steve Van Buren
RB	Tony Canadeo
E	Don Hutson
E	Jim Benton
E	Ken Kavanaugh

C	Clyde "Bulldog" Turner	RB	Chet Mutryn
G	Riley Matheson	E	Mac Speedie
G	Len Younce	E	Al Beals
T	Al Wistert	E	Dante Lavelli
T	Frank "Bruiser" Kinard	C	Bob Nelson
K	Roy Zimmerman	G	Bill Willis
P	Sammy Baugh	G	Bruno Banducci
Ret	George McAfee	T	Martin Ruby
		T	Nate Johnson
AAFC All-Decade Team		K	Frankie Albert
QB	Otto Graham	P	Glenn Dobbs
RB	Marion Motley	Ret	Chuck Fenenbock

Where They Played

Both the NFL and the rival AAFC were anxious to enter the booming California market. The Cleveland Rams moved to Los Angeles in 1946 and signed a lease at the spacious Los Angeles Memorial Coliseum. The official capacity was 92000, and while they didn't fill the place for every game, they did set attendance records.

Consider the sixth week of the 1949 season. The Rams drew 86080 fans for their contest against the Chicago Bears. That was more than all of the other NFL games that weekend combined.

NFL Attendance on October 30, 1949

Attendance	Game
86080	Bears at Los Angeles
37903	Philadelphia at Pittsburgh
21339	NY Giants at Chicago Cardinals
10855	Detroit at Green Bay
3678	Washington at NY Bulldogs

In 1940 two teams moved into new baseball parks built in their hometowns. The Lions moved from Titan Stadium to Briggs Stadium, home of baseball's Detroit Tigers. The Eagles moved from Municipal Stadium to Shibe Park, home to both the Phillies and Athletics.

Who Played the Game

The 1941 regular season ended on Sunday, December 7, with games played in Chicago, New York, and Washington, D.C. As news of the Japanese attack at Pearl Harbor was reported by radio, large contingents of servicemen in each stadium began to filter out of the stands as they received the call to report to their bases.

Thousands of Americans volunteered to enlist, and many more were drafted. Pro football players were well represented in both categories. More than 600 NFL players and coaches left the game to serve, a move that dramatically shrunk the talent pool.

One of the teams hit hardest by enlistment was the New York Giants. They lost twenty-seven players, including quarterback Ed Danowski and All-Pro guard Doug Oldershaw. After winning their division crown in 1941, the Giants slumped to 5-5-1 the following season. The Chicago Bears also lost some key people, including their three leading rushers, All-Pro tackle Joe Stydahar, and owner–head coach George Halas, who was summoned by the Navy mid-season.

The league's ten teams struggled not only to find enough players but also to find enough fans during the war years. Things got so bad that the Rams suspended operations for a year, opting not to field a team in 1943. The Steelers had to temporarily merge with other teams to keep from going under, pairing with the Eagles in 1943 and then the Cardinals in 1944. The Brooklyn Dodgers couldn't avoid that fate, and rather than fold completely, they merged with the Boston Yanks in 1945.

The overall declining quality of play was illustrated by the 1943 game between the Lions and the Giants, a game in which neither team managed to put any points on the scoreboard. It was the last scoreless tie in NFL history.

The end of the war, however, brought a rapid influx of talent. Not only were many former pro players returning to action, but so were dozens of college stars who had gone into service after graduation.

One of the biggest changes at the end of the war was the end of the color line. Although not officially banned from competing, African Americans had not appeared on NFL rosters between 1933 and 1945, and had played only sparingly before that. The integration of the military was forcing Americans to reconsider their segregated society, and the playing field was one of the most visible platforms for change.

When the Rams moved to Los Angeles in 1946, they faced incredible pressure from state and local government to add African-American players to their roster. It was essentially an ultimatum. The Rams obliged by signing two UCLA grads, end Woody Strode and halfback Kenny Washington. Strode was one of the great track-and-field athletes of the era, and he was a favorite to win Olympic gold in the decathlon before the war forced the cancellation of the 1940 games. Washington had led the nation in rushing as a senior in 1939, but he had been forced to play semi-pro football while the NFL's doors were shut.

The Rams opened that door, but integration was a remarkably slow process in the NFL. Strode was released by the Rams after just one season, leaving Washington as the league's only African-American player in 1947. Only two other teams, the Giants and the Lions, would integrate their rosters before the end of the decade. The Giants added defensive back Emlen Tunnell in 1948, while the Lions added three players, each of whom played just two seasons in Detroit.

The AAFC was much more willing to embrace African-American players. Six of the seven teams that lasted all four years of the league's existence had integrated rosters. Cleveland head coach Paul Brown was the first to welcome African Americans to his squad, adding Bill Willis and Marion Motley in 1946 and Horace Gillom in 1947. The team that took the biggest strides was the Los Angles Dons, who had eight different African-American players on their squad, including five during their final season in 1949.

How the Game Was Played

Most teams abandoned the single-wing offense during the forties, adopting the modern T-formation that had made the Bears so successful. One holdout, the Pittsburgh Steelers, stuck with the old system until 1952.

The overall impact of teams switching to the T-formation was an increased emphasis on the passing game. Quarterbacks such as Washington's Sammy Baugh and Chicago's Sid Luckman let the ball fly, and Green Bay's Don Hutson redefined the position of end, shattering all of the league's receiving records in the process.

Clark Shaughnessy, who had helped spawn this offensive revolution with the Bears, took his playbook to Los Angeles in 1948 as head coach of the Rams. He immediately kicked things up to a whole new level. Shaughnessy moved halfback Elroy Hirsch to a flanker position, creating a new variation of his offense with three ends. Rams end Tom Fears set an NFL record with 77 receptions in 1949, and Los Angeles won the division for the first of what would be three straight seasons on top.

Some teams continued to focus on the run, most notably the Chicago Cardinals. Owner Charlie Bidwill died before the start of the 1947 season, but not before assembling what everyone was calling the "Dream Backfield." During the war years, running back Marshall Goldberg had been the team's only star, but Bidwill added quarterback Paul Christman in 1945, fullback Pat Harder in 1946, and the much-coveted halfback Charley Trippi in 1947. All four men had been college All-Americans, and together they gave the Cardinals an offense that seemed unstoppable. Head coach Jimmy Conzelman found ways to spread the ball around and keep defenses from finding a way to slow the Cardinals down. The team piled up 282 rushing yards in the 1947 NFL championship game, beating the Eagles 28–21 for the title.

Player shortages led to a temporary rule that allowed free substitution. This enabled coaches to begin to develop different platoons for offense and defense, and for running and passing plays.

Helmets became mandatory in 1943, although most players were already wearing them by 1940. Eagles end Bill Hewitt was the last man to play with a bare head.

The Ultimate Sacrifice

Twenty NFL players were killed in action during World War II, including former All-Pros Al Blozis, Chuck Braidwood, Eddie Kahn, and Jim Mooney. Jack Chevigny, the one-time head coach of the Chicago Cardinals, was killed on Iwo Jima in 1945, along with players Jack Lummus and Howard "Smiley" Johnson. Lummus received the Medal of Honor for his heroism there, the highest military decoration awarded by the United States.

NFL Players Killed During World War II
- Mike Basca (HB, Philadelphia, 1941)
- Charlie Behan (E, Detroit, 1942)
- Keith Birlem (E, Cardinals/Washington, 1939)
- Al Blozis (T, Giants, 1942–1944)
- Chuck Braidwood (E, Portsmouth/Cleveland/Cardinals/Cincinnati, 1930–1933)
- Young Bussey (QB, Bears, 1940–1941)
- Ed Doyle (E, Frankford/Pottsville, 1924–1925)
- Grassy Hinton (B, Staten Island, 1932)
- Smiley Johnson (G, Green Bay, 1940–1941)
- Eddie Kahn (G, Boston/Washington, 1935–1937)
- Alex Ketzko (T, Detroit, 1943)
- Lee Kizzire (FB, Detroit, 1937)
- Jack Lummus (E, Giants, 1941)
- Bob Mackert (T, Rochester, 1925)
- Frank Maher (B, Pittsburgh/Cleveland Rams, 1941)
- Jim Mooney (E-FB, Newark/Brooklyn/Cincinnati/St. Louis/Cardinals, 1930–1937)
- Len Supulski (E, Philadelphia, 1942)
- Don Wemple (E, Brooklyn, 1941)
- Chet Wetterlund (HB, Cardinals/Detroit, 1942)
- Waddy Young (E, Brooklyn, 1939–1940)

Gus Sonnenberg is often included on the list of NFL players killed in action, but that's not accurate. He was on active duty during the war, but he died of leukemia at Bethesda Naval Hospital in 1944.

The AAFC Challenge

When the war ended, owners and fans were looking forward to the returning players and the impact they would have on boosting the quality of play. Unfortunately, that boon was almost immediately offset by the emergence of a rival league.

Several aspiring owners had attempted to bankroll new teams, but NFL commissioner Elmer Layden rebuffed them all. Times had been tight—first during the Great Depression and then during the war—and the owners who had survived those struggles were not anxious to let newcomers share in what looked to be a prosperous age for pro football.

Chicago sportswriter Arch Ward helped gather these spurned suitors together to form their own league. After two years of planning, the owners announced that their venture—dubbed the All America Football Conference—would take the field in 1946. A publicity campaign promised colorful uniforms and a variety of innovative offensive styles.

From the outset, it was clear that the AAFC was not content to exist peacefully alongside the NFL. They went head-to-head with the NFL by putting teams in Chicago and Cleveland, and two teams in New York. In each instance, the AAFC teams signed leases to play at stadiums that were larger than their NFL counterparts. This encroachment so worried Rams owner Dan Reeves that he decided to leave Cleveland and head to the west coast. The AAFC was already there, having placed teams in Los Angeles and San Francisco as well as staking their claim in Florida with a team in Miami.

The AAFC also launched a full-scale assault on the talent pool. About one hundred NFL veteran players opted to switch leagues, as did a number of college stars whose pro careers had been delayed by military service. Players like Glenn Dobbs, Frankie Albert, and Heisman Trophy winner Angelo Bertelli gave the new league instant credibility.

The AAFC also landed some high-profile coaches. Ray Flaherty, who had won two NFL titles with the Redskins, was signed as the head coach for the Yankees. Cleveland hired Paul Brown to lead their squad. He had coached Ohio State University to their first national championship in 1941, and was so popular in the state of Ohio that Cleveland fans voted to name their team after him.

Coach Brown assembled a roster that included six rookies who would eventually be inducted into the Hall of Fame. Among them were African-American players Marion Motley and Bill Willis, ensuring that the AAFC would be integrated right from the start.

The two leagues went head-to-head for four seasons, with both teams suffering the financial toll caused by rising player salaries and a divided fan base. Talk of merger between the rival leagues came to fruition in December 1949. The NFL agreed to take three franchises, and the first two were obvious choices. The Cleveland Browns had dominated their competition, winning all four AAFC title games with a roster overflowing with stars. The San Francisco 49ers were clearly the second best club, with both a competitive team on the field and strong ownership. The leading candidate for the third spot would seem to be the Buffalo Bills, but NFL owners were concerned about adding another small-market team (only Green Bay was smaller). Some were also concerned about Buffalo's harsh winter weather. Instead, they opted to add the Bal-timore Colts, a last-place team that seemed on the brink of bankruptcy.

The players from the New York Yankees roster were divvied up between the NFL's two existing teams, and the players from Buffalo, Chicago, and Los Angeles went into a dispersal draft.

Game-Related Deaths

The Chicago Cardinals' spirits were running high when they opened their 1947 title defense with a win against the Eagles. Their joy was short-lived, however. Tackle Stan Mauldin collapsed after the game and died in the locker room. The coroner later determined that the twenty-seven-year-old had died of a heart attack.

Mauldin is one of eight NFL/AFL players who have died after playing in a game or during practice. Five of them died from heart attacks, although in each case this appeared to be brought on not by physical trauma but by undiagnosed heart disease. Two players died after breaking their necks during a game.

Player Fatalities

Player	Team	Cause of Death
Stan Mauldin	1948 Cardinals	heart attack after game
Dave Sparks	1954 Redskins	heart attack after game
Howard Glenn	1960 NY Titans	broken neck during game
Stone Johnson	1963 Chiefs	broken neck, died ten days later
Chuck Hughes	1971 Lions	heart attack during game
J. V. Cain	1979 Cardinals	heart attack during practice
Korey Stringer	2001 Vikings	heatstroke during practice
Thomas Herrion	2005 49ers	heart attack after game

Great Sportswriting

I spent a lot of time looking at old newspapers on microfilm as part of my research for this book. One of the joys of that effort was discovering the quality of writing that appeared in the football coverage across the country during this time.

In those days, the local newspapers were often the only source for pro football news. There was no television coverage, and even the national sports magazines focused most of their attention on baseball and boxing.

Today we have an endless array of 24-hour sports channels and countless Internet sources, and while those outlets do a good job of reporting breaking news, sports reporters have largely stopped making any effort to be storytellers.

Consider these few sentences from the opening of a news account in the late forties. This is Wilfred Smith's description of a game between the Bears and crosstown rival Cardinals. It comes from the *Chicago Daily Tribune* on December 13, 1948:

> Here was one of the great games of professional football. Here was a battle of linemen whose fierce, reckless tackling was shudderingly effective. Here was a duel between magnificently accurate forward passers whose skill had to be seen to be believed.
>
> And transcending all else here were the champion Cardinals, so thoroughly outplayed in the first half they made only one first down by rushing, who rallied with furious determination to sweep the spectators to incessant waves of applause.

There's no need for modern writers to describe the action because all of their readers saw the game for themselves, either live or in countless highlights packages. Football columnists today are more likely to reel off one-liners or invent funny nicknames. They have to do something bold to attract attention, and the loudest voices build an audience even though in many cases they don't really have anything to say. It's a shame. There are still some good writers covering pro football, but it's the ones who act like standup comics that hold center stage.

The 1950s

Best Team Season
1951 and 1953 Cleveland Browns, 11-1

Best Team of the Decade
Cleveland Browns (88-30-2)

Winners of Multiple Championships
Cleveland Browns (1950, 1954, and 1955); Detroit Lions (1952, 1953, and 1957); Baltimore Colts (1958 and 1959)

Worst Team Season
1950 Baltimore Colts, 1-11; 1952 Dallas Texans, 1-11. Both teams folded after their dismal showing.

Worst Team of the Decade
Chicago Cardinals (33-84-3)

New Teams
Three teams joined the NFL in 1950, as part of the merger with the AAFC. They were the Cleveland Browns, San Francisco 49ers, and Baltimore Colts.

The Dallas Texans and a second version of the Baltimore Colts began play during the decade. See discussion below.

Defunct Teams
The players from the AAFC's New York Yankees were divvied up between the NFL's two teams in New York, the Giants and the Bulldogs, and Bulldogs owner Ted Collins also claimed the AAFC team's nickname and home stadium.

The Baltimore Colts folded after a dismal 1-11 season in 1950. They had been one of the three AAFC teams that joined the NFL that season. The Colts' players went to other teams in a dispersal draft.

The New York Yanks folded after the 1951 season, with owner Ted Collins selling his franchise back to the league. A few weeks later, it was sold to a group of investors in Dallas. In their eagerness to stake a claim in the state of Texas, the NFL failed to consider whether this move was economically viable. The tremendous popularity of college football in the area meant that smaller and smaller crowds were turning out to see the Dallas Texans play. By midseason, owner Giles Miller was unable to meet the payroll. The league took over the franchise, with the team playing its remaining home games in Akron, Ohio.

The following season, the remnants of the Dallas franchise were sold to Baltimore businessman Carroll Rosenbloom. He took the name of the recently defunct Colts, and before the end of the decade had turned a vagabond team into NFL champions.

There is some debate among historians as to whether the 1951 Yanks, 1952 Texans, and 1953 Colts represent the continuation of one franchise or three separate franchises. On the one hand, there's an argument to be made that this was one team because the rosters were largely the same. Key players like Buddy Young, George Taliaferro, and Hall of Famer Art Donovan played for each of the three teams in succession. On the other hand, the league considers each of these to be separate franchises because the ownership was different in each case. Either approach is a reasonable one, in my mind.

Significant Moves
None, unless you consider the Yanks/Texans/Colts scenario above to be a franchise relocating. This was a period of stability for the NFL, although some would prefer to call it stagnation.

Most Passing Touchdowns
Season: 32, Johnny Unitas, Colts, 1959
Decade: 151, Bobby Layne, Lions and Steelers

Most Rushing Yards
Season: 1527, Jim Brown, Browns, 1958
Decade: 7151, Joe Perry, 49ers

Most Receptions
Season: 84, Tom Fears, Rams, 1950
Decade: 404, Billy Wilson, 49ers

Best Coaching Record
.742, Paul Brown, 88-30-2, Browns

Biggest Player
Bears' center Earl Putnam is probably the first NFL player to acknowledge weighing over 300 pounds. He was 6-foot-6, 308 pounds.

Smallest Player
Billy Cross, a 5-foot-5, 150-pound halfback for the Cardinals. Steelers' kicker Tad Weed was 140 pounds and had what you'll have to agree is a name that does not conjure the image of a football player.

All-Decade Team
Offense
QB	Bobby Layne
RB	Joe Perry
RB	Hugh McElhenny
E	Billy Howton
E	Billy Wilson
E	Elroy Hirsch
C	Frank Gatski
G	Duane Putnam
G	Dick Stanfel
T	Lou Groza
T	Lou Creekmur

Defense
DL	Len Ford
DL	Andy Robustelli
DL	Leo Nomellini
DL	Gene Brito
LB	Chuck Bednarik
LB	Joe Schmidt
LB	Bill George
LB	Sam Huff
DB	Emlen Tunnell
DB	Warren Lahr
DB	Jack Christiansen
DB	Bobby Dillon

Special Teams
K	Lou Groza
P	Norm Van Brocklin
Ret	Emlen Tunnell

Where They Played

The addition of AAFC teams helped give the league a second franchise on the west coast. The San Francisco 49ers played their home games in Kezar Stadium, a venue with a capacity of 60,000 that had opened in 1925.

The Niners were one of just two NFL teams that weren't sharing a stadium with a Major League Baseball team. The other was the Green Bay Packers, who continued to play in the 6000-seat City Stadium—the football field at the city's East High School. The other owners complained about having to go there, not just because of the small gate receipts but also because of the lack of modern facilities.

The Packers were playing some of their home games in Milwaukee to accommodate larger crowds, and in the early fifties they made some minor upgrades at City Stadium. The other owners pressed the team for a more permanent solution, with some even arguing for the team to move to Milwaukee full-time. Fearful of losing their team, Green Bay residents approved a $960,000 bond measure in 1956 to build a new stadium. It opened a year later, and although it was at a different location, the folks christened the new place with the same old name, "City Stadium." That name was changed to Lambeau Field in 1965, after the death of team founder Curly Lambeau.

Who Played the Game

A huge wave of new talent hit the market at the end of World War II, and the creation of the All America Football Conference helped to soak up those players. But the death of the AAFC after the 1949 season caused a sudden contraction in the early fifties. The number of pro teams in the United States dropped from eighteen in 1948 to just twelve in 1951. The result was that a third of the talent pool (or roughly 180 players) were squeezed out of work.

African-American players continued to find more opportunities in pro football. By 1959, they accounted for roughly 12 percent of the NFL's roster spots.

How the Game Was Played

The style of play changed dramatically during the 1950s, largely due to the elimination of rules that limited substitutions during the course of the game. The teams experimented with this practice for the first time during the wartime player shortages, and they liked it so much that they eventually allowed it permanently.

For the NFL's first three decades, versatility was the most important trait for a player. Your starting quarterback had to be quick enough to play safety, your running backs tough enough to play linebacker. The downside to this approach was that a player with one specific skill—say blazing speed—might not be enough of an all-around player to crack the starting lineup.

With free substitution legalized, specialization became the norm. The most immediate impact came on defense, where coaches began to devise innovative approaches to slowing down the dominant passing games that had emerged from the modern T-formation.

Philadelphia coach Greasy Neale developed the Eagle Defense, spreading his five defensive linemen out along the line of scrimmage and using two linebackers to cover the short pass. He also created the first four-man secondary, largely in response to Paul Brown's multiple-formation offense, which had been devastating opposing defenses.

Another approach was the Umbrella Defense, created by New York Giants' coach Steve Owen and his defensive captain, Tom Landry. This utilized both the defensive ends and linebackers in pass coverage, allowing the Giants to completely smother their opponent's passing attack.

In Los Angeles, Clark Shaughnessy developed a 5-3-3 defense that combined the best elements of the Eagle Defense and the Umbrella Defense. And just as he had made motion a key element in developing the modern T-offense, he added stunts and shifts to the defensive side of the ball to keep opponents guessing.

Free substitution helped the passing game immensely because it allowed coaches to use quick players at offensive end who weren't big enough to play defense. Their speed could be used as a weapon, and many teams moved to formations that featured three ends and just two backs. To counter, Landry moved the Giants to a base 4-3-4 defense around 1954. There would be countless improvements to and variations on the three-end formation and 4-3-4 defense in the years that followed, but the basic approach of each has served as the foundation of offensive and defensive play for over fifty years.

The concept of the blitz was born in the fifties. It was originally known as a "red dog," and was only employed by the middle linebacker. By the end of the decade, teams were blitzing players from other positions and using players in combination.

Teams also began to use zone defenses in passing situations, although man-to-man coverage was still the norm throughout the decade.

The Slow Pace of Integration

Most folks know that Jackie Robinson broke baseball's color barrier. I think that fewer people realize how difficult it was to desegregate professional sports at a time when other institutions of segregation remained firmly entrenched. And I don't think that many folks realize how painfully slow the process of integrating pro sports really was.

The sports community was far ahead of the rest of American society in opening doors for African Americans. The color line was broken in pro football in 1946 and in Major League Baseball a year later, but other American institutions were much slower to react. President Truman ordered the integration of the armed forces in 1948, an order that was largely ignored until 1951. The Supreme Court's unanimous 1954 ruling in Brown v. Board of Education declared that segregated schools were not legal. Three years later, President

Eisenhower had to deploy members of the 101st Airborne Division to Little Rock, Arkansas, where Governor Orval Faubus was using National Guard troops to prevent black students from entering Little Rock High School. A similar showdown took place with Governor George Wallace in Alabama in 1962.

The so-called "Jim Crow Laws" perpetuated segregation throughout much of the south through the mid-1960s. This prompted the passage of the Twenty-fourth Amendment and the Civil Rights Act in 1964 and the Voting Rights Act in 1965. And of course, it wasn't as if this legislation suddenly ended all of the problems plaguing American society. Many public universities remained segregated until the mid-1970s, and issues of equality and discrimination remain to this day.

My point here isn't to launch a discussion of where race relations are today, but rather to give a sense for how strained they were in the 1950s when professional sports began to desegregate. Most aspects of American life were still segregated when baseball and football began to introduce African-American players. In many ways, the successful integration of the NFL and Major League Baseball helped to pave the way for the advances that follow.

But it is important to understand just how gradual the integration of professional sports really was. Just as the Brown v. Board of Education ruling didn't suddenly end segregation in the schools, neither did the arrival of Jackie Robinson in Brooklyn and Marion Motley in Cleveland mean that all the doors were suddenly open for African-American ballplayers.

Initially, NFL teams were much quicker to integrate than their baseball brethren. By 1950, thirty-three African-American players had participated in the NFL, compared to just twelve in major league baseball. By 1952, eleven of the NFL's twelve teams had integrated (the Redskins were the lone holdout), while just six of baseball's sixteen clubs had broken their color barriers.

Baseball also trailed pro basketball in its slow pace towards integration. The NBA was born in 1949 as a merger of two existing leagues—the

National Basketball League (NBL) and the Basketball Association of America (BAA). The BAA was largely comprised of teams in big cities, while the NBL thrived in niche markets like Sheboygan, Wisconsin; Waterloo, Iowa; and Anderson, Indiana. The merger created a new league with seventeen teams that began play in 1949.

By 1954, nine of those original NBA teams had folded—most of the small-town teams. Of the eight surviving teams, half had integrated by the 1951–52 season (as did several of the teams that would eventually fold). By the 1955–56 season, all of the NBA teams were integrated.

Baseball did catch up by the end of the decade, but the legend of Jackie Robinson has led most Americans to believe that baseball paved a road that other sports leagues followed. The truth is just the opposite.

I went back and looked at the four major sports leagues in North America and identified all of the African-American players who began their careers before 1960. I found 280 men, and the two tables that follow document their arrival on the scene. The first table shows how many African-American players made their debut each season, and the second number shows the number of African Americans who were active in any given season. (Note: The NFL column includes players in the AAFC from 1946 to 1949. For the NBA and NHL, the data appears in the year in which the season began. For example, the 1950–51 season is recorded as 1950.)

African Americans in Team Sports, 1946–1959

Player Debuts by Season

Year	NFL	MLB	NBA	NHL
1946	5	0	n/a	0
1947	6	5	n/a	0
1948	9	2	n/a	0
1949	7	4	0	0
1950	6	1	4	0
1951	0	8	3	0
1952	11	7	1	0
1953	8	12	3	0
1954	8	13	4	0
1955	15	12	6	0
1956	8	13	6	0
1957	12	10	5	1
1958	17	13	9	0
1959	9	16	6	0
Total	**121**	**116**	**47**	**1**

Active Players by Season

Year	NFL	MLB	NBA	NHL
1946	5	0	n/a	0
1947	9	5	n/a	0
1948	15	4	n/a	0
1949	19	9	0	0
1950	19	10	4	0
1951	17	19	6	0
1952	27	20	6	0
1953	29	25	7	0
1954	30	38	10	0
1955	41	44	12	0
1956	36	51	16	0
1957	42	53	16	1
1958	48	59	19	0
1959	49	69	24	0

To put those numbers in some context, it's important to also look at the number of teams in each league, and the number of roster spots that each league had available. In 1953, African-American players held roughly 7 percent of the NFL roster spots, compared to 4.5 percent in Major League Baseball and 6.5 percent in the NBA. By 1957, the percentage had grown to 10.0 percent in the NFL, 9.5 percent in baseball, and 16.7 percent in the NBA.

The other major team sport in North America was hockey, which I feel compelled to mention here for the sake of completeness. The National Hockey League's first black player—an African-

Canadian—was Willie O'Ree, who made his debut with the Boston Bruins on January 18, 1958. He played just two games before returning to the minors. He returned for a second stint during the 1960–61 season. O'Ree was the only black hockey player to appear in the NHL before 1974. According to the league, only seventeen black players appeared in the NHL between 1974 and 1991. Suffice it to say that diversity is a relatively recent circumstance for pro hockey.

The Northern Threat

The NFL instituted its annual player draft in 1936 as a way to help funnel more college players into the league. It was an effective strategy, if only briefly. During World War II, an increasing percentage of the players who were drafted by NFL teams never played, largely because they entered military service. The low point was 1944. Of the 330 players who were selected by NFL teams that year, 233 would never step onto an NFL field. That's more than 70 percent.

After enduring the player shortages caused by the war and spending four years fighting with the AAFC, the NFL quickly found another rival for the top college prospects: Canada.

It started in 1950, as scores of players from disbanded AAFC teams made their way north to continue their pro football careers. They were joined by others who were cast off by the NFL, and the sudden influx of American talent made a huge impact on the Canadian game. Eleven of the twelve spots on the 1950 Canadian All-Star team went to American players, including NFL stars like Edgar "Speedy Delivery" Jones from the Browns and former Giants quarterback Frankie Filchok.

The rules of the game were different up north, but the Canadians were willing to pay good money. By 1951, players under contract to NFL teams began to jump to Canada, lured by the promise of a bigger payday. Several teams filed lawsuits, but they were largely unable to stop the defections.

Rookies also began to use the threat of playing in Canada to gain leverage in salary negotiations.

In an era when most of a team's revenues came from ticket sales, the Canadian teams could compete financially with their American counterparts. That would all change when the money from television contracts started to pour in.

The First Television Wave

In 1950 there were roughly 3.6 million television sets in the United States. By 1959, that number had soared to nearly seventy million, and that huge new market was clamoring for something to watch.

Sports were a great fit for the new medium because of the preexisting interest in the competition itself as well as the ease with which sports programs could be broadcast. Unlike other forms of television entertainment, the producers of sports programs didn't need to write scripts, design costumes, or build sets. They basically just needed to show up and point their camera at an event.

Some sports like golf were not well suited to television, but others proved to be a perfect match. Boxing, with all of its action contained in a 20-foot-by-20-foot ring, was perhaps the best example. The rigid timing of rounds made it easy to insert frequent commercial advertisements, and while a baseball game might run well over two hours, a 15-round bout could be squeezed into one 60-minute broadcast. The popularity of boxing soared in the fifties, with fighters like Sugar Ray Robinson and Rocky Marciano becoming household names.

Football had a tougher time getting a foothold. The first NFL game was televised in New York in 1939, a time when there were only about 1000 television sets in the city. A handful of teams had begun to broadcast their road games in the late 1940s. The Los Angeles Rams sold the rights to broadcast all of their games in 1950—home and away. While this deal did bring in a new source of revenue, attendance for home games dropped by 50 percent. The NFL quickly implemented a black-out rule, prohibiting the broadcast of home games that weren't sold out, as well as blocking the broadcast of out-of-town games into a market where another NFL game was taking place.

In 1951, the DuMont Network paid $75,000 for the first national broadcast of the NFL championship game. Two years later, DuMont began broadcasting an NFL game on Saturday nights to a national network. This lasted through 1955; DuMont folded the following summer.

By then, most teams had deals in place with local stations to televise their road games. Several of them were more ambitious. The Browns essentially created their own network by making deals with stations across their region. The Colts and Steelers teamed up with NBC to produce a game of the week, broadcast nationally.

Being on the national stage helped pro football's popularity surge, and the pinnacle came with the 1958 championship game. Broadcast nationally by NBC, the game featured two of the league's most popular teams—the Baltimore Colts and New York Giants—and some of their biggest stars: Johnny Unitas, Ray Berry, Frank Gifford, and Sam Huff, to name just a few.

The game itself was a classic. It was a seesaw game, but the Giants rallied in the fourth quarter to take the lead. The Colts responded with a long drive and a game-tying field goal with just seven seconds left on the clock. This thrust the two teams into a sudden-death overtime—something that had never been seen before. After the Giants stalled on their opening possession, Unitas led the Colts on an 80-yard drive, capped by Alan Ameche's 1-yard touchdown plunge.

Louis Effrat covered the game for the *New York Times* and wrote that it was "easily the most dramatic, most exciting encounter witnessed on the pro circuit in many a season." He quoted commissioner Bert Bell, a veteran of more than twenty years in the NFL, as calling it the "greatest game I've ever seen."

That one game was like a boulder crashing into a lake, and the waves continued to ripple in the years that would follow. It brought a whole new group of fans to the game; it showed broadcasters and advertisers that there was a rapidly expanding audience; and it showed businessmen who weren't NFL owners that, for the first time, there was money to be made in pro football.

The 1960s

Best Team Season
NFL: 1962 Green Bay Packers, 13-1; 1968 Baltimore Colts, 13-1
AFL: 1967 Oakland Raiders, 13-1

Best Team of the Decade
NFL: Green Bay Packers (96-37-5)
AFL: Kansas City Chiefs (87-48-5); Los Angeles/San Diego Chargers (86-48-6)

Winners of Multiple Championships
Green Bay Packers won the NFL title five times (1961, 1962, 1965, 1966, and 1967) plus two Super Bowls (1966 and 1967). Three teams won multiple AFL championships: Dallas Texans/Kansas City Chiefs (1962, 1966, and 1969); Houston Oilers (1960 and 1961); and Buffalo Bills (1964 and 1965).

Worst Team Season
NFL: 1960 Dallas Cowboys, 0-11-1
AFL: 1962 Oakland Raiders, 1-13

Worst Team of the Decade
NFL: Pittsburgh Steelers (46-85-7); Washington Redskins (46-82-10)
AFL: Denver Broncos (39-97-4)

New Teams
The NFL expanded four times during the decade, adding the Dallas Cowboys (1960), Minnesota Vikings (1961), Atlanta Falcons (1966), and New Orleans Saints (1967).

The AFL added ten teams in the 1960s. The original eight were the Buffalo Bills, Boston Patriots, Dallas Texans, Denver Broncos, Houston Oilers, Los Angeles Chargers, New York Titans, and Oakland Raiders. The AFL expanded with the Miami Dolphins in 1966 and the Cincinnati Bengals in 1968.

Significant Moves
After forty years as Chicago's second team, the Cardinals moved to St Louis in 1960. Two of the original AFL teams pulled up stakes. The Los Angeles Chargers moved to San Diego in 1961, and the Dallas Texans moved to Kansas City and became the Chiefs in 1963. Also, the New York Titans changed their name to the Jets in 1963.

Most Passing Touchdowns
NFL Season: 36, Y. A. Tittle, Giants, 1963
AFL Season: 36, George Blanda, Oilers, 1961

NFL Decade: 207, Sonny Jurgensen, Eagles and
Redskins
AFL Decade: 182, Len Dawson, Chiefs (Dawson
also had 1 TD pass with the NFL Browns in 1960–61)

Most Rushing Yards
NFL Season: 1863, Jim Brown, Browns, 1963
AFL Season: 1458, Jim Nance, Dolphins, 1966

NFL Decade: 8514, Jim Brown, Browns
AFL Decade: 5101, Clem Daniels, Dallas Texans
and Oakland Raiders (Daniels also rushed for 37
yards with the NFL 49ers in 1968)

Most Receptions
NFL Season: 93, Johnny Morris, Bears, 1964
AFL Season: 101, Charley Hennigan, Oilers, 1964;
100, Lionel Taylor, Broncos, 1961

NFL Decade: 470, Bobby Mitchell, Browns and
Redskins
AFL Decade: 567, Lionel Taylor, Broncos and Oilers

Best Coaching Record
NFL: .745, Don Shula, 71-23-4, Colts; .742, Vince
Lombardi, 89-29-6, Packers
AFL: .639, Hank Stram, 87-48-5, Dallas Texans/
Kansas City Chiefs

Biggest Player
Defensive tackle Ernie Ladd was 6-foot-9 and
weighed as much as 315 pounds. Seven-footer
Richard Sligh appeared in eight games with the
Raiders in 1967, making him the tallest player in
NFL history.

Smallest Player
Return man Noland Smith of the Chiefs, who
weighed just 155 pounds.

All-Decade Team
NFL
Offense
QB	Sonny Jurgensen
RB	Jim Brown
RB	Jim Taylor
WR	Bobby Mitchell
WR	Carroll Dale
TE	Mike Ditka
C	Jim Ringo
G	Gene Hickerson
G	Jerry Kramer
T	Forrest Gregg
T	Dick Schafrath

Defense
DL	Bob Lilly
DL	Deacon Jones
DL	Merlin Olsen
DL	Alex Karras
LB	Wayne Walker
LB	Ray Nitschke
LB	Chuck Howley
LB	Maxie Baughan
DB	Willie Wood
DB	Herb Adderley
DB	Larry Wilson
DB	Erich Barnes

Special Teams
K	Jim Bakken
P	Bobby Joe Green
Ret	Abe Woodson

AFL
Offense
QB	Len Dawson
RB	Clem Daniels
RB	Paul Lowe
WR	Don Maynard
WR	Lance Alworth
TE	Billy Cannon
C	Jim Otto
G	Bob Talamini
G	Billy Shaw
T	Ron Mix
T	Jim Tyrer

Defense			DB	Dave Grayson
DL	Houston Antwine		DB	Johnny Robinson
DL	Jerry Mays		DB	Willie Brown
DL	Larry Eisenhauer		DB	Fred Williamson
DL	Ernie Ladd			
LB	Larry Grantham		Special Teams	
LB	Nick Buoniconti		K	Mike Mercer
LB	Tom Addison		P	Paul Maguire
LB	Mike Stratton		Ret	Speedy Duncan

Where They Played

The American Football League put teams in major markets, going head-to-head with the NFL in Los Angeles, New York, and the San Francisco Bay Area. They placed teams in markets that had lost pro football teams—Buffalo and Boston—and staked a major claim to the American west with teams in Dallas, Denver, and Houston.

The American south and west had been hotbeds for college football, and both rival leagues sought to stake their claims in the region. The NFL expanded four times in the decade, with three of those new teams going into the South: the Dallas Cowboys, Atlanta Falcons, and New Orleans Saints. The AFL's first expansion team was in Miami.

Many of the new teams moved into existing stadiums at nearby colleges: the Cotton Bowl in Dallas, Rice Stadium in Houston, Tulane Stadium in New Orleans, and Nickerson Field in Boston.

Multipurpose stadiums were a significant new development in the sixties, venues that were designed to host both football and baseball tenants. The first example of this architectural style was District of Columbia Stadium in Washington, D.C. (later renamed Robert F. Kennedy Memorial Stadium). The Redskins began playing there in 1961, and the local baseball team—the Senators—moved in the following spring. Busch Memorial Stadium in St. Louis was built to host both the football and baseball Cardinals.

New Stadiums Built in the 1960s

Year	Stadium	Location
1961	D.C. Stadium (RFK)	Washington
1964	Shea Stadium	New York
1966	Oakland Coliseum	Oakland
1966	Busch Memorial Stadium	St. Louis
1967	San Diego Stadium	San Diego
1968	Astrodome	Houston

American Football League teams would be the biggest beneficiaries of the multisport stadium trend. Shea Stadium opened in 1964 and played host to both the NFL's Jets and baseball's Mets. The Raiders moved into the new Oakland-Alameda County Stadium in 1966. The Chargers made the new San Diego Stadium (aka Jack Murphy Stadium) their home in 1967, joined by the expansion Padres in 1969. The fourth multisport venue was the Astrodome, which opened in Houston in 1965. Baseball's Astros moved in that summer, followed by the AFL's Oilers in 1968.

The Astrodome was the world's first domed stadium, and after it became clear that the grass would not survive, it became the first venue outfitted with an artificial playing surface. Developed by Monsanto, this fake grass was originally called "Chemgrass," but it quickly became known as "Astroturf." It was basically a plastic fiber carpet laid down over asphalt.

All three of these trends—multipurpose stadiums, domes, and Astroturf—would dominate the architectural planning that took place for the next ten years.

Who Played the Game

An awful lot more guys than had ever played before. The advent of the American Football League coupled with the addition of four NFL expansion teams caused the number of pro football teams to soar from eight in 1959 to twenty-six in 1968.

The players also benefited from larger rosters. In 1960, the NFL increased the roster size from thirty-six to thirty-eight in 1960, then to forty in 1964.

The bottom line: there were 288 jobs for players in 1959 compared to 1040 in 1969.

This rapid expansion naturally diluted the talent pool, because suddenly 750 men were on NFL rosters who wouldn't have been good enough to make the squad a decade earlier. On the positive side, it did allow certain types of players who had been previously ignored to get an opportunity. African-American quarterbacks, for example, whose numbers were steadily increasing in the college ranks. Marlin Briscoe became the first African-American starting quarterback in the pro game, leading the Denver Broncos as a rookie in 1968. The following year, James Harris began the season as Buffalo's starting quarterback, and while he didn't hold on to that job for long, he played well enough to stay in the NFL until 1981.

Players who were previously considered too small or too one-dimensional also started to get a chance to play. Players like Bob Hayes, a sprinter who had won two gold medals at the 1964 Olympics. He held several world records, and the Dallas Cowboys thought that his blazing speed could make an impact on the football field. It did, and Hayes led the team in both catches and receiving yards as a rookie. Opposing teams were forced to play zone defenses to keep him covered, and he helped the Cowboys become one of the dominant teams of the early seventies.

Before Hayes, the general consensus was that speed alone wouldn't make you an effective receiver. This was, after all, an era in which there were no rules that prohibited defenders from making contact with receivers down the field. Linebackers delivered stiff arms and defensive backs made bone-rattling hits to keep receivers from getting open. But Hayes was able to prove that the conventional wisdom was wrong, and opened the door for the generations of speedy receivers that followed.

How the Game Was Played

There were two very different trends that dominated the decade. The teams in the American Football League favored a much more wide-open game, with the balance shifting heavily toward the passing attack. Head coach Sid Gillman, who had been one of the NFL's great innovators in his tenure with the Rams, brought his system to the AFL as head coach of the Chargers. His strategy was to spread the field, both vertically and horizontally, forcing the defenses to stretch to their breaking point. Gillman led the Chargers to the AFL title game five times in the league's first six seasons. (They lost four times, but the point is that they got there.) Other AFL teams would adopt the same philosophy, most notably the Raiders and Jets.

In the NFL, more teams favored an offense based on a physical running game. The most successful of these was in Green Bay, where head coach Vince Lombardi used zone blocking and the power sweep to dominate the decade.

The Cleveland Browns took the same approach, although for them it was more about creating a system around a star runner than anything else. Eight times during the decade one of their running backs claimed the rushing title. Jim Brown led the league in rushing five times in a six-year span from 1960 to 1965. When he suddenly retired after the 1965 season, Cleveland's ground attack barely missed a beat. Leroy Kelly took over and finished second in rushing yards in 1966, and then claimed the crown in 1967 and 1968.

The Foolish Club

A lot has been written about the American Football League and its impact on pro football. There are at least a dozen full-length books on the subject, not to mention hundreds of articles and a handful of documentary films.

The league was started by a group of businessmen who grew frustrated at their inability to be considered for an expansion team in the National Football League. Other than absorbing three teams from the rival AAFC in 1950, the NFL had added just one expansion team since the mid-1930s. Fans in many cities were clamoring for a team of their own, and there were several potential owners who had enough financial clout to make a new team fly.

The most prominent of these was Lamar Hunt, the son of millionaire oilman H. L. Hunt. He was one of several bidders attempting to purchase the Chicago Cardinals in 1959, but when the Bidwill family decided to move their team to Chicago rather than sell it, Hunt had a brainstorm. He contacted the other suitors to pitch the idea of forming a new league. Three of those businessmen loved the idea, and within a few months the new league had ownership in place for teams in Dallas (Hunt), Denver (Bob Howsam), and Houston (Bud Adams).

By the summer of 1959, Hunt had also recruited owners in the two biggest American cities: Los Angeles (hotel magnate Barron Hilton) and New York (broadcaster Harry Wismer).

Wismer didn't have the personal wealth that his fellow owners had amassed, but he did have an idea that proved to be extremely valuable. He devised a plan for all of the teams to share the revenues from a national broadcasting contract. Since Wismer's team was in the country's largest television market, this seems like a rather generous proposal. He stood to lose the most in short-term cash flow, but Wismer realized that the success of the league hinged not on how strong their strongest teams were, but how strong their weakest teams were.

This gave the fledgling AFL an advantage over previous rivals right from the start. Ironically, Wismer would be the first of the AFL owners to run out of money, forcing him to sell the team after three seasons. Overall, however, the league was extremely stable.

Hunt and his fellow owners dubbed themselves "The Foolish Club," but it was their business acumen that enabled them to succeed. Most of the league's owners had made their fortunes outside of the sports world, and that experience helped guide the league through the inevitable tough times that marked their early years.

A mythology has grown over the years suggesting that the AFL thrived because of its willingness to be different. No doubt the league embraced a sense of showmanship, played an exciting style of football, and provided a stage for some colorful talented players. But what made the AFL thrive while every other rival failed was purely economics.

By the mid-1960s, it began to become clear that the AFL wasn't going to run out of money. Instead, it was the older league that faced growing financial pressures. The NFL had to compete with their younger rivals for a share of the lucrative broadcasting market, which by then had become their major source of revenue. Simultaneously, the competition for players was driving salaries up. It cost much more to sign the top college players each year, to say nothing of the rising salaries demanded by veteran players.

Things reached a head in 1965. The AFL owners got an infusion of cash when they signed a $36 million deal with NBC to broadcast their games. In March, they granted an expansion franchise to attorney Joe Robbie and television star Danny Thomas in Miami. Robbie and Thomas paid a $7.5 million expansion fee for their team, which would begin play the following year.

Those two deals brought an infusion of cash, and the AFL teams were ready to spend it. The money enabled them to sign some of the top college stars, like Alabama quarterback Joe Namath and Heisman Trophy winner Mike Garrett.

It was clear to the NFL owners that they weren't going to win a war of attrition, and they might not even win the war at all. Cowboys team president Tex Schramm reflected the views of many NFL executives when he worried that further battles might destroy both leagues.

So in April of 1966, Schramm and Hunt began secret meetings to negotiate the peace. By mid-May, the two leagues had hammered out a basic merger agreement. On June 8, 1966, in a press conference in New York, the merger of the two leagues was announced. The major points of the deal were:

- All existing franchises from both leagues would remain in operation.
- NFL Commissioner Pete Rozelle would remain as commissioner of the combined league.
- A championship game between the two leagues would be played each year, beginning at the end of the 1966 season.
- There would be a common draft after the 1966 season.
- Each league would continue under the terms of their existing TV contracts and keep their own money. (Each league's deal ran through the 1969 season.)
- Interleague games would be played during the preseason beginning in 1967. A common regular-season schedule would begin in 1970.
- AFL clubs would pay the NFL a total of $18 million over twenty years. This money would be used to compensate franchises that had to welcome a competing team into their market. The New York Giants would receive $10 million and the San Francisco 49ers would receive $8 million.

In order for the agreement to move forward, the leagues needed Congressional approval. Rozelle went to Washington to testify before the House's Subcommittee on Antitrust. The major concern of the committee members seemed to be keeping existing teams from moving. Naturally, they were looking out for the fans in their constituencies who would scream bloody murder if approving the deal meant losing the hometown team. Rozelle agreed to block any moves, so long as the league did not have to keep teams in stadiums deemed too small (defined as a seating capacity of less than 50000). As a result, the Bears moved from Wrigley Field to Soldier Field, and the Patriots moved from Boston's Fenway Park to a new stadium in nearby Foxboro. True to their word, not a single team left their hometown throughout the decade that followed.

The new league thrived. Revenues continued to grow and the owners had more cost certainty because they did not have to compete over players. Some have argued that the AFL teams could have gotten a better deal if they held out longer, but the reality is that everyone ended up in pretty good shape. The combined 26-team league wielded significant clout when it came to negotiating television contracts, and they quickly became the most powerful player in sports broadcasting.

The success of Lamar Hunt and his fellow owners prompted imitators to form rival leagues in other sports. The American Basketball Association launched in 1967, and the World Hockey Association took to the ice in 1972. In both cases, the new leagues adopted some of the AFL's strategies. They worked to make their style of play more exciting than their stodgy counterparts. They put teams in big cities that the older league had ignored. And they threw a lot of money after a handful of star players in order to get much-needed attention.

Those imitators never had the one thing that was most important for the American Football League: a steady stream of money. Both the WHA and ABA endured a series of franchise failures and relocations, and when all was said and done, only a handful of their teams were invited to be part of a merger.

The Compromise Commissioner

The birth of the AFL occurred at a time when the National Football League was in a bit of disarray. Commissioner Bert Bell had died suddenly on October 11, 1959. He suffered a massive heart attack while watching the Steelers and Eagles play in Philadelphia. Austin Gunsel, the league treasurer, was named as interim commissioner as the owners scrambled to find a replacement.

Some of the owners favored keeping Gunsel in the job permanently. He was a former FBI man and had been J. Edgar Hoover's administrative assistant. Bell hired him in the mid-fifties as head of the NFL's investigative department, a move made in response to a number of scandals that threatened to tarnish the league's image.

Another group of owners favored a different candidate, San Francisco attorney Marshall G. Leahy. The major sticking point seemed to be that Gunsel proposed to keep the league offices in Philadelphia, where they had been based during Bell's term. Leahy wanted to move them closer to his west coast home.

The two blocks of teams—one known as the "solid seven" and the other as the "fearless four"—debated the candidates for more than a week, and it became clear that neither side would budge. A three-fourths majority was required to select the new commissioner, and through twenty-three different ballots, neither Gunsel nor Leahy could muster the necessary votes.

With neither side willing to budge, Colts owner Carroll Rosenbloom offered a compromise candidate. That man was Pete Rozelle, the thirty-three-year-old general manager of the Los Angeles Rams. Rozelle was not well known outside of football circles, but he had spent six seasons with the Rams. He served as their public relations man from 1952 to 1954 before leaving to help promote the 1956 Olympics. He returned to the Rams the following year as their general manager. The team was losing money, as its five co-owners bickered over the day-to-day operations. Commissioner Bell used his influence to convince them to bring Rozelle in to keep the peace.

Some revisionist historians would credit Rozelle with turning that franchise around. He may have helped to stop the owners from quarreling with each other, but the Rams didn't exactly flourish on the field. After a modest improvement, the team slumped to 2-10 in 1959. He made what might be the most lopsided trade in football history, sending seven players and a draft choice to the Cardinals in exchange for aging halfback Ollie Matson.

While he may not have been a football genius, he sure knew marketing. He helped turn the Rams finances around by aggressively licensing his team's logos for merchandise, exploiting new streams of advertising revenue, and pursuing partnerships with local businesses.

It was Rozelle's marketing acumen and his diplomacy skills that made him an attractive candidate to the NFL owners in 1960. Maybe they knew that those were the skills they would need most in a leader in the coming years, or maybe they just got lucky. Either way, the fortunes of the National Football League changed dramatically that summer day in 1960 when the owners settled for Rozelle as their commissioner.

The 1970s

DECADE IN A BOX

Best Team Season
1972 Miami Dolphins, 14-0

Best Teams of the Decade
Dallas Cowboys (105-39-0); Miami Dolphins (104-39-1); Oakland Raiders (100-38-6). It was a decade for dynasties. While these three teams sported the best overall records, the Pittsburgh Steelers won four Super Bowls in a span of six seasons.

Winners of Multiple Championships
Pittsburgh Steelers (1974, 1975, 1978, and 1979); Dallas Cowboys (1971 and 1977); Miami Dolphins (1972 and 1973)

Worst Team Season
1976 Tampa Bay Buccaneers, 0-14

Worst Team of the Decade
New Orleans Saints (42-98-4)

New Teams
The Seattle Seahawks and Tampa Bay Buccaneers joined the league in 1976.

Significant Moves
After spending most of the sixties in Fenway Park, the Boston Patriots moved into their own stadium in 1971. Schaeffer Stadium was built in Foxboro, roughly thirty miles south of Boston and twenty miles north of Providence, Rhode Island. With the relocation, the team changed its name to the New England Patriots to reflect the broader geographical range of their fan base.

Most Passing Touchdowns
Season: 28, Terry Bradshaw, Steelers, 1978; 28, Steve Grogan, Patriots, 1979
Decade: 156, Fran Tarkenton, Giants and Vikings

Most Rushing Yards
Season: 2003, O.J. Simpson, Bills, 1973
Decade: 10539, O.J. Simpson, Bills and 49ers

Most Receptions
Season: 88, Rickey Young, 1978, Vikings
Decade: 432, Harold Jackson, Eagles, Rams, and Patriots

Best Coaching Records

.734, John Madden, 91-31-6, Raiders; .729, Tom Landry, 105-39-0, Cowboys; .726, Don Shula, 104-39-1, Dolphins

Biggest Player

Cowboys defensive end Ed "Too Tall" Jones was 6-foot-9 and 271 pounds. Chargers tackle Buddy Hardaway was the same height but weighed about forty pounds more. Gene Ferguson (6-foot-8 and 300 pounds) also spent two years with the Chargers.

Smallest Player

Jets receiver Eddie Bell was 5-foot-10 and weighed 160 pounds. Despite being so skinny, he survived seven seasons in the NFL. Running back Howard Stevens was 5-foot-5 and 165 pounds.

All-Decade Team

Offense

QB	Roger Staubach
RB	O.J. Simpson
RB	Larry Csonka
WR	Harold Jackson
WR	Gene Washington
TE	Raymond Chester
C	Jim Langer
G	Tom Mack
G	Larry Little
T	Art Shell
T	Ron Yary

Defense

DL	Joe Greene
DL	Alan Page
DL	Jack Youngblood
DL	L. C. Greenwood
LB	Jack Ham
LB	Isiah Robertson
LB	Chris Hanburger
LB	Bill Bergey
DB	Ken Houston
DB	Roger Wehrli
DB	Paul Krause
DB	Mel Blount

Special Teams

K	Garo Yepremian
P	Jerrel Wilson
Ret	Rick Upchurch

Where They Played

Increasingly, NFL teams were playing their games on artificial turf. At the end of the 1969 season, just one team—the Houston Oilers—played their home games on Astroturf. By 1979, the number had soared to twelve.

The spread of turf was largely due to a building boom. Between 1970 and 1976, ten new NFL stadiums were built, and all but one of them installed the green plastic carpet on their playing surface.

There were two architectural trends that dominated the era. Six multipurpose stadiums had opened in the sixties, and three more opened in the early seventies. Critics lamented that the new venues in Cincinnati, Pittsburgh, and Philadelphia looked nearly identical to the one that opened in St. Louis in 1966. To most observers, most of the nine stadiums that opened between 1964 and 1971 appeared to have been built from the same blueprint, with minor cosmetic variations. In reality, eight separate architectural firms designed them.

The critics called these cookie-cutter stadiums, because they all looked alike and seemed intentionally devoid of any distinguishing characteristics.

The other model that spawned copycats was the Houston Astrodome. The benefits of playing under a roof were readily apparent, particularly for teams in northern climates. Three new domed stadiums opened by 1976, located in Detroit, New Orleans, and Seattle. By the end of the decade, plans were under way for two more domed stadiums in Minneapolis and Indianapolis.

Who Played the Game

By the start of the 1970s, fewer players were leaving American colleges to play in Canada. The exceptions were players who were too small to compete in the NFL, and a handful of African-American quarterbacks, for whom the NFL market remained largely closed.

How the Game Was Played

The number of different playing styles was probably at its peak in the early seventies. The merger of the AFL and the NFL brought together teams that spanned the spectrum from wide-open passing attacks to ultraconservative running games. This created big challenges for defensive coaches, who had to prepare their squads to face all different kinds of opponents.

The merger also led to some cross-pollination, as young assistant coaches began to take head coaching jobs with NFL teams. Don Coryell, a disciple of San Diego's Sid Gillman, brought his high-flying offense to the St. Louis Cardinals. He stretched the field with his speedy receivers, and once the defense spread out, he would hand the ball to speedy halfback Terry Metcalf. The Cardinals won back-to-back division titles under Coryell's leadership.

He kicked his offense up another notch when he joined the Chargers at the end of the decade. Coryell turned his tight end into a primary receiver, making the passing game even more difficult to defend. Kellen Winslow became one of the league's most explosive receivers, and quarterback Dan Fouts broke nearly every passing record.

As passing attacks became more aggressive, defenses began to respond by removing linebackers during passing situations and inserting a fifth defensive back. This fifth man was dubbed the nickelback, and sometimes defenses would even use a sixth man called the dime back.

Defensive coaches had to come up with creative ways to defend against these passing attacks. In Miami, head coach Don Shula revived the Oklahoma defense, a scheme that had been developed by the legendary Bud Wilkinson at the University of Oklahoma in the 1940s. In its original incarnation, the Oklahoma defense featured five linemen with two inside linebackers. Shula turned Wilkinson's ends into linebackers who could help both against the run and in pass coverage. This system would come to be known as the 3-4 defense, and after the Dolphins dominated their opponents in the early seventies, other teams began to adopt it as well.

The NFL made a number of rule changes during the middle of the decade that helped shift the balance toward the offensive side of the ball, particularly in the passing game (see discussion below). There were also a number of changes aimed at increasing player safety, particularly in the aftermath of a devastating but legal hit that left New England receiver Darryl Stingley permanently paralyzed.

Other rules changes included the adoption of sudden-death overtime, moving the goal posts from the goal line to the back of the end zone, and shifting kickoffs from the 40-yard line to the 35. All three of these changes were adopted in 1974. The league also expanded its schedule from fourteen games to sixteen in 1978.

The Death of Defensive Dynasties

The AFL earned a reputation for high-scoring games and more wide-open offenses. But by the end of the sixties, the advantage in both leagues was shifting toward the defense. Scoring continued to drop after the merger, and owners worried that fan interest would wane if the trend continued. The chart, Points per Game, 1960–1979, shows the number of points scored per game in the ten years before and after the merger.

The league responded to the drop in scoring by instituting a number of rules changes that made life easier for players on the offensive side of the ball. It started in 1974 with two moves geared to help boost the passing game. First, the rules for offensive holding and illegal use of hands were

Points Per Game, 1960–1979

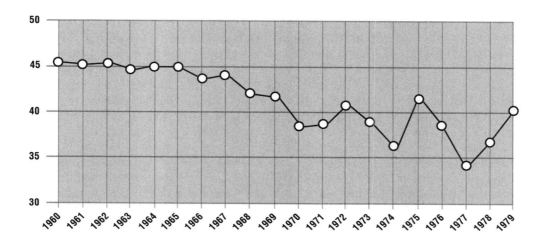

loosened and the penalties for those infractions were reduced from 15 yards to 10. Second, receivers were given a little more breathing room to run their patterns. Defenders could no longer roll-block or cut receivers, and the amount of contact they could make downfield was limited.

Those rules were expanded in 1977 and 1978, so that defenders could only make contact with receivers once, and only within 5 yards of the line of scrimmage. Pass protection was also strengthened by rules that allowed offensive linemen to extend their arms and use open hands for blocking.

The chart shows that these rules changes had the desired effect. Note the immediate upturn in scoring after they were implemented. If we continued the chart to the present day, you'd see that scoring has generally remained steady in the years that followed. Except for a brief dip in the early nineties, the average per game has remained between 40 and 45 points over the last twenty-five seasons.

Of course, while the folks on the offense were happy about theses changes, it made it more dif-

ficult for the guys on the other side of the ball. Defensive strategies are always changing, but the job of the defense has remained the same: Stop your opponent from scoring. There is a strong correlation between yards and points, but that correlation is not absolute. Teams with a high-scoring offense, like the Air Coryell Chargers or the Kurt Warner–era Rams, gave up a lot of garbage yards in the second half. With a Prevent defense, you're willing to give up short passes in the middle of the field, essentially trading those yards for time. It's not uncommon for a team to give up 50 or even 100 yards in a game this way. Those yards don't reflect a failure on the part of the defense, but rather a strategy. If you can keep the other team from scoring points, that's all that matters.

Another problem with yards as a metric is that some defenses employ a bend-but-don't-break strategy. They'll give up short plays, knowing that it's hard for the offense to maintain a long drive. At some point, there will be a stop . . . a penalty, an incompletion, or a turnover that stalls the drive. If the offense avoids mistakes and gets into the red zone anyway, then the defense stiffens and tries to force a turnover or a field goal. A great illustration of this approach was the 2001 Patriots, who finished 24th in yards allowed but were sixth in points allowed.

I'm not suggesting that yards are a meaningless measurement. They can tell us how a defense did what they did and where their strengths or weaknesses lay. By looking at points allowed, we really have our best view of the bottom line.

Since modern defenses aren't generally responsible for kick or punt coverage, we shouldn't hold them responsible for points scored on kick and punt returns. They are also not responsible for points the offense surrenders, either on interceptions or fumble returns. When we look at points allowed, we need to take this into account. To evaluate the defense, we count just the rushing and passing touchdowns and field goals that a team allows their opponents to score. The table below shows the fifteen stingiest defenses of the modern era.

Fewest Defensive Points Allowed Since 1950

Rank	Year	Team	Def Pts/G
1	2000	Ravens	9.56
2	1975	Rams	9.71
3	1970	Vikings	9.86
4	1977	Broncos	10.79
5	2000	Titans	10.81
6t	1978	Broncos	11.06
6t	2006	Ravens	11.06
8t	1971	Vikings	11.07
8t	1977	Rams	11.07
10	2002	Buccaneers	11.13
11t	2003	Buccaneers	11.25
11t	2005	Bears	11.25
13	1969	Vikings	11.29
14	1991	Saints	11.31
15	2001	Bears	11.31

You'll notice two clusters of teams. Seven of these teams played in the decade leading up to the rules changes of 1978. Seven played between 2000 and 2006.

The first group comprises three defensive units that stuck together over several seasons. You'll notice that the 1977–78 Broncos hold two spots on this list, the '75 and '77 Rams hold two spots, and the 1969–1971 Vikings hold three more. With great players like Lyle Alzado, Merlin Olsen, and Carl Eller, these teams reached and sustained a level of dominance over several seasons.

By contrast, many of the great defenses of more recent vintage were one-year wonders. The 2000 Ravens, the stingiest defense in history, gave up 5.5 more points per game the following year (9.56 to 15.06). The Bears went from being one of the great defenses of all-time to being a pretty lousy one. After surrendering just 11.31 points per game in 2001, they gave opponents 22.94 in 2002. There was an even bigger drop in Tennessee, where the Titans gave up twice as many points in 2001 (23.38) as they did the year before (10.81).

Bucking that trend has been the Tampa Bay Buccaneers, in large part because their defense has been built around stopping the passing game. The other great defenses from the 2000s focused on stuffing the run.

Why haven't we continued to see dominant defenses like we had in the seventies? The biggest reason is free agency. Any successful defense system relies on its members playing well as a unit, and that gets tougher and tougher when the faces are changing every year. Today's players just don't have the continuity and familiarity that they did in the seventies, and that's why it has become nearly impossible to build a defensive dynasty.

Parity Through Scheduling

There was another significant but generally overlooked change implemented in the seventies: the adoption of the imbalanced schedule. With the merger and expansion pushing the number of NFL teams to twenty-eight, it was no longer possible for a team to play every other team in a single season. In 1978, they introduced a scheduling formula that was based on the previous year's standings. The teams that finished at the top of the standings play each other, and the teams at the bottom play each other. Finish first in the AFC East, and your out-of-division opponents would consist of four first-place teams, a second-place team, and a third-place team. Finish fifth and you'd play two third-place teams, one fourth-place team, and four fifth-place teams. Lousy teams had a chance to do better the next year simply by playing weaker opponents.

The NFL abandoned this system in 2002, switching to a fixed schedule that ensured every team would play each of the other thirty-one teams in the league at least once every eight years. Teams within a conference now play each other at least once every four years.

With only a few years of data so far, it's difficult to understand exactly how much of an impact this change will have. But we can look at the old system and get a very clear picture of how well that worked. To understand how powerful the scheduling effects were, we simply look at how teams fared from one season to the next. Since the introduction of the sixteen-game schedule in 1978, seven teams have finished with a record of 1-15. The table below shows how they did in the season that followed:

Record of Teams One Year After 1-15

Year	Team	Record	Next Year
1980	Saints	1-15	4-12
1989	Cowboys	1-15	7-9
1990	Patriots	1-15	6-10
1991	Colts	1-15	9-7
1996	Jets	1-15	9-7
2000	Chargers	1-15	5-11
2001	Panthers	1-15	7-9

That's an average of nearly seven wins in the season following the 1-15 record, and it shouldn't be too surprising that all of these teams improved. But the amount of improvement was dramatic. Clearly, these teams couldn't have completely overhauled their roster, and simply adding a star college player from the top of the draft class can't account for teams improving by an average of six wins.

Just to demonstrate that it works the other way too, here are the sixteen teams that finished 15-1 or 14-2 under the imbalanced schedule.

Record of Teams One Year After 14-2 or 15-1

Year	Team	Record	Next Year
1979	Steelers	14-2	12-4
1984	Redskins	14-2	11-5
1985	49ers	15-1	10-6
1985	Dolphins	14-2	12-4
1986	Bears	15-1	14-2
1987	Bears	14-2	11-5
1987	Giants	14-2	6-10
1990	49ers	14-2	14-2
1991	49ers	14-2	10-6
1992	Redskins	14-2	9-7
1993	49ers	14-2	10-6
1999	Broncos	14-2	6-10
1999	Vikings	15-1	10-6
1999	Falcons	14-2	5-11
2000	Jaguars	14-2	7-9
2001	Rams	14-2	7-9

None of the teams won more games the following season, ten of sixteen (63 percent) saw their win total drop by 4 or more, and more than a quarter actually dropped so far that they had losing records.

Part of this is simply a statistical phenomenon called regression to the mean. Teams at the extreme ends of the spectrum will tend to be drawn back toward the center. Clearly, there was more at work than just that. If you look at how all teams have performed from one season to the next, about 65 percent of winning teams decline the following year and about 65 percent of losing teams improve. Here's a look at the results with the imbalanced schedule.

Record in the Following Year (1978–2002)

Wins	Worse	Same	Better
2–4	5%	11%	84%
5–7	30%	11%	59%
9–11	59%	11%	30%
12–14	77%	16%	7%
1–7	22%	11%	68%
9–15	64%	12%	24%

It's too soon to make any definitive statements about how the effects of parity have been impacted by the new schedule. After a few years, there's at least some anecdotal evidence to suggest that it will continue to serve as a tool to create competitive balance. Whether that holds true in the aggregate is something we won't be able to measure really well for several more years.

The 1980s

Best Team Season
1984 San Francisco 49ers, 15-1; 1985 Chicago Bears, 15-1

Best Team of the Decade
San Francisco 49ers (104-47-1)

Winners of Multiple Championships
San Francisco 49ers (1981, 1984, 1988, and 1989); Oakland/Los Angeles Raiders (1980 and 1983); Washington Redskins (1982 and 1987)

Worst Team Seasons
1982 Baltimore Colts, 0-8-1 (strike-shortened season); 1980 New Orleans Saints, 1-15; 1989 Dallas Cowboys, 1-15

Worst Team of the Decade
Tampa Bay Buccaneers (45-106-1)

Significant Moves
The Oakland Raiders moved to Los Angeles in 1982; Baltimore Colts moved to Indianapolis in 1984; St. Louis Cardinals moved to Phoenix in 1988.

Most Passing Touchdowns
Season: 48, Dan Marino, Dolphins, 1984
Decade: 220, Dan Marino, Dolphins

Most Rushing Yards
Season: 2105, Eric Dickerson, Rams, 1984
Decade: 11226, Eric Dickerson, Rams and Colts

Most Receptions
Season: 106, Art Monk, Redskins, 1984
Decade: 662, Art Monk, Redskins

Best Coaching Records
.669, Joe Gibbs, 91-45, Redskins; .665, Bill Walsh, 90-45-1, 49ers

Biggest Player
Here are the official weights as listed in the NFL's *1989 Fact and Record Book:* Dallas guard Nate Newton, 317; Chicago defensive tackle William Perry, 320. Newton was closer to 370, and as for Refrigerator Perry . . . well, I don't know what his lowest weight was during his NFL career, but Bears head coach Mike Ditka had complained to the press the previous year, "I don't want a 377-pound

defensive lineman." It had been a very long time since Perry had seen 320.

Smallest Player
Kick returners Gerald McNeil (5-foot-7, 145 pounds) and Reggie Smith (5-foot-4, 168 pounds)

All-Decade Team
Offense
QB   Joe Montana
RB   Walter Payton
RB   Eric Dickerson
WR   James Lofton
WR   Art Monk
TE   Ozzie Newsome
C   Dwight Stephenson
G   Randy Cross
G   John Hannah
T   Anthony Munoz
T   Jackie Slater

Defense
DL   Dan Hampton
DL   Randy White
DL   Howie Long
DL   (tie) Mark Gastineau, Ed Jones
LB   Lawrence Taylor
LB   Mike Singletary
LB   Harry Carson
LB   Rod Martin
DB   Ronnie Lott
DB   Deron Cherry
DB   Kenny Easley
DB   Gary Fencik

Special Teams
K   Nick Lowery
P   Rohn Stark
Ret   Mike Nelms

Where They Played

Yet another rival league was born in the eighties. The United States Football League operated from 1983 to 1985, and while it enjoyed some level of success, it ultimately failed in its efforts to force a merger.

NFL franchises were fairly stable throughout the sixties and seventies, but that all changed in the 1980s. Four teams moved from one part of town to another, while three more pulled up stakes and moved to another city altogether.

Finances were the key factor in each case, with teams looking for the increased revenue available from bigger venues or from modern additions like luxury boxes. The Dolphins and Vikings both moved into brand new stadiums, while the Jets and Rams found more suitable homes in existing buildings. For the Jets, that meant moving from Shea Stadium in Flushing, New York, to Giants Stadium in East Rutherford, New Jersey—about twenty-five miles to the west. For the Rams, the move took them about thirty-five miles southeast, from the Los Angeles Memorial Coliseum to Anaheim Stadium in Anaheim.

With the Rams gone, other teams immediately began to eye the Coliseum. Its 92000-seat capacity made it a lucrative venue, not to mention the 7.5 million residents living in the Los Angeles area. First among them was Al Davis, owner of the Oakland Raiders. Oakland had a population of roughly 1.7 million, but the Raiders were always competing for fans with the 49ers across the bay in San Francisco.

Davis knew a great opportunity when he saw it, and he quickly signed an agreement to move his team to Los Angeles. Such a move required approval by the league, specifically by three-fourths of the owners. When the matter came up for a vote, the tally was 22–0 against the proposal, with five owners abstaining.

Davis responded by filing an antitrust suit, asserting that the NFL was not a single business but rather twenty-eight separate entities that retained control over their own affairs, despite cooperating in some matters. Commissioner Pete Rozelle obviously disagreed, insisting that franchise stability was crucial to the success of the league as a whole. When one team moved, he argued, everyone suffered.

It took two years for the case to reach a resolution, but on May 7, 1982, a jury sided with Davis. It awarded the Raiders $35 million in damages (although a settlement reduced the amount to $18 million) and cleared the way for the team to move in time to play the 1982 season in Los Angeles.

The results of this case reverberated across the NFL landscape. Suddenly, other owners began to see relocation as a viable business strategy. Teams playing in older stadiums had new leverage to get upgrades made to their facilities, or more often to strengthen their efforts to get a new stadium built. There were plenty of outside cities anxious to make a lucrative offer to lure an NFL team within their borders.

One of the earliest tests of this strategy came in Baltimore. The Colts played in Memorial Stadium, a venue originally designed for baseball. One of the downsides to sharing a stadium with a baseball team was that they were often bumped in September while the baseball club finished its schedule. For a team like the Colts, this meant fewer home games in the nice weather and more in November and December, when the snow and cold might keep fans away.

Memorial Stadium was built in 1950, but age wasn't its primary drawback. Many of its design features made it a less than desirable environment for football. The upper deck, originally added to accommodate baseball fans, only covered the closed end of the horseshoe-shaped field. This meant a lot of seats behind home plate for Orioles games. For the Colts, it meant a plethora of end zone seats and a lot of empty space at the 50-yard line. The upper deck was supported by huge concrete pillars, which meant thousands of seats in the lower deck had obstructed views. Nearly half of the stadium's seats were benches with no backs, and 7000 more came in the form of temporary wooden bleachers at the north end of

the field. Bathroom facilities for fans weren't that great. Parking and traffic were a nightmare. There wasn't enough room to house either the Orioles or Colts front offices, and the two teams had to share a single locker room.

Colts owner Carroll Rosenbloom had been complaining about the stadium situation since the early sixties. He even toyed with the idea of building a new facility himself, but found he needed financial support from the city or state to make it happen. Local politicians were sympathetic to the problems inherent in the facility, and created an entity called the Maryland Sports Complex Authority, designed to "provide for a sports complex and related facilities in the greater Baltimore region." There was much talk but little action, and as the years went by, Rosenbloom lost patience. He sold the club to Robert Irsay in 1972.

Between 1966 and 1976, fourteen new stadiums were built to house NFL teams. That represented more than half of the league, and the folks in Baltimore wanted to get in on the action. The MSCA had drafted plans for a domed stadium—dubbed "Baltodome"—but the state legislature refused to approve funding. They were concerned that funding the project would require higher taxes, and the region was already suffering an economic downturn. Then in the fall of 1974, Baltimore voters passed a ballot measure called Question P, which actually prohibited the use of city funds to construct a new stadium.

Obviously, this did not make Irsay happy. He had anticipated the construction of a new stadium when he bought the Colts. While his public comments urged the MSCA to take action, he began to court offers from other cities. Among the acknowledged suitors were Phoenix, Indianapolis, Memphis, and Jacksonville. The latter was so impressive with their pursuit that Irsay reportedly said after a visit, "It's not a matter of if I'm leaving Baltimore but where I'm going."

That was mostly an idle threat until the Raiders won their lawsuit and moved to Los Angeles in 1982. The Colts signed a two-year lease to stay at Memorial Stadium through the 1983 season. Irsay continued to talk with representatives in other cities, and the lease expired with no progress being made toward a new football stadium in Baltimore.

During this time, the city of Indianapolis completed construction on a domed stadium, the Hoosier Dome. They didn't have a tenant, but they pulled out all the stops in their pursuit of the Colts. The facility was one of the first to feature a ring of luxury skyboxes, and the color scheme throughout was Colts blue. This made them the clear favorite in Irsay's mind.

Baltimore mayor William Donald Schaeffer and Maryland governor Harry Hughes scrambled to come up with an offer that would keep the Colts in town. When it began to look like those efforts might be unsuccessful, the mayor and governor opted for another strategy. They asked the Maryland legislature to enact legislation that would allow the city or state to seize the team through eminent domain proceedings. On March 27, 1984, the state senate did exactly that, an overplaying of their hand that forced Irsay to react dramatically.

With news of the resolution's passage in the headlines the following morning, Irsay feared that a seizure was imminent. He hastily concluded negotiations with representatives in Indianapolis and made plans for an immediate departure. Late that afternoon, eleven trucks from the Mayflower moving company were lined up at the team's headquarters in Owings Mills. Irsay's legal advisers were so concerned about seizure that they insisted the first truck be loaded with the team's critical legal and financial documents. They also ordered each of the trucks to take a different route out of town, fearing that local law enforcement would try to stop them. By ten o'clock that evening, the news media had been tipped off and had descended on the Colts' office complex to film the retreat. As snow flurries fell, the Mayflower fans departed and before the sun rose again, the Colts were gone.

To this day, people in Baltimore paint Irsay as the villain, and he certainly deserves his share of blame for uprooting a popular and beloved team. But in the twenty years that have followed, this scenario played itself out in other cities, and the outcome was often the same. The fans and politicians who refused to build a new stadium often watched helplessly as that team moved somewhere else.

Things were much less contentious when the Cardinals left St. Louis after the 1987 season. Owner Bill Bidwill, whose father had purchased the team in 1932, grew frustrated over his inability to convince local officials to build a new stadium. He was lured to Arizona and the cavernous Sun Devil Stadium, located on the campus of Arizona State University.

It wouldn't be fair to say that the folks in St. Louis were completely indifferent to the loss of their football team, but they took it in stride. In a poll conducted by the *St. Louis Post-Dispatch* that winter, fans were asked whether they were more upset by the loss of the football team or the departure of free agent first baseman Jack Clark from the Cardinals baseball team. Football prevailed, but just barely. The final tally was 51 percent to 49 percent.

Who Played the Game

At times, nobody played. The players went on strike twice during the decade. Business was booming for the National Football League and with soaring attendance and multimillion dollar television contracts, the players wanted to increase their share of the windfall. They also wanted to reap the same benefits as their baseball brethren, whose strong union had helped them achieve major gains. Midway through the 1981 season, baseball players went on strike to prevent owners from implementing a compensation system that they thought would dramatically weaken free agency. The players prevailed, and the baseball season resumed.

That emboldened the 1500 members of the NFL Players Association. With negotiations on their new collective bargaining agreement opening that winter, the players made an audacious proposal. They wanted the owners to agree to commit a fixed amount of gross revenues to player salaries—55 percent. The owners refused. The NFLPA wasn't nearly as strong as the baseball union, and NFL owners saw no reason to give ground.

After playing the first two weeks of the regular season, NFL players walked out. Their strike lasted for fifty-seven days, which was at the time the longest work stoppage in the history of professional sports. The players achieved some modest gains but not the kind of sweeping wage reforms they had sought. Instead, the owners agreed to raise minimum salaries and improve benefits.

Five years later, the players threatened to strike again over a number of issues, the most significant of which was free agency. The NFL had a system in place, but it provided that any team that signed a player must provide compensation to the player's former team. In practice, most teams viewed the compensation as too prohibitive a price to pay, and very little player movement was taking place. NFL players wanted the open market for player services that existed in baseball, not only for the freedom that it offered but also for the higher salaries that were sure to follow.

The average salary for baseball players rose from $51,501 in 1976 to $412,520 in 1986. The football players still lagged behind, with average salaries of about $90,000 in 1982 climbing to about $214,000 in 1987. The Player's Association argued that most of these increases had come due to competition from the rival USFL, and that gains had been relatively flat after that league's demise. With negotiations providing little progress toward those goals, the players threatened to strike during the 1987 season.

NFL owners vowed that they would continue to operate and play the schedule without them. Many viewed this as an empty threat, but a week after the player strike began, NFL teams returned to the field with replacement players. The quality of play was questionable, but the networks were obligated to broadcast the games, and fans who held tickets weren't getting refunds.

To counter this, NFL players decided to man picket lines, a move that quickly became a public relations nightmare. Local newscasts in every NFL city carried footage of the striking players harassing their replacements—cursing at them, spitting on them, vandalizing their cars. Whatever public support the players had quickly faded.

The solidarity among the striking players began to crack as well. That first week, a handful of players crossed the picket line to play. By the third week, that number had grown to nearly two hundred, and included many of the league's biggest stars. With their resolve crumbling, the players gave up and returned to work.

At the time, this seemed like a humbling defeat, but the players' failure in 1987 actually set them on the path to victory. They decertified their union and brought their case to federal court as a class-action suit. They eventually prevailed in that case in 1992, and the threat of more legal action brought both parties back to the negotiating table. By 1993, they'd hammered out an agreement that both sides were happy with, and they've continued to extend that agreement each time it expires. Players were granted liberal free agency in exchange for a salary cap. This allowed the teams to contain their costs while allowing individual players the opportunity to offer their services on the open market.

Each time this collective bargaining agreement expired, the players and owners simply decided to extend it. This happened most recently in 2006, when the agreement was extended through the 2011 season. That's a good indication of how mutually beneficial the system is, and it works for fans too. Unlike the systems used in baseball and basketball, it's unusual to see big stars change teams through free agency in football.

More important, this agreement helped provide pro football with labor peace in the 1990s, a tumultuous period where baseball, basketball, and hockey all suffered through devastating labor conflicts. A lengthy strike by baseball players shortened two seasons and prompted owners to cancel the 1994 World Series. The NBA (1998–99) and NHL (1994–95) each lost half a season due to a lockout. (Another NHL lockout cancelled the entire 2004–05 season.) The NFL, on the other hand, has now gone for more than two decades without a work stoppage.

How the Game Was Played

Rules changes in the late 1970s helped to open up the passing game, and a number of teams capitalized with aggressive aerial attacks. Many of these teams were in the AFC, such as the Chargers, Dolphins, and Broncos.

Some of the NFC teams resisted that trend and focused on their ground attack. Perhaps the most successful example was the Washington Redskins, who went to three Super Bowls in a six-year span. Head coach Joe Gibbs built an offense around the power running game, and the foundation was a massive offensive line known as "the Hogs." As if that wasn't enough, Gibbs often employed a two-tight end formation to increase the number of blockers and enhance pass protection. A staple of the playbook was the counter play, where the running back would start with a step in one direction before reversing and running in the other direction. Overaggressive defenders would be eaten alive, and often those who chose to stay in place would simply get run over.

To counter this, one team came up with a particularly innovative approach. Chicago's defensive coordinator Buddy Ryan dubbed it the 46 defense, after the uniform number of safety Doug Plank, who played a key role in the unusual scheme. The 46 started like a normal 4-3 alignment, but Plank moved closer to the line to play alongside middle linebacker Mike Singletary. Both outside linebackers would play right up on the line over the tight end, and the four defensive linemen would shift to the weak side. This left two corners in man coverage on wide receivers, a free safety playing deep for insurance, and eight men right on the line. Opponents didn't have anywhere to run, and if they tried to pass they would be faced with an overwhelming pass rush. The Bears went 15-1 in 1985 and stormed through the postseason, winning Super Bowl XX over the Patriots. Including the playoffs, the Bears held fourteen of their nineteen opponents to 10 points or less.

The Bears' success didn't spawn many imitators, because coaches figured out a way to counter the pressure that the 46 created. They simply spread their receivers out and threw quick passes.

Where Great Quarterbacks Come From

The 1983 draft featured a number of great players, including Eric Dickerson, Bruce Matthews, and Darrel Green. History, however, will remember it for what was regarded as the greatest crop of quarterbacks to come out of college in a single season. Six were taken in all, and as a group they combined for twenty-four pro bowl appearances and eleven Super Bowls.

Individually, however, the stories are much different. Three of those quarterbacks—John Elway, Jim Kelly, and Dan Marino—have been inducted into the Pro Football Hall of Fame. The other three had mixed success. Ken O'Brien spent eight years as the Jets starter but never became a star. Tony Eason took the Patriots to a Super Bowl in his third season, but only held on to the starting job for another year. Todd Blackledge struggled for a few years in Kansas City and never made much of an impact.

As Hamlet said, "there's the rub." For every superstar quarterback selected in the first round, it seems there's another example of a guy who never lived up to the expectations, and maybe even was a bust. And of course, people love to point out that Joe Montana wasn't selected until the third round, or that Tom Brady was a sixth-round pick.

This raises two fundamental questions: 1) How many good quarterbacks come from the top of the draft and how many are still available in later rounds, and 2) What are the odds that a quarterback taken at the top of the draft will pan out?

There are several variables that make it challenging to study these questions, but all of them are easy to address. First, you need to have an objective method for evaluating the quarterbacks. What precisely constitutes a bust and what constitutes a star? For the purposes of answering these questions, we don't need to concern ourselves with subtle distinctions. What we need is a method to group the quarterbacks into four or five broad categories.

Second, you need to account for changes that have occurred in the draft over the years. The number of rounds has decreased while the number of teams has increased. The No. 55 pick overall was a third-round pick in 1975 but a mid-second-round pick in 2005.

Third, you need to have a way to separate quarterbacks whose careers are just starting from those whose are over. Any statistical measure will be biased against the youngest players in your sample.

To accomplish this, I decided to look at all of the quarterbacks who made their debut between 1978 and 2002. Why those dates? Quarterbacks drafted after 2002 would have played no more than five seasons as this book goes to press, so it's far too early to include them. Labeling any of those guys a bust or a superstar at this point would simply be speculation. And by starting with 1978, that gives us an even twenty-five years. If we included guys before 1978, we'd also have to make adjustments for the switch from the fourteen-game schedule to sixteen, and if we went back into the 1960s we'd have to start accounting for differences between the two leagues. Using 1978 gives us a clean starting point.

Those time limits give us a group of 353 quarterbacks who were drafted by NFL teams and seventy-four who were undrafted and made their NFL debut in 1978 or later. That's a total of 427 quarterbacks during the twenty-five-year period.

Next, I came up with a quick-and-dirty method for ranking quarterbacks, based on career passing yards. I broke them into five categories. Superstars are players with at least 28000 career passing yards, and this includes guys like Dan Marino and John Elway. Starters had 15000 or more career passing yards. These tend to be quarterbacks who established themselves as quality starters, but weren't racking up a lot of Pro Bowl appearances. Examples would be Jay Schroeder and Mark Brunell. Reserves (5000 passing yards) are quarterbacks who may have spent a season or two as a starter but spent most of their career as a backup. Frank Reich and Jack Trudeau are two good examples. Fringe QBs (minimum 1 pass attempt) are guys who actually played in the NFL, but probably were never more than a backup or an emergency starter. Recent examples include Billy Volek and Jonathon Quinn. The last category we have is Bust, which is reserved for quarterbacks that were drafted but never attempted a pass in the NFL. These are guys you might not have heard of, unless you follow the college game, players like Giovanni Carmazzi or Dave Marler. It also includes drafted quarterbacks who simply opted not to play pro football, like Rick Leach.

For each player, then, I looked at the range of where they were drafted. I grouped players who were taken with the first twenty picks in a draft, then players picked between twenty-one and forty, and so on. Once I got above 100, I grouped them by fifty, and every player taken after the 300th pick (that's the discontinued tenth round or later) goes into the final group. Players who weren't drafted at all go into another group.

Now, I wouldn't argue that this is the most rigorous method for analyzing the success of pro quarterbacks, but for the purposes of this study it seems sufficient for grouping the players into broad categories. What we're looking for here are some general conclusions. I'm not asking whether Troy Aikman was better than Steve Young. It's enough to know that these two players are more similar to each other than to Erik Kramer and Jeff Blake.

The results appear in the table, Quarterbacks Drafted 1978–2002. It shows that since 1978, nine quarterbacks who were selected within the first twenty picks turned into Superstars. These were players like Troy Aikman, Jim Kelly, and John Elway. Fifteen players drafted that high became what we call Starters, guys such as Tim Couch, Kerry Collins, and Jeff George. Ten of the quarterbacks drafted in the top twenty are classified as Reserves, including Marc Wilson, Rick Mirer, and Todd Blackledge. Ten of the top twenty players only managed to qualify as Fringe QBs (Akili Smith, Andre Ware, and Heath Shuler). None of them was a Bust, at least by our definition, meaning that no quarterback drafted in the first twenty picks failed to attempt at least one pass in the NFL. In all, forty-four quarterbacks were drafted in the first twenty picks between 1978 and 2002.

If you read the chapter on Q-ratings, you'll recall that talent is not evenly distributed; there are

Range	20	40	60	80	100	150	200	250	300	300+	UND	Total	% QBs
Superstar	9	4	0	0	1	0	0	0	0	0	3	17	4.0
Starter	15	4	2	2	3	4	3	3	0	1	5	42	9.8
Reserve	10	3	7	3	5	7	5	4	2	0	3	49	11.5
Fringe	10	6	10	9	16	28	21	17	10	4	63	194	45.4
Bust	0	1	1	2	2	9	20	33	29	28	-	125	29.3
Total	44	18	20	16	27	48	49	57	41	33	74	427	
% QBs	10.3	4.2	4.7	3.7	6.3	11.2	11.5	13.3	9.6	7.7	17.3		

always more bad quarterbacks than mediocre ones, and more mediocre ones than great ones. Looking at the totals in the last column, you see that just 4.6 percent of the quarterbacks who were drafted or signed since 1978 qualify as Superstars, while nearly three-quarters (74.7 percent) fall into either the Fringe or Bust category. These guys come and go, but the great ones are hard to find.

If you're going to get a Superstar quarterback in the draft, you'd better show up early. Of the seventeen quarterbacks who qualify, only one great quarterback was drafted lower than fortieth. That was Joe Montana, grabbed at the end of the third round by San Francisco in 1979.

Looking a little further, you'll see that half of the quarterbacks who qualified as starters—15000 career passing yards—were taken within the first sixty selections. That equates to the first two rounds of the thirty-two-team draft. The conclusion is pretty clear: If you want a starting quarterback, you're most likely going to have to get him from the top of the draft.

This begs the next question, which is perhaps more important. How often do the quarterbacks taken with those high draft choices pan out? Looking at the first twenty picks, we find that approximately 55 percent of those quarterbacks become Superstars or Starters. That number drops to 44 percent for the next twenty picks, and then plummets to 10 percent for picks forty-one to sixty. The next table shows the likelihood of success with each range of draft picks.

Likelihood of Success Drafting a Quarterback

Based on 1978–2002 drafts

Range	Superstar or Starter	Reserve or Fringe	Bust
1–20	54.5%	45.5%	0.0%
21–40	44.4	50.0	5.6
41–60	10.0	85.0	5.0
61–80	12.5	75.0	12.5
81–100	14.8	77.8	7.4
101–150	8.3	72.9	18.8
151–200	6.1	53.1	40.8
201–250	5.3	36.8	57.9
251–300	0.0	29.3	70.7
300+	3.0	12.1	84.8
Total	13.8	56.9	29.3

The odds of finding a good quarterback drop dramatically after the first forty picks. While it's possible to find a Joe Montana with the eighty-third pick or a Tom Brady at number 199, the odds of landing a quality quarterback that late in the draft are pretty slim. You're more likely to end up with Mark Vlasic or Gino Torretta. The idea that you can get your next starter from the third round or even the late second is mostly wishful thinking. Sure, it can happen, just like it's possible to find a starter from the Arena League, but the odds aren't in your favor.

The 1990s

Best Team Season
1998 Minnesota Vikings, 15-1

Best Team of the Decade
San Francisco 49ers (113-47)

Winners of Multiple Championships
Dallas Cowboys (1992, 1993, and 1995); Denver Broncos (1997 and 1998)

Worst Team Seasons
1990 New England Patriots, 1-15; 1991 Indianapolis Colts, 1-15; 1996 New York Jets, 1-15

Worst Team of the Decade
Cincinnati Bengals (52-108)

New Teams
The league welcomed three expansion teams: the Carolina Panthers and Jacksonville Jaguars in 1995, and a new version of the Cleveland Browns in 1999.

Significant Moves
Los Angeles lost both of its teams in 1995, with the Raiders moving back up to Oakland and the Rams heading to St. Louis. The Cleveland Browns moved to Baltimore in 1996, changing their name to the Ravens. A year later, the Houston Oilers moved to Tennessee. After playing one season in Memphis they moved to Nashville and in 1999 changed their name to the Tennessee Titans.

Most Passing Touchdowns
Season: 41, Kurt Warner, Rams, 1999
Decade: 235, Brett Favre, Packers

Most Rushing Yards
Season: 2053, Barry Sanders, Lions, 1997; 2008, Terrell Davis, Broncos, 1998
Decade: 13963 Emmitt Smith, Cowboys; 13799, Barry Sanders, Lions

Most Receptions
Season: 123, Herman Moore, Detroit, 1995; 122, Cris Carter, Vikings, 1994 and 1995; 122, Jerry Rice, 49ers, 1995
Decade: 860, Jerry Rice, 49ers

Best Coaching Record
.719, George Seifert, 92-36, 49ers and Panthers

Biggest Player
Jerome Daniels (6-foot-5, 355 pounds) was a guard/tackle who lasted just one year with the

Where They Played

Nine new NFL stadiums opened during the nineties, and ground was broken for eight more that were completed between 2000 and 2003. That seems like an extraordinary amount of new facilities, but football's building boom was modest compared to the other major sports. Eight new baseball parks opened during the 1990s, as did twenty-nine arenas for use by NBA and NHL teams. As a group, the four leagues christened forty-six new buildings during the nineties. When all of their construction was finished in the mid-2000s, two-thirds of all their teams had a new place to play.

New Stadiums Opened from 1990 to 2007

League	2000s	90s	% of teams
NFL	9	9	53
MLB	9	8	57
NBA	5	11	79
NHL	4	10	73
NBA/NHL shared	0	8	
Total	**27**	**46**	**65**

The booming economy was the driving force behind most of the stadium and arena projects. With budget surpluses, taxpayers were more willing to provide public funds for such projects than they had ever been in the past. In some places, this spending bordered on wasteful. In Memphis, for example, the city spent $250 million to build FedEx Forum as a home for the Memphis Grizzlies basketball team. They did this despite the fact that the Grizzlies were playing in an arena that was built for them less than ten years earlier. The city of San Antonio built the Alamo Dome in 1993 and then the AT&T Center in 2001. The only major tenant in each case was the NBA Spurs, and each building cost local taxpayers between $175 and $200 million.

Those weren't the only communities to go hog wild. Seven cities each built three new sports venues: Philadelphia, Atlanta, Houston, Phoenix, Seattle, Cleveland, and Denver. I suppose you could even count the San Francisco–San Jose area as an eighth.

Aside from the fact that they had the money, why was there such a rush to spend public funds to build stadiums? One reason was the same old one, the idea that without a new place to play the economic pressures would force the hometown team to move. This tactic had been used, with varying degrees of success, since the 1950s.

But a new tactic emerged in the 1990s, an argument that a major league team made a significant impact on the local economy. Both local politicians and team owners made the case that a major league team creates jobs, attracts tourists, and generates tax revenues. Therefore, they argued, it's in the public's interest to pay for a new stadium.

In his 1997 book *Major League Losers,* Professor Mark Rosentraub blasted that idea, calling publicly funded stadiums nothing more than corporate welfare. While he acknowledged that sports teams made a real contribution to a community's quality of life, their contribution to the economy was much smaller than people thought. Rosentraub, director of the Center for Urban Policy and the Environment, argued that the craze for stadium building served only one purpose—to put money into the pockets of wealthy team owners. While most economists and scholars agreed with his conclusions, fans across the United States and southern Canada were not swayed by reason.

Three of the new NFL stadiums built in the 1990s were upgrades for existing teams. Aging facilities in Washington and Tampa were replaced with new ones, and a new domed stadium in Atlanta not only gave the Falcons a new home but also helped the city's bid to host the Summer Olympics.

In six other NFL cities, new stadiums were built to help land an expansion team or encourage an existing team to move there. Cleveland, Jacksonville, and Charlotte went the expansion route, while St. Louis, Baltimore, and Nashville lured teams away from other cities.

Who Played the Game

Underclassmen became eligible for the NFL draft in 1989, and a wave of college players began to seize the opportunity to come out early. By 2000, 472 players had opted to forgo their remaining college eligibility and declare for the draft. Nearly half of them (208, or 44 percent) went unselected.

Fifty-one of those eligible underclassmen were top ten picks, including six who were selected No. 1 overall.

How the Game Was Played

One system dominated most of the conversations about football strategy during the decades. The West Coast Offense helped the 49ers win four Super Bowls in the 1980s, and by the early 1990s a whole legion of imitators had been spawned.

The system was actually born in the early seventies in Cincinnati under a young assistant coach named Bill Walsh. He favored the vertical passing attack, but Bengals quarterback Virgil Carter did not have a very strong arm. Walsh devised a system of short, quick, timed throws, and the goal was to control the ball with the forward pass.

Rather than depending on big pass plays, the strategy relied on high percentage passing and an opportunistic running game. Critics called it a nickel-and-dime offense, but it enabled the Bengals to move the ball effectively, control the clock, and keep the opposing team's offense off the field. When defenses focused on stopping the pesky short plays, they created an opportunity for the big strike down the field.

Walsh spent a year as the San Diego Chargers offensive coordinator and two years as the head coach at Stanford. He implemented the Cincinnati offense in each place, but it didn't get a lot of attention until he became head coach of the San Francisco 49ers. Because Walsh spent those years in California, his system was dubbed the West Coast Offense. No matter what you call it, Walsh's system began to spread rapidly through both the college and professional ranks.

The West Coast Offense was based on four basic principles.

- Control the ball with the passing game. Walsh advocated a quick three-step drop and throwing a quick out or hitch or slant. In most coverages, the defense will allow you to complete these passes. That 5-yard play has a high likelihood of success, and there's little risk of a sack or interception. It's easier to gain 5 yards passing this way than to get a 5-yard rushing play. Timing is the key element, and the pass rush is mitigated by having the quarterback get rid of the ball almost immediately. In essence, the West Coast Offense is more about this basic philosophy than it is a collection of specific plays.

- Avoid tendencies. So much of what defenses do to prepare is to identify patterns in your offense. They notice things—that your team rarely throws on first down inside the 25 yard line; that if the tight end goes in motion you run the ball the other way; with a three receiver formation, you like to throw to the running back. With the West Coast Offense, you are prepared to throw the ball on any down and from any spot on the field. The defense has no idea what you're going to do in a given circumstance. They can't rely on nickelbacks or pass rushing specialists simply based on the down and distance.

- Spread the defense out, both horizontally and vertically. The field is 160 feet wide, and it makes sense to force the defenders to cover as much of that width as possible. Zone defenses get stressed as they get stretched, and the farther apart the defenders are, the easier it is for receivers to find a seam. Likewise, don't let the defensive backs become content. If they know your pass patterns are all within 15 yards of the line of scrimmage, the area they have to cover is dramatically reduced.

- Create mismatches. Using substitution, motion, and multiple formations, you can create mismatches or force the defense into predictable coverages. You try to get a linebacker covering a slot receiver or an undersized cornerback covering your tight end. These mismatches can lead to game-changing plays.

The philosophy is pretty simple, but putting the offense into place is difficult. Because the passing game is based on timing, a lot of practice and repetition is necessary before things start working consistently.

The complexity of the system meant that coaches couldn't simply take a playbook and implement the West Coast Offense. Because the timing and choreography are the heart of the system, not the plays, it takes an experienced coach to teach it. Across the league, teams began to hire head coaches who had been assistants under Walsh, eager for them to implement the West Coast Offense with their team. Among them were Mike Holmgren, George Seifert, Dennis Green, Brian Billick, Jim Fassel, Ray Rhodes, Bruce Coslett, and Sam Wyche. Those coaches spawned more protégés, and by the end of the nineties, half of the league was running some version of the West Coast Offense.

Can Scrambling Quarterbacks Win Championships?

In the mid-1990s, scrambling quarterbacks were all the rage. Many teams began to place a high value on having a signal caller who was not only mobile enough to escape a sack, but able to improvise and make something out of nothing. Paul Attner, the veteran football writer for the *Sporting News,* summed up the theory like this: "Confronted by quicker, strong defensive players, quarterbacks with legs have a better opportunity to find ways to make plays. And to win championships."

Scrambling quarterbacks were nothing new. The college ranks were full of them, but the conventional wisdom had long been that to play at the professional level, you had to learn to be a pocket passer.

This view clearly changed in the 1990s. Scramblers like Jeff Garcia, Steve McNair, and Kordell Stewart led their teams into the playoffs, and that just prompted teams to draft more scramblers—guys like Donovan McNabb, Daunte Culpepper, and Aaron Brooks. The following table shows just how dramatically this change swept through the league.

Quarterbacks with 400+ Rushing Yards in a Season

Decade	Number
2000s*	20
1990s	13
1980s	7
1970s	5
1960s	3
1950s	2
1940s	0

*through 2007

Still, while the consensus was that a scrambling quarterback could help to boost a struggling offense, there was considerable debate over whether a team could succeed in the long run with that kind of player under center.

Is a mobile quarterback necessary to win a championship? Obviously, the answer is no. Take a quick glance at the quarterbacks who have won recent Super Bowls, and you won't see a lot of mobility. What you'll find are the classic drop-back passers, guys like Tom Brady and Peyton Manning.

The table below shows how many rushing yards the winning quarterbacks for the 1990s Super Bowls had during the regular season. The trend got worse in the decade that followed. From 2000 to 2006, quarterbacks who won the Super Bowl averaged 49 rushing yards during the regular season, and none of them had more than 75.

Rushing Yards During Super Bowl Winning Season (1990s)

Quarterback	Year	Team	Rush	Yards	TDs
Kurt Warner	1999	StL	23	92	1
John Elway	1998	Den	37	94	1
John Elway	1997	Den	50	218	1
Brett Favre	1996	GB	49	136	2
Troy Aikman	1995	Dal	21	32	1
Steve Young	1994	Dal	58	293	7
Troy Aikman	1993	Dal	32	125	0
Troy Aikman	1992	Dal	37	105	1
Doug Williams	1991	Was	15	6	1
Phil Simms*	1990	NYG	21	61	1

* Phil Simms started fourteen games before suffering an injury. He did not play in Super Bowl XXV.

Young is the only one of this bunch who could be described as a pure scrambler. Elway was more mobile when he was younger, but by the time he won those two Super Bowls he was much more stationary.

Three hundred and fifty rushing yards in a season—that's slightly more than twenty yards a game if you play sixteen games in a season. That doesn't seem like a remarkably high threshold, but let's use that to identify quarterbacks who use their legs to help their team. Since the beginning of the Super Bowl era in 1966, quarterbacks have reached that mark in a season fifty-nine times. How many of those fifty-nine seasons ended with a trip to the Super Bowl? Exactly none.

If we use their regular season rushing totals to measure how much the Super Bowl quarterbacks contributed on the ground, the results become even clearer. The next table shows that Roger Staubach had the most rushing yards of any quarterback that went to the Super Bowl, and he was victorious in Super Bowl VI. Seven of the other top ten were not so lucky.

Most Regular Season Rushing Yards by Super Bowl QBs

Quarterback	Year	Team	Rush	Yards	TD	Res
Roger Staubach	1971	Dal	41	343	2	W
Steve McNair	1999	Ten	72	337	8	L
Ken Anderson	1981	Cin	46	320	1	L
Roger Staubach	1975	Dal	55	316	4	L
John Elway	1987	Den	66	304	4	L
Steve Young	1994	SF	58	293	7	W
John Elway	1986	Den	52	257	1	L
Jim McMahon	1985	Chi	47	252	3	W
Boomer Esiason	1988	Cin	43	248	1	L
John Elway	1989	Den	48	244	3	L

If you look at the eighty-four regular-season performances for quarterbacks who started a Super Bowl game, you find that less than half rushed for as much as 100 yards. Two-thirds rushed for less than 150 yards in their Super Bowl season. As to our original question, if we ask "can scrambling quarterbacks win championships?"— the answer clearly is "they haven't yet."

So why the fascination with scramblers? There's no question that quarterbacks who run with the ball can find regular-season success. Roughly 46 percent of teams with scrambling quarterbacks (based on this definition) reached the playoffs, compared to 34.5 percent with nonscrambling quarterbacks (see table below). About two-thirds of them finished with a winning record, compared to about a third of the non-scramblers.

What seems to be clear is that quarterbacks who run can win regular-season games, and they have been pretty successful at getting their teams into the post-season. As Paul Attner suggested, one of the assets these guys have is the ability to ad lib, to create something from nothing. Very often, the scrambling quarterbacks run so much because they don't have a lot of weapons around them. Their contributions help compensate for those sort of problems.

Attner theorized that quarterbacks who run are more likely to make plays against tough defenses. The evidence suggests that the opposite is true. In the postseason you face a good defense every week, and those teams are more likely to have the speed, strength, and discipline to contain a quarterback who likes to run. The ability to improvise is generally neutralized. All too often, when these quarterbacks are forced to stay in the pocket, they are less likely to make big plays downfield. Since their first instinct has been to run, they haven't developed the patience to stand up to the pressure, and let the receivers get open to make a play downfield.

If you don't have a dominant running back and your receiving corps isn't a serious threat, a scrambling quarterback adds a dimension to your offense that can help you win despite your offense's limited talent. However, if history is any indication, quarterbacks who run the ball can't translate that regular-season success into championships. The scramblers who did win Super Bowls—like Steve Young and John Elway—both got their rings later in their career, when they were running less and letting the players around them make more plays. That hasn't stopped NFL teams from continuing to salivate over scramblers, but maybe it should.

Team Success Based on Rushing Yards by Starting QB (1966–2007)

RushYds	Num	W	L	T	Pct	WinRec	Pct	Post	Pct
650+	6	46	46	2	.500	3	50.0	2	50.0
600-649	4	38	26	0	.594	3	75.0	3	75.0
550-599	3	27	21	0	.562	1	33.3	1	33.3
500-549	10	91	59	3	.605	7	70.0	4	40.0
450-499	9	87	57	0	.604	7	77.8	7	77.8
400-449	14	105	117	0	.473	6	42.9	4	28.6
350-399	14	116	93	5	.554	10	71.4	7	50.0
Total	**60**	**510**	**419**	**10**	**.548**	**37**	**61.7**	**28**	**46.7**
<350	1134	8540	8629	146	.497	528	46.6	391	34.5

The 2000s

DECADE IN A BOX

All figures are through the 2007 season.

Best Team Season
2007 New England Patriots, 16-0

Best Team of the Decade
New England Patriots (91-37); Indianapolis Colts (89-39);

Winners of Multiple Championships
New England Patriots (2001, 2003, and 2004)

Worst Team Season
2000 San Diego Chargers, 1-15; 2001 Carolina Panthers, 1-15; 2007 Miami Dolphins, 1-15

Worst Team of the Decade
Detroit Lions (40-88); Houston Texans (32-64); Arizona Cardinals (43-85)

New Teams
The Houston Texans were added as an expansion team in 2002. This brought the total number of teams to thirty-two and made it an opportune time to realign. The league switched from three divisions in each conference to four, and the Seattle Seahawks moved from the AFC to the NFC.

Significant Moves
The New Orleans Saints were displaced in 2005 after Hurricane Katrina ravaged the Gulf Coast region. The devastating storm struck less than two weeks before the start of the NFL's regular season. Massive flooding displaced most of the area's population, and the Saints home stadium—the Louisiana Superdome—was severely damaged. Strong winds had ripped holes in the roof and flooded the interior. Perhaps more significant, the building was being used as a shelter for thousands of local citizens who had been forced out of their homes.

After spending the first week of the season on the road, the Saints were scheduled to return home for a Week 2 game with the Giants. With the Superdome unavailable, the league moved the game to the Meadowlands, the Giants' home stadium.

The Saints made arrangements to play their next two home games at the Alamodome in San Antonio, drawing surprisingly large crowds of 58,688 and 65,562. In an effort to move closer to home, the Saints played their next four home games at Tiger Stadium on the LSU campus in Baton Rouge. The crowds there were much smaller. After drawing 61,000 for a late October game against the Dolphins, subsequent contests attracted less than 35,000 each. This prompted a return to San Antonio for their last scheduled home game, and attendance topped 63,000.

The Saints returned to New Orleans and a rebuilt Superdome in 2006, giving the struggling city's recovery effort a big emotional boost.

Most Passing Touchdowns
Season: 50, Tom Brady, Patriots
Decade: 254, Peyton Manning, Colts

Most Rushing Yards
Season: 2066, Jamal Lewis, Ravens, 2003
Decade: 10650, LaDainian Tomlinson, Chargers

Most Receptions
Season: 143, Marvin Harrison, Colts, 2002
Decade: 753, Torry Holt, Rams

Best Coaching Record
.719, Tony Dungy, 92-36, Buccaneers and Colts; .711, Bill Belichick, 91-37, Patriots

Biggest Player
Aaron Gibson was 6-foot-6 and 386 pounds when he came out of college. At least fourteen other players played multiple seasons weighing over 350 pounds during the decade.

Smallest Player
Kick returner Lamont Brightful (5-foot-10, 165 pounds)

All-Decade Team
Offense

QB	Peyton Manning
RB	LaDainian Tomlinson
RB	Tiki Barber
WR	Marvin Harrison
WR	Torry Holt
TE	Tony Gonzalez
C	Kevin Mawae
G	Will Shields
G	Alan Faneca
T	Walter Jones
T	Jonathon Ogden

Defense

DL	Jason Taylor
DL	Michael Strahan
DL	La'Roi Glover
DL	Warren Sapp
LB	Derrick Brooks
LB	Ray Lewis
LB	Joey Porter
LB	Zach Thomas
DB	Champ Bailey
DB	Ronde Barber
DB	Brian Dawkins
DB	John Lynch

Special Teams

K	Matt Stover
P	Shane Lechler
Ret	Dante Hall

Where They Played

Eight new stadiums opened between 2000 and 2003, remnants of the building boom that swept the country in the mid-1990s. All of them were football-only stadiums.

The Seattle Seahawks spent two seasons playing at the University of Washington's Husky Stadium while their new facility was under construction.

The Bears left Chicago for a year to play on the campus of the University of Illinois. While they were gone, Soldier Field was completely renovated, to the point that it could be considered a completely new stadium. A similarly thorough makeover occurred at Green Bay's Lambeau Field, although the Packers weren't forced to relocate during the construction.

Who Played the Game

At the beginning of the 1990s, roughly half of the NFL players were African-American. By 2002, that number had increased to over 70 percent. But at the same time, the league only had two African-American head coaches.

Public criticism began to mount in 2000, when ten head coaching positions were open and none was filled by an African American. Since Art Shell had become the NFL's first African-American head coach in 1989, eighty of the eighty-three openings were filled by white coaches.

The public outcry forced the NFL to examine its hiring policies to understand why minority coaches weren't getting coaching opportunities. What they found was interesting. The problem wasn't that teams were unwilling to consider African-American candidates. Rather, many teams simply didn't have a formal coaching search when they had an opening. They picked a guy who was already an assistant coach, or somebody who was a friend of the owner or general manager. It was a classic example of "the old boy's club." Promising candidates who didn't have the right connections were never getting a chance to compete for those jobs.

Steelers owner Dan Rooney proposed a simple solution, which came to be known as the Rooney Rule. It required that each team interview at least one minority candidate when it filled a head coaching vacancy, and the league would maintain a list of qualified candidates for teams to consult.

The rule was enacted in 2003, and it faced a challenge right away. After the 49ers fired head coach Steve Mariucci, Detroit's general manager Matt Millen leapt on the opportunity to hire him. He hastily arranged interviews with some other candidates to adhere to the letter of the rule. Several African-American coaches were invited to interview for the job, but they all declined, since it seemed clear that Millen has already made his decision. Because the hiring of Mariucci violated the spirit of the Rooney Rule, the Lions were fined $200,000.

The Rooney Rule made an immediate impact. In the five years before it was enacted, only one of the thirty-eight head coaching vacancies was filled by an African-American candidate (2.6 percent). In the five years that followed, the numbers rose to six of thirty-two (18.8 percent). Similar improvements followed for assistant coaches and front office staff.

How the Game Was Played

The obsession with the West Coast Offense began to cool somewhat. This was partly due to the realization that the system didn't work without the right personnel. Many of the teams who had embraced the West Coast Offense as a panacea began to revert to more typical offensive approaches.

Two defensive innovations took hold during the first part of the decade. One was the zone blitz, developed by Dick LeBeau when he was the Pittsburgh Steelers defensive coordinator. The foundation was a 3-4 alignment, but relying heavily on cornerbacks and safeties to bring pressure on the quarterback. Linebackers and even defensive linemen would drop into pass coverage, and it was very difficult for opposing quarterbacks and linemen to know where the blitz would be coming from. Blocking schemes based on assigning a lineman to a defender often broke down. By the middle of the decade, nearly a dozen teams were using the zone blitz.

The other major defensive innovation was the cover-2 defense, popularized by Tony Dungy of the Buccaneers. It was based on the two-deep safety coverage devised by Pittsburgh's Bud Carson when Dungy was a safety with the Steelers.

Dungy and his defensive coordinator, Monte Kiffin, created a base defense out of Carson's coverage scheme, adapting it to be used on every down. The purpose was to counteract the quick strike passes of the West Coast Offense, and it was very effective.

From a base 4-3 alignment, the field was divided into five short zones, each about seven yards deep. The three linebackers and two cornerbacks each played tight coverage against any receiver who came into their zone, and they could afford to be aggressive because they had help from the two safeties behind them. The general principle was to make a tradeoff between giving up the short gains and preventing any big plays.

The Death of Astroturf

Astroturf came to the NFL in 1969, when the Houston Oilers moved into the Astrodome. Although it was a brand name for a product developed by Monsanto, the popularity of Astroturf spawned imitators, and the term was eventually used as a generic name for any kind of artificial turf. By the end of the seventies, twelve of the league's twenty-eight teams were playing on the stuff.

Astroturf helped make it possible for teams to play indoors, and team owners loved the artificial playing surface because it was easier and less expensive to maintain than natural grass.

Players almost universally hated the stuff. It was essentially just plastic carpeting laid over asphalt, and this combination created several medical issues. Sliding would leave players with abrasions and the top layer of their skin missing. Not only were these injuries painful, they were also slow to heal and difficult to avoid. The even playing surface made footing more consistent, but cleats often got caught in the turf and caused serious knee injuries. Team medics complained that the hard undersurface led to an increase in the frequency and severity of concussions, and the players complained about the wear and tear it caused on their knees and feet.

Still, the number of stadiums with Astroturf grew, peaking in 1995 when fifteen of the league's thirty teams played their home games on the stuff. I don't think that anybody imagined in ten years Astroturf would be gone from the league completely.

The shift began in Lincoln, Nebraska, of all places, when the University of Nebraska installed a new artificial playing surface called FieldTurf.

Unlike Astroturf, this wasn't merely carpeting. The FieldTurf system had a base of sand and rubber several inches thick, with green fibers sticking up through it just like blades of grass. From a distance, it was tough to tell the difference between the new style of turf and natural grass. Many of the problems associated with the old turf were eliminated, and the players raved about it.

Seahawks owner Paul Allen took notice, and the following spring he paid for the new surface to be installed at Husky Stadium, where his team would spend two seasons. Both Seattle players and their opponents proclaimed their approval. The high point was during a late November game with the Broncos when a downpour soaked both teams. A grass field would have turned to mud, and an Astroturf surface would have been covered with standing water. The drainage system of the FieldTurf kept the field relatively dry, and the manufacturers couldn't have asked for a better way to advertise the benefits of their product. Veteran wide receiver Rod Smith was among the players singing praises afterward. "That grass was incredible—the best field I ever played on," he said. "It's better than grass. No ruts. They ought to install that field at every stadium." An annual poll of NFL players rated Husky Stadium as the league's best artificial playing surface.

The Seahawks were so impressed that they changed the plans for their new stadium, opting to install the FieldTurf instead of natural grass. The Lions did the same thing, and both stadiums opened in 2002. Over the next few years, seven other teams would switch from the Astroturf to FieldTurf (or one of the similar products made by other companies, brand names including Astro-Play, RealGrass, and SportExe). Four stadiums even tore up their natural grass fields to install the FieldTurf.

Fourteen teams played on artificial turf in 1999, and by 2003 just three remained. The lone holdouts played in domed stadiums, where a permanent installation of the new turf would make it difficult for other tenants to use the facility. That issue was resolved, and by 2005 AstroTurf had disappeared from NFL stadiums completely.

THE PLAYERS

Introduction to Player Comments

ASK TEN PEOPLE to name the greatest football player of all time and you're likely to get ten different answers. Of course, that's not a situation unique to football. If you ask about the greatest composer or the greatest U.S. president you will find the same lack of consensus. To paraphrase Clint Eastwood, opinions are like rear ends—everybody has one.

That sort of debate is one of the things that makes spectator sports so popular. One person might say that Brett Favre is the best quarterback who ever played. Someone else insists that nobody could hold a candle to Johnny Unitas. A spirited debate follows, with each fan tossing out evidence to support their man.

That's a fine way to pass the time, but, ultimately, even well-argued opinion is still just opinion. I'm more interested in finding objective answers, and that process has to start with asking some key questions. How do we define greatness? What are the attributes of players that we can measure? What aspects of player performance are most important? What considerations do we need to make to compare players from different eras? What are the limitations of the information available to us? By answering those questions, we can construct a framework for objective analysis.

Why is that important? First of all, because we all bring our own biases to the table. We all have opinions that are skewed by our own individual experiences and perspectives. Maybe you think Favre is better than Unitas because you never saw Unitas play. Maybe you think Unitas is better because you are a lifelong Colts fan. Those preconceptions skew your views of players. There's nothing wrong with that, but you're arguing from the heart rather than the mind.

Second, an objective process will open your eyes to players you might not have considered before. How many modern fans know about the exploits of players like Benny Friedman, Joe Schmidt, or Lenny Moore? An objective process can also help us to see past our preconceptions and learn new things about players we thought we knew. Is Joe Namath overrated? Is Phil Simms underrated?

Rather than start with a ranking of players and then attempt to justify my selections, I've started with a set of systems for player evaluation. I defined a set of criteria by which to evaluate players, developed tools and methods for measuring each set of criteria, and then determined how the players measured up.

Football is Not Baseball

Rating the players in these categories requires both raw data and methods for analyzing the data. Naturally, we turn toward baseball for help. Advanced statistical studies of baseball have been performed for more than fifty years, and some great models have been developed. It's been more than twenty years since Pete Palmer introduced his linear weights model in the 1984 book *The Hidden Game of Baseball*. During the eighties, Bill James unveiled his "Runs Created" system and other analytical methods in the annual *Baseball Abstract*. These two men have helped spawn a whole generation of analysts who have added even more tools to help evaluate the performance of baseball teams and their players.

Unfortunately, many of their methods and models don't apply to football so well. In baseball, the opportunities are distributed somewhat uniformly. If your shortstop is a lousy hitter, you can put him at the bottom of the batting order, but he will still come to the plate three or four times a game—500 times a year if he plays every day. In football, if your tight end is a lousy receiver, you can choose not to throw to him at all. If the left side of your line can't block, there's no rule that says you have to run in that direction. In football, the opportunities are not distributed uniformly. If you have a lousy quarterback and a great running back, you can run the ball fifty times a game and never pass. In baseball, you can't have a slugger like Manny Ramirez bat twenty-five times in a game and have a no-hit shortstop like Julio Lugo bat just once. You also can't bring Ramirez up to the plate every time the bases are loaded. In football, though, the Steelers could summon a bruising back like Jerome Bettis to pound the ball the ball into the line every time they were near the end zone.

Another problem in football analysis is separating the performance of teammates. Baseball is mostly a series of individual acts. It's clear that when a pitcher strikes somebody out or when a hitter knocks a home run, he deserves most of the credit. You can't do that with football players. Football is a team game, and when we try to isolate the performance of individual players, we are ignoring that central fact, or at the very least, trying to work around it. On every pass play, there are offensive linemen protecting the quarterback from getting sacked and creating passing lanes for him to throw. On every running play there are linemen and fullbacks and receivers who are making blocks and occupying defenders.

In the groundbreaking book *The Hidden Game of Football,* the authors recognized this dilemma. They wrote:

> The first thing that anyone must understand about football statistics is that they are not baseball statistics. While that may be obvious in detail—no one is likely to mistake an end run for a home run—it is less obvious in interpretation. Hence in scanning stat lines, we should not evaluate Terrell Davis's contributions to his team with the same cause-and-effect mind-set that we use for Mark McGwire's contributions to his.

Baseball analysis is based on the principle that you can isolate individual performances, and that just isn't the case for football.

Yet another problem is the great variety of jobs in football, and the fact that there are different statistical measures for each position. In baseball, hitters all accumulate statistics in the same categories, and you can use one number to evaluate them all. In football, you have a different set of statistics for each position. Kickers don't register sacks, offensive linemen don't intercept passes, and quarterbacks don't kick field goals. Each position has a different job, and different methods must be used to evaluate each position's performance.

One of the biggest challenges is the state of football statistics themselves, which are woefully inadequate for analysis. After more than eighty years of existence, the NFL still does not have a single statistic for measuring the performance of offensive linemen. Defensive players fare only slightly better.

You probably know that, but I bet that you didn't realize that there are important gaps for the so-called "skill position" players—quarterbacks, running backs, and receivers. For example, they don't keep track of when a player makes a first down. It's impossible to tell from the box score whether a fumble occurred on a running play, a pass play, or a kick return. If a quarterback kneels down on the ball to kill the clock, it's counted as a rushing attempt. That's ridiculous, and it makes it difficult for us to evaluate his performance as a ball carrier. They don't measure the distance of a kickoff—one of the simplest and most important pieces of special teams data. There's no record of how many times a player was called for a penalty—heck, the official NFL statistics don't even tell us how many of a team's penalties came against the offense, the defense, or special teams. They keep track of how many first downs a team makes, but they've never tracked first downs made by individual players. These are just a few examples of statistics that ought to be kept but aren't. They are easy to observe and would yield great insight, but they simply are not a part of the NFL's official record. And that makes the job of a football analyst that much more difficult. Imagine where baseball analysis would be if there were no distinction made between extra base hits, or if getting hit by a pitch was counted as a walk.

So, if you're familiar with the large body of analytical work in baseball, don't be disappointed that we don't have highly precise, supercomputer-generated models in football. It's not for a lack of effort, it's just that football is a very different game, and it's inherently more difficult to analyze individual players. The methods here are based on many years of research, analysis of play-by-play data from thousands of games, peer-reviewed studies, and an integration of the work by some of the best minds in the field of statistical analysis.

Adjusted Yards: A System for Evaluating Offensive Performance

Points are the best measure of team success in football. The team that scores the most points in a game wins, and there is a very strong correlation between a team's scoring and their win-loss record. Using the Pythagorean method, we can accurately predict how many games a team will win over the course of a season based on how many points they score and how many their opponents score.

Points, however, are not nearly as useful when assessing individual performance. If Giants running back Tiki Barber punches it in from the 1-yard line, should he get all of the credit for scoring that touchdown? What if an 80-yard pass from Eli Manning to Jeremy Shockey preceded the scoring play? Shouldn't those two get the lion's share of the credit, or at least some credit for setting up Barber's run?

Of course, there are a lot of ways that players contribute other than simply gaining yards. Some plays have a significant impact on the outcome of the game—an interception, for example. Just how should that figure into the mix? Using a linear weights model, we can assign values to those types of events, values that we determine from observation. I analyzed the play-by-play data and drive charts from more than a thousand NFL regular-season games to come up with the average value for each type of offensive event that could occur in a football game.

For example, my study revealed that the average cost of an interception turns out to be 35 yards. On average, surrendering an interception is the equivalent of a 35-yard play. The authors of *Hidden Game* pegged it at 50 yards, but a close reading reveals that their number was just an estimate, not an actual measurement. If 35 yards seems low, consider two things. First, a lot of interceptions occur in the second half when a team is trailing, on low-percentage high-risk plays, even Hail Mary plays. These plays really don't hurt a team that much. Second, the longer a pass is, the more likely it will be intercepted. There's not much difference between a punt and a third-down pass that is intercepted 40 yards down field.

What about fumbles? My analysis measures the average cost of a lost fumble as 40 yards. Losing a fumble is actually more costly than an interception for two reasons. First, because they tend to take place on more conservative plays when a turnover is more costly, and second, because they usually take place closer to the line of scrimmage or in the backfield.

Not all fumbles are lost, of course. Historically, a little more than half of all fumbles are recovered by the offense. In theory, you could say that a lost fumble costs the offense 40 yards, while a fumble recovered by the offense doesn't cost anything. There are three problems with this approach. First, a fumble is a bad play, and a player shouldn't be rewarded because his team happens to recover the ball. Second, the fumble usually shortens the play in progress. A mishandled snap or a botched handoff, for example, will result in a loss of yards rather than a gain. Third, the NFL has not historically recognized the distinction between a fumble that was lost and one that was recovered for individual player statistics. They record this information for each team, but not for each individual.

Besides turnovers, what else do we count? For a running play, we simply count each yard that they gain. It's a one-to-one deal.

Now we come to the part that may seem counterintuitive. How do we divvy up credit between quarterbacks and receivers on a passing play? Consider the quandary that existing football statistics create for us. Joe Montana throws a 12-yard pass to Jerry Rice. Montana is credited with 12 passing yards. Rice is credited with 12 receiving yards. Isn't that double-booking? Seems like Enron-style accounting to me. The net gain is 12 yards, not 24. The quarterback and the receiver should each receive credit for half of the total yards on each passing play.

There's one more important thing to include, and that's quarterback sacks. When a quarterback gets sacked, it's really no different than running for a loss. So we count it that way, subtracting the actual yards that a quarterback lost each time he was sacked. Before sacks became an official stat, if a quarterback was tackled for a loss it was counted as a running play. This makes it harder for us to analyze quarterbacks from that era—to know how elusive they were in the backfield, how good of a runner they were, and whether or not they were an effective scrambler. The overall picture is still complete, but our ability to understand their skills in specific areas is a little weaker.

Return Specialists

Special teams are too often ignored, and if I can have any impact on football analysis I hope to change that. The one thing I tried to do in my annual football books was to illustrate the major role that these guys play. We start by counting punt-return yards at face value. Kick returns are a little more complicated. Every team gets to return at least one kick each game, at the start of the first or third quarter. Every other kick return comes as the result of a defensive failure. If you're the kick returner for a team with a mediocre defense you're going to get a lot of returns, and thus, a lot of kick-return yards. If you return kicks for a team with a great defense, you don't get as many chances to return a kick. Consider two players from the 2007 season, New England's Ellis Hobbs and Miami's Ted Ginn, Jr., as shown in Table 1.

Ginn had more than 500 additional return yards, but that advantage comes from having so

TABLE 1			
2007 Kick Return Comparison			
Player	KR	KRYds	Avg
Hobbs	35	911	26.0
Ginn	63	1433	23.8

many opportunities. Hobbs was more productive with the kicks he fielded, based on his average.

There's also the nature of kickoff returns that we must consider. Generally, kickoffs are fielded near the goal line with nine or ten blockers in front of you and the nearest defender still 40 yards away. The first 20 yards of most kick returns is a gimme, and it wouldn't be fair to equate those yards with a 20-yard rush or a 20-yard pass play. Besides, a return man could simply let the ball bounce out of the end zone for a touchback and get 20 yards that way. So for kick returns, we only count what the player gains beyond 20 yards.

The solution is to ignore the first 20 yards of each kickoff. We do this by calculating the Adjusted Yards as Kick Return Yards minus (Kick Returns × 20). And in the example above, Hobbs ends up with 211 Adjusted Yards while Ginn had 173.

Adjusted Yards in Action

Okay, that about covers it. We can add all of these things together to calculate what we call Adjusted Yards. Here's the formula:

Adjusted Yards =
Passing Yards / 2
+ Receiving Yards / 2
+ Rushing Yards
+ Sack Yards x (–1)
+ Interceptions x (–35)
+ Fumbles Lost x (–40)
+ Punt Return Yards
+ Kick Return Yards – [Kick Returns x 20]
+ (Rushing TDs + Kick Return TDs + Punt Return TDs) x 10
+ (Passing TDs + Receiving TDs) x 5

So, let's take a look at one player and see how he rates. Table 2 contains the actual career statistics for Barry Sanders, from which we can calculate Adjusted Yards.

Not surprisingly, most of his contributions come from rushing the ball. Sanders did make some contributions as a receiver out of the backfield, and a handful of kick returns and pass attempts. Clearly, though, the majority of his Adjusted Yards are coming from just one column. For comparison, take a look at another player: quarterback Randall Cunningham (see Table 3).

TABLE 2

Adjusted Yards for Barry Sanders

Year	Rush Yds	Pass Yds	Rec Yds	Fum	Int	Sack Yds	PR Yds	KR	KR Yds	Pa/Re TDs	PR/KR/ Ru TDs	Adj Yds
1989	1470	0	282	10	0	0	0	5	118	0	14	1369.0
1990	1304	0	480	4	0	0	0	0	0	3	13	1529.0
1991	1548	0	307	5	0	0	0	0	0	1	16	1666.5
1992	1352	0	225	6	0	0	0	0	0	1	9	1319.5
1993	1115	0	205	3	0	0	0	0	0	0	3	1127.5
1994	1883	0	283	0	0	0	0	0	0	1	7	2099.5
1995	1500	11	398	3	0	0	0	0	0	1	11	1699.5
1996	1553	0	147	4	1	0	0	0	0	0	11	1541.5
1997	2053	0	305	3	0	0	0	0	0	3	11	2210.5
1998	1491	0	289	3	0	0	0	0	0	0	4	1555.5
TOTAL	**15269**	**11**	**2921**	**41**	**1**	**0**	**0**	**5**	**118**	**10**	**99**	**16118.0**

TABLE 3

Adjusted Yards for Randall Cunningham

Year	Rush Yds	Pass Yds	Rec Yds	Fum	Int	Sack Yds	PR Yds	KR	KR Yds	Pa/Re TDs	PR/KR/ Ru TDs	Adj Yds
1985	205	548	0	3	8	150	0	0	0	1	0	–66.0
1986	540	1391	0	7	7	489	0	0	0	8	5	311.5
1987	505	2786	–3	12	12	380	0	0	0	23	3	761.5
1988	624	3808	0	12	16	442	0	0	0	24	6	1226.0
1989	621	3400	0	17	15	343	0	0	0	21	4	918.0
1990	942	3466	0	9	13	431	0	0	0	30	5	1629.0
1991	0	19	0	0	0	16	0	0	0	0	0	–6.5
1992	549	2775	0	13	11	437	0	0	0	19	5	739.5
1993	110	850	0	3	5	33	0	0	0	5	1	242.0
1994	288	3229	0	10	13	333	0	0	0	16	3	491.5
1995	98	605	0	3	5	79	0	0	0	3	0	41.5
1997	127	501	0	4	4	60	0	0	0	6	0	47.5
1998	132	3704	–3	2	10	132	0	0	0	34	1	1600.5
1999	58	1475	0	2	9	101	0	0	0	8	0	339.5
2000	89	849	0	4	4	45	0	0	0	6	1	208.5
2001	40	573	0	4	2	66	0	0	0	3	1	55.5
TOTAL	**4928**	**29979**	**–6**	**105**	**134**	**3537**	**0**	**0**	**0**	**207**	**35**	**8872.5**

Cunningham, like other quarterbacks, has a more diverse statistical record than a running back like Sanders. He gains Adjusted Yards in several categories—and as one of the great scrambling quarterbacks, his contribution as a rusher is significant. But quarterbacks also score a lot of negatives—they're the ones who throw interceptions, and Cunningham threw a bunch early in his career. They also take sacks; Cunningham set an NFL record in his second season when he was sacked 72 times. As you'll see when we discuss the individual quarterbacks, the benefit that scramblers give you with their rushing yards is often offset by the cost in sack yardage. And of course, quarterbacks are also responsible for the majority of fumbles, since they handle the ball the most. They take the blame for botched snaps, sloppy handoffs, or just bone-jarring hits.

At this point, I suppose it's fair to raise the question of whether this system is fair to quarterbacks. Using Adjusted Yards as a barometer, nine of the top ten single seasons of all-time belong to running backs, with Barry Sanders and LaDainian Tomlinson appearing on our list twice (see Table 4). However, when you look at the career leaders in Adjusted Yards (see Table 5), you see that quarterbacks garner five of the top 10 spots. This helps to illustrate one of the fundamental truths about football. In the course of a season, it's the running backs who make the biggest difference. They tend to have higher peaks, but most of them burn out quickly. Quarterbacks, on the other hand, can play at or near their peak for many years, and so over the course of their careers, the best passers will end up with just as many Adjusted Yards as the best running backs.

TABLE 4

NFL All-Time Single Season Leaders in Adjusted Yards

Player	Year	Team	Rush Yds	Pass Yds	Rec Yds	Fum	Int	Sack Yds	Pa/Re TDs	PR/KR/ Ru TDs	Adj Yds
LaDainian Tomlinson	2006	SD	1815	20	508	2	0	0	5	28	2304.0
Terrell Davis	1998	Den	2008	0	217	2	0	0	3	21	2256.5
Barry Sanders	1997	Det	2053	0	305	3	0	0	3	11	2210.5
Tiki Barber	2005	NYG	1860	0	530	1	0	0	2	9	2185.0
Priest Holmes	2002	KC	1615	0	672	1	0	0	3	21	2136.0
Tom Brady	2007	NE	98	4806	0	6	8	128	50	2	2123.0
Barry Sanders	1994	Det	1883	0	283	0	0	0	1	7	2099.5
Larry Johnson	2006	KC	1789	0	410	2	0	0	2	17	2093.9
LaDainian Tomlinson	2003	SD	1645	21	725	2	0	0	5	13	2093.0
Marcus Allen	1985	LAR	1759	16	555	3	0	0	3	11	2049.5

Because the Adjusted Yards method combines all offensive yardages into one number, we get a more accurate way to compare players. Steve Young ranks 18th all-time in passing yardage, but he ranks fifth among quarterbacks based on raw Adjusted Yards. That's because it takes several of his other strengths into account. Young had one of the lowest interception percentages (7th all-time), scored more rushing touchdowns than any quarterback in history, and ranks second all-time in rushing yards by quarterbacks.

In this book, I'm rating and ranking players by position. In order to do that, it's necessary to separate special teams statistics from the equation. Danny White's performance as a punter or George Blanda's years as a place kicker should certainly be considered when weighing their individual contributions. When rating each of them as a quarterback, however, the yards accumulated in their kicking duties should not be included. The same holds true for running backs and wide receivers that returned punts or kickoffs.

Consider a player like Herschel Walker. When you take into account his rushing yards and his receiving yards, he ends up ranked 60th among all running backs. However, he's also 10th all-time in kick-return yards. While those yards helped his team and made him a more valuable player, they're not relevant when evaluating his skills as a running back.

It's also important to remember that adjustments must be made when using Adjusted Yards to compare players from different eras. A player from

TABLE 5

Career Leaders in Adjusted Yards

Rk	Player	Adjusted Yards
1	Emmitt Smith	19237.4
2	Dan Marino	17785.5
3	Walter Payton	16926.1
4	Barry Sanders	16117.8
5	Brett Favre	16102.0
6	Curtis Martin	15579.5
7	Marshall Faulk	15434.5
8	Joe Montana	14436.5
9	Steve Young	13872.1
10	John Elway	13838.9

the 1980s played a sixteen-game schedule, while players from the 1960s would play fourteen games per season and players in the 1950s played just twelve games a year. Looking simply at the raw totals would unfairly skew the rankings towards the more recent players. That's why the criteria that I use for ranking players in this books takes into account production on a per-game basis as well as in comparison to the other players of the same time.

Adjusted Yards for Kickers and Punters

The men who kick field goals and punt each make their own offensive contributions. Kickers convert field position into points, rescuing stalled drives if they make a field goal and squandering an opportunity if they miss one. Punters affect field position with the distance and placement of their kicks. My study has enabled us to come up with a method for measuring the contributions of both kickers and punters using Adjusted Yards.

For punters, we want to measure the two things they do. When a punter is called in to kick and the ball is on his team's side of the field, his job is to kick the ball as far downfield as possible. When a punter's team is across midfield, his job is to kick the ball as close to the goal line as possible without having the ball go into the end zone. To measure his performance in those short-distance situations, we assign a penalty of 20 yards for each touchback. When a punter puts a short kick into the end zone, that's an abject failure, and it carries one of the harshest penalties in football. The 20 yards assessed for a touchback is more severe than a personal foul penalty. On the other hand, if he can put the ball inside the 20, whether it rolls dead, bounces out of bounds, or is fielded by the return man, then that's a sign of success. Some of these punts are great, downed inches from the goal line. Others may barely cross the 20. We opt to take the average and credit 10 yards for a punt that is recorded as "inside the 20." To measure each punter's ability to kick for distance, we start with gross punting yards. Because the number of

punting opportunities is determined by the success of the offense, and because a certain distance on each punt is usually a given, we make the same sort of discount for punters that we make for kick returns. The precise formula is:

Adjusted Punting Yards =
Gross Punting Yards
+ Inside20 x 10
+ Touchbacks x (–20)
+ Blocked Punts x (–65)
+ Punts x (–35)
(divided by 2)

For kickers, they live and die on the success of their field goal kicks. Traditionally, they've been evaluated by field goal percentage, and frankly that's as useful as evaluating them by the number of letters in their last name. Not all field goal opportunities are created equal, and a guy who misses three kicks from 50 yards shouldn't be rated the same as a guy who misses three kicks from 25 yards.

There are two basic principles for evaluating their success. First, their performance must take into account the distance of their kicks. Making a longer kick is more valuable, and missing a shorter kick carries a stiffer penalty. Second, each kick is graded as 100 percent success or 100 percent failure. The kicker either ended the drive by putting 3 points on the board, or he ended it without scoring and turning the ball over to the opposing team.

For each field goal attempted, a kicker accrues Adjusted Kicking Yards (AKY) by making the kick, and he loses yards by missing the kick. Roughly speaking, there are 50 Adjusted Yards on the line for each attempt. If the line of scrimmage is the 2-yard line, for example, a successful kick is worth 2 AKY. The degree of difficulty is low, it's a high-percentage kick, and somebody else did the bulk of the work to get the field position that set up the 3 points. If a kicker misses the attempt from that distance, the penalty is 48 AKY. In that instance, not only has the kicker missed a kick he should never have missed, but he also squandered a scoring opportunity, where his team could have elected to go for it on fourth and goal from the two. Rather than use the precise distance for each kick, we group the field goal attempts into 10-yard segments. This eliminates some noise from the system, and more important gives us continuity between rating active kickers with kickers from earlier eras, for whom more precise records are not available. The precise formula is:

Adjusted Kicking Yards

FG Missed(0-19) x –48
+ FG Missed(20-29) x –42
+ FG Missed(30-39) x –32
+ FG Missed(40-49) x –22
+ FG Missed(50+) x –12
+ FG Made(0-19) x 2
+ FG Made(20-29) x 8
+ FG Made(30-39) x 18
+ FG Made(40-49) x 28
+ FG Made(50+) x 38

This is an admittedly imprecise system, based on assigning an average distance to each field goal attempt. Clearly, this overvalues some kickers who made frequent short attempts, and it undervalues those strong-legged kickers who made more long attempts. However, the sad truth is that the NFL did not publish this data for individual kickers until the 1980s, and we won't have a good understanding of earlier kickers until play-by-play researchers have reconstructed the statistics from those performances.

Adjusted Yards at the Team Level

Points are perhaps the ultimate measure of football performance, so it is worth asking how strongly Adjusted Yards correlates with points at the team level. I calculated the Adjusted Yards for each team since 1970—a total of 997 team seasons. Over that time period, teams scored an average of one point for every 13.35 Adjusted Yards. With that as a baseline, we can calculate how many points teams were expected to score based on their Adjusted Yards, and compare that to how many points they did actually score.

What I found was that the expected points based on Adjusted Yards was within a field goal per game for 66 percent of teams. The projection is within a touchdown per game for another 25 percent of teams. The standard deviation is about 3.7 points per game. This seems to be a good indicator of the effectiveness of the Adjusted Yards methodology.

Looking more closely at the teams for whom the difference was higher than a touchdown per game, I think I've identified the most significant factor: penalty yards. The method that the NFL uses now—and has for most of their history—is woefully inadequate when it comes to recording penalty yardage. While they count the number of yards an offense is penalized (for a false start or an illegal formation), they don't count the yards an offense gains due to defensive penalties (pass interference or off-sides). The same holds true for each team's defense; we know how many penalty yards they give up, but not how many they gain. This is an area that play-by-play data can help address, but right now it's creating a limitation for statistical analysis.

Adjusted Yards is a significant step for football analysis. What we have here is a tool that lets us evaluate both single-season performances and career performances. We can quickly and easily compare the performance of a power running back like Jerome Bettis with a multidimensional back like LaDainian Tomlinson. We have a good tool for analyzing an individual player's performance from one season to the next, to tell us whether he's improving or regressing. With some adjustments for differences from one era to another, we can compare the best seasons by Peyton Manning with those of Joe Montana or Johnny Unitas. Most significant, we have a single number that we can use to examine some of the more general football questions that need to be addressed. How well do quarterbacks drafted in the first round perform compared to those who aren't drafted at all? At what age do wide receivers peak, and are they ever productive as rookies? What effect does overwork have on running backs? Using Adjusted Yards, we have a way to answer all of these questions.

Q-ratings: The Grand Unified Theory of Statistical Analysis

Throughout this chapter, I presented a number of statistical methods for rating players. When you're doing analysis, one of the problems inherent with football compared to other sports is the number of different positions and the number of statistical categories. In hockey, for example, you have players and goaltenders. Individual statistics in baseball essentially consist of three sets of data—batting, fielding, and pitching. For basketball, there is just one set of data for all players, and that holds true for boxing, golf, auto racing, and most of the other major sports.

In football, there are ten different groups of positions—kickers, linebackers, and quarterbacks, to name just three. Each has their own type of statistics, with very little overlap between one group and the other. Kickers don't tend to accumulate sacks, quarterbacks don't often attempt field goals, and linebackers usually don't throw interceptions.

What we do in football, as we do in hockey and baseball, is develop different methods for rating players in different categories. We can use a tool like Line Scores to rate the offensive linemen, Adjusted Yards to rate the quarterbacks, and Pass Defender Score (PDS) to rate defensive players. Some of the methods that we develop may be more rigorous than others, but in the end, we have a yardstick for rating players against others in the same group—quarterbacks versus quarterbacks and linemen compared to other linemen.

As we develop a toolbox for rating these players, we begin to run into a problem. No matter how rigorous these individual tools are, the scales on which the ratings are made are unfamiliar. For example, Peyton Manning had 1641.5 Adjusted Yards in 2000. Is that a good season? A great one? It's not instinctive to know where that performance compares to historical totals. It doesn't register the way that 2000 rushing yards or 40 touchdown passes do. That's why I've developed a tool we call Q-rating.

The basic premise of the Q-rating is to grade each player on a scale from zero to ten, using his raw statistics and comparing him to other players at his position. The scale is based on all of the performances at that position during that season. A score of zero indicates the player didn't make any contribution, while a score of 10 represents the best performance for a player that season at that position.

The method for calculating the Q-rating is simple. Start with the player's raw score—Adjusted Yards for offensive players, Line Score for linemen, Pass Defender Score for defenders, etc. Then divide their raw score by the highest score at their position, and multiply by 10. Scores below zero are rounded up to zero. That's all there is to it. The steps below explain the method in more detail, starting with offensive players.

We compare each player's raw score (e.g., Adjusted Yards) for the season to the best total at that position for that season. For example, Jeff Garcia led all quarterbacks with 1963 AY in 2000, giving him a Q-rating for the year of 10.0. Peyton Manning's 1641.5 Adjusted Yards that season would result in a Q-rating of 8.4. Even if you're not familiar with Adjusted Yards, you know that a score of 8.4 on a scale of zero to 10 is pretty good.

Beyond the Bell Curve

When you calculate the Q-ratings for the entire league for a season, an interesting phenomenon is revealed. What you'll find is that the scores aren't distributed evenly. With a scale of zero to ten, you might intuitively expect an average score of five, with half of the players above and half below. However, that's not the way that talent is distributed in the NFL, or any other professional sport. There are a lot of guys who can make a minimal contribution on the field, guys like Maurice Hicks, who has spent several seasons with the San Francisco 49ers. In 2007, for example, he played in sixteen games, finishing the season with 21 carries for 117 yards and 14 catches for 86 yards. He gets a Q-rating of 0.7 for that performance.

Now, I don't want to offend Hicks by saying that guys like him are a dime a dozen, but he's one of 120 running backs that season who earned a Q-rating of 1.0 or below in 2007. That group accounted for 52 percent of all the running backs who had a rushing attempt or caught a pass in the NFL in 2007. (Another forty running backs spent time in the league that season without touching the ball. We don't include them for purposes of this discussion.) It's a lot harder to find a great running back. That year there were only two who earned a Q-rating of 8.0 or higher: LaDainian Tomlinson (SD) 10.0, and Brian Westbrook (Phi) 9.2. Talent is not evenly distributed in the NFL, or in other pro sports. If you graphed something that was normally distributed—say, the height of the women in your town—you'd get a chart that looked like a bell, what statisticians call the bell-shaped curve. Most of the values would be grouped in the middle, with fewer hits as you went towards the

extreme end of your scale. For example, a government study found that the average adult female in the United States is 5-foot-4, with 90 percent of women standing between 5-foot-1 and 5-foot-7.

More significant, with a normal distribution the shape of your graph would be pretty symmetrical. You would have about the same number of people above the midpoint as you do below the midpoint.

Why doesn't this happen in the National Football League? It's because the players in the league represent just the extreme right hand side of that bell curve. If you could measure the football talent of American males age 18–40, you'd probably get a bell-shaped curve. The guys on the extreme left would be those with some physical limitations, then those who had never played football, and as you approach the middle, that's where you'd find the average guy. Then as you got further to the right, there'd be the guys who played pretty well in high school. Further to the right, you'd find a

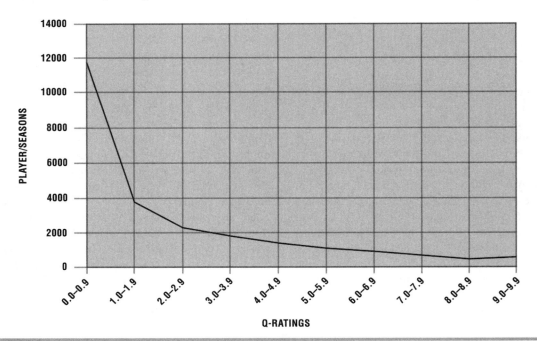

TABLE 6

Distribution of Q-ratings

smaller group of guys who played some college football, then a smaller group of guys who started at a Division-I school.

Beyond that you have a select group of guys who were the best high school player in their hometown and the star of their college team. Only some of that group gets a chance to play in the NFL, and so when we look at the distribution of talent in the league, we're seeing the extreme right end of that curve. The chart in Table 6 illustrates that quite clearly.

What you find is an average Q-rating of about 2.2, with roughly a third of the players below 1.0, another third between 1.0 and 3.9, and the final third spread out above that. Based on that, you can draw some general conclusions about the players in each group.

By default, you'll always have one player at 10 for each position each season. A Q-rating above 9 indicates an MVP-worthy season. Typically, there will only be a handful of other players in the league to score this high each season. A Q-rating between 7.0 and 8.9 usually indicates a player who had a Pro Bowl caliber season. He would likely be one of the top players on his team, and one of the best players at his position that season. Players in this range represent about 4 percent of the league in any given season.

Players who earn a Q-rating between 4.0 and 6.9 are generally those who played well enough to start all season. Roughly 14 percent of the players fall into this group.

Players who score between 2.0 and 3.9 tend to fall into one of two categories. They were either men who only played part of the season or men who played the whole season but played poorly. This group comprises another 18 percent of all NFL players.

The largest group of players—62 percent —will earn a Q-rating below 2.0. It's hard to score this low if you played a full season, primarily because performance at such a low level usually costs a player his job. Mostly, these were backups, part-time players, or others who saw limited and unremarkable action.

Cross-Era Comparisons

Using the Q-rating also helps us quickly put the raw score into some historical context. At first blush, Bobby Layne's 731.5 Adjusted Yards in 1958 pales in comparison to Drew Bledsoe's 998.5 AY in 1995. If you look closely, you'd notice that Layne only played ten games versus Bledsoe's sixteen. You might also know that teams threw the ball a lot more often when Bledsoe was playing than they did in Layne's day.

Using the Q-rating, we can quickly cut through those factors that bias the raw score and see how well each quarterback played compared to his contemporaries. In Layne's case, he had the best season of any NFL quarterback in 1958, edging Johnny Unitas (702.5) and Tobin Rote (660.0). Bledsoe ranked 20th among quarterbacks in 1995, far behind players like Bret Favre (1615.5) and Steve Young (1360.0).

Grand Unified Theory

There's no magic here. All that the Q-rating system does is convert other rating systems to an easy-to-understand scale. You can use it for basketball, hockey, or baseball to put measures like TENDEX, Adjusted Goals, or Runs Created on the zero to 10 scale. You can use it with other methods for rating football players too.

The key to remember is that what this system does is help you see how good a player was compared to his peers. A punter who earns a 9.0 rates as one of the best punters in the league that season, but that doesn't necessarily make him more valuable to his team than a running back that earns an 8.0 Q-rating. Those sorts of comparisons are better made with the raw numbers (or they just don't make sense).

This method brings all of the other ratings together in a straightforward way. If one wants to delve into the details of systems like Adjusted Yards, Pass Defender Score, or Line Scores, that option is still available. With Q-ratings, the science behind that is translated to one number for each player that is easy to understand.

Line Scores

Rating Offensive Linemen

We have great statistics for the so-called "skill" positions—passing, rushing, receiving—but there are no official statistics with which we can evaluate the play of offensive lineman. The offensive line works as a unit, and while we can discern significant differences from watching film, there's very little on the stat sheets that tell us who is a stud and who is a dud.

But we do have team statistics that can give us a good insight into how an offensive line performed. That works, not just because it's statistically convenient, but also because that is how the linemen work. An All-Pro center surrounded by overmatched guards and tackles can only do so much. The linemen need to work together as one.

Linemen have two jobs: to protect the quarterback when he drops back to pass and to provide holes for the running backs to go through. One of the things that becomes apparent when you watch linemen play is that these skills are not necessarily a package deal. Run blocking requires a lineman to make contact with an opposing defender and move him. This usually requires aggressiveness and pure physical strength. Pass protection is more of a reactive endeavor, relying on quickness and technique. Linemen can stop the defender by slowing him down, moving him in a different direction, or just physically stopping him in his path. It's not enough to simply keep the defender from touching your quarterback. Good pass blockers will maintain a pocket from which the quarterback can throw, and they will establish passing lanes, through which the ball can be thrown without being tipped.

Some individuals are ferocious run blockers but who can't keep your Aunt Marge away from their quarterback. Others protect their quarterback like secret service agents but can't get any kind of push at the line of scrimmage to open a hole. The ideal situation is to find five guys who excel at both facets of line play. The best offensive lines have four or five of those guys. More often, the skills are mixed within a unit. Perhaps the tackles are the keys to the pass protection, and the interior linemen—the guards and tackles—provide the run blocking.

For each team, we calculate a score for pass blocking, another score for run blocking, and a combined score, based on the percentage of the time that the team was involved in each type of play.

To grade pass blocking, we determine the team's sack rate—how often they gave up a sack. To grade their run blocking, we determine the average number of yards the team gained on each running play. These two components are combined into one overall score, with a weighting based on how often a team threw the ball and how often they ran with it.

The precise formulas are complex, and they are described below for those of you who are interested.

Team Ratings: Offense

Run Blocking Score

OLR = (RuYds / RuAtt) – 3.33 (or zero if <0)
OLRQ = OLR / YrMax x 10

Pass Blocking Score

OLP = [(PaAtt + PaSk) / PaSk] – 10 (or zero if <0)
OLPQ = OLPScore / YrMax x 10

Offensive Line Score

OLS = OLRQ x [RuAtt / (RuAtt + PaAtt + PaSk)] +
    OLPQ x [(PaAtt + PaSk) /(RuAtt + PaAtt + PaSk)]
Q = OLS / YrMax x 10

If you watch them closely and understand a little bit about their technique and responsibilities, you can come up with subjective ratings for individual offensive linemen. You can see what things each player does well, what his weaknesses are, and the type of defenders that he may be vulnerable to. That's what scouts and coaches do, and it's the best way for those folks to identify trouble spots, whether on their own line or their opponent's line. It's just not possible to grade individual offensive lineman subjectively, though. Certainly, none of the traditional statistics provide any insight into the performance of individual offensive linemen. The play-by-play data can help reveal some general trends, but I'd be misleading you if I suggested that we can rate the performance of individual linemen with any sort of scientific precision. Teamwork is an intrinsic part of the job, and pretending that the five linemen operate independently of one another retards our understanding. The best way to render objective ratings for them is as a group.

For a single season, this method is not that useful. A Hall of Fame center grades out the same as the other four men lined up next to him. On a macro scale—over the course of someone's career—we can draw a more meaningful distinction as the groups of players on each team change. We can also gain some measure of separation by including in our system a bonus for players who were named All-Pro at their position (i.e., the best player at his position in the league that year) and a longevity bonus for players with extraordinarily long careers.

Rating the Defensive Front

There are two basic defenses being played in the National Football League today: the 3-4 and the 4-3. There have been more than a dozen other variations throughout history, but with each one of those basic formations, the basic job of the linemen and linebackers has been the same: generate a pass rush, and stop the run. Those are essentially the same elements that the offense line is working to prevent, so we can use the same general approach to grade them a unit.

Team Ratings: Defense

Run Defense
RD = ABS [5.65 – (RuYds / RuAtt)] ^2
RDQ = RD / YrMax x 10

Pass Rushing
PD = ABS [40 – ([PaAtt + PaSk] / PaSk)] ^4.4
PDQ = PD / YrMax x 10
 Team Run Pct = RuAtt / (RuAtt + PaAtt + PaSk)
DefScore = (RD x TmRunPct) + [PD x (1 – TmRunPct)]
Q = DefScore / YrMax x 10

We use absolute value and an exponential factor to account for the fact that defensive stats are inverted relative to offensive stats. That is to say, the point of the offense is to gain yards while the purpose of the defense is to prevent them.

Pass Defender Scores

Defensive backs have a variety of duties, including rushing the passer and helping to defend the run. But by and large, their job is to defend the pass. Success in this area can be measured in different ways: interceptions and touchdowns allowed, completion percentage, and yards per play, just to name a few. In evaluating a defensive secondary, we can combine all of these elements by using the passer rating compiled by all of their opponents.

SecondaryScore = ABS [107 – QBRating]
Q = SecondaryScore / YrMax x 10

As with the players at other defensive positions and on the offensive line, we are using a team measure to evaluate individual players. Once again, this is in recognition of the fact that the secondary succeeds or fails as a group. In zone coverage, every player bears some responsibility for the outcome of the play, and the individuals must always be working together.

Summary of Methodology

Players are rated and ranked by position, using Adjusted Yards, Line Scores, and Pass Defender Scores as the raw measure for evaluation. With the Q-ratings, we put those raw numbers into appro-

TABLE 7

Priest Holmes Adjusted Yard and Q-rating Scores

Year-Tm	AY	Max-AY	Q
1997-Bal	0.0	2210.5	0.0
1998-Bal	1053.9	2256.5	4.7
1999-Bal	573.0	1920.0	3.0
2000-KC	639.0	1944.0	3.2
2001-KC	1792.0	1809.5	9.9
2002-KC	2136.0	2136.0	10.0
2003-KC	1995.0	2093.0	9.5
2004-KC	970.5	1869.5	5.2
2005-KC	574.5	2185.0	2.6
2007-KC	145.5	1890.0	0.8

priate historical context. To rate and rank the players here, I look at the Q scores they compiled for their best three seasons, their best six, and their best nine. Let's take a recent player like Priest Holmes, for example (see Table 7).

At his peak, Holmes was the best running back in the league. He ranked first in Adjusted Yards in 2002, was slightly behind Marshall Faulk in 2001, and finished second to LaDainian Tomlinson in 2003. The sum of his Q scores in those best three seasons was 29.4, and we'll call that Q(1–3). The Q(1–6), or sum of scores from his top six seasons, is 42.5, and the Q(1–9) is 48.9.

The scores are weighted, to avoid an overemphasis on outlying seasons. The weighting formula can be expressed in two forms.

Player Career Score = Q(1–3) + Q(1–6) x 1.25 + Q(1–9) x 1.5

or

Player Career Score = Q(1–3) x 3.75 + Q(4–6) x 2.75 + Q(7–9) x 1.5

The end result is a career score, which in the case of Holmes calculates to 155.8. Players at the skill positions are ranked using this Player Career Score. A list of the top players at each position is included in each chapter, with details available in the Records section at the back of this book.

Careers tend to be longer for quarterbacks than for the other skill position players, so we look at their best fifteen seasons rather than just the top nine. Also, we look at net wins for the seasons in which they were their team's starter (defined as seasons in which they led their team in pass attempts).

While I have generally argued that quarterbacks get too much credit for winning and too much of the blame for losing, what became clear to me as I reviewed the historical data was that the data suggested the opposite was actually true. The more I looked at the data, the clearer it became how much the shape of a quarterback's performance was affected by the context of his team. Some passers had to throw the ball more because their teams were always behind, and so the raw numbers look impressive even though they didn't translate into wins. By contrast, quarterbacks like Bob Griese and Terry Bradshaw didn't have to throw as much, because their teams had dominating defenses and good running games. Otto Graham is another great example of a guy whose individual numbers dropped off as his team got more dominant.

Two adjustments are added to this score for defensive players and offensive linemen. The adjustments are intended to help differentiate players from their teammates, as well as to draw on the evaluation of their performance provided by their peers. They get a bonus for playing in more than 150 games, the theory being that they can't stay around for that long unless their coaches have noticed a certain level of play. And for linemen, longevity itself is a virtue.

We also give them bonus points for being named to an All-Pro team, which generally recognizes them as the best player at their position in a particular season. Certainly, this recognition has always been subjective, and there are countless examples of players who have been overlooked or overrated. However, in the absence of other contemporary data, the All-Pro selections serve as a good commentary on whether an individual stood out.

Offensive Linemen

[(GS/G) x Career Score] + (WeightedAll-Pro) + (GP – 150)/3

Defensive Linemen & Linebackers

[(GS/G) x Career Score] + (WeightedAll-Pro)+ (GP – 150)/3

Defensive Backs

[(GS/G) x Career Score] + (WeightedAll-Pro) + (GP – 150)/3

In applying both of these adjustments, it's important to understand the context of this book. There have been more than 20000 players in NFL history, and we're not trying to draw subtle distinctions between No. 14617 and No. 14621. We're trying to separate the top 2 or 3 percent of players from the rest, and these methods help us to do that.

Special Problems With Early Players

For early players, coming up with objective ratings and rankings is even more difficult. There were no official statistics kept before 1932, leaving twelve seasons for which we have no data to work with at all. Subsequent research by David Neft and Richard Cohen reconstructed scoring data from newspaper box scores, as well as some playing statistics from selected games based on the available coverage. There are gaps, though, which prevent us from using the data in any comprehensive way.

For most seasons prior to 1950, each player participated on both the offense and defense. The rules discouraged substitution. When a player came out of the game, he could not return until the next quarter. So unless a starter was injured or tired, they generally stayed in for every play. In most cases, the lack of specialization makes it difficult to evaluate players in the same context as modern players. This problem is of course compounded by the aforementioned lack of statistics prior to 1932, thus affecting many players whose careers spanned into the forties.

Rather than completely ignore the players from the two-way era, I've made a special effort to separately recognize the standouts for whom there is an insufficient statistical record. There is a chapter on two-way players, which includes every player who was named an All-Pro at least four times between 1920 and 1945 and doesn't already appear as a rated player in other sections of the book.

Quarterbacks

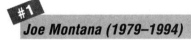

Joe Montana (1979–1994)

Why Joe?

Three simple reasons: His raw statistics, his rate statistics, and his ability to win.

Montana's raw numbers rank him as one of the top-ten passers ever. He didn't have a great arm, but when his team needed him to throw the ball, he could air it out with the best of them. Montana had 300 yards in a game 39 times and surpassed the 400-yard mark 7 times. When he retired he ranked 4th in passing yards and touchdowns.

The rate statistics help to prove that those numbers don't simply reflect a player who stayed around a long time. Montana ranks 3rd all-time in completion percentage, 4th in passer rating, and 9th in fewest interceptions per pass attempt. At his peak, he was the league's best quarterback.

Third, and perhaps most important, Montana was a winner. If you exclude the strike-shortened 1982 season, his team never finished worse than 10-6 in a year when he was the team's primary starter. They went to the playoffs in nine of those ten seasons, and won four Super Bowls in an eight-year span. Montana was named Most Valuable Player in three of those Super Bowls. "Some guys get tighter the bigger the game is, but Joe just seemed to get better," former 49ers guard Randy

Cross says. "If every game were a Super Bowl, Joe would have retired undefeated."

The time that he didn't win the Super Bowl MVP award might have been the best big game performance of his life. Trailing the Bengals 16–13, the Niners got the ball on their own 8-yard line with 3 minutes left to play. That's about as much pressure as an offense is ever going to face, but Montana kept his teammates focused by showing how calm he was. Rather than giving them a tense pep talk in the huddle, he pointed to a celebrity in the stands. "Hey, look. It's John Candy!" By showing his teammates that he was relaxed, he helped them to relax, and that enabled them to march 92 yards for the game-winning touchdown with 34 seconds to spare.

Of course, this was not his only great performance on the big stage. His composite Super Bowl statistics are amazing: 83 of 122 passes completed (68 percent) for 1142 yards, 11 TDs, and zero interceptions. Montana engineered 31 fourth-quarter comebacks during his career. The most memorable of his late game heroics came in the 1981 NFC title game, and would be remembered simply as "The Catch." Montana found receiver Dwight Clark in the corner of the end zone with 50 seconds left to upset the Dallas Cowboys.

Montana overcame two injuries that appeared to be career threatening. He ruptured a disc in the

1986 opener, and after surgery to repair it, doctors told him he might not be able to play again. Montana defied all expectations by returning two months later and showed no lingering effects.

A hard hit in the 1990 NFC championship game left him with what appeared to be a career-ending elbow injury. At the time, Montana already ranked among the top 10 all-time in passing yards and touchdowns, and with four Super Bowl rings, his place in Canton had been assured years earlier. He was thirty-four years old and everybody expected him to retire, but Montana spent two years rehabilitating and came back to play the 1992 season finale. By then, Steve Young was firmly entrenched as San Francisco's new starter. Montana's strong showing in that one game encouraged the Chiefs to trade for him. He spent two more productive seasons in Kansas City, taking his new team to the playoffs each year.

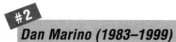

Dan Marino (1983–1999)

Maybe there's something in the water. There are twenty-three modern quarterbacks in the Hall of Fame, and six of them are from the same general area in western Pennsylvania. Marino, Johnny Unitas, and Jim Kelly were all born in Pittsburgh; Joe Montana hails from New Eagle; Joe Namath is from Beaver Falls; and George Blanda came from Youngwood. There are plenty of other notable passers from the region, including Johnny Lujack (Connellsville), Terry Hanratty (Butler), Babe Parilli (Rochester), and Marc Bulger (Pittsburgh). There's nothing to suggest any reason for this, but that sure is an awful lot of talent within a 40-mile radius

Marino was once of the most prolific passers in NFL history, ranking first all-time in pass attempts, yards, and touchdowns when he retired. In his first full year as a starter, he set single-season records for passing yards (5084) and touchdowns (48), and in 1986 he set the record for most pass attempts (623) and completions (378) in a single season.

The big knock against him, of course, is that he never won a Super Bowl. Marino had considerable success during the regular season, posting a 147-93 record as a starting quarterback and leading the Dolphins to a winning record in sixteen out of seventeen seasons. That level of success in undeniable, but his 8-10 record in the playoffs stands in stark contrast. In the minds of many, he made a career out of beating up on bad teams but couldn't win in the clutch. I don't think that's a fair conclusion at all.

First, Marino was always saddled with a one-dimensional offense, and teams that can't run the ball in the postseason always struggle. The Dolphins ranked in the bottom-half of NFL teams in rushing yards in fifteen out of seventeen seasons with Marino under center. They never ranked better than 13th, and only once had a running back reach the 1000-yard mark.

Second, those Dolphins teams almost always had a lousy defense. Their best unit was probably the 1990 defense, which ranked eighth in yards allowed. (They ranked in the top 5 in 1998 and 1999 when Jimmie Johnson was the head coach, but Marino was fading by that point.) If teams without a running game struggle in the postseason, teams with no running game and a lousy defense have no chance. The table below shows the score of the ten playoff games Marino lost. Even if you throw out the lopsided loss to the Jaguars at the bottom, Marino's Dolphins gave up an average of 31.4 points in the playoff losses. How could that be Marino's fault?

Dolphins Scores in Playoff Losses

Year	Opp	Score
1983	Sea	27–20
1984	SF	38–16
1985	NE	31–14
1990	Buf	44–34
1992	Buf	29–10
1994	SD	22–21
1995	Buf	37–22
1997	NE	17–3
1998	Den	38–3
1999	Jac	62–7

Marino lost a playoff game where his team scored 34 points. He lost two where he had three touchdown passes, and another where he threw for 422 yards. I don't think you can put all of the blame on his shoulders. In fact, I think a more realistic assessment of Marino's career would conclude that he helped a team that wasn't very good—and at times was downright lousy—to remain competitive. He led them to the AFC championship game in 1985, for example, with a 22nd ranked defense and the 18th ranked rushing offense. That team finished 12-4, and rather than blaming Marino for not taking them further, I think we ought to commend him for even getting them into the playoffs.

John Elway (1983–1998)

Like Marino, Elway was tagged for a long time with the label of a guy who couldn't win the big game. It was hogwash, of course. Elway took the Broncos to the Super Bowl three times early in his career, and he won a lot of games without much of a supporting cast around him. That changed late in his career, and if you made a graph of his career statistics, you'd see a sudden upswing around 1995. That's the year that Mike Shanahan arrived as head coach, and also the year that running back Terrell Davis joined the team. With a better crew around him, Elway had more success in the playoffs. Over his last three seasons, Elway and the Broncos went 39-9 during the regular season and 7-1 in the postseason.

Elway was originally drafted by the Baltimore Colts—a team that had finished the strike-shortened 1982 season without a win. In the weeks before the draft, Elway made it clear that he would not sign with the Colts. They went ahead and selected him anyway, and Elway remained firm in his stance. Five days later, the Colts realized they weren't going to change his mind and traded him to Denver. In exchange, the Colts received guard Chris Hinton, backup quarterback Mark Herrmann, the Broncos first-round pick in 1984 (which they would use to

select guard Ron Solt), and $1 million in guaranteed revenue from two preseason games scheduled in Denver. Hinton turned out to be a very good player in his own right, earning seven Pro Bowl invitations in a thirteen-year career. Solt was a pretty good player, and Herrmann was a decent backup.

Without their franchise quarterback, the Colts turned to young Mike Pagel, who spent three unimpressive seasons as their starter. By 1986, the team was ready to renew their search for a passer. Over the next five years, the Colts used two first-round picks and a second-round pick in a futile effort to find a starting quarterback (1986 2nd: Jack Trudeau; 1988 1st: Chris Chandler; 1990 1st: Jeff George). While all of them signed contracts, none of them made an impact. In the twelve years after trading Elway, the Colts made the playoffs just once, and that came with the help of replacement players during the 1987 strike. They never finished better than 9-7.

The Broncos, by contrast, went to the playoffs in Elway's rookie season, and advanced to the Super Bowl three times in the next six years. That's an important lesson in why there's so much angst over taking quarterbacks at the top of the draft. They may not always pan out, but when they do, they make an impact that lasts for a very long time.

Brett Favre (1991–2007)

Immaturity nearly ended Favre's career before it started. Drinking problems and drug abuse made his first season in the NFL a wasted one. His raw skills were clearly evident, and the young Favre thought that should be enough. Rather than working hard, he grumbled that he hadn't been handed the starting job, and that kind of attitude wore thin pretty quickly. Falcons' head coach Jerry Glanville shipped him off to Green Bay after one season, convinced that the kid's sloppy work habits and detached lifestyle would keep him from ever developing into a pro quarterback.

It's ironic then that Favre would eventually become the most reliable quarterback in NFL history, starting a record 273 consecutive games (including the playoffs). When he retired following the 2007 season, he held all of the significant career records for passers.

At his peak, he was arguably one of the top three or four quarterbacks in history. But there were times when he was just awful. In his late thirties, he threw a ton of interceptions, trying to force throws that he was no longer capable of making. He was picked off 29 times in 2005, the sixth-highest season total for a passer since the AFL/NFL merger. Favre threw four interceptions in a 2004 playoff loss to Minnesota. He had two regular-season games with at least four interceptions in 2005, and in his last six games in 2006, he threw 5 touchdowns and 11 interceptions. During the 2007 season, he became the all-time career leader in interceptions.

Favre was taking chances because he had no other option. After going to the Super Bowl in back-to-back seasons the offense regressed and the defense at times was downright horrible. He led the league in pass attempts in 2005 and 2006, finishing among the top five seven times in the decade from 1997 to 2006. More often than not, if Favre didn't make big plays, the Packers wouldn't win.

#5
Johnny Unitas (1956–1973)

You can't judge a quarterback based just on his raw numbers, and there's no better example of this point than Johnny Unitas. His records have all been eclipsed in the three decades since he retired, and the career totals look less impressive when compared to the inflated raw stats of modern players. Consider the pair of players whose career stats appear below.

Player	PaYds	PaTD	PaInt
A	46233	275	267
B	40239	290	253

One of those guys had a few more touchdowns, the other had more passing yards, but their stats are similar enough that at first glance they'd seem like comparable players. The truth is, one guy is Unitas (B), and the other is Vinny Testaverde (A). In fact, these two guys weren't really similar at all.

At his peak, Unitas was breathtaking. He threw touchdown passes in forty-seven straight games, a streak that stretched from 1956 to 1960. The Colts won two NFL championships during that five-year span and Unitas was twice named the league's Most Valuable Player. He would win that award two more times in the mid-sixties, and he would lead the Colts to another championship in 1970.

The question you have to ask with Unitas is whether a player's poor performances at the end of his career should count against him. Unitas suffered an elbow injury during the 1968 preseason, and while he continued to play for six more seasons, he probably shouldn't have. He did help lead the Colts to a Super Bowl win in 1970, but that team's success stemmed largely from its defense, and his own statistics were unimpressive. He threw more interceptions than touchdowns and averaged less than 150 net passing yards per game.

In the six years after the elbow injury, Unitas spent two seasons as a starter, two recovering from injuries, and two as a backup. He had always been prone to throwing interceptions because of his willingness to take risks down the field, but things got noticeably worse. In each of those six seasons he threw more interceptions than touchdowns, and the total for the period was 38 touchdowns and 64 interceptions. His completion percentage and yards per attempt also dropped significantly. The Colts missed the playoffs in three of those five seasons, and the Chargers finished 2-12 in the one year Unitas spent in San Diego.

That's why it's hard for me to make the case for Unitas as the best quarterback ever. We wouldn't ignore those subpar performances if they had come at the beginning of his career, or somewhere in the middle. I'm not sure why we can ignore them at the end.

Otto Graham (1946–1955)

Graham played ten seasons with the Cleveland Browns and led them to the championship game every year. The team had a record of 105-17-4 with Graham as their starter, and I don't have to tell you that's the best ever for a starting quarterback. Graham has more net wins than any player in NFL history.

Net Wins

1	Otto Graham	88
2	Joe Montana	81
3	John Elway	68
4	Brett Favre	66
5	Johnny Unitas	65
6	Tom Brady	60
7	Roger Staubach	54
8t	Terry Bradshaw	53
8t	Dan Marino	53
10	Bart Starr	51

He was a great passer, and in his prime he was as productive as anybody. Graham led the league in passing yards five times in his ten years in the league, even though the Browns great defense and outstanding running game often meant he was throwing less often. In his first season, he was averaging just 13.4 pass attempts per game. In his final season, he threw only 15.4 times per game. On both occasions, however, he led the league in yards per attempt.

Graham wasn't just a great passer, but a phenomenal all-around athlete who would do whatever it took to win. His 44 career rushing touchdowns is the highest total ever for a quarterback. We don't really know how good of a runner he was, because both the AAFC and the NFL counted sacks as running plays in those days. That means his career total of 405 rushes for 882 yards is significantly deflated.

Graham was twenty-five when he began his pro football career, having gone directly from college to serve in the Navy Air Corps. He announced his plans to retire after the 1954 season. He was thirty-four years old, and with some good business opportunities beckoning, it made sense to get out before his skills started to deteriorate. In the NFL title game, he threw for three touchdowns and ran for three more in a 56–10 drubbing of the Lions.

The next summer, Cleveland head coach Paul Brown convinced Graham to come out of retirement and play one more season by making him the league's highest-paid player—a one-year $25,000 contract. Graham went out on top—again—winning the league's MVP award and leading the Browns to another NFL title.

Between the time he left the Navy and joined the Browns, Graham spent a season playing pro basketball with the Rochester Royals. He was the sixth man on a team that won the 1946 league championship. That team featured four future basketball Hall of Famers: Bob Davies, Al Cervi, Red Holzman, and coach Les Harrison.

Steve Young (1985–1999)

Some guys are in the right place at the right time. Steve Young always seemed to be in the wrong place. It's hard to decide whether the struggles he went through made him a great quarterback, or if this Hall of Famer was robbed of some of his best seasons.

He started his pro career in the USFL, then spent two seasons with the woeful Tampa Bay Buccaneers, and finally served as Joe Montana's backup in San Francisco for four years. He was thirty years old before he got a chance to start for the Forty-Niners.

His critics dismiss him as a dink-and-dunk quarterback, a guy who benefited from playing in the 49ers West Coast offense. Those critics ignore the fact that his average of 8.0 yards per attempt ranks 6th all time. He never led the league in passing yards, but finished 2nd three times. He trailed

John Elway by seven yards in 1993 and finished 42 yards behind Bret Favre in 1998. The idea that Young made his living throwing 8-yard passes just isn't correct.

Young also led the league in touchdown passes four times, including his first three years as the San Francisco starter. From 1992 to 1994 he threw 89 touchdowns against 33 interceptions and averaged more than 3800 yards per season. That 1994 season was capped by Young's only Super Bowl win, where he threw a record six touchdown passes. His best season—his last full one—came in 1998, when he passed for 4170 yards, threw 36 TDs, and just 12 interceptions. He also ran for 454 yards and 6 touchdowns that year.

Critics of Young also like to point out that he inherited a great team when Montana was traded, but as I point out in my comments on George Seifert, the team was largely remade in the two seasons after Bill Walsh retired. About the only player Young and Montana both had to work with was Jerry Rice. Besides, if you do a side-by-side comparison, it's clear that Young wasn't simply riding a wave that Montana had created. In Montana's ten seasons as the starter, the Niners were 112-39-1, a .740 winning percentage. In Young's eight seasons as the starter, the team's record was 95-33, or .742 percentage. That's virtually identical.

If you look at their playing stats for the 49ers, Montana rates an edge because he played two more seasons than Young. But if you prorate the numbers to an equal number of passing attempts (Young/A), you'll see that Young was not only a more accurate passer, he was also getting more yards per pass play.

Player	Com	Att	Yds	TD	Int
Montana	2929	4600	35124	244	123
Young/A	3026	4600	37712	279	108
Young	2400	3648	29907	221	86

Young's mobility was all a major factor in his success. He ranks 1st all-time among quarterbacks with 43 rushing touchdowns and 2nd to Randall Cunningham with 4239 rushing yards.

The glaring difference between Montana and Young is their performance in the postseason. Young's postseason record was 8-6, and with the exception of the 6-touchdown performance in Super Bowl XXIX, he had a 14/13 touchdown-to-interception ratio in thirteen playoff games. Take out Montana's best playoff game—5 touchdowns in Super Bowl XXIV, and his ratio was still 40/21.

Peyton Manning (1998–2007)

Only two quarterbacks rank in the top 20 all-time in each of the four rate statistics for passers: completion percentage, yards per attempt, touchdowns per attempt, and interceptions per attempt. One is Steve Young, the other is Peyton Manning.

Rate statistics can go up or down, of course, but after ten seasons, Manning's raw statistics have already reached Hall of Fame levels. During the 2006 season, he moved past HOFers Jim Kelly and Troy Aikman in career pass attempts. In a similar amount of attempts, Manning threw for more yards, fewer interceptions, and a lot more touchdowns.

Player	Com	Att	Yds	TD	Int
Manning	3131	4890	37586	275	139
Kelly	2874	4779	35467	237	175
Aikman	2898	4715	32942	165	141

It's very likely that if he can avoid serious injury, Manning will finish his career at the top of these rankings, passing both Marino and Favre to set new career records for yards and touchdowns. In fact, it's reasonable to suggest that he will go so far beyond the current records so as to render them untouchable.

Fran Tarkenton (1961–1978)

A few writers have referred to Tarkenton as the first scrambling quarterback. That's not only historically inaccurate, but it creates an impression of him that may be misleading for those who never saw him play.

Sure, he scrambled a lot early in his career, running for his life with an expansion team in Minnesota. Later, when he was traded to the rebuilding Giants, his elusiveness in the backfield kept him from getting hurt and helped him get an otherwise moribund offense moving.

Unlike most quarterbacks labeled "scramblers," Tarkenton wasn't particularly quick, and he didn't take off like a running back. He dodged and danced and tried to avoid the pass rush long enough to get a pass away. With his skinny legs and jitterbug style, Tarkenton was able to escape often enough.

All of that hides the fact that he was a remarkably gifted passer. If he'd played on better teams and had the luxury of being a pure pocket quarterback, there's no telling what he might have done. Tarkenton was drafted by both the NFL's Vikings and the AFL's Boston Patriots. Things would have been very different had he elected to sign with the Patriots, a team with more talent and a much more explosive offense. Still, despite the fact that his team only finished with a winning record three times in his first eleven seasons, he became one of the most prolific passers in pro football.

Just when it looked like the Vikings were becoming competitive, Tarkenton was traded to New York. In his first year with the Giants he threw for a career-high 29 touchdowns, but a lousy running game kept the team from turning the corner. In 1972 he was shipped back to Minnesota, where head coach Bud Grant had turned the team into one of the NFC's best. Tarkenton helped lead the Vikes to the Super Bowl three times in a four-year span, but each time they lost.

He recovered from a broken leg in 1977, setting a career high with 3468 yards the following year. Age and the injury, however, had dramatically limited his mobility, and since he also threw 32 interceptions, it was less of a comeback than a farewell. Tarkenton retired after eighteen NFL seasons and headed for the broadcast booth.

It's worth noting that Tarkenton has had tremendous success as a businessman in his postplaying days and was an early pioneer in the computer software business.

#10
Roger Staubach (1969–1979)

In his first season as the Cowboys' starting quarterback, he won the Super Bowl and was named the NFL's Most Valuable Player. Not a bad debut, but unfortunately it didn't happen until he was twenty-nine years old.

Staubach's pro career was delayed by a four-year stint in the Navy, then two years as the backup behind Craig Morton. Once he finally got a chance to play, it was clear that he was going to be a star. Cowboys coach Tom Landry said, "Roger Staubach might be the best combination of a passer, an athlete, and a leader ever to play in the NFL." Now granted, Landry is not exactly an impartial observer, but Staubach's ability to excel in each of those roles was undeniable. In eight seasons as the Cowboys' starting quarterback, Staubach led his team to 23 come-from-behind victories, with 14 of them coming in the final 2 minutes.

Staubach missed most of the 1972 season with a separated shoulder, but returned to lead the league in touchdown passes in 1973. In his final season he set career highs with 3586 yards and 27 touchdowns, but that didn't dissuade him from walking away. Staubach finished among the top five in passing yards for six straight years but was never selected to an All-Pro team.

History has been pretty kind to Staubach. For many star quarterbacks, the regard with which they were held during their playing days fade as time passes. When their careers are viewed from some distance and their achievements are put into context, their luster fades. If anything, the regard for Staubach has grown as the years have passed.

#11
Len Dawson (1957–1975)

Dawson was a highly regarded college quarterback who washed out of the NFL after five lackluster seasons with the Steelers and Browns.

If this has happened just a few years earlier, that would have been the end of the story, but Dawson got a second chance in the American Football League and made the most of it. He joined the Dallas Texans in 1962, and under the tutelage of coach Hank Stram, Dawson finally blossomed. Together, they perfected an offense built around a moving pocket, and the pair won the AFL championship in their first season together. They would win two more AFL titles and a Super Bowl after the club moved north and became the Kansas City Chiefs. Dawson led the AFL in touchdown passes four times.

One of the reasons for Dawson's success was that he learned to become a great play-action passer. The Chiefs had explosive running backs like Abner Haynes and Mike Garrett, and Dawson understood that the threat of the running game helped soften the defense for the passing game. He didn't have the strongest arm, but he was an incredibly accurate passer and had the confidence to stay cool under pressure.

#12
Bobby Layne (1948–1962)

A tailback in college, Layne struggled in the pro ranks as the Bears tried to turn him into a T-formation quarterback. Like Len Dawson, Layne bounced around for a few years before he landed with a team that was a good fit. And like Dawson, it was an astute coach who saw the young man's potential and knew what to do with it.

Layne joined the Detroit Lions in 1950, where coach Buddy Parker had a plan. He knew that Layne's passing skills were raw but felt that his gutsy leadership and fearlessness could be invalu-

able when surrounded by other talented players. Layne was reunited with his friend and former high school teammate Doak Walker. Within a couple of years, the pair had become the best backfield in the league.

What he lacked in passing polish, Layne made up with pure bravado. Red Hickey, who coached the 49ers, said "as bad as he looked throwing the ball, he was a winner." Layne led the Lions to four NFL championship games in six seasons—all against the Cleveland Browns. The Lions won three out of four. Layne had a reputation for partying, which I guess was a polite way of saying that he drank a lot. An awful lot. There's one school of thought that says the alcohol helped to fuel his hard-driving personality and give him the sense of reckless abandon that made him a good leader. If you ask me, that's just hogwash. You can't tell me that guys like Layne or Mickey Mantle or Pete Maravich would have been lesser players if they were sober. There's a certain romanticism that has grown up around those guys, but the bottom line is that they were great players despite the fact that they had a drinking problem . . . not because of it.

Layne was injured during the 1958 season, and when backup Tobin Rote played well in his absence, the Lions decided to trade their veteran and stick with the younger player. Layne was reunited with coach Parker in Pittsburgh. The team finished with a winning record in Layne's first two seasons in Pittsburgh—the first back-to-back winning seasons in team history. Although he injected some much-needed excitement into a Steelers program with a long history of losing, it wasn't enough to get the team into the playoffs.

#13
Y. A. Tittle (1948–1964)

Tittle is best remembered today for an iconic photograph of defeat. In the image, Tittle is kneeling on the grass in the end zone, with a look of resignation on his face. A small trickle of blood runs down his forehead, symbolizing the sacrifice he has made, albeit a futile one.

In recent years I have developed an interest in the history of sports photography. I've spent considerable time reading about legendary photographers and the images they captured. There are usually great stories behind each one, and this one is no exception. The picture was taken by a man named Morris Berman, who was working for the *Pittsburgh Post-Gazette* at the time.

Some accounts have said that this photo came in the last game of Tittle's career, but that's not correct. It came earlier in his final season in a game against the Steelers. Tittle was trying to rally his team from behind, but that effort was thwarted when he was sacked by Pittsburgh defensive end John Baker. It was one of many frustrating afternoons for Tittle that season. The Giants finished 2-10-2 in what would be his last season.

Berman's editors didn't want to run the picture because it didn't have any action in it. They used it later, almost as an afterthought, and to their surprise people were captivated by the image. It would eventually win the National Headliner Award for best sport photograph in 1964. It remains one of the most well-known sports images.

When Berman died in 2002, the *Milwaukee Journal Sentinel* described the long-term effect of that photograph in their obituary of the photographer:

> The picture was not only an aesthetic success—capturing Tittle's failed last stand in the brutal world of pro football—but also helped change the way photographers looked at sports. While action shots were still a staple in newspapers and sports magazines, more subtle images that went beyond the action genre started to emerge.

Tittle's last NFL game actually took place in the Polo Grounds, a lopsided 52–20 loss to the Browns on a rain soaked field. A *New York Times* photographer took a memorable shot of him that day, sitting on the bench with his head bowed, towel in hand, his uniform wet and muddy.

#14 Norm Van Brocklin (1949–1960)

When Van Brocklin joined the Rams, the team already had a future Hall of Famer at quarterback. Bob Waterfield was only twenty-nine and led the team to an NFL championship in 1949, Van Brocklin's rookie season. It was clear that both players were gifted passers—maybe the best two in the league—but rather than decide between them, head coach Joe Stydahar had the two men share playing time. Both players hated the idea, but it worked. The Rams returned to the title game in 1950 with the league's top-ranked offense.

Van Brocklin wanted the job for himself, and he staked his claim in the 1951 season opener. With Waterfield sidelined by a minor injury, Van Brocklin completed 27 of 41 passes for 5 touchdowns and an NFL record 554 yards. That's a mark that's never been broken, and it helped Van Brocklin overtake his rival and become the lone starter. He led the Rams to the championship game again, facing the heavily favored Cleveland Browns. Van Brocklin's 73-yard touchdown pass to Tom Fears in the fourth quarter broke a 17–17 tie and gave the Rams the victory.

At the end of the 1957 season, Van Brocklin stunned everybody by announcing his retirement. "Nine years of football is enough," he declared, but the unspoken feeling was that three years under coach Sid Gillman was enough. What he really wanted was a change of scenery, and the Rams were happy to oblige. In May, they traded Van Brocklin to the last-place Philadelphia Eagles. Coach Buck Shaw built a team around a handful of veterans, and they improved from 2-9-1 to 7-5 in 1959. Things got even better in 1960, with Van Brocklin leading the Eagles to the NFL championship. Once again, he rallied his team for a fourth-quarter scoring drive to win the game. In doing so, he became the first quarterback to win NFL title games with two different teams.

Eagles head coach Buck Shaw retired during the off-season, and when the team named assistant Nick Skorich as his replacement, Van Brocklin was outraged. He claimed that Eagles' management had promised him he would succeed Shaw, a claim they didn't deny. Eventually he was asked to stay on as a player-coach, but Van Brocklin scoffed at the idea, saying "that stuff went out with Johnny Blood."

Van Brocklin left Philadelphia and spent the next fourteen seasons as an NFL head coach, first with the expansion Minnesota Vikings and later with the Atlanta Falcons. He suffered a number of illnesses after leaving the Falcons, including surgery to remove a brain tumor in the early 1980s. Asked about it, Van Brocklin joked, "it was actually a brain *transplant*. They gave me a sportswriter's brain to make sure I got one that hadn't been used."

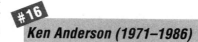

Steve McNair (1995–2007)

A great scrambling quarterback who could never seem to stay healthy. Coming out of a small school like Alcorn State, a lot of people wondered whether McNair could make a successful transition to the NFL game. He did, thanks in large part to the patience of Oilers head coach Jeff Fisher. While many young quarterbacks of the same era were rushed into the starting lineup, McNair spent most of his first two seasons watching and learning, taking over the starting job late in 1996.

McNair only missed eight games in his first seven seasons as a starter, but it seemed as if he was always playing through injuries that may have sidelined other players. The physical toll was largely the result of his choice to take off running, making him fair game for tacklers. He ran the ball 101 times in his first year as a starter, and at least 70 times in each of the next five seasons.

His playing style changed dramatically in 2003. He stopped scrambling, partly by design and partly as result of his physical limitations. As so often happens with scramblers, this shift in emphasis helped him become a more productive passer,

and he shared Most Valuable Player honors with Peyton Manning at season's end.

Ken Anderson (1971–1986)

Anderson's absence from the Pro Football Hall of Fame bothers me. Some men are overlooked for reasons that we can understand—their numbers understate their performance, they had off-the-field problems, or they spent their career stuck with a lousy team. Anderson suffered none of those calamities, but the selectors have largely ignored him.

The biggest reason? He had the misfortune of playing in the same division as the Pittsburgh Steelers in the 1970s. The Bengals finished with a winning record in each of Anderson's first six seasons, but each time they ended up behind the Steelers in the final standings. They finished 10-4 in 1976 and missed the playoffs. They finished 11-3 in 1975—the second-best record in the AFC—but the Steelers took the division crown at 12-2. Pittsburgh got home field advantage in the playoffs while the Bengals had to go on the road for their opening-round game with Oakland.

You have to know that team performance is the main reason why Steelers quarterback Terry Bradshaw breezed into Canton while Anderson has been largely ignored. It can't be about the individual performances. Their careers covered essentially the same time period, and Anderson was clearly the better passer.

Career Stats

Player	G	Yds	TD	Int	Rating
Bradshaw	168	27989	212	210	70.9
Anderson	192	32838	197	160	81.9

Bradshaw is just six months older than Anderson, although they entered the NFL a year apart. If you put them side by side from 1973 to 1982, the ten years when they were both starting, you'll find that Anderson had the better statistics in six or seven of those seasons. And while you might argue that the Steelers won more games than the Bengals in eight of those ten seasons, I'd counter that Bradshaw was surrounded by Hall of Famers—four on offense and four on defense—while Anderson didn't have any until the Bengals drafted tackle Anthony Munoz in 1980.

The bottom line, of course, is winning. The greatness of a quarterback is measured in large part by how far he took his team, and Bradshaw ended the decade with four Super Bowl rings. Anderson has none.

Anderson was the first West Coast quarterback, helping perfect Bill Walsh's short passing attack before it had even earned that name. This style of play—high percentage short passes—was less popular at the time than the vertical passing game, and the value of Anderson's contributions wasn't fully appreciated.

It also doesn't help that he's had such a poor track record as a quarterbacks coach after he retired. During his time on the staff in Cincinnati, he was responsible for two huge flops—David Klingler and Akili Smith—and then he went to Jacksonville where, under his guidance, Byron Leftwich failed to make significant progress.

#17
Sammy Baugh (1937–1952)

Baugh is widely regarded as one of the best punters in football history, probably the best in the premodern era from 1920 to 1959. He was also one of the best defensive backs of his time, and you can make a convincing case that his performance in those two areas was more than enough to merit his selection for the Hall of Fame.

No matter how great those accomplishments were, they're a mere footnote to what Baugh did as a quarterback. It wasn't just that he stood head and shoulders above the other passers of his day. His style of play revolutionized the game and helped the NFL begin to transform from a game predicated on running the ball to the modern-style passing attack. Before Baugh, teams would pass about eight times a game, usually in a desperate attempt to convert on third and long. Baugh helped to introduce the strategy of throwing on first and second down.

Having the idea was the easy part. Making it work was a different proposition, but Baugh had both a strong arm and the accuracy to hit receivers in stride. Defenses weren't sure how to react. They could no longer stuff the line of scrimmage with players and merely guess whether the offense was going to run left or right. Teams responded first by dropping players off the line of scrimmage—creating the linebacker position—and later by spreading defenders out wide to help the safety in pass coverage—creating what we'd call today the cornerback position. Other offenses began to change too. They began to abandon the single-wing offense, which had been a staple for two decades, in favor of the modern T that Baugh and the Redskins had perfected.

#18
Tom Brady (2000–2007)

In his first season in the NFL, Tom Brady threw for 6 yards in three attempts. Five years later he would hoist his third Super Bowl trophy. To say nobody saw this coming is an understatement indeed. Taking over for an injured Drew Bledsoe early in the 2001 season, there were mixed expectations for the inexperienced Brady. Going by his first two games as a starter, versus the Colts and Dolphins, respectively, it looked like the Patriots were in big trouble. Not until the Chargers came to town on October 14, 2001, did we see some signs of promise.

Brady's team began that day a run that ranks among the best in NFL history. From week five of the 2002 season through week seven of the 2003 season, Brady and the Patriots did not lose a single game, 21 games in total including two playoff games and a Super Bowl championship. His numbers weren't earth-shattering, but his ability to win games was undeniable.

I wonder whether we would have ever heard of Tom Brady if Patriots' starter Drew Bledsoe hadn't been knocked out of that game in 2001. Brady barely made the Patriots as rookie, ending up fourth on the depth chart behind Bledsoe, journeyman John Friesz, and prospect Michael Bishop. He beat Bishop out for the backup job during training camp in 2001, but nobody viewed Tom Brady as a star in waiting. I can't find any scouting reports from the era suggesting that his physical skills or any other attributes stood out. If Bledsoe had stayed healthy, Brady might have spent several seasons on the bench before being discarded in favor of another young passer. There are scores of young quarterbacks who follow this path, never getting much of an opportunity to do what Brady did. How many of them could have been great players if only they had been given a chance?

You could make a good case that Brady clinched a spot in Canton after winning three Super Bowls in his first four seasons. Any doubters were silenced after his 2007 season, arguably the best ever by a quarterback. His 4806 passing yards was the third highest total in NFL history, and his 50 touchdown passes set a new record. Brady's first seven seasons are enough to boost him to 18th in my rankings, and he's only thirty years old.

#19
Bart Starr (1956–1971)

Packers coach Vince Lombardi was fiery and intense. Quarterback Bart Starr was deliberative and calm. The more time I spend studying the Green Bay dynasty, the more convinced I become that this contrast between the two men was central to the team's success in the 1960s.

In an era when most coaches had taken over the play-calling duties, Lombardi let Starr run the offense. If you know anything about Lombardi and his reputation as a detail-obsessed perfectionist, you know what a measure of respect that decision was. Starr was praised by both teammates and opponents for his ability to know what opposing

defenses were going to do. This came as the by-product of relentless study. He had a file cabinet full of his own notes on opposing teams, gleaned from watching film and from his own experiences against those teams.

Others around him garnered much of the glory. Certainly Lombardi got his share of attention, as did the flamboyant Paul Hornung, the tough and gritty Jim Taylor, and others on both sides of the ball. Some have described Starr as being shy, which seems an unlikely attribute for a successful NFL quarterback. In his autobiography, teammate Jerry Kramer explained why it's more complex than that. "My emotions often ruled me. Bart ruled his. Emotional control is fundamental to understanding who Bart Starr is. It has cost him much yet given him more. It has cost him celebrity while giving him poise."

#20
Sid Luckman (1939–1950)

Sid Luckman arrived in the NFL at the same time as Sammy Baugh, and had a similar impact. Bears coach George Halas enlisted offensive guru Clark Shaughnessy to install the modern T offense, and by Luckman's second season the team was flying.

The two new passing stars met in the 1940 championship game, and Luckman's Bears trounced Baugh's Redskins with a 73–0 walloping that remains the most lopsided defeat in NFL history. The two quarterbacks would meet twice more in the title game over the next three seasons, with Baugh extracting some measure of revenge by winning in 1942, and Luckman prevailing again in 1943.

In all, Luckman led the Bears to four championships in seven seasons, while Baugh triumphed just once. Still, history regards Baugh as the better player. His individual statistics were a little better, but largely it stems from the perception that Baugh was the architect of the Redskins passing game while Luckman was just a tool used by his innovative coaches.

21

Jim Kelly (1986–1996)

Probably the best player to come out of the United States Football League. No, make that definitely.

One look at the numbers he posted in that rival league might make you gasp. In his first season, he threw for 5219 yards and 44 touchdowns. Both totals surpassed any single-season record set in the NFL. The following year his numbers dropped slightly, but were still remarkable (4623 yards, 39 touchdowns).

Folks in western New York were angry that Kelly spurned the Bills, but chances are, he was a better quarterback for having spent that time in the USFL. He would have gotten pummeled in Buffalo, playing for a lousy team in lousy weather, and who knows if he'd have been able to hold up long enough to become a great quarterback.

Kelly was of course a great passer, but what made him a Hall of Famer was his ability to remain calm under pressure. In the late eighties, Bengals coach Sam Wyche came up with a no-huddle offense that his team employed throughout the game. It was a strategy that teams had used for years in the fourth quarter when they were furiously trying to mount a comeback, helping them get as many plays off as quickly as possible. Wyche had a different strategy. He reasoned that by skipping the huddle and sending his players right to the line of scrimmage, he could prevent the defense from making frequent substitutions. If a team brought in an extra lineman on third and short, the Bengals would run the next play before their opponents could revert back to their base defense. It was sometimes effective, always infuriating, and, frankly, I'm not sure why more teams didn't emulate it.

The Bills were perhaps the only team to immediately adopt the no-huddle offense, and they dubbed their version the "K-Gun" in honor of Kelly. Unlike the Bengals though, Kelly's no-huddle offense wasn't so much about preventing substitutions as it was applying unyielding pressure. Opposing defenses quickly wore out, or grew confused about their assignments while trying to rapidly adjust to a wide variety of offensive formations.

That confrontational style of play suited Kelly perfectly. He was a physically aggressive quarterback who would rather overpower you than trick you. Kelly gets some of the blame for the Bills postseason failures, but, in fairness, injuries kept him from being more of a factor. He was knocked out of Super Bowl XXVII against Dallas early in the second quarter with a sprained knee. Injuries also kept Kelly out of the Bills' first two playoff games in 1992.

22

Daryle Lamonica (1963–1974)

When you think of the Raiders, you often think of wide-open offense with a lot of deep, risky passes. That image was effectively created during Lamonica's days with the team, from 1967 to 1974. It was a clear case of leveraging the weapons they had. Lamonica had a cannon for an arm and the confidence of ten men, so why not throw deep often?

Despite the aggressive passing game, Lamonica threw more touchdowns than interceptions in his six years as Oakland's starter. The Raiders won three consecutive division titles with him at the helm and made it to three AFL championship games, winning one in 1967. They followed that triumph with a trip to Super Bowl II, where they lost to the Packers.

Lamonica spent the first four years of his pro career in the AFL with the Buffalo Bills as a backup to Jack Kemp. While he did play quite a bit, he was never particularly effective. It's a perfect illustration of how a quarterback can excel in the right system and flounder in one that doesn't suit his strengths.

23

Roman Gabriel (1962–1977)

Early in his career, it looked like he was going to be a Hall of Fame caliber quarterback. At 6-foot-5 and 220 pounds, he was the biggest quarterback of his day, and he used his size to his advantage. Gabriel threw 25 touchdown passes and ran for six more in 1967, leading the Rams to the playoffs with an 11-1-2 record. He was named Most Valuable Player in 1969, and by then the Rams had become one of the best teams of the late sixties. But Gabriel floundered after that, and as the team's once fearsome defense regressed, the quarterback's performance suffered.

A trade to the Eagles in 1973 helped him get back on track, at least briefly. He was Comeback Player of the Year in 1973, but it was more of a last gasp than a return to glory.

#24
Randall Cunningham (1985–2001)

A vastly underrated quarterback who won two Most Valuable Player Awards eight years apart. Early in his career, he was a scrambler. If he hadn't been, he might not have survived. Behind a porous offensive line in Philadelphia in 1986, he was sacked 72 times even though he only took about half of the snaps. In 1990 he threw for 3466 yards and ran for 942—a record at the time for quarterbacks. Cunningham won his first MVP Award that year after leading his team to their third straight playoff appearance.

Injuries kept Cunningham out of action for two of the next three seasons. He suffered torn knee ligaments in the first quarter of the 1991 season opener and missed the rest of the year. He missed 12 games in 1993 after breaking his left leg. Once he returned, he was no longer an effective scrambler, and he struggled to adjust to his new limitations. After a lackluster 1994 season, Cunningham was benched in 1995 and out of football completely in 1996, cut loose by the Eagles and not offered a contract by any other team.

Cunningham would later say that sitting out a year was the best thing that could have happened to him. "I've been a Christian since 1987, but I was a hypocrite for a lot of that time. I was built up to be this superstar, and I spent all my time trying to live up to that . . . I needed to humble myself."

Eagles wide receivers coach Gerald Carr echoed those sentiments in a *Sports Illustrated* article: "He finally realized it wasn't all about Randall. Once he realized it wasn't all about him being a superstar, he became one."

Cunningham signed as a backup in Minnesota in 1997, and by then he had reinvented himself. After starter Brad Johnson broke his leg in the second game of the 1998 season, Cunningham took over and helped lead the Vikings to a 15-1 record. He set career highs in touchdowns (32) and yards (3404) while running for only 132, his lowest total for a full season. He won his second Most Valuable Player award that year, in what would prove to be his last season as a starter.

#25
Terry Bradshaw (1970–1983)

Bradshaw gets credit for some things that were accomplished by others, and he gets a pass on some of his poor performances because his teammates were able to overcome them.

That's not to say that I don't think Bradshaw was a great quarterback. He ranks 25th on my list, comfortably ahead of other players who are deserving Hall of Famers. But I've seen more than one ranking of quarterbacks that puts Bradshaw in the top ten, and I just think it's hard to make that case.

As I mentioned in my comments on Ken Anderson, Bradshaw had the great advantage of playing on a team with eight other Hall of Famers. He had a great running back to hand off to (Franco Harris), a pair of great receivers (John Stallworth and Lynn Swann), a legendary center (Mike Webster), and a defense that was consistently dominant.

The Steelers won an awful lot of games in the seventies, and while Bradshaw had a hand in many of those victories, there were times when he was more of a spectator. Early in his career, the Steelers were a running team. When they won their first Super Bowl in 1974, Bradshaw threw just seven touchdown passes during the regular season. When they won it again in 1975, he finished

14th in passing yards in an eighteen-team league. Bradshaw had two Super Bowl rings, but his career totals at that point showed 66 touchdowns and 90 interceptions.

The Steelers did start throwing the ball more later in his career, mostly in response to Franco Harris becoming a less dominating runner. He won the MVP Award in 1978 with a pretty good season, and he was just as good the following year.

In the end, I think you have to weigh both the good and the bad in evaluating Bradshaw's career. He threw an awful lot of interceptions because he took risks. They hurt his personal statistics, but because of the tremendous talent surrounding him, they were risks he could afford to take.

Donovan McNabb (1999–2007)

When the Eagles drafted Donovan McNabb with the second overall pick in the 1999 NFL draft, Philadelphia fans responded with boos. At the time, the negative reaction was understandable. The Eagles were a lousy team, and running back Ricky Williams was a more popular choice.

In the years that followed that draft day, McNabb's time in Philadelphia has been bittersweet. He endured public criticism from conservative commentator Rush Limbaugh and feuded with teammate Terrell Owens. Through it all, he led what many considered an otherwise lackluster offense and helped the Eagles reach the NFC championship game in four straight seasons.

One of the reasons the fans grew impatient with McNabb was that four of his first eight seasons ended early because of injury. The style of play that makes him a daring and exciting quarterback also resulted in his missing 20 percent of his team's games. Nobody questions his toughness. He threw 4 touchdowns in a 2002 game against the Cardinals, playing the whole game without realizing he'd broken his leg on the third play of the day.

This chapter is full of scrambling quarterbacks who had to stop running later in their career, and it certainly seems like that's the path McNabb is

heading down. I think the evidence suggests he's a good enough passer to make the transition. McNabb is the second-least-intercepted quarterback (per pass attempt) in NFL history, ranking behind Neil O'Donnell.

Troy Aikman (1989–2000)

There are some interesting similarities between Aikman and Terry Bradshaw. Both men were star quarterbacks in college drafted by teams at rock bottom. Both were the first of what would be an unusually large collection of great players, and both led their teams to a string of Super Bowl victories without posting fantastic statistics.

While the storylines are similar, Aikman and Bradshaw were very different players. Bradshaw was a gambler, a guy whose long passes were just as likely to be picked off as they were to produce a touchdown. Aikman took fewer risks, and while there were fewer big plays, there were also fewer turnovers.

The two played roughly the same number of games (168 for Aikman, 165 for Bradshaw), and a side-by-side comparison helps to illustrate the different playing styles. Bradshaw's edge in yards per attempt (7.2 to 7.0) shows that he was making more big plays, but by every other metric, Aikman was more productive.

Player	TD	Int	Att/G	Yds/G	Com Pct
Aikman	165	141	28.6	199.6	61.5
Bradshaw	212	210	23.2	166.6	51.9

Aikman was an All-Pro three times, though he never threw more than 16 touchdown passes in any of those seasons. In fact, he only threw 20 touchdowns one time in his career. He walked away from the game after suffering two concussions during the 2000 season—the count was four in his last two seasons and ten overall. That premature retirement and his relatively low seasonal totals kept him from accruing the kinds of career stats normally associated with great quarterbacks, but his record of success was undeniable.

John Hadl (1962–1977)

A prolific passer who thrived in Sid Gillman's offense, Hadl won two passing titles in the AFL and another in the NFL. The Chargers won the 1963 AFL Championship with veteran passer Tobin Rote at the helm, but that didn't discourage them from handing the job to the younger Hadl the following year. He didn't miss a beat, leading the Chargers back to the title game in 1964 and 1965.

As he got older, Hadl fell into a bad habit of forcing throws that he could no longer make. The result was an alarmingly high number of interceptions. He threw 32 in 1968, 25 in 1971, and 26 in a disastrous 1972 campaign that was his undoing.

#29

Warren Moon (1984–2000)

Frankly, I was surprised when Moon was selected for the Hall of Fame in his first year of eligibility . . . not because I didn't think he was overwhelmingly worthy, but because his was exactly the kind of career that the selectors had tended to overlook in the past. When he retired, he ranked 3rd all-time in passing yards and 4th in touchdown passes—impressive figures when you consider that he didn't reach the NFL until he was nearly twenty-eight years old.

Moon was a spectacular college quarterback, leading the Washington Huskies to a Rose Bowl victory over Michigan as a senior. He had a rifle arm, but none of the NFL teams were willing to draft him unless he changed positions. The league had seen a few other African-American quarterbacks, but teams were generally not willing to consider one as anything more than a novelty. With no other options, Moon went to Canada, where he took the league by storm. He led the Edmonton Eskimos to an unprecedented five straight Grey Cup victories, after which he announced his intention to play in the NFL. By then, it was hard to deny that he had the ability to play.

The Houston Oilers won a bidding war for his services, and while Moon struggled in his first few seasons, he eventually began to have the same kind of success in the states that he had in the CFL. The turning point was the Oilers adoption of the run-and-shoot offense, a system that largely ignored the running game and put the burden of the offense on the quarterback. Moon thrived in the run-and-shoot, setting a single-season record with 655 pass attempts in 1991.

The Oilers won with Moon, and he led them to the playoffs each year from 1987 to 1993. Despite all of their regular-season success, Moon never got his team to an AFC championship game. His playoff record in Houston was just 3-7.

Moon had two more 4000-yard seasons with the Vikings, and he had a phenomenal season in Seattle at the age of forty-one, throwing for 3678 yards and 25 touchdowns.

#30

Charley Conerly (1948–1961)

"Chuckin' Charley" loved to throw the ball, but because he had been a tailback in college he was also an effective runner. Conerly rushed for 5 touchdowns as a rookie and led the league with 2175 passing yards.

Conerly was throwing less by the mid-fifties, due largely to the conservative approach of head coach Jim Lee Howell and the emergence of a strong running game with Frank Gifford and Alex Webster. Conerly helped lead the Giants to the NFL championship game three times in four years, beating the Bears for the title in 1956. He was also on the losing side of the "Greatest Game Ever Played," the 1958 NFL championship game against Johnny Unitas and the Colts. While it was Unitas who rose to the top that day, Conerly played magnificently, at one point leading his team on a 95-yard drive to take the lead in the fourth quarter.

#31 John Brodie (1957–1973)

Brodie was a steady but unspectacular quarterback for the 49ers, and while he played well at times, the team went through the entire decade of the sixties without once reaching the playoffs.

Things changed with the arrival of coach Dick Nolan, and in 1970 Brodie had one of the best seasons of his long career. At thirty-five, he led the newly merged league in passing yards, touchdowns, and completions, and he won the Most Valuable Player Award. For three straight seasons Brodie led the Niners into the playoffs, but each time their quest for the Super Bowl ended with narrow losses to the Dallas Cowboys.

Brodie retired after a seventeen-year professional career, all with San Francisco. His post-NFL career was just as interesting. For years, Brodie was a prominent member of the Church of Scientology and its most visible spokesperson. In an interview with *Time* magazine, he said that when pain in his throwing arm threatened his career, he applied Dianetics techniques and soon was "zipping the ball" again like a young man. He eventually left the Church, telling the *Los Angeles Times* that some of his friends in Scientology were expelled and harassed during a power struggle with church management.

He also spent thirteen years playing professional golf on the Senior PGA tour, posting one tournament win and a dozen top ten finishes.

#32 Mark Brunell (1994–2007)

There's a picture I love from Packers training camp in 1994. It shows the four quarterbacks the team had on the roster standing together during a drill: Brett Favre, Ty Detmer, Kurt Warner, and Mark Brunell. Favre had spent two seasons as the Packers starter but had struggled—1994 would prove to be his breakout season. Detmer, winner of the 1990 Heisman Trophy, had spent two years as Favre's backup. Warner was an undrafted rookie with a rocket arm, and Brunell was the Packer's 5th-round pick from the year before. Looking back, I don't think anybody realized what an amazing collection of young quarterbacks the team had assembled.

Warner was used as a spare arm for passing drills, and he was released in mid-August without making much of an impression. But it was clear to most observers that both Detmer and Brunell had talent. When Favre threw for 3882 yards and 33 touchdowns that season, the two youngsters became expendable and other teams came calling. Detmer ended up in Philadelphia, spending two years as their starter before the Eagles drafted Donovan McNabb. Brunell went to the Jacksonville Jaguars, an expansion team that became competitive right away. He led the league with 4367 passing yards in 1996, leading the Jags to the AFC championship game in just their second season. Jacksonville made the playoffs in each of the next three seasons, finishing 14-2 in 1999 and advancing to the AFC title game again.

Brunell had a brief resurgence with the Washington Redskins, but he had become a less effective quarterback as his arm strength diminished. A series of knee injuries forced him to wear a brace while playing and eliminated whatever mobility he had possessed.

#33 Rich Gannon (1987–2004)

He started his career with the Minnesota Vikings and had limited success in two years as a starter. When Dennis Green arrived as the team's head coach, he decided he'd rather have a veteran quarterback and someone with a more fiery personality. Gannon was cut loose and spent the next several seasons as a backup. Twice during his career he went unsigned and sat out the entire season.

There's something to be said for karma, I suppose, because by the late 1990s, Gannon had become a grizzled veteran, developing a fiery competitiveness that teams were looking for. Injuries to starter Elvis Grbac made Gannon the Chiefs starter for most of the 1998 season, and he played well enough to attract an offer from the Raiders to become their starter the following year.

Moving from Kansas City's West Coast Offense to the vertical passing game in Oakland was a tricky adjustment, but by the end of that first season Gannon was flourishing. The Raiders advanced to the AFC championship game in 2000. His best season came two years later, when he was named MVP and led the Raiders to the Super Bowl. After one of the finest passing campaigns in league history, Gannon played horribly in the Super Bowl. Facing relentless pressure from the Tampa Bay defense, he threw 5 interceptions. Three of them were returned for touchdowns.

Gannon suffered a shoulder injury midway through the following season, and a neck injury the next year forced him to retire.

#34 Sonny Jurgensen (1957–1974)

A classic drop-back passer, Jurgensen got his start with the Philadelphia Eagles. That team won the NFL championship in 1960 with Norm Van Brocklin starting under center, but Jurgensen took over the following year after Van Brocklin's controversial retirement.

In his first year at the helm, Jurgensen destroyed nearly every team he faced. He set NFL records for passing yards (3723) and completions (235) and tied the mark for touchdown passes (32). The Eagles finished second despite their 10-4 record, and in the Playoff Bowl (a consolation game for second place teams) Jurgensen suffered a shoulder injury that would have long-term effects.

He led the league in passing again in 1962, although the shoulder was still bothering him. The following summer, he and a teammate left camp demanding more money. The owner relented, but Jurgensen reinjured the shoulder and the team fell to last place with a 2-10-2 record. A housecleaning followed, and Jurgensen was traded to Washington.

Although the team struggled, Jurgensen continued to be one of the league's leading passers.

When Otto Graham became Washington's head coach in 1966, he shifted the focus of the offense to a passing attack that could take advantage of Jurgensen's skills. The move paid off, and in 1967 Jurgensen set new single-season records for passing yards, attempts, and completions.

Injuries continued to dog him, and as the Redskins began winning in the early seventies, Jurgensen spent most of his time on the sidelines watching Billy Kilmer handle the quarterback's duties.

#35 Phil Simms (1979–1993)

Simms led the Giants to their first Super Bowl win in 1986, and four years later he had the team poised for a return. The team started the 1990 season 11-2 before Simms broke his foot in a game against the Bills. Backup Jeff Hostetler started the last two games of the season and led the Giants to a win in Super Bowl XXV.

Head coach Bill Parcells retired after that game, and when Ray Handley was tabbed to replace him, one of his first moves was to bench Simms and keep Hostetler as the starter. It was a curious move for several reasons. First, Simms had played well for several seasons and was well suited for the Giants ball control offense. Second, Hostetler hadn't done anything in seven seasons as Simms' backup to suggest he was a better player, and, frankly, he wasn't terribly impressive in the Super Bowl.

Hostetler threw just 13 touchdowns in his two seasons as the Giants starter. The Giants finished 8-8 as defending champs and 6-10 the following year, after which both the coach and his quarterback were shown the door.

Simms reclaimed the starting job in 1993 and had a pretty good season, helping to lead the Giants back into the playoffs with an 11-5 record. Fans can only wonder what might have happened in the Handley years if Simms had been allowed to stay under center.

Joe Theismann (1974–1985)

Most people probably don't know that Theismann was drafted not by the Redskins, but by the Dolphins in 1971. He chose not to play for Miami, opting instead to sign with the Toronto Argonauts of the Canadian Football League. He had three productive seasons in Canada, and by the time he returned to the states the Redskins owned his rights. Theismann was so eager to make the team that he offered to return punts if that would help him earn a roster spot. He spent four seasons as the backup to Billy Kilmer, finally earning the starting job in 1978 at the age of twenty-nine.

Theismann led his team to a victory in Super Bowl XVII, but his best season came a year later. In 1983, Theismann threw for 3714 yards and 29 touchdowns—both personal bests—and led the Redskins to a 14-2 record and another shot at an NFL title. Picked by many to dominate, the Redskins were upset in Super Bowl XVIII by the Oakland Raiders, losing 38–9. As some measure of consolation, Theismann received the league's MVP Award that season.

He was only six feet tall, small compared to most other NFL quarterbacks, and he didn't have the most powerful arm. Washington's coach Joe Gibbs helped to overcome these limitations by building a massive offensive line to protect him, a truly dominant running game, and a defense to keep opponents off the score board. Theismann was able to focus on his strengths: quick reads, attacking the flats, and escaping danger.

Anybody who saw the last play of Theismann's career will never forget it. During a nationally televised game, Giants linebacker Lawrence Taylor came around the left side on what was to have been a flea-flicker play. Charging in from the blindside on a blitz, Taylor grabbed Theismann's shoulders from behind and as the quarterback started to lean forward, Taylor fell with the full weight of his body onto Theismann's calf, bending him back awkwardly. The gruesome replay showed his leg being broken in at least two places. Taylor knew what had happened immediately and

leapt up, screaming frantically and gesturing wildly to the Redskins sideline to send in their medics.

Players break bones all the time in football, but we usually don't see it happen. During that *Monday Night Football* game, we saw it happen in graphic detail. We wanted to turn away because it horrified us, but at the same time we couldn't help watching it again and again. In an interview twenty years later, Theismann said he had never seen the replay. He said Taylor has told him he hasn't watched it either. I wish the rest of us could be so fortunate.

Dutch Clark (1931–1938)

Clark was one of the seventeen original members of the Pro Football Hall of Fame, and while I think he's regarded as the game's first great quarterback, it's hard to consider him in the same group with the rest of these guys. The game was so different, and the quarterback position in those days was so much different than what it is today.

Teams didn't throw much in those days, but Clark was the best of his era. In 1936 he completed 53.5 percent of his passes when the league average was 36.5. He called the plays on a Lions team that was full of stars. While he was unquestionably the team's leader, he was quiet and avoided the limelight.

The attribute most desired for players in the twenties and thirties was versatility, and Clark was one of the best. He could run, pass, play defense, and was the league's last drop-kicking specialist. He even spent his last two seasons as a player-coach.

Jim McMahon (1982–1996)

When the Bears selected McMahon in 1982, most of us figured he was a nice Mormon boy coming out of Brigham Young University. We were a little off in that assessment.

Perhaps the most free-spirited quarterback in history, McMahon spent his career fighting with his teammates, coaches, agent, media . . . really anyone who would listen. McMahon's most famous battles were with then NFL commissioner Pete Rozelle. When admonished by the league office for wearing a headband with a corporate logo on it, McMahon responded the next week with a homemade headband with the word ROZELLE scrawled in black marker. Character he did not lack.

McMahon did not lack talent either as he proved clearly in his time with the Bears. He had a knack for understanding the flow of a game and often called audibles at the line of scrimmage, turning the Bears offense into a highly dynamic, often surprising force.

It is interesting to scan through McMahon's year-by-year statistics. Looking only at the numbers, it is hard to see how he ever became a champion in 1985 and regarded as one of the best quarterbacks of his generation. In Chicago's 1985 15-1 season culminating in a Super Bowl championship, McMahon threw only 15 touchdowns along with 11 interceptions and passed for only 2392 yards. It is important to remember that the Bears had one of the greatest defenses in history during McMahon's tenure with the team and he simply didn't have to take a lot of chances, throw a lot of high-risk, high-reward passes. He also had Walter Payton behind him, relieving even more pressure he may have felt to carry the team on his back.

#39
Ken Stabler (1970–1984)

There is a group of folks—mostly Raiders fans—who feel that Stabler belongs in the Hall of Fame, and they can't understand why he's not there. Nothing I could say would convince his most hardcore supporters that it's anything other than Raider bias, but I think the reasons are fairly straightforward to any objective observer.

The case for Stabler basically consists of one argument: he was a winner. His win differential is +50 (104-54-1), which ranks 11th all-time. With Sta-

bler at the helm, the Raiders went to five straight AFC title games and won Super Bowl XI.

The case against Stabler is basically everything else. In those five seasons Stabler really only had two good years. In 1973, he only had 1997 yards passing in fourteen games. In 1975, he threw 16 touchdowns and 24 interceptions. In fifteen NFL seasons, he only finished with more touchdowns than interceptions five times, and one of those occasions was as a backup in 1972 when he finished with 4 and 3.

His defenders will say that the interceptions are a by-product of the Raiders' strategy. With a vertical passing game—the argument goes—you throw a lot of deep passes, and while you'll complete fewer of them and have more turnovers, those costs will be outweighed by the number of big plays you make. The theory might be sound, but it didn't work out that way for Stabler. While he did lead the league in touchdown passes twice, he never came close to leading the league in passing yards. Where was the payoff? More often than not, his inability to avoid turnovers cost them in big games.

The Raiders really got pass-happy in 1978, with Stabler's attempts jumping from 294 to 406, and then to 498 in 1979. The result was rather predictable—42 touchdowns and 52 interceptions over two seasons. That style of play is exciting, but ultimately it's not one that's likely to be successful unless your conversion rates are much higher. It's just like stealing bases in baseball.

If Stabler had won more than just one Super Bowl—or even if he had made it more than once, I think that Hall of Fame voters might be willing to overlook the interceptions and give him a shot. But since that's not what happened, I just don't see anything in Stabler's case that's compelling enough for him to get more serious consideration.

#40
Brad Johnson (1994–2007)

Got the job done everywhere he went, but nobody seemed to care. Johnson played well in two seasons as the Vikings starter, throwing for 3036 yards and 20 touchdowns in twelve starts in 1997. He broke his leg the following year, and when the team won with veteran Randall Cunningham under center, Johnson was out of a job.

Johnson moved to Washington and threw for 4000 yards in his first season as the Redskins starter, but a year later they dumped him for a bigger name—veteran Jeff George. Three years later he led the Buccaneers to a Super Bowl win, throwing for 3811 yards and a career-high 26 touchdown passes. Still, the team signed free agent Brian Griese during the off-season and turned the job over to second-year passer Chris Simms in early October.

While he was never a superstar, Johnson was a solid quarterback who got a raw deal more than once.

Bob Griese (1967–1980)

Griese never had great numbers, but then, he didn't need to. He didn't need to throw the ball all the time in order to win, because the Dolphins had a powerful running game and a stifling defense. Griese helped lead Miami to three straight Super Bowl appearances, but his numbers in those games reveal just how little the team relied on its passing game to win.

Game	Com	Att	Yds	TD	INT
VI (1971)	12	23	134	0	1
VII (1972)	8	11	88	1	1
VIII (1973)	6	7	73	0	0

That looks like the playing line for a quarterback who lost three Super Bowls, but in fact the Dolphins won in 1972 and 1973.

Griese was not physically imposing. The Dolphins listed him as 6-foot-1 and 190 pounds, and both figures were a little generous. He also wore glasses, which combined with his small stature made him look more like a bookkeeper than a quarterback

Milt Plum (1957–1969)

The Browns were hoping to draft a quarterback in 1957. They had the sixth overall pick and there were two can't-miss prospects coming out of college: Stanford's John Brodie and Purdue's Len Dawson. Both players were picked before the Browns' turn came, and so they had to settle for a running back, a kid named Jim Brown out of Syracuse.

Cleveland got their quarterback in the second round, Milt Plum from Penn State. He spent four years starting for the Browns, distributing the ball to Brown and another future Hall of Famer, wide receiver Bobby Mitchell. The Browns didn't pass much, but Plum was efficient. Although the NFL's passer rating system wasn't adopted until 1973, it's easy enough to calculate ratings for players from earlier seasons. Plum's 1960 season yields a 110.4 passer rating, which stood as the highest single-season total in league history until 1989.

Plum was traded to Detroit as part of a six-player swap prior to the 1962 season. The Lions didn't have much of a running game, which forced Plum to throw more often. He had a couple of good seasons, but struggled with injuries and lost his starting job twice.

Frankie Albert (1946–1952)

Without Frankie Albert's standout performances and immense popularity with the 49ers, it's unlikely the team would have been invited to join the NFL when the league absorbed the AAFC in 1950. It wasn't just that Albert helped the Niners win games, it was his exciting style of play.

Albert was a scrambler in college, leading Stanford's T-formation offense. He came out of college with the ability to read defenses and fool them into going one way when he planned on going the other. His lasting legacy is the bootleg play, which he invented and perfected while with San Francisco. Defenses never quite knew what Albert would do next, whether it was a quick pass or his patented bootleg. The left-handed Albert wreaked havoc on defenses in his seven pro seasons.

In the AAFC's four-year existence, the Niners were always overshadowed by the Cleveland Browns. Similarly, Albert lived in the shadow of their quarterback, Otto Graham. Still, Albert bested Graham for the league's Most Valuable Player Award in 1948. Like many star players from the AAFC, Albert had spent time in the military service after college. That's the main reason his pro career lasted just seven seasons.

#44
Frank Ryan (1958–1970)

Ryan was known as "the professor," and that wasn't just a nickname, it was his day job. He originally didn't want to play pro football because he planned to pursue a doctorate in mathematics, but the Rams convinced him to play for them while attending UCLA. He relented, eventually receiving his PhD with a thesis entitled "Characterization of the Set of Asymptotic Values of a Function Holomorphic in the Unit Disc." Don't feel bad, I don't know what that means either.

After being traded to the Browns, he began teaching undergraduate math classes at Case Institute of Technology. That made great fodder for sportswriters' jokes, but it was Ryan's performance on the field they should have been focusing on. He led the league in touchdown passes twice and led the Browns to an NFL championship in 1964.

Ryan made his first Pro Bowl appearance after that title win, and a hard hit by Baltimore's Gino Marchetti in the second half ruined his shoulder. He developed a sore elbow in training camp the next year, likely as a result of compensating for the shoulder pain. His numbers dropped dramatically in 1965, and while they rebounded the following year, the pain just got worse. He underwent surgery in 1967, but by the following season he had lost his job.

#45
Ed Brown (1954–1965)

Spent eight seasons with the Bears, earning two Pro Bowl invitations and leading Chicago to the title game in 1956. Brown had a well-deserved reputation as a gunslinger. He loved to throw long passes deep down the field, and while his completion percentages were always low, he often led the league in yards per completion. In fact his career average of 16.4 is the best for any player with at least 15000 passing yards. His best season came with the Steelers in 1963, when he threw for 2982 yards and 21 touchdowns

Brown was the starting quarterback for the undefeated 1951 University of San Francisco team, which included future pro football Hall of Famers Gino Marchetti, Ollie Matson, and Bob St. Clair. Because he was also the team's kicker and punter, he was known as "All Around" Ed Brown.

#46
Drew Bledsoe (1993–2006)

Bledsoe was a much-heralded passer coming out of college. He compiled great statistics as a professional because he was always in systems that threw a lot of passes, but that never translated to great success in terms of wins and losses. He helped the Patriots advance to the Super Bowl after the 1996 season, but in fourteen years in the NFL he only led his team to the playoffs two other times. It's telling that the Patriots offense surged after he was injured and Tom Brady took over. Bledsoe had become much less mobile in the pocket and had difficulty finding his receivers quickly.

In a six-year span he lost three different starting jobs, first in New England, then again after one big season in Buffalo, and finally in Dallas after a year and a half at the helm. The problems were the same each time, but teams kept falling in love with his arm strength and hoping somehow that would be enough. It never was.

Joe Namath (1965–1977)

Namath was born to play in New York. His larger-than-life personality might not have gone over well if he'd played in a place like St. Louis, but they loved him in the Big Apple.

Outside of New York City, there are some who have formed the opinion that Joe Namath made the Hall of Fame on the basis of one game: the Jets' shocking upset of the Colts in Super Bowl III. That just isn't the case. Namath was the AFL's best passer for his first five seasons—hell, he was better than anyone in the NFL at that time, too. He led the league in passing yards in 1966 and a year later became the first passer ever to surpass 4000 yards in a season.

It was his knees that kept him from staying at that level. He'd had three major knee surgeries by 1968, and although he was only 24 years old, there were signs that he was developing arthritis. He missed most of the 1970 season and then in 1971, blew out his left knee again trying to make a tackle during an exhibition game. He would spend most of the next five years in pain. His mobility was severely limited and he walked with a noticeable limp. He was barely adequate as a quarterback, and finally the Jets were forced to realize that the great passer wasn't going to return.

His completion percentage was never particularly good and he threw a lot of interceptions, particularly after his knees were shot. Of all the quarterbacks in the Hall of Fame, Namath's statistics are probably the least impressive. He was truly spectacular early in his career and dreadful in the later years. That's why the career totals don't give you an accurate picture at all.

While Namath gets the credit for delivering on his guarantee that the Jets would win, he didn't play particularly well in that game. He threw for 206 yards without a touchdown pass. Running back Matt Snell scored the Jets' only touchdown in the 16–7 win, and his tough running in the fourth quarter helped them control the clock and keep the Colts from coming back.

Matt Hasselbeck (1998–2007)

Oftentimes when you look at a quarterback's performance, you can see that a positive aspect of his play is simply a trade-off for a negative one. In Hasselbeck's case he's avoided interceptions but has taken an awful lot of sacks, often well behind the line of scrimmage. History shows that this is not a recipe for long-term success.

Hasselbeck was drafted by the Packers when Mike Holmgren was their head coach, and the pair was reunited in Seattle by a 2001 trade. The Seahawks coach announced that Hasselbeck would be his starter, which surprised nearly every one. Hasselbeck hadn't seen much action in his three years as a Packer backup, but Holmgren obviously saw something in the kid to suggest he could be a star. It took two seasons, but Hasselbeck finally put all of the pieces together in 2003 and earned his first Pro Bowl appearance. His father, Don Hasselbeck, played tight end in the NFL from 1977–1985, and his younger brother Tim has spent seven seasons as a backup quarterback in the league.

Billy Kilmer (1961–1978)

With running backs, it seems that if they're going to be stars then they are stars right from the very start. Quarterbacks are a much different breed, and for every young stud that fades to oblivion after a couple of promising seasons, there's a guy like Billy Kilmer. It took seven years for him to become a starter, and he had to overcome a number of challenges just to make it that far.

Kilmer was drafted by San Francisco, but he didn't fit into their shotgun offense very well. He spent most of his first two seasons playing halfback, leading the team with ten rushing touchdowns as a rookie and averaging 5.1 yards per carry in 1962. Late that year Kilmer broke his leg in a car accident after he fell asleep at the wheel and his car plunged into the San Francisco Bay. The injury sidelined him for more than a year, and he would see only limited playing time over the next three seasons.

His career got a boost when he went to New Orleans, having been selected in the expansion draft. Kilmer started training camp as the third quarterback, but injuries eventually pushed him into a starting role and he made the most of it. The Saints didn't win a lot of those games, but Kilmer was popular with the locals.

After four years in the Big Easy, Kilmer was traded to the Redskins. Once again, he was expected to be a backup but moved into the starting job when starter Sonny Jurgensen was injured. Over the next four seasons, a quarterback battle raged between the two players. Most observers acknowledged that Jurgensen was the better passer—his mechanics were better and he had a stronger arm—but the team won with Kilmer under center. The Redskins made the playoffs five times in Kilmer's six seasons as the primary starter, including a trip to the Super Bowl following the 1972 season.

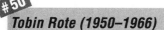

#50
Tobin Rote (1950–1966)

If you consider the arc that a quarterback's career makes, there are a few different shapes that most would take. You have the guys like Peyton Manning, who are superstars early on and just get better. You have a guy like Rich Gannon or Trent Green who doesn't hit his stride until he's in his thirties. You have a Kurt Warner who comes from nowhere to win an MVP Award, then just as quickly fades into oblivion. And you have a whole lot of journeymen who bounce around from team to team without ever making their mark.

Rote's career doesn't follow any of those patterns. He started with the Packers in the early 1950s, one of the best passers in a league where the running game still dominated. He led the league in adjusted yards in 1954 and 1956, and was 2nd in 1951 and 1955.

But in 1956, the Packers drafted Bart Starr, and the club decided to turn the reins over to

their promising young prospect. Rote was traded to Detroit, where he was expected to serve as a backup to Bobby Layne. When Layne broke his leg, Rote stepped in to guide the Lions to three straight wins to clinch a playoff spot. In the first round of the playoffs, he rallied the Lions from a 27–7 deficit to beat the Niners 31–27. Then he threw four touchdown passes in a 59–17 rout of the Browns in the NFL championship game.

Rote's success earned him the starting quarterback position, but both his teammates and the Detroit fans weren't happy with the development. The Lions regressed after the popular Layne was traded to Pittsburgh, and once again Rote found himself at the helm of a lousy team. After playing out his option, Rote went north to play in the Canadian league, where he set records and led the league in virtually every passing category.

He returned to the states to join the San Diego Chargers in 1963, leading a high-powered offense to an AFL championship. He was named the league's Most Valuable Player, finishing second in Adjusted Yards (behind Len Dawson).

Once again, however, Rote was pushed aside to make room for a younger quarterback. This time it was John Hadl, and although Rote helped lead the Chargers back to the title game in 1964, he was cut loose during the off-season.

Like Steve Young, Rote was a threat both on the ground and through the air. He led his team in rushing yards four times in addition to being one of the most productive passers of his era. Like Young, he won two league championships. But Rote is not regarded as a great quarterback because he left both championship teams a year after winning a title, and because he wasn't viewed as the central figure in his teams' success. He also suffers because his best years came with a bad Packers team at a time when quarterbacks were largely overlooked.

If he had spent his entire career with one team, he'd merit serious consideration for the Hall of Fame. If he had played in New York or Chicago, he might already be in.

Trent Green (1997–2007)

Green is one of several young quarterbacks who was discarded by the Redskins in the 1990s despite playing well. Green became the Redskins starter in 1998, throwing for 3411 yards and 23 touchdowns. That wasn't enough for head coach Norv Turner, who let Green walk as a free agent.

Other teams took interest, which was no surprise. Green had a strong arm and was a very accurate passer, which made him well-suited for playing the West Coast Offense. He signed a contract to be the Rams starter, but a knee injury knocked him out of action and opened the door for Kurt Warner in St. Louis. Two years later he was traded to the Chiefs, and he thrived in their short passing attack. He topped the 4000 yard mark for three straight seasons, even though his top receivers were usually his tight end and running back.

Jack Kemp (1957–1969)

Best remembered for his postfootball political career, Kemp was a heckuva quarterback and one of the leaders in players' efforts to organize a union. After bouncing around for a few years in the NFL, he found his home with Sid Gillman's Chargers. Kemp's strong arm made him a perfect fit for Gillman's downfield passing game. He was one of three quarterbacks to break the 3000 yard barrier in 1960, the first time that had been done.

The Chargers advanced to the AFL title game in each of their first two seasons, thanks largely to Kemp's aerial attack. Inexplicably, Kemp found himself on the waiver wire two games into the 1962 season. Gillman claimed that it was a clerical error, that he only intended to place Kemp on the injured list. The Buffalo Bills quickly placed their claim and for a mere $100, they had themselves a new quarterback.

Gillman appealed and tried to get the transaction rescinded, but it was too late. The situation became more painful when Kemp helped lead his

Bills to victory over the Chargers in the 1964 AFL Championship game, then again in 1965.

Kemp played in five of the first seven AFL championship games, and ended up as that league's most prolific passer. His totals of 3055 pass attempts, 1428 completions, and 21,130 yards all stand as the most in the AFL's ten-year history.

Jim Hart (1966–1984)

Jim Hart may be the best quarterback the Cardinals ever had. He is most definitely one of the most beloved players in franchise history. He had his best seasons from 1974 to 1976, leading his team to ten or more wins in each of those years and winning two division titles.

You can pretty much divide Hart's career into three sections. There's a five-year stretch from 1973 to 1978 when he played extremely well. That coincides exactly with the tenure of head coach Don Coryell. His wide-open passing attack encouraged Hart to throw the ball down the field, and Hart put up the best numbers of his career.

In the seven years before Coryell arrived, Hart was an unremarkable quarterback, never finishing with more touchdowns than interceptions and never leading his team anywhere near the playoffs. And in the six years after Coryell left St. Louis, Hart plummeted from Pro Bowl caliber play to being a marginal NFL starter.

Dan Fouts (1973–1987)

Like most quarterbacks who played in a vertical passing offense, Fouts ended up with a lot of yards and a lot of interceptions. He is one of five quarterbacks to throw for at least 4700 yards in a season, setting an NFL record with 4715 in 1980 and surpassing that with 4802 in 1981.

In each of those two seasons, however, he threw 24 interceptions, and that's the rub. The cost of all those turnovers didn't negate the gaudy yardage totals, but it was enough of a cost that it affected the team's ability to win games. This problem was particularly apparent in the postseason. Fouts averaged over 300 yards per game in his playoff appearances, but he threw 5 interceptions in two different playoff games, and the Chargers could never reach the Super Bowl.

Their best chance was probably in 1981, when the Chargers' explosive receiving game was complemented by the strong running of Chuck Muncie, who led the league with 19 touchdowns. The Chargers beat the Dolphins in their first playoff game and would face the Bengals in the AFC championship game. It had been unbearably hot and humid in Miami, but at kickoff in Cincinnati, the temperature was nine degrees below zero. Strong gusts off the Ohio River meant the wind chill was minus fifty-nine. It couldn't have helped when many of the Bengals players came out wearing short sleeves. Icicles were forming on Fouts's beard, and it didn't take long before the Chargers will to win seemed to disappear. Not that it would have mattered. The wind and the cold caused more than just psychological problems for the San Diego offense. Bengals general manager Mike Brown recalled "every time Fouts tried to throw a long pass, it would just die, like it would hit a glass partition."

And there's the other big caveat about the vertical passing game: it doesn't work so well when the weather gets ugly.

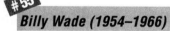

Billy Wade (1954–1966)

A great example of how much a team's style of play affects the performance of a quarterback. Wade spent seven seasons with the Rams, the last three as a starter in Sid Gillman's aggressive passing attack. The pace of play didn't suit Wade's strengths, and his stint as the team's starter was pretty frustrating. While he did rack up yardage, he threw too many interceptions and that kept the team from winning.

He went from the Rams to the Bears in 1961, and it was like he had become a different player.

Rather than throw deep passes all the time, the Bears played a short passing game. Because the Bears had such a strong defense, the pressure wasn't on Wade to be making big plays all the time. He could be successful by playing a disciplined game and avoiding turnovers. His first two years with the Bears were fantastic, and he led the Bears to an NFL championship in 1963. In that title game, he scored both of the team's touchdowns on quarterback sneaks en route to the 14–10 win over the Giants.

Craig Morton (1965–1982)

Morton led two different teams to the Super Bowl, first the Cowboys and later the Broncos. He liked to throw the deep pass, but unlike most of the gunslingers of his era, he used the play judiciously. Rather than throwing bombs all the time and hoping for the best, Morton preferred to pick his spots. As a result he never had gaudy passing statistics, but he didn't kill his teams with turnovers either.

Earl Morrall (1956–1976)

What a fascinating career. Over twenty-one seasons, Morrall played for six different teams, and while they all considered him more of a backup than a starter, he always performed exceptionally well when pressed into full-time duty.

The most notable of these occasions was in 1972 when he took over for an injured Bob Griese in Week 6. Morrall helped rally the Dolphins to a 24–23 victory over the Bills, then win their last eight games to become the first undefeated team in the modern NFL.

In 1968 he became the Colts starter when Johnny Unitas injured his elbow in the last preseason game. Morrall led the Colts to a 13-1 record and won the NFL title game before losing Super Bowl III to the Jets.

Morrall also had starting stints with the Steelers, Lions, and Giants, each of which lasted just one year.

White was an All-Pro punter and the last player to see significant action at another position while continuing his punting duties. He began his career as the Cowboys punter and backup quarterback to Roger Staubach. When Staubach retired after the 1979 season, White took over the starting job and continued to punt for the next five seasons.

White led the Cowboys to the NFC championship game in each of his first three seasons as their starting quarterback. He did not play well in any of those games—all losses—and became a scapegoat for the team's failure to return to the Super Bowl. His performance gradually declined after the 1983 season, although he remained the Cowboys starter until 1987.

Waterfield was the first rookie to win the league MVP Award and ended his first season with a 15–14 victory over the Redksins to win the NFL championship. In that game, Waterfield threw two touchdowns and thus began his love affair with Rams' fans. What stands out about that rookie season is Waterfield's 9.4 yards per attempt. With Waterfield averaging almost a first down per pass, it is understandable why the Rams had such success that season.

In 1946 the Rams moved to Los Angeles and Waterfield ended up sharing quarterback duties with Norm Van Brocklin. From 1949 to 1951, this duo led the team to the league title game each season, winning it all against the Browns in 1951. In both 1949 and 1950, Waterfield came off the bench late in playoff games to throw for 4 and 3 touchdowns, respectively, and send his team to the title game.

One of the first true deep passers, Waterfield was always exciting. He led the league in passing in both 1946 and 1951. His Hall of Fame candidacy was strengthened by his contributions as a kicker, punter, and defensive player.

Waterfield married actress Jane Russell while he was still in college, and his wife went on to become a huge movie star and one of the biggest sex symbols of the fifties. After he retired from football, Waterfield joined his wife in the movie business and became a successful film producer.

Kosar and the Browns pulled a fast one on the NFL and the Minnesota Vikings in 1985. They exploited a loophole in the rules for the NFL draft, with Kosar waiting until after the draft to announce his eligibility for the pros. This made him eligible to be chosen in the supplemental draft, and the Browns traded four draft picks (including No. 1 picks in both 1985 and 1986) so they could select Kosar. It was a match made in heaven as the Ohio native wanted to play for Cleveland and they really needed a good young passer.

Kosar was not a classic quarterback by any means. He threw sidearm most of the time. He was also terribly rigid, which made it difficult for him to escape pressure and avoid sacks. He overcame these limitations with his remarkable accuracy. At one point, Kosar threw 308 consecutive passes without an interception, an NFL record.

It was that lack of athleticism that I think hurt Kosar most in the NFL, keeping him from being a truly dominant passer. He had the ability to keep Cleveland in almost every game they played, but just imagine if he had been able to actually move out of the way of a pass rush once in a while.

George Blanda (1949–1975)

Blanda's longevity was amazing, but what a lot of people forget is his effectiveness for the bulk of his twenty-six years in the league. He began with the Bears in 1949 and became their starting quarterback by 1953, as well as a placekicker and linebacker. His career almost ended in 1958 when he retired, upset that head coach George Halas refused to use him as anything more than a place-kicker. If it had not been for the formation of the American Football League in 1960, we may never have heard from Blanda again.

It was not easy on Blanda when he became the quarterback and kicker for the AFL's Houston Oilers. He was quickly labeled a "reject" from the NFL and the press was merciless in their disapproval of his re-emergence in the "other" league. However, Blanda led the Oilers to the first two AFL championships and was named AFL Player of the Year in 1961.

Blanda ended up playing the entire ten years of the AFL's existence, switching teams in 1967 when he joined the Oakland Raiders. After eighteen years in the league, Blanda was expected to be a decent backup quarterback and the place-kicker for Oakland. He was definitely both. In 1970 Blanda came off the bench in five straight games to relieve Daryle Lamonica, producing four wins and a tie. He came off the bench again in the AFC title game against Baltimore, throwing 2 touch-downs and kicking a field goal to keep Oakland in the game, although they would eventually lose. Although he would only attempt 55 passes during the regular season, these heroics earned Blanda the 1970 NFL Most Valuable Player Award.

George Blanda holds many records, the most notable being his twenty-six years in the league. He also was the first player to score over 2000 points, the oldest quarterback to play in a title game (that 1970 game against the Colts when Blanda was forty-three years old), and is still the oldest player ever to play in an NFL game when he was forty-eight years old in 1975. Blanda did not really have

an abundance of natural skill, but his competitive spirit, his tenacity, and his refusal to let the fun end made him a legend both in and beyond his time.

Steve Grogan (1975–1990)

Grogan was one of the first modern running quarterbacks, gaining 2164 yards in his sixteen-year career. His 12 rushing touchdowns in 1976 are still the most in a single season by any quarterback. Like Steve Young and Randall Cunningham after him, Grogan used rushing as a weapon, not an escape plan.

His style of play made him extremely popular with the Patriots' blue-collar fans. He loved to deliver hits, and while that wasn't always a wise strategy, fans loved his linebacker mentality and toughness.

Kordell Stewart (1995–2005)

Stewart is wildly out of place on this list, but I can explain why he shows up. He had two pretty good years as a starter, beginning with his first year as the Steelers' starting quarterback. Stewart threw 21 touchdown passes and ran for 11 more while leading his team to the AFC championship game. Five years later, Stewart threw for 3109 yards and added 537 on the ground, and again took the Steelers to the AFC title game.

Everything in between was a mess, and that's why Stewart's inclusion here is so perplexing. His passing mechanics were inconsistent, and while he'd make big plays on occasion, there were games where everything just completely fell apart. Stewart just wasn't well suited to playing quarterback, and the Steelers kept hoping he'd become a better passer instead of simply capitalizing on the things that he was doing well.

His presence here is due largely to his contributions as a scrambler and only in small part due to what he did as a passer. Stewart had speed and athleticism, and he was able to use those skills to avoid the pass rush and to gain yards as a runner. The Steelers spent several years trying to improve his passing skills, but in retrospect, you have to wonder why they didn't just let him do what he did well and not ask him to throw the ball. Stewart might have had a better career if he'd moved to a position besides quarterback. He probably would have been a heckuva third-down back, catching passes and occasionally running out of the backfield.

Ace Parker (1937–1946)

Why haven't there been more quarterbacks in history with the nickname "Ace"? Clarence Parker stands out as the only one I can think of called by that name as well as being one of the first professional two-sport players, suiting up for both baseball's Philadelphia Athletics and football's Brooklyn Dodgers in 1937 and 1938.

Parker gave the NFL's Dodgers just what they needed to turn them from a miserable franchise into a contender, bringing both rushing and passing skills as well as receiving, placekicking, defensive play, and punting. In his second year with the team, Parker led the league in passing with 865 yards and two years later, he won the league MVP trophy. What is amazing is he broke his leg playing baseball that summer and had to play with a heavy brace for part of the football season. It is not as if Parker was a speed threat, but playing with a brace slowed him down even more. He still managed to throw for 817 yards that season and added 306 rushing and 139 receiving yards to once again be the offensive leader for the Dodgers.

Parker left professional sports in 1942 to enlist in the war and he would not return to football until 1945. He spent his last season in the AAFC with the New York Yankees, leading them to the 1946 championship game against the Browns.

Johnny Lujack (1948–1951)

Lujack led Notre Dame to a national championship as a sophomore in 1943, then promptly left school to serve in the Navy. When he returned from the war, the Chicago Bears used their first round pick to select him in the draft. Lujack opted to return to school, and over the next two seasons led the Fighting Irish to two more national championships. Lujack won the Heisman Trophy in 1947 and joined the Bears the following year. Lujack was an All-Pro defensive back during his rookie season, but in 1949 he became the starting quarterback, taking over for Glenn Davis.

The Bears were one of the few teams that had successfully made the forward pass the centerpiece of their offense in the 1940s, and Lujack picked up right where Sid Luckman left off. In a memorable performance against the Cardinals in a December 1949 game, Lujack threw for 468 yards in a 52–21 rout. That is a lot of yards in today's game, so just imagine the shock the Cardinals felt back in 1949.

He led the Bears offense for three years before bad knees forced his retirement from the league. He rated as the best quarterback in the league in every season from 1949 to 1951. If his knees had been able to hold up, Lujack would probably have been one of the great quarterbacks in league history. Since they didn't, he's remembered mostly as a college football star and not as a great pro passer.

Bert Jones (1973–1982)

For a three-year stretch, Jones was the best quarterback in football. He never really recovered from a shoulder injury in 1978, and a chronic back problem forced him to retire at thirty-one.

Jones is one of three quarterbacks in my top-75 whose father played in the NFL. Will "Dub" Jones was a fast, graceful halfback, who was an outstanding receiver. With the Browns in 1951, Jones scored 6 touchdowns in a game against the Bears—a feat only matched by Ernie Nevers (1929) and Gale Sayers (1965).

#67
Drew Brees (2001-2007)

The Chargers drafted Drew Brees in 2001 and made him their starter a year later. He struggled to make progress, and so the team drafted another quarterback in 2004. With promising rookie (Philip Rivers) poised to take his job, Brees suddenly blossomed, throwing for 3159 yards and 27 touchdowns. He was only 25, but at year's end he was named the Comeback Player of the Year.

It created a catch-22 for the Chargers. Did they stick with the kid who'd finally found his groove, or did they turn to the Rivers, the youngster who was earning millions to sit on the bench and watch? History suggested the younger option was usually the best one, so the Chargers let Brees leave as a free agent and made Philip Rivers their starter. It worked out well for everyone. Brees signed with the Saints, leading them to the NFC championship game in 2006 and throwing for more than 4400 yards in each of his first two seasons in New Orleans. Rivers was as good as promised, leading the Chargers to division titles in his first two seasons as the starter,

#68
Neil O'Donnell (1991–2003)

Relentlessly efficient, O'Donnell made a career out of avoiding risk at all costs. He threw fewer interceptions per pass attempt than any quarterback in history. Coaches often talk about wanting to have a quarterback who wouldn't kill their team with mistakes, but this isn't necessarily what they mean.

It was maddening at times to watch O'Donnell play, because his unwillingness to take any risks meant that he'd almost never make a big play.

A perfect example was the year he spent as the starter in Cincinnati. His numbers were respectable enough—15 touchdowns and 4 interceptions in thirteen games, but fans complained that his choices kept the team from winning. He'd dump the ball off on third down, taking a short completion that wasn't enough for a first down rather than risking something down the field. He finished with a passer rating of 90.2, which was sixth among NFL quarterbacks that year, but the team finished 27th in points scored.

Ironically, O'Donnell's best season ended with him throwing three interceptions in the Super Bowl. Two of them set up touchdowns by the Cowboys and led directly to Pittsburgh's 27–17 defeat.

#69
Jim Harbaugh (1987–2000)

A product of Michigan under Bo Schembechler, Harbaugh was a first-round pick of the Bears in 1987. He played behind Jim McMahon and Mike Tomczak until 1990 when he became the first-string quarterback for the Bears. Harbaugh never could capture the fan's love, often receiving the blame for falling short in the postseason.

It was with his next team, the Indianapolis Colts, that Harbaugh became known as "Captain Comeback." Taking over as the starter after a 1-2 start in 1995, Harbaugh led the Colts to come-from-behind victories in his first three starts. The entire season was a tapestry woven from grit and determination and nobody on the Colts characterized the team better than the tough-as-nails Harbaugh. The team advanced to the AFC championship game, propelled almost solely by Harbaugh's will to win. Although the Colts would lose that game, Harbaugh finished second in MVP voting and was named the Comeback Player of the Year.

The knock on Harbaugh was simply that his physical skills were inferior to his leadership abilities and all-around toughness. He often misread coverages and got himself in far too many third-and-long situations during his career. Without a powerful arm, he could not compensate for these weaknesses and when he was bad, he was really bad (just ask Chicago fans). However, when Harbaugh was good, he was outstanding and an absolute joy to watch.

#70 Kurt Warner (1998–2007)

At his peak, Warner was as good as any quarterback has ever been. Unfortunately, that peak was too short and came too late for him to rank with the all-time greats. If his story had been a Hollywood movie script, everybody would have dismissed it for being too unrealistic. Warner went from being completely unknown to being the league MVP and Super Bowl champion in a span of about four months.

Warner spent three seasons playing arena football and another year in Europe before finally reaching the NFL as a twenty-seven-year-old backup for the Rams in 1998. He became their starting quarterback by default the following year when starter Trent Green was hurt late in training camp. What happened next was astonishing. Warner absolutely dominated opposing defenses, throwing for 4353 yards and 41 touchdowns, easily enough to earn him his first MVP Award. The Rams had improved from 4-12 to 13-3, and Warner led the team to the Super Bowl. He capped his amazing season by throwing for 414 yards in the big game and leading the Rams to victory over the Titans. This last feat of the season added a Super Bowl MVP award to his collection. Only five other men have been both the league and Super Bowl MVP: Bart Starr, Terry Bradshaw, Joe Montana, Steve Young, and the only nonquarterback to win both awards, Emmitt Smith.

Before getting hurt in the middle of the 2000 season, Warner remained a force behind center, even as his team showed some leaks and got bounced from the playoffs early. In 2001 he returned with a vengeance, throwing for 4830 yards (the second-highest single-season total in history) and 36 touchdowns.

Teams couldn't figure out how to stop Warner or even slow him down, at least not until he faced the Patriots in Super Bowl XXXVI. The solution: get physical. New England slowed down the Rams receivers by pressing them at the line of scrimmage and keeping them from getting into their routes quickly. They also used the blitz to keep Warner from getting comfortable. The Patriots sacked him 3 times and forced 2 interceptions, limiting the Rams high-powered offense to just 17 points.

Warner was never a dominant quarterback again. After three incredible seasons, the bubble had burst. Some would say that the Patriots had simply provided a blueprint for stopping Warner. Others would suggest that a broken thumb in 2002 was his undoing. I think it was probably a combination of the two. Warner's mechanics seemed to be sound in his subsequent stints with the Giants and the Cardinals, but the results were merely ordinary.

#71 Jeff Garcia (1999–2007)

Garcia is yet another example of a quarterback who didn't get a shot coming out of college but ended up making a splash anyway. After he was spurned by NFL teams, Garcia spent five successful seasons in Canada, leading the Calgary Stampeders to a Grey Cup victory in 1998.

Garcia joined the 49ers in 1999 as a backup to Steve Young, taking over the starting job when Young suffered what would prove to be a career-ending concussion. In his first full season as a starter, Garcia threw for 4278 yards and 31 touchdowns. He earned the first of what would be three straight Pro Bowl appearances, and led the Niners to the playoffs in 2001 and 2002. Garcia became just the sixth quarterback in NFL history to throw 30 touchdown passes in back-to-back seasons. (The others are Steve Bartkowski, Brett Favre, Dan Fouts, Dan Marino, and Y. A. Tittle.)

Garcia's detractors complained about his lack of arm strength and said his success was due more to the Niners system than his own inherent ability. Both of those criticisms gained support after free agency took Garcia to the Browns and Lions, where his performance dropped off dramatically. Without a stellar cast around him, he was less than adequate. He found new life in Philadelphia in 2006, taking over for an injured Donovan McNabb to run a West Coast Offense nearly identical to the one he'd played in San Francisco. He moved to Tampa the following year and led the Buccaneers to a division title.

#72
Mark Rypien (1988–2001)

One of three quarterbacks with whom Redskins coach Joe Gibbs won a Super Bowl, Rypien was probably the least gifted of the bunch. However, he might have been the best fit for the coach's single-back passing attack. Rypien was adept at spreading the ball out to his quick receivers, and he helped lead the Redskins to a 14-2 record and a Super Bowl title in 1991.

Rypien's tenure in Washington was short. Gibbs retired a year after that Super Bowl win, and when the system changed Rypien was like a fish out of water. He would stick around the league for eight more years as a backup.

#73
Boomer Esiason (1984–1997)

A great left-handed quarterback and master of the play-action pass, Esiason led the Cincinnati offense to great heights in the late 1980s. He had a very strong arm and at 6-foot-5 and 240 pounds was pretty big for a quarterback.

Under head coach Sam Wyche, the Bengals played an up-tempo no-huddle offense, and Esiason thrived because of his ability to identify and exploit mismatches. He also developed several techniques for fooling defenders and making them think he handed the ball off when he still had it in his hand. With dangerous running backs like James

Brooks and Ickey Woods, the play-action pass became the centerpiece of the Bengals' attack.

A Long Island native, Esiason eventually got his wish to return home and play for the Jets. He struggled through three disappointing seasons there, playing for a different head coach each year.

Esiason showed some spark after leaving the Jets, throwing for 522 yards in a game for the Cardinals in 1996. A year later he returned to Cincinnati, taking over a 2-7 team and leading them to a 5-2 finish, throwing 13 touchdowns and just 2 interceptions. Esiason could have continued playing but opted to retire, joining the broadcast booth for *Monday Night Football*.

He holds most of the career records for left-handed quarterbacks, including most touchdown passes (247), passing yards (37920), and completions (2969).

#74
Babe Parilli (1952–1969)

An NFL journeyman who found a home in the American Football League. Parilli led the Boston Patriots to the AFL title game in 1963. His best season came a year later, when he led the league with 3465 passing yards and 31 touchdowns. He had never come close to those kinds of numbers earlier, and never reached them again.

#75
Dave Krieg (1980–1998)

Most folks would be shocked to know that Krieg ranked in the top ten in each of the major passing categories when he retired. While this can be partially attributed to his longevity, Krieg did have several very productive seasons during the 1980s that went largely unnoticed.

What stands out in most people's minds was a more dubious achievement. Krieg was one of the game's most frequent fumblers. He set records for most fumbles in a season (18 in 1989) and a career (153), although both marks have since been surpassed. This problem was generally attributed to his small hands, although his offensive line didn't help matters much. Krieg was sacked 494 times in his career, the third-highest total since the league began tracking sacks for quarterbacks.

Other Quarterbacks

 # 76. Bobby Hebert (1985–1996)

 # 77. Jay Schroeder (1985–1994)

 # 78. Jake Plummer (1997–2006)

 # 79. Elvis Grbac (1994–2001)

 # 80. Doug Flutie (1986–2005)

 # 81. Brian Sipe (1974–1983)

 # 82. Jim Everett (1986–1997)

 # 83. Greg Landry (1968–1984)

 # 84. Don Meredith (1960–1968)

 # 85. Wade Wilson (1981–1998)

 # 86. Ben Roethlisberger (2004–2007)

 # 87. Tommy Thompson (1940–1950)

 # 88. Daunte Culpepper (1999–2007)

 # 89. Michael Vick (2001–2006)

 # 90. Stan Humphries (1989–1997)

 # 91. Jay Fiedler (1998–2005)

 # 92. Jeff Hostetler (1985–1997)

 # 93. Ron Jaworski (1974–1989)

 # 94. Ken O'Brien (1984–1993)

 # 95. Kerry Collins (1995–2007)

 # 96. Vinny Testaverde (1987–2007)

 # 97. Jim Plunkett (1971–1986)

 # 98. Doug Williams (1978–1989)

 # 99. Bill Nelsen (1963–1972)

 # 100. Bernie Masterson (1934–1940)

Running Backs

Jim Brown (1957–1965)

If you want to talk about who the greatest running back in football history is, you don't have to start with Jim Brown, but Brown is where you'll inevitably end up. If you're going to select your "greatest player" based on your heart, based on a limited era of the NFL, or based on a preexisting belief, then you might come up with another name. But if you're objective, if you define a set of criteria by which to define greatness, you're going to see that Brown rises to the top in almost every discernable way.

It has been more than forty years since Brown took the field, which means that there are now two or three generations of football fans that never saw him play. Although I have made it a point to seek out game footage of Brown and other great players, I have to say that I never really saw him play either. There is a tremendous difference between seeing highlights of a player's career and living through his era. By experiencing the latter, you get to see the player when he was just average, or when he stumbled. You see the mediocre games, not just the handful of plays that stood out. You also know the era in which he played, the defenses that gave a player his biggest challenges, the importance of

that player within his own offense, and the stature of that player within the league.

Because I was born three years after Brown retired, I didn't experience any of these things. Still, I feel 100 percent certain in stating that Brown was the greatest running back of all time.

How could I possibly know?

There are many ways that one can define greatness, and there are many ways to measure great performance. For example:

- Outstanding performances in a single game
- Outstanding performances in a single season
- Career statistics
- Contributions to championship teams
- Honors received and recognition by his peers
- Impact on the game itself

In any of these ways of measuring, Brown comes out at the very top. As a rookie, he set the record for rushing yards in a single game. In his second season, he set the record for rushing yards in a season. When he retired, he had shattered the records for career rushing yards and touchdowns. Brown helped the Browns advance to the NFL title game three times, winning the championship in 1964. He was named the league's Most Valuable Player four times, was invited to the Pro Bowl every season he played, and led the league in rushing eight times in his nine NFL seasons.

But if all you know is these numbers, you really don't have an appropriate appreciation of Jim Brown's contributions as a football player.

Brown was one of the great athletes of the twentieth century, a multisport star at Manhasset High School and Syracuse University. The New York Yankees tried to sign him to play baseball. He was a track star in high school and college and considered running the decathlon in the 1956 Olympics. He led the Syracuse basketball team in scoring as a sophomore. He's in the Lacrosse Hall of Fame. (According to some sources, the rule requiring lacrosse players to keep their sticks extended from their body when carrying the ball was implemented to slow Brown down.) To understand the enormity of Brown's athletic talent, you have to start with the realization that football probably wasn't even his best sport.

Brown was an astonishing physical specimen. He had an 18-inch neck, broad shoulders, a barrel chest, and massive, powerful thighs. Author Terry Pluto described him as having "muscled legs like pistons and arms like jackhammers." He had a reputation for being a power runner, and at 6-foot-2 and 230 pounds it was a reputation he deserved. He was bigger than most linebackers, and certainly bigger than the defensive backs that tried to tackle him. But Brown was also nimble enough to avoid tackles and quick enough to outrun defenders in the open field. Nobody had ever seen that combination of speed and strength before, and he caused an immediate sensation when he joined the Browns as a rookie in 1957.

There might be a temptation to simply conclude that his physical gifts were what made him a great football player. To do that would be to miss what were probably his two most important characteristics: he was extremely intelligent, and he had an intense and unbreakable focus.

When there is going to be a collision, many backs will put their head down and brace themselves for the blow. Brown would attack the defender, delivering the blow himself. He had a fearsome forearm, and when he struck a would-be tackler with it, his goal was not so much to break a tackle but to hit the defender so hard that it dis-

couraged him from wanting to tackle Brown the next time.

That psychological aspect of his game might be the most underappreciated aspect of his career. Brown knew that, at its essence, football was a game of intimidation. For him, intimidation came not just from being a tough guy, but also from creating an outward appearance that suggested nothing could bother him. He didn't respond to taunting, he didn't engage in any flashy showmanship. When he was tackled, Brown would always get up deliberately, hesitantly, as if he were reassembling and collecting himself. He would slowly trudge back to the huddle. Why? Sometimes he would take a tremendous hit and need to get up slowly. But because he handled himself the same way every single time, nobody would know. Neither his teammates nor his opponents could tell when he was hurting.

Hall of Famer Chuck Bednarik, a linebacker who epitomized the tough football of the 1950s, described the frustration of playing against Brown. "You gang-tackled him, gave him extracurriculars. He'd get up slow, look at you, and walk back to that huddle and wouldn't say a word . . . just come at you again, and again. You'd just say, 'What the hell, what's wrong with this guy? For heaven's sake, when is he going to stop carrying the ball? How much more can he take?'"

In spite of his physical style of play, Brown had what you might call a Zen quality of calmness. He sat alone on the sidelines. Before games, he would be off by himself in the locker room, preparing for the game with quiet reflection. Visualization was an important part of his preparation, Brown later explained, but opponents and teammates alike were intimidated by his aloofness. Brown never argued with officials, even though he was a frequent victim of cheap shots. He never asked out of a game, and when he was injured, he wouldn't even let his fellow Browns know. He would come in hours before practice to get medical attentions, not wanting his teammates to ever see him in the trainer's room.

"Men deal with physicality," Brown said in a 2002 documentary film about his life. "The bottom line with a man is 'I'll kick your ass.' Most men would like to know that they are physical enough to bring it. In football, it's almost like brains don't count, emotions don't count, education doesn't count. The bottom line is 'I will bust you up. Can you stand this pressure?' And in my case, it was 'can you bring enough pressure to take my mind?' You can't bring enough pressure. You can't hurt me. You can't do anything to break my mind. And if you came to hurt me and you can't hurt me, I have won. It's just that basic."

Brown retired suddenly, at the age of twenty-nine. He had a lot of football left in him, but he felt there was nothing left to prove. He was right. He had won a championship, won MVP awards, and he held every rushing record in the book. More significantly for Brown, he had seen other star players hanging on after their skills had deteriorated, continuing to play until things got so bad they were benched. He wasn't going to let someone else decide when he was done. "I wanted to depart in style, on my own set of terms," Brown wrote in his 1989 autobiography *Out of Bounds*. "I wanted a career so consistent, production so constant, no one could [screw] with me the way they always do with an athlete who lingers too long. My first year in the NFL I led the league in rushing. My last year I was MVP. Bench *that!*"

Three numbers stand out. 1) He averaged 104 rushing yards per game—a rate of production that's never been matched. 2) He averaged 5.2 yards per carry—again, never been matched. 3) He missed zero games in nine seasons. That's simply astonishing when you consider the heavy load he carried and the intensity of the blows he endured.

In 1962, he played with a severely sprained—perhaps broken—wrist. It was the only time in his career he didn't lead the league in rushing (he finished 4th). The following season he played with a painful broken toe, but set an NFL record by rushing for 1863 yards in fourteen games.

There is no shortage of praise for Brown in the existing football literature. You won't find any books about the history of the game or its greatest players that aren't overflowing with quotes from his contemporaries. They rave about his athleti-cism, about his charisma, about his fierce competitiveness. But I haven't seen anyone talk about how he dramatically changed the style of offense played in the NFL. Before Brown, teams generally used a group of running backs to form their ground attack. They often had complementary skills, like the 49ers' Hugh McElhenny and Joe Perry. A team would typically have two backs combine for about 250 carries. Only eight backs had ever carried the ball 200 times in a single season, but Brown changed that. He averaged 262 rushes per season and changed the game by showing that one back could be used extensively, that a running game could be based on one dominant back. In the years since Jim Brown, the majority of teams have relied on one back to provide the bulk of their ground attack. He was pro football's first feature back. "When you have a Thoroughbred," coach Paul Brown said, "you run him."

Brown played at a time when all defenses focused on stopping the run, and, in particular, Cleveland's opponents were focused on trying to contain him. It rarely worked. He played in 118 regular season games and rushed for 100 yards or more 58 times (49.2%).

Brown left football for the movies, and in the ten years after he retired, Brown appeared in nineteen films. He parlayed his good looks and commanding presence into meaty roles in high-profile movies such as *The Dirty Dozen, Ice Station Zebra*, and *100 Rifles*. He was probably the first African-American sex symbol, and *New York Magazine* called him "the black John Wayne."

Brown's intimidating physical presence and his intensity made him a natural action hero, but it also led to some problems off the field. Brown has had several brushes with the law—seven by my count—mostly based on of accusations of violence against women. On the other hand, he's been an active leader in the African-American community. Shortly after leaving football, he founded an organization to help support African-American businesses. In the late 1980s, he created Amer-I-Can, a program that works to help rehabilitate gang members. Even as a college athlete, he realized that his success on the field made it possible for him to take a public stand for better treatment for minority athletes. One of the reasons the Cleveland Browns were so successful in the forties and fifties was that they were ahead of the rest of the league on issues of integration, and recognizing the contributions of African-American players. Brown deserves credit for his role in expanding that atmosphere during his time with the team and helping to empower his fellow athletes.

It's worth noting that two of his backups went on to have Hall of Fame careers. Bobby Mitchell was an underutilized back for four seasons in Cleveland. He emerged as a game-changing playmaker after he was traded to Washington in 1962. Leroy Kelly labored in Brown's shadow for two years, becoming the starter after Brown retired. You have to think that both men learned something while working with Brown, if only from just watching him play.

#2

Barry Sanders (1989–1998)

The most frustrating player in NFL history, both for the defenders who tried to stop him and for Lions fans who hoped his talent alone could carry the team to a championship. His unique running style made him one of the most exciting players of his day. Standing just 5-foot-8, Sanders didn't have the bulk to run over defenders. However, his blazing speed and his remarkable ability to stop on a dime and change direction made him a terror in the open field.

Hall of Fame linebacker Mike Singletary described it this way: "When you defend against Barry you have to start by finding him. Then you have to tackle with good technique. If you try to blast him, chances are he'll spin out of it, and you'll end up looking a little silly."

Sanders would have games where the defense would seem to have him bottled up. He'd get stopped for just 1 yard here, 2 yards there, and it looked like the defense had shut him down. Then all of a sudden he'd break a tackle and burst free for a huge gain. He'd end up with twenty plays where he did nothing, and two plays so spectacular that they made you forget the rest.

He rushed for 2053 yards in 1997, and it wasn't simply because the Lions kept giving him the ball. He actually had carried the ball more often in 1991, finishing with 505 fewer yards. He did the same thing in 1998. The difference in his 2000-yard season was his remarkable 6.1-yard rushing average. Sanders was just the third NFL player to average more than 6 yards per carry (with at least 150 rushing attempts).

Sanders surprised a lot of people with his sudden retirement just eighteen months after that record-breaking season. He left at the age of thirty-one, just 1457 yards shy of Walter Payton's NFL career rushing record. Sanders explained his departure with a simple statement: "My desire to exit the game is greater than my desire to remain in it."

No doubt his feelings were largely influenced by the Lions inability to build a better team around him. In Sanders's ten seasons, the Lions' regular-season record was 78-82, and they managed just one playoff win. Coach Wayne Fontes tried to keep opposing defenses from ganging up on Sanders by spreading the field with a run-and-shoot offense. By using four receivers and eliminating both the tight end and the fullback, all he accomplished was to leave Sanders more vulnerable to being stopped in the backfield. When Bobby Ross was hired to replace Fontes, he installed a more balanced offense, but the results weren't much different.

A study of the play-by-play data from Sanders's career reveals just how much this problem plagued him. The table above shows how many of his carries each season resulted in a loss of yards, and how many resulted in positive yardage. (For the purposes of this study, a play that netted zero yards is counted in the positive column.) In his first season, he was tackled for a loss on about 10 percent of his plays, and that number went steadily upward until it reached nearly 20 percent in his final season. One out of five times he touched the ball in his final season, Sanders was tackled behind the line of scrimmage, and yet he still gained nearly 1500 yards.

Sanders Gains/Losses per Season

Year	Gain	Loss	Pct
1989	251	29	10.4
1990	227	28	11.0
1991	296	46	13.5
1992	268	44	14.1
1993	206	37	15.2
1994	280	51	15.4
1995	260	54	17.2
1996	263	44	14.3
1997	287	48	14.3
1998	278	65	19.0
Total	**2616**	**446**	**14.6**

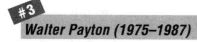

Walter Payton (1975–1987)

Payton was a quiet, humble superstar in an era when even the mediocre players bragged about their accomplishments. His even-tempered personality earned him the nickname "Sweetness," but there was nothing sweet about his running style. Payton wasn't big, but he was a punishing runner who relished the physical contact.

Despite battling the flu, Payton rushed for 275 yards in a 1977 game against the Vikings. The performance set a single-game record that stood until 2001. He had another memorable game against the Vikings two years later, when he caught, threw, and ran for a touchdown, a feat that has only been matched by six players.

Payton retired as the NFL's all-time rushing leader, but he was truly an all-around talent. Payton also had the most pass receptions by a running back when he retired (492) and ranked 5th in receiving yards (4538). His 8 touchdown passes are the most among modern running backs. He was a ferocious blocker, and he even served as the Bears' emergency punter.

Whereas Jim Brown would get up slowly following a tackle, Payton jumped up quickly to avoid taking any extra blows in the pileup. He ran with a unique, stiff-legged gait, running just on the balls of his feet. This helped him to make sharp cuts and spin out of tackles. Payton also felt that this would protect him from knee injuries because his feet were never firmly planted. Whether or not his theory was sound, Payton did remain healthy. He missed just one game during his career, the fifth game of his rookie season. He had suffered a calf bruise a week earlier against the Lions, and the team trainer insisted on holding him out.

My two most prominent memories of Payton take place off the field, after he retired. The first comes from his induction to the Hall of Fame in 1993. Previous honorees had asked former teammates or an influential coach for the honor of giving a speech about them just before their induction. Packers legends Forrest Gregg and Jim Taylor asked Marie Lombardi, the widow of their beloved coach. Mel Hein was introduced by a congressman. Blood McNally and Jimmy Conzelman were introduced by Supreme Court Justices.

But Walter Payton chose his twelve-year-old son for that honor, and in his acceptance speech he said that the thing he was most proud of was his two children, and the thing that he was most ashamed of was that his quest to match the feats of runners like Jim Brown and Gale Sayers made him neglect the people he loved the most.

Then in February of 1999, Payton announced that he'd been diagnosed with a rare liver disease. He spent his remaining months as an advocate for organ transplants before passing away that fall. Payton was just forty-five years old, and he was the first great sports star to pass away whose career I had witnessed.

Emmitt Smith (1990–2004)

There's no way of knowing for sure, but I'd wager that Smith could have made the Hall of Fame if he'd retired after just six seasons. He already had 96 touchdowns at that point, which was 6th on the all-time list, and his 8956 rushing yards put him at No. 12. Add in the fact that Smith was the key player on a team that won three Super Bowls in four seasons, and I think that his case for Canton would have been overwhelming.

Of course, Smith played nine more seasons, and although there's a tendency to think that the second part of his career was a letdown, it's only because he had attained such remarkable heights in those first six seasons. Smith ranked in the top 10 in Adjusted Yards for three of the next four seasons (he was 11th in 1997). So you have the first segment to his career when he was as dominant as anyone had ever been, and the second segment when he was less dominant but clearly still one of the NFL's top rushers.

Then his career entered a third phase, when the focus seemed to be on breaking Walter Payton's record for all-time rushing yards. Injuries sidelined him for the better part of 2003, but during the other four seasons in that stretch, he still averaged over 1000 yards per season.

Smith was a downhill rusher, a guy who liked to pound it out between the tackles. What set him apart from other power runners was his speed, his vision for the field, and his ability to cut back through gaps right as they appeared.

Smith was such a dominating runner in the early part of his career that we have largely overlooked how good he was as a receiver. From 1991 to 1995, he averaged 55 catches per season. He played a key role in the passing offense, usually the third choice for quarterback Troy Aikman after receiver Michael Irvin and tight end Jay Novacek.

#5
Eric Dickerson (1983–1993)

Three players set NFL records with their single-season performances in 1984. Dan Marino threw 48 touchdown passes, Art Monk caught 106 passes, and Eric Dickerson rushed for 2105 yards. The following summer, each of the three men sought to renegotiate their contracts to cash in on their suc-

cess. Monk quietly received a new contract from the Redskins. Marino held out of training camp, reporting a week before the opening game without a new deal, saying that it would be unfair to his teammates to stay away any longer.

Dickerson's holdout took a decidedly unfriendly tone, as both he and his agent traded barbs in the media with Rams owner Georgia Frontiere and team vice president John Shaw. He returned in time to play the Rams' third game, but he had a relatively disappointing season and the bad feelings that his holdout created would linger.

Just two years later, Dickerson was unhappy again, so unhappy that he suggested he wasn't able to give his best effort. Rams coach John Robinson suspended him, and on Halloween, Dickerson was traded to the Colts in a three-team deal that netted the Rams three first-round picks, three second-round picks, and two veteran players (running backs Greg Bell and Owen Gill). The Colts also gave up rookie linebacker Cornelius Bennett, a first-round draft pick whom they had been unable to sign.

The honeymoon in Indianapolis didn't last long. After his second full season there, Dickerson publicly criticized some of his teammates and demanded to be traded. He showed up two weeks late for training camp in 1990, failed his physical, and then was suspended when he refused to let team doctors reexamine him. He eventually reconciled with the team, but he was suspended again the following season after reportedly refusing to participate in practice. In four full seasons with the Colts, his yardage totals fell each season: 1659 in '88, 1311 in '89, 677 in '90, and 536 in '91. That's what we call a freefall, and by 1991 the Colts were fed up. They'd paid a heavy price to acquire the superstar and gotten nothing but headaches in return. When they dealt him to the Raiders on draft day 1992, all they got back were two low picks—a fourth rounder and an eighth rounder.

Dickerson's return to Los Angeles was disappointing, and his career ended a year later after playing four games with Atlanta. When he retired he ranked 2nd on the all-time rushing list, and his position on this list demonstrates how remarkable his career was. As with baseball's Mickey Mantle, however, there's a sense that he might have reached even greater heights if not for his own self-destructive behavior.

Holdouts and suspensions cost Dickerson fourteen games and undoubtedly diminished his performance in maybe a half-dozen more. His contract disputes and feuds with coaches and owners cost him a lot of games in his prime. In a 1991 interview with the *New York Times,* Walter Payton said that he believed Dickerson could have rushed for more than 20,000 yards if he had stayed in Los Angeles and avoided the controversies that surrounded his career. "He could have really set some records that no one could have reached," Payton said.

Though Payton's figure of 20,000 might have been a stretch, he did have a point. Dickerson was the kind of back who flourished on a grass field and in warm weather. The move to Indianapolis and the hard Astroturf surface of the Hoosier Dome wasn't in his best interest.

Dickerson was a remarkably durable running back. There have been twenty seasons where a player had 375 or more rushing attempts. In most cases, the heavy load from doing that just once dramatically shortened the player's career. Dickerson did it four times in six seasons and showed no adverse effects. Part of that can be attributed to the fact that he covered himself from head to toe in protective gear at a time when most other backs adopted a more minimalist approach. Among his accessories were goggles, elbow pads, gloves, and an unusually large mouthpiece that seemed to cover half of his face. Dan Pompei of the *Sporting News* said that Dickerson "looked like he had been dropped into the 1980s from the space age."

The other thing that kept Dickerson healthy was his unusual running style. He ran almost completely upright, with long strides that made it look as if he were much slower. When tacklers approached, he turned on a burst of speed that helped him avoid contact altogether. "I don't give players a chance to hit me," Dickerson explained. "I run upright mostly when I see daylight, so if you watch film you'll see I don't get hit in the chest much. Most of the hits I take come on top of the shoulder pads. I believe if I stay tall and run up high, I can see better."

Thurman Thomas (1988–2000)

The Bills of the early 1990s had a ton of talent, but Thomas was the best of them all. He was the final piece of the puzzle that transformed the Bills from a good team into a great one. A great all-around running back, Thomas is the only player to lead the league in yards from scrimmage (rushing plus receiving) four times. He's one of only four running backs to rush for over 1000 yards in eight consecutive seasons (Payton, Faulk, and Allen are the other three).

Thomas was poised to be the Most Valuable Player of Super Bowl XXV, but the Bills lost the game when kicker Scott Norwood missed a field goal with 8 seconds remaining. Thomas had rushed for 135 yards and a touchdown and had 5 catches for 55 yards in that game. When Norwood's kick sailed wide right, the award instead went to the Giants' Ottis Anderson. Thomas clearly outplayed Anderson (102 yards rushing, 1 catch for 7 yards), but the voters were apparently swayed by the final score.

Although Thomas continued to be one of the game's most dominating players during the regular season, his poor play in Super Bowls was a major factor in the Bills losing the next three. He missed the beginning of Super Bowl XXVI because he couldn't find his helmet. The Bills ran two plays from scrimmage before Thomas was able to get onto the field. He finished the game with just 10 carries for 13 yards as Buffalo was routed by Washington. Against Dallas in Super Bowl XXVII, Thomas rushed 11 times for 19 yards, and the following year he ran just 16 for 37.

Unfortunately, those failures on the big stage stick out in people's minds. They didn't keep him out of the Hall of Fame. But they are an unfortunate stain on his resume, and whether it's fair or not, he gets the lion's share of the blame for the Bills losing four straight Super Bowls.

Curtis Martin (1995–2005)

Steve Van Buren (1944–1951)

Does anyone think of Curtis Martin as one of the greatest backs in NFL history? I don't think so. The blogosphere is full of pundits who go so far as to say he's overrated. They claim that his numbers are inflated, that his success is the product of playing behind good offensive lines, or other such nonsense. Such views are the product of a media environment where only contrarian viewpoints are given, where the loudest voices are the only ones heard, and science and reason are discarded in favor of strongly held opinions.

The raw numbers are undeniable. Martin rushed for 1000 yards in each of his first ten seasons, a feat that only Barry Sanders has matched. He became just the third player to rush for more than 14000 yards, and when he retired his 90 rushing touchdowns ranked 10th all-time.

The argument against Martin appears to lie in the fact that he didn't have a period of sustained dominance. He won just one rushing title, which he didn't accomplish until he was thirty-one years old. He never won an MVP Award, and never did anything to emphatically stamp himself as the dominant running back of his time. What it boils down to, I think, is that Martin wasn't the kind of player who generated a lot of highlights in an era when that was the popular barometer of a player's success.

New York fans embrace guys with big personalities, larger-than-life figures like Joe Namath and Mickey Mantle. In contrast to those guys, Martin was relatively quiet. He was a humble, religious man, who preferred to let his on-field accomplishments speak for themselves. Martin might never have been the league's brightest star, but he was consistently among the top running backs in the game, and he maintained that level of play for a very long time. If that's not a great player, then I'm not sure what is.

He's No. 8 on my rankings but a guy that most modern fans won't know. Van Buren was the dominant running back of the post-war forties, a time when the league's talent levels were surging. He was a track star in college, but more often than not the Eagles used Van Buren as a battering ram. In his first six NFL seasons he won four rushing titles, leading the Eagles to three straight NFL title games. He scored the only touchdown in the 1948 championship game, a 7–0 win over the Cardinals played in a raging blizzard.

The following year's title game took place at the Los Angeles Coliseum, and a driving rain left the field in horrible shape. Van Buren led a group of players from both teams in urging the league to postpone the contest. While the mud was a real problem, the players were mostly concerned with the effects the weather would have on the size of the crowd. Their pay was based on a percentage of the gate, and fewer than 30,000 of the Coliseum's 90,000 seats were filled. Commissioner Bert Bell ignored their pleas, and Van Buren played the game in a rage. He rushed for 196 yards on the sloppy field and the Eagles won 14–0.

Van Buren retired as the league's all-time leader in rushing, but his name has now been largely erased from the record books.

NFL Career Rushing Yards Leaders

Player	Year Record Set	Career
Cliff Battles	1932	1932–37
Clarke Hinkle	1941	1932–41
Steve Van Buren	1949	1944–51
Joe Perry	1958	1948–63
Jim Brown	1963	1957–65
Walter Payton	1984	1975–87
Emmitt Smith	2002	1990–04

#9 Marshall Faulk (1994–2005)

There are a handful of players in NFL history who were better runners than Marshall Faulk, and a couple dozen who were better receivers. But there hasn't been anybody who did both things better.

Although the sudden fantastic play of quarterback Kurt Warner grabbed the headlines, it was the arrival of Marshal Faulk in St. Louis that turned the Rams into the "Greatest Show on Turf." Their aggressive passing attack wouldn't have been possible without the threat of Faulk on the ground.

Faulk's combination of size and speed made it very hard for defenses to cover him. Linebackers couldn't keep up with him, and safeties couldn't bring him down. Once he joined the Rams the problem was compounded even more. If teams used a combination of defenders to cover Faulk, that meant they'd have to leave receivers Isaac Bruce and Torry Holt in single coverage. And if they tried to cover all of the receivers, that left the middle of the field very vulnerable to the ground attack.

In 1998, Faulk finished 3rd among all players with 86 receptions, and he ranked 6th in rushing yards. In 1999, he set a new record for receiving yards by a running back, becoming just the second player to top the 1000-yard mark in rushing and receiving during the same season. His 2429 combined rushing/receiving yards that year were the most ever.

Top Receiving Seasons by an RB

Yards	Player	Year
1048	Marshall Faulk, Rams	1999
1027	Lionel James, Chargers	1985
1016	Roger Craig, 49ers	1985
962	Larry Centers, Cardinals	1995
941	Charlie Garner, Raiders	2002

Faulk ended his career with 767 receptions, more than such Hall of Fame receivers as James Lofton, Charlie Joiner, and Michael Irvin. Only Larry Centers had more receptions as a running back, but you could make the point that Centers functioned as more of an H-back or tight end. He had just 2188 rushing yards in his fourteen-year career, whereas Faulk ended with 12,279, 9th on the all-time list.

#10 LaDainian Tomlinson (2001–2007)

Chargers general manager John Butler had the first overall pick in the 2001 draft, and after failing to reach an agreement with quarterback Michael Vick, he traded the pick to Atlanta. The Falcons, like many other teams, coveted the young quarterback, but Butler really had his mind on another player. That was running back LaDainian Tomlinson, a versatile player who reminded Butler of a player he had built a team around when he was in Buffalo, a guy named Thurman Thomas.

Not only did the Chargers get their man, they got three draft picks and veteran receiver Tim Dwight from Atlanta for moving down. Three years later the Chargers would make a similar deal again, sending the rights to No. 1 overall pick Eli Manning to the Giants for the rights to the fourth pick, Phillip Rivers, and three additional draft choices.

In both cases, the Chargers leveraged their draft position to get extra value while still getting the player that they really wanted. In both cases that player turned out to have a better pro career than the player they passed on. Vick was tagged with the label "coach killer" and ended up in Federal prison after six seasons, while Tomlinson has established himself as one of the great running backs in NFL history.

Tomlinson catapulted himself into that elite company in 2006, when he set an NFL record with 31 touchdowns and was named the league's MVP. Even before that season his performances were establishing him as a standout. Tomlinson rushed for at least 1200 yards in each of his first six seasons, a feat matched by only one player (Eric Dickerson did it in his first seven years in the league). He reached 100 career rushing touchdowns faster than any other player, scoring at an unprecedented pace.

Highest Scoring Rate in First Six Seasons (minimum 50 games)

Player	G	RuYds	RuTD	RecTD	TotTD	TD/G
L. Tomlinson	95	9176	100	11	111	1.17
E. Smith	92	9223	97	7	104	1.13
S. Alexander	96	7817	89	11	100	1.04
M. Faulk	92	7801	65	30	95	1.03
P. Holmes	86	7078	79	6	85	0.99
J. Brown	78	8830	67	10	77	0.99
S. Van Buren	63	5089	58	3	61	0.97
L. Kelly	82	5923	67	12	79	0.96
J. Taylor	81	6774	70	7	77	0.95
L. Moore	73	3179	31	38	69	0.95

Because he catches so many passes, Tomlinson's statistics are going to look similar to versatile modern backs like Marshall Faulk and Priest Holmes. His running style, though, is more like that of Barry Sanders. Tomlinson is deceptively quick and has tremendous field vision, and he makes his big plays by finding small holes and bursting through them. The $64,000 question is whether the heavy load he's carried so early will shorten his career, or whether he'll enter into a second phase, like Emmitt Smith, where he's no longer setting records every year but still one of the top ten backs in the league.

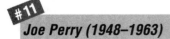

Joe Perry (1948–1963)

Perry is largely forgotten, but when he retired he had run for more yards and more touchdowns than any player in history. He started his career as a power runner, but later learned to take advantage of his speed and elusiveness. This explains how Joe, a big fullback, got the nickname "the Jet." It was rare for backs to rush for 1000 yards when teams were playing twelve-game schedules, but Perry did it back-to-back in 1953 and '54.

As I write this, Perry is still alive and living in Chandler, Arizona, with his wife, Donna. He turned eighty-one in January of 2008, and suffers from pugilistic dementia and short-term memory loss. Many people have pointed to him as one of the glaring examples of the inadequacies of the NFL pension system and, in a larger sense, of the incongruity of a league that generates six billion dollars of revenue a year while many of its former stars struggle to make ends meet. In a 2006 article on the subject, the *Baltimore Sun's* Ken Murray reported that despite playing pro football for sixteen seasons, Perry's pension was just $1,489 per month. Donna Perry told Murray: "People expect Joe, because he's in the Hall of Fame, to come and appear at different functions . . . [but] there's no money. We're on a fixed income, so we have to budget everything."

The NFL Player's Association, led by Gene Upshaw, has taken steps to help improve benefits, particularly for those like Perry who played before the pension plan was initiated in 1959. Many of his fellow Hall of Famers say that it's still not nearly enough. Howie Long, for one, said "it's the deep, dark secret nobody wants to talk about." In a 2005 interview with the *Charlotte Observer,* Long expressed his shock at how much players like Perry have struggled. "When I went to the Hall of Fame in 2000 and was inducted, it was a travesty the kind of carnage I saw out of these guys who were in their fifties and sixties, who had defined and in many ways laid the foundation for the NFL being what it is today. Many of them could barely rub two nickels together to get to Canton. Many of them couldn't afford to have their knee replaced or had fallen through whatever imaginary net there is from an economic standpoint. Not enough is being done."

Perry was inducted in the Hall of Fame in 1969.

#12 O.J. Simpson (1969–1979)

I was watching Game 5 of the 1994 NBA Finals when the folks at NBC interrupted their coverage to broadcast O.J.'s infamous low-speed freeway chase. Maybe you were too. Newspaper accounts revealed that 90 million Americans watched at least part of that surreal spectacle as it unfolded live on television.

Simpson's name conjures a whole different set of images today, and I suspect that ultimately he'll be remembered more for the crime he was accused (and acquitted) of than for his glory days on the gridiron.

Seven of the top 12 running backs on this list never played on a championship team, and Simpson was as deprived as any of them. He appeared in just one postseason game during his eleven-year career—a 32–14 loss to the Steelers in 1974. In his first three seasons, the Bills posted an 8-33-1 record, and while Simpson was the team's leading rusher, head coach John Rauch preferred to play a vertical passing game. The arrival of Lou Saban in 1972 thrust Simpson into the spotlight, and for the next four years he was dominating. Saban left in 1976 and Simpson tore up his knee, and both were basically done.

There is a growing sentiment in western New York to remove O.J. Simpson's name from the Bills' Ring of Honor at Ralph Wilson Stadium. I don't think that will ever happen, but it reflects the embarrassment that people in the area feel about his postfootball behavior. Simpson has become a pariah. Nobody wears his throwback jersey. Nobody wants to see highlight films of the Simpson era. For most people, the crimes he was accused of and his behavior in the decade that followed outweigh whatever positive things he accomplished on the football field.

#13 Leroy Kelly (1964–1973)

Kelly had the unenviable task of following the legendary Jim Brown in Cleveland. He'd spent two years returning punts and seeing spot duty in the backfield, and when Brown stunned everybody with his sudden retirement, Kelly was thrust into the starting role.

He couldn't have been more different than the man he was replacing. Brown was a power runner whose bread and butter was the sweep play. Kelly relied on his speed and quickness, and preferred trap plays. Brown was intense. Kelly was easygoing. Brown did one thing exceptionally well. Kelly was remarkably versatile.

The best way to follow in the footsteps of a legend is to have your own success, and that's just what Kelly did. Over the next four years, he was the league's best running back. Kelly won two rushing titles and led the league in rushing touchdowns three times. In 1967 he won the so-called rushing Triple Crown, leading the league in rushing yards, touchdowns, and rushing average. A year later, he was named Most Valuable Player after leading the Browns to the NFL championship game.

#14 Jim Taylor (1958–1967)

Taylor had the great fortune of playing for the Packers during the Lombardi era, but also the misfortune of playing in the NFL at the same time as Cleveland's Jim Brown. The two backs were similar in their playing style, brutally tough and fiercely intense. Taylor craved contact, relishing the opportunity to dish out punishment rather than receive it. "If you give a guy a little blast," Taylor said, "maybe the next time he won't be so eager. Football is a game of contact. You've got to make them respect you. You've got to punish them before they punish you."

Brown and Taylor were the league's most dominating backs in the early sixties, and there wasn't another player who was close enough to be considered in the same class as the pair. Over a five-year stretch from 1960 to 1964, Taylor won one rushing title and finished 2nd to Brown four times.

While Brown always seemed to best him when it came to individual honors, Taylor had the decided edge when it came to winning championships. The Packers won five titles in a seven-year stretch, plus the first two Super Bowls. Brown won just one championship during his career.

Although both men battled to be considered the NFL's top running back, Brown and Taylor met head-to-head only four times during their careers. The Packers won each time, and the table below shows their rushing statistics from each game.

Game	Score	Taylor	Brown
1961	W 49-17	21-158-4	16-72-0
1963*	W 40-23	13-45-1	11-61-0
1964	W 28-21	22-63-2	20-74-1
1965*	W 23-12	27-96-0	12-50-0

*postseason game

I'd like to tell you that these were all classic matchups but they weren't. Taylor had the best game of his career in the 1961 contest, and was named Most Valuable Player of the 1965 title game for his gritty performance.

#15

Edgerrin James (1999–2007)

Prior to the adoption of the sixteen-game schedule in 1978, just three men had rushed for 1500 yards in a season: Jim Brown (1958, 1963, 1965), O.J. Simpson (1973, 1975–76), and Walter Payton (1977). The new schedule boosted offensive totals simply by expanding the number of games each season by 12.5 percent.

But that increase in the number of games played each season can't account for the dramatic increase in the number of times the 1500-yard seasons have been happening. In the first two decades of the sixteen-game schedule, it occurred on aver-

age about 1.5 times per season. From 1998–2007, that rate has more than doubled.

1500-Yard Rushing Seasons by Decade

Decade	Times	Avg Per Yr
1978–87	17	1.7
1988–97	16	1.6
1998–07	34	3.4

Edgerrin James is part of a new breed of running backs who entered the league in the mid to late 1990s and starting piling up 1500-yard seasons like they were nothing. In his first seven seasons, he reached 1500 yards four times. Only three players have accomplished that feat: Walter Payton, Eric Dickerson, and Barry Sanders (who did it five times).

What's the root cause of this explosion? I think it's pretty clear. You gain more yards when you carry the ball more often, and while the early nineties saw many teams tilting toward the pass with variations of the West Coast Offense, a subtler trend has emerged. More teams have gotten away from the concept of a running back tandem or even a backup running back, and are turning to one player for the bulk of their running game.

Looking at the data in the table below, you'll see that the number of backs who carry the ball 250 times per season has risen dramatically.

Player/Seasons with 250+ Carries

Years	250+ Seasons	Avg Per Yr
1948–57	2	0.5
1958–67	13	1.3
1968–77	41	4.1
1978–87	83	8.3
1988–97	107	10.7
1998–07	164	16.4

You might be inclined to think that using backs more often means they'll burn out more quickly. In fact, if you look at all of the players who have had 250 carries in at least one season during their career, on average their careers lasted for 8.6 seasons. The average career length goes up the more often a back carries 250 times.

The evidence that overuse can dramatically shorten a career is overwhelming (see comments under Gerald Riggs). However, I think it's clear that NFL teams have learned they can safely use backs in a range that previously might have been considered overwork.

#16
Marcus Allen (1982–1997)

One of the great receivers out of the backfield and also one of the few backs who was able to remain productive well into his thirties. The reason for that, of course, was because of the way the Raiders abandoned him in the mid-1980s.

Flash back to 1983. It's Super Bowl XVIII, and Allen appears to be caught in the backfield. He turns back, cuts to the outside, finds an opening, and breaks free for a touchdown. It was a 73-yard gain—at the time the longest run in Super Bowl history. The Raiders won the game 38–9 as Allen finished with 191 yards.

In his first four years in the league, Allen led the NFL in touchdowns twice, won a rushing title, was named Rookie of the Year and earned a Most Valuable Player Award. Rather than continuing to build their offense around him, the Raiders decided to make him share the running back duties, first with Napoleon McCallum and then with Bo Jackson. The team was losing, and their best player wasn't getting much playing time.

Raiders owner Al Davis was clearly infatuated with Bo Jackson, and to some extent that explains why Allen's playing time was diminished from 1986 to 1990. Jackson's football career ended when he suffered a hip injury in a 1990 playoff game against the Bengals, however, and Allen never really got a chance to regain his starting job. The following year, Allen was still the No. 2 back, picking up carries behind free agent Roger Craig. In 1992, he fell to No. 3 on the depth chart behind Eric Dicker-son and Nick Bell. At that point, Allen's frustrations boiled over.

Allen lashed out in a startling interview with Al Michaels that aired at halftime of a Monday night game in December 1992. He claimed that Raiders owner Al Davis was out to get him. "I think he's tried to ruin the latter part of my career, tried to devalue me," Allen said. "He's trying to stop me from going to the Hall of Fame. They don't want me to play."

Davis denied the accusations, saying they reflected poorly on Allen. The interview didn't ultimately shed a lot of light on the situation, other than to reveal a bitter and long-simmering feud between Davis and Allen.

At season's end, Allen left as a free agent and signed with the division rival Kansas City Chiefs. Given a chance to play again, he led the league in rushing touchdowns and was recognized as the Comeback Player of the Year. Still just thirty-three, Allen wanted to prove that he still had some good football left in him. Although he didn't become the same kind of dominant back he had been in his early twenties, Allen was the leading rusher on a Chiefs team that went to the playoffs four times in five seasons.

The stat that gave Allen the most pleasure? I'd wager it was the fact that his Chiefs went 9-1 in games against the Raiders.

#17
Tuffy Leemans (1936–1943)

Over 55,000 fans showed up for the season finale at the Polo Grounds for "Tuffy Leemans Day." The Giants were honoring their star halfback before a game against the crosstown rivals from Brooklyn. The raucous celebration was interrupted when the public address announcer said over the loudspeaker: "All Navy men in the audience are to report to their posts immediately." The date was December 7, 1941, and the Japanese attack at Pearl Harbor had begun just moments before kickoff.

Like many other NFL players, Leemans chose to enlist in the service. A head injury in a game against the Bears left him deaf in one ear, however, and therefore he was unable to serve.

Leemans was a slashing runner who led the league in rushing as a rookie and helped lead the Giants to an NFL title in 1938. Although the statistics for the day are sketchy, he was probably the best punt returner of his era. He was named first- or second-team All-Pro seven times, but he wasn't elected to the Hall of Fame until 1978—thirty-five years after he retired.

#18
Lenny Moore (1956–1967)

ESPN.com's Jeff Merron ranked Moore 2nd on a list of the all-time underrated athletes. I think the main reason for this is that you don't know how to classify him. Was Moore a running back? Was he a receiver?

You can't really answer that question because he was neither. Moore played running back but was used primarily as a pass catcher. He would run the ball about 90 times a year, catch about 50 passes, and score about a dozen touchdowns. From 1956 to 1961, he split his time between the flanker position and halfback. The Colts won the NFL championship in 1958 and 1959.

Starting in 1962, he lined up exclusively in the backfield, and his productivity suffered. He was injured in 1963 but came back with the best year of his career in 1964. Moore was named league MVP after rushing for 16 touchdowns and scoring 20 overall.

From 1963 to 1965 he scored touchdowns in eighteen straight games, establishing a record that stood until LaDainian Tomlinson broke it in 2005.

#19
Ottis Anderson (1979–1992)

Anderson is the Dave Kingman of football. Dave Kingman, for those who don't know, was a Major League Baseball player who hit 442 home runs in his career. Despite those impressive power numbers, the voters showed no interest in selecting him for the baseball Hall of Fame. For two decades, he stood as the man with the most homers who wasn't in the Hall, the de facto definition of how good you could be without getting in. In Kingman's case, the voters rejection was based on a conclusion that he was a one-dimensional player. In Anderson's case, they seem to have concluded that he fell just below the threshold for induction. Anderson had some fantastic seasons with the Cardinals, which were largely overlooked because the team wasn't very good. He also spent a few productive seasons with the New York Giants, capped by his selection as MVP of Super Bowl XXV.

Late in that 1990 season he passed 10000 rushing yards, becoming just the 8th player to surpass that mark. All of the men ahead of him at the time (Payton, Dickerson, Dorsett, Brown, Harris, Riggins, Simpson) have been inducted into the Hall of Fame. By contrast, Anderson has never even been considered as one of the fifteen annual finalists. Like Kingman, he's been passed by a whole bunch of modern players, which makes his career totals look less and less significant with each passing year. By the end of the 2007 season, sixteen years after Anderson retired, fourteen more players had moved ahead of him.

#20
Tony Dorsett (1977–1988)

Things might have turned out very differently for Tony Dorsett. After winning the Heisman Trophy in 1977, he was widely considered the best prospect coming out of college. The teams with the first two picks were the Buccaneers and Seahawks, expansion teams who had a combined 1-27 record the year before. Both teams had a scarcity of talent. Had Dorsett gone to either place, he would have been the focus of the offense. However, with a lousy offensive line and no passing game to relieve the pressure, it's likely that Dorsett would have carried a heavy load but not achieved much success.

Instead, the Dallas Cowboys orchestrated a trade, sending three high picks to Seattle for the No. 2 overall pick and the right to select Dorsett. Rather than walk into a bad situation Dorsett went into the ideal one, an established team with a star quarterback, an established offensive line, and a championship-caliber defense.

He rushed for 1007 yards as a rookie and topped the 1000-yard mark eight times in his first nine seasons. The one year that he fell short was the strike-shortened 1982 season, when he led the league with 745 yards in nine games. He had good speed and great balance, and he had the patience to wait for things to develop in front of him before exploding forward. His most memorable run came in 1983, when he took a handoff in his own end zone on a broken play and scrambled 99 yards for a touchdown.

Dorsett's playing weight was listed between 183 and 193 in the various guides that I've looked at. Even at the high end of that range, he was small by the standards of his era. With a team like the Seahawks, I think he would have been asked to carry a very heavy workload, and he wouldn't have survived. Ricky Bell, who was taken ahead of Dorsett in the 1977 draft, lasted just four years as the centerpiece of the Tampa Bay offense. In Dallas, Dorsett didn't have to carry the offense all by himself, and as a result, he was able to stay healthy and be productive for a long time. He missed just three games in his first nine seasons in the league, and only once did the Cowboys ask him to carry the ball thirty times in game.

"If I wanted to risk Tony, I think he could gain as many yards as Payton and Campbell," Cowboys' coach Tom Landry explained. "But Tony is so much different than Earl, who is so big. Payton is probably the strongest little man I have ever seen. Then there is Wilbert Montgomery, who did get used a lot and got hurt. I don't want that to happen to Tony."

When Dorsett retired, he ranked 2nd all-time in rushing yards (12739) and in combined yards from scrimmage (16293), trailing Walter Payton in both categories.

Earl Campbell (1978–1985)

Campbell wasn't much of a receiver, which is about the only bad thing you can say about the guy. He ran for 74 touchdowns in his career but didn't catch a single touchdown pass.

There's an interesting grouping here, purely coincidental, of four guys who personified power football. Campbell ranks at No. 21, just ahead of Jerome Bettis, Larry Csonka, and Marion Motley from Nos. 24 through 26. Bettis played longer, Motley was a better all-around player, and Csonka won more championships. But none of those men dominated the league the way Campbell did.

He rushed for 1450 yards in 1978, earning both Rookie of the Year and Most Valuable Player Awards. Campbell's 19 rushing touchdowns in 1979 tied Jim Taylor's record for the most in a single season. The following year, Campbell rushed for 1934 yards, just 69 yards shy of O.J. Simpson's single-season record. You have to wonder how far Campbell might have pushed his total if not for a groin injury that sidelined him for most of one game and all of another. He had four 200-yard games that season, and during one stretch at midseason he averaged 179.3 yards per game.

Oilers head coach Bum Phillips described the huge impact that Campbell made on his team. "He is such a dominating runner that he makes linemen look better than they are, a quarterback look better than he is, and because he allows the offense to control the tempo of a game, the defense look better than it is."

After six seasons, Campbell was 9th on the all-time rushing list. He suffered a knee injury during the 1984 preseason that required surgery, and by the time he returned he was clearly worn out.

Ricky Watters (1992–2001)

A prototypical West Coast Offense running back, Watters may have been the best of the bunch. He rushed for 1013 yards as a rookie, and the following year he tied a playoff record by rushing for 5 touchdowns in a win over the Giants. A year later he scored 3 touchdowns in the 49ers' Super Bowl win over the Chargers.

Watters cashed in on that success by exploring free agency, signing a big contract with the Eagles. Three years later he moved on again, landing in Seattle. He spent three years starting for the Seahawks then lost his starting job and retired.

His career breaks down into three segments, each three years long. The table below shows his rushing and receiving totals each year, and as you can see, he was productive everywhere he went. The unfortunate truth is that despite those impressive numbers, he wore out his welcome everywhere he went.

Team	RuYds	RuTD	ReYds	ReTD
Niners	2840	25	1450	8
Eagles	3794	31	1318	1
Seahawks	3691	21	1373	4

Mike Freeman of the *New York Times* wrote this about Watters in 1996, his first season in Philadelphia: "Watters, off the field, is funny, charming, and nice. But when it comes to football he just can't keep quiet. On the field he is energetic to the point where he has become one of the biggest trash-talkers in the game. That fact has made him one of the more disliked players on the field." Watters's criticism wasn't just reserved for his opponents, though. He complained about his teammates and coaches, and eventually got the reputation for being selfish and childish. That's why despite rushing for 1242 yards and catching 63 passes in his last season, not one of the thirty-two NFL teams offered him a contract in 2002.

#23
Tiki Barber (1997–2006)

Most great running backs are stars from the very beginning of their careers, but Barber was one of the unusual cases that took a while to develop.

What's most remarkable about Barber was how he completely transformed himself mid-career, changing his playing style, his technique, and even his body, to go from being a part-time player to a dominating running back.

Because of his small stature, Barber was considered to be a third-down back when he came into the league. He was brought in to catch passes out of the backfield or to give the starter a breather, spending his first three seasons behind forgettable backs like Tyrone Wheatley, Gary Brown, and Joe Montgomery.

Barber blossomed in 2000 when he was paired with rookie Ron Dayne. The backfield duo, dubbed "Thunder and Lightning," combined for 1776 rushing yards and 13 touchdowns. The strong running game helped propel the Giants to the Super Bowl.

There was one problem that plagued Barber, however, and that was his inability to hold on to the football. From 2000 to 2003, Barber fumbled 35 times. Even though he was one of the league's most productive all-around running backs, the turnovers were killing his team. When Tom Coughlin became head coach in 2004, his biggest priority was to help Barber eliminate the fumbles and become more of a power runner.

The latter was accomplished through weight training, as Barber added bulk to his arms and upper body. Changing the way he ran with the ball cured the fumbling problem. Rather than holding it to his side under one arm, Barber cradled the ball across the top of his chest, wrapping it up with both arms when he was anticipating contact. He dropped from an average of 9 fumbles per season to just 3.

Barber also developed a modified stiff-arm technique that he says he copied from Emmitt Smith. Rather than using the stiff arm to keep an opponent at bay or knock him off balance, Barber used his hand to deflect the defender's leading arm. This made it difficult for the defender to strike at the football and very difficult to wrap Barber up for a tackle.

During the 2006 season, in what appeared to all observers to be the prime of his career, Barber announced he would leave football for a broadcasting career. It's a move that probably will cost him an invitation to the Hall of Fame, because he'll stop short of the career numbers that would push him into the upper echelon. Two or three more moderately good seasons would have pushed him into the top ten in rushing yards. Like others before him, he decided to walk away on his own terms, getting out while the decision was still his to make.

Jerome Bettis (1993–2005)

It's funny how sometimes a coach will look at a player who does one thing exceptionally well and then complain about all of the other things he doesn't do. That's what happened to Jerome Bettis when he was with the Rams. Things were great at first. As a downhill runner, he fit perfectly into the power running game that coach Chuck Knox loved to run. Bettis rushed for 1429 yards in 1993 and was named Offensive Rookie of the Year. He topped the 1000-yard mark again the following season, but then Knox got fired and Rich Brooks took over as the Rams head coach.

Brooks complained that Bettis was too slow and didn't really fit the kind of offense he wanted to run. Bettis didn't cut back through blocking lanes, he didn't juke and spin to make tacklers miss. He just ran right at them. Brooks sent Bettis to the Steelers for a paltry sum—two mid-round draft picks—and went about building his quick-pass attack. Brooks lasted just two seasons with the Rams, while Bettis continued what he did best, bowling over defenders in Bill Cowher's power running offense. Bettis had six straight 1000-yard seasons and established himself as the best big back of his era.

When injuries began to limit how often he could carry the ball, he became a short-yardage specialist and was very tough to stop. In the opening game of the 2004 season, Bettis scored 3 touchdowns on 5 carries, all from the 1-yard line. By mid-October he ranked 2nd in the league with 7 rushing touchdowns, even though he'd only had 37 carries.

Bettis's jovial personality made him a fan favorite, and he retired after the Steelers won Super Bowl XL.

Larry Csonka (1968–1979)

Csonka personified power football at a time when many teams were moving toward a passing game. At 6-foot-3 and 240 pounds, he was one of the biggest backs of his day. There was nothing subtle about his running style. He went straight ahead, running over any defender who got in his way. He topped the 1000-yard mark in three straight seasons from 1971 to 1973, helping to lead the Dolphins to the Super Bowl each time.

There was nothing fancy about Csonka's running style. He was just a bulldozer aimed right at the heart of the defense. He could be stopped if you were willing to focus all of your attention on him, but then the Dolphins would just run outside with Jim Kiick or Mercury Morris or throw it deep to Paul Warfield. The fact that Miami had such a diverse collection of talent made them stronger as a team and made each individual that much more dangerous.

Marion Motley (1946–1955)

In his 1971 book *The Thinking Man's Guide to Football,* legendary sportswriter Paul Zimmerman cast his vote for Motley as pro football's all-time best. "If there is a better football player who snapped on a helmet, I would like to know his name. [Jim] Brown was the best pure runner I've ever seen, but Motley was the greatest all-around player, the complete player." Zimmerman was a teenager when Motley was in his prime, and like the rest of us, I think his views were largely shaped by the fact that Motley was the game's biggest star during his formative years. Does that mean his opinion is off-base? Not necessarily.

There are a couple of problems we must confront when considering Motley's career. The first is that he didn't start playing pro football until after he'd turned twenty-six. Motley spent nearly five years after college serving in the U.S. Navy, costing him most of his prime football years. The second problem is that when he did turn pro, he started his career in the AAFC, a league that didn't have much competitive balance. Motley was an unstoppable avalanche, completely overwhelming opposing defenses. He averaged 6.2 yards per carry and helped the Cleveland Browns compile a 47-4-3 record and win all four AAFC championships. Some historians would argue that the Browns' dominance was due to the fact that most of the other teams in the rival league were less talented. Others would point to the Browns' continued success once they joined the NFL as evidence that they were simply an extraordinarily talented team.

Motley led the NFL in rushing yards in 1950, his (and the Browns') first year in the league. He was already thirty by this time, and injuries were beginning to take their toll. A bad right knee slowed him and his role in the Cleveland offense diminished over the next three seasons. Motley was forced to retire before the start of the 1954 season. He tried to come back a year later, playing just linebacker, and the Browns let him try, but he clearly wasn't up to the task. The Browns traded him to Pittsburgh, where he hobbled through five games as a blocking back before being released at the end of October.

League	RuAtt	RuYds	RuAvg	RuTD
AAFC	489	3024	6.2	26
NFL	339	1696	5.0	5
Total	**828**	**4720**	**5.7**	**31**

In the end, the numbers don't tell the whole story, of course. Motley lost years to military service on the front end and injuries on the back end, leaving just five full seasons for accumulating statistics. His career totals are too low to show up on the leader boards, and the only NFL records he holds are for yards per carry. You have to rely on anecdotal accounts from his contemporaries to get a real grasp for how good he was.

- Colts defensive tackle Art Donovan on Motley as a runner: "If you didn't stop him at the line of scrimmage you were in trouble."
- Hall of Famer Lou Groza on how hard Motley hit: "We were scrimmaging [in 1946] and I tackled Marion head-on. I felt like I was being hit by a truck. He had huge thighs. From that point on, I tried to tackle him from the side, drag him down. He was a load and he was fast."
- On his skills as a blocker, San Francisco defensive end Gail Bruce said: "You rush [quarterback Otto] Graham, and put on a move and beat your man and there's Motley waiting for you. Next play, you beat your man with a different move and there's Motley, waiting again. Pretty soon you say, 'The hell with it. I'd rather stand on the line and battle the first guy.'"
- Hall of Fame receiver Dante Lavelli: "Motley really built the passing attack for the Browns because of his blocking."
- Coach Paul Brown on Motley as a linebacker: "I've always believed that Motley could have gone into the Hall of Fame solely as a linebacker if we had used him only at that position. He was as good as our great ones."

In his book *Legends by the Lake,* John Keim concludes: "Motley's runs are legendary, handed down from generation to generation. They sound exaggerated. They weren't. The Hall of Fame has one film in which Motley grabs a swing pass, barrels over players down the sideline, loses his helmet and keeps running."

Motley basically invented the modern fullback position, the idea of a versatile power back who also caught passes. And of course, I haven't even mentioned the prominent role that Motley played in integrating professional sports. A year before Jackie Robinson broke baseball's color barrier, Motley was one of four African-American players to enter the pro football ranks in 1946. As with Robinson, Motley endured abuse and discrimination both on and off the field. He and teammate Bill Willis weren't allowed to play when the Browns played a game in Miami. If Jackie Robinson encountered harassment from other ballplayers on the diamond, you can only imagine what it must have been like for Motley playing a contact sport.

The more I think about it, the more I think that Zimmerman might just be right about Motley.

#27
Herschel Walker (1986–1997)

A victim of circumstance or bad choices? Take your pick. Walker won the Heisman Trophy as a junior at Georgia, and with nothing left to prove and the doors to the NFL closed to underclassmen, Walker jumped to the fledgling USFL. The new league had money to spend, and signing Walker gave them a marquee player for their first season. He dominated the league in his three seasons there, setting virtually every game, season, and career rushing record.

The table below shows the rushing and receiving totals he compiled in the USFL, along with the totals from his thirteen NFL seasons

League	RuYds	RuTD	ReYds	ReTD
USFL	5562	54	1484	7
NFL	8225	61	4859	21

I'm not suggesting that those two rows be added together. I purposely didn't do it here, and I'd encourage you not to even do it in your head. I'm not suggesting that Walker's USFL numbers be combined with his NFL totals either at face value or with some sort of formula designed to account for the USFL's lower level of competition.

What I am trying to do is illustrate that Walker most certainly spent his best years as a player outside of pro football's main arena. I don't know what kind of statistics he might have compiled in the NFL, and I'm not sure it's even worthwhile to wager a guess. My point is simply that most people consider Walker's NFL career to be a disappoint-

ment. He only reached the 1000-yard mark twice and was never the dominating kind of runner he had been in college or the USFL.

Part of that was because teams were hesitant to build their offense around him. The Cowboys and the Eagles both turned him into a hybrid back, often lining him up as a slot receiver or an H-back. Only three times in thirteen seasons did he get to carry the ball 200 times. I don't know whether it was because the heavy load of the USFL had worn him out or because his skills just weren't a good fit for the NFL, but in the end, Walker's opportunities were limited.

He's not a candidate for the Hall of Fame, but he might have been if he'd stayed in college another year and spent his first two pro seasons in the NFL.

#28
Floyd Little (1967–1975)

Little earned the nickname "The Franchise" because of the perception that he helped save the Broncos. Attendance was lagging, and the team had never had a winning season when he arrived in 1967. While he couldn't turn the team's fortunes around all by himself, his exciting style of play did help to energize the fans. Whether he single-handedly kept the team from leaving Denver is difficult to say, but the team didn't move, seating capacity at Mile High Stadium had to be expanded, and the franchise eventually flourished.

#29
Franco Harris (1972–1984)

When Harris was approaching Jim Brown's career rushing record, Brown was so outraged that he threatened to come out of retirement to prevent Harris from claiming the rushing crown. Brown was forty-eight years old at the time.

"What really bothers me," Brown told the *Los Angeles Times,* "is that I don't want certain guys to be considered heroes for things that are not right. . . . I've talked about him running out of bounds. My problems with him go way beyond football, but if Franco was running with full intensity, it wouldn't be an issue."

Harris fired back, and the two traded barbs in the media for several weeks. Brown was so upset that he challenged the thirty-four-year old Harris to race him in a 40-yard dash. Harris accepted (most likely to Brown's chagrin), and the pair met for a two-day, four-event competition in Atlantic City, televised nationally on the weekend before the Super Bowl. Brown bested Harris in racquetball and basketball, while Harris prevailed in a one-on-one football game, with Giants quarterback Phil Simms playing for both sides. When it came to the footrace, Brown pulled up midway with a sore hamstring, but still managed a time of 5.72 seconds. Harris finished in 5.16, enough to win the race but a dreadfully slow time for someone hoping to be productive in the NFL. Although Harris won the race, Brown proved his point.

Clearly out of steam, Harris was released by the Steelers and spent half a season with Seattle before calling it quits. In the end, he fell 192 yards shy of Brown's rushing mark. Walter Payton passed them both by the end of the 1984 season, and eight other players have passed Harris in the two decades since he retired.

Was Brown's criticism fair? Frankly, I agree with his conclusion that Harris didn't deserve to be considered one of the great running backs simply because he had hung around long enough. On the other hand, football is largely a game of attrition, and while there's something to be said for going all out when the game is on the line, there's also value in conserving yourself for the long haul.

The Steelers made the playoffs ten times in Harris's twelve seasons, and he was one of the major contributors to the team's success in the postseason. I count at least eight postseason games where he was a difference maker.

- Harris ran for three touchdowns in the second quarter of the divisional playoff game against Buffalo in 1974, putting the game out of reach.

- Scored a touchdown to tie the Raiders in the fourth quarter of the 1974 AFC championship game, then put the game away with a 21-yard touchdown run in the game's final minutes.
- Carried 34 times for 158 yards in Pittsburgh's 16–6 win over the Vikings in Super Bowl IX and was named the game's MVP.
- Set an AFC divisional playoff record with 153 rushing yards in win over Colts in 1975.
- Scored the go-ahead touchdown in fourth quarter of 1975 AFC title game against Oakland, finishing with 137 combined rushing/receiving yards in a frigid, windy contest.
- Rushed for 132 yards in just over a half of play in 1976 rout of Colts. Left the game in the third quarter with a rib injury.
- Scored at least 1 touchdown in each of their three playoff wins in 1978, including a 21-yard run in the fourth quarter of a Super Bowl game that went down to the wire.
- Caught 3 passes for 66 yards and scored on 2 short touchdown runs in Pittsburgh's Super Bowl XIV win over the Rams.

At the end of the day, Harris ended up with four Super Bowl rings. Brown won just one title in his career.

In the case of Harris, I think there was another reason that it made sense for him to avoid contact when possible. He fumbled an awful lot—90 times to be precise, which ties him with Tony Dorsett for the most fumbles by a running back in NFL history. If he had been a "head down and square your shoulders" kind of player, he would have fumbled even more.

Roger Craig (1983–1993)

In 1985, he became the first running back to gain 1000 yards rushing and receiving in the same season. He also became the first (and so far only) running back to lead the league in receptions.

Craig was perfectly suited for the so-called West Coast Offense that the 49ers ran in the eighties. He used his quickness to get open or to get outside on running plays. The inside running plays usually went to fullback Tom Rathman, a factor that I believe helped Craig avoid injuries during his prime.

He scored three touchdowns in Super Bowl XIX—1 on the ground and 2 through the air. Against the Bengals in Super Bowl XXIII, he ran for 74 yards and had 101 yards receiving.

Eddie George (1996–2004)

The Tennessee Titans rode George extremely hard on their road to the Super Bowl in 2000, giving him 403 carries and another 50 pass receptions. They continued to ride him hard in the years that followed, even though all evidence suggested he was worn out. The season after that Super Bowl appearance, George's rushing average had dropped to 2.98 yards per carry, the lowest ever for a back given at least 250 carries. The Titans weren't discouraged by his lack of success, giving him more than 300 carries in each of his last three seasons.

His supporters argue that the numbers didn't reflect his true value, because he gained the tough yards—short-yardage situations in the second half where a low rushing average didn't necessarily mean he wasn't a successful runner. I addressed those arguments in my annuals, demonstrating why the play-by-play didn't support those claims. George had just declined.

It doesn't really take any advanced mathematics to understand that when the league rushing average is 4.1 and your guy is getting just under 3.0, you aren't going to win by giving him 315 carries.

George was a dominating inside runner in his prime. From 1996 to 2000 he had thirty-one games with over 100 yards rushing, including the

postseason. After that 2000 season, he'd have just seven more. That, my friends, is what we call a drop-off.

John Riggins (1971–1985)

Running backs generally start out strong and fade as they approach the age of thirty. Riggins was a singular anomaly, posting his best season at the age of thirty-four. Among players who played at least twelve seasons, only he and John Henry Johnson gained more yards in seasons 7–12 than in their first six seasons. In Johnson's case, it was simply a matter of getting more playing time. For Riggins, it was about becoming a better, more powerful player.

Player	First 6	Next 6	Diff
John Henry Johnson	2196	4381	2185
John Riggins	4452	4984	532
Walter Payton	8386	7807	–579
Franco Harris	6295	5655	–640
Marshall Faulk	6701	5578	–1123
Tony Dorsett	7015	5724	–1291
Jerome Bettis	7372	5922	–1450
Emmitt Smith	8956	7231	–1725
Freeman McNeil	5320	2754	–2566
Marcus Allen	6151	3158	–2993
Thurman Thomas	7631	4307	–3324
Ottis Anderson	7364	2737	–4627

Riggins had two comebacks in his career. The first came after a knee injury in 1977, when he came back the following season to rush for 1014 yards. *Pro Football Weekly* named him the Comeback Player of the Year for that 1978 performance.

The second comeback came in 1981, when new Redskins coach Joe Gibbs convinced him to come out of retirement and return to football. A year earlier, Riggins had tried to renegotiate his contract, and when that effort failed, he left the team and went home to Kansas. Gibbs convinced him to return from exile, and he did, declaring to the Washington media, "I'm broke, I'm bored, and I'm back."

Riggins scored 13 touchdowns on just 195 carries in 1981, and a year later helped carry the Redskins to Super Bowl XVII. He ran 38 times for 166 yards—both of which set Super Bowl records—and was named the game's Most Valuable Player. The following season he ran for 24 touchdowns, shattering Jim Taylor's record of 19 set in 1962. Riggins finished with 104 rushing touchdowns, making him just the second man (after Jim Brown) to pass the century mark.

Bob Hoernschemeyer (1946–1955)

Began his career as a scrambling quarterback in the AAFC, but he was a better runner than he was a passer. When that league folded, Hoernschemeyer joined the Detroit Lions as a halfback and became one of the key players on a team that won two championships.

Lions coach Buddy Parker used Hoernschemeyer as a short-yardage specialist and receiver, pairing him with the more elusive Doak Walker in the backfield. Parker also liked to use Hoernschemeyer on the halfback option. In six NFL seasons Hoernschemeyer attempted 26 passes, completing 10 for touchdowns.

Corey Dillon (1997–2006)

Some sportswriters tried to brand Dillon as a troublemaker because he voiced his frustrations in Cincinnati. I think the record would show that he never did anything to create discontent in the locker room or to undermine his coaches. He was just tired of losing, and who could blame him?

Dillon rushed for 1000 yards in each of his first six seasons, but during that time the Bengals went 26-70. They never had a winning season, and the dysfunctional franchise didn't even seem to have a plan for turning things around. Dillon had a deep passion for winning, and he didn't feel like the organization around him shared that commitment.

He had his best season in 2004, after being traded to the Patriots. The thirty-year-old Dillon set career highs in rushing yards (1635) and touchdowns (12) and scored a fourth-quarter touchdown in the Super Bowl that turned out to be the game winner.

Fred Taylor (1998–2007)

Taylor earned his first Pro Bowl invitation in 2007, but history suggests that at the age of thirty-one, his best years were already behind him. I'm not sure that anybody today would consider him one of the best backs of his era, and I'm not sure there was ever a time when people looked at him that way. He was never named All-Pro, never led the league in anything. But during the 2007 season he passed the 10,000 yard mark. Maybe he's a guy we've overlooked?

Part of the reason has been that he's played his entire career in Jacksonville. While they've had their share of winning seasons there, the meaty part of Taylor's career came when the Jaguars were losing. He's also had a reputation for being injury-prone because he missed twenty-four games in his first four seasons. The local media dubbed him "Fragile Fred."

If you look beyond those early injuries, you see a guy who was awfully productive. He topped the 1000-yard mark seven times. In 2000, Taylor had nine consecutive games with at least 100 yards, the third-longest streak ever (Barry Sanders is first with fourteen consecutive 100-yard games; Marcus Allen had a streak of eleven games). His career average of 4.7 yards per carry ranks 5th all-time, and he's approaching the top ten in career rushing yards.

Career Rushing Average (min 2000 carries)

Jim Brown	5.2
Barry Sanders	5.0
Tiki Barber	4.7
Fred Taylor	4.7
O.J. Simpson	4.7

Taylor was never a superstar, but neither does he deserve to be remembered as "Fragile Fred." He was a good but not great running back who deserves a lot of the credit for Jacksonville's expansion team enjoying so many winning seasons so early in their existence.

Shaun Alexander (2000–2007)

A scoring machine, Alexander set an NFL record in 2002 when he scored 5 touchdowns in the first half of a game against the Vikings. The record for a game was 6, and with his Seahawks enjoying a 45–10 halftime lead, all eyes were looking expectantly toward Alexander in the second half. Minnesota's defense clamped down, however, holding him to 28 yards on 13 carries and stopping him on three straight plays inside the 10-yard line.

By the end of his sixth season, Alexander had 100 total combined rushing/receiving touchdowns. He set an NFL record in 2005 with 28 touchdowns, a mark that stood for only a year before LaDainian Tomlinson passed it.

Alexander won the Most Valuable Player award that season and led the Seahawks to their first Super Bowl appearance. However, he carried the ball 370 times that season, and the inevitable breakdown occurred the following season. Alexander missed nine games over the next two seasons, and saw his rushing average plummet from 5.1 to 3.5 yards per carry.

One of the things that worked against Alexander was his running style. He ran upright, which helped him see the field and find the cutback lanes. But it left him more vulnerable to big hits, and as

he gets older, it's going to be more difficult for a power runner who runs high to stay healthy.

Cliff Battles (1932–1937)

Five hundred dollars. That's the amount of money that prompted Cliff Battles to walk away from football in the prime of his career. He led the league in rushing yards as a rookie for the 1932 Boston Braves, becoming the first player to rush for 100 yards in a game. The following season, he posted the league's first 200-yard game, scrambling for 215 in a game against the Giants.

Owner George Marshall changed his team's name from Braves to Redskins, moved them to Washington, and added gunslinging quarterback Sammy Baugh. The combination of Battles running the ball and Baugh passing was nearly unstoppable. In their first year together, Baugh and Battles led the Redskins to an NFL championship. Battles had won his second NFL rushing title and held the record for career rushing yards. With all of those things in mind, Battles asked Marshall for a $500 raise on the $3000 yearly salary he'd been paid each year. Marshall refused, and Battles left the Redskins to become an assistant coach at Columbia University. He was just twenty-seven years old.

Priest Holmes (1997–2007)

How does a guy go from being a discarded backup with one team to being an MVP for another team in the span of a year? In the case of Holmes, the simple answer is that he went from a system that he wasn't well suited for him to one that highlighted his strengths. In Baltimore, they wanted a power back who could grind it out between tackles. In Kansas City, they took advantage of Holmes's speed and quickness and got him more involved in the passing game.

Holmes gained 1008 yards in his first season as a starter in Baltimore, but they wanted a big bruiser like Jamal Lewis who could pound the ball between tackles. He spent the next two seasons as a change-of-pace back before joining the Chiefs through free agency. Head coach Dick Vermeil was implementing the same offense he'd won a Super Bowl with in St. Louis, and he needed a versatile back to play the Marshall Faulk role. Holmes was a perfect fit. He lead the league in combined rushing/receiving yards for two seasons, then set an NFL record in 2002 with 27 rushing touchdowns.

Holmes is a great illustration of how players are helped or hindered by the system they play in. That doesn't mean that you could plug any back into the Chiefs offense and get a superstar. Rather, it shows that a player can thrive in a system that takes advantage of his abilities or wither in a system that asks him to do things he can never do well.

Clarke Hinkle (1932–1941)

The biggest rivalry in the 1930s was between the Bears and the Packers, and when they met head-to-head all eyes were on the teams' star fullbacks. Chicago's Bronko Nagurski was the personification of power football, but Green Bay's Clark Hinkle was much more versatile. He had an impressive combination of size and speed. He could also throw the ball, and he was the Packers punter and placekicker.

The Packers and Bears spent the decade vying for supremacy in the Western Division. Although the Packers were one of the league's best teams, they had a hard time getting past their rivals. During the regular season, Hinkle and his teammates were 4-8-1 against Nagurski's Bears, and those games usually meant the difference between 1st and 2nd place.

"When we played the Bears with Nagurski we put on all of the extra pads we could find," Hinkle said, "because when we took the field we knew both teams were there to commit mayhem. A couple of years ago a sportswriter asked me what was my greatest day in pro football and I told him, 'the day I heard Nagurski retired.'" That happened in 1937, and the Packers won the division the following two seasons, winning the league title in 1939.

Like many players, Hinkle left pro football in his prime for military service, and never returned. Although he never led the league in rushing in any of his ten seasons, he retired as the NFL's leader in career rushing yards.

Gerald Riggs (1982–1991)

Riggs was a workhorse back who carried a heavy load and paid the consequences. If you look at the list of players with the most rushing attempts in a single season, you see two things. First, it contains some pretty good players. Second, and more significant, most of the players on the list suffered breakdowns the following year or saw their productivity plummet.

Player	Year	Tm	Att	Yds
Larry Johnson	2006	KC	416	1789
Jamal Anderson	1998	Atl	410	1846
James Wilder	1984	TB	407	1544
Eric Dickerson	1986	LaRm	404	1821
Eddie George	2000	Ten	403	1509
Gerald Riggs	1985	Atl	397	1719
Terrell Davis	1998	Den	392	2008
Ricky Williams	2003	Mia	392	1372
Eric Dickerson	1983	LaRm	390	1690
Barry Foster	1992	Pit	390	1808
Eric Dickerson	1988	Ind	388	1659
Edgerrin James	2000	Ind	387	1709
Jamal Lewis	2003	Bal	387	2066

- Larry Johnson held out of training camp the year after he set an NFL record with 416 carries. He struggled early, then broke his foot and missed the second half of the season.
- Jamal Anderson carried the Falcons to their only Super Bowl appearance but shredded his knee 19 carries into his follow-up season. He returned for one more respectable season but the knee injuries did him in.

- Terrell Davis only made it through four games in his next season, and while he tried to stage a comeback for three years, he just couldn't overcome the knee injuries.
- Barry Foster suffered a season-ending injury midway through his follow-up season, and he played for only one more year after that.
- Edgerrin James also blew out his knee the following season, and although he came back, it took him two years to regain his form.
- Eddie George continued to play but his productivity plummeted. The year after his heavy season, his rushing average dropped to 2.98 yards per carry. It was the lowest total ever for a back with at least 250 carries, and he continued to play a major role in the Tennessee offense despite strong evidence that his skills had dramatically diminished.
- Ricky Williams quit football completely, and while his knees didn't give out he complained of being physically and mentally exhausted. He eventually returned for one season of backup duty but was not the same player.
- Jamal Lewis dropped from 2066 yards in 2003 to 1006 the following year, and dropped below 1000 in the following two seasons. His rushing average dropped from 5.3 to 3.4, and like so many of the other players on this list, he went from being a dominating back to being just an average one.
- The Buccaneers pulled some shenanigans to help Wilder become the first back to surpass the 400-carry mark. He carried the ball 365 times the following season, but those two years were essentially his entire career. He hung around five more years as a part-time player.
- Like Wilder, Riggs hung around for one more season of heavy work before injuries took their toll. He was able to prolong his career by becoming a short-yardage specialist with the Redskins.

Eric Dickerson is the anomaly here, since his name appears three times and he suffered neither debilitating injury nor dramatic drop-off in production. However, he did miss parts of three seasons due to contract holdouts and was suspended twice by the Colts. Like Ricky Williams, it seems that Dickerson found another method to let his body recover.

This is really just an anecdotal list, not a scientific study, but it at least suggests something about the damaging effects of overwork. What happened in most of these cases was a team found itself with a mediocre offense but a great running back. They kept giving the ball to him because he was moving the ball and scoring points, and as they began to win games they saw that a championship was within reach. With Davis and Lewis, that gambit paid off. With Anderson and George, their teams fell short but at least made it to the Super Bowl. With many other cases, the heavy load doesn't pay off for the team, and it shortens the length of the player's career or decreases his productivity.

#41
James Brooks (1981–1992)

I have no idea why the Chargers drafted Brooks in 1981. He was an elusive runner and a great receiver, but a complete mismatch for the offense that head coach Don Coryell was running. He preferred a big bruiser like Chuck Muncie, and Brooks saw limited action as a change-of-pace back and kick returner.

Muncie's career ended after the 1983 season, and rather than give Brooks a crack at the full-time job, Coryell traded him for another big, powerful back. Brooks went to the Bengals in a straight-up trade for fullback Pete Johnson, a past-his-prime and overweight fullback whose cocaine problems were bringing his career to an end. Johnson lasted just three games with the Chargers, while Brooks spent the next eight years catching passes out of the backfield and playing halfback in the Bengals two-back offense. The Chargers inherited a problem and the Bengals got a guy who would go to the Pro Bowl four times in five seasons.

Brooks posted three 1000-yard seasons, averaging more than 5 yards per carry each time. Teamed with Ickey Woods in 1988, the Bengals finished with the league's top-ranked offense and advanced to the Super Bowl. Brooks and Woods combined for 1997 rushing yards and 29 touchdowns.

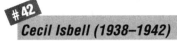

Cecil Isbell (1938–1942)

There are a handful of backs from the twenties and thirties that can't simply be labeled as either a quarterback or a running back. The role they played was really a hybrid, where they were called on to run with the ball and to pass it. Cecil Isbell is one of those characters. If I group him with the other quarterbacks, his ranking suffers. If I group him with the running backs, his passing exploits go unrecognized.

Isbell was drafted by the Green Bay Packers, who already had All-Pro passer Arnie Herber. Head coach Curley Lambeau moved Isbell to halfback, but Isbell played well when given a chance to throw the ball, and he gradually pushed Herber out of his job. While Herber would eventually go to the Pro Football Hall of Fame, it was Isbell who helped create the modern passing game through his work with receiver Don Hutson.

#43 Paul Lowe (1960–1969)

Lowe was one of just a handful of men to play in each of the AFL's ten seasons. He was an explosive back who had six games where he gained more than 100 yards on 14 carries or less. He averaged 4.9 yards per carry, the most in AFL history. Lowe played for the Chargers from 1960 to 1968, and was one of the key players on a team that advanced to the AFL championship game five times in six seasons.

#44 Clem Daniels (1960–1968)

The first great runner for the Oakland Raiders, Daniels not only ran well but was also an outstanding receiver. Originally signed by the Dallas Texans, he languished on the bench for a year before heading to Oakland, where he quickly established himself as one of the young stars of the new league. Daniels was the AFL Most Valuable Player in 1964, averaging 5.1 yards per carry and a remarkable 22.8 yards per reception. Daniels broke his leg late in the 1967 season, and didn't get to play with his teammates in Super Bowl II. He left the AFL the next year to play for the 49ers, but he still ended up with more rushing yards than any player in league history and more receiving yards than any other AFL running back.

#45 Ahman Green (1998–2007)

Green rushed for 100 yards in his first NFL game, getting some garbage time late in a 38–0 rout of the Eagles. Despite several long runs, his performance didn't garner much notice from the Seattle coaching staff. A third-round pick of the Seahawks, Green wasn't going to get playing time behind veteran Ricky Watters. When Seattle drafted Shaun Alexander in 2000, Green became expendable, and he was traded to the Packers

With that change in scenery came an opportunity to play, and Green made the most of it. In his first five seasons with the Packers he rushed for at least 1000 yards while averaging close to 60 catches a year. His best year came in 2003 when he rushed for 1883 yards, the 7th highest single-season total in history but only 2nd best that year (Jamal Lewis led the NFL with 2066). After that, injuries began to take their toll, as they usually do when a back touches the ball so many times.

#46 William Andrews (1979–1986)

Andrews is one of three Atlanta Falcons running backs whose careers were shortened because of overuse. There's really nothing to connect him and Jamal Anderson other than that end result. Andrews and Gerald Riggs, however, played at roughly the same time and for the same coach. Clearly, coach Dan Henning liked the idea of running with one horse until he dropped.

Andrews rushed for 1000 yards four times in his first five seasons, peaking with 1567 in 1983. During that season, he carried the ball 331 times and caught 59 passes, a pretty heavy load for a team that finished last in the NFC West. The following summer he tore up his knee pretty good, and while you can't draw a direct line between his workload in 1983 and the injury in 1984, it's at least a pretty strong inference. Andrews tore three ligaments as he planted his foot. He was not in contact with any other player.

Doctors told him that he might not walk again. To his credit, Andrews worked awfully hard and came back after missing two seasons. He looked remarkably good, but by then Henning was giving the ball to Gerald Riggs, over and over. . . .

Abner Haynes (1960–1967)

Haynes was the Rookie of the Year in the AFL's first season. His speed and quickness made him one of the era's most dangerous all-around backs. He led the league in rushing that year and added 55 receptions. Two years later, he was named Most Valuable Player and led his team to victory in the AFL championship game. He scored the only two touchdowns for the Texans in their upset of the Houston Oilers.

The following season, the Texans moved to Kansas City and became the Chiefs. Abner spent two seasons there before moving on to stints with the Broncos, Dolphins, and Jets. His 49 rushing touchdowns were the most by any AFL player.

Wilbert Montgomery (1977–1985)

Montgomery was a quick back, not particularly powerful, but what I remember most about him were the oversize shoulder pads he wore. They made him look bigger than he really was, which I suppose was the whole point.

He rushed for 1000 yards three times in a four-year stretch, falling short when the Eagles advanced to the Super Bowl in 1980. A knee injury sidelined him for part of that season, but he returned at full strength and torched the Cowboys by rushing for 194 yards in the NFC championship game. A knee injury during training camp in 1983 robbed him of much of his speed, and he retired after spending 1985 as a backup in Detroit.

Earnest Byner (1984–1997)

The Bill Buckner of football, a guy with a tremendous career who will always be best remembered for his miscue that cost his team a chance to win a championship.

As with Buckner, the criticism is both unfair and unwarranted.

With just over a minute left in the 1987 AFC championship game, the Browns had driven down to Denver's 8-yard line. They were poised to score a game-tying touchdown, when Byner took the handoff on a draw play and burst through a hole toward the end zone. Just before he got to the goal line, Byner was stripped of the ball by cornerback Jeremiah Castille. The Broncos recovered, and killed off the remaining time to preserve the victory and advance to the Super Bowl. The play would go down in football lore as simply "The Fumble."

Like Buckner's Red Sox, the Browns had gone a long time since winning their last championship, and it was easy for fans to pin their disappointments on a visible scapegoat. People remember that Buckner and Byner robbed their team of victory with their miscue, but in reality, each game would have merely been tied had they made their play. Both players were at least partially responsible for their teams advancing as far as they did, and while neither was a Hall of Fame player, both had very good careers.

Byner's best seasons came a few years later with the Redskins. He topped the 1000-yard mark in 1991 and 1992, falling 2 yards short in 1993. Byner was paired in the Washington backfield with veteran Gerald Riggs, who handled the short-yardage duties.

#50
Paddy Driscoll (1920–1929)

One of the best all-around backs of the 1920s, Driscoll's accomplishments go largely overlooked because of the lack of individual playing statistics from the era. There was nothing that he did not do well. He was an accomplished passer and runner. He was a marvelous punter. He set a record by drop-kicking four field goals in a game, one of which was a 50-yarder. And he was one of the best defensive players of the era.

The Pro Football Hall of Fame lists him as a quarterback, but that's not really accurate. He was a runner who occasionally threw the ball, not the other way around.

Driscoll was the biggest star on the Chicago Cardinals roster, the key player on the 1925 NFL championship team. When Red Grange and C. C. Pyle formed their rival American Football League in 1926, Driscoll was one of the first names on the list of stars they tried to sign. The NFL didn't want to lose him, but the Cardinals were struggling financially and couldn't match the offer Driscoll had received to jump. Instead, the Cardinals traded him to the cross-town rival Bears, a move that would have been inconceivable under any other circumstances.

Driscoll retired after four seasons with the Bears. He spent the next ten years coaching at the high school and college ranks before returning to the Bears as an assistant coach in 1941. He continued to work alongside Bears' owner George Halas in various capacities (including a successful stint as the team's head coach) until his death in 1968.

#51
Rick Casares (1955–1966)

When people think of powerful fullbacks, they often think of slow, plodding men who are more battering ram than athlete. The powerful running that Casares displayed with the Chicago Bears belied how gifted and diverse his physical talents were. At the University of Florida, he not only ran the ball but he also handled the kicking and punting duties and played some quarterback. He was captain of the basketball team, where he averaged 15.9 points and 11.4 rebounds for his career. Casares even had offers to pursue a professional boxing career, and he was a world-class javelin thrower.

In 2002, when Ohio State's Maurice Clarett sued for the right to join the NFL after just one season of college football, there was a lot of discussion about whether the time would ever come when football players could make the jump from high school directly to the NFL. The *Fort Worth Star-Telegram* assembled a group of scouts and recruiting analysts who concluded that only five players since 1950 had the physical skills necessary to make that jump: running back Herschel Walker, defensive lineman Andre Carter, wide receiver Randy Moss, linebacker Junior Seau, and Casares. That's how good he was.

The Bears have had so many great running backs in their history that it's easy to overlook this one. When he retired, he was the Bears' all-time leading rusher. Walter Payton would eventually pass him, as would Neal Anderson. The names of Bronko Nagurski and Red Grange ring out from the golden era, but Casares has been largely forgotten.

#52
Lydell Mitchell (1972–1980)

A pretty good runner and one of the best pass-receiving backs in NFL history. Over a four-year stretch, Mitchell averaged 1184 rushing yards and

65 catches per season. Twice he led all NFL players in receptions, and another time he tied for the lead in the AFC. He was the first Colts running back to top the 1000-yard mark, and he ranked among the league leaders in yards from scrimmage four times. Mitchell held out of training camp in 1978, angered that his relatively low salary didn't match his reputation as one of the league's best running backs. As often happens, there was a huge gap between what the team was offering and what he thought he was worth. Things got ugly between Mitchell and owner Robert Irsay, then they got nasty, and then they got downright out of control. The personal animosity spiraled out of control, and divorce was the only option. Just before the start of training camp, Mitchell was traded to San Diego.

He had one good season with the Chargers, but a knee injury during his first season led to a staph infection. Unable to walk for several months, Mitchell was never able to recapture his running ability.

#53
Neal Anderson (1986–1993)

Anderson was underrated because he followed Walter Payton, and anybody who does that is going to pale in comparison. There was a three-year stretch when he was considered one of the best running backs in the game. He was a good receiver, a powerful blocker, and he used his bursts of speed to get around the corner on outside runs. Anderson was also fond of diving into the end zone, especially if he was running down the sideline.

He earned All-Pro honors for his special-teams play as a rookie in 1986. The following year, the Bears moved him to fullback so that he could get some playing time with Payton starting at halfback. He took over the starting job in 1988, and for each of the next three years he topped the 1000-yard mark and scored double-digits in touchdowns. A hamstring injury in 1991 forced him to miss three games and limited his productivity, and he never really seemed to recover. His play went downhill,

and he was one of the scapegoats for the Bears' disastrous 1992 season. The team started 4-3, but lost eight of their last nine. In a desperate bid to stop the free fall, head coach Mike Ditka benched Anderson for the unremarkable Darren Lewis, but it made no difference.

#54
Larry Brown (1969–1976)

Brown joined the Redskins as an unheralded eighth-round draft pick in 1969. Washington had just hired Vince Lombardi to turn their sagging franchise around, and the legendary coach was looking for a great runner around whom he could build his famous power running game. Brown was thoroughly unimpressive, but Lombardi was watching closely and noticed that the rookie back was very slow out of the backfield. He watched more intently and realized that rather than listening to the quarterback's snap count, Brown was watching the linemen.

Lombardi suspected that Brown had a hearing problem, and tests confirmed it. Brown was completely deaf in his right ear. Lombardi petitioned the league for permission to install a hearing aid in Brown's helmet, and suddenly he was a different player.

Brown only weighed 195 pounds, but he charged through the line as if he weighed 250. He was one of the NFL's best runners for his first four seasons, winning a rushing title in 1970 and the Most Valuable Player Award in 1972.

#55
Jim Nance (1965–1973)

It's been nearly forty years since a running back from Syracuse University was selected in the first round of the NFL draft, but there was a time when the school was churning them out like clockwork. From 1957 to 1968—a twelve-year span—Syracuse University had six running backs drafted in the first round.

Year	Player	Pick	Team
1957	Jim Brown	1	Browns
1960	Gehrhard Schwedes	-	Patriots
1961	Art Baker	14	Eagles
1962	Ernie Davis	1	Redskins
1967	Floyd Little	6	Broncos
1968	Larry Csonka	8	Dolphins

Ernie Davis won the Heisman Trophy but died of leukemia before his rookie season started. Brown and Csonka are in the Hall of Fame, and Little was a star for Denver.

The one notable Syracuse back who's missing from this chain is Jim Nance, who slipped into the fourth round of the NFL draft by the Bears and the nineteenth round of the AFL draft by the Patriots. He ended up going to Boston, and after an unremarkable rookie campaign, he led the AFL in rushing in his next two seasons. His 1458 yards in 1965 was the highest single-season total in AFL history. The following year, he was named the AFL's Most Valuable Player by UPI, the AP, and the *Sporting News*.

After the 1971 season he was traded to the Eagles, but he refused to go and opted to retire instead. He came back briefly with the Jets in 1973 and spent 1974 playing for the Houston Texans/Shreveport Steamers of the World Football League (the club relocated midseason). Though he was well past his prime, Nance still finished 3rd in the league in rushing, a commentary on the league's relatively low quality of play.

#56
Hugh McElhenny (1952–1964)

Nicknamed "The King," McElhenny was a slashing runner with great speed. If you watch film of him playing, it won't take long before you see how similar he was to Barry Sanders. They both had that ability to stop on a dime and change direction. Both used a low center of gravity to help maintain their balance.

For most of the 1950s, the 49ers backfield consisted of three Hall of Famers: running backs McElhenny and Joe Perry, along with quarterback Y. A. Tittle. From 1954 to 1956 they were joined by another future Hall of Famer, John Henry Johnson. In the history of the league, I only count a dozen instances where a team had at least three skill position players bound for the Hall of Fame who stuck together for at least four seasons. They're listed in the table below.

Hall of Fame Trios (Three Skill Position Players on Same Team)

Years	Tm	Span	Players
12	Bal	1956–67	Johnny Unitas, Lenny Moore, Ray Berry
10	GB	1957–66	Bart Starr, Jim Taylor, Paul Hornung
10	Pit	1974–83	Terry Bradshaw, Franco Harris, John Stallworth (plus Lynn Swann 1974–82)
10	Dal	1990–99	Troy Aikman, Emmitt Smith, Michael Irvin
9	SF	1952–60	Y. A. Tittle, Joe Perry, Hugh McElhenny (plus John Henry Johnson 1954–56)
9	SD	1979–87	Dan Fouts, Charlie Joiner, Kellen Winslow
8	Cle	1946–53	Otto Graham, Marion Motley, Dante Lavelli
8	LaRm	1949–56	Norm Van Brocklin, Elroy Hirsch, Tom Fears
6	GB	1935–40	Arnie Herber, Clarke Hinkle, Don Hutson
5	GB	1930–35	Arnie Herber, Blood McNally, Cal Hubbard
5	Was	1964–68	Sonny Jurgensen, Bobby Mitchell, Charley Taylor
5	Mia	1970–74	Bob Griese, Larry Csonka, Paul Warfield

A lot of these trios, especially the ones near the top of the list, were the foundation of an NFL dynasty. Unitas and his crew won two championships, Starr's gang won three, and Bradshaw's Steelers won four. Despite their collection of starts, McElhenny and his teammates in San Francisco never won a league title, and only once qualified for postseason play. This was due in large part to a lousy defense, but more often the Niners' head coaches simply struggled to build a cohesive offense out of this collection of talent.

Curt Warner (1983–1990)

A slashing runner with an impressive combination of speed and power, Warner took the league by storm as a rookie. On his first NFL carry, he made a cutback at the line of scrimmage and rambled 60 yards. He would finish the season with an AFC-leading 1449 rushing yards and help lead the Seahawks to their first-ever playoff appearance. On the strength of their running game, Seattle advanced to the AFC championship game.

In the first game of his second season, Warner made a cut on the artificial turf of the Kingdome and tore up his knee. Even though the team certainly missed him, they still improved their record from 9-7 to 12-4. With Warner sidelined, they had to adopt a more balanced offense, and second-year quarterback Dave Krieg responded with 32 touchdown passes.

Warner returned strong the following season. He would top the 1000-yard mark in three of the next four seasons, finishing just short (985 yards) in the strike-shortened 1987 season.

Jamal Lewis (2000-2007)

Behind a strong line, Lewis could be dominating. He used his leg strength to drive through the line, and had the speed to make big plays once he got into the open. His arrival in Baltimore helped propel the Ravens to a championship in 2000. Lewis became just the second rookie to rush for 100 yards in the Super Bowl. Two years later, he broke the single-game record by rumbling for 295 yards in a Week 2 game against the Browns. In the rematch between the two teams later that season, Lewis rushed for 205 yards. That gave him a total of 500 yards against the Browns for the season. Lewis ended the 2003 season with 2066 yards, just 39 yards shy of O.J. Simpson's single-season record.

The following year, Lewis pled guilty to charges that he had tried to set up a drug deal. As part of his plea, he served his four-month sentence during the off-season. Still, the league suspended him for two games, and he missed two more because of an ankle injury. During the next two seasons his productivity dipped dramatically. He topped the 100-yard mark just four times between 2005 and 2006, before having a resurgence with the Cleveland Browns.

Terrell Davis (1995–2001)

One of the biggest debates in football these days is whether or not Davis belongs in the Hall of Fame. It's a debate that has less to do with Davis himself than with our concept of how to define greatness. There are a couple of ways to tackle the question, and both leave Davis inextricably linked with Gale Sayers. The two are linked because they were both remarkably good at their peak, and because they both had their careers cut short by knee injuries. Sayers is in the Hall of Fame, selected in his first year of eligibility, and he's the precedent that the Davis supporters cite to bolster their case. So let's start by looking at the case for Sayers.

Sayers was an incredibly elusive runner. He had the speed of a track star, but it was his ability to cut and find a hole that made him spectacular. "Just give me eighteen inches of daylight," he said. "That's all I need." During his rookie season, he tied an NFL record by scoring 6 touchdowns in a game against the 49ers. Four came on running plays. One came on an 80-yard screen pass. Another came on an 85-yard punt return. Sayers finished the season with 22 touchdowns, a record for rookies that has never been equaled. He led the league in rushing during his second season, and he was having his most productive season in 1968 when he suffered a serious knee injury. A hard hit by Niners safety Kermit Washington tore the ligaments in his right knee. Sayers rehabbed the knee and returned in 1969 to win his second rushing title. Then, during a preseason game in 1970, he injured ligaments in the other knee. He played a couple of games but was severely limited, and he opted for surgery. He never regained enough mobility to make it back, and he was forced to retire after a handful of carries in 1971.

Like Sayers, Davis was a game-changer. He rushed for a thousand yards as a rookie, then over the next three seasons had what might be the most dominating stretch a running back has ever had. He rushed for 1538 yards in 1996, 1750 in 1997, and 2008 in 1998, scoring 53 touchdowns in the process and leading the Broncos to back-to-back Super Bowl victories.

And like Sayers, Davis suffered first one knee injury and then another, bringing his career to an early end. Davis tore the ACL in his right knee early in 1999 while trying to make a tackle after an interception. It took two years for him to get all the way back, and for part of the 2001 season it looked like he had fully recovered. By the end of the year, though, he needed surgery on both knees, and his body just wouldn't let him continue.

Here are their career totals listed below.

	G	RuYds	RuTD	ReYds	ReTD	OtherTDs
Sayers	68	4956	39	1307	9	9
Davis	78	7607	60	1280	5	0

Sayers had 9 kick and punt returns for TDs and threw a touchdown pass, but when it came to rushing the ball, the totals for Davis are clearly better. Of course, the two played during different eras. Sayers played fourteen games a season while Davis played sixteen. Anytime you make cross-era comparisons, you have to account for a lot of differences when you're looking at the raw statistics. That's where the Q-ratings come in real handy.

Sayers

Year	G	RuYds	RuTD	ReYds	ReTD	AY	Q	Rk
1965	14	867	14	507	6	994.9	5.9	2
1966	14	1231	8	447	2	1468.9	10.0	1
1967	13	880	7	126	1	734.9	6.1	12
1968	9	856	2	117	0	689.3	5.1	10
1969	14	1032	8	116	0	902.5	7.9	4
1970	2	52	0	–6	0	9.0	0.1	131
1971	2	38	0	0	0	38.0	0.3	112

Davis

Year	G	RuYds	RuTD	ReYds	ReTD	AY	Q	Rk
1995	14	1117	7	367	1	1175.5	6.1	11
1996	16	1538	13	310	2	1633.0	10.0	1
1997	15	1750	15	287	0	1883.5	8.5	2
1998	16	2008	21	217	2	2256.5	10.0	1
1999	4	211	2	26	0	204	1.1	67
2000	5	282	2	4	0	264	1.3	55
2001	11	701	0	69	0	655.5	3.6	33

The Q-rating shows us how a player's performance stacked up against his contemporaries, with a score of 10.0 indicating he was the best in the league at his position. Sayers was the 1st- or 2nd-ranked back in his league twice, Davis three times. Sayers ranked 12th in his fourth-best season, Davis ranked 11th. Another way to look at it is to see what their Q-performances were in their best season, their second-best season, and so on.

	1st	2nd	3rd	4th	5th	6th	7th
Sayers	10.0	7.9	6.1	5.9	5.1	0.3	0.1
Davis	10.0	10.0	8.5	6.1	3.6	1.3	1.1

Sayers was substantially better in his fifth best season, but for both players, that was an injury-shortened season. The real difference between the players is how good they were in their second- and third-best seasons. In 1965, Sayers finished 2nd to Jim Brown in Adjusted Yards. It was Brown's best season and second-place was a long way back. In his third-best season, Davis finished 2nd in Adjusted Yards to Barry Sanders, who was having the best season of his career. Davis was the best back in the league in his second-best season, while Sayers spent just one season at the top of the heap.

My point here isn't to convince you that Davis was better than Sayers. I think taking an honest look at the data will leave a lot of people feeling that it's a much closer comparison than they thought. At his best, Davis was at least as dominant as Sayers was, and their careers both lasted almost exactly the same length. On top of that, Davis led his team to two championships, while the Bears never reached the playoffs, only twice finishing with a wining record during Sayers's career.

So the view that's usually expressed says that if Sayers is in that Davis has to be in. That's a dangerous path to head down, in my opinion, because it's advocating a view that says the barrier for entry should be as low as the worst mistake the Hall's selectors have made. I think most people would be surprised to know just how many people are in the Hall of Fame with extremely short careers, not to mention some players whose popularity far exceeded their actual accomplishments. Paul Hornung, for example, had 681 rushing yards in his best season. Doak Walker played six seasons and only amassed 1520 rushing yards. Both running backs are in the Hall of Fame. In fairness, both men also contributed on special teams, but there were plenty of players with much better credentials who haven't even had a sniff of Canton. If we induct every back who was better than Walker or Hornung, we're going to need to build another wing.

Davis shouldn't be considered for the Hall of Fame because he was better than Doak Walker or because he's as good or better than Sayers. He

should be considered because for three seasons, he was as good as any back who ever played.

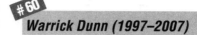

Warrick Dunn (1997–2007)

When Dunn left the Buccaneers after the 2001 season, he acknowledged that one of his reasons for leaving was so that he could be a feature back. In five seasons with Tampa Bay, he had shared the carries with fullback Mike Alstott. He signed a six-year contract with the Atlanta Falcons, where he was immediately paired with another big back, T. J. Duckett.

Duckett and Alstott were both big backs, and I suppose the theory was that pairing a powerful inside runner with a quick, elusive runner like Dunn would prove successful. It's a formula that has worked since the days of Bronko Nagurski and Red Grange. Dunn has gone to the playoffs six times in his ten NFL seasons.

For Dunn, there's a theoretical tradeoff. By taking fewer carries per season, he doesn't wear down as much. The result is a higher yards-per-carry average, and he plays more seasons, although his numbers each year aren't quite so high.

But there's another tradeoff too, and it's one that definitely doesn't work to Dunn's favor. When you're paired with a short-yardage specialist, the other guys are going to get the ball inside the 5-yard line, taking away many of your touchdown opportunities. The table below shows how those opportunities were distributed between him and the back he was paired with (Mike Alstott 1997–2001, T. J. Duckett 2002–05, Jerious Norwood 2006-07).

Over Dunn's career, the NFL average is 2.90 touchdowns per 100 carries. He's averaged just 1.89, while his backfield partners have averaged 4.22. Based on a rough calculation, I figure that the platoon system has cost him about 25 touchdowns over his career.

TDs by Dunn and his Partner

Year	Dunn		Partner	
	Att	TD	Att	TD
1997	224	4	176	7
1998	245	2	215	8
1999	195	0	242	7
2000	248	8	131	5
2001	158	3	165	10
2002	230	7	130	4
2003	125	3	197	11
2004	265	9	104	8
2005	280	3	121	8
2006	286	4	99	2
2007	228	4	102	1

#61
Freeman McNeil (1981–1992)

In a 2001 article, *Sports Illustrated* called McNeil "the most underrated running back in NFL history." At first glance, that seems like a huge stretch, and on second glance it's just as ridiculous. McNeil was a good player for a long time, but he was never a great one, and for most of his career he shared the running duties with somebody else.

The implication of the article, I think, was that he could have been great had he been allowed to carry the ball more. McNeil is one of the few players who averaged at least 4.0 yards per carry every year he played, and that rate of production could have made him a superstar if the Jets hadn't given so many carries to guys like Dwayne Crutchfield, Johnny Hector, and Roger Vick. At least, that's how the theory goes.

Over his first eight seasons, he got 43.2 percent of the rushing attempts that the Jets gave to their running backs. In those seasons he generally averaged about a half-yard more per carry than the other backs. The table below shows the rushing break down for each season.

Year	McNeil			Other Jets RBs			
	Att	Yds	Avg	Att	Yds	Avg	Pct
1981	137	623	4.55	388	1574	4.06	26.1%
1982	151	786	5.21	138	535	3.88	52.2%
1983	160	654	4.09	265	1250	4.72	37.6%
1984	229	1070	4.67	234	993	4.24	49.5%
1985	294	1331	4.53	239	901	3.77	55.2%
1986	214	856	4.00	239	811	3.39	47.2%
1987	121	530	4.38	233	863	3.70	34.2%
1988	219	944	4.31	266	1114	4.19	45.2%
1989	80	352	4.40	301	1199	3.98	21.0%
1990	99	458	4.63	339	1544	4.55	22.6%
1991	51	300	5.88	438	1743	3.98	10.4%
1992	43	170	3.95	338	1462	4.33	11.3%

As you can see, he only got half of the Jets rushing attempts twice. He led the league in rushing yards during the strike-shortened 1982 season, and in 1985, he ranked 5th with a career-high 1331 yards.

The idea of using two backs in tandem certainly wasn't one developed by the Jets. It's a model that has predominated since the end of the two-way era. The rationale is that a team's rushing attack can be more balanced if you pair two complementary players, typically one whose small but quick and another whose big and powerful. That's a model that fell out of favor in the late 1970s and early 1980s, as many teams focused on a one-man ground attack. Walter Payton regularly had 60 percent to 65 percent of the running back carries for the Bears. Houston's Earl Campbell was between 65 percent and 70 percent. Eric Dickerson was around 75 percent with the Rams.

But the reality is that McNeil simply couldn't carry that kind of workload. He was plagued by injuries throughout his career, and the Jets gave carries to his teammates because they had to. It doesn't make much sense to play the "what-if" game when we're talking about how good a player was. Whether you're talking about McNeil or Jim Brown or Gale Sayers, you have to judge a guy by what he actually accomplished. In McNeil's case, that means he was a pretty good back for a long time, but never a great one.

Two other things about McNeil are worth noting. From 1984 to 1985, he had eight consecutive 100-yard games against division opponents, a feat matched by only three other backs (Walter Payton 1976–77, Marcus Allen 1985–86, and Shaun Alexander 2004–05). Also, he was the lead plantiff in a 1992 suit by players against the NFL, which led to a verdict that the league's "Plan-B" free agency system violated antitrust laws. It helped open the door to true free agency in the league. While McNeil's claims for damages were denied, several other players received substantial settlements, and hundreds of players benefited from the new system over the next decade.

#62
Mike Pruitt (1976–1986)

Pruitt isn't a remarkably common name, I don't think. Not like Smith or Johnson or Williams. So it's a little unusual that the Cleveland Browns would end up with two guys named Pruitt in their backfield at the same time who weren't related to each other. Greg Pruitt, a speedy halfback from Oklahoma, joined the team in 1973. Mike Pruitt, a big workhorse who was a first-round pick out of Purdue in 1977.

The contrasting styles made the pair an effective one-two punch by 1978, but Mike became the full-time back when Greg injured his knee the following season. The younger Pruitt quickly became a favorite of new head coach Sam Rutigliano. He rushed for 1000 yards in four of the next five seasons, falling short during the strike-shortened 1982 campaign.

Pruitt was a powerful runner but also a pretty good receiver. He twice finished with more than 60 receptions in a season, leading all Browns with 63 catches in 1980. When Rutigliano was fired midway through the 1984 season, Pruitt's playing time

dwindled. He spent most of his last two seasons grinding it out with the Kansas City Chiefs.

#63
Mike Garrett (1966–1973)

He was the first in a string of great tailbacks from the University of Southern California. During a fifteen-year stretch, the school produced four Heisman Trophy winners: Garrett (1965), O.J. Simpson (1968), Charles White (1979), and Marcus Allen (1981). Two others—Anthony Davis (1974) and Ricky Bell (1976) finished as Heisman runners-up.

Garrett was small by NFL standards, at just 5-foot-9 and 185 pounds, but his jitterbug style worked perfectly well in the American Football League. He was one of the league's most productive backs, and he helped the Chiefs win two AFL Championships and a Super Bowl in his first four seasons.

A few months after that Super Bowl victory, Garrett announced that he was ready to quit football. "I just want to try something else," he explained, and that something else was baseball. The twenty-six-year-old said he intended to join the Los Angeles Dodgers at the end of the 1970 season, when his contract with the Chiefs expired. The football world was stunned, but his mind was made up.

Garrett vowed to play hard in his final year, but an ankle injury slowed him considerably and in October, the Chiefs traded him to San Diego for a second-round draft pick. Chargers general manager Sid Gillman was gambling that he could convince Garrett to abandon his baseball dreams, and that he could pick up on one the league's best rushers on the cheap. His gamble paid off. Garrett spurned the Dodgers on the eve of spring training and signed a new contract with the Chargers.

He spent three more seasons playing football then called it quits for good. After earning his law degree, Garrett returned to USC as athletic director, where he helped the school return to its status as one of the country's dominant football programs.

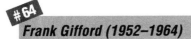

Frank Gifford (1952–1964)

A whole generation of fans know Gifford as a broadcaster on *Monday Night Football,* but he was one of the brightest stars in pro football during the 1950s. He started his pro career in the Giants secondary, even though he'd been a star tailback at USC. Gifford went to two Pro Bowls as a defensive back, but he would later say that he resented being switched to defense.

That changed in 1954 when Jim Lee Howell took over as head coach of the New York Giants and Vince Lombardi became the team's offensive coordinator. Gifford continued to play defense, but Lombardi loved Gifford's versatility and made him the cornerstone of his soon-to-be-famous ground attack. Playing both sides of the ball was a rarity by then, with teams abandoning the two-way platoon rules shortly after the end of World War II.

Gifford was not just a great runner but also a great receiver out of the backfield. His 5434 receiving yards was a team record that stood until 2003, and his 39 touchdown catches ranks 3rd all-time among running backs. He also threw 14 touchdown passes on halfback option plays.

Most TD Receptions by a RB

48	Lenny Moore
46	Joe Morrison
39	Frank Gifford
36	Marshall Faulk
36	Johnny Blood

His best season was 1956 when he was named league MVP and led the Giants to victory in the NFL championship game.

A vicious hit nearly ended his career and certainly derailed it. In a game against the Eagles in 1960, linebacker Chuck Bednarik blindsided

him after he caught a pass. It was a clean hit, but delivered with such ferocity that Gifford was knocked unconscious. There is a famous photograph of Bednarik celebrating the hit as he stood over the motionless Gifford. Three months later, he announced his retirement, though he did return a year later. He spent his final three seasons playing flanker, earning a Pro Bowl invitation at his third different position in 1963.

Tony Canadeo (1941–1952)

A tough and gritty running back, Canadeo was a star when the Green Bay Packers were at their worst. He joined the team in 1941, playing behind veterans Cecil Isbell and Clarke Hinkle. By 1943, he had replaced both men, leading the team in both passing and rushing. He spent the next two years in military service, and when he returned the team was no longer a championship contender.

As the Packers fell to 3-9 in 1948, coach Curley Lambeau turned to Canadeo as his only offensive weapon. By 1949, the playbook seemed to consist solely of "Canadeo Left" and "Canadeo Right." He ran 208 times for 1052 yards, becoming just the third player to pass the 1000-yard mark. An outstanding all-around player, he also returned kicks and punts and played stellar defense. The departure of Curley Lambeau at season's end, coupled with the addition of good young players like quarterback Tobin Rote and running back Billy Grimes, pushed Canadeo into a smaller role.

After retiring, he was a longtime broadcaster and served as a member of the Packers board of directors from 1955 to 1993. He was instrumental in the team's hiring of coach Vince Lombardi. The two shared a common heritage—both were Catholics of Italian descent—and they bonded while living in a Midwestern community that was very different from the big cities where they'd each grown up.

Canadeo was known as the "Gray Ghost of Gonzaga" because his hair went gray while he was still in college. He was inducted into the Pro Football Hall of Fame in 1974.

Clinton Portis (2002–2007)

In the mid-nineties, the Broncos had great success with their running game thanks to the work of line coach Alex Gibbs. He implemented a zone blocking scheme that helped them overwhelm opponents with their running game, and it seemed that their success continued no matter who the ball carrier was.

The Broncos drafted Portis in 2002, and he rushed for 1500 yards in each of his first two seasons. Rather than building the offense around him, the Broncos capitalized on Portis' strong performance by trading him to the Washington Redskins. In exchange, they acquired cornerback Champ Bailey to shore up their secondary. They also received a second round draft pick, which they used to select another running back (Tatum Bell).

The move seemed like a curious one from the Redskins perspective. Portis was an elusive runner who used his quickness to burst through cutback lanes. Washington preferred a more physical running game, for which Portis seemed ill-suited.

At the end of the day, the trade worked out well for both teams. Portis made the adjustment to the new style of offense, rushing for 1315 yards in his first year with the Redskins and 1516 yards the following season. In Denver, the Broncos used a different running back in each of the next three years, and each time, the new back rushed for more than 1000 yards.

Matt Snell (1964–1972)

The signing of Matt Snell by the New York Jets wasn't the first salvo fired in the war between the AFL and the NFL, but it was one of the biggest. Snell was drafted by both the Jets and the Giants after finishing his collegiate career at Ohio State. The Giants made a modest contract offer, but Jets owner Sonny Werblin made a splash, luring Snell away from his cross-town rivals with a substantially larger bid, and forcing football fans in the Big Apple to sit up and take notice. This laid the groundwork for his even bolder move to sign quarterback Joe Namath a year later.

Snell pounded the Houston Oilers for 180 yards in a game early in his rookie season. He was named the AFL's Rookie of the Year, finishing 2nd in rushing yards. His power running game helped soften up defenses and enabled the Namath passing attack to flourish.

Namath grabbed the headlines in 1968 with his bold prediction of victory over the Colts in Super Bowl III. It was Snell, though, who scored the Jets only touchdown in the game, and his powerful running helped the Jets to control the clock and keep the Colts offense off the field. Clinging to a 13–0 lead in the fourth quarter, the Jets didn't throw a single pass. Snell carried the ball thirty times for 121 yards to help preserve a 16–7 victory.

Don Perkins (1961–1968)

The first great back in what would be a remarkable string of Cowboys rushers. Perkins carried the load for the Cowboys in their early years, eventually helping them to rise from the depths of expansion to three straight appearances in the NFL championship game. When he retired he ranked fourth on the NFL's all-time rushing list. "I was small," the 5-foot-10, 205-pound Perkins once said, "but I was one that was afraid. When you're scared, you can run real fast."

Perkins was never spectacular but was quietly consistent. He earned six Pro Bowl invitations but never led the league in rushing, only posted ten games of 100 yards, and only occasionally broke free for a long gain.

Teammates and opponents described him as a great blocker. Later in his career he moved to fullback, where he opened holes for the young Dan Reeves. Perkins retired during training camp in 1969 after the Cowboys used their first-round draft pick to select Calvin Hill.

Chuck Muncie (1976–1984)

When Hank Stram became head coach of the New Orleans Saints, one of his first moves was drafting Chuck Muncie. A powerful back, Muncie teamed with the elusive Tony Galbreath to form a backfield tandem that was called "Thunder and Lightning." It was an effective pairing. In 1979, the duo combined to run for 1906 yards and scored 20 touchdowns.

Muncie was ravaged by off-the-field problems after that 1979 season. He was charged with battery after a daylong incident with his wife. Then his college roommate, Howard Strickland, alleged in interviews that Muncie hadn't attended a single class while at the University of California (a charge Muncie dismissed as "baloney.") He was traded to San Diego four weeks into the 1980 season, amid charges from the Saints that he had skipped practices and battled with coaches. Muncie agreed with the latter but said the claim that he had missed practice was "a bum rap." Moving from the sad-sack Saints to the high-flying Chargers offense revitalized Muncie's career. He rushed for 1144 yards and scored a league-leading 19 touchdowns in 1981, helping the Chargers advance to the AFC title game.

The following summer, he was called to testify in a trial that exposed cocaine use by NFL players, including Muncie and several of his ex-teammates in New Orleans. He was forced to acknowledge his own drug use, admitting that he spent $200 a week on cocaine. Muncie told a New Orleans paper that since being traded to San Diego he had "cut down his cocaine use." He went on to say that he still had a problem with alcohol and marijuana use. "I think the problem is not what it was, but it is still a small problem."

The Chargers sent him to a rehab clinic, but nobody was surprised that he lasted just one more season in the NFL.

Terry Allen (1991–2001)

I never went to medical school, but it's hard to be a serious student of pro football without having a cursory understanding of sports medicine. I can tell you that the anterior cruciate ligament is about an inch long, and that a torn ACL is the most common knee injury. From Red Grange to Gale Sayers, it has been the injury most likely to end a running back's career. Advanced imaging tools have made it easier for doctors to quickly diagnose torn knee ligaments, which is crucial because surgery must be done soon after the injury in order to be successful. Arthroscopic surgery has also shortened recovery times and increased success rates.

The most significant advancement in knee-ligament surgery has been a change in strategy. In the past doctors would sew the torn ligament back together, but today, they create grafts from existing tissue, essentially creating a new ligament rather than repairing one. The result is that players can come back from devastating injuries without necessarily seeing a decrease in their speed, strength, or ability to make cuts.

Terry Allen wasn't the first player to come back from an ACL injury, but I believe he was the first player to successfully return from reconstructive knee surgery twice. He injured the left knee during training camp in 1990, and spent his rookie season on injured reserve. Allen returned at full strength in 1991 and by the end of the season had taken the starting job from veteran Herschel Walker. He gained 1201 yards and scored 13 touchdowns in his first full season as a starter but injured his right knee in training camp the following July. Allen returned the following year and again topped the 1000-yard mark.

His best season came in 1996 when he rushed for 1351 yards and scored 21 touchdowns, at the time the 4th highest single-season total.

71

Tom Matte (1961–1972)

When starting quarterback Johnny Unitas and backup Gary Guozzo were both sidelined by injury, Colts head coach Don Shula turned to running back Tom Matte to be his emergency starter in the 1965 playoff game. Matte completed only 5 of 12 passes for 32 yards, but the Colts led 10–0 at halftime thanks in large part to his steady leadership. He carried the ball 17 times on rollouts and sneaks for 57 yards. The Colts lost in sudden-death overtime, but it was a memorable performance.

He started his career playing behind veteran backs Joe Perry and Lenny Moore—both Hall of Famers—but he was always an important contributor, catching passes out of the backfield and filling in when needed. Matte didn't have much speed, and Alex Karras of the Lions dubbed him "the Garbage Man" because of his slow but well-executed running. It was his ability to cut back against the grain that enabled him to gain yards. He was tremendously popular with teammates, opponents, and fans.

Matte became the Colts' primary ball carrier in 1967, and led the team in rushing from 1967 to 1969. He scored 3 touchdowns in the Colts' decisive victory in the 1968 NFL title game and rushed for 116 yards in Super Bowl III.

Matte's best season was in 1969, when he led the NFL in total yardage and combined rushing/receiving touchdowns. He tore knee ligaments early in the 1970 season, and was never able to return to the same form. Matte was traded to the Chargers in 1973, but he retired before training camp started.

72

Chris Warren (1990–2000)

Warren entered the league playing for Chuck Knox, a coach whose career was marked by an almost fanatical devotion to the running game. It's a bit surprising that in this environment, Warren languished on the bench for two years, doing little more than returning punts. Maybe it's because he was a fourth-round pick from Ferrum College, a small school in rural Virginia. Knox's team was struggling, and the running game was floundering as the coach struggled in vain to find a back to replace Curt Warner.

Tom Flores took over the head coaching duties in 1992, made Warren his starter, and the running game improved from 20th to 4th. Warren rushed for at least 1000 yards in each of his first four seasons peaking with 1545 yards in 1995. You have to wonder if Knox might have saved his job and pushed the Seahawks back into the playoffs if he had given Warren a chance rather than sticking with John L. Williams and Derrick Fenner.

Warren spent three good seasons as a third-down back in Dallas, and finished his career as an emergency replacement for Philadelphia in the 2000 playoffs.

73

Pete Johnson (1977–1984)

A massive fullback who seemed incapable of making a cut, Johnson powered through defenders with brute force at a time when smaller, speedier backs were in vogue. He was nearly unstoppable near the goal line, scoring 14 touchdowns in 1979 and 1983 and 12 in 1981, when he helped lead the Bengals to their first Super Bowl appearance.

He is probably best remembered, however, for his failure to score on three running plays close to the goal line in that game. With a first-and-goal from the 3-yard line, Johnson bulled his way to the 1-yard line, and then was stopped at the line on second down. After a third-down pass yielded no gain, the Bengals gave the ball to Johnson one more time, and he was again stopped short of the end zone. The fierce goal line stand proved to be the difference in a game which the Niners won 26–21.

Johnson played for Woody Hayes at Ohio State University, and he still holds school records for touchdowns in a career (56), a single season (25), and a single game (5). These gaudy totals came despite the fact that for his first three seasons, he was used primarily as a blocker for two-time Heisman Trophy–winner Archie Griffin. He reunited with Griffin in Cincinnati, but it was Johnson who played the lead role.

#74 Ken Willard (1965–1974)

Statistically similar to Floyd Little and Larry Brown, two running backs whose careers almost overlap with Willard's (see table below).

Little and Brown both relied on their speed, while Willard was more of a power runner.

He was San Francisco's best runner during the late sixties and when the team advanced to the NFC championship game in 1970 and 1971. With John Brodie at quarterback, the 49ers were focused on the passing game. Willard was a good change of pace, catching balls out of the backfield and getting tough yards in short-yardage situations.

#75 John Henry Johnson (1954–1966)

Most of the articles I've read about Johnson mention his blocking before they say anything about his skills as a runner. In his book *100 Greatest Running Backs,* Bob Carroll writes, "no back in football history has ever protected the quarter-

back better." Ron Smith, in *Heroes of the Hall,* said, "John Henry Johnson didn't simply block opposing defenders, he punished them with all of the ferocity he could muster."

Johnson didn't block in the way that many running backs do—pushing defenders with their hands. Rather, Johnson threw his elbows like they were sledgehammers. He drove his helmet into their ribs like a battering ram. Like Jim Brown, he delivered blows not simply to stop a defender on this play but to discourage him from approaching on the next.

He scored 9 touchdowns as a rookie with the Niners, joining a backfield that included Hugh McElhenny and Joe Perry. All three men—along with quarterback Y. A. Tittle—would end up in the Hall of Fame. Despite their undeniable talent, the Niners never reached the playoffs in the three years that the quartet played together.

Johnson was traded to Detroit in 1957, where he became the primary ball carrier and helped lead the Lions to victory in the NFL championship game. Three years later he joined the Steelers, where he had the best years of his career. He topped the 1000-yard mark in 1962 and 1964.

Others

 # 76. Jim Kiick (1968–1977)

 # 77. Mark Van Eeghen (1974–1983)

 # 78. Pat Harder (1946–1953)

 # 79. Johnny Strzykalski (1946–1952)

Comparison of Running Backs' Careers

Name	Career	RuAtt	RuYds	RuTD	RecNo	RecYds	RecTD	Fum
Willard	1965–74	1622	6105	45	277	2184	17	41
Little	1967–75	1641	6323	43	215	2418	9	32
Brown	1969–76	1530	5875	35	238	2485	20	40

80. Calvin Hill (1969–1981)

81. Rodney Hampton (1990–1997)

82. Dan Towler (1950–1955)

83. Stephen Davis (1996–2006)

84. Alan Ameche (1955–1960)

85. Andy Farkas (1938–1945)

86. Dub Jones (1946–1955)

87. Hoyle Granger (1966–1972)

88. George Rogers (1981–1987)

89. Charlie Garner (1994–2004)

90. Hewritt Dixon (1963–1970)

91. Garrison Hearst (1993–2004)

92. Chet Mutryn (1946–1950)

93. Ollie Matson (1952–1966)

94. Bill Dudley (1942–1953)

95. John L. Williams (1986–1995)

96. Alex Webster (1955–1964)

97. Eddie Price (1950–1955)

98. Gale Sayers (1965–1971)

99. James Wilder (1981–1990)

100. Chuck Foreman (1973–1980)

Wide Receivers

1

Jerry Rice (1985–2004)

When we talk about the shape of a player's career, we're generally talking about two different aspects of their performance: how good they were at their peak, and how long they were able to be productive. Rice scores phenomenally well in both categories. At his peak, he set single-season records in receptions, yards, and touchdowns. Rice ranked 1st in Adjusted Yards nine times in his first twelve seasons, a level of dominance over his peers matched only by two or three men in NFL history.

After he turned thirty-five, an age by which most NFL players have retired, Rice continued to play, adding another 499 catches, 6518 yards, and 43 touchdowns. At the age of forty, Rice had 92 catches for 1211 yards and was invited to the Pro Bowl. So when it comes to longevity, nobody played for as long or as well as Rice did.

Rice had tremendous receiving skills, but he also was blessed by being paired with some great quarterbacks. First it was Joe Montana then Steve Young with the 49ers, and when he joined the Raiders as a free agent, he teamed with Rich Gannon. Both teams played an offense skewed heavily to the passing game, but why wouldn't you do that with Jerry Rice in the lineup?

Some of his best performances came in big games. Rice had 11 catches for 215 yards in his first Super Bowl, and while people remember the last touchdown catch by John Taylor that clinched the victory, it was Rice's play earlier in the game that kept his team in the low-scoring contest. He had 148 receiving yards and 3 touchdowns in Super Bowl XXIV, and 149 yards and 3 touchdowns in Super Bowl XXIX. In all, he had eight 100-yard games in the postseason and scored 22 playoff touchdowns.

There's nothing that you can criticize about his first twelve seasons . . . they were nearly perfect. The only time you start to find any negatives is late in his career, when he missed parts of a couple of seasons due to injuries or started to slow down in his forties. Maybe you could say that he should have hung it up a year sooner than he did. But then, that's kind of like complaining about the eyebrows on the Mona Lisa.

2

Don Hutson (1935–1945)

Sports Illustrated's Peter King has written that he believes Hutson is the greatest player in NFL history. In studying the great players, King concluded that Hutson dominated his era more than any other athlete in any other sport. For example, he led the NFL with 74 receptions in 1942, and the next highest total for a player was 27 catches.

To a certain point, King is right. Hutson was so far ahead of his peers when it came to catching the ball. In eleven seasons, he led the league in receptions eight times and in receiving yards seven times. Twice, he was named the Most Valuable Player, and when he retired he held every significant receiving record.

While I agree that Hutson was one of pro football's greatest players, I can't agree with King's reasoning. There are two factors that contributed to Hutson's dominance over his peers, and I think they need to be included in the discussion. First, Hutson was a dominating receiver at a time when most teams didn't put much emphasis on their passing game. Hutson certainly helped change that, but he was playing a different game. The distance between him and his peers was as much about a new style of play as it was about superior skill.

Second, we have to acknowledge that the peak of Hutson's career came at a time when the level of play throughout the league was significantly deflated. Four of his six best seasons came between 1942 and 1945, when hundreds of the NFL's best players had been called into military service.

While these caveats are intended to counter the notion that Hutson belongs atop the list of great players, they aren't intended to knock him down very far. He was an innovator who helped show how and why the passing game could be a bigger part of the game.

Hutson was fast, but he didn't simply rely on his speed to get open. He used quick moves and changed speed to elude defenders. He created the idea of running preplanned pass routes, and many of those patterns he developed are still staples of the modern passing game. Hutson also pioneered the concept of timing patterns, running a precise number of steps and making a cut, so that the quarterback could release the ball before he turned.

As other teams adopted many of his strategies and techniques, defenses were also forced to adjust. At first, teams would use double or triple coverage against him, but eventually, they were forced to rethink their entire approach. The standard defense until the mid-thirties had seven linemen, two linebackers, and two deep backs, whose primary role was to serve as the last line of defense on running plays. In order to counter Hutson, teams started switching to a 6-2-2-1 defense, with two defensive backs assigned to cover the ends and a safety, who would help keep the offense from breaking a big pass play. Defensive ends also were used to help in pass coverage. The emergence of the passing game continued after Hutson left, as did the defensive counter-measures, but all of those changes in playing style have their roots with him.

Finally, it should be noted that since he played in the two-way era, Hutson excelled at other positions. He was one of the great defensive backs of his era, with 30 career interceptions. He also served as the Packers kicker, which led to one of his most memorable games. In a 1945 game with the Lions, he scored four touchdowns and kicked 5 extra points during the second quarter, a total of 29 points.

Marvin Harrison (1996–2007)

In an era when most wide receivers went to great lengths to draw attention to themselves, Harrison just went about his business quietly. "I've never been a loud guy," he said. "It's just the way I am. I'm not the type of guy who looks for a lot of attention on the field. Off the field I let my actions speak for themselves." A good receiver in his first three seasons, Harrison blossomed once Peyton Manning arrived, and together the pair became the most prolific quarterback-receiver duo in NFL history.

His best season came in 2002, when he set a new single season record with 142 catches. Harrison had at least 1000 receiving yards and 10 TDs in eight straight seasons, a feat that no other receiver has matched.

Steve Largent (1976–1989)

He didn't have blazing speed, wasn't blessed with intimidating size, and didn't have the infectious outgoing personality that might have made him a nationally recognized figure. What he had was great hands, an incredible work ethic, and patience. Even though he never had a great cast around him, Largent helped the expansion Seahawks become competitive in their third season.

His career almost ended before it started. Largent was drafted by the Houston Oilers but didn't make the team, and he was waived in August. Coach Bum Phillips thought he was too small and to slow to make it in the NFL. Before Largent cleared waivers, Phillips traded him to Seattle for an eighth-round pick. Given a chance to play, Largent proved Phillips wrong, finishing fourth in the AFC with 54 receptions that year, three more than any Houston player.

Largent had eight seasons of 1000 receiving yards in a nine-year stretch, missing the milestone when the player strike cut the 1982 season in half. When he retired in 1989, he held the NFL career records for receptions (819), receiving yards (13089), and touchdown receptions (100). All of those records were broken by Jerry Rice a few years later.

James Lofton (1978–1993)

Lofton's career had a great second act, which most likely is what clinched his spot in the Hall of Fame. He joined the Buffalo Bills after twelve NFL seasons, arriving just as the team emerged as an NFL powerhouse. Playing alongside Andre Reed in the Bills' K-Gun offense, Lofton helped provide the one thing they lacked, a deep threat in their passing game. He played a key role in their first Super Bowl run, catching 7 passes for 149 yards in their divisional playoff win over Miami and adding 113 yards and two more touchdowns in the conference championship victory against the Raiders.

The following year, at the age of thirty-five, Lofton earned a Pro Bowl invitation after posting his sixth 1000-yard season.

He spent his first nine years in Green Bay, and the Packers never had more than eight wins in any of those seasons. Their lone playoff appearance came after the strike-shortened 1982 season, and Lofton made the most of his opportunity. Against the Cowboys, Lofton caught 5 passes for 109 yards and scored two touchdowns. One of them came on a 71-yard reverse, which at the time was the longest running play in playoff history. Lofton made a huge impact during the Bills first Super Bowl run in 1990. In three postseason games, Lofton had 13 catches for 323 yards and scored three touchdowns.

Randy Moss (1998–2007)

Sometimes he was brilliant, sometimes he was petulant, and the frustrating thing was that you were never quite sure which guy you were going to get. Moss was the poster boy for a crop of bad-boy receivers who variously thrilled and aggravated their fans in the late 1990s and early 2000s.

On the field, Moss was spectacular. He made an immediate impact as a rookie, leading the league with 17 touchdown passes and racking up 1313 yards—at the time the second highest total ever for a rookie. Minnesota's passing offense went from mediocre to explosive, and the Vikings set an NFL record by scoring 556 points. In his first six seasons, Moss scored 76 touchdowns and finished in the top-five in receiving yards five times.

Off the field, Moss was never afraid to speak his mind, and oftentimes his comments were controversial. He had various scrapes with the law, acknowledged smoking marijuana, and on more than one occasion said that he wasn't always giving his best effort. Moss and the Vikings were happy to part ways after the 2004 season, and his career stalled after he was traded to the Oakland Raiders. He was reborn, however, after being traded to the New England Patriots in 2007. Teamed with quarterback Tom Brady, Moss set a new single season record with 23 touchdown receptions.

Lance Alworth (1962–1972)

A December 1961 article in *Time* magazine rated the college players who had just finished their senior seasons. One NFL scout offered this report on Alworth as part of his assessment of the ends: "Alworth didn't catch many at Arkansas. But he has tremendous speed—he runs the 100-yard dash in 9.6 seconds—and his performance as a breakaway running back shows that once he gets the ball, he can go the distance." That turned out to be a pretty good assessment, but on the other hand, the scout rated Alworth as the fifth-best receiver of the class.

The men rated ahead of Allworth? Gary Collins (Maryland), Bill Miller (Miami), Jerry Hillebrand (Colorado), and Jimmy Saxton (Texas). Collins was a two-time Pro Bowler who spent ten years with the Browns. Hillebrand switched to linebacker and played for three teams. Miller and Saxton had brief pro careers. None of them approached Alworth's level of success. Keep this in mind when you read the endless predraft prognostication from the self-appointed experts.

In retrospect, Alworth was perfectly suited for the Chargers and their high-flying passing game. His slender build and graceful running style were ideal for Sid Gillman's vertical passing game. Alworth was named Most Valuable Player in his first full season and the Chargers won the AFL title game 51–10. It was the first of seven straight 1000-yard seasons.

After a long and productive stint with the Chargers, Alworth joined the Cowboys in 1971. He teamed with speedster Bob Hayes and played a key role in the team's Super Bowl VI. Alworth was the first player from the AFL to be selected to the Hall of Fame, and perhaps the best receiver from a league where the passing game was king.

Don Maynard (1958–1973)

There are several players in the Hall of Fame who were initially overlooked or discarded by one team only to become a superstar somewhere else. In Maynard's case, it wasn't so much that his first NFL team didn't think he was a good player; they just didn't like him.

At a time when players were expected to have crew cuts and wear suits and ties, Maynard wore long sideburns and cowboy boots, marching to the beat of his own drummer. After Maynard's first season with the New York Giants, the team hired Allie Sherman as offensive coordinator. As Bill Ryczek described, in his book *Crash of the Titans,* that spelled trouble.

> Maynard's strange habits did not sit well with Sherman, a man who did not cotton to anyone who was 'different.' He was itching for an opportunity to rid himself of Maynard, and let it be known that he doubted Maynard had the intellectual capacity to play pro football.

Sherman cut Maynard a day after he muffed a punt in an exhibition game. Packers coach Vince Lombardi, who had been the Giants offensive coach in Maynard's rookie season, tried to convince him to come to Green Bay. Maynard opted instead to spend the season in Canada, returning the following summer to join New York's entry in the new American Football League. That team was known as the Titans from 1960 to 1962 before changing their name to the Jets.

The Titans first head coach was Hall of Fame quarterback Sammy Baugh, so it was no surprise that the team threw the ball early and often. In their inaugural season, Maynard and fellow receiver Art Powell became the first pair of teammates with 1000 receiving yards in the same season. They matched the feat again in 1962, with Maynard and George Sauer duplicating the feat again in 1967 and '68.

9

Terrell Owens (1996–2007)

Owens spent his first five professional seasons playing in the shadow of Jerry Rice, but he made a big statement at the end of their last season together. Rice was set to leave San Francisco through free agency, and in December of 2000, he played what everyone knew would be his last home game for the Niners. All eyes were on Rice, but Owens stole the day. He caught 20 passes, breaking the single-game record set by Tom Fears fifty years earlier. He racked up 283 yards—six shy of Rice's team record.

After the game, Owens said "what I did by no means overshadows No. 80 [Rice]. He's been a big part of my success." The humility of that moment seems a little strange in retrospect. For most of the rest of his career, Owens seemed to always be seeking the spotlight.

While he established himself as a bona fide star over the next few seasons, he feuded with head coach Steve Mariucci, and was publicly critical of quarterback Jeff Garcia. Owens complained that his numbers suffered because Garcia didn't have a strong arm, and that errant throws made Owens look like a worse receiver than he actually was.

Owens left the Niners on less than amicable terms, helping to orchestrate a trade to the Philadelphia Eagles. The new surroundings helped rejuvenate him, and Owens battled back from a broken ankle to help the Eagles with 9 catches for 122 yards in the Super Bowl loss to New England.

A year later he was unhappy again. Attempts to renegotiate his already lucrative contract were met with hostility, and he began to feud with teammates, including quarterback Donovan McNabb. The Eagles had little patience for his antics, suspending him twice during the 2005 season before eventually releasing him. He joined the Cowboys the following season, but the amount of controversy swirling around him didn't dissipate.

The question becomes whether a player like this helps or hurts a team, and I guess the answer is that it depends. All of the antics can be a dis-

traction, but they can also help take the focus and the pressure off of his teammates. If the reporters are always chasing a guy like T.O. for the latest soap-opera drama, that leaves the quarterback and the defensive captain and even the head coach to go about their preparations with less disruption. When a player is beleaguered by the press, his teammates can rally around him, and that camaraderie can carry over into their performance on the field. Obviously, when it becomes self-destructive or starts creating division in the locker room, it can be a bad thing. But sometimes a good team can benefit from having a lightning rod around to absorb all of the attention.

There's no doubt that he's one of the all-time greats, but I think the constant sideshow made it harder for folks to see that.

10

Michael Irvin (1988–1999)

The last great Cowboys player drafted by Tom Landry, Michael Irvin got off to a slow start in Dallas. His brash, cocky style might have played well at the University of Miami, but it didn't win him many fans in the Lone Star state. He caught only 32 passes in his rookie season, then missed parts of the next two with injuries.

By 1991, Irvin was healthy, and the Cowboys had built up their offense. With Troy Aikman at quarterback and Emmitt Smith in the backfield, the team was ready for a breakout season, and so was Irvin. He finally lived up to his nickname "The Playmaker," grabbing 93 passes for a league-leading 1523 yards. The Cowboys advanced to the Super Bowl, and Irvin's two first-half touchdown receptions helped the team jump out to a 28–10 halftime lead and beat the Bills.

Irvin topped the 1000-yard mark in each of the next four seasons, helping the Cowboys win two more Super Bowls. In 1995 he had a streak of eleven consecutive games with at least 100 receiving yards. He was a big, physical receiver who used his size to move defensive backs out of his way. He would push them to create separation, or pull them to knock them off balance. Irvin helped launch an era where big receivers were in vogue, but as other receivers began to emulate his style of play, the league cracked down, and officials began to call more offensive pass-interference penalties across the board.

Irvin's dominance came to a sudden end in 1996—and in retrospect, so did the Cowboys dynasty. Irvin was arrested at his thirtieth birthday party in March on charges of cocaine possession, and after pleading no contest he was suspended for the first five games of the season. The Cowboys offense struggled in his absence, losing three of their first four games and dropping from 7th to 26th in total yards. Irvin played well when he returned, and topped the 1000-yard mark in each of his next two seasons, but he never regained his perch as the league's best receiver, and the Cowboys didn't get back to the Super Bowl.

In a 1999 game at Philadelphia, Irvin suffered a spinal cord injury after a hard hit. Fans at Veterans Stadium cheered as he lay motionless on the field, and was later removed on a stretcher. The injury wasn't life-threatening, but it forced him to retire.

His work as a broadcaster has kept him in the spotlight, but two postretirement arrests for drug-related offenses hurt his candidacy for the Pro Football Hall of Fame. Irvin was too good to be kept out forever, but the blemishes caused voters to pass over him in his until his third year of eligibility.

#11 Harold Jackson (1968–1983)

Attended Jackson State University in Mississippi, a division 1-AA powerhouse which has produced a number of NFL stars. Its alumni include three Hall of Famers: Lem Barney (1966), Walter Payton (1974), Jackie Slater (1975).

Jackson had good hands and enough speed to get deep. He led the league in receiving yards twice while a member of the Eagles, and led in touchdown receptions in 1973 after being traded to the Los Angeles Rams. Jackson also spent four seasons with the Patriots.

His career numbers are good enough that he ought to have been considered for the Hall of Fame, but he's never been a finalist. I spent some time looking, but I couldn't find a single newspaper article advocating on his behalf. I looked through the archives of the *Philadelphia Inquirer* and the *Philadelphia News* and came up empty, and searches of other electronic databases turned up nothing. When he retired, Jackson ranked 2nd all-time in receiving yards, 7th in receptions, and 9th in touchdown catches. I'm not saying the guy should have been a first-ballot inductee, but I'm baffled that he's not even on the radar.

#12 Torry Holt (1999–2007)

Holt arrived in St. Louis at the same time as quarterback Kurt Warner and Marshall Faulk, and made just as big an impact. He had blazing speed, which is always an asset for a receiver, but it made him particularly dangerous in the Rams explosive passing offense.

Yards after catch has never been an official stat, and it's something that would be difficult to reconstruct going back in time. However, based on my own observations and the ten or so years for which I've tracked the number, Holt stands out as one of the players who gained the most yards after he caught the ball. I've watched a lot of game film, and it seems pretty clear to me that this is by design. That is to say that the Rams have taken advantage of his speed by putting him into the kinds of patterns, the kinds of matchups, and the areas of the field where he can get the ball in the open field and make plays.

#13 Jimmy Smith (1992–2005)

The presence of Jimmy Smith and Rod Smith so high on this list poses an interesting dilemma. That is to say at first glance, I'm not sure whether they ought to be ranked so high.

They're both here based on their numbers, of course, not because of my own personal opinions. Jimmy Smith, who spent the bulk of his career with the Jaguars, had nine 1000-yard seasons and ranks 10th all-time in receptions. Rod Smith had eight 1000–yard seasons with the Broncos and ranks 12th all-time in receptions. In terms of career yards and receptions, both rank among the all-time greats. The table below shows the wide receivers with at least 800 career receptions.

Player	Rec	ReYds	ReTD
Jerry Rice	1549	22895	197
Cris Carter	1101	13899	130
Tim Brown	1094	14934	100
*Marvin Harrison	1042	13944	123
Andre Reed	951	13198	87
*Isaac Bruce	942	14109	84
Art Monk	940	12721	68
*Keenan McCardell	883	11373	63
*Terrell Owens	882	13070	129
Jimmy Smith	862	12287	67
Irving Fryar	851	12785	84
Rod Smith	849	11389	68
Steve Largent	819	13098	100
Henry Ellard	814	13777	65
Keyshawn Johnson	814	10571	64
*Torry Holt	805	11864	71

* player was active in 2007

If I were to ask you, based on your own personal opinions, to go through that list and circle the names that you thought were Hall of Fame caliber receivers, and draw a line through the ones who weren't, I'd wager that most of us would end up with pretty similar lists. If you then took an index card and covered up the names, looking only at the numbers, I think you'll see why. It's the touchdown numbers. Most everyone's going to circle the six guys with 100 touchdowns. There will be some difference of opinion for the guys in the 80s, and very few of us will pick any of the guys in the 60s.

Here's another thing that's happening. In 1990 there were seven players with 10000 career receiving yards. At the end of the 2007 season, twenty-one more receivers had joined the club. That's created a sudden glut atop the leader boards, and not just for receivers. Over the same time period, the 10000-yard rushing club has grown from eight to twenty, and the 25000-yard passing club has swelled from twelve to twenty-nine.

You can see the effects on a season-by-season level too. The table below shows the number of 1000-yard rushers and receivers and the number of passers with 2500 yards each season, grouped by decade.

Decade	2500 Pass	1000 Rush	1000 Rec
1930s	0	1	0
1940s	9	4	6
1950s	7	6	10
1960s	80	31	75
1970s	65	79	30
1980s	155	101	118
1990s	185	128	170
2000s	169	147	165
projected	211	184	206

There are a lot of reasons for this general trend. Some of it has to do simply with expansion, or with the increase in numbers of games played per season. Improvements in sports medicine have played a role, I'm sure, as have a number of other factors. But regardless of the causes, the result is a whole lot more players with high career totals in the categories by which they're judged.

The system I use for rating players with Q-scores addresses this problem, I believe, by judging players within the context of their era. If the numbers are inflated across the board, the Q-scores don't overvalue them. People don't think of Rod Smith and Jimmy Smith in the same category as contemporaries like Terrell Owens and Randy Moss. Why not? The Smiths were both quiet guys, didn't seek out the limelight, and while they didn't get as much time on the highlight shows, they did put up very good numbers for a very long time.

The Hall of Fame will have to deal with this issue in the coming years, and I suspect that some worthy players from this era will be passed over, even though their resumes are clearly better than some of the players already inducted.

Isaac Bruce (1994–2007)

When you're looking at receiving stats, 1995 stands out as a strange year, and Bruce illustrates the case perfectly. He finished the season with 119 receptions in 1995, the 5th highest total to-date but only the 4th best among NFC receivers that year. This blip wasn't necessarily due to a sudden influx of great receivers, but rather the simple fact that teams were throwing the ball more. In 1995, teams averaged 34.79 pass attempts per game, the most ever. The table below shows the general trend upward in the three years leading up to that season, and the general trend downward afterwards.

League Pass Attempts per Game

Year	PA/G
1992	29.93
1993	32.17
1994	33.60
1995	34.79
1996	33.26
1997	32.77
1998	32.27

It was Bruce's second season in the NFL and his first year as a starter, and he set career highs in every receiving category that year (119 catches for 1781 yards and 13 touchdowns). Still, those phenomenal numbers were not good enough for Bruce to be one of the nine receivers invited to the Pro Bowl that season.

Tim Brown (1988–2004)

It took Brown five seasons to establish himself as a star receiver, but once he got started he just kept on going. He earned a Pro Bowl invitation as a rookie for his outstanding special teams play, excelling on punt returns and leading the league in kick-return yards and average. In the first game of the following season, he tore knee ligaments on a kick return, and it took him almost four years to get back to full strength.

That breakthrough season came in 1993 when he caught 80 passes for 1180 yards, the first of nine consecutive 1000-yard seasons. Brown was fast and elusive, but like Jerry Rice, much of his success stemmed from his hard work. He watched game film voraciously, looking for minor details in his performance that he could improve, or subtle weaknesses in a defensive back that he could exploit. And like Rice, he continued to be productive into his thirties. Brown led the league with 104 receptions when he was 31, and posted his ninth-straight 1000-yard season at the age of 35.

Rod Smith (1995–2006)

Smith was undrafted out of college, but the scouts couldn't overlook his remarkable speed. The Broncos signed him to their practice squad in 1994, and three years later he was a starter. The addition of Smith gave the Broncos offense a deep threat they'd been missing, and that added element helped propel the Broncos to back-to-back Super Bowl victories.

Speed—even blazing speed—can only get you so far as a receiver. Smith's success came in part because he developed the ability to run precise routes. He was also very physical despite the fact he was just 6-0. These two skills helped him become a polished possession receiver as he got older and his speed faded.

Smith led the Broncos in receiving for eight straight years, and would end his career with 849 receptions.

Cliff Branch (1972–1985)

The record books listed him as 5-foot-11 and 170 pounds, but both figures were exaggerations. Coach John Madden said he weighed closer to 155. Branch had Olympic-caliber speed, but he was pretty raw as a rookie. Over the next few years, he became a more polished receiver, learning to run precise routes and developing great hands.

Branch was the main offensive weapon on the Raiders team that advanced to five straight AFC championship games from 1973 to 1977. He was still the team's leading receiver when the team won Super Bowls after the 1980 and 1983 seasons.

Raymond Berry (1955–1967)

When people think of the 1958 championship game, the so-called "greatest game ever played," they typically think of fullback Alan Ameche falling across the goal line for the winning touchdown, or the cool leadership of quarterback Johnny Unitas. Nobody remembers that it was Berry who was the star of that game. He had two key receptions on that final drive for 33 yards, and ended the game with 12 catches for 178 yards. Without his performance, the New York Giants probably would have won that game.

Berry also had successful stint as head coach of the New England Patriots, compiling a 48-39 record in five-and-a-half seasons and winning the AFC championship in 1985.

Billy Howton (1952–1963)

Howton exploded on the scene with 1231 receiving yards and 13 touchdown receptions as a rookie in 1952. While he never reached those totals again, he was one of the most productive receivers of the 1950s. When he retired, Howton was the NFL's all-time leader in receptions (503) and receiving yards (8459), passing Don Hutson in both categories.

His best seasons came in Green Bay, but he left just as the Packers were beginning to get good. After one season with the Browns, he joined the NFL's expansion team in Dallas in 1960.

Gary Clark (1985–1995)

Clark teamed with Art Monk for eight years to form one of the great receiving duos of all time. Curiously, though, it was the Redskins No. 3 receiver who had a record-setting performance in Super Bowl XXII. The otherwise unheralded Ricky Sanders ended that game with 9 catches for a record 193 receiving yards in Washington's 42–10 rout of the Broncos. Clark had three catches for 55 yards in that game, while Monk was held to just 1 catch for 40 yards.

Henry Ellard (1983–1998)

The current trend is towards tall receivers who can outleap cornerbacks to make catches. Henry Ellard was only 5-foot-11, but he did that all the time. He had great speed and phenomenal leaping ability, enough to compete for a spot on the 1992 Olympic team as a triple-jumper when he was thirty-one years old.

There have been some great receivers on the Rams over the years, guys like Tom Fears and Elroy Hirsch and Jack Snow, but when Ellard retired he held all of the team's receiving records. He returned several years later as an assistant coach to tutor Torry Holt and Isaac Bruce, who ended up surpassing all of his team records.

#22
Paul Warfield (1964–1977)

He had blazing speed, but what made Paul Warfield so dangerous was that he played on teams where the offense was built around the power running game. When he first joined the Cleveland Browns, opposing defenses would have to focus on stopping Jim Brown's tough inside running. That softened things up for Warfield on the outside, and even though he didn't get the ball often, he usually made a big gain when he did get it. When Leroy Kelly replaced Brown at running back, the formula remained the same, and Warfield helped lead Cleveland to the NFL title game three times in six seasons.

The Browns stunned their fans in the spring of 1970, trading the twenty-seven-year old Warfield to Miami for a first-round draft pick. They felt an urgent need to improve at quarterback and had their hearts set on selecting Purdue's Mike Phipps. Warfield found himself in the middle of another power running game, using his elusiveness to make the occasional big play while the Dolphins ground it out with Larry Csonka. The team improved from 3-10-1 to 10-4 in Warfield's first season, and went to the Super Bowl in each of the next three years.

#23
Art Monk (1980–1995)

I originally wrote a long essay on why I felt Monk should be inducted into the Hall of Fame. It was a fairly thorough examination of his case, as well as a look at the arguments against his candidacy. The whole thing was rendered moot when Monk was named as a member of the Hall's 2008 class.

My argument in a nutshell was this. There's a case to be made for every player, and they all fall into three categories. The first is what you'd call the no-brainers. Guys like Jerry Rice, Joe Montana, or Jim Brown, who each compiled a body of work that makes an overwhelming case for their induction. I'm not sure that any of these candidates require much discussion.

There's a second, much larger group of candidates that I'd call the gray zone. There are arguments both for and against their selection, and while there is consensus that they were good players, the debate centers on the question of whether they were good enough.

And then there is the third category, which I think is the most difficult group of players to weigh. In this category, the question is about whether that *type* of player is worthy of induction. That's the discussion that's obviously taken place about special teams players as a group, since only one had been inducted in the Hall's first forty-six classes. It's a discussion that frankly hasn't taken place with regard to some other players such as Ken Anderson or Bob Hayes, whose careers have been under appreciated because their style of play was different than their contemporaries. Clearly, this is the category that Monk falls into. He was essentially a possession receiver in the era before the West Coast Offense became the vogue. Rather than giving him credit for what he did do, those who made a public case against him knocked Monk because he was not a prototypical deep threat receiver.

Instead, Monk was a big physical receiver who made his living making tough catches over the middle. He didn't have great speed, but he ran crisp routes and could work the seams in a zone defense as well as anyone. Monk also mastered the technique of using his body to shield smaller defensive backs, putting himself in a position where the defender was powerless to prevent the pass from being completed. He also drew a lot of praise for a contribution that never shows up on the stat sheets and often goes completely overlooked—his downfield blocking.

Even though Monk lined up as a wide receiver, his role was really more like that of a tight end. He used his physicality to catch passes. He went inside and over the middle most of the time. He was asked to block a lot. All of those things make him a different creature than the typical speed receiver, guys who stayed outside, used their speed to get open, and weren't expected to contribute as a blocker.

In that context, I think that all of the objections to Monk's induction are mitigated. His 940 career catches put him in the middle of a logjam of receivers, but he'd stand out among tight ends. His yards per catch look a lot better in that context as well. I haven't heard anyone else suggesting that we consider Monk as a hybrid tight end, but coach Joe Gibbs, hinted at it in interview with Washington sportswriter Gary Fitzgerald: "What has hurt Art—and I believe should actually boost his credentials—is that we asked him to block a lot," Gibbs said. "He was the inside portion of pass protection and we put him in instead of a big tight end or running back. He was a very tough, physical, big guy."

There's another issue that's worked against Monk, and that's a huge misconception about how good someone has to have been to be worthy of the Hall of Fame. Imagine for a minute that they stopped playing football today, and you were charged with the task of building a new Hall of Fame from scratch. Based on the body of work since 1920, how many players would you want in your Hall? If your definition of a Hall of Famer was players who dominated the era in which they played, how many would that be? Fifty? Maybe one hundred?

What if instead, I told you that your Hall had to have 300 members? You couldn't possibly fill that roster with players who dominated their era. Only so many players can reach that threshold of greatness. You'd have to start adding guys who were dominant for three or four seasons, or who were the third or fourth best player at their position for a decade.

That's where we are. The Hall's rules mandate the selection of at least 4 candidates per year, and the average has been about 5.3 inductees per class. At this rate, Canton will receive its 300th member in 2108, ten years from now.

This rate of selection translates to roughly fifty players per decade. Take any decade and pick the best player at each position. That doesn't even get you halfway there. You need thirty more players per decade, and you're not going to find thirty more guys who dominated their era.

In that context, it's hard for me to understand why it took so long for Monk to be inducted, and why some of the people with a vote lobbied so hard to keep him out. Is he one of the four or five best receivers who ever played? Clearly not. Was he one of the four or five best receivers of his era? Clearly he was.

#24
Drew Pearson (1973–1983)

Pearson was not drafted out of college, probably because he didn't have the kind of blazing speed that had become the vogue among NFL receivers in the early seventies. He's often described as a great "clutch" receiver, which I suppose is a reference to his making some big plays in big games. The most notable was in the 1975 playoff game against the Vikings, when he caught a 50-yard Hail Mary pass from Roger Staubach to give the Cowboys a stunning upset win.

But Pearson never had 100 yards in a playoff game, and only scored a touchdown in 5 out of the 20 postseason games he played. Besides the Hail Mary pass in 1975, his only other notable playoff performance came in 1980. Down 27–17 to the Falcons, Pearson caught two fourth-quarter touchdown passes to help the Cowboys rally for the win.

I don't say this to denigrate Pearson, but rather to point out how abstract and meaningless the idea of a "clutch" player is. It's meant to say "this guy didn't make a lot of big plays, but he made some important ones." Or more specifically, "even though the statistics don't show this guy as a great player, I know in my heart that he is."

Pearson led the league in receiving once, went to three Pro Bowls, and was the offensive captain for a Cowboys team that went to three Super Bowls in four years. He was selected by the Hall of

Fame as one of the four best receivers of the 1970s. Regardless of what he did in "big games," he was a great receiver.

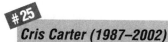

Cris Carter (1987–2002)

Philadelphia Eagles head coach Buddy Ryan has been ridiculed for years for a comment he made in 1990, and a move that might seem foolish in retrospect. At the end of training camp, he cut Cris Carter, a young receiver who had shown flashes of brilliance in his first three seasons. Why did you just cut a guy who caught 11 touchdown passes last year, the press wanted to know. "Because all he does is score touchdowns," the coach replied.

What he meant, of course, was that Carter worked hard to make plays inside the 20-yard line, but that he couldn't be counted on the rest of the time. Ryan never gave a more detailed explanation, but years later Carter himself would acknowledge he had problems with drug and alcohol abuse. Carter recounted how he constantly clashed with the disciplinarian coach, and how being cut in 1990 forced him to confront the poor choices he had made in his personal life. He joined the Minnesota Vikings and refocused himself.

Over the next twelve seasons, Carter improved to become one of the game's top receivers. He set a single-season record with 122 catches in 1994 and from 1993 to 2000 he had eight straight 1000-yard seasons. Some folks in Philadelphia lamented his departure and wondered how their fortunes might have changed if Carter had put up those kinds of numbers in an Eagles uniform rather than with the Vikings. But the reality is that if he'd have stayed, he probably would have self-destructed, and he certainly would never have developed into one of the game's most prolific pass catchers. Being released forced him to develop a strong work ethic, and ultimately that's what led to his success.

When he retired he ranked 2nd all-time in receptions and receiving touchdowns.

Art Powell (1959–1968)

At 6-foot-3 Powell was tough to cover. His great speed made it even harder. Powell had the great fortune of playing for two teams who liked to throw the ball. With the New York Titans under coach Sammy Baugh, Powell and Don Maynard formed one of the most prolific receiving duos in pro football history. He later joined the Oakland Raiders and the high-flying vertical passing game of coaches Al Davis and John Rauch. He retired with 81 touchdown receptions, which ranked 3rd all-time.

Del Shofner (1957–1967)

Perhaps he should be regarded as a tight end. Shofner is one of those hybrids in an era when the tight end position was beginning to be developed, but I think it makes more sense to consider him in the same group as the receivers of his day. He got his start with the Rams but really came into his own with the New York Giants, and during the early 1960s he was one of the leading receivers in the NFL.

Gene Washington (1969–1979)

Just so we're clear, there were two pretty good receivers named Gene Washington, and their careers overlapped way too much for most of us to be expected to keep the two men straight. Both played for the NFC in the Pro Bowl in 1969 and 1970.

The older Gene Washington went to Michigan State and spent most of his career with the Vikings. The younger Gene Washington went to Stanford and spent nine seasons with the San Francsco 49ers. It's this younger man that ranks 28th on our list of wide receivers. He went to four straight Pro

Bowls, leading the league in receiving yards in 1970 and in receiving touchdowns in 1972.

After his playing career ended, Washington took a job in the league office, eventually rising to the role of Director of Football Operations, responsible for overseeing what happens on the field on a day-to-day basis. He's the most prominent minority working in any North American sports league, and he has helped open doors for other African Americans, both in league positions and in management positions with the league's teams.

In his frequent speaking appearances, Washington tells young people that rather than looking to athletes or entertainers as role models, that they should look to prominent African-American businessmen, like Richard Parsons (CEO of Time Warner), or Stanley O'Neal (CEO of Merrill Lynch). Those folks not only make a lot more money than athletes or rap stars, they wield real power and can help change the playing field by creating opportunities for others.

#29 Charley Taylor (1964–1977)

Taylor was a running back when he was named the NFL's Rookie of the Year in 1964, but it was clear from the outset that his future was as a receiver. He rushed for 755 yards that season, but what caught people's attention was his 53 catches for 814 yards. It was an NFL record for catches by a running back, and it marked the first time in twenty years that a rookie had finished in the top-ten in both rushing and receiving.

Midway through his third season, Taylor switched from the backfield to split end. He finished the year with a league-leading 72 catches for 1119 yards and 12 touchdowns. All of those figures were career highs, but Taylor continued to be one of the league's top receivers through the mid-1970s.

Taylor spent his entire career with the Redskins, and was inducted into the Hall of Fame in 1984.

#30 Andre Reed (1985–2000)

Reed is an interesting test case for Hall of Fame voters, who passed over him in 2007 in his first year of eligibility. He ranked 3rd all-time in catches when he retired, and 6th in both receiving yards and touchdowns. Reed is the first receiver who played primarily in the 1990s to come up for consideration, and when they're considering his candidacy, the voters will have to think not just about Reed but about the context for evaluating receivers of this era in general.

Time will not be on his side, and I suspect that if he's not picked in 2009, he'll probably never get in. By then, we'll have a flood of guys like Tim Brown and Cris Carter to clutter the field.

What should help Reed, in my opinion, is that unlike some of the other receivers from the 1990s, he wasn't what critics like to call a "compiler," a player who racked up gaudy numbers without necessarily helping his team win, or someone who was mediocre but stuck around for a long time. Reed was a key member of the Bills team that won four straight AFC championships, best known for making tough catches over the middle. Despite taking a lot of blows, he only suffered one serious injury (in 1995).

He had a lot of big games in the postseason, including twice grabbing 8 passes in a Super Bowl game. His most notable performance came in the opening round of the playoffs in 1992, when the Bills rallied from a 35–3 deficit to beat the Houston Oilers. Reed had 8 catches for 136 yards and 3 touchdowns in one of the most remarkable comebacks in sports history.

#31 Joey Galloway (1995–2007)

Galloway is a great example of a player whose raw skills leave scouts with their mouths hanging open, but whose inability to translate those natural gifts into dominating on-field performances exasperated coaches. His blazing speed was the reason why the Seahawks grabbed him with the eighth overall pick in the 1995 draft. He topped the 1000-yard mark three times in his first four seasons, and also returned 4 punts for touchdowns. Galloway was probably the fastest player in the league, but while he could outrun most cornerbacks, he didn't add any other skills to his repertoire. His routes were sloppy and he had a hard time shaking off defenders who got physical with him. In short, he was a big-play guy but never a go-to guy.

A contract dispute led him to hold out for the first eight weeks of the 1999 season, and at season end the Seahawks traded him. Cowboys' owner Jerry Jones was tantalized by Galloway's speed and convinced that he could become a better all-around player. Dallas surrendered two first round picks (which the Seahawks used to select RB Shaun Alexander and WR Koren Robinson) and signed Galloway to a seven-year contract for $42 million. It was a deal they would almost immediately regret.

Galloway tore his ACL in the season opener and missed the rest of the 2000 season. After quarterback Troy Aikman retired, the Cowboys struggled to find a replacement. The Dallas offense wasn't helped by a one-dimensional deep-threat receiver, and Galloway's contract was killing their salary cap. They traded him to Tampa Bay for disgruntled wideout Keyshawn Johnson after the 2003 season.

Galloway had a bit of a resurgence with the Buccaneers, I think in part because it was the first time he'd been in an offense that took advantage of his style of play. Through the 2007 season, he'd posted six 1000-yard seasons and ranked pretty high on the all-time leaders list for receiving yards and touchdowns (23rd and 21st, respectively). Despite those numbers, he was never invited to a Pro Bowl. As he approaches the end of his career, there's a nagging sense that if he hadn't relied solely on his speed, he could have been one of his era's great all-around receivers.

John Gilliam (1967–1977)

Gilliam might be better remembered if he had spent the bulk of is career with one team. Instead, he played for five different NFL teams in an eleven-year career. He also spent part of one season with the Chicago Winds of the World Football League.

A second round draft pick for the New Orleans Saints, Gilliam returned the opening kickoff in the team's inaugural game 94-yards for a touchdown. His speed made him a dangerous return man and a deep-threat receiver.

His most productive seasons came with the Vikings, where he spent four seasons and earned a Pro Bowl invitation each year. In a 1973 playoff game, he caught 2 fourth quarter touchdown passes from Fran Tarkenton to help the Vikings come from behind and beat the Redskins.

Mark Clayton (1983–1993)

After playing sparingly as a rookie, Clayton caught 18 touchdown passes in his sophomore season, setting a new NFL single-season record. He had become the favorite target of quarterback Dan Marino, and the prolific duo led the Dolphins to the Super Bowl that year.

Clayton and fellow receiver Mark Duper came to be known as "The Marks Brothers." Both were relatively small receivers, just 5-foot-9 and roughly 180 pounds. Both used their speed and quickness to get open, and each benefited from having an equally electrifying receiver on the other side.

Clayton finished with 81 career touchdowns, and his other numbers are comparable to or better than many of the receivers already in the Hall of Fame. However, Clayton hasn't garnered much support as a candidate in his own right. I suspect that the voters dismiss his numbers as being a by-product of playing with a great quarterback. I'm not sure that makes much sense, and neither does Clayton. "I caught more touchdowns and more receptions from

Marino than he threw to anybody," he argued in 2003. "So if he's in there, I had a nice, big hand in helping him get in there. Somebody had to be catching his throws. They didn't catch themselves."

Wes Chandler (1978–1988)

Originally a draft pick of the New Orleans Saints, Chandler went to San Diego in a mid-season trade in 1981. The Chargers had lost their top receiver, John Jefferson, after a bitter holdout, and needed a playmaker to fill the gap in their explosive passing game.

Chandler made an immediate impact. In the opening round of the playoffs that year, he returned a Miami punt 56 yards for a touchdown and caught 6 passes for 106 yards. His best season came the next year, in 1982, when he led the league in receiving yards (1032) and touchdown catches (9). In that strike-shortened season, Chandler averaged 129 yards per game—a mark that still stands as the all-time record.

Chandler represented his Chargers' teammates in the player's union and after the 1987 strike, many of the players who held that role found themselves being cut or traded. Chandler was just one example, sent to the 49ers just three months after he was elected to the union's executive committee. He retired after four games with San Francisco, citing tendonitis in his knee.

Chad Johnson (2001-2007)

When ESPN was filming a preseason segment on Bengals head coach Marvin Lewis in 2003, they caught him in a private exchange with receiver Chad Johnson. Never shy, Johnson told his coach "I want to be the best of all time. I want to be better than [Jerry] Rice." Lewis restrained a chuckle, and replied "I know, and we're going to help you."

It was way too early (not to mention ridiculous) for Johnson to compare himself to Rice, but

clearly he was ambitious. He became one of the league's most prolific receivers, averaging nearly 1400 yards over the next five seasons and earning Pro Bowl invitations each year.

The late 1990s and early 2000s were an era dominated by prima donna receivers. Guys like Terrell Owens, Randy Moss, and Keyshawn Johnson petulantly demanded center stage. When you considered that at their best, these guys would touch the ball about six times per game, the ratio of disruption to production was astonishing.

Johnson loved the spotlight, but for the most part his antics were fun as opposed to angry. He concocted elaborate post-touchdown celebrations, such as a mock-proposal to a Bengals cheerleader, or donning a Santa cap and passing out wrapped gifts to fans in the stands. Some people found that grating, but personally, I prefer those types of shenanigans to shouting matches with coaches and pouty press conferences.

Drew Hill (1979–1993)

Hill spent his first six seasons with the Rams, where he used his speed and quickness to become a dangerous return man. With an offense built around the running game, Hill didn't get much of an opportunity to use his skills as a receiver. He was used as an occasional deep threat, but never caught more than 19 passes in a season.

That all changed when he was traded to Houston in 1985. The team needed some weapons for quarterback Warren Moon to throw to, and acquired Hill to be one of the primary targets in a new wide-open passing attack. In his seven years with the Oilers, Hill averaged 1068 receiving yards per season, leading the team for five straight seasons.

Harold Carmichael (1971–1984)

On November 4, 1979, Carmichael caught a 5-yard hitch pass from quarterback Ron Jaworski. After being tackled, he got up to find owner Leonard Tose rushing across the field towards him on a golf cart, with Harold's wife and infant son sitting next to him. The catch itself wasn't that spectacular, but the Eagles' owner stopped the game to commemorate the fact that Carmichael had caught a pass in 106 consecutive games, a new NFL record. Tose presented Carmichael's wife with 106 red roses and unveiled a huge trophy, one that local reporters measured at 23 feet 9 inches.

It was a fitting tribute for the tallest receiver of his day. Carmichael stood 6-foot-8, towering over most of the cornerbacks that he faced. The Eagles thought he was best suited to play tight end, but after spending his rookie season at that position it was clear that he lacked the bulk to be effective. In a game against the Cowboys, Carmichael was manhandled by middle linebacker Lee Roy Jordan, and it was clear that he would never survive in the trenches.

He moved back to receiver the next season and, by his third season he was flourishing. He led the NFL in receptions and receiving yards in 1973, and became a fan favorite with his touchdown celebrations, including one where he'd spin the ball as if he was rolling dice.

Carmichael's production would sag in the years that followed, the consequence of playing on a losing team with a lousy offense. But he did enjoy a resurgence after the arrival of head coach Dick Vermeil and the emergence of Jaworski at quarterback.

He extended his streak of games with a reception to 127, before being shut out in a game against the Cowboys in December 1980. He left the game early in the second quarter with an injury and didn't return. The record was subsequently broken by Art Monk (183), and later by Jerry Rice (274).

Gary Garrison (1966–1977)

The Chargers have had a string of great receivers in their history. Garrison is among them, but he has been largely forgotten because his career fell between two Hall of Famers—Lance Alworth and Charlie Joiner. Garrison played at the tail end of the Sid Gillman era and retired just before Don Coryell arrived. It's a stretch of time that unfortunately coincided with the longest playoff drought in team history.

Garrison paired with Lance Alworth to form one of the most prolific receiving duos of the late sixties. In 1968, the two became the third pair of teammates to top the 1000-yard mark in the same season. After Alworth was traded to the Cowboys in 1971, Garrison had some of the most productive years of his career. Over a five year stretch, Garrison went to the Pro Bowl or AFL All Star game four times.

He had long hair late in his career, but when it was shorter, I thought Garrison was a dead ringer for Kirk Douglas. Take a look at his 1971 football card and tell me that he doesn't look like Spartacus.

Fred Biletnikoff (1965–1978)

He didn't have great speed and he wasn't very big, but Biletnikoff had an uncanny knack for getting open. He also was one of the early proponents of Stickum, an industrial adhesive that he slathered all over his hands and arms. He'd keep a stash on his socks too, so he could reapply the stuff to his hands when it wore off. A handful of other players followed his lead, but when teammate Lester Hayes started slathering his entire body with Stickum, the league banned its use.

Biletnikoff played a key role in the Raiders high-flying pass offense, and some of his best performances came in big postseason games. He caught 7 passes for 168 yards and 3 touchdowns in an opening round win over the Chiefs in 1968. A week later, he had seven catches for 190 yards in a narrow loss to the Jets. The Raiders went to the playoffs ten times in an eleven year stretch, but only reached the Super Bowl once. Biletnikoff was named Most Valuable Player of that game, setting up 3 touchdowns with catches that put the Raiders inside the 2-yard line.

When he retired, Biletnikoff held the record for most playoff catches, receiving yards, and touchdown catches. He still shares the record for touchdowns in a playoff game with 3.

#40
Charlie Joiner (1969–1986)

Joiner started his career with the Oilers and came into his own under offensive coordinator Bill Walsh in Cincinnati. After Walsh left the Bengals to become an assistant in San Diego, he helped arrange a trade to bring Joiner to the Chargers.

He had impressive speed, but the Chargers had other receivers who could stretch the field. They used Joiner as a possession receiver, taking advantage of his ability to read defenses and find soft spots in their zone coverage. His steady presence helped San Diego integrate younger receivers into the "Air Coryell" offense, players like John Jefferson, Wes Chandler, and Kellen Winslow.

Joiner topped the 1000-yard mark four times, and when he retired his record of 750 receptions was the most of all-time. He played 18 seasons before retiring, the most ever by a wide receiver.

Others

 # 41. Herman Moore (1991–2002)

 # 42. Stanley Morgan (1977–1990)

 # 43. Sterling Sharpe (1988–1994)

 # 44. Bobby Mitchell (1958–1968)

 # 45. Mac Speedie (1946–1952)

 # 46. Tony Hill (1977–1986)

 # 47. Irving Fryar (1984–2000)

 # 48. Mel Gray (1971–1982)

 # 49. Dave Parks (1964–1973)

 # 50. Otis Taylor (1965–1975)

 # 51. Mark Duper (1982–1992)

 # 52. Bob Hayes (1965–1975)

 # 53. Hines Ward (1998–2007)

 # 54. Jim Benton (1938–1947)

 # 55. John Stallworth (1974–1987)

 # 56. Anthony Carter (1985–1995)

 # 57. Keyshawn Johnson (1996–2006)

 # 58. Eric Moulds (1996–2007)

 # 59. Anthony Miller (1988–1997)

 # 60. Jimmy Orr (1958–1970)

 # 61. Andre Rison (1989–2000)

 # 62. Dante Lavelli (1946–1956)

 # 63. Rob Moore (1990–1999)

 # 64. Roy Green (1979–1992)

 # 65. Nat Moore (1974–1986)

 # 66. Billy Wilson (1951–1960)

 # 67. Rich Caster (1970–1982)

 # 68. Joe Horn (1996–2007)

 # 69. Elroy Hirsch (1946–1957)

 # 70. Keenan McCardell (1992–2006)

 # 71. Ken Burrough (1970–1981)

 # 72. Terry Glenn (1996–2007)

 # 73. Ernest Givins (1986–1995)

 # 74. John Jefferson (1978–1985)

 # 75. Isaac Curtis (1973–1984)

Tight Ends

1

Tony Gonzalez (1997–2007)

Most of the evidence suggests that professional football is the most popular spectator sport in North America. That wasn't always the case, of course. Baseball was first in the American mind for nearly a hundred years. In the twentieth century, there were times when boxing ran a close second. Basketball has had its peaks and valleys. So has tennis. At different times, other athletic pursuits have vied for the public's attention as well.

The different sports have even competed with each other for the top athletes. Sandy Koufax was a college basketball star at my alma mater, the University of Cincinnati, but when he left school it was to play professional baseball. In the 1970s, Dave Winfield of the University of Minnesota and Colorado's Dave Logan pulled off the trifecta, being drafted by pro football, baseball, and basketball teams. Bo Jackson chose baseball over football after he won the Heisman Trophy in 1985. Eight years later, Charlie Ward passed on the NFL to play point guard for the New York Knicks.

There's nothing new about multisport players, or about top athletes being forced to choose one sport over another. One of the trends that we saw in the late 1990s was that power forwards from top basketball programs were being recruited by the NFL to play tight end. Gonzalez was a second-team All-American as a junior on the University of California's football team in 1996. That winter he played a key role in the basketball team's impressive tournament run, stepping up his game after Ed Gray, the Golden Bears' leading scorer, broke his foot. Gonzalez helped lead the team into the Sweet Sixteen and then declared his eligibility for the NFL draft.

Tony Gonzalez was not the first player to take this path, but he was the one who had the most success. Unlike the plodding but powerful tight ends that typified the late 1980s and early 1990s, Gonzalez represented a new breed—tight ends who were too big and too fast for traditional defenses to cover. This opened the door for other players like Antonio Gates and Marcus Pollard, guys who a decade earlier probably would have continued their careers in the NBA. Instead, the agility and quickness that those players honed on the hardwood was put to use on the gridiron.

Gonzalez was the first (and so far the only) tight end with 100 catches in a single season. During the 2007 season, he passed Shannon Sharpe for the most career catches and touchdowns by a tight end, and also moved within 78 yards of Sharpe's mark for receiving yards by a tight end.

Shannon Sharpe (1990–2003)

I suppose you could write a whole book on the history of the tight end—why the position initially developed, how it evolved, the different types of tight ends that have emerged over the years, and the various ways that defenses have adjusted. Nobody would read a book on so narrow a topic of course, but there's enough detail and enough subtlety in the story to fill hundreds of pages.

There have been three major developments that we should look to for the basis of our evaluation of tight ends throughout history. The first is the emergence of the tight end as a receiver, which began in earnest during the early 1960s. The mind-set shifted from the idea that the tight end was an extra blocker to the idea that he was an extra receiver. Teams started to look for big guys who could catch the ball, because this created mismatches with the defense. Guys like John Mackey and Mike Ditka were really tough to tackle, especially in the open field.

A second shift happened in the mid-eighties, as the West Coast Offense began to be widely adopted. The role of the tight end began to diminish, as many of the blocking and pass-catching duties were shifted from the tight end to the fullback. Players like Tom Rathman and Darryl Johnston were the ones catching passes in the flat and sealing the corner with their blocking on outside run plays. Some teams reverted to a power running game where tight ends were almost exclusively used for blocking, while others experimented with the run-and-shoot offense, which eschewed the tight end completely.

The third major change took place in the 1990s, when the tight end began to re-emerge as a major part of the offense. Rather than look for a player who could both block and catch passes, most teams split the position into two roles. There were blocking tight ends and receiving tight ends, and two guys would replace each other as the situation dictated. What this meant was that a receiving tight end didn't need to carry the bulk necessary to block 300-pound linemen, so the position could be stocked with smaller but stronger and more athletic players.

The key figure in that last shift was Shannon Sharpe, who emerged as a new kind of offensive weapon with his play for the Broncos. He was just 6-foot-2 and 225 pounds, which most people considered too small to play tight end in the NFL. But he had the speed, strength, and agility to create havoc for defenders. Sharpe credited his strength to a rigorous weight-training regimen, something he copied from his older brother Sterling.

"In college, I started lifting weights and changing my body," Sharpe said, "and I was hooked. I was like an addict. When my teammates were going to parties at 10 o'clock at night, I'd be in the weight room. Eventually, football was like a by-product, because I would've rather lifted than play football. Football allowed me to do what I really, really loved to do: lift weights."

Sharpe's breakout season came in 1992, his third season with the Broncos. In an otherwise tumultuous season for the organization, he emerged as the favorite target for quarterback John Elway. Sharpe led the team in receptions—something he would do each year between 1992 and 1996. Although he was never too shy to sing his own praises, his performance in the 1993 playoffs was what really catapulted him into the national spotlight. Against the rival Los Angeles Raiders, Sharpe had 13 receptions for 156 yards and a touchdown.

The arrival of wide receiver Rod Smith helped take some of the pressure (and defensive attention) away from Sharpe in the late nineties, but he continued to play a key role on the Broncos team that won back-to-back Super Bowls in 1997 and 1998. After an injury-plagued 1999 season, Sharpe joined the Baltimore Ravens as a free agent in 2000. He returned to form, leading the Ravens in receptions, receiving yards, and receiving touchdowns. With running back Jamal Lewis, Sharpe helped key the team's ball control offense. He had two touchdown catches in the Ravens Super Bowl run—including a 96-yarder in the AFC title game.

Ozzie Newsome (1978–1990)

Newsome and Kellen Winslow redefined the position in the eighties, ushering in what I'd call the second generation of tight ends. It wasn't simply that teams were finding tight ends who could also catch the ball, they were making them a bigger part of their offensive strategy as well. A look at the aggregate data shows that trend clearly. A look at the average number of catches each team had by their tight ends shows how it spikes in the 1980s. But what's really telling is not just that average, but how many catches the league's leading tight end had. Here is where you can clearly see the tight ends emerge as premier receivers.

Average Team TEs

Year	Rec	Yds	TD
1960	7.5	129.7	0.7
1970	33.4	465.8	3.7
1980	47.5	611.4	5.1
1990	38.8	441.7	3.2
2000	50.4	521.9	4.1

League's Leading TE

Year	Rec	Yds	TD
1960	43	804	5
1970	47	687	9
1980	89	1290	9
1990	59	747	7
2000	93	1203	9

Newsome tormented opposing teams who tried to defend him. Typically, defenses used a linebacker to cover the tight end, but Newsome's speed made that difficult. He was simply too fast, and if he was able to get separation at the line of scrimmage, the linebacker would never catch up with him. Some teams tried to adjust by using a strong safety—who was often fast enough to stay

with Newsome but had trouble tackling him in the open field. He would just muscle past those guys.

Newsome led the Browns in receiving each year from 1981 to 1985, setting a team record with 89 receptions in 1983. His numbers dropped in the years that followed, but that was more a function of the offense improving than Newsome declining. The Browns advanced to the AFC title game three times in a four-year span, with Newsome playing a key role. He caught at least one pass in 150 straight games, which was the second-longest streak to that point in NFL history.

Jackie Smith (1963–1978)

Smith is most remembered for dropping what would have been a game-tying touchdown pass in the third quarter of Super Bowl XIII. He spent fifteen seasons with the St. Louis Cardinals and held all of the lifetime records for tight ends—480 receptions, 7918 yards, and 40 touchdowns. But the Cards had only been to the playoffs twice during his career, and Smith joined the Dallas Cowboys as a blocking tight end in hopes of finally winning a championship.

Smith did not catch a single pass during the regular season, but he did catch three passes in the Cowboys' first round playoff win over the Falcons. Then came that fateful play against the Steelers in the Super Bowl. Trailing 21–14, the Cowboys drove to the Steelers' 10-yard line late in the third quarter. On third down and 3, Smith broke free and stood wide open in the end zone. Dallas quarterback Roger Staubach saw him and threw a perfect pass, but Smith dropped it. The Cowboys had to settle for a field goal and went on to lose by four points—precisely the difference between scoring that touchdown and settling for the kick.

The man who had a reputation for being a sure-handed receiver was the center of attention after the game, with the media converging on him in the locker room, anxious for an explanation. "I just missed it," Smith admitted. "I slipped a little, but still should have caught it. I've dropped passes before, but never any that was so important. Maybe I should have tried to catch it with my hands only, but in that situation you try to use your chest. Then I lost my footing, my feet ended up in front of me and I think the ball went off my hip."

Staubach tried to take some of the heat off of Smith's shoulders. "If you're casting blame, it's 50 percent my fault and 50 percent Jackie's. I know one thing, the play wasn't a failure for lack of experience because we're the two oldest guys on the team."

It was the last game Smith ever played, and it's a shame for him to be remembered for that one play. He was a ferocious blocker and a great pass catcher. Smith also had more speed than contemporaries Mike Ditka and John Mackey, which made him more of a big-play receiver.

Pete Retzlaff (1956–1966)

A tweener, the kind of guy who makes it difficult to rate and rank guys by position, Retzlaff spent his first two seasons as a running back, then switched to wide receiver and later moved to tight end. I'd argue that he has to be included with the tight ends for a number of reasons. Retzlaff played a key role in the development of the tight end position. He was one of the first to play the position as it emerged in the early sixties, and he really had his best success there. Perhaps most significant, he is the only tight end to win a Most Valuable Player Award.

That honor came late in his career, in 1965, when he finished with 66 catches for 1190 yards and 10 touchdowns. More than forty years later, the yardage total still stands as the 5th best season total for a tight end. Retzlaff played an important role on the 1960 Eagles team that won the NFL championship, leading the team in receptions and receiving yards.

One of the prominent figures in the early days of the NFL Player's Association, he served as president for several years and lobbied for the development of a pension plan. He also spent four years

as the general manager of the Eagles under owner Leonard Tose.

Kellen Winslow (1979–1987)

Winslow was the best pass catcher ever to play tight end. He was tall and strong and had tremendous speed. This not only made him a threat to run deep routes, but also made him capable of making big gains after he'd caught the ball.

One of the strategies the Chargers employed to help Winslow was the use of a second tight end whose job was primarily blocking. This freed Winslow up to focus on his pass-catching duties, and kept him from getting worn down in the trenches. San Diego head coach Don Coryell developed this system, and one of his assistants, a young running backs coach named Joe Gibbs, would later take the two–tight end offense to Washington.

In 1980, Winslow led the NFL with 89 catches and amassed 1290 yards, a single-season record for tight ends that still stands. His numbers over a four-year stretch were remarkable, especially if you prorate his totals for the strike-shortened 1982 season.

Winslow's Receptions

Year	Rec	Yds	TD
1980	89	1290	9
1981	88	1075	10
1982*	96	1282	11
1983	88	1172	8

*9 game totals prorated for 16 games

Before 1980, no tight end had caught more than 75 passes in a season. Winslow was doing that every year.

Winslow's peak was amazing but it was short. A knee injury, which had sidelined him as a rookie, was reaggravated in 1984. He missed fifteen games over the next two seasons, and when he returned he had lost much of his speed. When Al Saunders took over as Chargers head coach in 1987, Winslow's role in the new offense diminished, and he was unceremoniously dumped at the end of the season.

Mike Ditka (1961–1972)

The first pure tight end, and the man who defined the position for several generations. Ditka was the league's Rookie of the Year in 1961, and he was unquestionably the league's best tight end in each of his first four seasons. He was the Bears' biggest offensive weapon in those days and led the team in receptions and scoring when they won the NFL championship in 1963. Ditka's best seasons came in Chicago, but he also spent two seasons with the Eagles and another four with the Cowboys.

Ditka deserved to be elected to the Hall of Fame not only for his outstanding performances on the field but also for his role as an innovator in creating the tight end position. His candidacy was largely ignored for more than a decade, not gaining any serious momentum until after he'd returned to the Bears as head coach and won a Super Bowl.

In their groundbreaking book *The Hidden Game of Football,* authors Bob Carroll, John Thorn, and Pete Palmer devoted an entire chapter to the Hall of Fame, and the criteria by which some questionable players got in while some seemingly obvious choices were snubbed. In conclusion, they offered a somewhat tongue-in-cheek list of the things a retired player could do to boost his chances. Among them were "stay alive," "stay in the limelight after you retire," and "let others say how good you were. If you say it, no one will believe you and you'll be a bore." Ditka succeeded on all three counts, and that's why he became the first tight end elected to Canton.

Todd Christensen (1979–1988)

Originally a fullback, the Raiders thought his blocking and receiving skills would be put to better use as a tight end. It wasn't until his fifth season

that Christensen emerged as a big-time player. He had 92 catches, making him just the second tight end (after Kellen Winslow) to lead the league in that category. Christensen was the Raiders' leading receiver for four straight years, including their 1983 Super Bowl–winning season.

Jerry Smith (1965–1977)

Smith spent thirteen seasons with the Washington Redskins, playing for coaches Otto Graham, George Allen, and Vince Lombardi. He tied the NFL single-season record for touchdown receptions by a tight end with 12 in 1967. Smith also retired as the all-time leader with 60 touchdown catches, a mark that stood until Shannon Sharpe edged past him in 2003.

In August of 1986, Smith announced that he was battling AIDS. Just forty-three years old, his weight had dropped from 210 pounds to 150, and he was getting weaker with each passing day. The stunning announcement came in an interview with the *Washington Post.* Rock Hudson had died less than a year earlier, and both the public and the medical profession were still struggling to understand the disease. There was a huge stigma for those who acknowledged they were infected.

Smith had been diagnosed the previous December but understandably didn't want people to know. In the article, he expressed concern that his invitation to be honored by the Redskins as a member of the team's "Hall of Stars" that summer might be rescinded. He waited until he was confined to the hospital, when he couldn't hide it any longer.

Eventually, Smith decided that while letting the public know might affect how people viewed him personally, it would ultimately help educate people about AIDS. "I want people to know what I've been through and how terrible this disease is," Smith told the *Post.* "Maybe it will help people understand. Maybe it will help with development in research. Maybe something positive will come out of this."

He was the first athlete—active or retired—to publicly acknowledge that he'd contracted AIDS. The backlash that Smith feared never came. On the contrary, his friends and teammates rallied around him. Some might expect that football players—hard-nosed tough guys—would not want to stand up for a teammate player who'd contracted a disease primarily associated with drug addicts and homosexuals. But as Ira Berkow wrote in the *New York Times,* the courage to do something like that was one of the things that made football players excel in the first place. "It's the courage of character, the courage not to accept stereotypes. It's the courage of true virility. Perhaps it is true, as Leo Rosten wrote in *Captain Newman, M.D.,* that 'it is the weak who are cruel, and that gentleness is to be expected only from the strong.'"

Smith died seven weeks after the *Washington Post* article was published. Despite his prolific career, he has never been included as a finalist on the ballot for the Pro Football Hall of Fame.

#10 Riley Odoms (1972–1983)

In his autobiography titled *They Call Me Assassin,* notorious Raiders safety Jack Tatum says that the best hit of his career came at the expense of Broncos tight end Riley Odoms. "I heard Riley scream on impact and felt his body go limp," Tatum recalled. He had delivered a blow called "The Hook," a forearm to the head whose purpose was, he said, "to strip the receiver of the ball, his helmet, his head and his courage."

Although Odoms was uninjured on that particular play, the incident gives you a flavor for what it was like to play tight end during the seventies. Until the NFL changed its rules in 1978, defenders were relatively free to make contact with receivers down the field. Physical contact was the preferred method for disrupting receivers in their routes and discouraging them from coming over the middle. That's one reason why so few tight ends from the sixties and seventies had long careers.

Odoms lasted twelve seasons in the NFL—all with the Denver Broncos. Unfortunately, his least productive year as a starter came in 1977, the year that the Broncos made their first Super Bowl appearance.

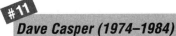

#11 Dave Casper (1974–1984)

Different than most tight ends of his day because of his size, Casper weighed 255 pounds when he reported to training camp as a rookie. He had been an outstanding blocker at Notre Dame, but the Raiders considered moving him to the offensive line. The following year he showed up thirty pounds lighter, making a clear statement that he wanted to remain at tight end.

Casper was regarded as a great blocker and a clutch receiver. He had 5 touchdowns in the Raiders two playoff games in 1977, including 3 in a double-overtime win against the Colts. The marathon game ended with his 10-yard touchdown catch, but he would be best remembered for a 41-yard catch that set up a game-tying field goal as regulation time expired. The play went down in football lore as "The Ghost to the Post," a reference to his nickname and the pattern that he ran.

During the 1980 season, Casper was traded to the Houston Oilers. He was reunited there with Ken Stabler, the longtime Oakland quarterback who had been traded to the Oilers himself during the off-season. The pair had two productive seasons together, though their only playoff appearance ended in a loss to their former Raiders teammates.

#12 Jay Novacek (1985–1995)

Under head coach Jimmy Johnson, the Dallas Cowboys transformed themselves from a league-worst 1-15 record in 1989 to a playoff berth in 1991, and from there they would go on to win three Super Bowls in four seasons. Much of the focus on that turnaround has fallen on the flurry of trades that Johnson made and the remarkable success they had in the draft. Adding players like Troy Aikman, Emmitt Smith, and Michael Irvin certainly can affect that kind of change.

Often overlooked is the signing of tight end Jay Novacek through Plan B free agency. The addition of a receiving threat at tight end helped to give second-year quarterback Troy Aikman an option underneath. It's difficult to conclude there was a direct cause and effect, but Aikman's play improved dramatically after Novacek arrived.

The popular perception is that Novacek was an unspectacular player with the Cardinals who was transformed into a star by the Cowboys. The reality is that he was already a pretty good receiver—particularly in 1988. The Dallas coaches recognized this and put him into a system that took better advantage of his skills. "I was pretty much just as good a player with the Cardinals as I was with the Cowboys," Novacek said years later. "I was just put in a different situation with the Cowboys."

#13
Ben Coates (1991–2000)

Like Novacek, Coates played a key role in helping a young quarterback develop and lead a team to the Super Bowl. He was in his third season when the Patriots drafted Drew Bledsoe, and he quickly became the young passer's favorite receiver. Coates led the team with 53 receptions during Bledsoe's rookie season, and the following year set an NFL record for tight ends with 96 catches.

Coates was the Patriots' leading receiver in their Super Bowl XXXI loss to the Packers, with 6 catches for 67 yards and a touchdown. He made another Super Bowl appearance four years later, as a backup with the Ravens. The Giants focused their efforts on containing starter Shannon Sharpe, holding him to just 1 catch in the big game. Coates had 3 catches for 30 yards and ended his career after winning the title.

If he had been in better shape at the end of his career, Coates might have pushed his statistical totals

high enough to make a case for the Hall of Fame. He caught at least 60 passes in five straight seasons, and ranked 5th all-time among tight ends with 499 catches and 50 touchdowns when he retired.

#14
Keith Jackson (1988–1996)

To say that Jackson made a splash in his NFL debut would be a huge understatement. The record for receptions by a rookie tight end was 56, a mark that had stood for twenty-seven years. Jackson shattered it, reigning in 81 catches in his first season with the Eagles.

His totals would drop, however, in each of the next five years. Although he made the Pro Bowl in four of his first five seasons, injuries began to rob him off his speed. At 6-foot-2 and 250 pounds, Jackson was just too big for most opponents to cover, but what made him so dangerous was his ability to split the zone in the middle of the field.

Jackson spent his most productive years in Philadelphia and Miami, but had a brief and interesting resurgence in two seasons with the Packers. Green Bay head coach Mike Holmgren devised a devastating two–tight end approach, teaming Jackson with another Pro Bowl tight end, Mark Chmura. This formation was used to devastating effect in the 1996 playoffs, creating matchup problems by lining both tight ends up on the same side, or occasionally having both of them split out wide. Either alignment forced the middle linebacker to commit to pass coverage, which opened things up for the Packers otherwise unspectacular running back Edgar Bennett. While it would be hard to describe this as the centerpiece of the Packers Super Bowl run, it was a significant piece of the puzzle.

#15
Raymond Chester (1970–1981)

Arguably the second-best tight end in the history of two different teams, the Raiders and the Colts.

Chester caught 22 passes in his first three seasons with the Raiders, but he was traded to Baltimore after owner Al Davis drafted Notre Dame's star tight end Dave Casper. Chester played a key role in the Colts offense, and the team made three straight playoff appearances.

Chester longed to return to Oakland, and he did in 1978, where he and Casper shared playing time. When Tom Flores became the head coach in 1979, he found a way to get both tight ends involved in the offense, and they formed what was undoubtedly the greatest tight end tandem in history. They combined for 115 catches, 1483 yards, and 11 touchdowns, and both men made the Pro Bowl. Casper was bigger, but Chester had more speed, and although neither man was particularly happy about the arrangement, it worked.

The arrangement lasted only one year. Casper was traded to the Oilers midway through the following season. Chester was thirty-two years old by this point, and beginning to show the effects of age. He retired after the 1981 season, but returned eighteen months later with the Oakland Invaders of the United States Football League. He was named as the USFL's top tight end by the *Sporting News,* and went on to play a significant role in the Invaders' front office.

Wesley Walls (1989–2003)

Walls languished in San Francisco for four years, sometimes injured and otherwise ignored. After five years with the Niners, he joined the Saints as a free agent. He set a team record for receptions by a tight end in 1995, then parlayed that success into a big free agent contract with the Panthers. He flourished in Carolina, becoming one of the league's most prolific tight ends. Walls scored ten touchdowns in 1996, but his best year came in 1999. He set career highs in every statistical category, and his 12 touchdowns tied the single-season record for tight ends shared by Mike Ditka (1961) and Jerry Smith (1967).

Steve Jordan (1982–1994)

Caught 68 passes for the Vikings in 1985 without scoring a single touchdown. That's one of those statistical anomalies that leaps out at you, even though it's more a coincidence than anything else. In general, tight ends tend to have a higher number of touchdowns per reception than other receivers because of their usefulness in short-yardage situations.

A lot of this comes down to how a team decides to use their tight end. The table below shows four players who rank pretty close in total receptions. You can see that Smith had significantly more touchdowns in roughly the same number of catches as Jordan and Wycheck. Coates nearly doubled their totals. If we calculate the number of touchdowns they scored for each 50 receptions, the difference is clear.

Player	Rec	TD	TD per 50 Rec
Frank Wycheck	505	28	2.77
Ben Coates	499	50	5.01
Steve Jordan	498	28	2.81
Jackie Smith	480	40	4.17

None of these four players represents the extremes. Jim Mandich of the Dolphins had 23 touchdowns on just 121 career receptions—a rate of 9.5 touchdowns per 50 receptions. Don Warren of the Redskins scored seven touchdowns on 244 catches—a rate of 1.43.

Bob Trumpy (1968–1977)

At 6-foot-6, Trumpy was remarkably tall compared to other tight ends of his era. Jerry Smith was 6-foot-2, while Mike Ditka and John Mackey were 6-foot-3. Looking at all of the tight ends who retired before 1980, the only tight end taller than Trumpy was 6-foot-10 Morris Stroud, a college basketball star who was used mostly as a field goal–

blocking specialist. Stroud had only 54 catches in five seasons with the Chiefs.

When I was nine years old my family moved to Cincinnati. It was the first time I'd lived in a city with major league sports teams, and it didn't take long for me to become completely obsessed with the Reds and Bengals. Two moments stand out from that fall, and both of them have to do with Bob Trumpy.

The first came in a November game against the Dolphins, a game played during a driving rainstorm. Trailing 17–16, the Bengals called a flea-flicker play. Quarterback Ken Anderson handed the ball off to running back Archie Griffin, who turned and pitched it to receiver John McDaniel. He then handed the ball back to Anderson, who heaved the ball to Trumpy in the end zone for the game-winning touchdown.

Needless to say, I was completely mesmerized by that play. The paper the next morning was full of photos and diagrams, and I think that burst of excitement helped recapture the attention of local fans. The Bengals had gone into the game with a losing record, but the win started a four-game winning streak. A win over the Steelers in December put them into a tie for first place, although a loss in the season finale resulted in a second-place finish.

The other moment came a few weeks after the flea-flicker play. My parents were watching the game on television when Trumpy was injured and had to be carried off the field on a stretcher. "Is that Bob Trumpy?" my mother asked. No nine-year-old boy thinks that his mother knows anything about sports, so I was surprised when she not only knew the player by name but also rattled off the name of the college he had attended. It turned out that Trumpy had been a high school classmate of my mother's in Springfield, Illinois.

I'd like to say that Trumpy became one of my favorite players, but I'm fairly certain that injury marked his last appearance on an NFL field. He did, however, become an extremely popular radio talk-show host the following year, and I listened with rapt attention every night for four hours, calling in as often as I could get past his screeners.

Mark Bavaro (1985–1994)

A big, physical tight end, Bavaro was a key figure in the rise of the New York Giants during the mid-1980s. He led the team in receptions and receiving yards in 1986, helping lead the team to its first Super Bowl victory. The Giants trailed the Broncos at halftime of that game, but the tide turned when Bavaro caught a 13-yard touchdown pass on the Giants first possession of the third quarter. They went on to score 30 points in the second half—a Super Bowl record.

Bavaro's ability to catch passes over the middle opened things up for the outside receivers. His blocking was also important to the Giants' power running game and helped the team win a second Super Bowl title four years later.

He suffered a knee injury in a 1989 game against the Chargers. Bavaro tried to tough it out, but all the willpower in the world won't help you overcome torn ligaments. He had surgery during the off-season, and was a less dominant player after he returned. His numbers dropped significantly in 1990, and after missing the 1991 season, he hung on for three more years in Cleveland and Philadelphia.

Charlie Sanders (1968–1977)

Sanders spent his entire career with the Detroit Lions, leading the team in receptions five times. His toughness was legendary, and he helped define the way tight ends were used in the modern offense with his willingness to catch passes over the middle.

He was finally selected for the Hall of Fame in 2007, thirty years after he retired. During his playing days, he was recognized by his peers as one of the game's best tight ends—as evidenced by his seven Pro Bowl invitations and his two All-Pro selections. After his career ended, however, he suffered in the voting process. One reason was that he played on a team that didn't have much success. The Lions finished with a losing record six times in his ten seasons, and made just one playoff appearance. Because he didn't play on a bigger stage, it was easier for the memories of him to fade for people outside of Detroit.

Although Sanders compared favorably to the other tight ends of his era, the Hall's induction of several of his contemporaries made his candidacy more difficult too. Mike Ditka, John Mackey, and Dave Casper all preceded him into the Hall, and it seems clear in retrospect that the selection committee had a hard time with the idea of choosing a fourth tight end from the same era.

#21
Brent Jones (1987–1997)

Jones was smaller than the typical tight end of his era, but he was a perfect fit for San Francisco's West Coast Offense. He could use his speed to get open over the middle, on the quick outside route, or even down the field. Jones also had great hands, and became a trusted target, first for Joe Montana and then later for Steve Young.

During eleven seasons with the 49ers, Jones appeared in twenty-one postseason games, including three Super Bowls. His career almost ended before it started. Jones was a fifth-round draft pick of the Pittsburgh Steelers in 1986, but a week after draft day he was involved in a serious auto accident. A drunk driver struck his car, and Jones sustained a neck injury that kept him out of action for his rookie season. The Steelers cut him loose during the offseason, and he signed with the 49ers as a free agent.

#22
Jim Mitchell (1969–1979)

Known affectionately as "Pork Chop," Mitchell was a fan favorite in the early days of the Atlanta Falcons franchise. He was invited to the Pro Bowl after his rookie season, and the following year led the team in both receptions and receiving yards.

During a nationally televised game with the 49ers in 1973, Mitchell got into a scuffle with teammate Art Malone in the huddle. The two were arguing over a muffed play, and the pair had to be separated after they started exchanging blows. The Falcons lost that game, but the incident helped bring the team together. They won their next seven games and finished with a 9-5 record.

#23
John Mackey (1963–1972)

Mackey was the first great tight end, and when he retired he was considered the model for what all young tight ends should aspire to. He had the perfect blend of power and quickness, but it was his breakaway speed that made him standout. In 1966, for example, he scored 9 touchdowns, and 6 of them came on plays of more than 50 yards. Traditional defenses were inadequate for a player like Mackey, because linebackers were too slow to keep up with him and defensive backs often weren't strong enough to tackle him without help.

Mackey led the Colts in receiving yards as a rookie in 1963, and he was invited to the Pro Bowl five times in his first six seasons. He also played in two Super Bowls, scoring a 75-yard touchdown on a tipped pass in Baltimore's 16-13 win over the Cowboys in Super Bowl V.

Mackey was the first president of the Players' Association, and he was instrumental in leading a strike at the start of training camp in 1970. He later filed a lawsuit challenging the so-called "Rozelle Rule," which allowed the commissioner to order a team signing a free agent to give players as compensation to his former team. This effectively made it impossible for players to move freely from one team to another. Mackey prevailed in federal court, although it would take another decade for players to achieve any real measure of free agency. His union activism was probably the main reason that he had to wait twenty years to be selected for induction in the Hall of Fame.

#24 Frank Wycheck (1993–2003)

Wycheck was the key figure in one of the most memorable moments in playoff history, the Music City Miracle. A field goal gave the Buffalo Bills a 16-15 lead over Wycheck's Tennessee Titans with sixteen seconds left in the 1999 AFC Wildcard game. Lorenzo Neal fielded the subsequent kickoff and handed it to Wycheck. As the Bills defenders approached him, Wycheck threw the ball across the field to teammate Kevin Dyson, who ran 75-yards down the sideline for the game-winning touchdown as time expired. The Bills argued that Wycheck's toss had been an illegal forward pass, but a review of instant replay upheld the call, and the Titans emerged with a dramatic victory.

The Titans went on to win the AFC title game and advance to the Super Bowl.

Wycheck led the Titans in receptions each season from 1996–2000, playing a key role in the development of quarterback Steve McNair as a reliable outlet receiver. He caught sixty passes or more for five straight seasons and earned three Pro Bowl invitations.

#25 Billy Cannon (1960–1970)

Cannon won the 1959 Heisman Trophy as a halfback at Lousiana State University, and was the subject of an intense bidding war between the NFL and the fledgling American Football League. Legend has it that Houston Oilers owner Bud Adams signed Cannon to a contract in the end zone following LSU's victory in the 1959 Sugar Bowl. The NFL's Los Angeles Rams alleged that he'd also signed a contract with them, but the Oilers prevailed in a court battle.

The signing generated huge amounts of publicity and gave the AFL a much needed dose of credibility. Cannon's presence also helped to make the Oilers one of the league's most formidable teams. With the league's most prolific offense, they won the first two AFL championship games. Cannon led the AFL in rushing in 1961.

The Oilers traded him to Oakland in 1964, and head coach Al Davis felt Cannon's blend of size and speed would make him well suited to playing tight end. He was right. Within a few years, Cannon emerged as one of the best of his era. He caught 10 touchdown passes in 1967 and appeared in three more AFL title games with the Raiders.

Others

 # 26. Bob Tucker (1970–1980)

 # 27. Rodney Holman (1982–1995)

 # 28. Mickey Shuler (1978–1991)

 # 29. Willie Frazier (1964–1975)

 # 30. Antonio Gates (2003-2007)

 # 31. Jim Whalen (1965–1971)

 # 32. Milt Morin (1966–1975)

 # 33. Dave Kocourek (1960–1968)

 # 34. Henry Childs (1974–1984)

 # 35. Preston Carpenter (1956–1967)

 # 36. Charle Young (1973–1985)

 # 37. Eric Green (1990–1999)

 # 38. Jackie Harris (1990–2001)

 # 39. Russ Francis (1975–1988)

 # 40. Ted Kwalick (1969–1977)

 # 41. Todd Heap (2001–2007)

 # 42. Fred Arbanas (1962–1970)

 # 43. Jerome Barkum (1972–1983)

 # 44. Jimmie Giles (1977–1989)

 # 45. Alge Crumpler (2001–2007)

 # 46. Jeremy Shockey (2002–2007)

 # 47. Freddie Jones (1997–2004)

 # 48. Doug Cosbie (1979–1988)

 # 49. Paul Coffman (1978–1988)

 # 50. Tony McGee (1993–2003)

Offensive Linemen

#1

Jim Otto (1960–1974)

There is a Catch-22 with offensive linemen. They play an integral role in the offense, but they are largely anonymous. On the one hand, this would be a great opportunity to expand on who the great linemen were and what made them great. On the other hand, I'm not sure if the average fan is that interested in reading about them in great detail.

Jim Otto is one of those great characters that most football fans have heard about, although very few can tell you anything about him other than the fact that he played for the Raiders. When he first came to the NFL, Otto weighed just over 200 pounds. That size disadvantage forced him to develop his footwork and use his speed to contend with much bigger defenders. He eventually bulked up to about 250, but he was still able to cover more range as a blocker than most other centers. Otto set the tone for the Raiders as a collection of tough, scrappy, blue-collar players who didn't fit pro football's conservative mold. That's a persona that Raiders players continue to embrace to this day.

Oakland had the AFL's most productive offense in 1969 and 1970, and they remained No. 1 after joining the NFL in 1970. While the team never led the league in rushing yards, they were in the top ten every year that Otto played. The low totals were mainly a function of Oakland's vertical passing offense; the Raiders had just one 1000-yard rusher in their ten AFL seasons. A better measure of their run blocking was their rushing average, and the Raiders led the AFL in yards per run three times.

Later in his career, Otto helped to mentor two younger linemen who would end up in the Hall of Fame: tackle Art Shell and guard Gene Upshaw.

#2

Bruce Matthews (1983–2001)

Matthews was the premier lineman of his era, a player who was among the best all-time at the two diverse skills of pass blocking and run blocking.

This diversity enabled him to play all five positions on the offensive line. Matthews started at right guard as a rookie, but the Oilers moved him to center the following year. He spent his third season at right tackle, and his fourth at left tackle. Matthews would eventually find his home in the interior line. He was a consensus pick for All-Pro at guard six times and three more times at center.

With Mathews as the anchor of their line, the Oilers made the playoffs each year from 1987 to 1993. Although many linemen in his era absorbed pass rushers or pushed them out of the way, Matthews was much more aggressive. He preferred to attack defensive linemen rather than reacting to their moves.

3

Gene Hickerson (1958–1973)

With the induction of Bruce Matthews and Gene Hickerson in 2007, the number of offensive linemen in the Hall of Fame rose to forty-eight. If you take all the modern quarterbacks and running backs combined you'll get exactly the same number. If nothing else, this shows you the high regard that the Hall has had for linemen.

Unfortunately, I'm not sure the standards they've used to choose those linemen have always been consistent. Hickerson is No. 3 in my rankings, yet he waited for more than thirty years before he was selected. Even if you exclude the players who are still active or aren't yet eligible, there are still six linemen in my top-25 who haven't been invited to Canton. We should debate the merits of each guy individually, of course. However, with forty-eight linemen already in and so many strong candidates being overlooked, I think it's time to step back and look at how we should be rating and ranking offensive linemen.

I don't want this book to be seen as a rant against the Hall's voting process, but rather as a call for football historians to approach their work with some sort of consistent methodology. Whether you like my tools for measuring players or you prefer someone else's, there has to be some deliberative process.

It's hard to wrap your head around the problem when you consider how many candidates the Hall of Fame voters have to deliberate. So let's make it simpler. Imagine for a moment that you're asked to decide between two players for a spot in the Hall of Fame. They both played the same position at roughly the same time. Let's say Hickerson and Jerry Kramer. What criteria would you use to weigh the two?

That's essentially the dilemma that the Seniors Committee faced in selecting their two finalists in January 2007. When asked how they did it, committee member Don Pierson of the *Chicago Tribune* said his deliberation was "based on Pro Bowls and testimony I've seen and heard over the years." With all due respect to Pierson, there ought to be more to the selection process than that.

Look, I realize that there are no individual statistics available to judge offensive linemen, but there has to be a better process for picking Hall of Famers than simply counting Pro Bowl appearances and collecting quotes. Finding those two things is easy. Roger Brown, a great defensive tackle with the Lions and Rams says, "Jerry Kramer was head and shoulders above Gene Hickerson." Hall of Famer Bob Lilly says that Hickerson was "the premier pulling guard of his era." Jethro Pugh of the Cowboys says, "I think they were almost equal." I respect their opinions, because those men had to face both Kramer and Hickerson, but even well-respected opinions should not be the foundation of our research.

In my mind, the measure of success for offensive linemen is simple. Their job is to help the running game with their blocking and to protect their quarterback on passing plays. The NFL did not track quarterback sacks on the team level until 1963, so that limits our ability to rate linemen from earlier seasons on their pass-protection abilities. But we can discern who the best run blockers were by looking at team rushing stats back to 1932. I'd love it if we had better data to work with, but that's what we have. While it might be inadequate for making fine distinctions between players or looking at short time spans, it's more than adequate for separating the studs from the duds over the course of their careers.

In Hickerson's case, the evidence makes a compelling case. In his first ten seasons, the Browns led the league in rushing yards six times, and had the league's highest rushing average seven times. He blocked for two Hall of Fame running backs— Jim Brown and Leroy Kelly. (You could even argue that he blocked for a third, Bobby Mitchell, although Mitchell had his best seasons after he was traded to the Redskins.)

The Browns ran their sweep play with Hickerson pulling out and leading the way. He didn't just push defenders out of the running lane. He flattened people. I won't claim that Hickerson made Jim Brown a great runner, but you have to believe he made Brown better. You also have to credit Hickerson for the fact that Cleveland continued to be the league's top-ranked rushing offense in the years after Brown retired.

Hickerson started to get the recognition he deserved once Brown was gone. He was voted to play in the Pro Bowl for six consecutive years (1965–1970), and when the league picked its All-Sixties team, Hickerson was one of two guards selected.

#4
Jackie Slater (1976–1995)

Slater was a great pass blocker, in part because of his long arms and remarkable upper body strength. The scouting reports described him as a "technician," which often is code for a player who gets too fancy. In Slater's case, it was a compliment on his meticulous technique. He could outmuscle defenders when he needed to, but more often he relied on balance, good hands, and strong footwork.

Of course, Slater was also a dominating run blocker. During the course of his career he opened holes for seven different 1000-yard rushers. The most notable of those was Eric Dickerson, who rushed for a rookie-record 1808 yards in 1983 and set the single-season record with 2105 a year later.

Slater became the first NFL player to spend 20 seasons with one team. In more than 40 percent of his games (107 out of 259), a running back rushed for over 100 yards.

#5
Gene Upshaw (1967–1981)

At 6-foot-5, Upshaw was taller than most other guards of his era. Raiders owner Al Davis says that he drafted Upshaw so he would have somebody to block Kansas City's Buck Buchanan, a 6-foot-7 terror. "I figured we'd better get some big guy who could handle him," Davis explained.

He and Buchanan had some classic battles, and Upshaw quickly established himself as one of the league's best all-around linemen. In his second season, the Raiders led the league with a 4.6-yard rushing average. A year later, they allowed just 12 sacks in fourteen games. The strong play of Upshaw and his teammates on the line helped propel the Raiders to the AFL title game in each of his first four seasons. Upshaw would appear in three Super Bowls, losing in Super Bowl II but winning rings after the 1976 and 1980 seasons

Upshaw was active in union activities during his playing career, and shortly after retiring he became executive director of the NFL Player's Association. He led an unsuccessful player strike in 1987, then spent two years pursuing antitrust claims against the league in court. Ultimately, Upshaw prevailed, and he forged an agreement with new commissioner Paul Tagliabue that has worked quite well. In the twenty years that have followed, the NFL has not had a work stoppage. The NBA, NHL, and Major League Baseball all endured costly strikes during the 1990s and saw their popularity (and profitability) plummet in the aftermath. The combination of free agency and a salary cap gave both owners and players a system that they could live with, and the game's popularity (and profitability) have soared.

Upshaw has also been harshly criticized for failing to provide better retirement benefits for those players who retired before the pension system was created. There are Hall of Fame players in their sixties who receive pensions of less than $200 a month, many of whom are overwhelmed by their medical bills. Upshaw responded to his critics by saying the union had spent millions of dollars on players who weren't actually members of the pension plan. In fairness, it's an incredibly complex and complicated issue, but it's hard to reconcile a league that generates billions of dollars in revenues each year with the image of these neglected stars.

#6
John Hannah (1973–1985)

One of the great run blockers, Hannah attacked defenders with brute strength. He was an All-Pro for ten consecutive seasons, widely recognized during his career as the best guard of his era. The Patriots power running game thrived with Hannah controlling the middle of the field or pulling on sweeps. The Patriots rushed for an NFL record 3165 yards in 1978, and I'd bet that even Patriots fans won't remember who their running backs were that season without looking them up. It was all about the blocking.

Hannah used his forearm to dispatch defenders who stood in his path. His love for football may have been genetic. His father Herb played tackle for the New York Giants and his younger brother Charley spent ten years in the NFL with the Raiders and Buccaneers.

#7
Will Shields (1993–2006)

Shields earned eleven Pro Bowl invitations and didn't miss a single game in fifteen years with the Chiefs. During that time, Kansas City finished in the top-five in rushing yards eight different times.

While some guards use their upper bodies to drive, Shields used his legs. If he got a defender squared up he could push the pile back. He was a good pass blocker early in his career, but began to struggle with one-gap pass rushers as he got older.

#8
Randall McDaniel (1988–2001)

McDaniel had one of the most awkward stances I've ever seen for a lineman. He crouched with his left leg bowed way out to the side. If you didn't already know he was one of the greats, just looking at him lining up would make you conclude he didn't know what he was doing. McDaniel looked like he couldn't possibly generate any push from that position, but he was one of the most powerful run blockers of the nineties.

The unusual stance came as the result of a knee injury early in his career. McDaniel simply couldn't bend the knee, and the only way he could get low enough was to lean over to the side. It seemed to work. Defenders had a hard time reading him, figuring out what McDaniel was going to do by the way he lined up. After his knee recovered, McDaniel stuck with the stance.

With McDaniel anchoring the line, the Vikings became an offensive juggernaut in the late 1990s, capped by an astonishing 1998 season in which they scored an NFL-record 556 points. During his thirteen-year career, McDaniel blocked for five different 1000-yard rushers and four 3,000-yard passers.

#9
Jim Ringo (1953–1967)

An undersize center, Ringo became a star with the pre-Lombardi Green Bay Packers. Those were some pretty bad teams, but Ringo earned All-Pro honors and Pro Bowl invitations when the team finished 3-9 in 1957 and 1-10-1 in 1958.

Once Lombardi arrived, Ringo really began to flourish. His speed and agility made him ideally suited to the coach's power running game. In fact, you could make the case that Lombardi built that offense around Ringo. His ability to make the cut-off blocks on the sweep play helped Paul Hornung become a productive NFL back and later, propelled Jim Taylor to the Hall of Fame.

His relatively small stature didn't mean that Ringo lacked power. He attacked middle linebackers on straight-ahead running plays, cutting them off before they could reach the ball carrier.

The Packers won the NFL championship in 1961 and 1962, and a year later Ringo was traded to the Eagles. There's a story about how that transaction happened, that Ringo walked into Lombardi's office with an agent, asking for a substantial raise. Agents were new to the sports world, and the conservative Lombardi wasn't too happy to have this intermediary present. Lombardi excused himself, left the room for a few minutes, and returned to tell the agent, "go talk to the Eagles about it. Mr. Ringo has been traded to Philadelphia."

It's a great story that illustrates Lombardi's no-nonsense management style, but it didn't actually happen that way. Ringo wanted to go back to the Philadelphia area, his home, and Lombardi felt that an aging Ringo needed to be replaced. It was a deal that made both parties happy, not to mention the Eagles. In return, the Packers netted All-Pro linebacker Lee Roy Caffey and a first-round draft pick, which they used to select punter/fullback Donny Anderson.

Lombardi was the one who perpetuated the myth about the Ringo trade, partly to bolster his image and partly to discourage other players from playing hardball in negotiations.

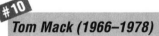

Tom Mack (1966–1978)

Mack had a rare combination of size and speed. He was strong enough to steamroll defenders, but also quick enough to lead a runner around the outside on a sweep. Mack went to eleven Pro Bowls in his thirteen-year career, and helped lead the Rams to eight division titles.

It was the Rams defense that got most of the attention in those years, but the consistently strong running game was what kept the team in the play-offs. Mack anchored a line that made it possible to run the ball well despite a lack of stars in the backfield. He also helped improve the pass protection, dropping their sack totals from an average of 56.3 in the three years before he arrived to 20.0 per year at his peak.

George Allen was the Rams head coach when Mack arrived, a man whose strategy was to stock-pile veteran players. Mack was one of just two rookies who stuck on the roster in 1966, and it's a testament to his skill that Allen made him a starter so quickly.

Ron Mix (1960–1971)

People who don't follow football have a perception of lineman as big dumb brutes. In my experience, they're often the smartest guys on the team. Mix was a great example of that. He was nicknamed "The Intellectual Assassin" because of his cerebral approach to the tackle position. He also earned his law degree while playing for the San Diego Chargers.

Mix says that he originally intended just to play pro football for a year or two, to earn some money while he continued his education. As he began to have success at the pro level, he says that he began to enjoy the game more. He anchored the Chargers line and helped them to dominate the AFL's Western Division. Legend has it that he was called for a holding penalty just twice in ten years. Mix was named All-AFL in each of his first nine seasons, eight times at tackle and once as a guard.

After an injury-plagued 1969 season, Mix retired to pursue a political career. Nothing substantial materialized, and he returned after a year off to play one more season with the Raiders.

Anthony Munoz (1980–1992)

I'd like to say that Munoz changed the way the tackle position was played. However, it's more accurate to say that he played the game on a completely different level than those that came before him, and while those that followed aspired to Munoz's standard, none have reached it.

Munoz was massive—6-foot-6 and 280 pounds—but he had the agility of a running back. His remarkable footwork and balance made him tremendously athletic. The speed pass rushers couldn't get around him. Munoz had an interesting technique for dealing with them. Rather than trying to counter their moves with his own technique, Munoz would simply back off after the initial contact and let the defender do his thing. Then he would pounce, using his quickness and agility to get right back in the guy's face and take him where he wanted him to go.

As a run blocker, Munoz was overwhelming. He could block straight-on, he could pull and trap, he could do it all. Several times a game he would pancake somebody, driving them completely off their feet and onto the ground. From 1986 to 1989, the Bengals had the league's most productive running game, and Munoz was the primary reason. Although the team struggled to win consistently during the eighties, they reached the Super Bowl twice during the decade. Each time, their power running game was the foundation of their success.

#13 Lou Groza (1946–1967)

Groza is one of a handful of players in pro football who was truly great at two different positions. Because he was an exceptional kicker, people tend to overlook just how dominating he was as a lineman.

The Browns offense dominated the AAFC for four seasons and didn't lose any momentum when they joined the NFL in 1950. After winning every AAFC championship, the Browns advanced to the NFL title game seven times in their first eight seasons after the merger.

The contributions of offensive linemen were rarely recognized in the forties and fifties. For Groza, it was even more difficult to get attention on a team that was overflowing with stars. He didn't receive All-AAFC honors as the league's best tackle in any of the league's four seasons, and didn't win All-NFL until 1951. Groza began to stand out as the Browns started running the ball more, but the increased exposure of the National Football League had a lot to do with it, too. Groza was a consensus All-Pro six times from 1951 to 1957.

A back injury kept him out of action in 1960, and when he returned he could no longer play the line. He spent seven seasons as a kicking special-ist, earning the nickname "Lou the Toe." Although he got much more notoriety as a kicker than he ever did as a tackle, Groza preferred to be remembered as a lineman who just happened to kick.

#14 Forrest Gregg (1956–1971)

Gregg was a tall agile blocker who used his athleticism to handle bigger defenders. He played right tackle for Vince Lombardi's Packers, winning five NFL championships in seven years.

He wasn't strong enough to outmuscle linebackers or defensive linemen, so Gregg relied instead on great footwork and his remarkable ability to maintain his balance. His agility served him well in 1965 when he moved from tackle to guard, filling in for an injured Fuzzy Thurston. Although he had never played the position before, Gregg was a first-team All-Pro selection. He earned the honor five times at tackle.

Gregg spent his last few seasons in Green Bay as a player-coach, and would go on to spend eleven seasons as an NFL head coach with three different teams. His best success came in Cincinnati, where he led the Bengals to the Super Bowl in his second season at the helm.

In 1980, the Bengals had the No. 3 overall pick in the draft, and some within the organization wanted to select USC tackle Anthony Munoz. Others were concerned about a knee injury the young man had suffered as a senior, worried that the hype exceeded the skill. Gregg silenced them all by saying he'd find out for himself how good the kid was. Gregg flew to California and went on the field with Munoz to run through some drills. He'd lost some of his quickness at 47 years old, but he could tell right away the kid was going to be a great one. He was right of course. Gregg rebuilt the Bengals with a powerful offense line, adding not just Munoz but also guard Max Montoya and center Dave Rimington during his short tenure.

#15
Dick Schafrath (1959–1971)

Schafrath earned six straight Pro Bowl invitations and teamed with guard Gene Hickerson to help give the Browns the most dominating ground attack in the sixties. Schafrath was a great downfield blocker who helped Hall of Fame backs Jim Brown and Leroy Kelly turn short runs into long ones.

While most linemen labor in obscurity, Schafrath got attention for some of the crazy things he did off the field. He once wrestled a bear. He liked to enter eating competitions. He became the first person to canoe across Lake Erie. To win a bet, he ran nonstop from Municipal Stadium in Cleveland to his high school in Wooster, Ohio—a distance of seventy miles.

#16
Willie Roaf (1993–2005)

Roaf has a decent shot at being elected to the Hall of Fame, and he would become the first player inducted in Canton who spent most of his career with the Saints. Roaf spent nine seasons there, earning seven Pro Bowl invitations but only reaching the playoffs once.

He was remarkably strong, using his legs to drive blocks and using his arms to control pass rushers. He understood the importance of blocking angles as well as any lineman of his era, knowing that he could deflect and redirect defenders past the pocket.

Roaf will be best remembered for opening holes for running backs like Ricky Williams, Priest Holmes, and Larry Johnson. He was underrated as a pass blocker, though, helping journeymen quarterbacks like Jim Everett and Trent Green play their best football when they were in their mid-thirties.

#17
Jim Tyrer (1961–1974)

Life after football isn't always easy. Players who accomplish great things on the field, like Jim Tyrer did, find that success off the gridiron can be more elusive.

For fourteen seasons with the Chiefs, he was hailed as one of the game's great linemen. He earned All-Pro honors for ten straight seasons, first in the AFL and then in the post-merger NFL. Tyrer won three AFL titles and went to two Super Bowls with the Chiefs, playing a key role in their 23–7 upset of the Vikings in Super Bowl IV.

After retiring, the glory faded, and while several of his teammates found successful careers as coaches, broadcasters, or businessmen, Tyrer struggled. He turned down an offer from the Chiefs to work as a scout, opting instead to work as a salesman. The low wages and grueling travel wore him down, and over the next few years he tried his hand at several businesses, all of which failed.

The debt grew and so did his frustration. It came to a head in 1980, five years after he'd retired. Tyrer spent the afternoon at the Chiefs' game with his ten-year-old son. After returning home, he waited until his family went to bed, then fatally shot his wife, Martha, before turning the gun on himself. Tyrer left behind four children, including seventeen-year-old son Bradley, who hid under his bed for an hour after he heard the gunshots, fearing that intruders had come into the house.

Washington Post Ken Denlinger put the tragedy into perspective when he wrote: "There were so many contradictions, so much irony. The largest Chief was the weakest, the most outwardly secure the most inwardly bedeviled. The pride that made Tyrer a special football player might well have cost him his life."

The murder-suicide helped open people's eyes to the struggles of athletes in adjusting to life after athletics. It also prompted NFL teams to be more cognizant of mental health issues.

Tyrer's tragic end overshadowed his accomplishments as a player. He was a finalist for the Hall of Fame in 1981, a few months after his death. In the twenty-five years that have followed, his name hasn't appeared on the ballot again.

Lomas Brown (1985–2002)

One of the premier tackles of the nineties and a blocker who helped spring undersized running back Barry Sanders. With the Lions spread offense, most of their running plays went to the outside, and Sanders had his greatest success running behind Brown on the left side.

Brown wasn't always overpowering but he was tenacious, staying with his blocks until the ball carrier had gone past. He was also an outstanding pass blocker, although the Lions never had much success with their passing game.

After eleven seasons with the Lions, Brown bounced around for seven more years. He started at left tackle for the Giants in Super Bowl XXXV and won a ring as a backup with the Buccaneers two years later.

Bruno Banducci (1944–1954)

The Cleveland Browns dominated the AAFC for four seasons, but the 49ers were a not-too-distant second. While the Browns' passing game soared, San Francisco won games with their dominating ground attack. They led the AAFC in rushing yards three out of four seasons, then finished first in the NFL each year from 1952 to 1954.

Guard Bruno Banducci was the cornerstone of the offensive line that made that possible. In fact, in his nine seasons with the 49ers, the team ranked 1st or 2nd in rushing yards eight times, and led the league in rushing average six times. We don't have sack statistics from the era, but one researcher who

reviewed the games from 1954 reports that Banducci and his teammates allowed just 8 sacks in 1954. That would have been the all-time record until the Dolphins surrendered 7 in 1988.

Banducci only went to one Pro Bowl, but he was named All-Pro seven times. The year after he retired, the Niners rushing offense fell apart, even though the backfield still featured three future Hall of Famers (Joe Perry, Hugh McElhenny, and John Henry Johnson).

Mike Webster (1974–1990)

Webster anchored the Steelers line for fifteen years. He was an All-Pro nine times and played in each of the Steelers four Super Bowl championships. He was perhaps the best ever at the cut-block, where instead of attacking a player's upper body, you dive at his ankles. If the defender is looking into the backfield, he won't see it coming, and before he knows what hit him he's on the ground. In the years since Webster retired, the technique has become controversial although it remains legal. When done incorrectly—or maliciously—the cut block can shred a knee or break a leg.

Webster's stellar career was overshadowed by his tragic life after football. Like many former players, his body had been worn out and used up. The toll on his brain was more troubling. By his early forties he was showing signs of dementia and symptoms of Parkinson's disease. He had suffered seizures and was taking a cocktail of medication for anxiety and depression.

When Webster died in 2002 at the age of fifty, the official cause of death was a heart attack. An investigative report by ESPN's Greg Garber helped tell the sad story of his life after football. Webster had been homeless in the last few years of his life, spending his days at the Amtrak station in Pittsburgh "glassy-eyed like a punch-drunk boxer, huddled alone, staring into space at night." He slept in an old pickup truck, with a garbage bag taped up over the broken back window. He'd go for days without eating, often telephoning friends and family late at night and rambling incoherently.

Everyone had tried to help him . . . friends, family, teammates, even fans. But they couldn't prevent the onetime star from meeting such a tragic end.

#21 Larry Little (1967–1980)

Little was a devastating run blocker who helped make the Miami ground attack so dominant in the early seventies. The Dolphins were equally successful giving the ball to a power runner like Larry Csonka or to a speedster like Mercury Morris, thanks in large part to Little's diverse skills as a blocker.

He was an outstanding pulling guard who excelled at making blocks in the open field. He was fast, and when he got his 265-pound frame moving, the momentum would hit defenders like a runaway bus.

#22 Walt Sweeney (1963–1975)

Sweeney played alongside tackle Ron Mix on the right side of the Chargers line for his first six years. During that time, the team led the league in rushing twice and passing once. Sweeney was a big powerful blocker who was named All-Pro six times. He spent his last two seasons with the Redskins as a member of George Allen's "Over the Hill Gang."

In 1997, Sweeney won a judgment against the NFL in federal court for $1.8 million. He claimed that his post-football life had been ruined by drug addiction, a problem that began when trainers began giving him amphetamines before games and depressants to bring him down afterward.

The case provided an interesting footnote to the story documented in the 1976 book *The Nightmare Season*. The book was written by Arnold Mandell, a psychiatrist who gained notoriety at the time for his work with the Chargers. He was hailed as the first "football psychiatrist," and profiled on

60 Minutes and in *Reader's Digest*. Mandell tried to help the team play better by administering mood-altering drugs, and commissioner Pete Rozelle eventually banned him for prescribing them to eleven players.

#23 Larry Allen (1994–2007)

Allen combined brute strength with a nasty on-field demeanor, intimidating opponents both physically and psychologically. "Basically I try to go out there and punk them, make them quit," Allen said of his Sunday routine. "It's either him or me and it's not going to be me." Defenders dreaded having to face him, even going so far as to feign injury to get out of the assignment. Michael Strahan of the division rival Giants said, "The saddest thing is how many players will watch him on film during the week and then, as the game gets closer, they pull up with some mysterious injury or flu or something. We call that catching 'Allen-itis.'"

Allen was a seven time All-Pro and went to eleven Pro Bowls, moving between four different positions on the offensive line. At the age of thirty-four, Allen won the "Strongest Man" competition during the 2006 Pro Bowl weekend. He defended that title a year later, beating out a group of competitors who were significantly younger than him.

#24 Roy Foster (1982–1993)

Foster is one of the most overlooked linemen of the modern era. I think this is largely due to the fact that he spent half of his career lined up next to Hall of Fame center Dwight Stephenson. For nine straight years (1982–1990), the Dolphins gave up the fewest sacks of any NFL team. That nine-year stretch began the year Foster joined the Dolphins and ended the year after he left.

A third of that streak came after Stephenson had retired, which I think stands as strong evidence of Foster's individual contribution. In the first year after Stephenson retired, Foster and his teammates set an NFL record by yielding just 7 sacks in sixteen games. They went nineteen consecutive games without allowing a sack, a streak that stretched from until October 2, 1988, to October 29, 1989.

Foster left Miami as a free agent after the 1990 season to join the 49ers. San Francisco's sack total dropped from 37 to 24 in Foster's first year in the lineup. It was with the Niners that Foster could finally showcase his skills as a run blocker. That had been his biggest strength in college, where he opened holes for Heisman Trophy–winners Marcus Allen and Charles White at USC. The Dolphins had never run the ball well during Foster's tenure, mostly because they were so focused on their passing game.

Joe DeLamielleure (1973–1985)

His teammate Reggie McKenzie got more press, but DeLamielleure came to be recognized as the best player on Buffalo's vaunted offensive line. The Bills linemen earned the nickname the "Electric Company" because "they turned the Juice loose." The Juice was O.J. Simpson, who became the first player to top the 2000-yard mark in 1973.

DeLamielleure was an All-Pro at guard nine times, helping the Bills lead the NFL in rushing yards in 1973 and 1975. He was traded to the Browns in 1980, and while there he earned a reputation as a strong pass blocker. He helped the Browns get to the playoffs twice in four seasons.

Others

 # 26. Kevin Mawae (1994–2007)

 # 27. Duane Putnam (1952-1962)

 # 28. Dan Dierdorf (1971–1983)

 # 29. Gary Zimmerman (1986–1997)

 # 30. Tom Nalen (1994–2007)

 # 31. Winston Hill (1963–1977)

 # 32. Richmond Webb (1990–2002)

 # 33. Ray Brown (1986–2005)

 # 34. Bob Brown (1964–1973)

 # 35. Nate Newton (1986–1999)

 # 36. Jim Langer (1970–1981)

 # 37. Steve Wisniewski (1989–2001)

 # 38. Tom Banks (1971–1980)

 # 39. Bob Young (1968–1981)

 # 40. Ken Iman (1960–1974)

 # 41. Len Rohde (1960–1974)

 # 42. Ed White (1969–1985)

 # 43. Ernie McMillan (1961–1975)

 # 44. Bob St. Clair (1953–1963)

 # 45. Jerry Kramer (1958–1968)

 # 46. John Wooten (1959–1968)

 # 47. Conrad Dobler (1972–1981)

 # 48. Mike Munchak (1982–1993)

 # 49. Dwight Stephenson (1980–1987)

 # 50. Art Shell (1968–1982)

Defensive Linemen

1

Bruce Smith (1985–2003)

Smith retired with the NFL record for sacks, amassing 200 in his nineteen-year career. He had at least 10 sacks in fourteen seasons and was a key member of a Buffalo Bills defense that went to four straight Super Bowls. Smith was big and strong, but the secret to his success as a pass rusher was his remarkable speed. Early in his career, he would beat tackles to the outside just with his quickness, and it didn't take long for teams to start double-teaming him on every down. To compensate, Smith developed an inside move that was equally dangerous.

His best season came in 1990, when he registered 19 sacks and helped lead the Bills to their first Super Bowl appearance. In that game, he registered a safety by sacking Giants quarterback Jeff Hostetler in the end zone. He also made a key tackle on a fourth-down play near the end of the third quarter, stopping Ottis Anderson for a 2-yard loss to give the Bills possession.

The *Associated Press* named Smith as the Defensive Player of the Year that season, an award he would win again in 1996. Only six players have received that honor more than once.

Although he is best known for his prowess in sacking the quarterback, Smith was equally phenomenal against the run. Typically, the strategy for blocking a defensive end on a running play is to move him to the outside. That didn't work against Smith. He had an unusual stance, standing somewhat upright with his legs far apart. This enabled him to control his center of gravity unusually well for a big man. It wasn't enough to simply bump him out of the running lane. You had to block him and keep blocking him, otherwise Smith would fight his way through traffic and make the tackle. He also refused to rely just on his speed or his strength to get separation, the way that so many defensive linemen do. He had great hand techniques and a number of moves that helped him shed blockers.

2

Reggie White (1985–2000)

True free agency began in the NFL in 1993, and the biggest player on the market was Eagles defensive end Reggie White. His resume included seven Pro Bowl appearances and the 1987 Defensive Player of the Year Award. Every team was interested, and some teams pulled out all the stops in their courtship of the thirty-one-year-old star.

Critics of the new free agency agreement warned that the top players would quickly migrate to the teams in big cities, where larger revenue streams would allow them to offer bigger contracts. White confounded those critics by signing with the Packers, who played in the NFL's smallest market. He had said that his priorities were winning a Super Bowl and establishing a ministry that would help the African-American community of an inner city. Green Bay didn't seem to offer either of those things, but what they could offer was a significant amount of money. The team's four-year $17 million contract was significantly more than most other teams could put on the table.

Why did he pick the Packers? White's public explanation was "God told me to come to Green Bay." The message was clear: Green Bay was a great place to be, a strong organization on the verge of winning. Other players soon followed White, signing free agent contracts with the Packers. Among them were established stars such as tight end Keith Jackson, defensive linemen Sean Jones and Santana Dotson, linebacker Seth Joyner, and return man Desmond Howard. Four years after White arrived, the Packers made the first of what would be two straight Super Bowl appearances, and each of those free agent additions made a significant impact on one or both of those teams.

In the twenty-five years before White came to Green Bay, the Packers had enjoyed just six winning seasons. They had a winning record in each of the six seasons White played in Green Bay, and have had just one losing record in the seven years since he retired. That, my friends, is what we call a turning point.

White died suddenly at the age of forty-three from respiratory disease (specifically sarcoidosis). He had suffered from sleep apnea for several years, a disease that afflicts many football players because of their size. His untimely death helped to raise awareness about the health challenges that NFL players face after their retirement.

Merlin Olsen (1962–1976)

A gentle giant, Olsen was a member of the Rams' dominant defensive line that came to be called "The Fearsome Foursome." Olsen and Rosey Grier were the tackles with Deacon Jones and Lamar Lundy playing end. All were great players, but it was the steady consistent play of Olsen in the middle that made it possible for the other players to wreak havoc on the outside.

He was agile and fast for a player his size, but Olsen was most often praised for his intelligence. He earned a master's degree in economics while he was playing for the Rams, and his ability to dissect the offense and identify screens and draw plays gave opposing teams fits.

With Olsen leading the league's stingiest defense, the Rams went to the playoffs in 1967 and again in 1969. They won the NFC West title four straight times from 1973 to 1976, ranking 1st in run defense three times and ranking in the top five in sacks each year. After he retired, Olsen remained in the public spotlight as a pitchman for FTD florists and a color commentator on NBC's pro football coverage. He also had a successful acting career, appearing for five seasons on the popular show *Little House on the Prairie* and playing the title role in the series *Father Murphy*. He also appeared in a number of motion pictures, mostly Westerns, including John Wayne's *The Undefeated*.

Bob Lilly (1961–1974)

In the 1960s, teams would run the ball about 60 percent of the time. Cowboys head coach Tom Landry believed that the key to success was to stop the run on first and second down, and to do that he developed his Flex Defense. Lilly had been a defensive end in college, but Landry moved him inside to tackle, where his quickness made him perfectly suited for Landry's scheme.

The Flex Defense was essentially a zone defense against the run. By moving Lilly back from the line of scrimmage a step or two, it helped to improve his pursuit angles. Lilly's job was to read the play and react, plugging the gap in front of him if the ball carrier was coming or pursuing him to the outside on a sweep play. Typically, NFL teams would put their faster linemen at the end and their run stuffers in the middle. Using Lilly inside created headaches for opposing teams, because they couldn't seem to find a way to neutralize him.

The expansion Cowboys struggled in their first few seasons, but by 1964 their defense was among the best in the league. By 1966, they had reached the NFL championship game, and they would return to the NFL or NFC title game five times in the next seven seasons. More than any other single player, Lilly personified the relentless fury of the Cowboys defense that was responsible for that success.

Joe Greene (1969–1981)

Greene appeared in a memorable Super Bowl commercial near the end of his career. In it, he's limping down the tunnel toward the locker room after a game, worn out and somewhat dejected. A young boy offers him his bottle of Coca-Cola, which he begrudgingly accepts. As he drinks it, his mood is transformed. As the kid slinks away, Greene calls out to him and tosses his jersey to the kid in thanks.

The commercial played off of the reputation Greene had earned as the toughest, gruffest guy in football. His nickname was "Mean Joe" Greene after all, although his first name was actually Charles; the moniker was a reference to his college team, the North Texas State Mean Green.

Greene was a hard hitter, but he used his quickness as much as his strength to neutralize blockers. He developed the technique of lining up at a sharp angle in the guard-center gap—as opposed to lining up with his shoulders square with his opponent's. This helped to disrupt the opponent's blocking assignments and disguised his intentions.

The Steelers defense ranked among the top ten each year from 1972 to 1979, and Greene was both their best player and their emotional leader. The Steel Curtain defense peaked in 1976, when they held their last nine opponents to a total of 28 points, notching 5 shutouts in what was arguably the best defensive performance of the modern era. The Steelers won four Super Bowls in that six-year stretch, and Greene was twice named as the NFL's Defensive Player of the Year.

Randy White (1975–1988)

A few months after Bob Lilly retired, the Cowboys used their first-round draft pick to select White from the University of Maryland. At first, they tried using him at middle linebacker, but it soon became clear he was better suited to playing on the line. He moved back to defensive tackle, and in many ways picked up right were Lilly left off. The two were similar in size and temperament, and both served as the anchor of an aggressive defense.

White earned the nickname "Manster"—as in half man, half monster. Teammates and opponents agreed that off the field, he was one of the nicest guys around. On game day, between the lines, he was just plain mean. From 1975 to 1982, the Cowboys played in six of eight NFC championship games and three Super Bowls. White was named co-MVP of Super Bowl XII (with teammate Harvey Martin).

According to John Turney's research, White registered 111 sacks in his career. That's the most ever for a defensive tackle.

Alan Page (1967–1981)

Page is one of only four defensive players who have been named as the NFL's Most Valuable Player. He earned that honor in 1971, when the

Vikings defense allowed a league-low 139 points in fourteen games. From 1968 to 1977, the team compiled a record of 104-35-1, thanks largely to Page and his teammates on a defense dubbed "The Purple People Eaters."

He had long arms, which he used to get separation from offensive linemen and to block passes. Page often lined up in a three-point stance—as opposed to the four-point stance favored by most defensive linemen of his era. This helped him to take better advantage of his speed and quickness. He was the first defensive tackle to establish himself as an outstanding pass rusher. His massive wingspan also helped him excel at blocking punts and field goal attempts, which he did 28 times during his career.

Many players put on weight as they get older, especially linemen, but Page actually got slimmer. He dropped from 245 pounds to 220 in his last few seasons, due largely to his obsession with long-distance running. One report said that he was running eighty miles a week. Page completed his first marathon in 1979, reportedly the first NFL player to do so.

Somehow, between his constant running and his day job playing football, Page also found time to attend law school. He joined a Minneapolis law firm in 1979, and later served as assistant attorney general. In 1993, he was elected to a seat as an associate justice of the Minnesota Supreme Court.

#8

Jack Youngblood (1971–1984)

The Los Angeles Rams played in the NFC championship game five times during Youngblood's career, winning just once. That helps you begin to understand why in 1979, when the Rams won and advanced to the Super Bowl, Jack Youngblood insisted on playing even though he'd broken his leg two weeks earlier.

The injury occurred in the opening round of the playoffs against Dallas, but Youngblood played the rest of that game, and played the NFC championship game against Tampa Bay a week later with his left leg wrapped in tape and splints. Youngblood led a defense that held the Buccaneers to just 7 first downs and 181 yards of offense in a sloppy, 9–0 victory. According to newspaper reports, he took no pain medication other than aspirin. He was willing to endure the agony because he couldn't imagine watching from the sidelines. "If I had a breath in my body, I swore I was going to play," Youngblood told reporters afterwards. "I've known what it felt like to be a loser. Now I know what it feels like to be a winner."

Youngblood played every defensive play in Super Bowl XIV, and the Rams defense stifled Pittsburgh's offense for three quarters before running out of steam. None of the postgame reports mentioned it, but it seems from my viewing of the film that Youngblood might have also broken his left hand in that game.

It was this toughness that earned him national recognition, but he was one of the best defensive players of his era. Sacks were not an official statistics until 1982, but unofficial numbers suggest he was the leading pass rusher of his era. Youngblood also had a habit of screaming like a banshee as he approached the quarterback. This often caused the quarterback to flinch or misfire on his throw even when Youngblood didn't make contact in the backfield.

Youngblood missed just one game in his fourteen-year career, the next-to-last game in his final season. He was named All-Pro nine times and elected to the Pro Football Hall of Fame in 2001.

#9

Deacon Jones (1961–1974)

If you look at highlight films or read newspaper accounts of NFL games from the forties and fifties, you're struck by how infrequently you'll come across any mention of defensive players. The story of a game was told through the scoring plays and the big gains that offensive players made. Unless a defender scored a touchdown, he received little attention.

That all started to change in the sixties, and Deacon Jones was one of the main reasons. He was an unknown player from an obscure little college, but he was determined to make a name for himself in the NFL. He even gave himself a nickname, fearing that nobody would remember a player named David Jones.

He also helped coin a term that described what he did best, the quarterback sack. "You know, like you sack a city," Jones explained. "You devastate it." By giving a name to it, Jones helped bring attention to a particular aspect of defensive play. At the time, the only official statistic kept for individual defensive players was interceptions, and that wasn't a very meaningful statistic for defensive linemen.

Although people started noticing the contributions of pass rushers in the mid-sixties, it wasn't until 1982 that the NFL adopted the sack as an official statistic. That's why you won't find the name Deacon Jones anywhere in the record book. Officially, his sack total is zero.

Football historian John Turney made an attempt to rectify that injustice. In the mid-nineties, he started collecting the unofficial play-by-play accounts that NFL teams make for each of their games. He contacted every NFL team, and with research partner Nick Webster, he traversed the country, visiting the teams and mining their archives for these nuggets of historical data. Turney tells me that between these play-by-plays and the NFL Films archive, he's been able to gather play-by-play accounts from 99 percent of the games played back to 1970, and about 95 percent of the games in the 1960s.

The play-by-play data is immensely valuable because it helps us reconstruct some of the statistics that the NFL didn't keep at the time. For example, the league didn't begin tracking a team's third-down efficiency until 1981. With the play-by-play data, it's easy to go back and make a record of things like that, as well as crediting individual player's who converted a first down. The data would let you count touchbacks or kick inside the 20 for punters. The bit of Turney's research that has attracted the most attention is the sack records.

Sacks are one of the most popular defensive statistics, and it's easy to tell from the play-by-play when a quarterback was tackled for a loss.

The official record shows twenty-one players with at least 100 NFL sacks. Turney's research has turned up twenty-two more, and he's confident that if he could find more play-by-play records, he'd find more unheralded defenders. "I'd love to get a complete total for guys like Len Ford, Gino Marchetti, and Gene Brito," he told me. "But the data from the 1950s is incomplete, and there are even minor gaps in the sixties and seventies."

Here is Turney's list of the top ten all time sack leaders. Official sacks are the ones counted by the NFL since 1982 and unofficial are the ones counted by Turney in 1981 and earlier.

All-Time Sack Leaders

Rank	Total	Unofficial	Official	Player
1	200.0	–	200.0	Bruce Smith
2	198.0	–	198.0	Reggie White
3	173.5	173.5	–	Deacon Jones
4	160.0	–	160.0	Kevin Greene
5	150.5	–	150.5	Chris Doleman
6	150.5	126.5	24.0	Jack Youngblood
7	148.5	148.5	–	Alan Page
8	142.0	7.5	132.5	Lawrence Taylor
9	137.5	–	137.5	John Randle
10	137.5	–	137.5	Richard Dent

The year-by-year record for Jones is quite simply astounding. Despite playing fourteen-game seasons, Jones registered yearly sack totals of 26 (1967), 24 (1968), and 22 (1964). In the more than twenty years since the NFL has been keeping track, no player has had more than one season of 20 sacks in a sixteen-game schedule. Jones did it three times in a five-year span, despite playing fewer games per season.

Deacon Jones Career Statistics

Year	Team	Sacks
1961	LARm	8.0
1962	LARm	9.0
1963	LARm	4.0
1964	LARm	22.0
1965	LARm	18.0
1966	LARm	16.0
1967	LARm	26.0
1968	LARm	24.0
1969	LARm	15.0
1970	LARm	12.0
1971	LARm	4.5
1972	SD	6.0
1973	SD	5.0
1974	Was	3.0

The award for Defensive Player of the Year wasn't given until 1972, but I feel pretty strongly that he would have won it at least twice (1967 and 1968) and perhaps as many as three more times (1966, 1969, 1970). Jones set the standard for modern defensive end play. He was fast and very mobile for his size, which was in stark contrast to the plodding, stay-at-home defensive ends that were typical in his era. Jones's greatest asset was the sprinter-like speed that allowed him to roam from sideline to sideline, delivering what he called "civilized violence." In an effort to control Jones, teams used double- and triple-teams, but that strategy simply freed teammate Merlin Olsen to make plays. Jones also popularized the head slap, a maneuver that later was outlawed by the NFL.

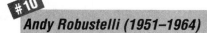

Andy Robustelli (1951–1964)

The record will show that Robustelli is one of four players in my top ten defensive linemen who got their start with the Los Angeles Rams. Merlin Olsen, Jack Youngblood, and Deacon Jones all played for the team at a time when their offense defined them. When Robustelli joined the Rams in 1951, their strength was their high-flying offense. They won the NFL championship in Robustelli's rookie season and advanced to the title game again four years later. It wouldn't be accurate to say that he was underrated, because he was named All-Pro twice in five seasons. However, Robustelli was definitely under-appreciated on a team where offense came first.

He wasn't particularly big for a defensive end, but he was strong and quick. Robustelli had a knack for finding the ball, which made him equally effective in stopping the run and rushing the quarterback.

After the 1955 season, the Rams traded Robustelli to the New York Giants. The Connecticut native longed to play for an east coast club, where he could look after his growing sporting goods business. The Rams were happy to oblige, worrying that at thirty, his skills were beginning to fade.

To the contrary, Robustelli was reborn with the Giants, whose defense was the foundation of their success. He played with renewed vigor, helping the Giants win their first world championship since 1938. Robustelli was the keystone of a smothering defense that advanced to the NFL title game five more times in the seven years that followed. He was named All-Pro seven times with the Giants and was selected Most Valuable Player in 1962, the first defensive player to win the award.

#11
Chris Doleman (1985–1999)

During the late 1980s, many of the teams that had adopted the 3-4 defense began to switch back to the 4-3 defense. As they did this, they found that they missed the speed off the edge that they were getting from the outside linebacker. To compensate, they began to convert outside linebackers into defensive ends, and Chris Doleman was the player who made that conversion most successfully.

He recorded 11 sacks in 1987, the first of eight seasons in which he would reach double digits. Doleman's best season came in 1989 when he led the league with 21 sacks, one shy of Mark Gastineau's single-season record. Despite his success, I'm not sure he was ever regarded as the best pass rusher of his era. He never achieved the stardom of players like Lawrence Taylor or Reggie White.

Doleman spent his first nine seasons with the Vikings before leaving a free agent in 1993. He had tried to leave after the 1989 season, arguing that he wasn't bound by the option clause in his standard player's contract. The league disagreed, and Doleman filed a lawsuit to plead his case. Although it was unsuccessful, he eventually agreed to return to the Vikings with a contract that made him the highest-paid player in team history.

#12 Dan Hampton (1979–1990)

There were a lot of colorful figures on the 1985 Bears defense, often regarded as one of the best defenses in pro football history. While the rest of the guys were inking endorsement deals or filming a music video for the "Super Bowl Shuffle," Hampton preferred a simpler, no-nonsense approach. He wasn't interested in the trappings of success; he just wanted to win, and he would do whatever it took.

Midway through that 1985 season he switched from right tackle to left end, a move that allowed rookie William "the Refrigerator" Perry to get in the lineup. That move was an example not just of Hampton's unselfishness but also his versatility. In his twelve-year career, he spent six seasons at tackle and six at end, earning All-Pro honors at both positions.

#13 Carl Eller (1964–1979)

Overshadowed by younger teammate Alan Page, Eller had to wait twenty-five years after his retirement before he was inducted into the Hall of Fame. Page and Eller formed one of the most prolific pass-rushing duos in pro football history, and helped lead a Vikings defense that dominated the late sixties and early seventies.

Eller was named All-Pro each year from 1967 to 1973, and recorded 44 sacks during a three-year period from 1975 to 1977. His 23 career fumble recoveries was the 3rd most in NFL history when he retired.

Shortly after leaving football, Eller acknowledged that he'd struggled with cocaine addiction during his playing days. In a June 1982 interview with the *New York Times,* he described how his drug use ruined his playing ability:

> Cocaine robbed me of my upper-body strength and it took away my stamina. When I first came into the league, I could stay on the field all afternoon. But after using cocaine, I lost my strength quickly and I would get irritable if we had to stay out there long. In my prime, I could take up the slack and sometimes turn things around by myself. After cocaine became a habit, I had to look to other people for help. I stopped making the most vicious tackle, I lost my sense of intimidation.

Eller wasn't coming out just to tell his own story. He believed that cocaine use was a growing problem for pro football players and he urged the league to do something about it. Eller helped to develop the NFL's first Employee Assistance Program, and later started his own counseling center.

#14 Howie Long (1981–1993)

Long was a troubled kid who grew up in a rough part of Boston, the product of a broken home. His parents had split up, and he spent most of his childhood being shuttled back and forth between relatives. He fought hard to overcome these challenges, earning a scholarship to Villanova, the prestigious Roman Catholic university. His clean, chiseled good looks and quiet demeanor made him seem polished and civilized.

Then he was drafted by the Oakland Raiders.

The Raiders defense had a well-deserved reputation for being wild and crazy. Veteran linemen John Matuszak and Lyle Alzado played with an intensity that seemed at times to leave them out of control. Long would later describe how much he felt out of place as a rookie, and how his confidence wavered when he had to line up across from great players like Art Shell and Gene Upshaw in practice.

Although his teammates challenged him, it wasn't out of a desire to break his spirit. Rather, it was to help unleash the intensity they knew he had within him. It worked. Long recorded 7.5 sacks as a rookie, and by his third year he had become the best player on that Raiders defense. His best season came in 1983 where he registered 13 sacks—including 5 in one game—and helped lead the Raiders to a 38–9 victory over the Redskins in the Super Bowl.

Of all the players I have studied on film, Long was the best at using his hands to create leverage. His trademark was the rip move. From a crouched position, he'd bring his arm under a blocker's arm—an uppercut to the armpit. This move would lift the opposing lineman off his feet or at least knock him off balance, and at that point the battle was over. Long also developed the hump move, which was later emulated with great success by Reggie White. The hump is actually a combination of moves, starting with a quick step to the outside. When the tackle slides out to mirror the defender's movement, Long would club him with his inside arm. If timed right, the tackle's momentum would carry him outside while Long slipped inside.

#15 Ed Jones (1974–1989)

The nickname was inevitable. Listed variously at 6-foot-9 or 6-foot-10, Jones complained that his uniform pants were too short during one of his first college practices. A teammate replied, "they're not too short, you're too tall," and from that day forward, he was known as Ed "Too Tall" Jones.

His height was a great asset, making him a major obstacle for opposing quarterbacks. Often, a team puts its best pass rusher at right end so that they can pursue the quarterback from his blind side. Jones spent his entire career lined up on the left side, which meant he was usually in the quarterback's field of vision. As a result, he deflected a lot of passes. The Cowboys went to three Super Bowls in Jones's first five seasons, and Jones was emerging as a star on one of the league's most dominating defenses. That's why it was so surprising when Jones announced his decision to retire at the age of twenty-eight to pursue a boxing career. Basketball might have made more sense, but Jones professed a passion for the sweet science. After training for almost a year, he entered the ring for a debut bout that was broadcast on national television. The more charitable boxing writers described Jones as clumsy. The legendary Red Smith was more blunt: "[H]e cannot box, he cannot punch, and his chin gives off a musical tinkle when tapped."

Jones fought six bouts, winning five of them by knockout. However, his carefully selected list of opponents offered little competition, and the public's interest in his efforts waned. The Cowboys were happy to welcome Jones back to their lineup, and he picked up right where he left off. To many observers, he seemed to play with a fierce intensity that hadn't been visible prior to his boxing foray. He earned All-Pro honors in 1981 and 1982, becoming one of the most dominant defensive players in the league. With a revitalized defense, the Cowboys advanced to the NFC championship game in the first three seasons after Jones returned. He retired in 1989 after fifteen seasons with the Cowboys—more than any other player.

#16 Alex Karras (1958–1970)

The Detroit mob was at its peak in the 1960s, and bookmaking was one of its major money earners. Two of the city's biggest sports stars were caught up in the action, accused both of having business ties to local organized crime figures and placing illegal bets. Denny McLain won thirty-one games in 1968 and led the Tigers to a World Series win, but his ties to the Detroit crime syndicate would end his career just as it was reaching its peak.

A *Sports Illustrated* cover story accused McLain of running a bookmaking operation, and alleged that his 1967 foot injury (which caused him to miss six starts and cost his team the pennant) was the result of an attack by a mob enforcer. McLain denied both charges, but he was suspended, and he was out of baseball entirely at the age of twenty-eight.

Karras had a similar problem. NFL Commissioner Pete Rozelle had launched an investigation in 1963 to look into allegations of gambling by players. Some of the wilder allegations included claims that games had been thrown, point shaving had occurred, and that star players feigned injury to avoid playing in big games. The investigation found no evidence of that, although Rozelle did fine five members of the Detroit Lions for placing bets on an NFL playoff game between the Packers and the Giants. Green Bay running back Paul Hornung, who had been the main subject of many of the allegations, was suspended after Rozelle found evidence that he'd bet on dozens of games during the 1960, 1961, and 1962 seasons. The evidence also showed that Karras had placed bets on NFL games as far back as the 1958 season.

More troubling was the fact that Karras was co-owner of a sports bar called Lindell's AC, which was widely known as the center of the mob's illegal bookmaking operation in Detroit. Although initially defiant, Karras eventually agreed to sell his interest in the bar and stop associating with individuals termed as "known hoodlums." Hornung and Karras were both suspended indefinitely, but applied for reinstatement a year later. Rozelle ended the suspensions after meeting with each man and concluding "they now have a clear understanding of the seriousness of the offenses and the circumstances that brought them about." Publicly, both men expressed their apologies for their transgressions and said that being forced to

confront their bad behavior was the best thing that ever happened to them.

Because I have written extensively about Pete Rose, I'm often asked about the seeming incongruity between his case and that of Karras and Hornung. There are striking similarities, of course, especially between Rose and Karras. Both were gamblers, and both were running with a bad crowd. Both were confronted with overwhelming evidence of their guilt and had to balance the threat of punishment by their commissioner with ongoing investigations by local and federal law enforcement. Both received an indefinite suspension from the game for their transgressions, with the opportunity to apply for reinstatement after one year.

Of course, the two men handled their situations differently. Rose was recalcitrant, stubbornly refusing to acknowledge he'd done anything wrong. Karras was apologetic, righted his wrongs, and asked forgiveness.

I don't know either Rose or Karras, and I can't claim to understand what's in their heart. However, I don't believe that they necessarily chose different paths because they had a different moral compass. I think it comes down to the fact that each man faced that crossroads with different motivations. Karras was just twenty-eight, a three-time Pro Bowler at the peak of his talents. His career was on the line, and he took the steps necessary to save it.

By contrast, Rose was forty-seven years old when he was summoned to the commissioner's office and confronted with evidence of his wrongdoing. Although he was still serving as manager of his hometown Cincinnati Reds, he'd been retired as a player for two years. What he had left to salvage was his legacy, one that would be tarnished if he acknowledged gambling. In retrospect, his decision to remain defiant was horribly misguided. Rose's reputation was destroyed anyway, and his fifteen-year campaign of denial only made things worse.

Redemption is a complicated subject. I believe it requires not just admitting that you did something wrong, but doing things to make up for your shortcomings. Rose never did that, opting instead to paint himself as a martyr fighting against injustice. McLain certainly did nothing to redeem himself. His transgressions only got worse after he was kicked out of baseball. Karras and Hornung, on the other hand, took steps to earn their forgiveness. Hornung overcame the rumors that he'd given less than his best effort by producing clutch performances in big games for the Packers. Karras had to battle his reputation as a shady character by changing his lifestyle. The public perception of him changed because he changed his behavior.

Karras parlayed his new image into a successful acting career after he retired from the game in 1970. His portrayal of Mongo, the deputy sheriff in the classic comedy *Blazing Saddles* is unforgettable, and he later starred as an adoptive father in the long running sitcom *Webster*.

#17
Michael Strahan (1993-2007)

Strahan set the single-season sack record in 2001, but not without creating some controversy. Heading into the last game of the season against the Packers, he had 21.5 sacks—one shy of Mark Gastineau's record.

With three minutes left in the game, Strahan still hadn't recorded the milestone sack. With his team comfortably ahead, Green Bay quarterback Bret Favre called a running play but kept the ball, scrambled towards Strahan's side of the field, then slid to the ground. Strahan fell on top of him for the record breaker, and as the crowd acknowledged the moment, Favre hugged him.

The move irritated Favre's teammates and his head coach. The next day, Mike Freeman of the *New York Times* wrote "it would have been better for Strahan not to get the record than to get it like this." Favre denied that he had given Strahan the sack, but as Freeman reported, "he could barely do it with a straight face."

Strahan was a more productive pass rusher after he turned thirty, although he missed parts of two seasons due to injuries during his mid-thirties.

Age	Seasons	Games	Sacks	Sacks per 16G
to 29	1993-2000	119	62.0	8.3
30+	2001-2007	97	79.5	13.1

Strahan was equally adept at defending the run and rushing the passer. He faced double-teams throughout most of his career, but his variety of skills made it possible for him to adapt his style of play depending on the opponent. He could use his speed and finesse moves, or he could overpower blockers with his brute strength.

#18
Ron McDole (1961–1978)

The American Football League had a reputation as an offensive league, but the Buffalo Bills of the mid-sixties were one of the great defensive teams in history. They registered 50 sacks in 1964 and had a streak of seventeen straight games without allowing a rushing touchdown. The keystone of that defense was Ron McDole, a defensive end from the University of Nebraska. His nickname was the Dancing Bear, a testament to his agility and quick footwork. On the strength of their defense, the Bills tied for the division title in 1963 and won the AFL championship in 1964 and 1965.

McDole ended his career with 12 interceptions, which remains as the all-time record for a lineman.

#19
Steve McMichael (1980–1994)

Perhaps best remembered today as a professional wrestler, McMichael was a key member of the stifling Bears defenses of the mid-eighties. It was the ends and the linebackers who got most of the glory in Chicago's 46 defense, but none of that would have been possible without the constant pressure from the tackles. McMichael used his size and strength to help control the center of the line, keeping blockers away from middle linebacker Mike Singletary. He was also one of the best inside pass rushers of his era, using a series of agile moves to get into the backfield.

McMichael had 1 of the Bears' 7 sacks in Super Bowl XX and helped hold the Patriots to just 7 rushing yards for the game. He spent his final season (1994) with the Green Bay Packers, starting alongside Reggie White. After retiring from the NFL, he spent four years as a professional wrestler. Using the name Mongo, he won the World Championship Wrestling Heavyweight Championship in 2001.

#20 Gino Marchetti (1953–1966)

He enlisted in the army right out of high school, and Marchetti was just seventeen years old when he fought in the Battle of the Bulge. After that, playing in the trenches of the NFL couldn't have been so tough by comparison. Players from his era like to tell tales of Marchetti playing a game with a separated shoulder, returning to action a week after having surgery for appendicitis, or of breaking his leg in the 1958 championship game and refusing to be taken for medical treatment, watching the classic double-overtime victory from a stretcher on the sidelines.

Marchetti basically invented the position of defensive end at a time when two-way play was coming to an end. He was a relentless run stuffer, but his major innovation was the concept of using the end to rush the quarterback. Prior to that time, ends tended to be big, plodding brutes, but Marchetti had speed and agility.

He was one of the most dominant players of his era and is regarded by many historians as the best defensive end in pro football history. I think that's a hard case to support. Sure, he changed the game, and he was a great player. Even in his own era, however, I have him ranked behind Doug Atkins and Andy Robustelli. And the fact remains that in the forty years since he retired, we've seen other spectacular defensive ends. When players like Marchetti or Don Hutson or Benny Friedman create a new style of play, part of their success is

due to the fact that opposing teams haven't found a way to counter the new strategy. The novelty of Marchetti's ability stood out in the fifties, but defensive ends in later years faced more complex blocking schemes and shouldered more complicated assignments. Marchetti may have been the first great defensive end, but that doesn't mean he was the last.

#21 Doug Atkins (1953–1969)

A prolific pass rusher who was the cornerstone of the great Bears defenses of the early sixties, Atkins was also a basketball star in college and a champion high jumper. His leaping ability came into use on the football field, where he often would hurdle over opposing blockers to get into the backfield. He would sometimes attack by pushing the blocker straight back into the quarterback.

Atkins was a free spirit who played for two no-nonsense coaches, first Paul Brown in Cleveland and then George Halas in Chicago. His easy-going approach irked both men, but his passion on the field was undeniable. Atkins spent his last three seasons with the expansion New Orleans Saints, where he quickly became a fan favorite.

#22 Richard Dent (1983–1997)

Dent was the leading pass rusher on the vaunted Bears defense of the 1980s. He led the league with 17.5 sacks in 1985, and he was a terror during the postseason. In the wild card game against the Giants, Dent forced a pair of fumbles and registered 3.5 sacks. He had another sack and forced fumble in the NFC championship game, and was named MVP of Super Bowl XX with 2 forced fumbles and 1.5 sacks.

Dent was named All-Pro five times with the Bears before leaving as a free agent. He won another Super Bowl ring with the 49ers after the 1994 season, though injuries limited him to just two games. He spent his last few seasons as a pass rushing specialist. Dent ranked 3rd all-time in sacks when he retired.

Buck Buchanan (1963–1975)

Buchanan was a multi-sport athlete at Grambling, starring on the basketball and track teams and playing both offense and defense on the football team. He had tremendous speed, and at 6-foot-7 and 270 pounds, also had the size to be a disruptive presence on the defensive line. Buchanan was the first player selected in the 1963 AFL draft, and he spent his rookie season playing both end and tackle for the Kansas City Chiefs. He eventually settled in at right tackle, earning All-Pro honors for eight straight years, from 1964 to 1971.

The Chiefs strong defense helped them win the AFL Championship in 1966, and four years later they beat Minnesota in Super Bowl IV. Buchanan manhandled Mick Tinglehoff, the undersized Vikings center, in that game. He and his teammates shut down the Vikings running game and battered quarterback Joe Kapp. The Chiefs were 12.5 point underdogs, but they walloped the Vikings by a score of 23-7.

Rosey Grier (1955–1966)

Grier was part of two great defensive lines, each of which earned the nickname "Fearsome Foursome." The first instance was with the Giants in the late fifties. Grier teamed with ends Andy Robustelli and Jim Katcavage and tackle Dick Modzelewski to anchor a dominating defense. In Grier's nine seasons with the Giants, the team advanced to the NFL championship game six times.

In 1964, Grier was traded to the Rams, where he joined Deacon Jones, Merlin Olsen, and Lamar Lundy on the starting line. The "Fearsome Foursome" nickname apparently went with him, as well.

Between both teams, Grier was named All-Pro at defensive tackle for seven straight years. He went into show business after retiring from football, making guest appearances on dozens of television shows and hosting his own variety show. Grier also served as a bodyguard for his friend Robert Kennedy during the 1968 presidential campaign, but he was with the Senator's wife, Ethel, on the night that Kennedy was assassinated in Los Angeles. Grier rushed forward when he heard shots being fired, grabbing the gun and subduing assassin Sirhan Sirhan.

L. C. Greenwood (1969–1981)

There were a lot of stars on the Pittsburgh Steelers of the 1970s, and the quiet Greenwood was mostly overshadowed by his teammates. The only thing he did to stand out was to wear gold shoes on the field. The rest of the Steelers wore plain black.

Greenwood was 6-foot-6 and used his long arms to block the quarterback's passing lanes. He also had tremendous speed, which he used to get around defenders and into the backfield. With teammates like Joe Greene, Jack Ham, and Jack Lambert helping to anchor the Pittsburgh defense, Greenwood could freelance and take chances as a pass rusher. He was at his best in the big games. In Super Bowl IX he knocked down three Fran Tarkenton passes, and a year later he sacked Roger Staubach three times in Super Bowl X.

Others

 # 26. Elvin Bethea (1968-1983)

 # 27. Jim Katcavage (1956-1968)

 # 28. Lyle Alzado (1971-1985)

 # 29. Roger Brown (1960-1969)

 # 30. William Fuller (1986-1998)

 # 31. John Randle (1990-2003)

 # 32. Jason Taylor (1997-2007)

 # 33. Larry Brooks (1972-1982)

 # 34. Ted Washington (1991-2007)

 # 35. Jim Marshall (1961-1979)

 # 36. Clyde Simmons (1986-2000)

 # 37. Jethro Pugh (1965-1978)

 # 38. Harvey Martin (1973-1983)

 # 39. Henry Jordan (1957-1969)

 # 40. George Andrie (1962-1972)

 # 41. Jerry Mays (1961-1970)

 # 42. Houston Antwine (1961-1972)

 # 43. Ray Childress (1985-1996)

 # 44. Bryant Young (1994-2007)

 # 45. Coy Bacon (1968-1981)

 # 46. Henry Thomas (1987-2000)

 # 47. Dwight White (1971-1980)

 # 48. Claude Humphrey (1968-1981)

 # 49. Warren Sapp (1995-2007)

 # 50. Willie Davis (1958-1969)

Linebackers

#1

Junior Seau (1990–2007)

Before we talk about Seau, I'm obligated to start with some discussion about how linebackers are rated and ranked, and why a guy who's on the top of many other lists of linebackers ranks at 50 here instead of No. 1.

As far as I know, there has only been one book dedicated exclusively to the subject of NFL linebackers. It's called *The Gridiron's Greatest Linebackers*, written by Kansas City sportswriter Jonathan Rand in 2003. He has Chicago's Dick Butkus rated as the No. 1 linebacker of all-time. Rick Korch wrote a book called *The Truly Great* in 1994, which ranks players by position. He has Butkus as the top inside linebacker, with Lawrence Taylor ranked first among outside linebackers. The *Sporting News* published "Football's 100 Greatest Players" in 1999 with Butkus ranked as the ninth-best player overall, second to Lawrence Taylor (whom they put fourth overall) among linebackers.

Rand described Butkus as "without peer at his position." Korch called Butkus "the meanest linebacker to ever play." In the *Sporting News* book, Ron Smith wrote: "A ball carrier who fell into the grasp of his long, thick arms could expect to be squeezed into submission."

That's the problem with trying to rate and rank players without defining any objective criteria. All you have to work with are anecdotes, quotes, and lavish praise that sounds great but doesn't really tell you anything about the player or his contributions.

It's difficult to come up with ways to measure linebackers objectively. Part of the problem is the lack of individual statistics, and part of the problem is the inability to separate the performance of an individual from the other players around him. This issue applies to all football players, but the group it affects most is linebackers. We have to judge them in the context of the team they played for, and by that measure, it's hard to find any data to support the claims for Butkus being the clear and obvious pick for greatest linebacker of all-time.

The Bears never made the playoffs during Butkus's career, and they only finished with a winning record twice (one of which was a 7-6-1 record in 1967). They never finished as the league's top-ranked defense—either against the run, the pass, or overall. They finished in the bottom half of the NFL's defenses five out of nine seasons. They were pretty good against the run at times, but other times they got steamrolled.

When you try to find specific ways in which Butkus helped his team to win, or at least helped limit the number of yards and points the Bears gave up, it's impossible. Admittedly, some of this is due to the inherent difficulties of rating individual defenders, but we don't find it so hard to build a compelling case for other linebackers from the same era.

When watching film or reading contemporary accounts of Butkus, it's clear that he was all over the field making plays. But how much of that was due to the fact that he was a star, and how much of that was just because the rest of the defense stunk?

You'll only find a couple of nuggets of factual information in all of the praise heaped on Butkus, and when you try to verify them you run into problems. For example, Korch concluded that "teams didn't run on the Bears because of Butkus." That's one of those kinds of comments that is easy to throw around, but it simply wasn't true. Teams *loved* to run the ball against the Bears, and they did it more and more as Butkus got older.

The chart below shows how often teams ran the ball against the Bears during the Butkus era, specifically showing the percentage of all plays they faced that were running plays. You can see that in 1965, the Bears ranked first out of fourteen NFL teams with only 45.3 percent of the play against them coming on the ground. But every year after that, teams ran against the Bears at a rate that exceeded the league average.

Year	Run %	LgAv	Rank/Total Teams
1965	45.3	50.4	1 / 14
1966	51.7	49.2	11 / 15
1967	50.3	49.5	10 / 16
1968	54.1	51.9	9 / 15
1969	57.2	49.7	16 / 16
1970	51.3	51.7	14 / 26
1971	56.6	53.6	19 / 26
1972	56.6	55.6	17 / 26
1973	62.7	57.1	25 / 26

If you take anything away from reading this book, I hope it's an appreciation for how impor-

tant it is to use objective criteria to rate NFL players. Some of the methods are admittedly rudimentary, and the statistical record has some sizable gaps. But it's the twenty-first century—the computer age, for Pete's sake—and we've got to approach our study of pro football history with something more than compilations of quotes from teammates and platitudes about how "tough" guys were. Players aren't great just because other people say they are. They're great because we can point to specific evidence of what they did and describe how that helped their team.

Like Butkus, Junior Seau played most of his career with a lousy team. In his thirteen seasons with the Chargers, the team finished with a winning record just three times. During that time, however, the San Diego run defense ranked in the top five in seven different seasons, including the 1994 season that ended with the Chargers' first Super Bowl appearance.

Seau's best season came in 1998, when he helped the Chargers hold opposing runners to a league-low 2.7 yards per carry. He blitzed a lot for an inside linebacker, leading the team in sacks in back-to-back seasons in 1996 and 1997. His critics said that he freelanced too much, blitzing when the play called for him to stay in coverage or going out of position trying to make a play. His coaches didn't seem to mind, because Seau made big plays often enough to compensate for the times he guessed wrong. A great example of that was the 1994 AFC championship game, where he made 16 tackles and helped the Chargers upset the Steelers. Pittsburgh had the league's top-ranked running game, but Seau almost single-handedly shut down running back Barry Foster, holding him to 47 yards on 20 carries.

Seau moved to the outside late in his career, but even during his days with the Dolphins and Patriots, he helped his team get better against the run. The Dolphins run defense improved from 3.8 to 3.3 yards per carry in Seau's first year in Miami. He played a key role for the undefeated Patriots team in 2007, finishing second on the team in tackles.

Mike Singletary (1981–1992)

The Bears have a lineage of great middle linebackers that started with Bill George in 1955 and can be traced all the way to Brian Urlacher in the present day. Mike Singletary was the best of the bunch. From 1984 to 1986, the Bears were the top-ranked defense in the NFL, and Singletary was at the center both literally and figuratively.

When he first came into the league, Singletary was a ferocious run stuffer, but he struggled in pass coverage. Bears defensive coordinator Buddy Ryan took him out of the game in passing situations. This infuriated Singletary, but served as motivation for him to improve his coverage skills. It didn't take long for him to become a great all-around player.

In fact, Buddy Ryan developed the 46 defense in large part because of Singletary's ability to single-handedly dominate the middle of the field. He might team with a cornerback to cover the slot receiver. He might cover the tight end or have zone coverage responsibilities for crossing patterns underneath. He might key the run or even blitz. Singletary could do it all, and his ability to do so many things from the middle was what made Ryan's innovative defense possible.

The Bears defense ranked 1st or 2nd in yards allowed for five straight seasons, consistently stuffing their opponents' efforts to run the ball and unleashing a relentless pass rush that made it all but impossible to throw the ball. Singletary was named NFL Defensive Player of the Year twice—first in 1985 and again in 1988. He's one of only six players to win that award more than once.

Lawrence Taylor (1981–1993)

The 1981 draft class included four future Hall of Famers on the defensive side—Lawrence Taylor (No. 2, Giants), Ronnie Lott (No. 8, 49ers), Mike Singletary (No. 38, Bears), and Howie Long (No. 48, Raiders). All of them were great, but none of them changed the game the way that Taylor did.

Before Taylor, the star linebackers played in the middle, but LT showed that you could be a dominating player from the outside as well. He redefined the position of outside linebacker in the 3-4 defense, mostly by being aggressive instead of simply reading the play and reacting.

Taylor had tremendous quickness, which is what enabled him to be so disruptive even though he lined up on the outside.

Teams learned that it was better to run at him than away from him. Niners head coach Bill Walsh used a guard to block Taylor on every play, a strategy that most other teams copied. Joe Gibbs of the Redskins adopted the H-back and designed his two-tight end offense specifically to keep Taylor away from his quarterback.

Still, Taylor was an unstoppable force who made an immediate impact. The Giants defense improved from 24th to 3rd in yards allowed, and reduced their points allowed from 425 in 1980 to 257 in 1981. He was not only named Rookie of the Year but also Defensive Player of the Year. He would go on to win the latter award a record three times and in 1986 he became the first defensive player to be unanimously voted as the league's Most Valuable Player.

As great as he was at defending the run, Taylor got more attention for his skills at rushing the passer. He led the league with 20.5 sacks in 1986 and had 142 for his career (including 9.5 unofficially as a rookie; sacks did not become an official statistics until the following season.)

I feel confident that Taylor would rank 1st overall among linebackers if he hadn't missed so many games in his prime. Players' strikes in 1982 and 1987 cost him eleven games, and he missed another four games while suspended for failing a drug test in 1988. In a 2003 appearance on the television program *60 Minutes,* Taylor described how his cocaine use had consumed him in the early years of his career. He cleaned up after his suspension, knowing that another failed test would end his career. However, he wrote in his biography that he looked forward to resuming his drug use when his playing days ended. "I saw coke as the only bright spot in my future," he wrote.

#4
Jack Ham (1971–1982)

The Pittsburgh Steelers of the 1970s were famed for their great defense, dubbed the "Steel Curtain." Two of their linebackers rank among my top ten with a third—Andy Russell—checking in at No. 26.

Ham played the strong side in Pittsburgh's 4-3 defense, a position that traditionally focused on stopping the run. Strong side linebackers were usually pretty big, but Ham didn't play the power game. His greatest asset was his tremendous speed, and with defensive linemen L. C. Greenwood and Mean Joe Greene playing in front of him on the left side, Ham was less concerned with confronting big blockers and was free to roam. He had a great knack for finding the ball carrier through the crowd, and opposing teams were often forced to run away from Ham toward their weak side.

His speed also made him unusually effective in pass coverage. Ham had 32 interceptions in his career, and at times was used like an extra defensive back. He dislocated a toe on his left foot in 1979 during the next-to-last game of the season in Houston. The injury forced him to miss the playoffs and Super Bowl XIV, and when he returned the following year he clearly wasn't the same. He no longer had the strong burst of speed that let him get outside, and once teams saw this they started running around him. Ham continued for three more seasons, but his play didn't improve and he opted to retire. "The films don't lie," he said. "There has been a drop-off. It hasn't been getting any better or worse, so I decided it was time to quit."

Ham was generally overshadowed by other, more colorful players on the Pittsburgh defense . . . guys like Greene, Jack Lambert, and Mel Blount. At his peak, though, I think Ham was the best player of that whole bunch.

#5
Ted Hendricks (1969–1983)

At 6-foot-7 and 214 pounds, Hendricks didn't look like he could play linebacker in the NFL. Although he appeared to be skinny, he was deceptively strong, and he used his massive wingspan to envelop ball carriers. He also used his long arms to deflect throws and obstruct the passing lanes.

Hendricks played for three different teams and represented each one in the Pro Bowl. His best years came with the Oakland Raiders, where he was not so much a linebacker as he was a freelance disruptor. Hendricks would line up in a different position on every down, moving around before the snap to confuse the offense and disrupt their blocking assignments.

The Raiders won three Super Bowls with Hendricks, allowing 14, 10, and 9 points. Hendricks also played for the Colts in Super Bowl V, a game that they won 16–13.

#6
Derrick Brooks (1995–2007)

"Who's my favorite player? Mister Derrick Brooks." That's the refrain of a song that Brooks taught a busload of school kids in a television commercial for the United Way. It's a silly little spot, but years later it still pops into my head every time I see him.

Brooks was the key figure on a Tampa Bay defense that dominated opponents in the early 2000s. Their offense was generally inept, however, which kept the team from making much progress in the playoffs.

The Buccaneers defense seemed to take things into their own hands in 2002. It wasn't enough simply to stop their opponents from scoring. The defense had to score points themselves. Brooks scored 4 touchdowns during the 2002 regular season. One came on a fumble recovery and 3 were on interception returns, the latter establishing an NFL record for linebackers.

Tampa Bay's defense was even more explosive in the playoffs. In three postseason games, the defense scored 4 more touchdowns while surrendering just 3. In the closing minutes of Super Bowl XXXVII, Brooks intercepted a Rich Gannon pass and returned it 44 yards for a touchdown to quash the Raiders comeback. He capped his 2002 season by being named the NFL's Defensive Player of the Year.

The Buccaneers defense ranked 21st overall in 1994, so they went into the draft looking for help on that side of the ball. With their two first-round picks, they landed Brooks (No. 28) and defensive tackle Warren Sapp (No. 12). Two years later, the Bucs defense ranked third and they remained in the top ten for nine straight seasons. Sapp and Brooks made a combined seventeen Pro Bowl appearances.

#7
Chuck Howley (1958–1973)

Howley began his career with the Chicago Bears, and a knee injury early in his second season prompted him to retire. After sitting out a year, Howley attempted a comeback with the Dallas Cowboys. Much to everybody's surprise, his speed had returned, and he became the cornerstone for coach Tom Landry's "Doomsday Defense."

Like most outside linebackers of the era, Howley's first job was to defend the run. From 1964 to 1972, the Cowboys ranked 1st in run defense five times and ranked 2nd three times. He was named Most Valuable Player of Super Bowl V—the first time a defensive player earned the honor and the only time it was given to a member of the losing team. Howley put on a one-man show, harassing the Colts offense all day. He intercepted two Johnny Unitas passes and recovered a fumble, although the Cowboys fell short in the final score.

Dallas returned to the big game the following year, and Howley turned in another big performance. He recovered a fumble at midfield to set up the Cowboys' first score. In the fourth quarter, Howley killed a Miami drive by intercepting a pass and returning it 41 yards. He appeared to be heading in for a touchdown, but with no defenders around him, Howley began to stumble at the 20-yard line, eventually coming to rest at the Miami 9. He jumped up and spiked the ball, throwing it to the ground with both hands in disgust at his tumble. Quarterback Roger Staubach threw a touchdown pass three plays later to seal the victory and give the Cowboys their first championship. There's no way of knowing for sure, but I suspect that if Howley had been able to stay on his feet and get into the end zone, he'd have won the Super Bowl MVP Award again. Instead, the honor went to Staubach, who had completed just 12 passes for 119 yards.

#8
Jack Lambert (1974–1984)

Lambert was the middle linebacker for the dominant Steelers teams of the seventies, joining them as part of their amazing 1974 draft class. Pittsburgh selected four future Hall of Famers with their first five picks that year, including Lambert, Lynn Swann, John Stallworth, and Mike Webster.

The defense was already good, but Lambert was the missing piece that helped push them over the top. They were the league's stingiest defense in 1974 and again in 1976.

Lambert was named Defensive Player of the Year in 1976, leading what many would argue was the greatest defense in NFL history. The team started 1–4 and saw quarterback Terry Bradshaw go down with neck and wrist injuries. The defense stepped up, and over the last nine weeks Lambert and his teammates allowed just 2 touchdowns.

Most middle linebackers are run stuffers, and with Lambert in the lineup the Steelers were always one of the toughest teams to run against. What set him apart from the great linebackers of the sixties was his pass coverage ability and his remarkable range. "I try to get to the football," Lambert said, "as opposed to the Butkus and Nitschke types who stood in the middle and dared you to knock them down. If I can run around a blocker and make a tackle, I'll do it."

#9 Rickey Jackson (1981–1995)

When Jackson joined the Saints they were an awful mess. In 1980, the team started 0-14 and finished the season with just one win, a 21–20 victory over the Jets.

The Saints' fortunes began to turn in 1981 with the addition of Jackson and fellow rookie George Rogers, the Heisman-winning runner from South Carolina. Jackson registered 8 sacks as a rookie, and by the mid-eighties had established himself as one of the league's premier linebackers. Through his first five seasons he'd recorded 47.5 sacks, just 3 less than another member of the 1981 draft class, Lawrence Taylor.

Jackson wasn't as good at defending the run as Taylor was, but he was in the same league as Taylor as a pass rusher. Jackson finished with 136 sacks while Taylor had 142 in his career. The biggest difference, of course, was that Taylor was playing in New York for a perennial playoff team, while Jackson labored in obscurity in the Deep South.

By the late eighties, the Saints had surrounded Jackson with other talented linebackers, and collectively they were known as the Dome Patrol. The Saints posted the first winning season in franchise history in 1987, and didn't have another losing season until the year after Jackson retired.

#10 Harry Carson (1976–1988)

Carson was the first inside linebacker in the Hall of Fame. Unlike the middle linebackers in the 4-3 defense, the inside linebackers in the 3-4 defense had to be equally talented against the run and the pass. Lawrence Taylor always got more press, but it was Carson on the inside who made the Giants defense consistently good. Taylor brought excitement, but it was Carson who brought stability.

He was elected to the Hall of Fame in his thirteenth year of eligibility, but years of being passed over made Carson a vocal critic of the Hall's voting process. At one point, he even asked that his name be taken off the ballot. He felt that it was unfair to have members of the media casting votes, rather than former players and coaches, who could better appreciate the true contributions a candidate made.

Some dismissed these complaints as sour grapes, but Carson was absolutely right. The selection process is fraught with politics, with some longtime members of the selection committee wielding virtual veto powers over nominees they dislike. Too often, marginal candidates are elected because of a strong lobbying effort by powerful supporters. And just as often, strong candidates are ignored because they don't have that kind of personal support.

#11 Ray Lewis (1996–2007)

There was a time when I thought Lewis would end up as the greatest linebacker ever. That hasn't happened, I think in part due to a shoulder injury he suffered in 2002. After that, he seemed to have a harder time shedding blockers. A hamstring injury in 2005 also seemed to slow him. Still, he's 11th all-time in my rankings and as of this writing, probably has clinched a spot in the Hall of Fame.

Lewis was the Defensive Player of the Year in 2000 and was named Most Valuable Player of Super Bowl XXXV. That Ravens defense set an NFL record for fewest points allowed in a season (165), fewest rushing yards in a sixteen-game season, and recorded 4 shutouts, 1 shy of the post-merger record. He won another Defensive Player of the Year Award in 2003.

#12 Joe Schmidt (1953–1965)

In the early fifties, most teams played a basic 5-2 defense, with a middle guard in the center of the line as a run stuffer. As offenses began to employ more spread formations and use slot backs, the middle of the field was left open for the passing attack. To respond, some defenses moved that middle guard back a few steps. From that perspective, they could read and react to the play, dropping into pass coverage or pushing up to stop the run.

Detroit's Joe Schmidt was one of the first to make the move, helping to invent the position that would come to be known as middle linebacker. The Lions won two championships with Schmidt manning the middle, first in 1953 and again in 1957. He was a great tackler, but what made him successful was his ability to diagnose plays and get to the ball. Schmidt was helped by having two great defensive tackles in front of him to occupy blockers—Alex Karras and Roger Brown. That left Schmidt free to make plays.

In 1960, Schmidt became the first defensive player to be named Most Valuable Player. It was an interesting selection, more a testament to Schmidt's overall impact than anything. The Lions finished 7-5 that year, and while the defense played well as a unit, it wasn't particularly dominating.

After retiring, Schmidt spent six seasons as the Lions head coach. He led the team to the playoffs in 1970, but retired two years later, complaining that coaching was no longer fun. He compiled a 43-34 record in six seasons, and none of the twelve coaches that have followed him has done better than his .558 winning percentage.

#13
Nick Buoniconti (1962–1976)

A five-time AFL all-star with the Patriots, Buoniconti was best known as a member of the Dolphin's "No-Name Defense" of the early seventies. At just 5-foot-11, he was smaller than most middle linebackers of his era. But he was aggressive, both against the run and the pass. He would throw himself into the scrum with reckless abandon, and his ball-hawking instincts resulted in 32 career interceptions.

Buoniconti was the leader of that great Miami defense, and the only member to make the Hall of Fame. The Dolphins had the league's top-ranked defense in 1972, a major reason the team went undefeated. The defense was probably better the following year, when Miami won its second-straight Super Bowl.

#14
Sam Huff (1956–1969)

Another legendary middle linebacker from the fifties, some have argued that Huff was overrated because he played in New York. There's no doubt that Huff got more press than any other defensive player up to that point. He was the subject of a *Time* magazine cover story in 1959, and was featured in a 1960 television special on CBS called *The Violent World of Sam Huff*.

In fairness, though, Huff deserved most of the attention he was getting. In his first eight seasons, the Giants advanced to the NFL championship game six times, and their stingy defense played a major role. From 1958 to 1960 they were the league's best all-around defense, and the tough, hard-hitting Huff was one of the main reasons.

Further evidence of his impact was how quickly the defense fell apart after he was traded to the Washington Redskins in 1964. And his new team went from being one of the league's worst defenses to one of the best. He spent his last season as a player-coach under Vince Lombardi.

#15
Bobby Bell (1963–1974)

Bell was an extremely athletic outside linebacker, with a combination of size and speed that was deadly. He was quick enough to cover receivers down the field and big enough to fend off linemen trying to block him. Most teams tried to double-team him on running plays, usually with the tight end.

He started off as a defensive end, but moved to outside linebacker in coach Hank Stram's "stack defense"—which was the precursor to the 3-4 defense. Bell didn't blitz the quarterback much, but he was incredibly disruptive from the outside.

#16
Wayne Walker (1958–1972)

Walker was an outside linebacker who spent his entire career with the Lions. His best years were from 1964 to 1966, when the Lions were arguably the NFL's best defense. Walker played alongside two outstanding middle linebackers, first with Joe Schmidt, and later Pro Bowler Mike Lucci. Having that help inside let him be more aggressive.

Walker's college roommate was Jerry Kramer, who would become one of his fiercest rivals as a lineman for the Green Bay Packers. When he retired, Walker had played more games at linebacker (200) than any other NFL player.

#17
Lee Roy Jordan (1963–1976)

Jordan was the leader of the Cowboys Doomsday Defense, which ranked first against the run for four straight years, 1966 to 1969. While most NFL teams of the era relied on tough physical play, the Cowboys trademark was their speed. Jordan was listed in the Dallas media guide at 215 or 220 pounds, but he was probably much closer to 200. What he lacked in size he made up for with remarkable range. That let him close quickly on running plays and cover the middle of the field on pass plays.

Jordan intercepted 34 passes in his career, including three in a 1973 game against the Bengals.

#18
Larry Grantham (1960–1972)

A five-time AFL all-star with the New York Titans/Jets, Grantham played right outside linebacker. He was one of the backbones of a defense that reached the Super Bowl in 1968. People think of Namath and his guarantee when they remember that game, but the brash Jets quarterback had thrown more interceptions (17) than touchdowns (15) during the regular season, and the Jets offense produced just 1 touchdown against the Colts in the Super Bowl. It was the defense that got them to the big game, and the defense that was responsible for winning it.

The 1968 Jets were the AFL's stingiest offense, ranking 1st against the run and 2nd against the pass. Grantham called the defensive signals during the Super Bowl, and the Jets kept the heavily favored Colts out of the end zone until late in the fourth quarter.

#19
Isiah Robertson (1971–1982)

The Rams defenses of the sixties and seventies featured some great defensive linemen. Robertson joined the team as they were transitioning from Deacon Jones and Coy Bacon to Jack Youngblood and Fred Dryer. While the men up front were getting all the glory, the linebackers also played an important role in the success of the Rams defense.

Robertson was the best of the bunch. He was named Defensive Rookie of the Year in 1971 and was a first- or second-team All-Pro each year from 1971 to 1977. The Rams' stingy run defense helped them win seven straight division titles and advance to the NFC title game five times in six years. His 59-yard touchdown return of an interception in the 1974 playoff game against Dallas sent his team to the NFC championship game.

#20
Cornelius Bennett (1987–2000)

One of the key members of the Buffalo team that went to four straight Super Bowls, Bennett joined the Bills midway through the 1987 season. He was part of a three-way trade that sent star running back Eric Dickerson to Indianapolis. Bennett had been the second pick in the 1987 draft but couldn't reach agreement with the Colts on a contract.

The trade came on Halloween, with half the season gone. In his first game for the Bills, he came off the bench to record a sack and two quarterback pressures. That was enough to convince the Bills he was ready to start, and Bennett would end the season with 8.5 sacks in eight games.

He blossomed in 1988 and so did the Bills, who won their first division title in eight seasons. His ability to create havoc on the outside made it hard for teams who wanted to constantly double-team defensive end Bruce Smith. When they did, it just created opportunities for Bennett to make plays.

Bennett joined the Atlanta Falcons as a free agent in 1996 and three years later had the dubious distinction of becoming the first player to lose five Super Bowls. He spent his last two seasons with the Colts, the team he had spurned as a rookie. He retired with 71.5 sacks and 26 fumble recoveries, placing him third in fumble recoveries in NFL history.

Bill George (1952–1966)

George was the first middle linebacker, creating the position in 1954 by moving off the line in Chicago's 5-2 alignment to play a few yards off the line of scrimmage. He grew frustrated at being taken out of plays by opposing centers, and quickly learned that he could play a bigger role in the passing defense from his new vantage point.

He was named first-team All-Pro each year from 1955 to 1961, and again in 1963 when he helped lead the Bears to the NFL championship. It was to be his final hurrah. George struggled with injuries over the next two seasons and became expendable when the Bears drafted Dick Butkus in 1965. He spent his final season playing MLB behind the Los Angeles Rams' "Fearsome Foursome."

Chris Hanburger (1965–1978)

Redskins fans have devoted so much energy to complaining about Art Monk's omission from the Hall of Fame that they have overlooked Hanburger. If you ask me, the case for Hanburger's selection is a much easier one to make.

He had a unique playing style. Well, maybe not completely unique, but it was unusual. Hanburger tackled guys high, hitting them in the chest rather than the legs. Pop Warner coaches tell you to hit low because you'll knock the ball carrier off balance, and that's how you make a tackle. Hanburger was more interested in knocking the ball loose, and if he couldn't do that, he was strong enough to wrap his arms around a guy and pull him down.

He had his best years as the defensive captain for George Allen's Over the Hill Gang, which from 1971 to 1974 was extremely tough against the run. Hanburger was a five-time All-Pro at outside linebacker, but I suspect that two things have kept him from getting serious consideration for the Hall of Fame. One is that he played for some bad Redskins teams and never won a Super Bowl. The other, and unfortunately more difficult to overcome, is that he had an antagonistic relationship with the media. In 2005, *Washington Post* writer (and member of the Hall's selection committee) Len Shapiro summed it up clearly. "He was extremely media unfriendly, and some people have long memories."

Ray Nitschke (1958–1972)

I'm not sure I'm prepared to say that Ray Nitschke was overrated, and I certainly would not say it to his face. He was without a doubt the fiery leader of the Packers defense that won five championships in a seven-year stretch from 1961 to 1967. But was he one of the top two or three linebackers of all-time, as many would have you believe?

I could fill pages with quotes from the players of his era about how tough Nitschke was, how mean he was, and how his ferocious hits made players dread going over the middle. NFL Films has some great footage of him in action, especially from a 1966 game against the 49ers. "This is the face of a tiger," booms the voice of narrator John Facenda, as we see a close-up of Nitschke's snarling face, "and this, the action of a tiger." We see Nitschke explode through the line to tackle running back Ken Willard in the backfield, then another shot of him waylaying receiver Dave Parks with a vicious shoulder blow after a catch over the middle.

Highlights are easy. It's harder to find evidence that Nitschke was consistently the best linebacker in the game. At times, the Packers defense was lousy against the run. They ranked thirteenth out of fourteen teams in yards allowed in 1965, and thirteenth of sixteen in 1967. As the middle linebacker, Nitschke certainly bears the brunt of the responsibility for those struggles. The NFL started tracking quarterback sacks for teams in 1963, and the Packers were never great in that category either. Green Bay's offense was so dominating during this era that they could still win, but we can't ignore that their defense struggled at times.

And then we have to deal with how his contemporaries judged him. In a fifteen-year career, Nitschke was only selected to one Pro Bowl, and he was a first team All-Pro only twice. Year in and year out, the top honors for NFL middle linebackers went to Nitschke's competitors: Detroit's Joe Schmidt, Chicago's Bill George and Dick Butkus, or Atlanta's Tommy Nobis.

Nitschke is a deserving Hall of Famer, and don't think for a minute that ranking No. 23 on my list means I think he was a slouch. But the conventional wisdom for years has been that Butkus and Nitschke were without question the game's best linebackers. I just don't see any evidence to support those claims.

Derrick Thomas (1989–1999)

Thomas was the best defensive player on a Chiefs team that won more games in the 1990s than anyone else. He made an immediate splash as a rookie, and in his second season led the league with 20 sacks. Thomas set an NFL record that year by notching 7 sacks in a game against the Seahawks.

A car accident in January 2000 left Thomas paralyzed from the waist down, and he died from complications of his injuries the following month. At the time of his death, his 126.5 career sacks were the fourth highest total for a linebacker. Thomas was probably a year and a half from breaking Lawrence Taylor's mark of 142.

Chuck Bednarik (1950–1962)

A tough holdover from the two-way era, Bednarik is perhaps best remembered for the iconic photograph taken after he'd knocked Giants halfback Frank Gifford unconscious. Gifford lay motionless on the ground while Bednarik stood over him, yelling and gesturing.

Although a handful of modern players have dabbled with playing both offense and defense, Bednarik was the last player of his era to play both offense and defense full time. He played his entire fourteen-year career with the Eagles and missed just three games.

Bednarik won two NFL championships with the Eagles. The first, in 1949, came largely because of the strong play of the defense. The second, in 1960, came in spite of the Eagle's defense.

Others

26. Andy Russell (1963–1976)

27. Rod Martin (1977–1988)

28. Jack Pardee (1957–1972)

29. Zach Thomas (1996–2007)

30. Leslie O'Neal (1986–1999)

31. Seth Joyner (1986–1998)

32. Wilber Marshall (1984–1995)

33. Maxie Baughan (1960–1974)

34. Robert Brazile (1975–1984)

35. Brad Van Pelt (1973–1986)

36. Matt Millen (1980–1991)

37. Steve Nelson (1974–1987)

38. Dave Edwards (1963–1975)

39. Willie Lanier (1967–1977)

40. Clay Matthews (1978–1996)

41. D. D. Lewis (1968–1981)

42. Dave Robinson (1963–1974)

43. Pat Swilling (1986–1998)

44. Jack Reynolds (1970–1984)

45. Greg Lloyd (1988–1998)

46. Randy Gradishar (1974–1983)

47. Jerry Robinson (1979–1991)

48. Bill Romanowski (1988–2003)

49. Tom Addison (1960–1967)

50. Dick Butkus (1965–1973)

Defensive Backs

#1

Rod Woodson (1987–2003)

The term "shutdown cornerback" gets tossed around a lot. In theory, it means a defender whose coverage is so strong that the opposing quarterback can't ever get the ball to his man. If you listen to the television commentators, they'll have you believe that there are about twenty-five of these guys playing in the league at any given time. The reality is that this kind of player comes along once or twice in a decade. It requires the speed to keep up with a receiver in the open field, but more than that, it requires the quickness to catch up with a receiver who has made a move. It requires strength, especially if you're going to match up with a big receiver.

To be a great coverage cornerback requires one other intangible skill, something that I think you'll find in baseball's great closers, or hockey's great goalies: the ability to forget a bad play.

Rod Woodson did that as well as anybody, and he had all of the physical skills too. He played for ten years in the tough AFC Central, a division that was filled with physical teams who liked to play smashmouth football.

He suffered a devastating knee injury in the first game of the 1995 season. There was some fear that it might end his career, but Woodson fought

hard and rejoined the Steelers in time to play in Super Bowl XXX. At the time, it was reported that Woodson was the first player in NFL history to tear his anterior cruciate ligament and return in the same season. I'm fairly certain that feat was first achieved by Red Grange in 1927, but only because the Galloping Ghost played through his injury rather than get treatment. Regardless, Woodson's comeback was remarkable. Not only did he make it back, he continued to play at a remarkably high level as well. In fact, Woodson's interception rate increased after the knee injury, from .27 per game to .33 per game. That's an increase of 1 interception per sixteen games.

After leaving the Steelers, Woodson eventually made the transformation from cornerback to free safety. He won a Super Bowl with the Ravens in 2000, playing a key role on their smothering defense. He also returned to the Super Bowl with the 2002 Raiders.

Woodson retired with 79 interceptions, second-best all-time and 2 shy of Paul Krause's career record. His 12 interception returns for touchdowns broke Ken Houston's all-time record of 9, a mark that was later tied by Deion Sanders. Woodson also had 20 fumble recoveries, the 3rd-highest total for a defensive back.

There were three Pro Bowl–caliber defensive backs named Woodson playing in the late 1990s and early 2000s—Darren Woodson, a strong safety with the Cowboys, and Charles Woodson, the Heisman Trophy–winning cornerback from the Oakland Raiders.

Deion Sanders (1989–2005)

Sanders was a ten-time consensus All-Pro, earning the honor more times than any other defensive back in history. He also received All-Pro honors in four different seasons as a return specialist.

That's an amazing accomplishment when you consider that Sanders spent most of his football career being distracted by baseball. He made his major league debut with the Yankees the summer before his first NFL training camp, a pre-emptive attempt by the Bronx Bombers to get Sanders to forgo football altogether. It didn't work, but he stuck with it for nine big league seasons.

Sanders was a decent baseball player. He led the National League in triples in 1992 and finished 2nd in stolen bases twice. Sanders did this despite the fact that he would leave his baseball team when the football season started, or at times splitting his time between the two sports. In 1992, he played an afternoon game with the Falcons at Miami, and then flew to Pittsburgh for the Braves playoff game that night against the Pirates.

Deion's nickname was "Primetime," but more often than not he was a distracting sideshow. If he had committed to baseball full time, he might have become an All-Star. If he had committed to football full time, I have no doubt he'd have been a better football player. He was tremendous in coverage, but everyone acknowledged he was a lousy tackler. Sanders could control half of the field with his cover skills, but he wasn't much help if the ball went somewhere else.

He was a guy that you either loved or hated. His teammates loved him, especially when he joined a team like the 49ers or Cowboys and helped them win a Super Bowl. But Sanders's brash personality and need for the spotlight alienated many others. He clashed with some members of the press,

including a bizarre locker-room incident in 1992 where he threw buckets of ice water at Tim McCarver three times during a live broadcast.

In the end, while many considered him a prima donna, you can't overlook his numbers. His 303 interception return yards in 1995 is the second-best ever, and many consider it a more impressive performance than Charlie McNeil's 349 in the 1961 AFL. Sanders ranks 4th all-time with 77 interceptions, and he tied Rod Woodson's record with 12 returns for touchdowns. Sanders also caught 3 touchdown passes and returned 9 kicks for touchdowns (6 punts, 3 kickoffs).

Paul Krause (1964–1979)

Krause set the all-time record with 81 career interceptions, a mark that has stood for more than twenty-five years despite the increasing role of the passing game and the advent of sixteen-game schedules.

In his rookie season, Krause intercepted passes in seven straight games and led the NFL with 12. He had another streak of six straight games with an interception in 1968.

Some critics complained that Krause's interceptions were largely a function of playing center field in the Vikings' zone defense. That never made much sense to me. First of all, he intercepted plenty of passes in his first four seasons with the Redskins. Second, I've never thought it seemed fair to criticize a guy for not doing things that he wasn't asked to do. Criticize his limitations, sure, but why knock a guy for the role he was asked to play? Krause was a natural ball hawk and his coaches found a way to take advantage of that.

If you want to find fault with Krause, then blame him for sticking around for so long in pursuit of the record. He inched toward Emlen Tunnell's interception record with 2 interceptions in 1976 and 2 more in 1977. He was still 1 shy of Tunnell's career mark heading into the 1978 season. No longer a starter, Krause did not intercept a pass all year. He returned for another try in 1979, finally tying the mark in a Week 5 game at Detroit. Krause broke the record—and added 1 more for good measure in a Week 14 loss to the Rams.

Willie Brown (1963–1978)

The AFL was a passing league, and during the sixties defenses had a hard time keeping up with all of the offenses that liked to air the ball out. That's part of the reason Brown's outstanding play at cornerback made a huge impact. He was an end in college converted to defensive back by the Houston Oilers. The move didn't seem to be working, and the Oilers cut him loose during training camp. He hooked on with the Denver Broncos, and by his second season Brown had become a star. He had 9 interceptions in 1964, and although the Broncos struggled to win games, he earned the first of what would be nine Pro Bowl invitations.

A trade sent Brown to Oakland in 1967. The Raiders made their first playoff appearance that year and would advance to the AFC championship game nine times in the next eleven years. Brown had 7 interceptions in the postseason, including 1 in Super Bowl XI that he returned 75 yards for a touchdown.

Brown claims to have invented bump-and-run coverage, and if he didn't he certainly perfected it. He would hit the receivers hard on every play, disrupting their timing and preventing them from running their route. Doing that is easy, but it only works if you can maintain your coverage after you've hit the receiver. Brown had great quickness and an uncanny ability to shadow receivers step-for-step.

In large part because of Brown, the NFL adopted a rule in 1978 that prohibited defenders from making contact with receivers more than 5 yards past the line of scrimmage. It was Brown's final season, but he managed to get his hits in within the 5-yard limit. He had just 1 interception that year, but he became the first player in NFL history to pick off at least 1 pass in sixteen consecutive seasons.

Ken Houston (1967–1980)

Here is the perfect example of why it doesn't make sense to rank defensive backs solely by individual statistics. Houston had just 49 interceptions in his fourteen seasons. Part of that was due to the fact that opposing teams avoided throwing in his direction. The other part was the way he was used at safety.

When you look at the team stats it becomes clear what an impact he had on stopping the passing game. Houston's teams regularly finished among the leaders in opponent's passer rating, ranking in the top six in ten of his fourteen seasons. Opposing quarterbacks were held to a low completion percentage, produced relatively few yards, and over the course of Houston's career had a 200/313 ratio of touchdowns to interceptions.

When he did get his hands on the ball, Houston knew what to do with it. He scored 9 touchdowns on interception returns—the all-time record when he retired and still the 3rd best total in history. Four of them came with the Oilers in 1971, still the NFL's single-season record.

Houston was traded to the Redskins in 1973, joining head coach George Allen's collection of veterans dubbed the "Over The Hill Gang." He nabbed 6 interceptions that season and recovered 5 fumbles.

Willie Wood (1961–1971)

When people think about the Packers dynasty of the sixties, they think about the leadership of Vince Lombardi and Bart Starr, or Jim Taylor running behind that great offensive line. But people rarely think about Green Bay's outstanding secondary, which played just as large a role in allowing the Packers to dominate the decade.

The Packers pass defense ranked 1st or 2nd in the NFL for eight straight years, and they were No. 1 each year from 1964 to 1968. Wood led the league with 9 interceptions in 1962, and made a key play in the first Super Bowl. The Packers had a slim 14–10 lead over the Chiefs at halftime, and Kansas City started the third quarter with an impressive drive. On a third-down play at midfield, Wood stepped in front of tight end Fred Arbanas to intercept a pass, returning it 45 yards to the Kansas City 5-yard line. Green Bay scored one play later to take a 21–10 lead, which completely changed the momentum of the game.

Wood was a quarterback in college, the first African-American quarterback in the Pacific Ten Conference. When he left the University of Southern California, nobody was interested in him. You had to be white to play quarterback in the NFL in those days, and so despite his success in the college ranks, Wood wasn't drafted by either an NFL or AFL team.

Wood would later break significant barriers as the first African-American head coach in pro football during the modern era. He led the World Football League's Philadelphia Bell in 1973, and later became the first African-American coach in the Canadian Football League.

#7
Mel Blount (1970–1983)

Blount was one of the great bump-and-run defenders, a big, strong cornerback who intimidated opposing receivers with his physical style of play.

One of the things that you begin to notice if you study defensive backs is that they rarely excel in a vacuum. If they don't have a good defense around them, they have less freedom to be aggressive and try to make big plays. When the defense in front of them is struggling, defensive backs have to devote more focus to helping against the run, and that makes it harder to make a big impact in the passing game.

Fortunately for Blount, he was surrounded by a cast of stars. Three of his teammates on defense are in the Hall of Fame, and seven others were recognized as All-Pros.

#8
Johnny Robinson (1960–1971)

Robinson is the highest-ranked player on my list who is eligible but not in the Hall of Fame. He was a finalist six times during the 1980s, but support seemed to disappear after 1986. I haven't been able to find out for sure, but I suspect that one of the writers who covered the AFL left the board of selectors in 1987, and clearly nobody else on the board took up his case.

He started his career as a running back but switched to safety and quickly established himself as one of the best. The Chiefs defense ranked 1st or 2nd overall for six of the AFL's ten seasons, and Robinson was one of the main reasons. He led the AFL with 10 interceptions in 1966, and led the merged AFL-NFL again in 1970.

In Super Bowl IV, Robinson made two big plays. His early fumble recovery and fourth-quarter interception helped the Chiefs stifle the Vikings offense, holding them to a single touchdown.

#9
Herb Adderly (1961–1972)

His tremendous speed made him a natural for the cornerback position, but Adderley entered the NFL as a halfback. He had been an All-Conference runner at Michigan State, but he wasn't going to find much playing time with the Packers behind stars Jim Taylor and Paul Hornung.

Green Bay coach Vince Lombardi knew his skills would make him a good defensive back, and it didn't take long for Adderley to prove his coach right. He was a consensus All-Pro in his second season and became a key member of the Packers stifling pass defense.

Adderley played in four of the first six Super Bowls, two with the Packers and two with the Dallas Cowboys. He is one of only three players to play on six NFL championship teams.

10

Carnell Lake (1989–2001)

Lake didn't intercept a ton of passes, but he made a big impact as a free safety for the Pittsburgh Steelers. Defensive coordinator Dick LeBeau—a great defensive back in his own day—developed the zone blitz defense, a system that relied heavily on Lake to pressure the quarterback.

He registered 21 sacks with the Steelers and 24 overall, which ranks 2nd all-time among defensive backs. Lake was strong against the run, and his coverage skills were good enough that he occasionally moved to cornerback, but he made his biggest impact on the safety blitz.

Most Sacks by a Defensive Back

30	Rodney Harrison (1994–2007)
24	Carnell Lake (1989–2001)
20	LeRoy Butler (1990–2001)
20	Ronde Barber (1997–2007)
17	Keith Bostic (1983–1990)
17	Lawyer Milloy (1996–2007)

Lake's career was shortened by an injury originally diagnosed as a high ankle sprain. It turned out to be a stress fracture, and a series of surgeries were unable to alleviate the pain. He even tried a bone graft, which forced him to sit out the entire 2000 season, but that didn't resolve the problem.

He was named as one of four safeties for the All-Decade team for the 1990s, but the injury likely robbed him of the longevity necessary for a strong Hall of Fame candidacy.

11

Dick "Night Train" Lane (1952-1965)

There's nothing like starting strong. Lane intercepted 14 passes as a rookie, setting a single-season record that has stood for more than fifty years. Not bad for an undrafted free agent, especially when you consider the NFL played a twelve-game schedule in those days.

Lane was bigger than most of the receivers he was covering and faster than many of them too. He was noted as a vicious tackler, with a signature move that was dubbed "the Night Train Necktie." Lane would basically clothesline the ball carrier, hitting him in the neck and head with his forearm. If the man didn't fall, Lane would wrap him up and take him down. The league eventually banned the move because it was too dangerous.

After two years with the Los Angeles Rams, Lane was traded to the Cardinals. He earned All-Pro honors in each of his six seasons there and continued to excel in six more years with the Detroit Lions.

Lane's life story is fascinating. According to his obituary, he was abandoned as a baby and taken in by a widow who found him crying in an alley. Despite his hard-luck background, he went to junior college and then spent four years in the army. After being discharged, he talked his way into a tryout with the Rams in 1954 by showing off a scrapbook of newspaper clippings describing his gridiron exploits in high school.

While playing with the Lions, Lane married legendary jazz singer Dinah Washington. Tragically, she died of an accidental drug overdose just six months into their marriage. After Lane retired as a player, he was the road manager for comedian Redd Foxx and later served as a college coach.

12

Ronnie Lott (1981–1994)

Lott began his career as an outstanding cornerback, and then switched to safety in 1985. His hard-hitting aggressive style was better suited to that position, and he would eventually receive All-Pro honors at both free safety and strong safety.

He won four Super Bowls with the Niners, notching 9 interceptions in twenty postseason games. His best season was 1986 when he led the league with 10 interceptions despite missing two games due to injury. He led the league again in 1991 as a member of the Los Angeles Raiders.

Emlen Tunnell (1948–1961)

Tunnell was the first great safety and the first African American inducted into the Pro Football Hall of Fame. Because of his military service, he was twenty-six years old as a rookie with the Giants in 1948.

To counter the growing success of NFL passing attacks, Giants coach Steve Owen developed the "umbrella defense." This was basically a 6-1-4 formation, adding a fourth defensive back where teams had traditionally used just three. They were spread out in the shape of an umbrella, with Tunnell at the top.

It helped the Giants contain the seemingly unstoppable aerial attacks of the Cleveland Browns. Tunnell and the Giants finished with the league's top-ranked defense in 1951 and again in 1956, when they won the NFL championship.

Tunnell was often referred to as the Giants "offense on defense" because of his ability to create turnovers, as well as his outstanding skills as a punt returner. He returned 3 punts for touchdowns in 1951 plus a 100-yard kickoff return for a score the same season.

Early in his fifth season, Tunnell became the all-time leader in interceptions with 36 (breaking the mark set by his former teammate Frank Reagan). He would expand his record to 79 by the time he retired.

Dave Grayson (1961–1970)

Grayson holds the AFL career record for interceptions and had the longest return—99 yards—in the league's ten-year history. He began his career with the Dallas Texans, helping them claim the 1962 AFL championship with a dramatic double-overtime win against the Raiders. His interception of a George Blanda pass in the second quarter set up a Dallas touchdown.

He was traded to the Raiders for Fred Williamson prior to the 1965 season, and Grayson would have his best seasons in Oakland. He led the league with 10 interceptions in 1968, and helped the Raiders win AFL titles in 1967 and 1969.

Eric Allen (1988–2001)

Allen shares the record for touchdowns by interception in a season (4) and in a single game (2). Both feats were accomplished during the 1993 season. He also had 3 interception returns for touchdowns in 2000, at the age of thirty-five.

He was a key figure in the Philadelphia Eagles defenses of the early 1990s. That unit was the league's stingiest in 1991, but before the team could make a Super Bowl run, most of the stars left as free agents. The domino effect started with the departure of Reggie White, and Eric Allen was among the players who quickly followed. He spent three unremarkable seasons with the Saints and finished his career with the Raiders.

Yale Lary (1952–1964)

Lary was one of the first free safeties, although that term didn't come into common use until much later. He had a fascinating playing style that I think was unique in his day. He'd lurk downfield, watching the receivers run their patterns but not getting too close. This created the illusion that they were open, but just as the quarterback would pull the trigger, he would pounce. Lary's quick burst would close the gap, and often he would arrive before the ball did.

After helping lead the Lions to championships in 1952 and 1953, he spent the next two years serving in the army. He helped the Lions win another title in 1957. While he never led the league in interceptions, he finished 2nd twice and was named All-Pro at safety nine times.

Lary was also a great punter, leading the league in punting average three times. He narrowly missed a fourth punting title in 1964. His contemporaries rave about his ability to punt the ball high and keep opponents from making significant returns. The term "hang time" hadn't been coined yet, but I'm confident that if we can reconstruct the play-by-play accounts from his career, our appreciation of his abilities will only grow.

Darrell Green (1983–2002)

One of the fastest men ever to play pro football, Green confounded his critics who said that his size would keep him from being an effective cornerback. At just 5-foot-8, he was four to six inches shorter than the era's leading receivers, such as Michael Irvin, Jerry Rice, or Cris Carter.

But Green held his own, and while he wasn't able to outleap six-footers for balls in the air, he was adept at stepping in front of receivers to beat them to the ball. While most cornerbacks attacked a short passing game by getting physical at the line of scrimmage, Green played close to the line. He knew that he could smother them on short patterns, and that he had the speed to recover if they decided to go deep. By cheating up to the line, he could also break up screen passes or run down ball carriers in the backfield.

Green showed off his blazing speed in his first NFL game, chasing down Tony Dorsett of the Cowboys to prevent a touchdown. He raced past two teammates to catch Dorsett after a 77-yard run, and Dallas had to settle for a field goal.

As he got older, Green naturally lost some of his speed, but he never slowed to the point that he had to stop playing cornerback. He spent twenty seasons in the NFL, all with the Washington Redskins. Green finished with 54 career interceptions

and 4 fumble recoveries for a touchdown, the latter a record for defensive backs.

John Lynch (1993–2007)

Lynch is a hard-hitting strong safety who came to prominence with the Tampa Bay Buccaneers. It was there that head coach Tony Dungy and defensive coordinator Monte Kiffin perfected the cover-2 defense, which would later become known as the Tampa-2. In that system, the two safeties play a deep zone with the corners and linebackers playing a tighter zone coverage underneath. To succeed with this scheme, you need safeties who can keep everything in front of them and make tackles in the open field—both against speedy receivers and against bulkier running backs.

Lynch fit the bill perfectly, and he was one of the main reasons why the Buccaneers defense was so dominating in the late 1990s and early 2000s.

Where most defensive backs would go for the interception, Lynch preferred to deliver a big blow. He liked to creep up to the inside part of his zone so he could crunch receivers or tight ends coming over the middle.

He joined the Broncos as a free agent in 2004 and moved to free safety. Lynch's chief asset in Denver was his ability to read the play and call out adjustments to his teammates.

Tim McDonald (1987–1999)

When McDonald retired, his former coach Bill Walsh praised him as one of the best players of his era. "There are those who would state flatly that he was the best strong safety to ever play the game," Walsh mused. It's tough to argue with that conclusion.

In his first six seasons with the Cardinals, McDonald was selected as an All-Pro four times.

He really flourished after moving to San Francisco as a free agent, playing strong safety in the team's cover-3 defense. The cornerbacks and free safety each covered the deep zone while McDonald moved up as the eighth man in the box. McDonald was an aggressive defender who was terrific against the run. His physical style of play also made him very effective in covering bigger receivers man-to-man.

McDonald was one of a string of great safeties that came out of the University of Southern California in the 1980s, a list that also includes Dennis Smith, Ronnie Lott, and Mark Carrier. Among the other notable safeties the school has produced are Hall of Famer Willie Wood, Troy Polamalu, Sammy Knight, and Jason Seehorn.

Emmitt Thomas (1966–1978)

Thomas led the league in interceptions twice and still ranks in the top ten with 58 for his career. He spent his entire career with the Chiefs, winning an AFL championship in 1966 and a Super Bowl in 1969.

It has been nearly thirty years since he retired as a player, and during that time Thomas has been one of the most successful assistant coaches in the NFL ranks. In my annuals, I compiled basic statistics for offensive and defensive coordinators, just based on how their units performed. I never went back much further than the late 1990s, but I'd wager that if I did, Thomas would rank as one of the great defensive coaches of all time. He had successful stints with five different teams, most notably the Redskins and Eagles.

Thomas was in his mid-fifties before the Rooney Rule went into effect, which requires NFL teams to interview minority candidates every time they have an opening for head coach. Based on my rudimentary research, I think the first time he was considered for a top job was in 1997, when he interviewed with the Giants and Rams. Thomas got

another shot with the Ravens in 1999, but he was never a front-runner for any of those jobs. Now in his mid-sixties, those calls won't be coming anymore.

It's a shame, because his resume is impeccable, and by all accounts he was a great teacher. If he'd have been born ten or fifteen years later he might have made a pretty good head coach.

Pat Fischer (1961–1977)

Fischer wasn't very big, just 5-foot-9 and maybe 170 pounds soaking wet, but he was one of the hardest hitting cornerbacks of his era. Most of the bump-and-run defenders used their size and strength to combat receivers. Fischer had to rely on his toughness and tenacity.

He had eight interceptions in 1963 and ten the following year, leading to the first of six All-Pro selections. The Cardinals traded Fischer to Washington in 1968, where he quickly became a fan favorite. He thrived as part of coach George Allen's "Over the Hill Gang," before injuries knocked him out of action for good in 1977. When he retired, Fischer ranked 7th all-time with 56 career interceptions.

Donnie Shell (1974–1987)

Shell joined the Steelers as an undrafted free agent in 1974. He played linebacker in college, but at 5-foot-11 and 190 pounds, was too small to play that position in the NFL. The Steelers turned him into a defensive back, and by his third season he was a starter. Over the course of his career, he intercepted 51 passes, a figure which still stands as the most ever by a strong safety.

Even though he was in the secondary, he played like a linebacker. Shell was terrific at defending against the run, and one play stands out in my memory as an example of what a hard hitter he was. In a 1978 game against the Oilers, Shell came flying out of the secondary to meet Earl Campbell at the line of scrimmage. Campbell was the biggest, strongest running back in the league, but Shell knocked him flat, and Campbell didn't get up. Houston's battering ram left the game with broken ribs, and the Steelers went on to win the game 13-3.

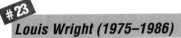

Louis Wright (1975–1986)

Wright was an eight-time All-Pro cornerback who spent his entire career with the Denver Broncos. He was part of the Orange Crush defense that led the Broncos to Super Bowl XII following the 1977 season, and also a member of the 1986 team that advanced to Super Bowl XXI. Both teams had outstanding run defenses, which left most opponents trying to pass the ball. Wright's ability to smother receivers with his man-to-man coverage made that a difficult alternative to pursue.

Warren Lahr (1949–1959)

The NFL expanded it's annual draft to 32 rounds during the forties in an attempt to help teams find more players. In practice, I think it had the opposite effect. With that many picks, there was no pressure to get it right, and rather than invest in scouting, most teams just picked a lot of guys and hoped that a few happened to pan out. Occasionally, one of those names selected late in the draft turned out to be a pretty good player. As longtime scout Bucko Kilroy acknowledged, "We were still drafting guys sight unseen. That's why a lot of last-rounders made it."

The lowest draft pick to actually play in the pros was George Groves, selected 327th by the Bears in 1945. He played nine games for two different AAFC teams. Tackle Bill Fischer was the 300th pick in 1947, and he was a two-time All-Pro

with the Chicago Cardinals. Ralph Earhart scored touchdowns rushing, receiving, and on a punt return after the Packers made him the 296th pick in 1948.

But among the 32nd round picks, the best was undoubtedly Warren Lahr. A graduate of Case Western, he was selected by Pittsburgh as the 293rd pick in 1947. A knee injury forced him to miss his rookie season, and the Steelers cut him loose during the offseason. Lahr signed with the Cleveland Browns and became a key member of one of the most dominant teams of the era. He intercepted 44 passes in 11 seasons, and in both 1950 and 1951 he returned two interceptions for touchdowns. He was named All-NFL six times as a defensive halfback, before moving to safety later in his career.

After he retired, Lahr was a longtime color commentator on CBS television broadcasts of NFL games.

Lemar Parrish (1970–1982)

Parrish went to six Pro Bowls as a member of the Bengals and two more with the Redskins, so it's hard to say that he was overlooked. Still, I can't help but feel he's been largely forgotten. Parrish was one of the NFL's great cornerbacks of the seventies, an exciting player who could hurt you in a lot of different ways. In his first five years in the league he scored 6 touchdowns on defense and 5 more as a return specialist.

He was traded to the Redskins with Coy Bacon for a first-round draft pick in 1978, and a year later had a career-high 9 interceptions.

Others

 # 26. Gary Fencik (1976–1987)

 # 27. Mel Renfro (1964-1977)

 # 28. Mike Haynes (1976-1989)

 # 29. Jimmy Patton (1955-1966)

 # 30. Erich Barnes (1958-1971)

 # 31. Ronde Barber (1997-2007)

 # 32. Eugene Robinson (1985-2000)

 # 33. Le Roy Butler (1990-2001)

 # 34. Jimmy Johnson (1961-1976)

 # 35. Richie Petitbon (1959-1972)

 # 36. Roger Wehrli (1969-1982)

 # 37. Jake Scott (1970-1978)

 # 38. Ken Riley (1969-1983)

 # 39. Albert Lewis (1983-1998)

 # 40. Johnny Sample (1958-1968)

 # 41. Aeneas Williams (1991-2004)

 # 42. Jack Christiansen (1951-1958)

 # 43. Eddie Meador (1959-1970)

 # 44. Steve Atwater (1989-1999)

 # 45. Deron Cherry (1981-1991)

 # 46. Larry Wilson (1960-1972)

 # 47. Billy Thompson (1969-1981)

 # 48. Darren Woodson (1992-2003)

 # 49. Lem Barney (1967-1977)

 # 50. Mike Wagner (1971-1980)

Kickers

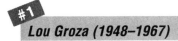

1

Lou Groza (1948–1967)

Groza preferred to think of himself as an offensive lineman who just happened to kick. He did double duty for thirteen seasons, and after a 1960 back injury returned as a kicking specialist only.

Would he have made the Hall of Fame if he hadn't been a kicker? Probably, yes. He was an awfully good tackle for a Browns team that relied heavily on its running game.

Would he have made the Hall of Fame if he had *only* been a kicker? That's a tougher question to answer, not because you can't make the case that he was one of the greatest field goal kickers ever, but because the Hall has largely ignored kickers and punters, especially those like Groza who also played a second position.

Although the Browns often had a potent offense, they attempted more field goals than the other teams of their era. At a time when kickers missed more attempts than they made, the sure-footed Groza gave the Browns a reliable option when their drives stalled in enemy territory. Rather than going for it on fourth and long, as was the standard practice at the time, they'd bring out Groza to kick.

In 1953, for example, Groza converted 23 of 26 attempts, a success rate of 88.6 percent. The other kickers in the league were a combined 74 for 184, or 40.2 percent. It wasn't just that he kicked more often: Groza was often called to kick with the game on the line. His most memorable clutch kick came in the 1950 NFL championship game. Groza's 16-yard field goal with 28 seconds left on the clock gave the Browns a 30–28 victory over the Rams, Cleveland's first NFL title after the AAFC-NFL merger.

Groza used a specialized kicking tee and a strip of tape, six feet long, that he would lay on the ground to help line up his kick. Both items were banned in 1956, a rule that would come to be known as the Lou Groza Rule. The change had little affect on Groza, who continued to be one of the league's best kickers for ten more seasons.

2

Matt Stover (1991–2007)

From 1999 to 2001 Stover set an NFL record by making field goals in thirty-eight consecutive games. The Ravens of that era had a great defense but their offense often struggled to score points. In those three seasons, eleven of the Ravens wins came by 7 points or less, and Stover often played a deciding role.

This was never more evident than in a five-game stretch during the 2000 season when the Ravens didn't score any touchdowns. Stover kicked

14 field goals in those five games, accounting for all of his team's points in the month of October.

October 2001 Ravens

Week	Score	Opponent
5	W 12–0	Cleveland
6	W 15–0	Jacksonville
7	L 10–3	Washington
8	L 14–6	Tennessee
9	L 9–6	Pittsburgh

The Ravens offense came to life after that loss to the Steelers, winning their last seven games en route to their first Super Bowl victory. There were four other times that season—including in the AFC championship game—when the offense scored just 1 touchdown and counted on Stover to do the rest. The Ravens won all four of those games.

Morten Andersen (1982–2007)

Andersen appears to be giving George Blanda a run for his money as the oldest player in NFL history. He has said repeatedly that he intends to play until he is fifty, and there's no reason to think he can't. Andersen turned forty-seven in 2007 and completed 84.3 percent of his field goals that season—five points better than his career average.

While durability has become his trademark, that certainly wasn't a label he earned at the outset of his career. On his first NFL play, Andersen sprained his ankle on a kickoff and was out of action for the next eight weeks. With the exception of the players' strikes, Andersen didn't miss another game for twenty years.

John Carney (1988–2006)

Carney almost didn't make it in the NFL. He was undrafted then cut from his first training camp. He finally hooked on as a replacement player during the 1987 strike. Over the next couple of years, he found opportunities only when another kicker was injured mid-season. It wasn't until his fourth year of bouncing around that Carney found a home and a job of his own. Joining the Chargers in Week 5 of the 1990 season, he went on to convert 19 of 21 field goal attempts, setting a team record for field goal percentage (90.5 percent).

After ten seasons with the Chargers, he moved to New Orleans and continued to be one of the league's most consistent kickers. Surprisingly, he was only invited to one Pro Bowl in his career.

Gary Anderson (1982–2004)

Anderson set an NFL record in 1998 by converting all 35 of his field goal attempts. It was the most in history without a miss. Prior to his feat, the record for most attempts without a miss in a single season was 17.

There was a time when he was the most accurate kicker in NFL history, but rate statistics almost always go down when you get older. Anderson played until he was forty-five, and while that hurt his percentages, his longevity helped him retire as the all-time leader in points, field goals, and attempts.

Anderson also set an NFL record by scoring 164 points with the Vikings in 1998, most ever by a kicker. He topped the 100-point mark fourteen times in his career, more than any other player.

He'll be forever tied with kicker Morten Andersen in the collective memory of football fans, and not just because they have similar surnames. Both kickers came into the league in the same year and were among the best kickers in the game for two decades. The two men rank 1st and 2nd in nearly every kicking category in the record book.

They were very different, though. Morten Andersen is a big strong Dane with dirty blonde hair. He boomed his kicks with a powerful leg. Gary Anderson was smaller, a dark-haired South African who made up for his lack of leg strength with his remarkable accuracy.

Jan Stenerud (1967–1985)

The Pro Football Hall of Fame has largely ignored special teams players, but Jan Stenerud was selected in his first year of eligibility. It's a testament not only to the quality of his performance but also to the impact he had on the game.

Pete Gogolak became the first soccer-style kicker in the pro ranks in 1964. It looked strange at first to see a field goal kicker using the side of his foot, but Gogolak had moderate success, enough at least for coaches to consider other sidewinders for kicking jobs. Stenerud was the first to become a bona fide star, and his success helped bring the era of straight-ahead kickers to an end. That breed was extinct by the early 1980s.

Chiefs coach Hank Stram, a former kicker himself, was completely enamored when he saw Stenerud kicking for Montana State University. Stram used a third-round draft pick to grab him in 1966, a year and a half before he finished school.

Stenerud was phenomenal on field goals, but he changed the game with the way he boomed kickoffs through the end zone. After a few seasons, the NFL responded by moving the kickoff point back from the 40-yard line to the 35.

He kicked a 57-yard field goal in his first NFL game, and on three different occasions Stenerud made 5 field goals in a single game.

Nick Lowery (1978–1996)

Lowery joined the Chiefs in 1980, replacing Jan Stenerud. He would break most of Stenerud's team records and go on to surpass most of his career totals as well. Early in his career, Lowery passed Rolf Benirschke's high mark for field goal percentage, eventually pushing the career record from 72 percent to over 80 percent.

He was one of the leading kickers of that transitional era when teams began to understand the contributions of the kicking game to winning. It wasn't just that teams were grasping this as an abstract concept, but that they were devoting more resources to improving special teams play. This manifested itself in many ways, not the least of which was more practice time. In the sixties and seventies, a kicker might get five snaps with the center and holder at the end of practice on Friday. Typically, the snapping duties were handled by the starting center while the quarterback served as the holder, and so their practice time was limited. By the early nineties, many teams were beginning to employ long snappers who played only on special teams. Some also began to assign the holding duties to a punter or backup quarterback. Because these guys didn't need to participate in other practice sessions, kickers suddenly had the opportunity to take forty or fifty practice snaps a day. The efficiency of the snap-place-kick routine improved dramatically, and field goal percentages went up across the board.

Jason Elam (1993–2007)

In 1998, Elam tied Tom Dempsey's 1970 record for the longest field goal in league history, nailing a kick from 63 yards out. Dempsey's kick was dramatic, coming with 2 seconds left in a game that his Saints trailed 17–16. It passed over the crossbar with about a foot to spare, and his teammates stormed the field to celebrate the remarkable victory. Elam's kick came at the end of the first half in a game that his team led 24–10. While the achievement was noted, it was almost as an afterthought. In a closer game, Elam likely wouldn't have even been given the opportunity to attempt that kick.

There have only been a handful of field goals attempted from that far out. Teams are generally discouraged from attempting such long kicks by a couple of rule changes that have occurred since Dempsey's record-setter. In 1974, the league moved the goalposts from the goal line to the back of the end zone, adding 10 yards to each field goal attempt. Beginning in 1994, when a team missed a field goal attempt, their opponents would take possession from the spot of the kick rather than the line of scrimmage, a difference of roughly 7 yards. Both of these moves forced teams to change their strategy when it came to attempting long field goals.

In the thirty-five years after Dempsey's kick, only three other men had made field goals of 60 yards or more. None played a decisive role in the game: Besides Elam's long kick, the other two came in a losing effort. I wrote in one of my football annuals that 60-yard field goals were probably extinct. The penalty for missing one was pretty high—the opponent would get the ball at midfield or in your own territory. Strategically a punt was always preferable unless the game was on the line, in which case a pass play had a much higher level of success.

Then a strange thing happened in 2006. Two kickers made field goals of 60 yards or more, and both swung the outcome in the final seconds of the game. The first came in late October, when Matt Bryant of the Buccaneers kicked a 62-yarder as time expired to beat the Eagles. Five weeks later, the Titans' Rob Bironas kicked one from 60 yards with less than 10 seconds remaining in the game. That gave Tennessee a 20–17 win against the divisional rival (and eventual Super Bowl champions) Indianapolis Colts.

Longest Field Goals

Yds	Kicker	Tm	Score	Opp
63	Tom Dempsey	NO	W 19–17	Det
63	Jason Elam	Den	W 34–27	Jac
62	Matt Bryant	TB	W 23–21	Phi
60	Steve Cox	Cle	L 9–12	Cin
60	Morten Andersen	NO	L 17–20	Chi
60	Rob Bironas	Ten	W 20–17	Ind

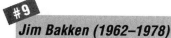

Jim Bakken (1962–1978)

The life of a field goal kicker is all about opportunities. As with punters, they only get a chance to come on to the field when their offense fails. Bakken spent his entire career with the St. Louis Cardinals,

appearing in just two playoff games in his seventeen seasons. While the losing couldn't have been much fun, it gave him plenty of opportunities to kick.

In a 1967 game against the Steelers, Bakken attempted 9 field goals and made 7 of them, setting new records in each category. He kicked 6 later that season in a game against the Falcons.

Jeff Wilkins (1995–2007)

Currently the second-most accurate kicker in NFL history, among players with at least 125 attempts. Wilkins tied an NFL record in 2003 by kicking 39 field goals. That year, he also pulled off an interesting feat in a game with the Arizona Cardinals. Wilkins kicked a field goal as time ran out in the first half, kicked another to tie the game as time expired in the fourth quarter, then ended the game with a field goal in overtime. It's the first and only time a player has made three period-ending field goals in an NFL game.

Others

 # 11. Don Cockroft (1968–1980)

 # 12. Jason Hanson (1992–2007)

 # 13. Adam Vinatieri (1996–2007)

 # 14. Mike Vanderjagt (1998–2006)

 # 15. Garo Yepremian (1966–1981)

 # 16. Al Del Greco (1984–2000)

 # 17. Eddie Murray (1980–2000)

 # 18. Norm Johnson (1982–1999)

 # 19. Pete Stoyanovich (1989–2000)

 # 20. Bobby Layne (1948–1961)

 # 21. John Kasay (1991–2007)

 # 22. Jim Turner (1964–1979)

 # 23. Ryan Longwell (1997–2007)

 # 24. Fred Cox (1963–1977)

 # 25. George Blanda (1949–1975)

Punters

Dave Jennings (1974–1987)

Ask anybody who the greatest punter in NFL history is and you will get the same answer: It was Oakland's Ray Guy. Ask them why, and they won't be able to tell you. They certainly wouldn't be able to construct a case based on statistics. Although he is universally acclaimed as the greatest punter in history by those who saw him play, Guy doesn't hold any punting records—either single-season or career. And while a portfolio documenting Guy's case for the Hall of Fame would be overflowing with quotes and anecdotes, you would not be able to include a statistical analysis showing why Guy was better than all other punters. There's just no way that you can spin the data to support that conclusion.

In Guy's defense, you might argue that the root problem is that existing statistics aren't robust enough to identify the things that he did well. However, the league made net punting yards, touchbacks, and punts inside the twenty official statistics in 1976, and we have that data for most of Guy's career. What else should we be measuring that we're not? Guy's supporters would say hang time, but that's a metric for scouts, not analysts.

The theory is that by punting the ball high in the air, your coverage team has an opportunity to get down the field and tackle the defender before he can make a return. If that theory is true, then it should be reflected in your net average. In the eleven seasons that we have those figures for Guy, he never once led the league in net average. Among qualifying punters (minimum 250 career punts), Guy ranks 44th in gross punting average and 103rd in percentage of touchbacks versus punts inside the twenty.

I'm not trying to denigrate Ray Guy or to build up a case against him. All I'm saying is that we ought to at least have the conversation. Conventional wisdom has anointed him as No. 1, and the discussion has pretty much ended without any attempt at real analysis.

As I discussed in the introduction, depending on where the line of scrimmage is when they come on to the field, punters either kick the ball as far as possible or kick it as close to the goal line as possible without having the ball go into the end zone. In theory a team could employ two different punters—one who specializes in each of those skills, but in reality, teams rely on their punter to do both.

Dave Jennings was not the best punter at either of those skills, but he was very good at both, and his ability to do both kinds of punting extremely well makes him the highest-rated punter of all time. He ranked in the top ten in gross average for eight straight years, and in the top five for punts inside the 20 in five straight seasons. For a six-year period from 1977 to 1982, Jennings ranked 1st or 2nd in adjusted punting yards each season. It was perhaps the most dominant stretch ever for a punter, but since it came during a streak of eight straight losing seasons by the Giants, Jennings's feats were largely overlooked.

That's where part of the problem lies. Punting becomes more important on a losing team because an unproductive offense stalls more frequently, and the punters have more opportunities to do their thing and impact the game. In 1977, for example, the Giants finished with a 5-9 record and Jennings punted 100 times—the second-highest total in the league. Ray Guy only punted 59 times, as his Raiders went 11-3.

I keep coming back to Ray Guy, not simply because he's the presumed standard bearer, but also because the careers of Jennings and Guy overlap almost perfectly. Guy came to the NFL one year earlier than Jennings and retired one year earlier. In their fourteen seasons, Jennings had more punts for more yards, with fewer touchbacks and more punts inside the 20. Maybe that's not enough to end the discussion over who was better, but if you're open-minded, it ought to at least be a good starting point.

back in short-yardage situations. He had trouble following his blockers. Once when the Chiefs were backed up against their own goal line they gave the ball to Wilson. In those days, the goal posts were in the end zone, and he ran directly into an upright, a thunderous collision that resulted in a safety.

It was also an era when teams were beginning to realize the value of kicking and punting and that having a specialist for those duties gave them an advantage against teams who used a lineman or whomever they could find on the roster that was willing. Wilson quickly established himself as one of pro football's best punters, leading the AFL in punting average in 1965 and 1967. After the AFL and NFL merged, Wilson led the league another two times. His four punting titles is a feat matched only by Sammy Baugh.

In 1969, the Pro Football Hall of Fame asked a panel of historians to select an all-time American Football League team, and they chose Wilson as the best punter in the league's ten-year history. He played in two AFL championship games and two Super Bowls, averaging 46.5 yards on 22 punts. That's the highest average for a punter in championship games, although the NFL requires a minimum of 25 punts to be eligible for the official record.

Wilson attended the University of Southern Mississippi, the same school that would later produce Ray Guy.

#2
Jerrel Wilson (1963–1978)

His friends and teammates all called him "Duck," but fans dubbed him "Thunderfoot." Teammate Len Dawson used to say that Wilson kicked balls so hard he thought that eventually one would explode. Wilson was a running back and linebacker in college, a big strong guy with tremendously powerful legs. Drafted by the AFL's Kansas City Chiefs, Wilson saw occasional duty as a full-

#3
Bobby Walden (1964–1977)

Walden started his career in Canada, then joined the Minnesota Vikings in 1964. He led the league in punting as a rookie with a 46.4-yard average—a rookie record that still stands. After four years with the Vikings, he moved to Pittsburgh and served as the Steelers' punter for ten seasons. Walden led the league in adjusted punting yards four times in a three-year stretch.

Bobby Joe Green (1960–1973)

Green was not the first player hired purely as a kicking specialist, but he was the first one to make a significant impact. Green was among the leaders in punting average each season throughout the 1960s. By the end of the decade, most other NFL teams had followed suit.

While he was a trendsetter in one regard, he was the last of his kind in another. Green was the last NFL player to take the field without a facemask, a practice he continued until he retired in 1973. Most other players had adopted the facemask by the mid-fifties. The NFL made them mandatory for all players starting in 1954, but since punters and kickers weren't considered "real" players, they were exempt until the mid-1970s.

Rohn Stark (1982–1997)

In his first five seasons, Stark led the league in punting average three times. He finished 2nd and 3rd in the other two seasons. At the end of the 1986 season, his career average was 45.16, the best average in NFL history (ahead of Sammy Baugh's 45.1 career mark).

Players went on strike the following season, sitting out for four weekends before returning. When Stark came back, he had completely fallen apart. In the first six games back, he averaged an anemic 37.3 yards per kick. He had 4 punts in that stretch that traveled less than 30 yards, and at one point had 9 straight punts of less than 40 yards.

In an interview with Len Pasquarelli of the *Sporting News,* Stark blamed his troubles on the layoff. "Because of some of the weather conditions during the strike, I started kicking across the ball too much," he explained. "When you do that, the ball takes off at an angle instead of downfield." Stark continued to struggle with his mechanics and

finished with an average of 40 yards per punt—20th among kickers that year.

Stark rebounded somewhat in 1988, but never returned to the ranks of the NFL's top punters. His average over the rest of his career fell to 42.7, which more often than not left him below the top ten.

Sean Landeta (1985–2005)

Landeta started his pro career in the USFL, playing in all three league championship games as a member of the Philadelphia/Baltimore Stars. He went on to a twenty-one-year NFL career, winning two Super Bowls with the New York Giants. He was a first-team All-Pro three times in the NFL and twice in the USFL.

The Pro Football Hall of Fame selected him as the punter of the decade for both the 1980s and 1990s. The moment that I'll always remember was not such a glorious one, however, an infamous play from his first NFL season. It was a 1985 playoff game against the Bears at Soldier Field, and the winds were howling. Landeta was back to punt, but as he dropped the ball the wind caught it, blowing it hard enough that he completely missed it with his foot. Shaun Gayle of the Bears scooped it up and ran in for the game's first touchdown. The Giants went on to lose that game 21–0.

Paul Maguire (1960–1970)

Best known today as a color commentator, Maguire retired as the most prolific punter in NFL history. He was one of the last punters to also play defense full time—a starter at right linebacker in his days with the Chargers.

Contemporary accounts describe him as a master of the "coffin corner" kick, but we don't yet have statistics (for touchbacks, net yards, or punts inside the 20) from that era to back that up. He ranked in the top three in gross average six times in his eleven seasons, which suggests that if nothing else, he had one of the strongest legs of his era.

Maguire played in six AFL title games—three with the Chargers and three with the Bills.

Rich Camarillo (1981–1996)

Camarillo had the longest punt in Super Bowl history, a 62-yarder that pinned the Bears at their own 4-yard line. But nothing could stop the Bears in Super Bowl XX. They marched 96 yards for a touchdown on their way to a 46–10 trouncing of Camarillo's New England Patriots.

He had some good years with the Patriots, but really flourished during his five seasons with the Phoenix Cardinals. Camarillo set a record with 35 punts inside the 20 in 1994, and led the league in both gross average (1989) and net average (1991) in separate seasons.

Sammy Baugh (1937–1952)

Baugh retired with a gross average of 45.1 yards per punt, setting an NFL record that has stood for over fifty years. Glenn Dobbs of the AAFC averaged 46.4, but played just four seasons and fails to qualify for most leader lists. The most serious threat to Baugh's record comes from Shane Lechler, who as of this writing has just completed his eighth season with the Oakland Raiders. Through the 2007 season, Lechler's average stands at 46.5, although as with most rate statistics, it's virtually certain that this figure will drop as more time passes.

Punting stats were not kept as part of the official record until 1939, so we have no idea how well Baugh performed in his first two seasons in the NFL. It's possible that his average would be even higher if we had data from the 1937 and '38 campaigns.

Another one of Baugh's punting records is unlikely to be broken. In 1940 he averaged 51.4 yards per punt. In the last forty years, only two other punters have averaged more than 48 yards in a season.

Darren Bennett (1995–2005)

One of the best ever at dropping the ball inside the 20-yard line. The Australian-born punter had 261 punts inside the 20 and only 62 touchbacks, the third-best ratio of all-time.

In the early nineties, Bennett was a star of Australian Rules Football, a sport that resembles rugby more than football. While on his honeymoon in California in 1994, he telephoned the San Diego Chargers to ask for a tryout. The coaches obliged, and were so impressed that they signed him to the practice squad. After spending a season in NFL Europe, he took over the punting duties for the Chargers.

Most NFL punters used a spiral technique on their punts, while Bennett used the drop punt, which is the more common style in the Australian game. While his kicks tended to have less distance, the end-over-end backward spin meant the ball would bounce straight up or back toward him when it hit the ground.

Bennett's success prompted other Australian players to compete for jobs as NFL punters. Among the imports were Ben Graham of the Jets and Mat McBriar of the Cowboys.

Others

 # 11. Rick Tuten (1989–1999)

 # 12. Ray Guy (1973–1986)

 # 13. Chris Gardocki (1992–2006)

 # 14. Tommy Davis (1959–1969)

 # 15. Jim Arnold (1983–1994)

 # 16. Brad Maynard (1997–2007)

 # 17. Sam Baker (1953–1968)

 # 18. Todd Sauerbrun (1995–2007)

 # 19. Don Chandler (1956–1966)

 # 20. Mark Royals (1987–2003)

 # 21. Reggie Roby (1983–1998)

 # 22. Mike Horan (1984–1999)

 # 23. Norm Van Brocklin (1949–1960)

 # 24. Jeff Feagles (1988–2007)

 # 25. Tom Tupa (1989–2004)

Return Specialists

RETURNING KICKOFFS AND returning punts require different physical skills and different techniques. Through the 2007 season, more than 6200 players have returned kicks or punts in an NFL game, but only 30 percent of them have done both. Only fifty-six players in NFL history have returned at least 100 kickoffs and 100 punts. For that reason, we need to evaluate players in the two categories separately.

But there is another, even bigger challenge. The majority of return men have also played another position. Even in the present day, return duties are often handled by younger players who serve as a nickelback, a fourth receiver, or a backup running back. As their play at that position improves and they move into the starting lineup, they tend to stop playing on special teams. The result is that a number of players who were dazzling return men for a brief time suffer from their small sample size, players such as Travis Williams, Jack Christiansen, or Bobby Mitchell.

What I've done in this section is rank the top kick returners and the top punt returners separately. I've also included a combined ranking to recognize that handful of players who did both things exceptionally well.

Kick Returners

#1 Abe Woodson (1958–1966)

Arguably the NFL's first return specialist, Woodson was a defensive back with tremendous speed. He used bursts of acceleration to break free from defenders. Woodson led the league in kick return average three times—a feat no player has matched—and his career average of 28.7 is the highest in league history (with a minimum of 100 returns). Woodson also led the league in punt return average in 1960.

#2 Glyn Milburn (1993–2001)

As I mentioned in the introduction, most of the players who have success as return men get moved to other positions. Invariably, teams want to take advantage of those skills at positions they deem more important, usually at wide receiver or in the defensive secondary. But there have been three recent returners who were able to keep special team jobs despite their success. They are Brian Mitchell, Alan Rossum, and Glyn Milburn. All three rank in my top fifteen for both kick returns and punt returns. Mitchell was head and shoulders above everyone else at punt returns. Rossum is similarly more productive on punts than kickoffs. But Milburn was much better at kick returns.

Milburn played for four teams in his nine-year career, finding his best success with the Chicago Bears. In 1995, he set the NFL record for all purpose yards in a game. Pressed into action at running back, Milburn gained 131 yards rushing, 45 yards receiving, and 228 on kick and punt returns. His 404 total yards broke the mark of 373 yards set by Billy Cannon in 1961.

In 1998 he scored 2 touchdowns on kick returns and another on a punt return.

One of the most prolific return men in history, Milburn ranks fourth all time in kick-return yards and third in combined kick and punt returns.

The Bears cut him suddenly a few years later after he fumbled 2 kickoffs in the same game. One ball hit him in the facemask; the other he just coughed up. Although he spent the rest of the season returning punts for the Chargers, Milburn never returned another kickoff in the NFL.

Brian Mitchell (1990–2003)

The most prolific returner in NFL history and the only man to make my top-five list for both kicks and punts. He's firmly atop the leader board in nearly every return category in the NFL's record book. When the Hall of Fame voters eventually come to their senses and realize that special teams players deserve a place in Canton, Mitchell should be the overwhelming first choice.

Mitchell never had blazing speed, but he was incredibly elusive. He had good field vision and was able to find the holes as they developed. The other thing he did better than most return men of his day was to get up the field quickly. That sounds obvious, but if you watch closely you'll notice a lot of less-experienced players hesitate after they

catch the ball. They scan the field, looking for their blockers and trying to see where the defenders are. As a result, Mitchell would gain yards even when he didn't break free for a touchdown. In explaining why he signed Mitchell, Giants General Manager Ernie Acorsi said, "You don't win championships with an occasional 80-yard return but with 9- and 12-yard returns all season."

Mitchell was also an outstanding third-down back, catching 255 passes and rushing for 12 touchdowns in his career. He rushed for 109 yards and a touchdown in the Redskins 1992 playoff win over the Vikings.

Dante Hall (2000–2007)

Over a nine-game stretch at the end of the 2002 season and the beginning of the 2003 season, Hall scored 3 touchdowns on kickoff returns and 4 more on punt returns. Only about a dozen return men had scored that many in their careers, and nobody had returns for touchdowns in more than two consecutive games.

After that, teams just stopped kicking to him. In six of his next nine games, he watched as his opponents kicked every punt out-of-bounds or found other ways to keep the ball out of his hands. They couldn't do that forever, and Hall would score at least one return touchdown in each of the next three seasons. In 2005 he tied the record set by Ollie Matson (and shared by three others) by scoring his 6th touchdown on a kick return.

Hall has blazing speed and great moves in the open field. On one memorable kickoff return against the Broncos in 2003, Hall appeared to be hemmed in by the coverage team. He juked left, then right. He took a stutter step and ran back 4 or 5 yards toward the goal line. Just when it looked like he had run out of places to go, Hall came back to the left side at full speed. He blew past the Denver defense as if he'd been shot out of a rocket, looping to the outside and running 93 yards for a touchdown.

Mel Gray (1986–1997)

"Never think and always move." That's how Gray described his strategy for returning kicks. In 1991 he became the first player to lead the NFL in both kick return average (25.8) and punt return average (15.4). He started his pro career in the USFL before playing twelve seasons in the NFL, mostly with the Lions. He also led the league in punt return average in 1987 while playing with the Saints.

There was another pretty good football player with the same name. The other Mel Gray was a four-time Pro Bowl wide receiver who played from 1971 to 1982 with the St. Louis Cardinals.

Others

- **# 6.** Terrence McGee (2003–2007)
- **# 7.** Tyrone Hughes (1993–1998)
- **# 8.** Michael Bates (1993–2003)
- **# 9.** Timmy Brown (1959–1968)
- **# 10.** Gale Sayers (1965–1971)
- **# 11.** Buddy Young (1947–1955)
- **# 12.** Lynn Chandnois (1950–1956)
- **# 13.** Joe Arenas (1951–1957)
- **# 14.** Allen Rossum (1998–2007)
- **# 15.** Josh Cribbs (2005-2007)

Punt Returners

Brian Mitchell (1990–2003)

Running backs return kicks while cornerbacks and receivers return punts. That's a huge generalization, but it's a good way to look at the different skill sets that are required for the two different jobs. Punt returners have to catch the ball in the open field and advance with little blocking. Kick returners have a wall of blockers in front of them and need to find an opening, either through the heart of the defense or around them.

Mitchell stands as an anomaly, however, because he was a running back who excelled at returning punts. Most punt returners rely on their speed to elude tacklers, but Mitchell preferred to steamroll them. In a 2002 interview, he claimed to have broken the arms of at least five opponents who tried to arm tackle him. "I have a linebacker's mentality," Mitchell said. "I am trying to give it to them more than they are to me."

His size was what made him so durable. The speediest punt returners were all too small to survive the return game for long. His longevity also helped him amass numbers that are unlikely to be equaled. He had 463 punt returns for 4999 yards—no one else has more than 75 percent of those totals.

Mitchell led the league in punt return average in 1994, and returned nine punts for touchdowns in his career—second only to Eric Metcalf.

Dave Meggett (1989–1998)

Meggett led the league in punt return yards as a rookie, earning a Pro Bowl invitation at the end of the 1989 season. Over his first four seasons with the Giants, he caught 10 touchdown passes and ran for another. He compiled 129 all-purpose yards in the team's 20–19 win over the Bills in Super Bowl XXV.

In 1993 Meggett became one of the few players in the modern era to record at least 300 yards in four different categories: rushing (329), receiving (319), kick returns (403), and punt returns (321).

After six seasons with the Giants, Meggett signed with the Patriots as a free agent, reuniting with head coach Bill Parcells. He had several productive seasons in New England, but his career ended abruptly after a series of off-the-field incidents in 1998. Meggett was arrested in Toronto in February, prompting the Patriots to release him.

The charges were later dropped, and Meggett got a second chance with the Jets that fall. During the team's Week 2 trip to Baltimore, Meggett was arrested a second time. Nobody else would sign him after that.

Jermaine Lewis (1996–2004)

The Ravens of the late 1990s boasted an offense that avoided mistakes and played things close to the vest. It was up to the defense and special teams to be aggressive, and more often than not, they produced the big plays. Jermaine Lewis made an immediate impact as a punt returner, leading the league in return average twice in his first five seasons. His blazing speed made him a threat to score every time he touched the ball. Lewis is one of three players in NFL history to twice return 2 punts for touchdowns in the same game.

He made several big plays in Super Bowl XXXV. Lewis returned a punt 43 yards in the first quarter to set up the Ravens' first touchdown of the game. Then the Giants got a big boost of momentum in the third quarter when they returned a third-quarter kickoff for touchdown and closed the deficit to 10 points. But Lewis burst their bubble seconds later, returning the ensuing kickoff 84 yards for a touchdown to make the score 24–7 and put the game out of reach.

A year later, the Ravens left Lewis unprotected in the expansion draft, and the Houston Texans were thrilled to take him. It seemed an odd choice given Lewis's high-salary-cap figure and the Texans' plethora of needs. Surrounded by an inexperienced supporting cast and ravaged by injuries, Lewis was a shadow of his former self. After suffering through a disappointing season in Houston, Lewis was released. He signed a three-year $4 million contract with Jacksonville but could not regain his form as one of the league's top return

specialists. He suffered a torn ACL in his left knee in his second game with the Jaguars. The following year he suffered two concussions and was forced to retire.

Billy Johnson (1974–1988)

Billly "White Shoes" Johnson was fast, but it was his showmanship that made him so exciting. He wasn't the first player to celebrate a touchdown, but he took his celebrations to a whole new level. It started with his knees flying back and forth in opposite directions as he held the ball aloft. He'd pass it behind his back or between his legs, finishing it off with a spike or by tossing the ball into the stands. His Houston Oilers teammates learned to wait until the theatrics were over to offer their end zone congratulations. Johnson called his dance the "White Shoes Wiggle."

Johnson's speed sometimes got him into trouble. Any coach will tell you it's not a good idea to run backwards to avoid tacklers, but Johnson did it all the time. "Billy is an equal-opportunity runner," joked Oilers head coach Bum Phillips. "He gives everyone an equal chance to tackle him."

He tied an NFL record with 4 returns for touchdowns in 1975 (3 on punt, 1 on a kickoff). Injuries forced him to miss most of two seasons, and Johnson spent a year with the Montreal Alouettes of the CFL before joining the Atlanta Falcons in 1982. The following year he won the NFL's Comeback Player of the Year Award. In addition to being one of the league's best return men, he caught a career-high 64 passes.

Johnson played six more seasons in Atlanta, retiring just shy of his thirty-seventh birthday after a one-game stint with the Redskins in 1988. His 11.8-yard career average for punt returns is the 6th best of all time.

Eric Metcalf (1989–2002)

Metcalf holds the NFL record with 10 career touchdown punt returns. As a running back, Metcalf caught 31 touchdown passes in his career and rushed for another 12. He's the only NFL player with more than 7000 combined return yards and 7000 combined rushing/receiving yards.

He was part of one of the most infamous trades in NFL history, The San Diego Chargers traded Metcalf along with two first-round picks and a second-round pick to the Arizona Cardinals in 1998, a deal they made in order to move up one spot in the draft order. Why was San Diego so anxious to jump from the third overall pick to the second? They wanted to draft Washington State quarterback Ryan Leaf, a man who would go down as perhaps the biggest draft bust ever.

Others

- **# 6.** Vai Sikahema (1986–1993)
- **# 7.** Tim Brown (1988–2004)
- **# 8.** Desmond Howard (1992–2002)
- **# 9.** Darrien Gordon (1993–2002)
- **# 10.** Rick Upchurch (1975–1983)
- **# 11.** J. T. Smith (1978–1990)
- **# 12.** Glyn Milburn (1993–2001)
- **# 13.** Kelvin Martin (1987–1996)
- **# 14.** Troy Brown (1993–2007)
- **# 15.** Allen Rossum (1998–2007)

Combined KR/PR Rankings

- **# 1.** Brian Mitchell (1990–2003)
- **# 2.** Billy Johnson (1974–1988)
- **# 3.** Abe Woodson (1958–1965)
- **# 4.** Vai Sikahema (1986–1993)
- **# 5.** Speedy Duncan (1964–1974)
- **# 6.** Dave Meggett (1989–1998)
- **# 7.** Glyn Milburn (1993–2001)
- **# 8.** Alvin Haymond (1965–1973)
- **# 9.** Rick Upchurch (1975–1983)
- **# 10.** Emlen Tunnell (1948–1959)
- **# 11.** Dante Hall (2000–2007)
- **# 12.** Mel Gray (1986–1997)
- **# 13.** George McAfee (1940–1950)
- **# 14.** Mike Nelms (1980–1984)
- **# 15.** Al Carmichael (1953–1960)
- **# 16.** Tim Brown (1988–2004)
- **# 17.** J.T. Smith (1978–1990)
- **# 18.** Jermaine Lewis (1996–2004)
- **# 19.** Andy Farkas (1939–1945)
- **# 20.** Desmond Howard (1992–2002)
- **# 21.** Woodley Lewis (1950–1958)
- **# 22.** Allen Rossum (1998–2006)
- **# 23.** Ron Smith (1966–1974)
- **# 24.** Dick Todd (1939–1948)
- **# 25.** Jon Arnett (1957–1966)

Two-Way Era Players

LAWRENCE RITTER'S *Glory of Their Times* might be the best baseball book ever published. After the death of Ty Cobb in 1961, it occurred to Ritter that some of the great players from baseball's golden age were old men, and he resolved to interview as many of them as he could before it was too late. Over the next five years, Ritter crisscrossed the country recording oral histories, and the stories that those men told formed the book.

Not only was it a best seller, it prompted a surge of interest in baseball's dead-ball era as well. Four of the twenty-two men who told their stories would later be inducted into baseball's Hall of Fame, and two of them—Goose Goslin and Rube Marquard—directly credited Ritter's book for the renewed interest in their careers. *Glory of Their Times* was rereleased in the mid-eighties with additional interviews added, and the recordings of the original interviews were released on a CD box set in the late nineties.

I'd love to say that there's an analogous book for pro football, a volume that contained oral histories from great early players like Mel Hein, Benny Friedman, and Johnny "Blood" McNally. It doesn't exist, and it's too late to get started. Most of the guys who played in the twenties and thirties are dead, and an awful lot of the players from the forties and fifties are gone too.

Chris Willis, head of the Research Library at NFL Films, did the next best thing a few years ago, collecting oral histories and interview transcripts that hadn't been previously published and putting them into a book called *Old Leather*. It contains some fascinating stories of pro football's early days, but frankly, reading it only reminds me of all the other stories from that era that have been lost or forgotten.

The players from pro football's early decades have never received their proper due, and I have to admit that they are underrepresented in my rankings. There are four major reasons why this has happened, both here and in general. The biggest reason is that the league did not keep any official statistics prior to 1932. For a lot of those players, we simply don't have any statistics with which we can measure their level of performance. For others, we have only a partial record of their career because they started playing before 1932.

Second, many of the players who started their careers in the mid-thirties had their careers interrupted by military service. More than six hundred NFL players served during World War II. While our evaluation of them does benefit from the availability of individual playing statistics, the loss of playing time during their peak seasons makes those numbers suffer in comparison to players from later years.

Third, when looking at players from the two-way era, it's hard to sort them by position in a way that cleanly matches up with the players of the modern era. For example, the quarterback position as we know it didn't exist until the Bears introduced the modified T-formation offense. Players from this era typically played every down—offense, defense, and special teams. Diversity was the most important trait. The best players were able to do a lot of things well, but very few stood head and shoulders above the crowd in any one area.

Finally, a lot of players ended their careers prematurely because they simply got better job offers. The National Football League wasn't necessarily the destination of choice for great athletes. Baseball was by far the more popular sport in pre-war America, and a number of pro football players abandoned promising football careers to play in the major leagues. More often, pro football players left their teams for more lucrative jobs in the private sector. There wasn't a lot of money to be made playing pro football in those days, and it wasn't unusual for a star player to walk away from his team in search of a little more money.

There are at least a dozen players from this era who overcame all of these issues to earn a ranking in the preceding chapters. Nevertheless, I felt that it was important to acknowledge the other great two-way players here. What I did was to compile a list of the players who were named All-Pros at least four times between 1920 and 1945. The selection of those postseason all-star teams aren't without their biases, but they serve as a pretty good way to identify the great players—or at least the players that were perceived as great players during their day.

I can't say that this method does a great job of ranking players in the right order. However, I'm confident that it does a good job of identifying the best fifty players of the era. The players are ranked by position based on number of All-Pro selections, and in the case of a tie, the number of NFL games they played is used to further refine the rankings. I've sorted them into five groups based on their offensive positions: backs, ends, tackles, guards, and centers. The listing also shows the years that their career spanned. For many of these players, there were years within that span when they did not play in the NFL. For the sake of simplicity, I've just mentioned the start and end date without regard to those gaps.

Backs

Bronko Nagurski (1930–1943)

Nagurski was a big bruising back who would burst through the line of scrimmage and bowl over defenders. His toughness was legendary, and he was the NFL's first great power runner.

There is a great book by Jim Dent called *Monster of the Midway* that recounts how Nagurski came out of retirement in 1943 to help lead the Bears to the NFL championship. The legendary fullback had been retired for five seasons, but player shortages during the war were making it hard for some teams to compete. The Bears didn't just need warm bodies, they needed somebody whose name would sell tickets, and there was no bigger star in Bears' history than Nagurski.

At the age of thirty-five, Nagurski's body could no longer take the heavy toll of running the ball, but he volunteered to come back and play on the offensive line. At the end of the season, the Bears needed a win in their final game to clinch the division title. After three quarters they trailed the Cardinals by a touchdown. Nagurski switched to fullback, and led the Bears on a 62-yard drive that tied the game. He continued to bull his way through the line on Chicago's next possession, setting up the winning touchdown. At the end of the day, Nagurski had run 16 times for 84 yards in one quarter of play, and the Bears went on to win the championship.

When Nagurski first retired, he had become a professional wrestler, and after his brief return to the Bears in 1943, he returned to the ring. Nagurski wrestled until 1960, retiring a three-time world heavyweight champion at the age of fifty-two.

Ken Strong (1929–1947)

In an era before specialization, Strong did everything exceptionally well. He was a powerful blocker, a tremendous runner, a solid passer, and one of the best kickers of his era. In 1939, sportswriter Grantland Rice argued that Strong ranked with Jim Thorpe as the game's greatest player. Rice said:

> Considering the test of both college and pro football, I'd say the battle of the swift and strong was among Ken Strong, Jim Thorpe, and Ernie Nevers, with Bronko Nagurski close up. Strong and Thorpe had greater variety; this gives them the edge. I mean everything that belongs to football—running, blocking, tackling, passing, and every type of kicking.

Strong spent his prime years toiling in obscurity for the Staten Island Stapletons. He was a superstar surrounded by stiffs, a one-man show on a team that rarely finished above .500. When the "Stapes" folded, Strong joined the New York Giants. His best year might have been 1934, when his steady running on an icy field helped the Giants win the NFL title game. A broken back forced him to retire after the 1939 season, but he returned during World War II as a kicking specialist.

Benny Friedman (1927–1934)

Omitting Friedman from the initial class at the Hall of Fame in 1963 was a big mistake, and it's hard to believe that it took more than forty years for that mistake to be corrected. While other teams were grinding it out on the ground, Friedman was flinging the ball all over the field. At a time when the rules discouraged passing, Friedman offered an exciting option. He was one of the great players from pro football's first decade, and his passing

skills dramatically changed the way the game was played.

Friedman broke the single-season record for touchdown passes as a rookie with 11, and three years later he threw 20. Nobody else in the league threw more than 6. He was finally invited to Canton in 2005, more than twenty years after his death.

Ward Cuff (1937–1947)

A tough multiposition player, Cuff played nine seasons for the Giants and was a key member of their 1938 championship team. He was a standout defensive back, but also one of the Giants' best offensive players. Cuff retired as the leading scorer in team history, and had led the Giants in both rushing and receiving. He also led the league in field goals four times—a number bested only by Lou Groza.

Verne Lewellen (1924–1932)

Lewellen may have been the league's first great pass receiver, but it's hard to know for sure. Eight of his nine seasons came before the league started keeping statistics, so we're left mostly with anecdotal commentary. Lewellen spent nine seasons with Curley Lambeau's Packers, a team that loved to throw the ball. He was also one of the league's best runners and an outstanding punter. He capitalized on his popularity when he ran for district attorney in 1928, serving two terms while continuing to star for the Packers.

Ace Gutowsky (1933–1938)

The Detroit Lions of the 1930s used a single-wing offense that was so prolific on the ground that they came to be known as the "Infantry Attack." Tailbacks Dutch Clark and Glenn Presnell were flashier, but Ace Gutowsky was their workhorse. The Russian-born fullback was the one they turned to when the ball was near the goal line. In 1936, the Lions rushed for a combined 2885 rushing yards, a record that would stand until 1972. Gutowsky was the Lions' leader that season with 827 yards, just 3 behind league leader Tuffy Leemans. He retired as the all-time leading rusher in Lions history, a spot he would hold until the mid-1960s.

#7
Glenn Presnell (1931–1936)

Like Ace Gutowsky, Presnell played in the shadows of Hall of Fame teammate Dutch Clark. Of the three, however, Presnell was probably the best all-around player. He booted a 54-yard field goal in 1934, a record for the longest kick that stood until 1953. He led the NFL in scoring in 1935 as the Lions won their first NFL championship. Presnell was still making appearances and giving interviews in his late nineties. He died in 2004, six weeks after his ninety-ninth birthday.

#8
Johnny Drake (1937–1941)

Selected in the first round of the 1937 draft by the expansion Cleveland Rams, Drake was a powerful fullback who twice led the league in rushing touchdowns. A foot injury sidelined him for parts of two seasons, and he was forced to retire after just five years in the league. He spent his off-seasons working as a night watchman and appearing in Hollywood Westerns.

#9
Ernie Nevers (1926-1931)

Nevers was one of the great college football stars of the 1920s, but he stunned everybody when he decided to sign with the Duluth Eskimos. Not only were they a largely unsuccessful team, but they also played all of their games on the road. An injury sidelined him after two seasons with the Eskimos, and when he returned in 1929, he signed with the Chicago Cardinals. It was still a one-man show, best illustrated by the game against the Bears in which Nevers scored all of his team's points (6 touchdowns and 4 extra points) in a 40–6 victory.

#10
Red Grange (1925–1934)

Harold "Red" Grange was undoubtedly the greatest college football star of the 1920s, and he did more than any other player to help elevate the fledgling NFL onto the national stage. As an actual player, however, his achievements don't rank him among the greatest pro football players of the era.

His first pro season started on Thanksgiving Day in 1925, and while record crowds came out to see him play, the Bears actually fell out of contention after he arrived. Playing a rigorous schedule, Chicago went 3-3-1 with Grange in the lineup, and finished in 7th place—their worst showing to date.

Grange spent the next few months barnstorming, playing games in the South and on the west coast. Seeing the big crowds that were coming out to watch him play, Grange decided he wanted to form his own team (and keep the lion's share of the gate receipts). He arranged a lease for Yankee Stadium, but Giants owner Tim Mara argued that he held the exclusive rights for playing in New York, and the other owners reluctantly backed him.

Undaunted, Grange simply formed his own league—dubbed the American Football League. It fielded three teams in New York City, and went head-to-head with existing NFL teams in Chicago, Cleveland, and Philadelphia. The NFL countered by expanding and increasing their efforts to sign college stars, particularly those from schools on the west coast. In the end, there simply wasn't enough talent to sustain two leagues, and the AFL folded at year's end.

Grange returned to the NFL in 1927, but in his fourth game of the season, he shredded his knee. Newspaper accounts from the time don't describe the incident in great detail, perhaps because the seriousness of the injury wasn't apparent at the time. Grange later recounted, "I went up for a pass and when I came down, I caught my cleats in the sod and George Trafton . . . fell over me." He refused to have surgery, even though he was clearly hampered by the injury. When it failed to respond to treatment, he opted to sit out the 1928 season. When he returned with the Bears in 1929, he was clearly not the same player. He had not only lost much of his speed, but his ability to make cuts was gone as well, and by that point he was a good but not spectacular runner.

In 1930, the Bears signed fullback Bronko Nagurski, and Grange gradually got less and less playing time. He continued to be effective on defense, but he was never again a dominating runner.

Before his knee injury, Grange played just nine NFL games. He was perhaps the first—though certainly not the last—superstar whose accomplishments were curtailed because of an injury. His impact on the game, however, is undeniable.

Jack McBride (1925–1934)

A power runner and a fair passer, McBride was a star for the New York Giants in the late 1920s. After spending a year with Providence and two more with the Brooklyn Dodgers, McBride returned to the Giants in 1932. He was one of the best punt returners of the era, developing a unique style that others tried to emulate. McBride would position himself very deep, then time it so he would catch the punt while running at top speed. Often, he would run right past the defenders who were charging downfield to cover the punt.

Joey Sternaman (1922–1930)

A great all-around player, Sternaman was the Bears quarterback for most of the twenties. In 1924 he led the league in scoring with 75 points, 27 from field goals and the remaining 48 points from touchdowns (four rushing and one each receiving, passing, punt return, and interception return).

Bill Shepherd (1935–1940)

A big fullback for the Lions' dominating rushing attack of the mid-thirties. After Dutch Clark retired, Shepherd became the team's top back, leading the Lions in rushing in 1938 and 1939. He was also an exceptional punter.

Ends

Lavvie Dilweg (1926–1934)

Like his teammate, Verne Lewellen, Dilweg worked as an attorney throughout his playing career. He later served in Congress and was appointed to a state department position by President Kennedy. Dilweg was one of the best defensive ends of his era and also an outstanding receiver on a Packers team that liked to throw the ball more than most.

Ray Flaherty (1926–1935)

Inducted to the Hall of Fame as a coach, Flaherty was also an outstanding pass receiver for eight NFL seasons. He was named All-NFL twice and played in the first three NFL championship games with the New York Giants. He retired after the 1935 season to become head coach of the Boston Redskins. The Giants honored him by retiring his uniform number, the first NFL player to receive that tribute.

Bill Hewitt (1932–1943)

Hewitt was the last NFL player to take the field without a helmet, which serves today as a good illustration of his reckless style of play. He was called the "Offside Kid" because he got into the opponent's backfield so quickly that they were convinced he was offside. Hewitt's best years came with the Bears, where his lateral helped them win the 1933 championship game.

Bill Smith (1934–1939)

Without a good nickname, a guy named Bill Smith isn't going to be remembered. It doesn't help that he also played with a lousy team. Smith was the leading receiver for the Chicago Cardinals of the 1930s and also led the NFL in field goals in 1935.

George Wilson (1937–1946)

Pass-catcher for the Bears who posted his best seasons during World War II. The Bears appeared in four straight NFL title games from 1940 to 1943, winning three times. Wilson was head coach of the Detroit Lions from 1957 to 1964, leading his team to a league championship in his first season. He also was the first head coach for the Miami Dolphins, serving in that post for four seasons.

Luke Johnsos (1929–1936)

For the years that we do have individual playing statistics, we know that Johnsos scored 20 touchdowns on 58 receptions. That's what we call converting your opportunities. When Bears head coach George Halas entered the navy in 1942, he tabbed his two assistants, Johnsos and Hunk Anderson, to run the team. The team advanced to the league championship twice in the three years that Johnsos was co–head coach, winning in 1942 to cap an undefeated regular season.

Duke Hanny (1923–1930)

Played end opposite from George Halas with the Chicago Bears and later joined the Providence Steam Roller. Legend has it that he asked Halas for permission to miss a game so that he could get married that afternoon. Halas refused, so Hanny showed up, started a fight with an opposing player on the opening kickoff, and was promptly ejected from the game. Problem solved, and off he went to his wedding.

Red Badgro (1927–1936)

Badgro got his start in the NFL playing for Red Grange's New York Yankees squad. He left football to spend two seasons playing baseball with the St. Louis Browns. When he returned to the gridiron with the New York Giants in 1930, he re-established himself as a big-play receiver on the league's best team. He was named All-Pro four times in five seasons, finishing his career with the Brooklyn Dodgers.

Tillie Voss (1921–1929)

Football's first true journeyman, Voss played for eleven different NFL teams in nine seasons. His longest stint was two years with the Chicago Bears. Voss also played center for several American Basketball League teams from 1925 to 1930, including the Brooklyn Arcadians and the Washington Palace Five.

Guy Chamberlin (1920–1927)

Chamberlin was likely the best coach of the 1920s, in an era when most of the coaches were also players. He won four titles with three different teams (Canton, Cleveland, and Frankford). Chamberlin's secret to success was building the team around himself. He had size and speed and could dominate on both sides of the ball.

Perry Schwartz (1938–1946)

Schwartz was a prolific pass catcher for the Brooklyn Dodgers and was the favorite target for quarterback Ace Parker. After spending four years in the military, he came back to play one more season in the AAFC, reuniting with Parker to play for the New York Yankees.

Paul Goebel (1923–1926)

Probably the best player in the brief history of the hapless Columbus Tigers. He jumped ship to play with Red Grange's New York team in 1927, where he was largely ignored. Goebel was a collegiate star at Michigan, and after leaving the NFL he spent more than twenty years as a college football referee.

Tackles

Link Lyman (1922–1934)

His given name was William, but I suspect he received the nickname Link as a reference to Lincoln, Nebraska, the city where he attended college. Lyman was a key figure on the Canton Bulldogs team that won back-to-back championships in 1922 and 1923. He followed coach Guy Chamberlin, first to Cleveland in 1924 (where the pair won another title) and then to the Frankford Yellow Jackets in 1925. Lyman joined the Chicago Bears for Red Grange's barnstorming tour following the 1925 season, and spent the rest of his NFL career there. Lyman won his fourth NFL championship with the Bears in 1933 and retired a year later.

Lyman is credited with inventing the tactic of shifting along the line of scrimmage, an effort to confuse the offensive linemen charged with blocking him. He would slide along the line, moving from one gap to another just before the ball was snapped. Prior to that, opposing linemen would just line up squarely across from each other, much like Civil War soldiers.

Turk Edwards (1932–1940)

An immovable lineman, Edwards excelled on both sides of the line of scrimmage. He was a hardhitting linebacker and a steamrolling offensive tackle. He starred with the Braves/Redskins, earning All-Pro honors at tackle each year from 1932 to 1939. His toughness was legendary, but he tore knee ligaments during a pregame coin toss in 1940, an injury that proved to be career ending.

Cal Hubbard (1927–1936)

At 6-foot-4 and 250 pounds, Hubbard was a powerful lineman, but he was noted for his remarkable speed and quickness. He starred at end for the Giants before switching to tackle after he was traded to the Packers in 1929. Hubbard retired from football in 1936 and became a legendary baseball umpire. He is the only individual inducted in both the baseball and pro football Halls of Fame.

Bruiser Kinard (1938–1947)

One thing's clear just from looking at the players in this chapter: They had some great nicknames in those days. If a guy is regarded as one of the great tackles of his era despite being just 6-foot-1 and weighing 215 pounds, you have to figure he was a hard hitter. Kinard held his own with the bigger linemen he faced off against and used his speed to outmaneuver them. He played six seasons with the Brooklyn Dodgers before being called to military service, returning for two more seasons with the AAFC's New York Yankees.

Duke Slater (1922–1931)

One of the few African-American players from the NFL's first decade, Slater played in the NFL from 1922 to 1931. As a star tackle at the University of Iowa, he was one of the few players who elected not to wear a helmet. It helped fuel his tough, rugged persona, but in later years he acknowledged it was a style born of his impoverished upbringing. In high school, his parents couldn't afford to buy him both a helmet and a pair of cleats, so they bought the shoes and advised him to be careful to avoid injury. Once of the iconic photographs from college football history shows the bareheaded Slater clearing a hole for running back Gordy Locke by blocking three Notre Dame defenders.

Slater entered the NFL twenty-five years before Jackie Robinson broke baseball's color barrier, and you have to imagine that he suffered all of the same indignities, insults, and outright hostility. Of course, the opportunities for abuse had to have been greater while playing a contact sport.

As far as I know, there's no significant film footage of Slater playing, but you can get a sense for how good he was by looking at some of the accomplishments of the teams he played on. With Slater leading the way, the Rock Island Independents scored 9 rushing touchdowns in a 1921 game, a record that's never been broken. When Ernie Nevers scored 6 touchdowns in a 1929 game, it was Slater's blocking that made it possible. In its coverage of that game, the *Chicago Herald Examiner* reported, "Duke Slater... seemed the dominant figure in that forward wall which had the Bear front wobbly. It was Slater who opened the holes for Nevers when a touchdown was in the making."

Slater was one of the inaugural members of the College Football Hall of Fame, but the call from Canton never came. His name was mentioned as a "strong candidate" for pro football's second Hall of Fame class in 1963, and he was a finalist in 1970 and 1971. Slater's teammate Fritz Pollard, the first African-American to play and first to coach in the NFL, was finally inducted in 2006. The honor came twenty years after Pollard died and nearly eighty years after his career ended. It took too long to correct that oversight, and Slater's exclusion is just as egregious.

George Christensen (1931-1938)

During the thirties, the Lions had one of the great running attacks in NFL history, and Christensen was one of the main reasons. In 1936, the Lions rushed for 2885 yards, an NFL record that would stand until 1972. Not to be confused with Jack Christiansen, the Lions Hall of Fame defensive back of the 1950s.

Joe Stydahar (1936–1946)

Chicago's first-ever draft pick, Stydahar's massive size was just what the Bears needed to keep their power running game going. He was named All-Pro as a rookie in 1936 and each year after through 1940. Stydahar later served as head coach of the Rams and Cardinals.

George Musso (1933–1944)

At 262 pounds, Musso was one of the largest players in the NFL during the 1930s. He was the captain of a Bears team that dominated the decade. Musso was the first player to be named All-Pro at two positions, first as a tackle then as a guard.

Gus Sonnenberg (1923–1930)

Sonnenberg starred for the Providence Steam Roller, but he was best known during his era as a professional wrestler. Using the name "Dynamite" Gus Sonnenberg, his patented move was a flying tackle. This involved first headbutting his opponent and then smashing him again in the stomach as he was falling. Sonnenberg won the world championship in 1929 and drew huge crowds for his matches across the country. He married a movie star, made a fortune, and lived the high life, but died at the age of forty-four after a long battle with leukemia.

Buford "Baby" Ray (1938–1948)

At 6-foot-6 and 250 pounds, Ray was one of the biggest players of his day. He played eleven years for Curly Lambeau's Packers, leading a dominating line that was credited for winning the 1939 championship game against the Giants.

Chet Adams (1939–1950)

A Cleveland native, Adams played first for the Cleveland Rams and later the Cleveland Browns. He also spent a year in Green Bay, earning All-Pro honors for Curly Lambeau's Packers. Adams once bragged about his healthy lifestyle, boasting that he drank thirteen bottles of milk for lunch each day.

Frank Cope (1938–1947)

Cope was a mainstay on the New York Giants, teaming with Al Blozis, Len Younce, and Mel Hein to form the toughest line of the era.

Lee Artoe (1920–1948)

In addition to being an outstanding linebacker for the Bears, Artoe was one of the strongest-legged kickers of his day. He kicked a 52-yard field goal in 1940 that still ranks as one of the longest in team history. What makes this feat amazing is that his poor eyesight made it impossible for him to see the goalposts he was aiming at. His teammates would have to help him line up, and afterward he'd ask them, "Did I make it?"

Lou Gordon (1930–1938)

Gordon was one of the few Jewish football stars from the 1920s. He liked to say that Benny Friedman "might be the smartest Jewish football player, but I was the toughest." His skills stood out on a Chicago Cardinals team that didn't win many games, and he later won a championship while playing with the Packers.

Pete Henry (1920–1928)

Jim Thorpe may have been the Canton Bulldogs biggest star, but Henry was their anchor. Hailed by the legendary Walter Camp as "the greatest lineman of all time," he excelled on both offense and defense. Henry also set records for the longest punt (94 yards) and longest drop-kick field goal (40 yards). His given name was Wilbur but most people knew him as either "Fats" or "Pete."

Howard "Cub" Buck (1920–1925)

The rivalry between the Packers and Bears has always been intense, but never more so than during Buck's era. In the first-ever meeting between the two teams, Chicago guard John "Tarzan" Taylor sucker punched Buck, breaking his nose. A few years later, Buck returned the favor, breaking the arm of one of the Bears' players as the Packers beat Chicago for the first time.

Guards

Danny Fortmann (1936–1943)

In eight NFL seasons, Fortmann was first- or second-team All-Pro every year. He was only nineteen years old when he was drafted and weighed just over 200 pounds, but his toughness and determination made him a star. While playing for the Bears, he pursued (and received) his medical degree at the University of Chicago.

Mike Michalske (1926–1937)

A fullback in college, Michalske used his size and speed to become one of pro football's premier guards. After starting his career with the NFL's New York Yankees, he joined the Packers and anchored a line that won three straight championships from 1929 to 1931. "Iron Mike" was the first guard elected to the Hall of Fame.

Ox Emerson (1931–1938)

Emerson teamed with tackle George Christensen on the Lions overpowering line in the 1930s. His combination of size and speed made him a devastating blocker, leading the way on off-tackle plays and sweeps. Emerson retired after the 1937 season to serve as an assistant coach for Brooklyn, but a rash of injuries to his squad forced him back into action for one more season.

Riley Matheson (1939–1948)

Matheson was one of the great defensive players of the forties. He played linebacker but liked to drift back into the secondary, trying to remain unseen and intercept passes. Matheson played eight of his ten seasons with the Rams, first in Cleveland and then in Los Angeles. He joined the Lions in 1943, along with some of his teammates, when the Rams suspended operations for the season, and earned All-AAFC honors playing his final season with the 49ers.

Al Nesser (1920–1931)

Nesser's first pro football experience came in 1910, when he joined his five older brothers to form the core of the Columbus Panhandles. In the book *Their Deeds and Dogged Faith*, Mike Rathert and Don Smith wrote that, "next to the Canton Bulldogs of the Jim Thorpe era, they were probably the best-known team of the pre-NFL years." Historian Bob Carroll described them as "burly boilermakers" and notes, "if they lost as often as they won, they usually left their opponents battered." Nesser joined the Akron Pros for the NFL's inaugural season. After that team folded, he played for the New York Giants, where he played a key role on the 1927 championship team.

Zuck Carlson (1929–1936)

Played guard and linebacker for the Chicago Bears. Carlson and his teammates starred in a 1934 short film by Oscar-winning director Pete Smith called *Pro Football*. The Bears ran through various plays, which were shown first at regular speed and then again in slow motion. I'm not sure if this served as a direct inspiration for the work of Ed Sabol and other groundbreaking football filmmakers, but it does stand as a fascinating snapshot of a great football team.

Ed Healey (1920–1927)

Pro football didn't begin with the NFL, of course, and a number of players in those early years were already veterans of existing pro teams. Healey was twenty-five when he joined the Rock Island Independents and quickly emerged as one of the league's best linemen. In 1922 Chicago's George Halas paid $100 to acquire Healey for the Bears, making him the first player ever sold for cash. After retiring, Healey was a long-time assistant coach at Notre Dame.

Jim McMillen (1924–1928)

After former NFL star Gus Sonnenberg became the world champion of pro wrestling in 1929, a number of other football players tried to follow in his footsteps. While McMillen never won a champion-

ship belt, he did become one of the top wrestlers of the 1930s. He played with Red Grange at the University of Illinois and was an All-Pro in each of his five seasons with the Bears.

Walt Kiesling (1926-1938)

A rugged, hard-hitting lineman, Kiesling spent thirty-four years in the NFL as a player and coach. Most of his career was spent toiling for losing teams, but he did win a championship with the Packers in 1936 and was a key member of the undefeated 1934 Bears.

Augie Lio (1941-1947)

Lio was one of the great college players of the late 1930s, a bruising blocker and prolific place kicker for the Georgetown Hoyas. He played three seasons for the Detroit Lions in the early forties, then bounced around with three other teams. After retiring, he spent thirty-seven years as a sportswriter covering the New York Giants for the *Passaic Herald and News*.

Al Graham (1925-1933)

In the mid-twenties, there were still a number of strong teams playing outside of the NFL. One of the hotbeds for semi-pro ball was in the Ohio Valley, and that's where Al Graham came to prominence. He didn't play college ball, but at the age of eighteen he was a star with the Middletown Miamis. His standout play earned him a contract with the NFL's Dayton Triangles, a team that was better financed but less competitive. In Graham's five seasons with them, the hapless team managed a record of 2 wins, 30 losses, and 3 ties. He would go on to play with the Portsmouth Spartans, Providence Steam Roller, and Chicago Cardinals, but none of those teams fared much better.

Russ Letlow (1936-1946)

Letlow was drafted by the Packers in 1936, their first ever draft pick. He was one of the great defensive guards of his era, playing in four NFL championship games in his first six seasons.

Joe Kopcha (1929-1936)

Kopcha played five seasons over seven years, a bruising lineman with the Chicago Bears. He took two years off to attend medical school, and later asked Bears' owner George Halas to trade him to Detroit so he could pursue an internship there. Halas obliged, but Kopcha helped the Lions defeat the Bears late in the season and knock them out of the playoffs. During his playing days, he developed a new type of shoulder pads to better protect the shoulder joint—an innovation that was quickly adopted by all of the manufacturers. "Shoulder pads in those days were nothing more than epaulets—like a hotel doorman wears. I resurrected a set to actually fit my shoulders and protect my collar bone and the acromio-clavicular joint," he explained years later. "I didn't even get a consulting fee," Kopcha said. "But, what-the-heck. There's a lot of guys walking around today *without* banged up shoulders who otherwise might be crippled. That's a terrific reward!"

Denver "Butch" Gibson (1930-1934)

With center Mel Hein and tackle Lee Grant, Gibson helped form the most powerful line of his era. He spent just five seasons with the Giants but earned All-Pro honors four times.

Orville Tuttle (1937-1946)

The Giants won three NFL championships in a four-year stretch between 1938 and 1941, and Tuttle helped solidify the team's five-man defensive line. Tuttle spent five years in the Navy before returning to the Giants for the 1946 season.

Centers

Mel Hein (1931–1945)

When the NFL decided to give out an official award for Most Valuable Player, Hein was the first recipient. When the Pro Football Hall of Fame opened, he was one of eleven players in the inaugural induction class. That's the esteem with which Hein was held. He was the iron man of his generation, playing every down of every game. Hein once called a timeout so that trainers could fix his broken nose without having to miss a play.

In the single-wing era, centers snapped the ball directly to tailbacks. It was much like the modern-day shotgun formation, and bad snaps were a frequent problem. Hein took a scientific approach, developing techniques for snapping that are still used today. He was the first center to pull off the line and block for backs on outside running plays. He was the first lineman to drop back to protect the passer from rushing linemen.

It should also be mentioned that Hein was an outstanding linebacker who had the agility to cover even the speediest receivers of the day. He finished with 19 career interceptions.

Hein retired after the 1941 season to coach at Union College. When the war started, player shortages hit the Giants hard, and Hein was persuaded to return. He spent weekdays at the college and joined the Giants for games on Sunday. He played four more seasons, twice earning All-Pro honors.

George Trafton (1920–1932)

Halfback Red Grange, who played both with and against George Trafton, called him "the toughest, meanest, most ornery critter alive." Teammates loved his intense competitiveness. Opponents hated it. After one particularly fierce contest, fans in Rock Island chased him from the field, hurling rocks at his cab as he scrambled to escape.

His reputation for rough play was well deserved, but he also possessed tremendous skill for the game. Unlike most centers of the day he preferred to snap with one hand, believing that with his other hand free he'd be quicker to engage defenders. Trafton was one of the first defensive players to roam on defense, and he was renowned for his ability to block punts.

Bulldog Turner (1940-1952)

There are only four centers in the Hall of Fame whose careers took place mostly before 1950. Two of those men, George Trafton and Clyde "Bulldog" Turner, played for the Chicago Bears. Their careers span the two-way era, and their presence helps explain why the Bears were one of the most dominant teams of the era.

Growing up in Sweetwater, Texas, Turner longed to play college football. He was a pretty good halfback, but he was much too small even by the standards of the 1930s. He weighed just 155 pounds when he graduated high school, too small to attract the interest of any major college football program. It was 1935, the height of the Depression, and like most other young Texans, he got work tending cattle. The life of a cowboy helped Turner became tough and muscular, and he was able to make the football team at Hardin-Simmons, a small Baptist college in Abilene. Through a series of fortunate events, Turner found himself playing in the East-West All-Star Game a few years later, played a great game, and ended up drafted by George Halas to play for the Bears.

Turner's speed and smarts helped make up for his lack of size. He was a hard hitter, a fantastic blocker, a great tackler, and an emotional leader. At the end of his rookie season, the Bears trounced the Redskins 73–0, and Turner got into the action by returning an interception 24 yards for a touchdown. In 1947 he intercepted a pass from Sammy Baugh that he returned 96 yards, changing speeds and making cuts to elude would-be-tacklers as he made his way down the sideline. Turner led the league with 8 interceptions in 1942.

He got his wish to play halfback in a 1944 game. It was the season finale, and the Bears were beating the winless Card-Pitts—a combined squad from the Chicago Cardinals and Pittsburgh Steelers. On his first carry, he ran 48 yards for a touchdown.

Nate Barragar (1930–1935)

After starring at the University of Southern California, Barragar broke into the league with the Minneapolis Red Jackets, who promptly folded. He joined the Frankford Yellow Jackets in 1931, and that team, too, ran out of money and closed up operations. Barragar's luck changed when he joined the Green Bay Packers, with whom he spent four and a half seasons.

After football Barragar went into the movie business, working as assistant director on film classics like *Gunga Din*, *Hondo*, and *Sands of Iwo Jima*. He also worked in television on such shows as *The Adventures of Superman*, *Bonanza*, and *Have Gun Will Travel*.

Charley Brock (1939–1947)

Brock was one of the anchors of the Green Bay Packers line in the 1940s, earning All-Pro honors five times in nine seasons. He helped to lead the team to championships in 1939 and 1944. That was the era of Don Hutson, and the Packers loved to throw the ball. Often, their opponents were forced to do the same thing. Brock and his teammates were opportunistic ball hawks, making plays and forcing turnovers. In 1943, the Green Bay defense set an NFL record by intercepting 9 passes in a game against the Lions. Brock had 4 interceptions that year, and the Packers set a team record with 42 steals. Fumble recoveries weren't an official statistic until 1945, but Brock led the league in 1945 and 1946.

Frank Bausch (1934–1941)

One of the early stars on the Boston Redskins, Bausch's blocking helped make Cliff Battles one of the premier rushers of the era. He later joined the Bears, where he played with future Hall of Famers Danny Fortmann and Bulldog Turner.

PART 3
THE COACHES

Coaches

THE DUTIES OF an NFL head coach have changed dramatically over time, and that makes it difficult to make meaningful comparisons between men from different eras. But the main goal of a head coach has always been the same: to win.

In search of an objective method for rating coaches, it makes sense to start by asking a fundamental question: What matters? What does a successful coach do? He must be a leader. He's got to build a good staff of assistants. To some extent, he's got to evaluate talent and put a good team together. A coach must decide who will be his starters and devise offensive and defensive strategies. A coach has to teach his players. During games, he must call plays, make substitutions, manage the clock, and make strategic and tactical decisions. All of these things are important, but they are nearly impossible to measure.

What about judging a coach by his team's statistical performance? You could look at how his offensive and defensive units ranked. You could look at numbers such as point differential and net yardage or other statistical criteria. There are all kinds of reasons that these stats can be misleading, and all kinds of reasons that the credit for these things should be given to somebody besides the head coach. In my mind, it all comes down to winning games. Ultimately, there is no better measure of a coach's performance than the bottom line.

Stat geek guru Bill James wrote a whole book about analyzing baseball managers. He looked at the simple methods that we had been using to rank managers—career wins, winning percentage, games above .500, even simply championships won. Any of these single methods is fatally flawed, James argued, and what was needed was a system that recognizes various levels of accomplishment. In the James system, managers received points for posting a winning record, winning the division, winning the league championship, winning the World Series, winning 100 games, and finishing 20 games over .500. With these six criteria, James rated each manager on a scale from zero to six each season, with the cumulative total providing a career total.

James concluded that this system appeared to work pretty well for rating the best baseball managers of all time. A similar system would no doubt identify the best pro football coaches of all time. We can take the six criteria that James outlined and adapt them for football. My system for yearly coaching performance awards points as follows:
- One point for finishing the season with a winning record
- One point for earning a playoff berth
- One point for winning 65 percent or more of his regular season games

- One point for advancing to the Super Bowl or league championship
- One point for winning the Super Bowl or league championship

For seasons prior to 1960, a league championship is counted the same as a Super Bowl win. For the seasons from 1960 to 1965, winning an NFL or AFL championship is counted the same as a modern conference championship, and since those two champions didn't meet in a Super Bowl game, each team is awarded half a point in the "Super Bowls Won" category.

There's not a lot of subtlety in this system. If a coach finishes with a losing record, he earns no points for the season. About half of the coaches fall into this category each season, and more than half of the coaches in history have finished their careers without scoring a single point. Marion Campbell, for example, spent nine seasons as an NFL head coach and never finished better than 5-11. Dan Henning spent seven seasons with Atlanta and San Diego and finished below .500 every time.

As you can see, the points are heavily skewed toward playoff success, and that's by design. After all, how successful can you call a coach like Norv Turner, who went to the playoffs only one time in seven seasons with the Redskins? The first job of a modern coach is to get his team to the playoffs; absent that, win totals are essentially meaningless.

To a great extent, that's what coaches are paid to do each season—win enough games to qualify for the playoffs, and then advance as far as they can. When George Halas led his Bears to the NFL championship in 1933, the postseason consisted of one game Today, twelve teams qualify for the playoffs. That's more than one-third of the league, and there are four rounds of playoff games before a champion is crowned. Postseason performance, therefore, is one of the most significant proving grounds for NFL coaches, one that all too often is overlooked.

Analyzing single-season coaching performances is a completely different proposition, one I explored at depth in my annuals (*Pro Football Prospectus* and *Pro Football Forecast*). The system

above doesn't provide enough detail to show significant differences between coaches on different teams for one season. The best way to do that is to look at how a team performed versus their previous season. An 8-8 finish by a team that was 4-12 the year before is a significant improvement, where an 8-8 finish that follows a 12-4 season reflects poorly on the coach. So many variables can enter into this sort of analysis, including strength of schedule, injuries, and even the statistical tendency for bad teams to improve and good teams to regress.

Our goal here is not to discern minor differences between coaches, but rather a coarse method for separating the legends from the merely good, the average from the lousy. Over the course of a coach's career, this method does a good job of doing that.

One of the things that becomes apparent when you look at coaching careers is how few good ones there are. More than half of all pro coaches get three years or less as a head coach. Less than a hundred men have coached for as long as five seasons, and we're not talking simply about their tenure with one team. The ratio of flops to successes among the head coaching ranks is about two-to-one.

One important note before we get to the actual rankings. I have included a somewhat subjective measure here, a bonus for a coach's innovations and contributions to the game that go beyond his win-loss record. Tom Landry gets extra credit for developing the 4-3 defense, a scheme that was eventually adopted by every other NFL team. Bill Walsh is recognized for his offensive innovations, which influenced strategies for the next twenty-five years, and gave birth to a family tree of new head coaches. This reflects an important role that coaches have played but which is not specifically reflected by their win-loss record.

These points weren't awarded just off the top of my head. I did a pretty rigorous review of what was written about each coach by his contemporaries, looking for specific citations of his innovations or contributions that had a significant impact on the way the game was played. Points were awarded based on some specific criteria I came up with and a scale for measuring their ultimate impact. It's subjective, but based on a defined methodology.

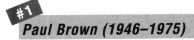

#1
Paul Brown (1946–1975)

There are several categories in which you can judge a coach's contributions, and I'm hard-pressed to think of one in which Brown wouldn't rate head and shoulders above everybody else. He had unparalleled success leading his teams on the field. Brown's Cleveland teams won seven league championships—including five in a row—and played in eleven championship games. He also took an expansion team in Cincinnati to the play-offs in its third season.

Brown's eye for talent was uncanny. Among the players that he brought into the NFL were Otto Graham, Jim Brown, and Lou Groza—each among the best ever to play their position. Another six of his players won league or conference rookie of the year honors during his tenure with the Bengals. The number of legendary coaches who got their start under Brown, either as assistant coaches or as players, is extraordinary. It includes Hall of Famers Don Shula, Chuck Noll, Weeb Ewbank, and Bill Walsh. Twelve of the first forty Super Bowls were won by coaches who got their start under Brown, and another six were won by coaches who got their start under one of Brown's protégés.

With the possible exception of Walter Camp, nobody made as many contributions to the game as Brown did. Brown pioneered the use of game film to study opponents. He was the first to have a full-time staff of assistant coaches. He studied play-calling tendencies and adopted the practice of scripting plays at the beginning of the game. He introduced the use of messenger guards to relay plays from the sidelines. A list of Brown's innovations goes on and on. In fact, most of the things that professional coaches do today derive from practices that he pioneered.

Brown also made significant contributions to integration, signing fullback Marion Motley and center Bill Willis to contracts in 1946—helping to integrate pro football a year before Jackie Robinson made his debut with the Brooklyn Dodgers. The success of Motley and Willis (both would eventually be inducted into the Hall of Fame) encouraged other teams to pursue African-American players and helped spur fan interest in the fledgling AAFC.

Of course it should not be forgotten that Brown founded two of the NFL's existing franchises, one bearing his name and the other playing in a stadium that bears his name. No other coach has had such a significant impact in so many different ways. His success in Cleveland helped make the AAFC-NFL merger necessary, breathing new life into pro football and adding excitement to a game that was stagnating in some ways.

When the AAFC and NFL merged for the 1950 season, the new league kicked off its season by having their respective champions meet in the season opener. Brown's team had won four straight titles, but many observers felt that his team couldn't be nearly so dominant against NFL competition. Cleveland answered those critics by trouncing the NFL-champion Eagles 35–10 in Philadelphia. Eagles coach Greasy Neale was undaunted, dismissing the Browns by saying "all they do is pass the ball." When the two teams met again in December, Brown called nothing but running plays, and his Browns won the rematch without throwing a single pass.

Paul Brown's personality has been described as prickly. He was intensely serious about his work and didn't tolerate any sort of monkey business. It was refreshing to see him soften a bit at the end of his career. In 1988, Bengals rookie Ickey Woods gained popularity for his touchdown celebration—dubbed the "Ickey Shuffle." Brown was famous for discouraging players from engaging in such demonstrations, telling them "if you reach the end zone, act as if you've been there before." The league cracked down on Ickey and other players, ruling that they would be penalized for "unprofessional demonstration" if they continued their end zone celebrations. Woods moved his touchdown dances to the sideline, explaining that he was following Brown's orders. When a disbelieving press asked Brown for confirmation, he expressed his appreciation for Ickey's enthusiasm. Then the straightlaced and frail eighty-year-old Brown demonstrated his own version of the Ickey Shuffle for the news cameras.

George Halas (1920–1967)

George Halas didn't invent the game of football, but he might as well have. Papa Bear's figure looms so large over the pro game that it's hard to imagine that the National Football League would even exist without his influence.

His career spanned three separate eras, from the birth of the NFL to the age of television, and throughout those years he was always one of the league's premier coaches. In the days before the NFL played postseason games, Halas claimed the league title twice. His Bears dominated the league in the thirties and forties, appearing in eight of the first fourteen NFL championship games and winning five times between 1933 and 1946.

That team earned the name "Monsters of the Midway" for their ferocious defense, but it was Halas's offensive innovations that had the most profound impact on the game. In collaboration with his assistant Ralph Jones and University of Chicago coach Clark Shaughnessy, Halas refined the T-formation offense and ushered in the modern era of football.

The new offense made the quarterback the center of the offense for the first time. By splitting the ends out wide and putting players in motion, it helped open up the game tremendously. For the first time, speed and deception drove offensive strategy rather than just brute strength.

Halas retired from coaching three times, including midway through the 1942 season when he re-enlisted in the navy. He served as a lieutenant commander with the Seventh Fleet in the South Pacific, but still kept tabs on the Bears, issuing directives by telegram. Halas retired for good in 1967, having spent forty seasons as a head coach.

As a team owner, Halas was an early proponent of revenue sharing, understanding the importance of competing with other teams on the field and cooperating with them off the field. He was responsible for dozens of innovations that helped shape the way coaches did their job. Halas introduced the concept of daily practices and assistant coaches, and turned the position of head coach into a professional job.

Halas won his fifth NFL championship in 1963, thirty years after winning his first. Both victories came against the New York Giants.

Vince Lombardi (1959–1969)

Lombardi is viewed as the master motivator, but he was also an incredible innovator. As an offensive line coach at Army, he developed the concept of zone blocking. While most offenses had their linemen engage defenders man-to-man, Lombardi had them work together as a unit.

The concept in a nutshell is for two offensive linemen to double-team a defender. This allows each blocker to be more aggressive, knowing that he has help. It also creates movement and opens running lanes for the ball carrier. Because a two-on-one attack can quickly neutralize a defender, the second blocker can slide free and engage one of the linebackers. It sounds complicated, but when it is well executed it can be devastating. For the running back, their job becomes simple: run to daylight.

As an assistant coach with the New York Giants, Lombardi ran the offense and helped the team win a championship in 1956, hurtling running back Frank Gifford to stardom. The coach's success continued in Green Bay, where he took over a team that was 1-10-1 and led them to the NFL title game two years later. Lombardi helped Jim Taylor to become one of the league's top rushers, and he assembled what may have been the best offensive line in football history. Center Jim Ringo and tackle Forrest Gregg ended up in the Hall of Fame. Guards Fuzzy Thurston and Jerry Kramer were both named All-Pros at least five times, and tackle Bob Skoronski was a Pro Bowler and team captain.

In large part because of his devastating line, Lombardi's signature play became the Green Bay Sweep. The center and tackles sealed off defenders in the middle, while both guards and a blocking back led the charge around one end. "There's nothing spectacular about it," Lombardi said. "It's my number-one play because it requires all eleven men to play as one to make it succeed, and that's what 'team' means." The job for the ball carrier, typically Taylor or Paul Hornung, was simply to read the blocks and hit the hole that was created.

The power sweep symbolized Lombardi's general philosophy. It was simple, it required teamwork, and it stressed execution of fundamentals. The Packers ran this one play over and over, and for nearly a decade opposing defenses struggled in vain to stop it.

#4

Tom Landry (1960–1988)

As a player-coach with the New York Giants, Landry invented the 4-3 defense. The innovation created the position of middle linebacker, and helped the Giants advance to the NFL title game three times in four seasons. Within a few years, most other teams had adopted the 4-3, and it became the standard for the next two decades.

Landry became head coach of the expansion Dallas Cowboys in 1960, where he developed a variation of the 4-3 called the Flex Defense. He moved defensive linemen off the line of scrimmage in various combinations, creating what was in essence a zone defense against the run.

Offensively, he overwhelmed opponents with a seemingly endless variety of formations. In a typical game, the Cowboys might line up in thirty different formations, making it impossible for opposing defenses to figure out what play they were running by seeing where the players were lined up. Landry revived the use of man-in-motion

to further this cause, as well as a pre-snap shift, where his offense would line up in one formation then quickly shift to another. He also brought back the widespread use of the shotgun formation to help protect his quarterback.

Most Postseason Wins

Rank	Wins	Coach
1	21	Tom Landry
2	19	Don Shula
3	17	Joe Gibbs
4	16	Chuck Noll
5	15	Bill Belichick

Landry coached the Cowboys in 37 postseason games, the most by any coach. His 21 playoff wins is also the all-time record.

The team struggled in the mid-1980s, suffering three straight losing seasons and falling to 3-13 in 1988. Some folks thought the game had passed him by, but the bigger problem was the rapid departure of star players and the inability of general manager Tex Schramm to replace them. Maybe it was time for Landry to go, but the way that he was dismissed was disgraceful. New owner Jerry Jones publicly courted Landry's replacement before he had even closed the deal to buy the team. When he finally delivered the news in person, Landry reportedly wept. Hours later, at a press conference to announce he had bought the team and fired Landry, Jones was gleeful and opened by saying, "It's like Christmas." Everybody was stunned. For many people, Tom Landry was the Cowboys, and after spending twenty-eight years building the team, he should have been sent out with some fanfare.

#5

Don Shula (1963–1995)

From 1971 to 1992, Shula led his Dolphins to the AFC championship game seven times. You can do the math . . . that's an average of once every three seasons. Critics would argue that when he retired, Shula had gone more than twenty years without winning a championship. His supporters, on the other hand, would point out that despite the shortage of titles, the team was always competitive under Shula. Only twice in twenty-six seasons did Shula's Dolphins finish with a losing record.

In the first part of his career, Shula's teams were known for their strong running game and stifling defenses. It was much different in the second half of his career. The Dolphins went seventeen years—from 1979 through Shula's retirement after the 1995 season—without a single running back reaching the 1000-yard mark. Five times in his last ten seasons, the Dolphins finished with a defense ranked among the bottom five.

Of course, the event that divides Shula's career into two distinctly different segments is the arrival of quarterback Dan Marino in 1983.

The Marino years were tough on Shula. After losing the Super Bowl to the Niners in 1984 and the AFC title game to the Patriots a year later, the Dolphins went into a funk. Over the next four seasons the team went 30-33, with the league's most prolific offense and a horrible defense. When a team throws the ball so much and scores so many points, there's a tendency to suggest that the defensive woes are just an artifact of your offensive strategy. If you throw the ball a lot and score a lot of points, it forces other teams to be aggressive and take chances throwing the ball. In the case of those Dolphins teams, it was a porous run defense that really was the major problem. Opposing teams tried to control the clock and keep the ball out of Marino's hands, and more often than not, that made the Dolphins the team that was forced to rally from behind. The division-rival Jets were a great example of a team that employed that strategy successfully. For four straight years, the Dolphins lost games to the Jets despite scoring at least 30 points, including a memorable 51–45 shootout in 1986.

Shula Comparison

Category	Before Marino	With Marino
Seasons	20	13
Winning Pct.	.721	.614
Super Bowls	5	1
Top-10 Rush Offense	15	0
Top-10 Defense	16	2

Shula knew how to work with quarterbacks. After all, he went to an NFL championship game or Super Bowl with five different passers—Johnny Unitas, Earl Morrall, Bob Griese, David Woodley, and Marino. The lack of balance on the offense made it impossible to compete for a title with Marino, no matter how well he threw the ball.

#6
Steve Owen (1931–1953)

Owen is largely forgotten, and I'm not entirely sure why. He was a tremendous innovator, developing both the A-formation offense and the Umbrella Defense. Owen invented what's now called the safety blitz, and he pioneered the strategy of settling for field goals instead of always going for it on fourth down. On the field, his Giants teams dominated the league for nearly two decades.

He introduced the use of a two-platoon system, giving his players a rest at a time when most players played on both sides of the ball for the entire game, which as you might expect, left them exhausted by the fourth quarter. Rules of the time severely limited substitution. If a player came out of the game, he couldn't return until the next quarter. Subs generally would enter the game only if a starter was hurt or tired. Owen developed two full squads of eleven, and would play each for half a quarter. Because his players were usually fresher, Owen always had an advantage.

Until the mid-forties, most teams played the same basic defense. Owen introduced his Umbrella Defense to counter the Cleveland Browns' aggressive passing attack. He was much less willing to modernize his offense. Every other team had adopted the T-formation by the early thirties, the first offense that used a quarterback. Owen stuck with his version of a single wing offense—without a quarterback—until 1949. His A-formation featured an imbalanced line, with four linemen on one side of the center and two on the other. The center would snap the ball directly to one of three backs. Fans complained that it was outdated and ultraconservative, but the Giants were winning a lot of games with it. The NFL began playing a championship game in 1933, and the Giants appeared in eight of the first fourteen contests.

The most memorable might have been in 1934 in a contest that came to be known as "The Sneakers Game." A freezing rain left the field at the Polo Grounds covered in ice, and the slippery field made it hard for the Giants offense to get moving. At halftime, Owen sent his equipment manager to nearby Manhattan College to borrow thirty-five pairs of sneakers. With the new footwear, the Giants rallied back with 27 unanswered points in the second half for a commanding 30–13 win.

#7
Chuck Noll (1969–1991)

A relatively quiet man, Noll preferred to stay out of the limelight. His aloof demeanor masked a quiet intensity. He didn't show a lot of emotion on the sidelines, but that didn't mean he lacked passion. If a player screwed up on the field, he didn't need to yell at them—his displeasure was communicated with a stare. Steelers guard Chuck Wolfley said, "being on the wrong end of a Chuck Noll glare was all the motivation you needed."

Noll was relatively unknown when he took the Steelers head coaching job in 1969, but his pedigree was impressive. He had spent seven seasons in the NFL playing for Paul Brown in Cleveland, winning two NFL championships After his retirement, he joined Sid Gillman's staff in San Diego, serving as defensive backfield coach for a Chargers team that advanced to five of the first six AFL

championship games. From there, he joined Don Shula's staff in Baltimore, culminating with the loss in Super Bowl III.

When Noll joined the Steelers, he was taking over a team that had never gone to the playoffs. In thirty-six seasons, the club had only finished with a winning record eight times. The Steelers didn't just need a new coach, they needed someone who could transform the organization. Noll was the right man for the job.

Shortly after he was hired, Noll sat down with owner Art Rooney, Jr., and told him that the key to turning the franchise around was to find the right kind of players. They needed to be good athletes, but more important, they needed to have the right attitude. Noll later summarized his approach:

> There are many impediments to winning, and most of them lie in the area of attitude. Nothing impedes problem solving more than a lousy attitude, and attitudes are like a virus—they're contagious. A bad one can spread through a locker room in a hurry. But a good attitude can be passed around as well. That's what I was looking for—a nucleus of players with the ability to win and an attitude to match. On every team, there is a core group that sets the tone for everyone else. If the tone is positive, you have half the battle won. If it is negative, you are beaten before you ever walk on the field.

From the outset, Noll believed that the team should be built through the draft, and that the Steelers should focus on players who came from successful college programs, teams that had instilled in those players the attitude that Noll was looking for.

That first season, the Steelers finished 1-13, but Noll had found a gem in his first draft—lineman Joe Greene. The draft yielded two more future Hall of Famers the following season—Terry Bradshaw and Mel Blount—along with Jack Ham in 1971 and Franco Harris in 1972. In 1974, Noll landed four more players who were Canton-bound: Lynn Swann, Jack Lambert, John Stallworth, and Mike Webster.

That's nine Hall of Famers in six seasons. With such an impressive assembly of talent, it's not particularly surprising that the Steelers went on to dominate the rest of the decade, winning four Super Bowls in a span of six years.

One might say that with such a great team playing for him, Noll couldn't help but win. In my mind, this points to one of the most important questions with regard to pro football: Are great players found or are they made? If you believe they are found, then you have to conclude that the Steelers scouts and front office staff possessed a keen insight that the league's other teams were missing. Only four of the nine Hall of Fame players that they drafted were picked in the first round. Webster, one of the greatest centers of the modern era, was a fifth-round pick. Did the other twenty-five teams simply overlook these great prospects? Or rather, did the Steelers turn less-than-stellar college players into NFL stars?

What happened in Pittsburgh in the early seventies is, in my mind, the strongest evidence that great players are developed. That doesn't mean that players don't come into the league with some degree of athletic ability, and it doesn't mean that a great coach can turn lousy players into Hall of Famers. I believe that players need to be nurtured, they need to be instructed, and they need to be put into systems and situations for which they are well suited. Chuck Noll clearly did this with his players in Pittsburgh, and the evidence lies not only in the number of players he sent to the Hall of Fame but also the number of games his teams won.

As remarkable as the Steelers' success was in the seventies, the subsequent letdown was inevitable. A collection of great young players eventually becomes a collection of aging players, and it's impossible to replace them all simultaneously. Between 1981 and 1983, all of the key members of the dynasty (except Webster) retired, and the draft yielded no stars.

In the twelve seasons after that fourth Super Bowl win, Noll compiled a rather pedestrian record of 93-92. Maybe Noll ran out of steam. I think it's more accurate to say that he had a harder time developing talent in the free-agency era. His late-eighties drafts did yield players like Rod Woodson, Greg Lloyd, Dermontti Dawson, and Neil O'Donnell—all of whom played a role in the Steelers resurgence in the nineties.

Noll's twenty-three-year tenure as head coach of the same team was exceeded only by three men: George Halas of the Bears (thirty years), Green Bay's Curley Lambeau and Tom Landry of the Cowboys (twenty-nine years each).

Joe Gibbs (1981–2007)

I'm not really sure why Joe Gibbs decided to come back to the NFL after an eleven-year retirement. Having already been enshrined in the Hall of Fame, he had nothing more to prove. His competitive drive was being fueled by his second career as the owner of a successful stock car racing team. His coaching resume could only be marginally enhanced by another Super Bowl title, and anything less would just serve as a disappointing epilogue to an otherwise spectacular career. His return ended after four seasons, posting a modest 30-34 record.

Gibbs earned a reputation as an offensive genius, in part due to the fact that he won three Super Bowls with three different quarterbacks. He was an assistant under Don Coryell, architect of the aggressive passing attacks that ushered in a new era of offensive strategy. When Gibbs became head coach of the Redskins in 1981, he incorporated some of Coryell's ideas, but largely developed his own new system based on a power running game. With a strong offensive line (known affectionately as "The Hogs") and Hall of Fame back John Riggins, Gibbs won the Super Bowl in his second season and took them back again in his third season. The signature play was the counter trey, where the right side of the line would block to the left, but the left guard and tackle would pull to the right. The running back would start with a step to the left, giving the impression the play was going in that direction. Then he would cut back to the right, with two linemen leading the way. The misdirection play was tough to stop for even the most disciplined defenses.

In the early 1980s, Gibbs developed a one-back offense in an attempt to better protect his quarterback. The system grew largely in reaction to one player, linebacker Lawrence Taylor of the rival New York Giants. Gibbs used two– and three–tight end formations to provide maximum protection. He also employed a lot of pre-snap shifts and motion to create confusion and mismatches. While the strategy was largely successful, it didn't stop Taylor from ending quarterback Joe Theismann's career with a crushing hit in 1985.

#9
Curley Lambeau (1921–1953)

When people think of the Packers, they think of legendary coach Vince Lombardi. But whose name is on the stadium in Green Bay? Curley Lambeau.

Lambeau was co-founder of the Packers in 1919 and helped the team join the NFL in 1921. He was a player-coach from 1921 to 1928, favoring a passing offense at a time when the rules favored the running game. He was the first coach to make the forward pass a significant part of his strategy.

When he stopped playing, the team really took off. Lambeau added three players in 1929 who made a huge impact: running back Johnny Blood and linemen Cal Hubbard and Mike Michalske. The Packers were crowned as league champions for each of the next three seasons, making them the NFL's first real dynasty. After signing receiver Don Hutson in 1935, Lambeau was able to take his passing game to new heights. Hutson rewrote the record book, and the Packers won three NFL championship games in an eight-year span (1936, 1939, and 1944).

Lambeau was squeezed out during a restructuring of the Packers board in 1949. He spent two seasons with the Cardinals and another two with the Redskins, but couldn't help turn either franchise around.

#10
Sid Gillman (1955–1974)

One of the greatest offensive innovators in football history, Gillman developed offenses that stretched the field horizontally with spread formations and vertically with deep passes. All of the major offensive innovators of the last forty years have built on his work, from Al Davis to Don Coryell to Bill Walsh. "God bless those runners because they get you the first down, give you ball control and keep your defense off the field," Gillman once said, "but if you want to ring the cash register, you have to pass."

Gillman coached the Los Angeles Rams for five years, leading them to the NFL championship game in his first season. In 1960, he moved across town to take over the Chargers, a team in the new American Football League. His wide-open passing offense was nearly unstoppable. The Chargers advanced to the AFL championship game five times in their first six seasons. They lost twice to the Bills and twice to the Oilers, beating the Boston Patriots 51–10 in the 1963 title game.

Gillman resigned as coach of the Chargers midway through the 1969 season, suffering from a stomach ulcer and chest hernia. He returned in 1971, but was fired midway through the season. Gillman resurfaced with the Oilers for a season and a half, winning Coach of the Year honors after the team improved from 1-13 to 7-7. With that, he called it quits. "Coaching is a young man's game," Gillman said on announcing his retirement. "You can't do this job unless you dedicate your whole life, 365 days, 24 hours a day, to it. Give me a coach who goes on vacation and I'll give you a loser."

Gillman is the only coach inducted into both the College and Pro Football Hall of Fame.

11

Bill Belichick (1991–2007)

I wrote a piece about Belichick in one of my annuals in which I described his coaching style: "He is like oatmeal: bland, tasteless, unattractive. . . . yet nourishing, substantial and enough to get by on. He meets the recommended daily allowances." This was after he'd won his first Super Bowl, mind you. Despite his success, he's never been very demonstrative. His answers at press conferences never offer the slightest insight as to what's going on. Even his sideline demeanor is boring.

Belichick isn't really an innovator in the sense of bringing a fresh new approach to one aspect of the game. Rather, he has adopted Paul Brown's approach of relentless study, eliminating the guesswork, and making a science out of the game. "There probably isn't one thing we do as the New England Patriots—other than maybe a technological improvement—that [Paul Brown] didn't do thirty years ago," Belichick explained. "The same things he did with the Cleveland Browns, that's what we do here in terms of preparation, in terms of fundamentals, in terms of the basic strategy of the game, how to coach the team, or how to prepare the team."

This approach to the game isn't revolutionary, but it can give a coach a slight edge in a very competitive marketplace. In the era of free agency and the salary cap, it's not enough to simply identify talent. Everybody can see who the superstars are. The trick is to find players at the next level down, guys with good skills who aren't going to cost an arm and a leg. Belichick won three Super Bowls in four seasons, and you can make a reasonable case that he did it with no more than one potential Hall of Famer (quarterback Tom Brady). Rather than trying to build a team around two or three great players, Belichick assembled a roster of B-plus talent, finding players with the specific skills needed to thrive in his system. Belichick did a great job of finding undervalued talent (the 2007 trade for Randy Moss is a great example), and the Patriots amassed a huge number of compensatory draft picks each year by letting veterans leave through free agency. In an era when free agency and the salary cap made it difficult for most teams to retain talent, Belichick found ways to work the system to his advantage.

Despite the Patriots loss in Super Bowl XLII, Belichick's 15-4 record in the playoffs makes him the second most successful postseason coach in NFL history.

Best Postseason Win Percentage (minimum 10 games)

Rank	Pct	W-L	Coach
1	.833	10-2	Vince Lombardi
2	.789	15-4	Bill Belichick
3	.727	8-3	Tom Flores
4	.714	10-4	Bill Walsh
5	.708	17-7	Joe Gibbs

Belichick came to prominence as a defensive coordinator under Bill Parcells with the New York Giants. He was the architect of game plans that helped stifle the high scoring offenses of the Denver Broncos (Super Bowl XXI) and Buffalo Bills (Super Bowl XXV). His Patriots did the exact same thing against the Rams' "Greatest Show on Turf" in Super Bowl XXXVI.

Some critics point to his struggles during his first head coaching stint in Cleveland, but that's not really fair. Belichick inherited a team that was 3-13 and had them in the playoffs within four years. He took a lot of flack for his decision to release popular quarterback Bernie Kosar, but it was clearly the right move. In 1994, the Browns had the league's stingiest defense, and Belichick had the team moving in a positive direction. When Art Modell announced on November 6, 1995, that he was moving the team to Baltimore, the organization just disintegrated. The team lost seven of eight games after the announcement, and Belichick was criticized for losing control of his team. When asked years later what lessons he learned from his time in Cleveland, he replied curtly, "Not to move your team to another city in the middle of a season."

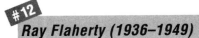

Ray Flaherty (1936–1949)

In just seven seasons as head coach of the Redskins, Flaherty took his team to the NFL championship game four times. Three times they faced the Chicago Bears, the most dominant team of the era. In the 1937 title game, Flaherty introduced a new play that helped propel his team to victory—a quick pass behind the line of scrimmage that would later come to be known as the screen pass.

Flaherty's rookie quarterback, Sammy Baugh, had taken the league by storm with his passing prowess. Heading into the big game, Flaherty knew the Bears would focus all of their efforts on getting to Baugh in the backfield. The quick screen passes confounded the Bears and led to three long touchdown plays. Flaherty's team won 28–21.

The Redskins beat Chicago for another title in 1942, but it's the one title game that Flaherty lost to the Bears that people most remember—the infamous 73–0 drubbing in 1940.

After retuning from military service during the war, Flaherty joined the AAFC as head coach of the New York Yankees. He was popular in the Big Apple, having been a two-time All-Pro in nine seasons playing for the Giants. It was also a major coup for the fledgling league to sign a coach of such stature. He won two division titles in two seasons before stepping down.

Bill Parcells (1983–2006)

The only man to lead four different teams to the playoffs, Parcells is the quintessential nineties coach. At each of his stops, he brought sweeping changes to the organization that employed him. He didn't simply introduce a new playbook, he gave the team a whole new way of doing business.

Parcells took over a Patriots team that had gone 2-14 and led them to the playoffs in his second season. The Jets improved from 1-15 to 9-7 in his first season at the helm, and the Cowboys from 5-11 to 10-6.

At a time when many teams were turning toward the West Coast Offense, Parcells adopted a more conservative approach. Each of his teams followed the same basic blueprint. It started with a power running attack led by a veteran quarterback. By avoiding turnovers and penalties, Parcells played a game that was predicated on ball control and field position. On the other side of the ball, Parcells stuck with the 3-4 defense long after most teams had abandoned it.

Parcell's personal style was just as old-school as his playbook. His stern, disciplinarian approach rubbed some players the wrong way. "If you're sensitive, you will have a hard time with me," he said. "The only players I hurt with my words are the ones who have an inflated opinion of their ability. I can't worry about that."

Bill Walsh (1979–1988)

Despite a relatively short tenure, Walsh was one of the most influential coaches in football history. He developed and popularized what came to be known as the West Coast Offense while he was an assistant coach with the Bengals from 1968 to 1975. Sid Gillman had first used the style of play in the late fifties, but Walsh perfected it in Cincinnati with quarterback Ken Anderson.

When Bengals coach Paul Brown retired after the 1975 season, he named line coach Tiger Johnson as his successor. Walsh was bitter, not just because he was passed over for the job, but because he felt that Brown had undermined his attempts to land a head coaching job with another organization. He left on bad terms, spent a year as an assistant with the Chargers and then two years as head coach at Stanford University.

He finally got his chance to be an NFL head coach in 1979, taking over a 49ers team that had just finished 2-14. The organization was in disarray, having gone through five coaches in four seasons. The front office was a shambles, with absentee owners in Ohio unable to effectively run a business in California. Walsh transformed the organization, bringing in experienced football men to run the front office, rebuilding the scouting staff, and starting to sort through the messy roster he inherited.

Walsh drafted players like Joe Montana, Dwight Clark, Ronnie Lott, and Keena Turner. By his third season, the Niners had the league's No. 2–ranked defense and were running Walsh's offense to perfection. They finished 13-3 and won Super Bowl XVI against Walsh's old team, the Bengals.

He would win two more Super Bowls over the next seven years, retiring after beating the Bengals in the big game for a second time. Walsh had nothing left to prove, and he was elected to the Hall of Fame a few years later.

His accomplishments with the 49ers were remarkable, and his contributions to the modern passing game are undeniable, but, frankly, his record on the field keeps him from being considered in the same class as the very best of the best . . . guys like Brown, Halas, and Lombardi.

First, Walsh only coached ten seasons, and two of those seasons were shortened by the strike. Both times, he benefited. The Niners were one of the few teams that had key players stay on the job during the 1987 strike, and one of only three teams that won all three of the games played with replacement players (San Diego and Washington were the others). In 1982, coming off their first Super Bowl win, the team stunk. They couldn't run the ball and the defense fell apart, and a strike-shortened season probably trimmed four or five losses from Walsh's final tally.

In his first four seasons, Walsh's 49ers compiled a record of 24-33. In his last six seasons, the Niners made the playoffs every year and won two Super Bowls. But only twice did one of Walsh's teams finish with more than ten wins, and from 1985 to 1987 they suffered double-digit losses in their opening playoff game. I'm not trying to suggest that Walsh wasn't a great coach, but only that he had some vulnerabilities.

Walsh played a key role in developing three Hall of Fame–caliber quarterbacks—everybody knows what he did with Montana. I'm convinced that Ken Anderson will eventually be enshrined in Canton, and Walsh deserves much of the credit for his success. Nobody has really given Walsh the proper credit for his work with Dan Fouts during their season together in San Diego. Fouts had spent five seasons in the NFL before Walsh arrived, throwing 57 interceptions and just 34 touchdown passes. With Walsh coaching him in 1978, Fouts set career highs in yards and touchdowns, and would go on to lead the NFL in passing yards for each of the next four seasons.

In his 1990 autobiography, Walsh wrote an entire chapter called "The Care and Feeding of Quarterbacks." He begins by saying "probably more drafting mistakes are made on quarterbacks than any other position." Walsh owes much of his success to the astute selection of Anderson in 1971 and Montana in 1979—both third-round picks. However, as general manager of the 49ers, he misfired badly in 2000 with his selection of Hofstra QB Giovanni Carmazzi. Walsh thought he saw something in the small-college player that would make him a star. There was a hidden gem in that draft, but it wasn't Carmazzi (who would never play a down in the NFL). It was Tom Brady, selected in the sixth round by New England.

#15
Hank Stram (1960–1977)

On the sidelines of Super Bowl IV, the Chiefs players noticed that coach Hank Stram was acting strangely. Running back Mike Garrett described him as "unusually animated." Quarterback Len Dawson noted how odd it was for Stram to keep calling him over to discuss the play-calling strategy, particularly since Dawson called his own plays. Stram was engaging everybody in conversation, cracking jokes with the officials, and explaining every decision he made in great detail to anybody who would listen.

It wasn't until the following April that everyone figured out what was happening. Stram had been wired for sound by the folks at NFL Films. The result was some remarkable footage, a detailed inside glimpse at a major sporting event. The finished product was unforgettable. Strolling the sidelines with the game plan rolled up in his hands, Stram exhorted his players by calling out: "Just keep matriculating the ball down the field, boys."

Leading 9–0 in the second quarter, Stram called for a play named "65 toss power trap." He sent receiver Gloster Richardson in with the play, and then paced the sidelines repeating the call over and over again for the benefit of the players on the sidelines. The play resulted in a touchdown run by Mike Garrett, and Stram cackled with glee: "I told you that baby was there."

Stram was the first head coach of the AFL's Dallas Texans, and he stuck with the team when they moved to Kansas City and became the Chiefs in 1963. He was the only coach whose tenure spanned the AFL's entire ten-year existence. During that time, he won three AFL championships in addition to the Super Bowl IV triumph. His use of a multiple formation offense was a great example of the innovations that helped the AFL develop an exciting level of play and attract widespread fan interest.

#16
Dan Reeves (1981–2003)

Dan Reeves and Bud Grant are virtually tied in my rankings, and they are the highest rated coaches on this list who didn't win a championship. They appear just ahead of another coach whose resume is missing a league title, Marv Levy.

Levy and Grant are both in the Hall of Fame, as is one other coach who didn't win a title: George Allen. I think Reeves will eventually join them.

One of the biggest arguments against Reeves is his relatively low winning percentage, which suffered greatly in the second half of his career. Over his last eight seasons, Reeves compiled a record of 60-80—and that's including a 14-2 season with the Falcons in 1998. After leaving Denver, he made just three playoff appearances in eight seasons.

Dan Reeves Versus Hall of Fame Coaches Without a Championship

Win Pct	Coach	Career record
.705	George Allen	116-47-5
.620	Bud Grant	158-96-5
.563	Marv Levy	142-110-0
.535	Dan Reeves	190-165-2

Like Levy and Grant, Reeves was 0-4 in Super Bowls. But what makes him stand apart is that he took two different teams there. He won Coach of the Year honors with three different teams (Denver-1985, NY Giants-1993, Atlanta-1998)—only Dick Vermeil and Chuck Knox did that. His ability to be successful with three different teams—and three different *kinds* of teams—will be what eventually gets him enshrined at Canton.

#17
Bud Grant (1967–1985)

Harry "Bud" Grant is best remembered today as a coach who lost four Super Bowls.

While he failed at that task, he succeeded at just about everything else in his career.

Grant was a three-sport star at the University of Minnesota, and was selected as the No. 1 pick in the 1950 NFL draft by the Philadelphia Eagles. He opted to play pro basketball instead, and spent two seasons as a forward with the Minneapolis Lakers. He played with some great players, including future Hall of Famers George Mikan, Vern Mikkelsen, Jim Pollard, and Slater Martin—a group that won the 1950 NBA championship.

He joined the Eagles in 1951, playing sparingly, but in 1952 he finished second in the NFL with 997 receiving yards. Grant parlayed that success into a lucrative contract offer from the Winnipeg Blue Bombers of the Canadian Football League. He was an All-Star three times in his four seasons up north before retiring to become Winnipeg's head coach. From 1956 to 1966 he led the team to the championship game six times and won four Grey Cups.

In 1967, he returned to Minnesota as head coach of the Minnesota Vikings. The team hadn't made much progress in six seasons under Norm Van Brocklin, but Grant turned them into division champs in his second year. A year later they won the NFL championship game and advanced to the Super Bowl against the Kansas City Chiefs. In a span of eight seasons, Grant would take the Vikings to the Super Bowl four times. Each time, he would come up short against a Hall of Fame coach—Hank Stram, Don Shula, Chuck Noll, and John Madden. The Vikings were dominating during that stretch, compiling a record of 87-24 and winning seven division titles.

Rather than being wedded to one playing strategy, Grant adapted his style based on his players. He built a dominating running game around backs Bill Brown and Dave Osborn when he first took over the team. A few years later, the Vikings traded for quarterback Fran Tarkenton and drafted running back Chuck Foreman, and Grant implemented a short-passing game. In the mid-1970s, the team added receivers Ahmad Rashad and Sammy White. Grant took advantage of their speed with a big play passing offense.

Grant and Warren Moon are the only two individuals in both the Pro Football Hall of Fame and the Canadian Football Hall of Fame.

#18
Marv Levy (1978–1997)

The perfect example of why second chances matter, Levy was sixty-one when he was named head coach of the Buffalo Bills. For nearly thirty years, he had been a successful coach at the college level, in the USFL, and in the Canadian Football League. Although he'd spent three years as a special teams coach on George Allen's staff, Levy was best known to most people for the five unremarkable seasons he spent as head coach of the Kansas City Chiefs. His lack of success there didn't keep the Bills from hiring him as their head coach midway through the 1986 season.

Levy took over a team had finished 2-14 two seasons in a row, but there was some good young talent in place. Defensive end Bruce Smith and receiver Andre Reed were in their second pro seasons, and Jim Kelly had just joined the Bills after spending three years in the USFL. In Levy's third season the Bills drafted running back Thurman Thomas and finished 12-4, winning the division crown.

The Bills lost the AFC championship to the Bengals in 1988, and Levy noticed how that team used its no-huddle offense to keep defenses off balance. A year later, he developed his own version of the system, dubbed the K-Gun Offense (the "K" standing for Kelly). When the Bills fell behind in a playoff game against the Browns the following season, Levy started the second half playing a two-minute offense. The team didn't huddle, Kelly called the plays from the line of scrimmage, and they were frequently snapping the ball before the defense had a chance to get resituated. Although the Bills lost that game, Kelly ended up throwing for over 400 yards, and Levy realized that he needed to unleash the massive collection of firepower he had assembled.

Levy tailored the fast-paced offense around Kelly, Reed, and Thomas, and the next year the Bills started their run of four straight Super Bowl appearances. When Levy retired after the 1997 season he was seventy-two years old—tying him with George Halas as the oldest coach in NFL history.

#19
Mike Shanahan (1988–2007)

Like Bill Belichick and Marv Levy, Shanahan had mediocre results in his first stint as an NFL coach. And like those other two men, Shanahan flourished in a more favorable environment.

Shanahan had great success as a quarterbacks coach and offensive coordinator, working first with John Elway in Denver and then with Steve Young in San Francisco. When he became head coach of the Broncos in 1995, he installed his own variation of the Niners' West Coast Offense. Shanahan's version was run-heavy, featuring zone blocking, cut-back lanes, quarterback rollouts, and the occasional deep pass.

The changes yielded immediate results. After going 8-8 in Shanahan's first season, the Broncos finished 13-3, 12-4, and 14-2 over the next three seasons, winning two Super Bowls. However, it was after that remarkable run that the real magic of Shanahan's offensive innovations began to be revealed. From 1998 to 2006, six different running backs were plugged into that offense and each posted a 1000-yard rushing season (Terrell Davis, Olandis Gary, Mike Anderson, Cliton Portis, Reuben Droughns, and Tatum Bell).

Shanahan has been criticized for his lack of playoff success after Elway retired (one playoff win from 1999 to 2007), but frankly, he has never gotten the credit he deserves. He already ranks in the top twenty for career wins, and he's had just one losing season in thirteen years with the Broncos.

#20
Bill Cowher (1992–2006)

Cowher finally got his ring in his fourteenth season. Only seven coaches had that many years under their belt without a title (Reeves, Knox, Schottenheimer, Grant, Levy, Mora, Coryell). Cowher had done just about everything else, but like so many others, had trouble converting the consistent regular season success into postseason triumph.

The one constant throughout Cowher's time with the Steelers was change. The organization hadn't been a major player on the free-agent market. More often than not, top players were leaving Pittsburgh for more money with other teams. After the Steelers reached the Super Bowl in 1995, Cowher had to endure the defection of quarterback Neil O'Donnell, who cashed in on his success by signing a big contract with the Jets. Linebacker Kevin Greene, safety Rod Woodson, and tackle Leon Searcy would soon follow. It seemed as if Cowher was constantly trying to plug holes in his lineup, but somehow the Steelers were always competitive. In his fifteen seasons, the team finished with a winning record eleven times.

One of the secrets to the Steelers' success was the close relationship between Cowher and the Rooney family, which owns and runs the team. There was a level of trust, and because Cowher felt secure, he was not afraid to make decisions that might not pay off immediately. In an environment where coaches are always under the microscope and one bad season can get you fired, Cowher had a unique advantage.

Cowher's prominent chin and his severe expression on the sidelines created the impression that he was a stern disciplinarian, but he was in fact a player's coach. He was unforgiving of players who screwed up their assignments or made a dumb decision on the field, but he was also their biggest cheerleader.

#21
Mike Holmgren (1992–2007)

After having some remarkable success in Green Bay, Holmgren resigned because the Packers weren't willing to let him serve the dual role of head coach and general manager. Many coaches have argued that it's unfair to be held responsible for the performance of the team if they aren't allowed to choose which players are on the roster. It's an argument that gets harder to support as free agency and the salary cap have placed limits on the flexibility that teams have with regard to personnel. What's more, both jobs have become so complicated and time consuming that it's hard for one person to do both things well. (It was a bit ironic then that after the Packers let Holmgren leave over the issue, they let new head coach Mike Sherman wear both hats from 2001 to 2004.)

Holmgren served as GM and coach in Seattle, and made some player moves that raised eyebrows. He traded for a raw young quarterback named Matt Hasselbeck and dumped prolific running back Ricky Watters for the younger Shaun Alexander. After four mediocre seasons, Holmgren relinquished his GM duties, and that's when the Seahawks really started to take off. Hasselbeck and Alexander blossomed. The team reached the playoffs in 2003, Holmgren's first year as just the coach, and two years later advanced to the Super Bowl.

Is Holmgren a great coach? I think you can make a pretty strong case, and taking a second team to the Super Bowl boosted his Hall of Fame chances. But I think his record also suggests that teams are better served by letting their coaches focus on coaching and by getting good people—different people—to run the front office.

#22 Tony Dungy (1996–2007)

Another guy tagged with the label of "can't win in the playoffs" for the longest time. Even though he won the Super Bowl after the 2006 season, he didn't overcome the sentiment that he'd failed to capitalize on several other good opportunities.

Dungy has had great regular-season success with two different teams. In Tampa Bay, he won by building a formidable defense. In Indianapolis, he has been the architect of an explosive offense. In both places, his inability to advance in the postseason was incredibly frustrating.

Part of the problem, frankly, was that most of those playoff teams didn't win enough games during the regular season to earn the right to play their postseason games at home. Through 2005, Dungy's postseason record was 4–1 at home, 1–7 on the road. Given a chance to play the AFC title game at home, Dungy's 2006 team capitalized and finally got through to the big game.

When the 2005 Colts got to mid-November without losing a game, Dungy announced that he was more concerned about getting his team ready for the playoffs than he was with finishing undefeated. He announced that he planned to rest some of his starters after the team clinched home field advantage throughout the playoffs. This rankled some folks, but it was the right approach, of course.

The sudden death of Dungy's son in late December of that season dealt a huge blow, not just to the coach but also to the entire organization. Although the team said all of the right things

about keeping their focus despite the tragedy, they lost three of their next four games (including the opening round of the playoffs) after starting the season 13–0.

In 2006, the team's regular-season record was less spectacular, but once the playoffs started the team was hitting on all cylinders. It was as if Dungy had learned to conserve something for the month of January. His Colts finished with the league's worst run defense during the regular season, but stiffened in the playoffs. The ability to make those adjustments in the postseason was a contrast to earlier coaching performances, when Dungy's critics claimed that he got more conservative in the postseason.

#23 George Seifert (1989–2001)

Some folks point to Seifert's accomplishments in eight seasons with the 49ers as overwhelming evidence of his greatness, while others dismiss him as a caretaker coach who simply capitalized on a remarkable confluence of circumstances. If you're going to analyze NFL coaches, you have to start with Seifert . . . not because he's the best coach in history, but because the way you answer the fundamental questions about his performance will shape the way that you analyze every other coach.

Here are the four questions that have to be asked:

1. To what extent does a coach get credit or blame for the quality of the team that he inherits?

In the vast majority of cases, a head coach begins his tenure with a losing team, often one that has serious problems. It is precisely because the team is in such dire straits that the previous coach got fired. Occasionally, though, a coach inherits a team that's in much better shape. Seifert got the job in San Francisco because Bill Walsh retired after the 1988 season, becoming the first in a string of head coaches to walk away from Super Bowl teams over the next decade. It was a move repeated by the winners of the next four Super Bowls, and those teams weren't always able to continue their success after the coaching change.

- Bill Parcells retired from the Giants in 1990, having won two Super Bowl titles in his last five seasons. His successor, Ray Handley, went 14-18 in two seasons, and the team made just one playoff appearance over the next six years. Parcells walked away from another Super Bowl team in New England in 1996, and the team's record got worse in each of the four seasons after he left.

- Joe Gibbs retired in 1992, a year after winning his third Super Bowl in Washington. It took seven years before the Redskins made it back to the playoffs.

- Jimmy Johnson bailed out of Dallas in 1993 after winning back-to-back Super Bowls. The momentum continued with Barry Switzer at the helm, as the team won another Super Bowl two years later. Things fell apart shortly thereafter, and the team has now gone eleven years without winning a playoff game.

- Dick Vermeil retired after winning a super Bowl with the Rams in 1999. He was replaced by Mike Martz, who returned to the Super Bowl two years later, but after reaching the playoffs in his first two seasons, Martz's team began to regress, finishing with a winning record just once more in the next four years.

So inheriting a Super Bowl team has been something of a mixed bag. Some of the subsequent coaches have had initial success, but none have been able to sustain that success.

That is where Seifert stands apart. Dismiss his first-year Super Bowl win if you like. Say that Seifert won a championship with Walsh's team, and that any halfway competent coach probably could have done the same thing. But Seifert kept his team at those heights for a long time. In eight seasons, he took his team to the playoffs seven times, and the one season that they missed out they still finished 10-6. Contrast that with Walsh, who had a losing record three times, and only finished better than 10-6 three times in ten seasons. Clearly, any

objective analyst has to recognize that Seifert took Walsh's teams to heights they had not previously reached.

But more significantly, we need to acknowledge that the idea that Seifert simply continued to win with a team that Walsh built simply isn't true. By the end of Seifert's second season, the core of the team that Walsh had built was gone. Offensive lineman Harris Barton retired, running back Roger Craig was worn out, and quarterback Joe Montana suffered a career-threatening injury that eventually led to his being traded. Within two years of taking the job, Seifert lost three Pro Bowlers from the defense—defensive backs Ronnie Lott and Eric Wright and linebacker Keena Turner. Three more would leave over the next two seasons (defensive linemen Charles Haley, Michael Carter, and Pierce Holt), with linebacker Bill Romanowski and guard Guy McIntyre jumping ship a year later.

With the exception of wide receiver Jerry Rice, Seifert's 1992 team bore little resemblance to the roster that Walsh had left behind. Over the next five seasons, Seifert compiled a record of 60-20 with a team largely of his own design, advancing to the conference championship game three times and winning another Super Bowl. (And it's worth noting that in Seifert's two Super Bowl wins, the Niners scored 55 and 49 points.)

Look at his year-by-year record and draw your own conclusions, but I think it's pretty clear. A lousy coach who takes over a Super Bowl team will drive it into the ground. A mediocre coach who takes over may have some initial success but ultimately the team will regress back to the middle of the pack. Only a truly gifted coach can take over a great team and take it to even higher levels, maintaining that success for a long time. That's what Seifert did.

The Niners were 12-4 in Seifert's last season with San Francisco. Three years later, they were 4-12. If Seifert were merely along for the ride, you wouldn't have expected the team to fall as far and as rapidly as they did after he was fired. On the contrary, I think that's a pretty good indicator of how much he really contributed to San Francisco's success.

2. How much credit should a coach get for winning with great players, and how much blame should he get for losing with lousy players?

This is a question whose answer has changed in the modern era, I believe. There was a time when great players were a reflection of the coach's ability to scout, develop, and teach young players and turn them into productive professionals. Once free agency and the salary cap entered the picture, I don't believe that those skills mattered as much any more. A guy like Chuck Noll or Tom Landry could nurture players for years, bringing them along slowly until a job opened up or until their skills progressed to a point that they forced the coach to give them more playing time. The rapid turnover in the free-agency era made that sort of patience impossible. Players have to produce quickly—often immediately—or someone else will take their place.

Sometimes a coach benefits from a great player falling into his lap, a once-in-a-decade kind of talent that you can build a team around like Jim Brown or Lawrence Taylor or Bret Favre. But these days, a coach has to assemble a team to fit his system or design a system to fit his existing players, and do that within the constraints of the marketplace. It's that effort that defines a modern coach, and we have seen that the great ones are able to win with different players and different types of teams. Seifert continued to win as his roster turned over.

3. When a coach has success with one team but not another, how does that affect our overall evaluation of him?

This is the other big knock against Seifert, and probably the one that carries the most weight. Seifert was dumped by the 49ers after eight seasons. He didn't get along with owner John York and was unceremoniously fired after a season in which his team finished 12-4. A year later, Seifert took the reigns of the Carolina Panthers. He finished 8-8 and 7-9 in his first two seasons before everything fell apart in 2001. Seifert inherited a lot of personnel problems that he simply wasn't able to address

adequately. In his third season, the Panthers won their season opener but lost all the rest of their games, finishing with a 1-15 record and becoming the first team in NFL history to rank dead last in both offense and defense. It was an unmitigated disaster.

There have been plenty of other examples of coaches who struggled with one team after having had great success with another.

- Tom Flores won two Super Bowls with the Raiders but managed just fourteen wins in three seasons with the Seattle Seahawks.
- Mike Ditka won 106 regular season games with the Chicago Bears but couldn't get the New Orleans Saints to finish any better than 6-10 in three seasons.
- Bobby Ross was 47-33 in San Diego (including an AFC championship) but was just 27-30 in Detroit.
- Bum Phillips had a 55-35 record with the Oilers and won four playoff games but was just 27-42 in New Orleans.

In each of these cases (and plenty of others), the coaches' failures in their second stop completely changed the public perception of them. It's puzzling, because coaches who stink at one job and then excel at another (Levy, Shannahan, Belichick) are given a pass, while guys who soar first then stumble seem to be dismissed.

4. How much credit does a head coach get for the accomplishments of his supporting staff or the decisions made by the front office?

Shortly after the Panthers fired Seifert, Joel Buschbaum of *Pro Football Weekly* wrote: "In San Francisco, Seifert had great assistant coaches, great players and a strong front office. In Carolina, he had a mediocre staff, less than mediocre front office in large part because Seifert was just the coach in San Francisco and called the shots in Carolina. He was in over his head doing so."

Some of the personnel moves that Seifert made in Carolina seemed curious at the time, particularly the string of decisions that resulted in twenty-nine-year-old rookie Chris Weinke becoming the Panthers starting quarterback in 2001. With the benefit of some hindsight, however, it's clear that the lack of talent on that 1-15 roster was more about the players that Seifert had inherited than the players he had brought in himself.

Look at the horrible first-round picks the Panthers made in the four years before Seifert arrived.

- 1995—Quarterback Kerry Collins battled alcoholism and feuded with teammates before essentially quitting midway through his fourth season.
- 1996—Running back Tim Biakabutuka never played well enough to become a starter, let alone an impact player. He was drafted ahead of backs like Eddie George and Stephen Davis.
- 1997—Receiver Rae Carruth played just one full season before being charged with (and eventually convicted of) arranging the murder of his girlfriend.
- 1998—Defensive lineman Jason Peter managed just seven sacks in four injury plagued seasons.

At the end of Seifert's final season, it looked like his team was completely devoid of talent. Looking back now, it's clear that Seifert had put some pretty good pieces in place. Just two years after he left, the Panthers were in the Super Bowl, and sixteen of the twenty-two starters in that game were holdovers from the Seifert era. Among the players that Seifert drafted in his three seasons were WR Steve Smith, DE Mike Rucker, DT Kris Jenkins, LB Dan Morgan, and DB Deon Grant—all of whom played a major role on the 2003 Super Bowl team. Seifert deserves a lot of the blame for Carolina's disastrous 2001 season, but he also deserves at least some of the credit for the success the team had after he left.

Everybody talks about the coaching tree—guys who serve as an assistant under a great coach and go on to do great things themselves. There are four men who served as coordinators or assistants under Seifert in San Francisco who went on to be head coaches and took their teams to a Super Bowl: Mike Holmgren, Mike Shannahan, Jon

Gruden, and Jeff Fisher. I suspect that says something about Sefiert's eye for talent, too.

So where does that leave us in our evaluation of George Seifert? In my mind, he's the most underrated coach of the free-agency era. First, he suffers greatly in comparison to the guy he succeeded. Walsh was a great innovator. Seifert was not. Walsh shaped the game of football for a generation. Seifert was a pretty good defensive coordinator, and he had considerable success as an assistant coach, but nothing that he did changed the way the game was played.

If you believe in context, you have to believe that there's a pretty strong case to be made for Seifert's greatness. Placed into an ideal situation in San Francisco, he took a team to heights that no other coach has ever reached. Placed into a lousy situation in Carolina, he kept a team afloat for two years before it sunk, but built enough of a foundation for the next coach to turn things around. As time passes, I hope people will begin to recognize how remarkable a coach Seifert really was.

George Allen (1966–1977)

Although a glimpse at his record shows just two coaching stints, Allen was fired four times in his NFL career. Rams owner Dan Reeves dismissed him after three seasons in Los Angeles. Despite posting a 29-10-3 record in three seasons, Allen exerted complete control over the organization, a situation that grated on the owner. Reeves said "it's more fun to lose than to win with George Allen." The players, however, loved their coach and led an open revolt, calling a press conference to announce that they wouldn't perform without their chosen leader. Reeves relented, and let him return. Allen led the Rams to records of 11-3 and 9-4-1 before being fired again two years later.

The coach took his act to Washington, where he continued to win ball games and continued to feud with ownership. Redskins owner Edward Bennett Williams grew increasingly uncomfortable with the amount of control Allen had over personnel and financial matters. That led to an acrimonious departure after the 1977 season. Allen returned to the Rams in 1978, but his intense style and grueling practices irked the players, who led another revolt—this time, against Coach Allen. Carroll Rosenbloom, the new owner of the Rams, fired Allen after just two exhibition games. Both Rosenbloom and Allen agreed that the arrangement had been a colossal mistake.

Allen first showcased his innovative defensive philosophies with the Bears, where he spent seven years as an assistant under George Halas. Chicago won the 1963 championship, and Allen's work with players like Dick Butkus, Richie Petitbon, and Doug Atkins was a major factor. By the time he had become a head coach, Allen advocated a "future is now" policy to building his teams. He constantly traded draft picks for veteran players, and his strategy was mostly successful. In twelve seasons, his teams never finished with a losing record, and Allen retired with the fourth-highest winning percentage in NFL history.

In Washington, Allen added so many veteran players that his team was nicknamed the "Over the Hill Gang." He acquired many of the players he had coached with the Rams—including defensive standouts Richie Petitbon, Jack Pardee, and Diron Talbert. In all, he made eighty-one trades during his seven seasons with Washington. The Redskins had managed just one winning season in the fifteen years before he arrived, but finished above .500 each year under Allen and made five playoff appearances, including a trip to Super Bowl VII.

#25

John Madden (1969–1978)

If you're involved in most professional sports, either as a player, a coach, or a journalist, you spend just as much time on airplanes as you do at the actual game. Madden's well-publicized dislike for flying hasn't kept him from remaining in the business. Stories have been published about Madden surviving a crash, or enduring a bad flight, but that's not the case at all. It stems from having what Madden describes as a "full-blown panic attack"

during a 1979 flight, after which he vowed not to get back on a plane again.

He traveled by train for a while before switching to a private bus, which has come to be known as the Madden Cruiser. This unique method of transportation has brought him some notoriety and made it possible for him to keep working as a commentator, but I suspect it has also helped to cultivate his broadcasting style and approach to the game.

In a 2003 article, Madden explained: "I used to get on the airplane, then I'd get off the airplane. I'd go to the hotel and the stadium, then back to the airplane. I traveled all over, but I didn't see anything. Now, I do. . . . This is seeing our country. I've always said a congressman should ride across country. Not drive, because you can't see when you drive, you have to ride. You have to be a witness to America."

The Hall of Fame doesn't induct broadcasters, but I suspect that if we were to make a list of the men whose broadcasting careers made the biggest impact, Madden's name would have to be in the top five. Through 2008, he has won fourteen Sports Emmy Awards and received the prestigious Pete Rozelle Radio-Television Award. Some coaches influence a generation of coaches that come after them. Madden has influenced a whole generation of color commentators.

Oh, yeah, Madden was one heckuva coach too. Just looking at the numbers, it's hard to understand why it took twenty-five years for the HOF voters to realize he was worthy of being inducted. In ten seasons with the Raiders, he compiled the highest winning percentage in NFL history. He led the Raiders to the AFC championship five straight times (1973 to 1977), though his team lost four of those games. A commanding win over the Steelers in the 1976 title game propelled the Raiders to the Super Bowl, where they walloped the Vikings 32–14.

Madden was a successful defensive coordinator at San Diego State University, and was the Raiders linebacker coach for two years before being named head coach in 1969. At thirty-two, Madden was the youngest coach in the NFL. He retired after just ten seasons, citing health concerns. He had battled stomach ulcers, and said that doctors had told him the stress of coaching gave him "the body of a seventy-year-old man."

Weeb Ewbank (1954–1973)

With a career record just one game above .500, Ewbank has the lowest winning percentage of the twenty-one coaches in the Hall of Fame. All those losses racked up because he signed on to coach two expansion teams. He took over the Colts in their second season, and later joined the New York Jets in their fourth season. Each time, he inherited a losing team and turned them into champions.

The key move in each instance was the acquisition of a great quarterback. In Baltimore, it was Johnny Unitas. With the Jets, it was Joe Namath. Each time, Ewbank acquired and nurtured a young passer, built a solid team around him, and led the team to a title.

Ewbank was the first (and to date the only) NFL coach to win championships with more than one team. He was also the winning coach in what were arguably the two most significant games in NFL history. The first was the 1958 championship game, where the Colts beat the Giants in the first sudden-death overtime in football history. The second was Super Bowl III, where the AFL champion Jets upset the heavily favored NFL champion Colts, a game in which Joe Namath had guaranteed victory.

Ewbank was the losing coach in another memorable game, a 1968 matchup between the Jets and Raiders that came to be known as the Heidi game. In a hard-fought contest, the lead bounced back and forth. With 1:05 left on the game clock, the Jets kicked a field goal for a 32–29 lead. After the ensuing kickoff, the NBC broadcast went to a commercial, and when it returned, they started airing a movie adaptation of the classic children's book *Heidi*. Millions of fans missed the dramatic finish that followed. The Raiders scored two touchdowns in the game's final minute to win, but most fans didn't learn about the comeback until they read the paper the next day.

The Colts won back-to-back titles under Ewbank in 1958 and 1959, but fans grew restless when the team couldn't return to those heights. Though the Colts didn't finish with a losing record in any of the next three seasons, Ewbank was fired after the 1962 season and replaced by Don Shula. A similar fate befell Ewbank in New York. After winning Super Bowl III in 1968 and advancing to the playoffs again in 1969, the Jets regressed. After missing the playoffs for the next four seasons, Ewbank retired.

Buddy Parker (1949–1964)

A *Los Angeles Times* article from 1965 described Parker as "often quixotic, rarely colorless, and yet a sound gridiron strategist when the occasion demanded." In Detroit, Raymond "Buddy" Parker developed what would come to be known as the 2-minute offense. Quarterback Bobby Layne ran it to perfection, and opposing defenses simply couldn't keep up. With an explosive offense and stifling defense, the Lions advanced to the NFL championship game in three straight seasons, meeting the Cleveland Browns each time. The Lions beat an injury-ravaged Cleveland team for the title in 1952, and came back to beat the Browns in a 17–16 thriller a year later. The Lions lost to Cleveland in the 1954 title game.

Parker stunned everybody when he resigned suddenly at the end of the 1957 preseason. At a "Meet the Lions" banquet to introduce the players to the community, he expressed his disgust at the state of the team and said that he was through with football in Detroit. "I can't handle this team," he told reporters later that evening. "It's the worst team I've ever seen in training camp."

George Wilson, a longtime Parker assistant, was named head coach the following day, and he adamantly disagreed with Parker's assessment of the club. "This team is farther advanced than any other Lion team in my nine years," concluded Wilson, adding, "I think Parker was using this excuse to cover up his real reason for quitting."

Wilson was right on both counts. Parker signed a lucrative contract to coach the Pittsburgh Steelers two weeks later, after reportedly spurning an offer to replace Weeb Ewbank as coach of the Colts. Whether Parker had these offers lined up before he resigned is a mystery, but it certainly didn't take him long to find a new job.

As for the state of the team, Wilson's assessment proved to be more accurate than Parker's. The team that Parker said was the worst he'd ever seen would go on to win the NFL championship. The Lions had two great quarterbacks—Layne and Tobin Rote—and Wilson used them in tandem until Layne broke his leg in November. The strong play of Rote, along with veteran fullback John Henry Johnson, helped lead the Lions back to the NFL title game, where they destroyed the Browns 59–14.

Buddy Parker would spend nine years with the Steelers, constantly trading his draft picks for veteran players that he thought would put the team over the top. He acquired his old quarterback, Bobby Layne, in a 1958 trade, John Henry Johnson in 1960, and Gene "Big Daddy" Lipscomb in 1961. None of these moves paid off, and despite some winning seasons, the Steelers never made the playoffs under Parker.

He quit the job in Pittsburgh abruptly too. After the Steelers lost four exhibition games in 1965, he walked away, and never coached in the NFL again.

#28
Greasy Neale (1941–1950)

Earle "Greasy" Neale played with Jim Thorpe on the pre-NFL Canton Bulldogs, and spent eight seasons as an outfielder with the Cincinnati Reds—including the infamous 1919 World Series. His unfortunate nickname came from childhood. He tagged a neighborhood boy with the nickname "Dirty," and that kid retaliated by calling Neale "Greasy." The name stuck. When he joined the coaching staff at Yale University in 1934, school officials asked reporters to refrain from using the nickname. The

coach dismissed that request. "Yale or no Yale, if you fellows want to call me Greasy, go ahead."

Neale became head coach of the Philadelphia Eagles in 1941, and his innovations there changed the game of football. Most teams were using a basic 6-2-2-1 defensive formation, with two defensive halfbacks and a safety bearing the primary responsibility for stopping the pass. This was a largely ineffective strategy against the growing number of offenses who were adopting Clark Shaughnessy's T-formation passing attack. To counter that, Neale developed what was called the "Eagle Defense," a 5-2-4 formation that eliminated an interior lineman (known at the time as a middle guard, or what we would call today a nose tackle). Neale replaced that lineman with another defensive halfback, essentially creating the modern position of cornerback. Under Neale's system, the defense could cover receivers man-to-man, rather than always relying on zone coverage.

He also had his ends or linebackers make contact with the receivers at the line of scrimmage to disrupt their timing and keep them from getting downfield quickly. Neale's Eagle Defense was a forerunner of the 4-3 defense, developed a few years later by Tom Landry and which would become the standard for all NFL teams for the next three decades.

Neale used his own variation of the T-formation to build Philadelphia's offense. It was centered around Steve Van Buren, the most dominating runner the league had seen to date. The Eagles led the league in scoring in 1944 and 1945, and by 1947 they were in the playoffs—the first postseason appearance in franchise history. After losing the 1947 title game to the Chicago Cardinals, the Eagles returned for a rematch in 1948. The field at Shibe Park was blanketed by several feet of snow, which made play nearly impossible. Officials couldn't use chains for measurements and the sidelines were marked by a series of ropes and stakes. Neither team could mount much of an offense, and a fourth-quarter touchdown run by Steve Van Buren provided the game's only scoring.

A year later, the Eagles were even better. Neale's team averaged more than 30 points a game and gave up a league-low 134 (the Steelers were the next lowest with 214). Philadelphia shut out the Rams 14–0 and won their second straight championship.

Eagles owner Lex Thompson sold the team after the 1949 season. Neale had been friends with Thompson since his time at Yale, and Thompson was a hands-off owner, content to let Neale do his thing. That changed when James P. Clark bought the team. After losing a close game to the Giants in November, Clark stormed into the locker room and berated the coach in front of his players. Neale was irate, and the two men nearly came to blows. When the season ended two weeks later, Clark fired the most successful coach in his franchise's history. Over the next thirty years, they would make just one playoff appearance.

One more interesting note about Neale: He hated to fly. As a result, the team took trains to every road game—something his players universally despised. "God almighty, I hated those train trips," explained Hall of Fame linebacker Chuck Bednarik. "Here I was, a man who had flown thirty missions over Germany in World War II, had gotten shot at, and survived. So you know, he should have felt safe flying on the same plane with me." It took three and a half days to get from Philadelphia to Los Angeles. Neale would stop along the way, have his team get off to practice for an hour or so, and then get back on.

#29
Marty Schottenheimer (1984–2006)

Schottenheimer's teams didn't have a losing record until his fifteenth season, but they repeatedly fell short in the postseason. He was unceremoniously dumped after four full seasons in Cleveland, despite making the playoffs each year. It was two spectacular postseason losses that led to his dismissal, games that would come to be remembered as simply "The Drive" and "The Fumble."

In the 1987 AFC championship game, Schottenheimer's Browns led the Broncos 20–13 with a little over five minutes left in regulation. Denver muffed the ensuing kickoff and recovered at their own 2-yard line. Quarterback John Elway methodically picked the Cleveland defense apart, leading a fifteen-play drive that was capped by a 5-yard touchdown pass with 37 seconds left. Denver won the game with a field goal in overtime.

A year later, the two teams met again in the AFC title game. Cleveland rallied from a 21–3 halftime deficit to tie the game in the fourth quarter. After Denver retook the lead with 4 minutes remaining, Cleveland quarterback Bernie Kosar tried to produce his own memorable drive. The Browns marched down to the Denver 8-yard line, and Ernest Byner took a handoff around the left side, on his way to what would be a game-tying touchdown. At the 3-yard line, Denver safety Jeremiah Castille stripped the ball loose. Denver recovered and held on for the victory.

These two losses were especially demoralizing because the Browns had come tantalizingly close to victory each time. Schottenheimer's departure was more about cleansing their spirit than anything else.

Schottenheimer continued to have success in Kansas City, finishing with a winning record nine out of ten seasons and reaching the playoffs seven times. Twice, however, the Chiefs finished with the league's best record only to be bounced in the first round of the playoffs. The same thing happened to Schottenheimer's Chargers in 2006. Only Shula and Landry have lost more playoff games than Schottenheimer, but, of course, those two coaches have each also won a pair of Super Bowls.

Coaches with Losing Playoff Records (min 10 games)

Win Pct	Coach	W-L
.200	Steve Owen	2-10
.278	Marty Schottenheimer	5-13
.333	Dennis Green	4-8
.389	Chuck Knox	7-11
.400	John Robinson	4-6
.455	Bud Grant	10-12

Tom Flores (1979–1994)

Despite winning two Super Bowls, Flores not only hasn't been inducted into the Hall of Fame, he isn't even considered a serious candidate. There are three reasons for this. One is that he was a quiet, unassuming guy. The Hall tends to favor guys with big personalities—no matter whether they were friendly or confrontational. The second thing is that after his successful run with the Raiders, he spent three pretty miserable seasons in Seattle. The Seahawks fell from 7-9 to 2-14 in his first year at the helm, and finished 6-10 in each of his next two seasons.

Those issues could be dealt with, but the third reason is the biggie, and it's one that I suspect will ultimately be too big of a hurdle to overcome. That's the impression that he was just a puppet of owner Al Davis. It's not fair, but his unassuming personality and his struggles in Seattle only add fuel to the fire. John Madden was tagged with the same label, which is why it took twenty-five years for him to be inducted into the Hall of Fame.

Dick Vermeil (1976–2005)

Who says tough guys can't cry? Vermeil wasn't afraid to break down in tears at a press conference, a symbol of how passionate he was about his players.

When he took over the Eagles in 1976, Vermeil got a team that had been to the playoffs just once in twenty-five years. He helped build a strong 3-4 defense around veterans like Bill Bergey and Claude Humphrey. He also traded for Ron Jaworski, a backup quarterback with the Rams, and drafted running back Wilbert Montgomery, giving the Eagles the building blocks for a formidable offense. Vermeil led the Eagles to the Super Bowl in 1980, but resigned two years later saying that he was burned out. It was a term that most people hadn't heard before, but fellow coaches knew the effects that the long hours could have on a man's psyche.

He spent the next fourteen years in the broadcasting booth, returning to coach the St. Louis Rams in 1997. He was roundly criticized for stocking his coaching staff with assistants who were in their sixties, longtime veteran coaches like Jim Hanifan and Bud Carson. The team stumbled to 5-11 and 4-12 finishes in his first two seasons. I have read some sources that report the Rams wanted to fire Vermeil after the 1998 season but didn't because they couldn't agree on the terms of a contract buyout. If that's true, it turned out to be a remarkable stroke of luck. Two things happened during the off-season that changed the course of the franchise. On the eve of the draft, the Rams acquired running back Marshall Faulk from the Colts for a second- and fifth-round draft pick. Then, after free-agent quarterback Trent Green injured his knee late in training camp, the Rams were forced to start the season with a guy that nobody had ever heard of, Kurt Warner. Faulk flourished in the Rams offense, posting career highs in both rushing yards and receiving yards. Warner had one of the best seasons ever for a pro quarterback, making the phenomenal leap from backup quarterback to league MVP. The Rams improved from 4-12 to 13-3 and won the Super Bowl. Dick Vermeil went out on top, announcing his retirement two days after winning the big game.

He would return a year later with the Chiefs, leading them for five years before retiring again. Vermeil has a Super Bowl ring, but at the end of the day, he's still a guy whose career record is just a little bit above .500.

Mike Ditka (1982–1999)

For an entire generation of football fans (and maybe two), Mike Ditka personifies the word "toughness." One of my favorite stories about him is probably apocryphal, but it illustrates his fiery style well. The Bears were losing a game at halftime, and the coach was disappointed with his team's effort. As he stood to address his players, he plunged his arm into a bucket of water and emerged with a snapping turtle clamped tightly to his hand. As the turtle bit into his hand, and with blood streaming down his arm, Ditka lectured his team on the need for them to be tougher. "Any one of you can do the same thing if you are as determined as I am." And with that, he asked for a volunteer to step forward and show his own toughness.

One voice spoke up, massive defensive tackle William Perry, who came to stand next to the coach. As Ditka tried to pry the turtle loose from his hand, Perry said, "No need to remove the turtle, Coach. Just stick out your other hand and I'll bite that one instead."

Ditka managed an uncomfortable co-existence with his defensive coordinator, Buddy Ryan. Both men were made from the same mold, and that made it hard for them to get along. In retrospect, I think they genuinely disliked each other, but each recognized the other's skills, and they were able to make things work. The 1985 Bears were one of the most dominating teams in NFL history, with Ryan's stifling 46 defense and an offense built around running back Walter Payton.

The Bears didn't have a losing record in Ditka's first six full seasons, but I remember an outburst in the locker room after his team suffered a close loss to the Buccaneers in 1989. "I don't think this team's good enough to win another game," he concluded. It was surprising, because the Bears were 6-4, and had gone 52-11 over the previous four seasons. But Ditka was right. The Bears lost their last six games to finish 6-10. He cleaned house at the end of the season, and the rebuilt team finished 11-5 in each of the next two years.

Ditka was fired at the end of the 1992 season, a move that I think the Bears quickly grew to regret. He resurfaced with the New Orleans Saints in 1997, but the fifty-eight-year old coach didn't have the patience to rebuild the team properly. He traded all of the team's draft picks in 1999 for the right to draft Heisman Trophy–winner Ricky Williams. It was a bold move, but a ridiculous miscalculation. The most common mistake that teams make is thinking that one great player is all they need to get to the Super Bowl. First, they are almost always underestimating the deficiencies of their own team. Second, they overestimate the impact that one player can have. This was certainly the case with Williams, a back whose physical skills were unquestioned, but who didn't have the psychological makeup to take on the kind of burden that Ditka had saddled him with.

The move was a disaster. Williams lasted just three seasons in New Orleans, but the bigger problem was the loss of draft picks in what turned out to be a very deep pool of college prospects. Ditka failed to understand that in the era of free agency, the draft provides a vital flow of mid-level talent. Sure, superstars usually come from the top of the draft, but most of your starters come from the middle rounds. When you give those picks away, you'll spend the next few seasons stocking the rest of your lineup with players you pluck from the waiver wire.

Ditka would later describe his time in New Orleans as the worst three years of his life. It was a forgettable chapter for a franchise with its share of bad memories.

Chuck Knox (1973–1994)

Knox retired with more wins than any other coach who hadn't won a championship. In his first stint with the Rams, he advanced to the NFC title game in three straight seasons but couldn't win. He got there with the Bills in 1981 and again with the Seahawks in 1983, but each time his teams fell one game short of the Super Bowl.

His offensive strategy was called "Ground Chuck" because of its reliance on the running game. He also was able to build stingy defenses, which ranked in the top ten in eleven of his twenty-two seasons.

After five seasons with the Rams, Knox had compiled a record of 52-15-1, taking the team to the playoffs every year. He wasn't getting along with team owner Carroll Rosenbloom, however, and moved to Buffalo to take over the Bills in 1978. He signed what was a huge contract at the time—$1.2 million for six years. That job also ended when he feuded with owner Ralph Wilson over a contract extension.

Knox headed to Seattle and turned the Seahawks into contenders, taking them to the playoffs for the first time in franchise history. After some initial success, the team leveled out, finishing 9-7 or 7-9 for five straight seasons. He returned to the Rams for three more years but couldn't recapture any of the glory from his first stint with the team.

The big criticism of Knox is that he never got to the Super Bowl, though the Rams and Bills each made it to the big game within a few years after he left.

#34
Don Coryell (1973–1986)

We talk about coaching trees in football. Like family trees, they show us how one coach influenced the assistants that worked under him, and thus trace the impact that one coach can have on future generations.

There are two Hall of Fame coaches in Coryell's tree. Joe Gibbs and John Madden both worked under Coryell at San Diego State, and Gibbs was also an NFL assistant with Coryell in St. Louis and San Diego. It's interesting to note that while Coryell was a major innovator, neither of these coaches really followed in his footsteps. Both incorporated some aspects of the "Air Coryell" offense, but they couldn't really be described as Coryell disciples. Madden was primarily a defensive coach, and his teams ran more than they passed. Gibbs developed a one-back offense, and his teams were more about power football than airing it out.

Coryell had already embraced an aggressive passing game as head coach at Whittier College in the late fifties, and he took things to a different level when he moved to San Diego State University in 1961. Unable to compete for recruits with nearby powerhouses USC and UCLA, Coryell focused on recruiting junior college players. That strategy, combined with his innovative offense, was an unparalleled success. In one span from 1965 to 1970, the Aztecs went 54-1-1. His team shared a stadium

with the San Diego Chargers, and Coryell spent a lot of time watching their practices and comparing notes with Chargers coach Sid Gillman.

In 1973, Coryell became head coach of the St. Louis Cardinals, a franchise with just two playoff appearances in their fifty-three-year history. By his second season, the Cardinals were division champions. Coryell stretched the field with his receivers, and when defenses committed themselves to deep coverage, he'd give the ball to speedy halfback Terry Metcalf.

One of Coryell's greatest innovations came after he left St. Louis and took over the Chargers in 1978. He developed the role of the tight end as a primary receiver. He actually used two tight ends. One, typically Eric Seivers, would line up next to the tackle, and play the traditional blocking role that most tight ends played. The other, usually Kellen Winslow, was a motion tight end—Coryell called him an H-back. He would line up in the slot, split wide, in the backfield, opposite Sievers, or anywhere.

Winslow led the league in receptions during his first full season, and the Chargers offense exploded. They led the league in passing yards seven times in eight years (finishing 2nd in 1984). Quarterback Dan Fouts became just the second passer to top the 4000-yard mark, setting a new NFL record with 4082 in 1979. He upped the mark to 4715 in 1980, and 4802 the following year. But it wasn't just about flinging the ball downfield. As Fouts described it, it was more about using the pass to gain small chunks of yards: "When Coryell was in high gear, defenses were very predictable. We threw a lot on first down because teams played zone 90 percent of the time on first down. So they're playing zone, and you run these little read screens or dink-and-dunk things, and all of a sudden, you're second-and-2 without even breaking a sweat."

Coryell was able to take Gillman's aggressive passing strategies to new heights because of two significant rule changes in 1978, which allowed offensive linemen to extend their arms and open their hands, and prevented defenders from making contact with receivers more than five yards past the line of scrimmage. As much as anybody, Coryell exploited these rule changes and took advantage of the extra time they gave the passing game.

The Chargers advanced to the AFC championship game twice, but both times, his high-flying offense couldn't overcome an equally porous defense. In Coryell's first full season with the Chargers, the defense ranked 2nd in yards allowed. Within two years, they'd fallen to 26th in a twenty-eight-team league, and the Chargers stayed in the bottom five from 1981 to 1986.

Injuries caused the Chargers' vaunted air attack to deteriorate, and defenses began to catch up with Air Coryell. The Bears 46 defense, for example, started out as a way for an undermanned Chicago team to keep the Chargers passing game in check. San Diego's 1986 season started out with a rousing 50–28 win over the Dolphins, but the Chargers lost their next seven games and Coryell called it quits. He later acknowledged he was burnt out. ""The last couple of years, I figured I'd die if I didn't get out of football," Coryell said. "We hadn't lost before, and I couldn't take it."

Coryell is in the College Football Hall of Fame, and was the first coach (and to date the only one) to win 100 games in both college and the NFL.

#35
Blanton Collier (1963–1970)

Following the legendary Paul Brown is an overwhelming task, but Collier succeeded. He gave his players more freedom both on and off the field, which made him immensely popular. More important, he helped get the Browns back to the pinnacle of success, and Cleveland fans widely regard the Collier era as the golden age in Browns history.

The team had missed the playoffs in its last four seasons under Coach Brown. Collier remedied that in his first season, as he turned Jim Brown loose. The twenty-seven-year-old running back dominated opponents in 1963, rushing for an NFL record 1863 yards in fourteen games. A year later, the Browns advanced to the NFL championship

game where they trounced the heavily favored Colts 27–0.

Collier led the team to the title game in 1965, losing 23–12 to Green Bay. Jim Brown's sudden retirement didn't stop Collier from winning. The Browns reeled off four more winning seasons, advancing to the NFL championship game again in 1968 and 1969.

Though he was always a somewhat quiet man, Collier didn't reveal until later in his career that he suffered from a hearing disability. By the end of his career, he was almost completely deaf. It had become increasingly difficult for him to communicate with his players. Although newspaper accounts at the time don't mention his hearing loss as a factor in his retirement, you have to believe it was a major factor.

#36
Jimmy Johnson (1989–1999)

Johnson will probably never get into the Hall of Fame because he committed two deadly sins. He quit a team that was at the top, and when he came back with another team he couldn't match the same level of success. When that happens, people inevitably draw the conclusion "this guy's not as good as we thought he was." Others get the credit for building the first team, or people say anybody can win with the players he had. Neither is really true. If it weren't for the brevity of his coaching tenures, it would be clear that Johnson was a great coach.

The Cowboys were 1-15 in Johnson's first season but won the Super Bowl just three years later. Many observers credit the turnaround to a trade that sent running back Herschel Walker to the Minnesota Vikings. In his 1993 book, Johnson devoted a whole chapter to the deal, and its title—"The Great Train Robbery"—is an apt description. Walker was the best player on the team that Johnson took over, maybe their only good player, but Johnson quickly concluded that he could not be part of their turnaround. "Herschel Walker is a good football player. He is not a great football player. He can be made to look great, if you're willing to build your entire offense around him, as Vince Dooley was at the University of Georgia in the early 1980s and Tom Landry was at Dallas in 1988. I was not willing to do that."

Johnson wisely surmised that the team needed help in a lot of areas, and that trading their one valuable commodity could yield enough talent to start turning the team around. After shopping Walker around to several teams following the 1989 season, he struck a deal with Minnesota general manager Mike Lynn, swapping Walker for five unremarkable players and a first-round draft pick in 1992.

The press lambasted the Cowboys for the deal. Randy Galloway of the *Dallas Morning News* wrote: "The Vikings got Herschel Walker. The Cowboys got nothing more than a huge handful of Minnesota smoke. And who knows if there'll ever be any fire." Frank Luska of the *Dallas Times-Herald* compared the loss of Walker to a noted Dallas historical site. "As the Cowboys continue their purge of treasured landmarks, the blessing is that they do not own John Neely Bryan's Cabin. Else it, too, would be traded, probably for a bag of beans and a cow to be named later."

What the sports reporters didn't realize was that there were conditional draft picks associated with each of the players the Cowboys acquired. If those players were not on the roster by February 1, Dallas would receive the corresponding draft picks. That turned into a bonanza for the Cowboys, because most of the players in the deal were essentially straw men. Johnson wanted the draft picks, and he ended up with first- and second-round picks in 1990 and 1991, and first-, second-, and third-round choices in 1993. Among the players those picks led to were running back Emmitt Smith, safety Darren Woodson, and defensive tackle Russell Maryland.

Johnson made another big trade that has gone largely forgotten. After drafting quarterback Steve Walsh in the supplemental draft, he sent him to the Saints for three picks, a first- and third-rounder in 1991 and a second-round pick in 1992.

Obviously, the flood of draft picks had a lot to do with the Cowboys turnaround, but they are only part of the story. As Johnson himself pointed out, the Rams made a similar deal when they traded Eric Dickerson to the Colts in 1988, but their extra draft picks didn't yield a crop of star players.

I think the biggest innovation Johnson brought was his approach to the draft and his realization that it was the key to replenishing the depleted talent levels of the Dallas roster. He brought an economist's approach to the NFL draft. The prevailing strategy at the time was to draft the best player available when it came your time to pick. But what if the best player available was somebody you didn't want? What if the player you really wanted was the tenth-best player remaining on your draft board? Should you go ahead and take him, or wait until the next round and hope he was still available? Johnson dismissed both options and advocated a third: Trade up or down a few spots in the draft to maximize your value. This was a tricky proposition, and to be successful it was going to require more science than art.

Rather than speculating on how much draft picks were worth, Johnson studied it. Looking at historical data, he developed what came to be known as the draft value chart. He assigned a relative value to each slot in the NFL draft, so that he could determine whether he was coming out ahead or behind in a proposed swap of picks. Let's say he wanted to move up from the twenty-first pick to the sixteenth to take a player he really coveted. According to his research, the twenty-first pick is worth 800 points and the sixteenth pick is worth 1200. The other team asks for your third-round pick in exchange—say the eighty-fifth pick overall, which is worth 165 points. You're coming out way ahead. The projected value of the player you'll get at No. 16 is going to be more than the combined value of the two players at No. 21 and No. 85. Within a decade, every organization had adopted the same methodology.

In five seasons with the Cowboys, Johnson made fifty-one draft-day trades. At first, a lot of people dismissed his machinations as making trades for trades' sake, but over time, they began to see the advantage of his approach. Especially after they saw how those machinations built an impressive collection of talent that won three Super Bowls in four seasons.

Johnson revolutionized the way that football organizations approach talent acquisition. That, more than his two Super Bowl rings with Dallas or his three trips to the playoffs with the Dolphins, will be his legacy.

#37 Tom Coughlin (1995–2007)

Coughlin was the first coach of the Jacksonville Jaguars, leading the team to the AFC championship game in just their second season of existence. Over the next three years, the Jaguars posted a 36–12 record, winning three straight division titles and advancing to the conference championship again in 1999.

How does an expansion team pull things together so quickly? The Jags did it largely by spending on free agents, and by the end of the 2000 season they found themselves in trouble. The salary cap was $62 million and they headed into the 2001 season with a payroll of $98 million—a record $36 million over the cap. They had no choice but to start shedding most of the players that had made them so successful, and the results were somewhat predictable. Jacksonville finished 6–10 in each of the next two seasons, and Coughlin lost his job.

Coughlin's reputation as a strict disciplinarian was appealing to the Giants, who had fallen apart in 2002. Ownership felt like they needed a hardliner to take control of the veteran squad. This approach didn't sit well with many of the Giants veteran players. Tiki Barber announced that he was retiring midway through the 2006 season. In a book he published the following year, he said Coughlin's coaching style was largely what drove him to retire during what seemed like the prime of his career. "[Coughlin] robbed me of what had been one of the most important things I had in my life, which was the joy I felt playing football," Bar-

ber wrote. "I had lost that. He had taken it away." Defensive end Michael Strahan skipped training camp the following summer. He said that he was mulling over retirement, but most observers felt he was simply avoiding the tough regimen of Camp Coughlin. Strahan returned a few days before the season opener.

Despite the unhappiness of his players, Coughlin's team started 5–2 in his first year at the helm and advanced to the playoffs in each of the next four seasons. By his own admission, he softened his approach a bit in 2007. He loosened curfews and cut down on the number of two-a-day practices. He created a player's council, to get feedback from the rank and file. He shocked everyone when he staged a casino night during mini camp, and again during training camp when he cancelled meetings one night and took the entire team to a local bowling alley. These things helped the team pull together, and after going 7–1 on the road during the regular season, the Giants won three road playoff games en route to their upset of the heavily favored Patriots in Super Bowl XLII.

#38 Jimmy Conzelman (1921–1948)

Conzelman was a key figure in the earliest days of the league: a star player, a successful coach, and even a team owner. He bounced around with several teams before buying a franchise in Detroit. The Panthers were successful on the field but drew little support from fans in the Motor City, and the club folded after two seasons.

He spent the next four seasons as a player-coach with the Providence Steam Roller. In 1928, Conzelman was sidelined by a knee injury but continued coaching. The defense was dominating, allowing just 42 points in eleven games, and Providence finished with a league-best 8-1-2 record. Before 1932, NFL teams didn't play for a championship: They simply named the team with the best record as champion. Providence was named champion in 1928, and they were the last team to be given an NFL title that isn't still in the league.

Conzelman pursued other interests throughout the thirties, including serving in the front office with baseball's St. Louis Cardinals. He was lured back to football in 1940 as coach of the hapless Chicago Cardinals. The end of the war brought a sudden influx of playing talent, and owner Charlie Bidwill opened his checkbook to compete with his new crosstown rival, the Chicago Rockets of the AAFC. The Cards signed college-star Charley Trippi, who joined with Paul Christman, Pat Harder, and Marshall Goldberg to form what was called "The Dream Backfield." Conzelman led the team to a 9-3 record in 1947 en route to a win over Philadelphia in the championship game.

A year later, Conzelman's Cardinals finished 11-1 and met the Eagles for a championship rematch. A blinding snowstorm made for a messy game, and a fourth-quarter touchdown gave the Eagles a 7–0 victory. Despite the team's success, Conzelman left after the season ended, largely because he felt that the death of Bidwill in a plane crash had left the organization in disarray. He was right, of course. It was nearly thirty years before the Cardinals returned to the playoffs.

#39
Andy Reid (1999–2007)

In his first seven seasons as the Eagles head coach, Reid showed a propensity for calling pass plays. He threw the ball on 58.5 percent of his teams plays, the highest percentage of any coach in NFL history with at least 100 games. The median for the rest of the league over the same time period was 43.8 percent. What caused this great imbalance? Part of it was Reid's apparent lack of confidence in his running backs, but the main reason seemed to be an infatuation with the skills of quarterback Donovan McNabb.

There's no doubt that McNabb's versatility made him a dangerous player. His ability to run with the ball, avoid the pass rush, and make passes down the field helped the Eagles win a lot of games. However, Reid's unwillingness to commit to a ground game left them vulnerable at times.

The lack of balance made the play-calling more predictable, and in turn that made it easier for good defenses to focus on containing McNabb.

To a large extent, Reid's success in Philadelphia has come from the team's focus on targeting offensive and defensive linemen early in the draft. After selecting McNabb in the first round of the 1999 draft, the Eagles used five of their next seven first-round picks on linemen. From 2000 to 2006, the Eagles sent five different linemen to the Pro Bowl.

#40
Jim Lee Howell (1954–1960)

Howell had the shortest career of any coach to make my top fifty list. He took over as head coach of the New York Giants when Steve Owen retired. Owen was both popular and successful, and after twenty-four seasons at the helm, it couldn't have been easy for Howell to follow.

His greatest move was in his choice of assistants, hiring Vince Lombardi, the head coach at West Point, to run his offense and tabbing veteran defensive back Tom Landry to coach the defense. As a player-coach, Landry invented the 4-3 defense. Lombardi installed his patented power running game, and thus Howell created the practice of having an offensive and defensive coordinator.

While many fans decried the Giants' approach on both sides of the ball as too conservative, they couldn't argue with the results. The team's record improved from 4-8 to 7-5 in Howell's first year at the helm, and two years later the Giants won the 1956 NFL championship with a 47–7 thrashing of the Bears.

Howell's deep Arkansas drawl and steady disposition often created the impression that he was more of a bystander than an active participant in the team's success. "I just blow up the footballs and keep order," he said.

He clearly had a great eye for talent. Besides hiring Landry and Lombardi as coaches, he drafted six future Hall of Famers: Rosey Brown, Frank Gifford, Sam Huff, Don Maynard, Andy Robustelli, and Emlen Tunnell.

Howell led the Giants to the NFL championship game three times in seven seasons, including a loss to the Colts in the 1958 match dubbed "The Greatest Game Ever Played." After Lombardi left for Green Bay in 1959 and Landry became head coach of the Cowboys in 1960, Howell decided to retire. He moved into the Giants front office, where he remained until his retirement in 1981.

#41
Lou Saban (1960–1976)

The word that best describes Saban is "enigmatic." He won two AFL championships in his first stint with the Buffalo Bills but appeared to grow restless after that, hopping from job to job and never staying in one place for very long.

Saban was an All-Pro linebacker for the Cleveland Browns, serving as captain for head coach Paul Brown on a team that won four AAFC championships. He retired after just four seasons to pursue a coaching career. After ten seasons as a college coach, he was tapped as the first head coach of the Boston Patriots. Fired midway through the 1961 season, Saban was quickly hired as director of player personnel in Buffalo. He started assembling an impressive array of talent, plucking overlooked quarterback Jack Kemp off the Chargers roster, luring running back Cookie Gilchrist down from Canada, and drafting future stars like Tom Sestak and Daryle Lamonica. In 1962, he took over the coaching reigns and set a new tone for the organization. Saban stressed the fundamentals, running his training camp like a drill instructor and forcing his players to run drills over and over until they got it right. By his third season in Buffalo, the Bills were the best team in the AFL. With a dominating running game and a strong defense, the Bills won back-to-back championships in 1963 and 1964.

Whereas most coaches used the preseason as a way to get veteran players in shape, Saban opted to use the exhibition games to get a good look at his rookies and other untested players. It not only gave him a chance to evaluate their skills, but it also gave them some much-needed experience so that when they were pressed into action, they were better prepared.

Saban was adamant that his players do things his way, and when they didn't, he reacted sternly. He suspended Cookie Gilchrist in the middle of the 1964 season after the team's biggest star showed up for a key game with a hangover. The Bills were 9-0, but Gilchrist's lackluster performance led to the team's first loss. At the end of the season, Gilchrist was traded to Denver.

A week after the Bills won their second-straight AFL championship, Saban jumped ship and headed to the University of Maryland. "I came to a crossroads," he would later explain. "I began to wonder where I was going with it. I often wondered if I could go ahead with four kids with this lifestyle."

It's an unsatisfying explanation, and frankly somewhat bizarre. Saban would continue to coach into his eighties but never stayed at one job very long. A psychiatrist might call that a lifestyle of avoidance, always leaving town before the novelty of his arrival had worn off, before he could be held accountable for the work he had done.

Saban spent just one season at Maryland, returning to the AFL as head coach of the Denver Broncos. Fired after four and a half losing seasons, he returned to Buffalo and built an offense around running back O.J. Simpson. Over the next five seasons, Simpson was dominating, but the defense was mediocre and the offense was simply a one-man show. The Bills made just one playoff appearance in Saban's second stint with the team, and he resigned midway through the 1976 season. Though he would continue to coach past the age of eighty, he would never return to the NFL.

I'm not sure if even Saban can recall all of the places he's coached, but some accounts say that he served twenty-two different teams in the twenty-five years after he left the NFL. His longest stint came at Canton Tech, a two-year school near the New York–Ontario border, where he spent five seasons. An exact account is difficult, given his penchant for sometimes leaving a job before he actually started. He quit as head coach of Alfred State before coaching a game, and left the post of athletic director at the University of Cincinnati after just nineteen days. He coached high school teams in his late sixties, spent four games coaching in the Arena League, and even spent two years in Major League Baseball, working for George Steinbrenner as president of the New York Yankees.

A nostalgic folklore has grown up around Saban painting him as a hired gun, the kind of guy who would come in, save a football team, and leave it for somebody else to run. But the reality is that he usually left his employers high and dry, departing suddenly without putting the pieces in place for the organization to continue without him. That reputation, along with a career record below .500 will keep him out of the Hall of Fame.

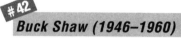

Buck Shaw (1946–1960)

A three-time All America tackle for Knute Rockne's Notre Dame squad, Lawrence "Buck" Shaw rose to national prominence as head coach at Santa Clara University in the late 1930s. Tall and slender with silver hair, he wore dark suits and horn-rimmed glasses and carried himself with a genteel manner that made him look more like a businessman than a football man. He earned the nickname "Silver Fox," as much for his appearance as for his quietly aggressive style.

Shaw was in his mid-forties when he was lured away from the college ranks to join the fledgling AAFC, where he served as the first head coach for the San Francisco 49ers. He built a passing offense around quarterback Frankie Albert, and the team compiled a record of 38-14-2, finishing in 2nd place each year behind the Cleveland Browns. After the AAFC merged with the NFL, Shaw led the Niners to a winning record in four of their next five seasons. Owner Tony Morabito concluded that despite that success, Shaw would never win a title, so he fired him. (The Niners wouldn't reach a championship game until Super Bowl XVI, twenty-seven years later.)

After spending a couple of seasons coaching at the Air Force Academy, Shaw returned to the pro ranks as head coach of the Philadelphia Eagles in 1958. He took over a team with a moribund offense that had suffered three-straight losing seasons. His first move was to find a quarterback to run his passing game, acquiring veteran Norm Van Brocklin in a trade with the Rams. Although the team had some good young talent, they stumbled to a 2-9-1 finish. After a 20–0 thrashing in the season finale, the normally affable Shaw erupted. He closed the locker room and lambasted his players, many of whom (according to press reports) had been out carousing the previous night. "This has never happened to me before," Shaw told them. "It will never happen again. Maybe you don't have any pride, I do. I'll be here again next year, but some of you may not."

The outburst shocked the players, and many of them returned with a renewed sense of purpose the following season. They improved to 7-5 in 1959 and a year later, they were the NFL's best team. With thirty-four-year-old Van Brocklin's leading the offense and thirty-five-year-old Chuck Bednarik leading the defense, the Eagles finished 10-2 and beat the Packers in the NFL championship game. Shaw retired after the game, having proven that he could win the big game after all.

Dennis Green (1992–2006)

Green was one of the first of what would be a flood of head coaches who emerged from the tutelage of Bill Walsh. He installed the West Coast Offense in Minnesota, and it was an immediate triumph. The Vikings went to the playoffs eight times in his first nine seasons as their coach.

Green had a penchant for finding veteran quarterbacks to run his offense, and more often than not they had great success. Warren Moon had back-to-back 4000-yard seasons and tied his career high with 33 touchdown passes when he was thirty-nine years old. Randall Cunningham was thirty-five when he had the best year of his career, winning MVP honors in 1998. That Vikings squad finished 15-1 and set an NFL record for the most points scored in a season.

That team lost in the NFC championship game, the first team in league history to win fifteen games but not claim the crown. Ultimately, that was the biggest criticism of Green. Despite all of his regular-season success, his teams couldn't get to the Super Bowl.

Jon Gruden (1998–2007)

Gruden became an NFL assistant with the 49ers at the age of twenty-seven, and quickly rose through the ranks with stints in Green Bay and Philadelphia that established him as a bright young coaching star. He was just thirty-four when he was named head coach of the Oakland Raiders, and by his third season he had his team in the AFC championship game.

But things were uneasy in Oakland. Owner Al Davis wasn't sure he wanted to give the young coach the power or the money that he craved, and so a deal was orchestrated that sent Gruden to Tampa Bay. The Buccaneers traded four high-draft picks (two first-rounders and two second-rounders) plus $8 million to the Raiders in exchange for the rights to the coach, whom they promptly signed to a five-year $17.5 million contract.

It was an incredibly steep price to pay, but the initial returns were promising. In his first year at the helm, Gruden did what his predecessor, Tony Dungy, could not, namely win playoff games. He led his new team to the Super Bowl where they soundly defeated his old team. Critics, however, minimized Gruden's accomplishment, saying that he won with a team that was built by Dungy. Some, including a few of the Buccaneers' players, credited the team's success to the smothering defense that Dungy had built, a defense which accounted for three of the team's six Super Bowl touchdowns.

Whether that criticism was fair or not, it has been bolstered by Gruden's subsequent inability to build on that initial success. Through 2007, his record is 36–44 since winning that Super Bowl.

Jim Mora (1986–2001)

"Uh, playoffs? Don't talk about playoffs. Are you kidding me? Playoffs? I just hope we can win a game, another game."

Mora's infamous postgame explosion was a classic, one that still gets plenty of airplay. It came in 2001 after a tough loss that dropped the Colts' record to 4-6. It was, however, the comments that he made right before those that would get him fired. Asked about the performance of his quarterback, a young Peyton Manning, Mora was blunt in his assessment:

> You can't turn the ball over five times like that. Holy crap! I don't know who the hell we think we are when we do something like that. Unbelievable! Five turnovers! One of 'em . . . we've thrown 4 interceptions for touchdowns this year. That might be an NFL record. Hell, we've still got six games left . . . no telling what might happen. That's pitiful. I mean it's absolutely pitiful to perform like that. Pitiful! If our defense hadn't played half way decent against a great offensive football team they might have scored 60 . . . All I know is we threw 4 interceptions and fumbled once. One interception they returned for a touchdown. Three others were in our end of the field where they scored points. That's all I know. That's inexcusable. Inexcusable!

Although Mora would later say that the words "pitiful" and "inexcusable" were directed at his entire team, not just his quarterback, that's not how the press or the public interpreted them. It soon became clear that it wasn't how Manning had interpreted them either, and he didn't take kindly to the public admonishments. It was the strained relationship more than the losing season that caused Mora to be canned six weeks later.

Of course, everything Mora said was true, and while it may not have helped soothe Manning's ego to be so harsh, I for one thought it was refreshing to hear a coach admit that his team stunk rather than mouthing platitudes.

It wasn't the first time he expressed himself so forcefully. After his Saints played poorly in a loss to the Panthers in 1996, he made plain his disgust with the way the team had played:

> We just got our ass totally kicked. We couldn't do diddly-poo offensively. We couldn't make a first down. We couldn't run the ball. We didn't try to run the ball. We couldn't complete a pass. We sucked! [In] the second-half, we sucked. We couldn't stop the run. Every time they got the ball they went down and got points. We got our asses totally kicked in the second half. It was a horseshit performance in the second half. Horseshit! I'm totally embarrassed and totally ashamed. Our coaches did a horrible job. The players did a horrible job. We got our asses kicked in the second half. It sucked.

Mora resigned three days later.

#46
Jeff Fisher (1994–2007)

In his 2007 book *The Paolantonio Report*, ESPN personality Sal Paolantonio ranked Fisher as the second-most overrated coach in NFL history, behind Norv Turner. Ironically, both coaches took their teams to the playoffs the same year his book came out.

Calling someone overrated is usually a sportswriter's trick that starts with the false premise that the individual in question is rated highly in the first place. Do Fisher's contemporaries regard him as a good coach? Sure. But is he considered to be one of the best coaches of his time? In an era when Belichick, Dungy, Holmgren, Parcells, and Gibbs were all active, that would be a huge stretch. Fisher isn't in the same class as those guys, and I don't think anybody ever argued that he was.

Part of the problem with Paolantonio's assessment is that it focuses too much on the problems the Titans had in the three seasons immediately preceding the release of his book. From 2004–2006, Fisher's team finished with records of 5–11, 4–12, and 8–8. It's easy to look at those three seasons and conclude he's not doing a good job. But that's one of the problem with subjective rankings—they're biased toward the present.

With a little more distance, the reason for the Titans downturn is pretty clear. It wasn't that Fisher suddenly forgot how to coach; it was that he lost all of his star players all at once. Seven Pro Bowl players left during the span, either due to salary cap issues or because age had caught up with them. All of the core members of the offense (Steve McNair, Eddie George, Derrick Mason, Bruce Matthews, and Frank Wycheck) departed, and rather than attempt a quick fix, the Titans rebuilt their team with young stars like Vince Young, LenDale White, and Albert Haynesworth.

Knock Fisher for having two losing seasons during the rebuilding process if you like, but you have to acknowledge that he came out on the other side with a playoff team. It's not that dissimilar from what he did earlier in his career. He took over a Houston Oilers team that was 1–9, and had them up to 7–9 the following year. By 1999, the team was 13–3 and went to the Super Bowl.

#47
Potsy Clark (1931–1940)

Clark served in both world wars, seeing combat as a field artillery officer in France during the first and with the submarine corps in the Pacific during the second. In between, he served as head coach of the Portsmouth Spartans and followed them when they moved north to Detroit and became the

Lions. The team finished with a winning record in each of his six seasons and claimed the league title with a victory over the Giants in 1935. Clark later spent several seasons in Brooklyn but couldn't turn the Dodgers into winners. He also served as head coach at six different colleges, including powerhouses Nebraska and Kansas.

#48
Wally Lemm (1961–1970)

Lemm was a long-time college coach and served as a defensive coordinator in the NFL. He joined the Houston Oilers in that capacity during their inaugural season, helping the team to win the American Football League's first championship. Despite that success, he retired at season's end, heading back home to Libertyville, Illinois, to open a sporting goods business.

The following year, the Oilers got off to a slow start, winning just one of their first five games. Owner Bud Adams fired head coach Lou Rymkus and asked Lemm to return and take over. He agreed, and the team was rejuvenated with Lemm at the helm. The team won all of their remaining nine regular season games and then beat San Diego for a second straight AFL championship.

Although he agreed to a contract extension after the title game, Lemm decided he wanted to work closer to home, and bolted the Oilers for the head coaching job with the St. Louis Cardinals. In a curious twist, the Oilers hired the man that Lemm replaced, Cards coach Pop Ivy.

Lemm spent four seasons with the Cardinals and had mixed success, then returned to Houston in 1966. He helped turn the struggling Oilers around, leading them back to the AFL title game in 1967 and another playoff berth in 1969.

#49
John Robinson (1983–1991)

Robinson was a highly successful college coach, leading the University of Southern California to a national championship in 1978. His trademark was the one-back running game, and two of his backs won the Heisman Trophy—Marcus Allen and Charles White.

He brought his system to the NFL with the Los Angeles Rams in 1983, and landed a great running back—Eric Dickerson—in that spring's draft. The team improved to 9–7 and earned a wild card berth, and the following year Dickerson set the NFL single season rushing record with 2105 yards.

Robinson led the Rams to the playoffs in six of his first seven seasons, twice advancing as far as the NFC championship game. After a couple of losing seasons, the Rams fired Robinson, and he returned to Southern Cal for another stint as head coach of the Trojans.

#50
Brian Billick (1999–2007)

Billick earned a reputation as an offensive genius as an assistant coach with the Minnesota Vikings. Under his guidance, the Vikings set an NFL record by scoring 541 points in 1998. What made this run so remarkable was that Billick kept building his offense around older quarterbacks that had been discarded by other teams. The first was 38-year-old Warren Moon, who matched his career high with 33 touchdown passes in 1994. Then there was Randall Cunningham, given up for dead a few years earlier but reborn in Minnesota. Cunningham was 35-years old in 1998 when he led the Vikings to a 15–1 record and was named Most Valuable Player.

Billick parlayed that success into a head coaching job with the Baltimore Ravens, winning a Super Bowl in his second season. But throughout his tenure, Billick struggled to get the Baltimore offense going, and at times they were downright awful. They almost always had a dominating defense, but Billick's supposed offensive genius never rubbed off on the Ravens.

One of the biggest problems was his inability to find a quarterback. Billick had a different starting quarterback in each of his first four seasons with the Ravens, with eight different players taking their turn at the job. Each one was a veteran castaway, but Billick couldn't recapture any of the magic he'd worked in Minnesota.

Others

 # 51. Allie Sherman (1961–1968)

 # 52. Bobby Ross (1992–2000)

 # 53. Jack Pardee (1975–1994)

 # 54. Ted Marchibroda (1975–1998)

 # 55. Wade Phillips (1985–2007)

 # 56. Steve Mariucci (1997–2005)

 # 57. Bum Phillips (1975–1985)

 # 58. Dave Wannstedt (1993–2004)

 # 59. Mike Sherman (2000–2005)

 # 60. Hunk Anderson (1942–1945)

 # 61. Luke Johnsos (1942–1945)

 # 62. Barry Switzer (1994–1997)

 # 63. Mike Martz (2000–2005)

 # 64. George Wilson (1957–1969)

 # 65. Mike Holovak (1961–1976)

 # 66. Ray Malavasi (1966–1982)

 # 67. Joe Stydahar (1950–1954)

 # 68. Raymond Berry (1984–1989)

 # 69. Wayne Fontes (1988–1996)

 # 70. Art Shell (1989–2006)

 # 71. Roy Andrews (1924–1931)

 # 72. Guy Chamberlin (1922–1927)

 # 73. Forrest Gregg (1975–1987)

 # 74. Jim Fassel (1997–2003)

 # 75. John Rauch (1966–1970)

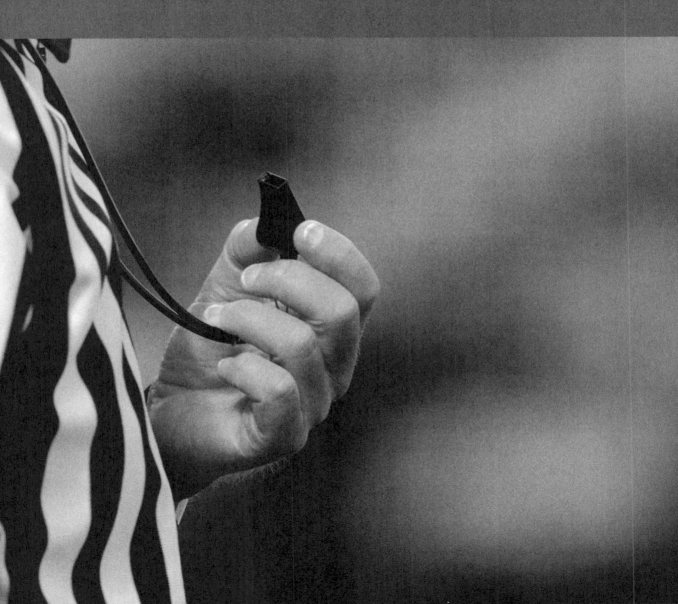

PART 4

THE RECORDS

About the Football Project

DURING THE SUMMER of 2000, I read an article in *Pro Football Weekly* about Reggie White becoming the NFL's all-time sacks leader. Noted football researcher John Turney described the problem that this situation created. Because sacks had not been kept as an official statistic until 1982, all the men who played before that were being shortchanged in the record book.

Turney described how he and a partner, Nick Webster, collected play-by-play accounts from NFL teams in an effort to reconstruct the sacks record for pre-1982 players. This yielded fascinating insight into the performances of players like Deacon Jones, Bob Lilly, and Alan Page and their contributions as pass rushers.

This article got me to thinking that there was a lot more of the historical record that we could reconstruct, and that there were many more insights to be gained. I knew that the NFL compiled these play-by-play accounts each week during the season—they call them "Game Books"—but it never occurred to me that they were available for past seasons until I read about Turney and Webster. I began to reach out to folks in the football research community and quickly learned that many other people had done their own research with these play-by-plays.

Unfortunately, what I learned was that after these researchers had done all the legwork to col-lect those documents, the game sheets generally just sat in a drawer collecting dust. Each researcher used the information for whatever specific task he or she was interested in but never shared the raw material with others. Anybody interested in researching another topic would have to redo all of the same legwork to collect those game reports again. It made sense to me to coordinate that effort, not just to archive the play-by-play accounts but also to digitize them and make them freely available to other researchers.

The Retrosheet Model

Baseball folks had been working on a similar task for years, an effort that was conceived by Bill James as "Project Scoresheet" in the mid-eighties. Baseball author and researcher Gary Gillette oversaw the complex task of finding volunteers to score each and every major league game, enter the play-by-play into a computer, and proof the resulting data. Their work provided a wealth of data for writers, researchers, and analysts who wanted to learn more about specific players and the game in general.

While teams of volunteers continue to collect play-by-play accounts of current baseball games, David Smith organized others to start working their way back in time. This group, called "Retrosheet," started soliciting teams, journalists, and official scorers for their game accounts. By 2007, about 300 volunteers had participated and their database included more than fifty complete seasons worth of play-by-play data—roughly 170,000 games in all.

Since I've been active with Retrosheet (and Project Scoresheet before that), I knew that the task of compiling play-by-play accounts for baseball is an arduous task. However, there are three key differences that make the task easier for football. First, the league and teams keep the play-by-play data themselves, so we can work with them to collect the source material. Some newspapers carried play-by-play accounts, especially in the years before World War II. As a result, much of the play-by-play data already exists. It's simply a matter of collecting and compiling that information, Second, the volume of NFL games is significantly less—sixteen NFL games per season today versus 162 for baseball teams, so there's much less work to be done inputting the games. There were roughly 10,000 regular and postseason football games from 1960 to 2005. If we did 10,000 baseball games, we'd only cover three years.

Third, expansion (both with teams and schedules) means that the vast majority of NFL games has been played in recent years. By a rough calculation, half of the games in NFL history have taken place since 1978. If we can get all of the games back to 1960 (which I think is feasible), we'd have 77 percent of all NFL/AFL games ever played.

Birth of the Football Project

In the mid-1990s, I compiled a database of baseball statistics from existing sources and made it available on the Internet free to anybody who wanted to use it. My hope was to provide a valuable reference source and encourage new research, and I think I was successful in that goal. The database became the underlying data source for seminal Web sites like Baseball-Reference.com and later editions of the massive encyclopedia, *Total Baseball*, and made it possible for scores of

researchers to perform analysis that hadn't been possible before.

There weren't any similar sources for football, and while there is an active research community, nobody else was working on compiling the game's play-by-play data. So shortly after reading the Turney article, I enlisted my friend and colleague Todd Greanier to start the process of collecting and digitizing this data. By the end of 2001, we had four or five recent seasons compiled. The following year, he and I created the annual preview book, *The Pro Football Prospectus*, and used that data as the foundation of our analytical work. Over the next few years, we were able to provide some insight into areas of the game that had not been subject to much analysis, such as play-calling in the red zone, performance trends by age, and overall special teams play.

I always knew that the real valuable insights would come from a much broader dataset, allowing us to focus more on the players of the past than simply those who were currently active. What started as a two-man effort has grown in the last few years, and by the summer of 2008 we had about fifty volunteers helping us collect the game books, input them into our database, and create tools for working with the raw data.

What's the goal of this effort? It will help improve the historical record by helping us identify errors in recordkeeping. It will give us a more detailed insight into the careers of specific players and specific teams, and it will help us to understand more about how and why players succeed and teams win. With the proper data, we can analyze strategies and tactics and figure out whether the conventional wisdoms are correct. That's the kind of basic science that football research has been lacking, and the widespread availability of more raw data will make that sort of work possible.

Just as important, the play-by-play data will help us reconstruct some of the statistics that the NFL didn't keep at the time. For example, the league didn't begin tracking a team's third-down efficiency until 1981. With the play-by-play data, it's easy to go back and make a record of things like this, as well as crediting individual players who converted a first down. The data would let us count things like touchbacks or kicks inside the 20 for punters. I'm not a big fan of trying to count subjective things—like the number of times a team blitzed or a receiver dropped a pass. But there are all sorts of indisputable events that have already been measured on a per-play basis, but never collected together by team, season, or player.

For example, I have long believed that there was value in grouping plays based on length. In other words, we know that Barry Sanders averaged 5 yards per carry in his career. How often did he get stopped for a loss? How often did he break runs of more than 10 yards? These seem like basic questions to ask about a running back. We know how many of Mickey Mantle's hits were home runs and how many were singles, but we don't have the same level of detail for football players.

Our knowledge of special teams players is woefully inadequate, especially with regard to kickers and punters. Play-by-play data would allow us to examine field goal percentages from different distances. As it stands now, there's no distinction made between knocking one in from 50 yards and dinking one through from 20. Likewise, broad measures like gross and net average do very little to tell us about the performance of punters.

So much of player performances is based on context—the down, distance, and location of the ball on each play. The play-by-play data lets us delve into differences in player performance based on those different situations. How often did Earl Campbell convert on third-and-short plays? How many of Bruce Smith's sacks knocked the opponent out of field goal position? What percentage of Steve Young's completions came on passes of less than 10 yards?

We can't answer any of those questions today, but ten years from now I hope we can. If you're interested in helping the effort, or if you're just interested in browsing through our data, please visit our Web site at http://footballproject.com.

Player Records

Quarterbacks

Troy Aikman (27)											
Year	Team	PaYds	PaTD	PaInt	PaSkYds	RuYds	RuTD	Fum	APaY	ARuY	Q
1989	DAL	1749	9	18	155	302	0	6	-78.8	276.0	1.4
1990	DAL	2579	11	18	288	172	1	5	243.2	165.3	2.5
1991	DAL	2754	11	10	224	5	1	4	704.6	8.8	5.4
1992	DAL	3445	23	14	112	105	1	4	1086.6	103.9	7.1
1993	DAL	3100	15	6	153	125	0	7	1001.9	105.1	7.2
1994	DAL	2676	13	12	59	62	1	2	849.9	66.1	5.0
1995	DAL	3304	16	7	89	32	1	5	1207.0	33.0	7.7
1996	DAL	3126	12	13	120	42	1	6	824.2	35.8	7.0
1997	DAL	3283	19	12	269	79	0	6	817.9	68.6	6.3
1998	DAL	2330	12	5	58	69	2	3	879.6	81.4	5.4
1999	DAL	2964	17	12	130	10	1	8	710.9	6.1	4.9
2000	DAL	1632	7	14	91	13	0	2	192.8	10.2	1.0

Hall of Fame? Yes

Pro Bowl Appearances: 6

All-Pro Selections: Consensus - 0, Total - 3 (1993-1995)

Awards: MVP, Super Bowl XXVII - 1992; Walter Payton NFL Man of the Year - 1997

Frankie Albert (43)

Year	Team	PaYds	PaTD	PaInt	PaSkYds	RuYds	RuTD	Fum	APaY	ARuY	Q
1946	SF	1404	14	14	–	–10	4	–	282.0	30.0	4.4
1947	SF	1692	18	15	–	179	5	–	411.0	229.0	5.3
1948	SF	1990	29	10	–	349	8	–	790.0	429.0	10.0
1949	SF	1862	27	16	–	249	3	–	506.0	279.0	6.2
1950	SF	1767	14	23	–	272	3	4	24.9	280.6	5.1
1951	SF	1116	5	10	–	146	3	0	233.0	176.0	7.1
1952	SF	964	8	10	–	87	1	3	101.3	84.9	4.2

Hall of Fame? No

Pro Bowl Appearances: 1

All-Pro Selections: Consensus - 1, Total - 4 (1946-1949)

Awards: None

Ken Anderson (16)

Year	Team	PaYds	PaTD	PaInt	PaSkYds	RuYds	RuTD	Fum	APaY	ARuY	Q
1971	CIN	777	5	4	159	125	1	5	–60.5	110.0	0.6
1972	CIN	1918	7	7	155	94	3	5	406.9	111.1	5.9
1973	CIN	2428	18	12	163	97	0	5	534.7	83.3	8.8
1974	CIN	2667	18	10	292	314	2	3	674.2	321.3	10.0
1975	CIN	3169	21	11	247	188	2	4	914.6	190.9	10.0
1976	CIN	2367	19	14	235	134	1	3	442.7	134.8	5.0
1977	CIN	2145	11	11	197	128	2	5	359.3	134.2	5.4
1978	CIN	2219	10	22	237	167	1	8	–142.9	152.4	0.1
1979	CIN	2340	16	10	324	235	2	1	538.7	252.3	6.8
1980	CIN	1778	6	13	174	122	0	1	252.0	120.0	2.6
1981	CIN	3754	29	10	140	320	1	5	1348.7	313.3	10.0
1982	CIN	2495	12	9	154	85	4	1	801.3	122.2	9.4
1983	CIN	2333	12	13	187	147	1	4	434.7	146.8	3.6
1984	CIN	2107	10	12	191	64	0	1	453.9	62.6	2.8
1985	CIN	170	2	0	16	0	0	1	40.1	–1.1	0.3
1986	CIN	171	1	2	4	0	0	0	16.5	0.0	0.1

Hall of Fame? No

Pro Bowl Appearances: 4

All-Pro Selections: Consensus - 2, Total - 4 (1974-1975; 1981-1982)

Awards: Walter Payton NFL Man of the Year - 1975; AP NFL Offensive Player of the Year - 1981; Most Valuable Player (AP) - 1981; Most Valuable Player (Bell) - 1981; NEA NFL Player of the Year - 1981; PFW/PFWA Offensive Player of the Year - 1981; *Sporting News* NFL Player of the Year - 1981; UPI AFL/AFC Player of the Year - 1981; Comeback Player of the Year - 1981; PFW/PFWA Comeback Player of the Year - 1981

Sammy Baugh (17)

Year	Team	PaYds	PaTD	PaInt	PaSkYds	RuYds	RuTD	Fum	APaY	ARuY	Q
1937	WAS	1127	8	14	–	240	1	–	113.5	250.0	3.9
1938	WAS	853	5	11	–	35	0	–	66.5	35.0	1.9
1939	WAS	518	6	9	–	46	0	–	–26.0	46.0	0.2
1940	WAS	1367	12	10	–	16	0	–	393.5	16.0	6.1
1941	WAS	1236	10	19	–	14	0	–	3.0	14.0	2.7
1942	WAS	1524	16	11	–	61	1	–	457.0	71.0	6.5
1943	WAS	1754	23	19	–	–43	0	–	327.0	–43.0	3.4
1944	WAS	849	4	8	–	–38	0	–	164.5	–38.0	3.2
1945	WAS	1669	11	4	–	–71	0	5	595.3	–87.1	10.0
1946	WAS	1163	8	17	–	–76	1	7	–186.1	–89.8	8.8
1947	WAS	2938	25	15	–	47	2	15	556.0	30.8	10.0
1948	WAS	2599	22	23	–	4	1	7	328.0	10.5	4.8
1949	WAS	1903	18	14	–	67	2	0	551.5	87.0	9.3
1950	WAS	1130	10	11	–	27	1	6	11.1	27.8	0.7
1951	WAS	1104	7	17	–	–5	0	6	–226.7	–20.6	0.7
1952	WAS	152	2	1	–	1	0	1	13.3	–0.1	0.2

Hall of Fame? Yes

Pro Bowl Appearances: 5

All-Pro Selections: Consensus - 6, Total - 9 (1937-1938; 1940-1943; 1945; 1947-1948)

Awards: None

George Blanda (61)

Year	Team	PaYds	PaTD	PaInt	PaSkYds	RuYds	RuTD	Fum	APaY	ARuY	Q
1949	CHIB	197	0	5	–	9	1	0	–76.5	19.0	0.6
1950	CHIB	0	0	0	–	0	0	0	0.0	0.0	0.0
1950	BAL	0	0	0	–	0	0	0	0.0	0.0	0.0
1951	CHIB	0	0	0	–	0	0	0	0.0	0.0	0.0
1952	CHIB	664	8	11	–	104	1	0	–13.0	114.0	1.6
1953	CHIB	2164	14	23	–	62	0	3	246.7	55.3	4.1
1954	CHIB	1929	15	17	–	41	0	3	345.0	34.3	4.6
1955	CHIB	459	4	7	–	54	2	0	4.5	74.0	1.8
1956	CHIB	439	7	4	–	47	0	2	77.9	43.8	1.2
1957	CHIB	65	0	3	–	–5	1	0	–72.5	5.0	0.0
1958	CHIB	19	0	0	–	0	0	0	9.5	0.0	0.1
1960	HOU	2413	24	22	76	–60	4	8	231.5	–36.7	4.8
1961	HOU	3330	36	22	–	12	0	3	980.8	10.2	10.0
1962	HOU	2810	27	42	–	6	0	2	2.6	5.5	0.1
1963	HOU	3003	24	25	–	1	0	8	469.1	–1.6	5.9
1964	HOU	3287	17	27	–	–2	0	7	538.0	–3.9	8.3
1965	HOU	2542	20	30	–	–6	0	2	249.6	–6.6	3.9
1966	HOU	1764	17	21	–	1	0	3	137.5	0.0	1.4
1967	OAK	285	3	3	19	0	0	0	33.5	0.0	0.4
1968	OAK	522	6	2	19	0	0	1	187.3	0.0	2.0
1969	OAK	73	2	1	4	0	0	1	1.7	–0.4	0.0
1970	OAK	461	6	5	37	4	0	1	29.8	3.4	0.3
1971	OAK	378	4	6	26	0	0	1	–46.4	0.0	0.0
1972	OAK	77	1	0	19	0	0	1	16.7	0.0	0.2
1973	OAK	0	0	0	0	0	0	0	0.0	0.0	0.0
1974	OAK	28	1	0	0	0	0	0	19.0	0.0	0.2
1975	OAK	11	0	1	8	0	0	1	–40.7	0.0	0.0

Hall of Fame? Yes

Pro Bowl Appearances: 4

All-Pro Selections: Consensus - 1, Total - 7 (1961-1963; 1966-1967; 1970; 1973)

Awards: UPI AFL/AFC Player of the Year - 1961; Most Valuable Player (Bell) - 1970; *Sporting News* AFC Player of the Year - 1970; UPI AFL/AFC Player of the Year - 1970; Walter Payton NFL Man of the Year - 1974

Drew Bledsoe (46)

Year	Team	PaYds	PaTD	PaInt	PaSkYds	RuYds	RuTD	Fum	APaY	ARuY	Q
1993	NE	2494	15	15	99	82	0	8	399.5	60.5	3.0
1994	NE	4555	25	27	139	40	0	9	979.4	19.1	5.4
1995	NE	3507	13	16	170	28	0	11	662.1	15.1	4.2
1996	NE	4086	27	15	190	27	0	9	1115.8	14.2	9.3
1997	NE	3706	28	15	258	55	0	4	1057.7	47.3	7.8
1998	NE	3633	20	14	295	44	0	9	790.0	25.5	4.6
1999	NE	3985	19	21	342	101	0	8	711.6	79.9	5.4
2000	NE	3291	17	13	264	158	2	9	678.7	150.8	4.2
2001	NE	400	2	2	21	18	0	1	81.6	15.4	0.7
2002	BUF	4359	24	15	369	67	2	11	982.7	69.8	6.1
2003	BUF	2860	11	12	371	29	2	15	120.5	22.5	0.9
2004	BUF	2932	20	16	215	37	0	9	446.6	21.4	2.3
2005	DAL	3639	23	17	295	50	2	17	404.2	30.3	3.0
2006	DAL	1164	7	8	107	28	2	3	115.0	43.0	0.8

Hall of Fame? Not eligible until 2011

Pro Bowl Appearances: 4

All-Pro Selections: Consensus - 0, Total - 2 (1994; 1996)

Awards: None

Terry Bradshaw (25)

Year	Team	PaYds	PaTD	PaInt	PaSkYds	RuYds	RuTD	Fum	APaY	ARuY	Q
1970	PIT	1410	6	24	242	233	1	3	−451.9	229.2	0.0
1971	PIT	2259	13	22	287	247	5	7	−110.2	264.7	1.8
1972	PIT	1887	12	12	237	346	7	4	210.0	392.5	6.9
1973	PIT	1183	10	15	186	145	3	3	−172.4	157.9	0.0
1974	PIT	785	7	8	104	224	2	1	10.6	236.9	2.5
1975	PIT	2055	18	9	290	210	3	6	296.4	216.1	4.6
1976	PIT	1177	10	9	164	219	3	7	−84.2	212.7	1.1
1977	PIT	2523	17	19	235	171	3	10	79.9	167.6	2.7
1978	PIT	2915	28	20	222	93	1	8	379.8	78.7	4.9
1979	PIT	3724	26	25	196	83	0	10	537.2	66.8	5.2
1980	PIT	3339	24	22	245	111	2	13	297.3	93.4	2.7
1981	PIT	2887	22	14	155	162	2	7	653.5	157.0	4.9
1982	PIT	1768	17	11	131	10	0	5	259.0	4.0	2.7
1983	PIT	77	2	0	0	3	0	0	48.5	3.0	0.3

Hall of Fame? Yes

Pro Bowl Appearances: 3

All-Pro Selections: Consensus - 1, Total - 3 (1975; 1978-1979)

Awards: Most Valuable Player (AP) - 1978; Most Valuable Player (Bell) - 1978; MVP, Super Bowl XIII - 1978; MVP, Super Bowl XIV - 1979

Tom Brady (18)

Year	Team	PaYds	PaTD	PaInt	PaSkYds	RuYds	RuTD	Fum	APaY	ARuY	Q
2000	NE	6	0	0	0	0	0	0	3.0	0.0	0.0
2001	NE	2843	18	12	216	43	0	12	431.7	7.8	3.3
2002	NE	3764	28	14	190	110	1	11	929.4	92.6	5.9
2003	NE	3620	23	12	129	63	1	13	893.1	36.7	5.8
2004	NE	3692	28	14	162	28	0	7	1076.2	5.8	5.4
2005	NE	4110	26	14	188	89	1	4	1354.4	91.6	10.0
2006	NE	3529	24	12	175	102	0	12	849.3	62.2	4.7
2007	NE	4806	50	8	128	98	2	6	2019.0	104.0	10.0

Hall of Fame? Not eligible (active)

Pro Bowl Appearances: 4

All-Pro Selections: Consensus - 1, Total - 2 (2005; 2007)

Awards: MVP, Super Bowl XXXVI - 2001; MVP, Super Bowl XXXVIII - 2003; Most Valuable Player (AP) - 2007; AP NFL Offensive Player of the Year - 2007

Drew Brees (67)

Year	Team	PaYds	PaTD	PaInt	PaSkYds	RuYds	RuTD	Fum	APaY	ARuY	Q
2001	SD	221	1	0	12	18	0	2	28.7	12.8	0.3
2002	SD	3284	17	16	180	130	1	2	912.2	134.8	6.0
2003	SD	2108	11	15	178	84	0	5	217.0	73.5	1.9
2004	SD	3159	27	7	131	85	2	7	1090.5	73.6	5.9
2005	SD	3576	24	15	223	49	1	8	852.3	46.7	6.2
2006	NO	4418	26	11	105	32	0	8	1550.9	10.1	8.0
2007	NO	4423	28	18	109	52	1	9	1265.5	50.1	6.2

Hall of Fame? Not eligible (active)

Pro Bowl Appearances: 2

All-Pro Selections: None

Awards: Comeback Player of the Year - 2004; PFW/PFWA Most Improved Player of the Year - 2004

John Brodie (31)

Year	Team	PaYds	PaTD	PaInt	PaSkYds	RuYds	RuTD	Fum	APaY	ARuY	Q
1957	SF	160	2	3	0	0	0	0	−15.0	0.0	0.0
1958	SF	1224	6	13	59	−12	1	6	−97.6	−16.4	0.0
1959	SF	354	2	7	−	6	0	0	−58.0	6.0	0.0
1960	SF	1111	6	9	−	171	1	1	233.7	177.8	5.7
1961	SF	2588	14	12	141	90	2	1	766.6	106.4	9.3
1962	SF	2272	18	16	359	258	4	8	21.7	263.3	3.3
1963	SF	367	3	4	5	63	0	1	17.6	58.9	0.8
1964	SF	2498	14	16	178	135	2	11	168.2	127.8	2.7
1965	SF	3112	30	16	101	60	1	4	890.7	64.3	10.0
1966	SF	2810	16	22	165	18	3	4	391.8	46.2	5.0
1967	SF	2013	11	16	129	147	1	3	258.7	150.8	3.5
1968	SF	3020	22	21	159	71	0	4	572.4	64.6	6.6
1969	SF	2405	16	15	134	62	0	1	584.7	60.8	6.7
1970	SF	2941	24	10	67	29	2	1	1134.4	48.1	10.0
1971	SF	2642	18	24	111	45	3	3	344.1	70.9	4.8
1972	SF	905	9	8	39	8	1	0	178.5	18.0	2.3
1973	SF	1126	3	12	29	16	1	0	129.0	26.0	2.2

Hall of Fame? No

Pro Bowl Appearances: 2

All-Pro Selections: Consensus - 1, Total - 2 (1965; 1970)

Awards: Most Valuable Player (AP) - 1970; NEA NFL Player of the Year - 1970; PFW/PFWA Offensive Player of the Year - 1970; *Sporting News* NFC Player of the Year - 1970; UPI NFL/NFC Player of the Year - 1970

Ed Brown (45)

Year	Team	PaYds	PaTD	PaInt	PaSkYds	RuYds	RuTD	Fum	APaY	ARuY	Q
1954	CHIB	283	3	1	–	36	0	0	121.5	36.0	1.9
1955	CHIB	1307	9	10	–	203	2	4	244.0	195.6	10.0
1956	CHIB	1667	11	12	–	164	1	3	387.9	154.8	5.6
1957	CHIB	1321	6	16	–	129	1	5	−17.5	114.2	1.8
1958	CHIB	1418	10	17	–	94	3	4	38.1	105.5	2.0
1959	CHIB	1881	13	10	–	108	1	7	454.5	91.1	6.3
1960	CHIB	1079	7	11	–	89	2	2	136.5	102.2	3.3
1961	CHIB	742	4	11	–	18	0	1	−16.8	15.0	2.2
1962	PIT	726	5	6	–	−8	0	1	155.0	−8.5	1.7
1963	PIT	2982	21	20	–	20	2	5	729.2	33.1	7.8
1964	PIT	1990	12	19	–	110	2	5	224.7	114.2	3.1
1965	PIT	123	0	5	–	−1	0	2	−189.3	−5.2	0.0
1965	BAL	81	1	0	24	−2	0	1	−7.6	−5.6	0.1

Hall of Fame? No

Pro Bowl Appearances: 2

All-Pro Selections: None

Awards: None

Mark Brunell (32)

Year	Team	PaYds	PaTD	PaInt	PaSkYds	RuYds	RuTD	Fum	APaY	ARuY	Q
1994	GB	95	0	0	16	7	1	1	−1.6	10.1	0.0
1995	JAC	2168	15	7	238	480	4	5	505.6	490.4	6.2
1996	JAC	4367	19	20	257	396	3	14	826.7	360.8	9.7
1997	JAC	3281	18	7	189	257	2	4	1151.4	262.1	10.0
1998	JAC	2601	20	9	172	192	0	3	807.1	178.4	5.6
1999	JAC	3060	14	9	174	208	1	6	892.8	196.2	7.4
2000	JAC	3640	20	14	289	236	2	7	882.9	234.1	5.7
2001	JAC	3309	19	13	387	224	1	8	609.4	212.1	6.0
2002	JAC	2788	17	7	210	207	0	5	841.4	189.6	5.9
2003	JAC	484	2	0	46	19	1	1	169.2	25.8	1.2
2004	WAS	1194	7	6	105	62	0	6	93.8	45.2	0.7
2005	WAS	3050	23	10	213	111	0	11	672.3	75.7	5.2
2006	WAS	1789	8	4	1	34	0	5	602.6	24.9	3.2
2007	WAS	0	0	0	0	0	0	0	0.0	0.0	0.0

Hall of Fame? Not eligible (active)

Pro Bowl Appearances: 3

All-Pro Selections: None

Awards: Pro Bowl MVP - 1996; Byron "Whizzer" White Award - 2002

Dutch Clark (37)

Year	Team	PaYds	PaTD	PaInt	PaSkYds	RuYds	RuTD	Fum	APaY	ARuY	Q
1931	POR	–	1	–	–	–	9	–	5.0	90.0	10.0
1932	POR	272	2	8	–	461	3	–	–134.0	491.0	6.9
1934	DET	383	0	3	–	763	8	–	86.5	843.0	10.0
1935	DET	133	2	4	–	427	4	–	–63.5	467.0	10.0
1936	DET	467	4	6	–	628	7	–	43.5	698.0	10.0
1937	DET	202	1	3	–	468	5	–	1.0	518.0	10.0
1938	DET	50	1	2	–	25	0	–	–40.0	25.0	0.0

Hall of Fame? Yes

Pro Bowl Appearances: None

All-Pro Selections: Consensus - 6, Total - 6 (1931-1932; 1934-1937)

Awards: None

Charley Conerly (30)

Year	Team	PaYds	PaTD	PaInt	PaSkYds	RuYds	RuTD	Fum	APaY	ARuY	Q
1948	NYG	2175	22	13	–	160	5	5	576.4	187.8	8.8
1949	NYG	2138	17	20	–	42	0	4	306.1	30.8	4.9
1950	NYG	1000	8	7	–	22	1	2	234.7	21.5	3.6
1951	NYG	1277	10	22	–	65	1	4	–190.3	65.2	2.9
1952	NYG	1090	13	10	–	115	0	1	225.9	109.5	5.4
1953	NYG	1711	13	25	–	91	0	5	–139.8	76.3	0.0
1954	NYG	1439	17	11	–	107	1	3	312.3	104.7	5.1
1955	NYG	1310	13	13	–	10	0	4	114.7	1.1	2.6
1956	NYG	1143	10	7	–	11	0	0	376.5	11.0	4.0
1957	NYG	1712	11	11	–	24	1	11	112.7	7.3	2.2
1958	NYG	1199	10	9	–	–17	0	3	221.8	–24.3	2.7
1959	NYG	1706	14	4	–	38	1	2	708.7	42.3	8.7
1960	NYG	954	8	7	40	1	0	6	38.3	–19.2	0.3
1961	NYG	634	7	8	134	16	0	4	–204.5	–1.5	0.0

Hall of Fame? No

Pro Bowl Appearances: 2

All-Pro Selections: Consensus - 0, Total - 3 (1956-1957; 1959)

Awards: Most Valuable Player (AP) - 1959; NEA NFL Player of the Year - 1959

Randall Cunningham (24)

Year	Team	PaYds	PaTD	PaInt	PaSkYds	RuYds	RuTD	Fum	APaY	ARuY	Q
1985	PHI	548	1	8	150	205	0	3	−244.2	178.2	0.0
1986	PHI	1391	8	7	489	540	5	7	−223.9	537.0	2.3
1987	PHI	2786	23	12	380	505	3	12	296.8	467.1	5.4
1988	PHI	3808	24	16	442	624	6	12	606.6	621.4	9.8
1989	PHI	3400	21	15	343	621	4	17	365.9	558.1	6.7
1990	PHI	3466	30	13	431	942	5	9	704.2	924.8	10.0
1991	PHI	19	0	0	16	0	0	0	−6.5	0.0	0.0
1992	PHI	2775	19	11	437	549	5	13	225.7	513.8	4.4
1993	PHI	850	5	5	33	110	1	3	138.0	104.0	1.6
1994	PHI	3229	16	13	333	288	3	10	550.6	274.6	4.5
1995	PHI	605	3	5	79	98	0	3	−40.2	81.7	0.3
1997	MIN	501	6	4	60	127	0	4	−44.1	102.1	0.4
1998	MIN	3704	34	10	132	132	1	2	1465.5	136.6	9.1
1999	MIN	1475	8	9	101	58	0	2	285.1	54.4	2.3
2000	DAL	849	6	4	45	89	1	4	133.1	75.4	1.1
2001	BAL	573	3	2	66	40	1	4	25.0	30.5	0.4

Hall of Fame? No

Pro Bowl Appearances: 4

All-Pro Selections: Consensus - 3, Total - 4 (1988; 1990; 1992; 1998)

Awards: Most Valuable Player (Bell) - 1988; Pro Bowl MVP - 1988; Most Valuable Player (Bell) - 1990; PFW/PFWA Offensive Player of the Year - 1990; UPI NFC Offensive Player of the Year - 1990; Comeback Player of the Year - 1992; PFW/PFWA Comeback Player of The Year - 1992; Most Valuable Player (Bell) - 1998

Len Dawson (11)

Year	Team	PaYds	PaTD	PaInt	PaSkYds	RuYds	RuTD	Fum	APaY	ARuY	Q
1957	PIT	25	0	0	1	31	0	1	−4.5	19.0	0.3
1958	PIT	11	0	2	11	−1	0	0	−75.5	−1.0	0.0
1959	PIT	60	1	0	–	20	0	1	9.5	5.5	0.2
1960	CLE	23	0	0	24	0	0	1	−49.6	−2.9	0.0
1961	CLE	85	1	3	19	−10	0	0	−76.5	−10.0	0.0
1962	DTX	2759	29	17	–	252	3	11	537.5	234.0	10.0
1963	KC	2389	26	19	–	272	2	4	514.7	276.8	10.0
1964	KC	2879	30	18	–	89	2	15	420.4	48.1	7.4
1965	KC	2262	21	14	–	142	2	7	500.6	127.4	10.0
1966	KC	2527	26	10	–	167	0	5	859.1	151.4	10.0
1967	KC	2651	24	17	–	68	0	6	623.2	55.3	8.1
1968	KC	2109	17	9	0	40	0	4	677.6	26.9	7.4
1969	KC	1323	9	13	89	3	0	0	162.5	3.0	1.9
1970	KC	1876	13	14	277	46	0	5	43.2	38.8	0.7
1971	KC	2504	15	13	303	24	0	8	260.2	12.8	3.1
1972	KC	1835	13	12	255	75	0	2	230.9	71.6	3.5
1973	KC	725	2	5	104	40	0	4	−58.6	32.1	0.0
1974	KC	1573	7	13	199	28	0	6	−62.8	18.3	0.0
1975	KC	1095	5	4	196	7	0	4	81.3	2.2	0.8

Hall of Fame? Yes

Pro Bowl Appearances: 7

All-Pro Selections: Consensus - 2, Total - 5 (1962; 1964; 1966; 1968; 1971)

Awards: AFL All-Star Game Offensive MVP - 1968; MVP, Super Bowl IV - 1969; Walter Payton NFL Man of the Year - 1973

John Elway (3)

Year	Team	PaYds	PaTD	PaInt	PaSkYds	RuYds	RuTD	Fum	APaY	ARuY	Q
1983	DEN	1663	7	14	218	146	1	6	−60.2	134.7	0.5
1984	DEN	2598	18	15	158	237	1	14	214.2	178.8	2.2
1985	DEN	3891	22	23	307	253	0	7	684.1	232.4	7.4
1986	DEN	3485	19	13	233	257	1	8	858.3	238.7	8.3
1987	DEN	3198	19	12	138	304	4	2	1066.8	333.4	10.0
1988	DEN	3309	17	19	237	234	1	7	584.9	218.1	6.4
1989	DEN	3051	18	18	298	244	3	9	362.8	239.4	4.4
1990	DEN	3526	15	14	311	258	3	8	744.4	261.2	6.2
1991	DEN	3253	13	12	305	255	6	12	536.0	267.3	6.2
1992	DEN	2242	10	17	272	94	2	12	−133.7	71.7	0.0
1993	DEN	4030	25	10	293	153	0	8	1199.2	130.8	8.6
1994	DEN	3490	16	10	303	235	4	11	774.7	232.3	5.4
1995	DEN	3970	26	14	180	176	1	9	1109.4	161.6	7.9
1996	DEN	3328	26	14	194	249	4	6	892.1	266.9	9.5
1997	DEN	3635	27	11	203	218	1	11	962.0	190.5	8.2
1998	DEN	2806	22	10	135	94	1	7	773.8	78.9	4.9

Hall of Fame? Yes

Pro Bowl Appearances: 9

All-Pro Selections: Consensus - 4, Total - 5 (1986-1987; 1993; 1996-1997)

Awards: Most Valuable Player (AP) - 1987; UPI AFC Offensive Player of the Year - 1987; Walter Payton NFL Man of the Year - 1992; UPI AFC Offensive Player of the Year - 1993; MVP, Super Bowl XXXIII - 1998

Boomer Esiason (73)

Year	Team	PaYds	PaTD	PaInt	PaSkYds	RuYds	RuTD	Fum	APaY	ARuY	Q
1984	CIN	530	3	3	52	63	2	4	−12.9	58.9	0.3
1985	CIN	3443	27	12	289	79	1	9	811.5	65.0	7.0
1986	CIN	3959	24	17	194	146	1	12	870.5	116.9	7.3
1987	CIN	3321	16	19	209	241	0	10	508.0	201.0	5.1
1988	CIN	3572	28	14	245	248	1	5	1010.0	239.4	10.0
1989	CIN	3525	28	11	288	278	0	8	937.5	250.0	8.7
1990	CIN	3031	24	22	198	157	0	11	272.2	112.3	2.4
1991	CIN	2883	13	16	190	66	0	10	377.3	45.2	3.2
1992	CIN	1407	11	15	150	66	0	12	−364.8	34.3	0.0
1993	NYJ	3421	16	11	139	118	1	13	791.0	84.4	5.6
1994	NYJ	2782	17	13	134	59	0	11	472.3	33.7	2.7
1995	NYJ	2275	16	15	198	14	0	12	35.5	−7.0	0.2
1996	ARI	2293	11	14	109	52	1	5	410.6	53.9	3.8
1997	CIN	1478	13	2	43	11	0	1	652.6	9.4	4.7

Hall of Fame? No

Pro Bowl Appearances: 4

All-Pro Selections: Consensus - 2, Total - 2 (1988-1989)

Awards: Most Valuable Player (AP) - 1988; PFW/PFWA Offensive Player of the Year - 1988; *Sporting News* NFL Player of the Year - 1988; UPI AFC Offensive Player of the Year - 1988; Walter Payton NFL Man of the Year - 1995

Brett Favre (4)

Year	Team	PaYds	PaTD	PaInt	PaSkYds	RuYds	RuTD	Fum	APaY	ARuY	Q
1991	ATL	0	0	2	11	0	0	0	−81.0	0.0	0.0
1992	GB	3227	18	13	208	198	1	12	602.2	167.2	4.6
1993	GB	3303	19	24	199	216	1	14	200.7	172.8	2.4
1994	GB	3882	33	14	188	202	2	7	1166.0	204.0	7.4
1995	GB	4413	38	13	217	181	3	8	1423.9	191.6	10.0
1996	GB	3899	39	13	241	136	2	11	1042.6	121.9	9.5
1997	GB	3867	35	16	176	187	1	7	1119.7	169.8	9.1
1998	GB	4212	31	23	223	133	1	8	933.3	122.7	6.0
1999	GB	4091	22	23	223	142	0	9	782.8	126.7	6.2
2000	GB	3812	20	16	236	108	0	9	865.2	92.8	4.9
2001	GB	3921	32	15	151	56	1	16	847.2	23.3	6.3
2002	GB	3658	27	16	188	73	0	10	832.6	56.4	5.1
2003	GB	3361	32	21	137	15	0	5	775.6	7.9	4.9
2004	GB	4088	30	17	93	36	0	4	1350.5	31.5	6.9
2005	GB	3881	20	29	170	62	0	10	466.6	50.9	3.6
2006	GB	3885	18	18	134	29	1	8	959.7	27.8	5.1
2007	GB	4155	28	15	93	12	0	9	1257.5	−6.0	5.9

Hall of Fame? Not eligible until 2013.

Pro Bowl Appearances: 9

All-Pro Selections: Consensus - 5, Total - 7 (1995-1997; 2001-2003; 2007)

Awards: AP NFL Offensive Player of the Year - 1995; Most Valuable Player (AP) - 1995; Most Valuable Player (Bell) - 1995; PFW/PFWA Offensive Player of the Year - 1995; *Sporting News* NFL Player of the Year - 1995; UPI NFC Offensive Player of the Year - 1995; Most Valuable Player (AP) - 1996; Most Valuable Player (Bell) - 1996; PFW/PFWA Offensive Player of the Year - 1996; *Sporting News* NFL Player of the Year - 1996; UPI NFC Offensive Player of the Year - 1996; Most Valuable Player (AP) - 1997 (tie)

Dan Fouts (54)

Year	Team	PaYds	PaTD	PaInt	PaSkYds	RuYds	RuTD	Fum	APaY	ARuY	Q
1973	SD	1126	6	13	129	32	0	2	−68.4	29.4	0.0
1974	SD	1732	8	13	99	63	1	4	203.3	61.7	2.7
1975	SD	1396	2	10	197	170	2	3	52.4	178.6	2.1
1976	SD	2535	14	15	220	65	0	8	286.3	51.2	2.9
1977	SD	869	4	6	77	13	0	4	15.2	5.3	0.2
1978	SD	2999	24	20	130	43	2	10	408.4	44.1	4.8
1979	SD	4082	24	24	195	49	2	13	629.2	45.8	5.8
1980	SD	4715	30	24	210	15	2	11	1033.2	19.3	7.2
1981	SD	4802	33	17	134	56	0	9	1489.2	43.8	9.2
1982	SD	2883	17	11	94	8	1	2	969.6	15.9	10.0
1983	SD	2975	20	15	107	−5	1	5	762.1	−1.6	4.7
1984	SD	3740	19	17	228	−29	0	8	829.6	−36.0	4.4
1985	SD	3638	27	20	135	−1	0	13	611.5	−13.5	4.8
1986	SD	3031	16	22	173	−3	0	4	493.9	−4.4	3.6
1987	SD	2517	10	15	176	0	2	10	219.5	8.0	1.6

Hall of Fame? Yes

Pro Bowl Appearances: 6

All-Pro Selections: Consensus - 3, Total - 6 (1979-1983; 1985)

Awards: Sporting News AFC Player of the Year - 1979; UPI AFL/AFC Player of the Year - 1979; AP NFL Offensive Player of the Year - 1982; NEA NFL Player of the Year - 1982; PFW/PFWA Offensive Player of the Year - 1982; UPI AFL/AFC Player of the Year - 1982; Pro Bowl MVP - 1982 (tie)

Roman Gabriel (23)

Year	Team	PaYds	PaTD	PaInt	PaSkYds	RuYds	RuTD	Fum	APaY	ARuY	Q
1962	LARM	670	3	2	–	93	0	2	212.1	80.9	3.4
1963	LARM	1947	8	11	–	132	3	10	271.4	119.1	4.0
1964	LARM	1236	9	5	–	5	1	9	153.7	–10.7	1.3
1965	LARM	1321	11	5	–	79	2	5	364.0	75.5	4.6
1966	LARM	2540	10	16	–	176	3	10	406.3	159.7	6.5
1967	LARM	2779	25	13	–	198	6	5	880.3	237.2	9.5
1968	LARM	2364	19	16	226	139	4	6	270.6	159.9	4.5
1969	LARM	2549	24	7	112	156	5	7	779.4	184.1	10.0
1970	LARM	2552	16	12	134	104	1	6	576.8	99.2	5.7
1971	LARM	2238	17	10	200	48	2	9	310.4	51.6	4.2
1972	LARM	2027	12	15	102	16	1	6	216.1	16.4	2.7
1973	PHI	3219	23	12	219	10	1	10	695.0	10.5	10.0
1974	PHI	1867	9	12	259	76	0	6	68.2	67.3	1.4
1975	PHI	1644	13	11	131	70	1	5	179.0	72.0	2.3
1976	PHI	476	2	2	111	2	0	9	–279.8	–11.2	0.0
1977	PHI	15	0	0	0	0	0	0	7.5	0.0	0.1

Hall of Fame? No

Pro Bowl Appearances: 4

All-Pro Selections: Consensus - 1, Total - 2 (1968-1969)

Awards: Most Valuable Player (AP) - 1969; Most Valuable Player (Bell) - 1969; NEA NFL Player of the Year - 1969; PFW/PFWA Offensive Player of the Year - 1969; *Sporting News* NFL Player of the Year - 1969; UPI NFL/NFC Player of the Year - 1969; Comeback Player of the Year - 1973; PFW/PFWA Comeback Player of The Year - 1973

Rich Gannon (33)

Year	Team	PaYds	PaTD	PaInt	PaSkYds	RuYds	RuTD	Fum	APaY	ARuY	Q
1987	MIN	18	0	1	0	0	0	0	−26.0	0.0	0.0
1988	MIN	90	0	0	22	29	0	0	23.0	29.0	0.4
1990	MIN	2278	16	16	188	268	1	10	118.8	230.2	2.1
1991	MIN	2166	12	6	91	236	2	2	770.4	247.8	7.7
1992	MIN	1905	12	13	177	187	0	5	206.3	161.2	2.2
1993	WAS	704	3	7	87	88	1	3	−69.4	82.4	0.1
1995	KC	57	0	0	0	25	1	0	28.5	35.0	0.4
1996	KC	491	6	1	42	81	0	1	163.0	76.5	2.0
1997	KC	1144	7	4	86	109	2	5	210.9	99.1	2.2
1998	KC	2305	10	6	155	168	3	9	514.9	160.6	3.8
1999	OAK	3840	24	14	241	298	2	8	1013.6	293.9	8.9
2000	OAK	3430	28	11	124	529	4	9	1040.3	514.7	7.9
2001	OAK	3828	27	9	155	231	2	13	1110.3	199.7	9.5
2002	OAK	4689	26	10	214	156	3	9	1576.1	160.4	10.0
2003	OAK	1274	6	4	90	18	0	2	358.9	16.1	2.3
2004	OAK	524	3	2	17	26	0	3	77.7	18.3	0.5

Hall of Fame? Not eligible until 2009

Pro Bowl Appearances: 4

All-Pro Selections: Consensus - 3, Total - 3 (2000-2002)

Awards: Most Valuable Player (Bell) - 2000; Pro Bowl MVP - 2000; Pro Bowl MVP - 2001; Most Valuable Player (AP) - 2002; Most Valuable Player (Bell) - 2002; PFW/PFWA Offensive Player of the Year - 2002; *Sporting News* NFL Player of the Year - 2002

Jeff Garcia (71)

Year	Team	PaYds	PaTD	PaInt	PaSkYds	RuYds	RuTD	Fum	APaY	ARuY	Q
1999	SF	2544	11	11	94	231	2	5	668.7	230.3	6.1
2000	SF	4278	31	10	155	414	4	7	1539.7	423.3	10.0
2001	SF	3538	32	12	114	254	5	9	1078.1	260.9	9.8
2002	SF	3344	21	10	93	353	3	2	1263.4	373.6	9.4
2003	SF	2704	18	13	104	319	7	9	566.7	346.1	5.7
2004	CLE	1731	10	9	99	169	2	9	182.0	148.5	1.7
2005	DET	937	3	6	34	51	1	1	203.0	57.5	1.8
2006	PHI	1309	10	2	1	87	0	6	420.9	59.6	2.5
2007	TB	2440	13	4	104	116	1	4	895.7	111.3	4.7

Hall of Fame? Not eligible (active)

Pro Bowl Appearances: 3

All-Pro Selections: None

Awards: PFW/PFWA Most Improved Player of the Year - 2000

Otto Graham (6)

Year	Team	PaYds	PaTD	PaInt	PaSkYds	RuYds	RuTD	Fum	APaY	ARuY	Q
1946	CLE	1834	17	5	–	–125	1	–	827.0	–115.0	10.0
1947	CLE	2753	25	11	–	72	1	–	1116.5	82.0	10.0
1948	CLE	2713	25	15	–	146	6	–	956.5	206.0	9.5
1949	CLE	2785	19	10	–	107	3	–	1137.5	137.0	10.0
1950	CLE	1943	14	20	291	145	6	6	–146.6	162.1	0.3
1951	CLE	2205	17	16	371	29	3	7	9.2	26.3	0.6
1952	CLE	2816	20	24	242	130	4	4	282.6	153.4	7.1
1953	CLE	2722	11	9	245	143	6	8	581.7	157.3	10.0
1954	CLE	2092	11	17	197	114	8	3	214.0	169.0	4.7
1955	CLE	1721	15	8	241	121	6	7	209.8	105.7	7.2

Hall of Fame? Yes

Pro Bowl Appearances: 5

All-Pro Selections: Consensus - 9, Total - 10 (1946-1955)

Awards: UPI NFL/NFC Player of the Year - 1953; *Sporting News* NFL Player of the Year - 1955; UPI NFL/NFC Player of the Year - 1955

Trent Green (51)

Year	Team	PaYds	PaTD	PaInt	PaSkYds	RuYds	RuTD	Fum	APaY	ARuY	Q
1997	WAS	0	0	0	0	0	0	0	0.0	0.0	0.0
1998	WAS	3441	23	11	338	117	2	14	591.7	97.8	3.9
2000	STL	2063	16	5	145	69	1	3	680.0	70.5	3.8
2001	KC	3783	17	24	198	158	0	11	525.0	132.2	4.8
2002	KC	3690	26	13	141	225	1	1	1341.4	232.6	9.1
2003	KC	4039	24	12	130	83	2	5	1398.6	93.9	9.3
2004	KC	4591	27	17	227	85	0	11	1186.4	67.1	6.3
2005	KC	4014	17	10	204	82	0	8	1237.5	62.5	9.0
2006	KC	1342	7	9	127	59	0	5	79.8	43.2	0.6
2007	MIA	987	5	7	53	32	0	2	144.1	28.4	0.8

Hall of Fame? Not eligible (active)

Pro Bowl Appearances: 2

All-Pro Selections: None

Awards: None

Bob Griese (41)

Year	Team	PaYds	PaTD	PaInt	PaSkYds	RuYds	RuTD	Fum	APaY	ARuY	Q
1967	MIA	2005	15	18	240	157	1	3	98.8	155.7	3.0
1968	MIA	2473	21	16	372	230	1	1	373.3	236.2	6.4
1969	MIA	1695	10	16	289	102	0	5	–137.8	88.3	0.0
1970	MIA	2019	12	17	282	89	2	5	9.7	91.8	0.9
1971	MIA	2089	19	9	248	82	0	9	246.5	52.0	3.4
1972	MIA	638	4	4	45	11	1	0	154.0	21.0	2.0
1973	MIA	1422	17	8	75	20	0	5	251.7	9.3	3.7
1974	MIA	1968	16	15	202	66	1	5	147.8	65.2	2.1
1975	MIA	1693	14	13	131	59	1	2	256.6	62.9	2.9
1976	MIA	2097	11	12	266	108	0	3	306.0	99.5	3.5
1977	MIA	2252	22	13	303	30	0	6	248.7	19.3	3.0
1978	MIA	1791	11	11	165	10	0	3	284.6	5.9	3.1
1979	MIA	2160	14	16	223	30	0	4	212.1	24.9	2.0
1980	MIA	790	6	4	89	0	0	1	156.4	–0.4	1.1

Hall of Fame? Yes

Pro Bowl Appearances: 8

All-Pro Selections: Consensus - 2, Total - 5 (1968; 1970-1971; 1973; 1977)

Awards: NEA NFL Player of the Year - 1971; *Sporting News* AFC Player of the Year - 1971; Most Valuable Player (Bell) - 1977

Steve Grogan (62)

Year	Team	PaYds	PaTD	PaInt	PaSkYds	RuYds	RuTD	Fum	APaY	ARuY	Q
1975	NE	1976	11	18	207	110	3	6	−11.9	117.9	1.0
1976	NE	1903	18	20	155	397	12	6	−15.6	479.1	4.0
1977	NE	2162	17	21	155	324	1	7	40.9	289.1	3.6
1978	NE	2824	15	23	184	539	5	9	200.8	526.2	7.8
1979	NE	3286	28	20	341	368	2	12	319.7	330.3	5.6
1980	NE	2475	18	22	138	112	1	4	273.1	108.4	2.6
1981	NE	1859	7	16	137	49	2	5	78.7	59.4	0.9
1982	NE	930	7	4	48	42	1	2	237.2	46.8	2.9
1983	NE	2411	15	12	195	108	2	4	516.3	117.7	3.9
1984	NE	444	3	6	45	12	0	4	−164.3	−1.7	0.0
1985	NE	1311	7	5	86	29	2	6	215.2	23.3	1.9
1986	NE	976	9	2	31	23	1	2	358.3	26.7	2.9
1987	NE	1183	10	9	55	37	2	8	−14.5	23.0	0.1
1988	NE	834	4	13	77	12	1	2	−171.9	18.9	0.0
1989	NE	1697	9	14	64	19	0	3	223.4	15.1	1.7
1990	NE	615	4	3	68	−5	0	1	116.0	−6.5	0.7

Hall of Fame? No

Pro Bowl Appearances: None

All-Pro Selections: None

Awards: None

John Hadl (28)

Year	Team	PaYds	PaTD	PaInt	PaSkYds	RuYds	RuTD	Fum	APaY	ARuY	Q
1962	SD	1632	15	24	–	139	1	8	–226.3	106.3	0.0
1963	SD	502	6	6	–	26	0	0	71.0	26.0	1.2
1964	SD	2157	18	15	124	70	1	6	333.1	66.9	6.3
1965	SD	2798	20	21	–	91	1	9	461.4	76.7	8.6
1966	SD	2846	23	14	–	95	2	4	903.4	100.3	9.9
1967	SD	3365	24	22	91	107	3	6	721.2	118.3	10.0
1968	SD	3473	27	32	110	14	2	6	413.2	22.3	4.6
1969	SD	2253	10	11	190	109	2	3	490.0	120.5	7.2
1970	SD	2388	22	15	327	188	1	3	340.7	189.6	4.5
1971	SD	3075	21	25	145	75	1	4	468.7	78.8	6.3
1972	SD	2449	15	26	187	99	1	7	–61.9	94.0	0.4
1973	LARM	2008	22	11	126	5	0	1	564.9	3.1	8.1
1974	LARM	680	5	6	36	28	0	2	45.7	21.3	0.7
1974	GB	1072	3	8	70	–3	0	4	47.4	–9.4	0.4
1975	GB	2095	6	21	284	47	0	7	–207.8	33.3	0.0
1976	HOU	634	7	8	123	11	0	2	–126.9	6.9	0.0
1977	HOU	76	0	3	26	11	1	1	–128.9	16.9	0.0

Hall of Fame? No

Pro Bowl Appearances: 6

All-Pro Selections: Consensus - 1, Total - 4 (1965-1966; 1968; 1973)

Awards: AFL All-Star Game MVP - 1969; Walter Payton NFL Man of the Year - 1971; *Sporting News* NFC Player of the Year - 1973; UPI NFL/NFC Player of the Year - 1973

Jim Harbaugh (69)

Year	Team	PaYds	PaTD	PaInt	PaSkYds	RuYds	RuTD	Fum	APaY	ARuY	Q
1987	CHIB	62	0	0	45	15	0	0	−14.0	15.0	0.0
1988	CHIB	514	0	2	49	110	1	1	104.2	113.8	1.7
1989	CHIB	1204	5	9	106	276	3	2	140.9	291.1	3.1
1990	CHIB	2178	10	6	206	321	4	8	444.4	319.6	4.7
1991	CHIB	3121	15	16	163	338	2	6	701.9	328.6	7.8
1992	CHIB	2486	13	12	167	272	1	6	506.9	256.1	4.5
1993	CHIB	2002	7	11	210	277	4	15	−73.7	233.1	1.0
1994	IND	1440	9	6	72	223	0	1	449.0	217.0	3.6
1995	IND	2575	17	5	219	235	2	4	839.5	234.4	6.6
1996	IND	2630	13	11	190	192	1	8	516.4	170.6	5.6
1997	IND	2060	10	4	256	206	0	4	538.9	191.1	5.2
1998	BAL	1839	12	11	145	172	0	7	200.3	141.2	1.9
1999	SD	2761	10	14	208	126	0	12	284.8	93.7	2.6
2000	SD	1416	8	10	96	24	0	5	115.8	10.2	0.6

Hall of Fame? No

Pro Bowl Appearances: 1

All-Pro Selections: Consensus - 1, Total - 1 (1995)

Awards: UPI AFC Offensive Player of the Year - 1995; Comeback Player of the Year - 1995 (tie); PFW/PFWA Comeback Player of the Year - 1995

Jim Hart (53)

Year	Team	PaYds	PaTD	PaInt	PaSkYds	RuYds	RuTD	Fum	APaY	ARuY	Q
1966	STL	29	0	0	21	0	0	0	−6.5	0.0	0.0
1967	STL	3008	19	30	219	36	3	5	136.0	60.0	1.7
1968	STL	2059	15	18	129	20	6	3	232.0	73.5	3.2
1969	STL	1086	6	12	100	16	2	1	14.5	34.5	0.5
1970	STL	2575	14	18	216	18	0	6	281.9	7.6	2.4
1971	STL	1626	8	14	139	9	0	2	147.9	5.1	1.8
1972	STL	857	5	5	56	17	0	3	110.5	9.0	1.4
1973	STL	2223	15	10	168	−3	0	2	589.2	−3.7	8.3
1974	STL	2411	20	8	134	21	2	5	696.3	36.2	7.4
1975	STL	2507	19	19	43	7	1	7	369.0	8.5	3.4
1976	STL	2946	18	13	132	7	0	4	819.1	3.9	7.2
1977	STL	2542	13	20	89	18	0	5	352.8	12.2	4.0
1978	STL	3121	16	18	166	11	2	5	648.8	26.7	7.2
1979	STL	2218	9	20	183	11	0	5	74.4	8.1	0.7
1980	STL	2946	16	20	292	11	0	4	404.0	8.0	2.8
1981	STL	1694	11	14	119	2	0	4	134.8	0.2	0.8
1982	STL	199	1	0	0	0	0	0	104.5	0.0	1.1
1983	STL	592	4	8	99	12	0	5	−253.8	2.8	0.0
1984	WAS	26	0	0	0	−6	0	0	13.0	−6.0	0.0

Hall of Fame? No

Pro Bowl Appearances: 4

All-Pro Selections: Consensus - 1, Total - 1 (1974)

Awards: PFW/PFWA Offensive Player of the Year - 1974; UPI NFL/NFC Player of the Year - 1974; Byron "Whizzer" White Award - 1976

Matt Hasselbeck (48)

Year	Team	PaYds	PaTD	PaInt	PaSkYds	RuYds	RuTD	Fum	APaY	ARuY	Q
1999	GB	41	1	0	9	15	0	1	–9.4	0.9	0.0
2000	GB	104	1	0	2	–5	0	0	55.0	–5.0	0.3
2001	SEA	2023	7	8	251	141	0	6	299.6	116.9	3.0
2002	SEA	3075	15	10	143	202	1	5	936.0	195.5	6.5
2003	SEA	3841	26	15	246	125	2	4	1129.2	135.3	7.9
2004	SEA	3382	22	15	155	90	1	5	931.2	89.8	5.1
2005	SEA	3459	24	9	154	124	1	4	1231.8	122.7	9.4
2006	SEA	2442	18	15	229	110	0	3	442.1	104.9	2.8
2007	SEA	3966	28	12	204	89	0	9	1161.1	66.9	5.8

Hall of Fame? Not eligible (active)

Pro Bowl Appearances: 3

All-Pro Selections: Consensus - 1, Total - 1 (2005)

Awards: None

Brad Johnson (40)

Year	Team	PaYds	PaTD	PaInt	PaSkYds	RuYds	RuTD	Fum	APaY	ARuY	Q
1994	MIN	150	0	0	5	–2	0	0	70.0	–2.0	0.4
1995	MIN	272	0	2	18	–9	0	2	–16.7	–24.3	0.0
1996	MIN	2258	17	10	119	90	1	5	563.9	81.1	5.3
1997	MIN	3036	20	12	164	139	0	4	885.2	128.1	7.2
1998	MIN	747	7	5	30	15	0	1	167.6	10.9	1.0
1999	WAS	4005	24	13	177	31	2	12	1032.2	29.3	7.2
2000	WAS	2505	11	15	150	58	1	5	443.3	57.2	2.5
2001	TB	3406	13	11	269	120	3	4	963.7	140.3	8.0
2002	TB	3049	22	6	121	30	0	8	992.1	21.4	5.8
2003	TB	3811	26	21	111	33	0	6	959.3	23.2	6.1
2004	TB	674	3	3	55	23	0	2	115.4	19.6	0.7
2005	MIN	1885	12	4	134	53	0	5	539.2	42.3	4.0
2006	MIN	2750	9	15	200	82	1	9	356.0	71.0	2.2
2007	DAL	79	0	0	9	–5	0	0	30.5	–5.0	0.1

Hall of Fame? Not eligible (active)

Pro Bowl Appearances: 2

All-Pro Selections: None

Awards: None

Bert Jones (66)

Year	Team	PaYds	PaTD	PaInt	PaSkYds	RuYds	RuTD	Fum	APaY	ARuY	Q
1973	BAL	539	4	12	126	58	0	0	−256.5	58.0	0.0
1974	BAL	1610	8	12	328	279	4	4	−44.9	300.9	2.6
1975	BAL	2483	18	8	325	321	3	1	690.9	346.6	9.4
1976	BAL	3104	24	9	284	214	2	4	927.8	219.2	10.0
1977	BAL	2686	17	11	221	146	2	2	747.0	161.0	10.0
1978	BAL	370	4	1	62	38	0	1	74.3	31.7	1.1
1979	BAL	643	3	3	77	40	1	0	154.5	50.0	1.8
1980	BAL	3134	23	21	262	175	2	1	647.1	192.9	5.8
1981	BAL	3094	21	20	263	85	0	3	574.0	80.0	3.9
1982	LARM	527	2	4	72	73	0	0	61.5	73.0	1.4

Hall of Fame? No

Pro Bowl Appearances: 1

All-Pro Selections: Consensus - 1, Total - 2 (1976-1977)

Awards: AP NFL Offensive Player of the Year - 1976; Most Valuable Player (AP) - 1976; NEA NFL Player of the Year - 1976; UPI AFL/AFC Player of the Year - 1976

Sonny Jurgensen (34)

Year	Team	PaYds	PaTD	PaInt	PaSkYds	RuYds	RuTD	Fum	APaY	ARuY	Q
1957	PHI	470	5	8	88	–3	2	0	–108.0	17.0	0.0
1958	PHI	259	0	1	29	1	0	1	27.2	–0.7	0.4
1959	PHI	27	1	0	0	0	0	0	18.5	0.0	0.2
1960	PHI	486	5	1	45	5	0	3	78.0	–5.0	1.0
1961	PHI	3723	32	24	211	27	0	6	741.5	16.0	8.1
1962	PHI	3261	22	26	212	44	2	4	465.6	56.9	6.0
1963	PHI	1413	11	13	111	38	1	1	158.0	45.5	2.1
1964	WAS	2934	24	13	–	57	3	3	1019.9	79.1	10.0
1965	WAS	2367	15	16	–	23	2	6	469.4	32.1	5.3
1966	WAS	3209	28	19	210	14	0	5	674.6	8.9	7.8
1967	WAS	3747	31	16	157	46	2	5	1117.0	60.5	10.0
1968	WAS	1980	17	11	183	21	1	2	429.0	29.0	4.8
1969	WAS	3102	22	15	322	156	1	2	736.7	163.3	9.3
1970	WAS	2354	23	10	214	39	1	4	570.6	46.4	5.2
1971	WAS	170	0	2	8	29	0	1	–29.3	25.3	0.0
1972	WAS	633	2	4	21	–5	0	4	15.3	–14.8	0.0
1973	WAS	904	6	5	114	7	0	1	154.0	6.3	2.2
1974	WAS	1185	11	5	69	–6	0	2	325.3	–7.8	3.2

Hall of Fame? Yes

Pro Bowl Appearances: 5

All-Pro Selections: Consensus - 1, Total - 5 (1961; 1964; 1966-1967; 1969)

Awards: None

Jim Kelly (21)

Year	Team	PaYds	PaTD	PaInt	PaSkYds	RuYds	RuTD	Fum	APaY	ARuY	Q
1986	BUF	3593	22	17	330	199	0	7	721.9	178.6	6.7
1987	BUF	2798	19	11	239	133	0	6	645.1	118.4	5.6
1988	BUF	3380	15	17	229	154	0	5	754.9	140.5	7.2
1989	BUF	3130	25	18	216	137	2	6	619.5	141.5	5.5
1990	BUF	2829	24	9	158	63	0	4	910.6	53.9	5.9
1991	BUF	3844	33	17	227	45	1	6	1034.1	45.9	8.2
1992	BUF	3457	23	19	145	53	1	8	732.8	43.7	4.6
1993	BUF	3382	18	18	171	102	0	7	719.0	83.0	5.2
1994	BUF	3114	22	17	244	77	1	11	409.7	65.3	2.6
1995	BUF	3130	22	13	181	20	0	7	768.5	10.5	4.8
1996	BUF	2810	14	19	287	66	2	9	178.7	70.3	2.0

Hall of Fame? Yes

Pro Bowl Appearances: None

All-Pro Selections: Consensus - 1, Total - 3 (1990-1992)

Awards: Pro Bowl MVP - 1990

Jack Kemp (52)

Year	Team	PaYds	PaTD	PaInt	PaSkYds	RuYds	RuTD	Fum	APaY	ARuY	Q
1957	PIT	88	0	2	22	−1	0	1	−79.3	−6.2	0.0
1960	LA	3018	20	25	341	−103	8	9	93.9	−83.9	0.2
1961	SD	2686	15	22	−	105	6	10	290.3	122.7	4.2
1962	SD	292	2	2	−	28	1	2	18.1	25.9	0.6
1962	BUF	636	3	4	−	56	1	1	157.5	61.5	2.8
1963	BUF	2914	13	20	−	226	8	10	469.7	258.3	9.2
1964	BUF	2285	13	26	−	124	5	7	51.4	140.1	3.0
1965	BUF	2368	10	18	−	49	4	9	275.1	58.7	5.2
1966	BUF	2451	11	16	−	130	5	7	466.6	153.9	6.1
1967	BUF	2503	14	26	−	58	2	14	−98.7	28.2	0.0
1969	BUF	1981	13	22	187	124	0	8	−192.0	94.5	0.0

Hall of Fame? No

Pro Bowl Appearances: 7

All-Pro Selections: Consensus - 2, Total - 5 (1960-1961; 1963; 1965-1966)

Awards: None

Billy Kilmer (49)

Year	Team	PaYds	PaTD	PaInt	PaSkYds	RuYds	RuTD	Fum	APaY	ARuY	Q
1961	SF	286	0	4	71	509	10	8	–146.3	388.0	2.6
1962	SF	191	1	3	17	478	5	5	–42.8	375.5	4.4
1964	SF	92	1	1	13	113	0	3	–26.0	43.3	0.4
1966	SF	84	0	1	12	23	0	0	–5.0	23.0	0.2
1967	NO	1341	6	11	147	142	1	5	–15.0	135.5	1.0
1968	NO	2060	15	17	170	97	2	5	151.6	105.4	2.7
1969	NO	2532	20	17	212	18	0	5	364.6	12.4	3.9
1970	NO	1557	6	17	155	42	0	4	–94.3	34.8	0.0
1971	WAS	2221	13	13	110	5	2	2	534.5	21.0	6.4
1972	WAS	1648	19	11	67	–3	0	1	427.5	–3.5	4.9
1973	WAS	1656	14	9	88	10	0	6	263.6	1.4	3.8
1974	WAS	1632	10	6	96	27	0	3	442.8	24.2	4.7
1975	WAS	2440	23	16	138	34	1	3	520.5	40.5	5.1
1976	WAS	1252	12	10	125	–7	0	3	97.7	–13.7	0.7
1977	WAS	1187	8	7	180	20	0	4	55.4	13.1	0.8
1978	WAS	316	4	3	22	1	0	1	11.8	0.2	0.1

Hall of Fame? No

Pro Bowl Appearances: 1

All-Pro Selections: Consensus - 0, Total - 2 (1972; 1975)

Awards: None

Bernie Kosar (60)

Year	Team	PaYds	PaTD	PaInt	PaSkYds	RuYds	RuTD	Fum	APaY	ARuY	Q
1985	CLE	1578	8	7	121	−12	1	14	−47.3	−51.7	0.0
1986	CLE	3854	17	10	274	19	0	7	1119.8	7.7	8.4
1987	CLE	3033	22	9	129	22	1	2	1105.3	29.2	8.1
1988	CLE	1890	10	7	172	−1	1	0	578.0	9.0	4.7
1989	CLE	3533	18	14	192	70	1	2	1098.8	75.8	8.5
1990	CLE	2562	10	15	220	13	0	6	351.1	7.9	2.2
1991	CLE	3487	18	9	232	74	0	10	905.7	55.5	7.3
1992	CLE	1160	8	7	126	12	0	1	210.1	10.9	1.3
1993	CLE	807	5	3	128	19	0	4	48.4	6.1	0.4
1993	DAL	410	3	0	4	7	0	2	145.7	−2.7	0.9
1994	MIA	80	1	1	0	17	0	0	10.0	17.0	0.1
1995	MIA	699	3	5	28	19	1	3	48.4	22.1	0.4
1996	MIA	208	1	0	34	6	0	0	75.0	6.0	0.7

Hall of Fame? No

Pro Bowl Appearances: 1

All-Pro Selections: Consensus - 0, Total - 1 (1987)

Awards: None

Dave Krieg (75)

Year	Team	PaYds	PaTD	PaInt	PaSkYds	RuYds	RuTD	Fum	APaY	ARuY	Q
1980	SEA	0	0	0	6	0	0	0	–6.0	0.0	0.0
1981	SEA	843	7	5	85	56	1	4	49.6	52.9	0.6
1982	SEA	501	2	2	117	–3	0	5	–114.5	–15.0	0.0
1983	SEA	2139	18	11	279	55	2	10	118.3	53.5	1.1
1984	SEA	3671	32	24	314	186	3	11	437.3	180.2	3.4
1985	SEA	3602	27	20	448	121	1	11	372.9	106.1	3.9
1986	SEA	2921	21	11	281	122	1	10	531.0	100.5	4.7
1987	SEA	2131	23	15	247	155	2	11	12.9	130.6	1.0
1988	SEA	1741	18	8	92	64	0	6	370.3	42.2	3.3
1989	SEA	3309	21	20	289	160	0	18	100.5	110.0	1.5
1990	SEA	3194	15	20	360	115	0	16	12.5	75.7	0.5
1991	SEA	2080	11	12	216	59	0	6	228.5	49.5	2.1
1992	KC	3115	15	12	323	74	2	10	519.2	64.3	3.5
1993	KC	1238	7	3	138	24	0	6	192.7	2.3	1.3
1994	DET	1629	14	3	100	35	0	4	534.3	20.2	3.0
1995	ARI	3554	16	21	380	29	0	16	122.5	8.5	0.8
1996	CHIB	2278	14	12	104	12	1	6	455.0	12.6	3.8
1997	TEN	2	0	0	0	–2	0	0	1.0	–2.0	0.0
1998	TEN	199	0	0	15	–1	0	3	–21.7	–14.8	0.0

Hall of Fame? No

Pro Bowl Appearances: 3

All-Pro Selections: Consensus - 0, Total - 1 (1984)

Awards: None

Daryle Lamonica (22)

Year	Team	PaYds	PaTD	PaInt	PaSkYds	RuYds	RuTD	Fum	APaY	ARuY	Q
1963	BUF	437	3	4	–	8	0	1	72.0	5.3	1.2
1964	BUF	1137	6	8	–	289	6	6	150.6	276.9	6.7
1965	BUF	376	3	6	–	30	1	2	–77.0	30.0	0.0
1966	BUF	549	4	5	–	6	1	2	47.2	8.3	0.5
1967	OAK	3228	30	20	334	110	4	3	615.5	144.5	9.1
1968	OAK	3245	25	15	224	98	1	4	845.1	101.4	10.0
1969	OAK	3302	34	25	100	36	1	1	807.2	44.8	10.0
1970	OAK	2516	22	15	127	24	0	0	716.0	24.0	6.3
1971	OAK	1717	16	16	172	16	0	3	88.3	14.2	1.2
1972	OAK	1998	18	12	136	33	0	5	339.6	26.4	4.2
1973	OAK	614	2	8	87	–7	0	3	–164.5	–12.5	0.0
1974	OAK	35	1	4	14	–3	0	2	–200.1	–14.4	0.0

Hall of Fame? No

Pro Bowl Appearances: 5

All-Pro Selections: Consensus - 3, Total - 5 (1967-1970; 1972)

Awards: UPI AFL/AFC Player of the Year - 1967; PFW/PFWA Offensive Player of the Year - 1969; UPI AFL/AFC Player of the Year - 1969

Bobby Layne (12)

Year	Team	PaYds	PaTD	PaInt	PaSkYds	RuYds	RuTD	Fum	APaY	ARuY	Q
1948	CHIB	232	3	2	–	80	1	3	–32.1	66.7	0.5
1949	NYB	1796	9	18	–	196	3	10	–25.8	164.8	2.0
1950	DET	2323	16	18	–	250	4	13	166.9	215.9	6.4
1951	DET	2403	26	23	–	290	1	8	256.2	250.3	8.9
1952	DET	1999	19	20	–	411	1	5	244.6	371.9	10.0
1953	DET	2088	16	21	–	343	0	8	146.3	265.7	5.6
1954	DET	1818	14	12	–	119	2	2	487.7	130.3	7.6
1955	DET	1830	11	17	–	111	0	4	231.5	94.5	7.4
1956	DET	1909	9	17	–	169	5	3	317.9	202.7	5.3
1957	DET	1169	6	12	–	99	0	3	104.6	86.9	3.6
1958	DET	171	1	2	–	1	0	1	–12.0	–2.8	0.0
1958	PIT	2339	13	10	96	153	3	6	577.6	153.9	10.0
1959	PIT	1986	20	21	–	181	2	2	295.3	194.0	5.7
1960	PIT	1814	13	17	–	12	2	1	344.3	29.0	5.2
1961	PIT	1205	11	16	–	11	0	4	–49.7	3.1	0.0
1962	PIT	1686	9	17	–	25	1	7	29.9	18.1	0.5

Hall of Fame? Yes

Pro Bowl Appearances: 5

All-Pro Selections: Consensus - 1, Total - 6 (1952-1954; 1956; 1958-1959)

Awards: None

Sid Luckman (20)

Year	Team	PaYds	PaTD	PaInt	PaSkYds	RuYds	RuTD	Fum	APaY	ARuY	Q
1939	CHIB	636	5	4	–	42	0	–	203.0	42.0	2.9
1940	CHIB	941	4	9	–	–65	0	–	175.5	–65.0	2.7
1941	CHIB	1181	9	6	–	18	1	–	425.5	28.0	10.0
1942	CHIB	1023	10	13	–	–6	0	–	106.5	–6.0	4.3
1943	CHIB	2194	28	12	–	–40	1	–	817.0	–30.0	10.0
1944	CHIB	1018	11	12	–	–96	1	–	144.0	–86.0	1.4
1945	CHIB	1727	14	10	–	–118	0	4	464.2	–137.8	6.4
1946	CHIB	1826	17	16	–	–76	0	7	214.6	–100.4	6.0
1947	CHIB	2712	24	31	–	86	1	2	315.0	93.6	7.1
1948	CHIB	1047	13	14	–	11	0	1	62.5	9.2	1.0
1949	CHIB	200	1	3	–	4	0	1	–37.0	1.8	0.0
1950	CHIB	180	1	2	–	1	0	0	25.0	1.0	0.4

Hall of Fame? Yes

Pro Bowl Appearances: 3

All-Pro Selections: Consensus - 6, Total - 9 (1940-1948)

Awards: Most Valuable Player (Carr) - 1943

Johnny Lujack (65)

Year	Team	PaYds	PaTD	PaInt	PaSkYds	RuYds	RuTD	Fum	APaY	ARuY	Q
1948	CHIB	611	6	3	–	110	1	1	210.2	115.4	4.6
1949	CHIB	2658	23	22	–	64	2	2	606.2	82.3	10.0
1950	CHIB	1731	4	21	–	397	11	2	93.7	492.9	10.0
1951	CHIB	1295	8	8	–	171	7	2	347.3	224.9	10.0

Hall of Fame? No

Pro Bowl Appearances: 2

All-Pro Selections: Consensus - 1, Total - 4 (1948-1951)

Awards: None

Peyton Manning (8)

Year	Team	PaYds	PaTD	PaInt	PaSkYds	RuYds	RuTD	Fum	APaY	ARuY	Q
1998	IND	3739	26	28	109	62	0	3	793.4	59.1	4.8
1999	IND	4135	26	15	116	73	2	6	1330.9	78.6	9.6
2000	IND	4413	33	15	131	116	1	5	1527.3	114.2	8.4
2001	IND	4131	26	23	232	157	4	7	894.5	181.0	7.8
2002	IND	4200	27	19	145	148	2	6	1199.0	154.0	7.8
2003	IND	4267	29	10	107	26	0	6	1592.9	15.0	10.0
2004	IND	4557	49	10	101	38	0	5	1881.8	28.7	9.6
2005	IND	3747	28	10	81	45	0	5	1395.6	31.9	9.9
2006	IND	4397	31	9	86	36	4	2	1875.6	72.9	10.0
2007	IND	4040	31	14	124	−5	3	6	1329.6	16.4	6.3

Hall of Fame? Not eligible (active)

Pro Bowl Appearances: 8

All-Pro Selections: Consensus - 4, Total - 7 (1999-2000; 2003-2007)

Awards: Most Valuable Player (AP) - 2003 (tie); Most Valuable Player (Bell) - 2003; *Sporting News* NFL Player of the Year - 2003; AP NFL Offensive Player of the Year - 2004; Most Valuable Player (AP) - 2004; Most Valuable Player (Bell) - 2004; PFW/PFWA Offensive Player of the Year - 2004; *Sporting News* NFL Player of the Year - 2004; Pro Bowl MVP - 2004; Byron "Whizzer" White Award - 2005; Walter Payton NFL Man of the Year - 2005; MVP, Super Bowl XLI - 2006

Dan Marino (2)

Year	Team	PaYds	PaTD	PaInt	PaSkYds	RuYds	RuTD	Fum	APaY	ARuY	Q
1983	MIA	2210	20	6	80	45	2	5	731.8	48.2	4.8
1984	MIA	5084	48	17	120	−7	0	6	1838.1	−18.1	10.0
1985	MIA	4137	30	21	157	−24	0	9	981.8	−39.3	7.6
1986	MIA	4746	44	23	119	−3	0	8	1354.9	−8.9	10.0
1987	MIA	3245	26	13	77	−5	1	5	1025.7	−0.2	7.3
1988	MIA	4434	28	23	31	−17	0	10	1133.7	−29.7	8.8
1989	MIA	3997	24	22	86	−7	2	7	989.3	6.2	7.3
1990	MIA	3563	21	11	90	29	0	3	1294.9	25.6	8.1
1991	MIA	3970	25	13	182	32	1	6	1243.7	31.3	9.7
1992	MIA	4116	24	16	173	66	0	5	1251.6	59.4	7.8
1993	MIA	1218	8	3	42	−4	1	4	350.7	−2.7	2.3
1994	MIA	4453	30	17	113	−6	1	9	1320.6	−8.1	7.1
1995	MIA	3668	24	15	153	14	0	7	1002.5	8.0	6.2
1996	MIA	2795	17	9	131	−3	0	4	880.9	−7.4	7.2
1997	MIA	3780	16	11	142	−14	0	8	1132.3	−23.3	7.8
1998	MIA	3479	23	15	178	−3	1	9	804.5	−6.0	4.5
1999	MIA	2448	12	17	66	−6	0	5	426.1	−9.1	2.8

Hall of Fame? Yes

Pro Bowl Appearances: 9

All-Pro Selections: Consensus - 6, Total - 8 (1983-1986; 1988; 1992; 1994-1995)

Awards: Sporting News NFL Rookie of the Year - 1983; AP NFL Offensive Player of the Year - 1984; Most Valuable Player (AP) - 1984; Most Valuable Player (Bell) - 1984; NEA NFL Player of the Year - 1984; PFW/PFWA Offensive Player of the Year - 1984; *Sporting News* NFL Player of the Year - 1984; UPI AFC Offensive Player of the Year - 1984; UPI AFC Offensive Player of the Year - 1994; Comeback Player of the Year - 1994; PFW/PFWA Comeback Player of the Year - 1994; Walter Payton NFL Man of the Year - 1998

Jim McMahon (38)

Year	Team	PaYds	PaTD	PaInt	PaSkYds	RuYds	RuTD	Fum	APaY	ARuY	Q
1982	CHIB	1501	9	7	196	105	1	1	318.3	111.3	4.4
1983	CHIB	2184	12	13	266	307	2	4	294.1	304.7	3.8
1984	CHIB	1146	8	2	48	276	2	1	463.3	287.9	4.2
1985	CHIB	2392	15	11	125	252	3	4	620.8	262.6	7.2
1986	CHIB	995	5	8	40	152	1	1	167.4	157.1	2.4
1987	CHIB	1639	12	8	136	88	2	2	390.4	101.1	3.5
1988	CHIB	1346	6	7	79	104	4	6	166.0	117.0	2.3
1989	SD	2132	10	10	167	141	0	3	488.6	131.7	4.5
1990	PHI	63	0	0	7	1	0	0	24.5	1.0	0.2
1991	PHI	2239	12	11	128	55	1	2	591.7	60.0	4.9
1992	PHI	279	1	2	25	23	0	0	49.5	23.0	0.4
1993	MIN	1968	9	8	104	96	0	4	498.6	82.4	3.8
1994	ARI	219	1	3	23	32	0	1	−48.9	27.4	0.0
1995	GB	6	0	0	0	0	0	0	3.0	0.0	0.0
1996	GB	39	0	0	0	−1	0	1	−0.5	−21.0	0.0

Hall of Fame? No

Pro Bowl Appearances: 1

All-Pro Selections: Consensus - 0, Total - 1 (1985)

Awards: Comeback Player of the Year - 1991

Donovan McNabb (26)

Year	Team	PaYds	PaTD	PaInt	PaSkYds	RuYds	RuTD	Fum	APaY	ARuY	Q
1999	PHI	948	8	7	204	313	0	8	−202.4	261.5	0.4
2000	PHI	3365	21	13	262	629	6	7	825.6	654.7	7.5
2001	PHI	3233	25	12	273	482	2	8	771.2	459.3	9.0
2002	PHI	2289	17	6	166	460	6	6	647.0	486.5	6.5
2003	PHI	3216	16	11	253	355	3	9	733.7	341.9	6.7
2004	PHI	3875	31	8	192	220	3	8	1324.7	225.8	7.8
2005	PHI	2507	16	9	112	55	1	8	606.5	45.0	4.5
2006	PHI	2647	18	6	140	212	3	3	953.9	231.6	6.1
2007	PHI	3324	19	7	227	236	0	9	956.7	204.3	5.5

Hall of Fame? Not eligible (active)

Pro Bowl Appearances: 5

All-Pro Selections: None

Awards: None

Steve McNair (15)

Year	Team	PaYds	PaTD	PaInt	PaSkYds	RuYds	RuTD	Fum	APaY	ARuY	Q
1995	HOU	569	3	1	63	38	0	3	95.1	24.4	0.7
1996	HOU	1197	6	4	45	169	2	7	210.9	141.6	2.9
1997	TEN	2665	14	13	190	674	8	16	235.7	635.8	6.2
1998	TEN	3228	15	10	176	559	4	5	988.6	573.4	8.8
1999	TEN	2179	12	8	74	337	8	3	696.1	396.4	7.4
2000	TEN	2847	15	13	141	403	0	12	492.7	332.8	4.2
2001	TEN	3350	21	12	251	414	5	5	936.6	436.4	10.0
2002	TEN	3387	22	15	121	440	3	9	847.1	420.4	7.3
2003	TEN	3215	24	7	108	138	4	12	935.4	138.2	6.7
2004	TEN	1343	8	9	95	128	1	5	119.8	119.7	1.2
2005	TEN	3161	16	11	134	139	1	7	878.5	132.0	7.0
2006	BAL	3050	16	12	84	119	1	7	844.9	105.1	4.9
2007	BAL	1113	2	4	85	32	0	8	35.7	17.8	0.3

Hall of Fame? Not eligible (active)

Pro Bowl Appearances: 3

All-Pro Selections: Consensus - 0, Total - 1 (2003)

Awards: None

Joe Montana (1)

Year	Team	PaYds	PaTD	PaInt	PaSkYds	RuYds	RuTD	Fum	APaY	ARuY	Q
1979	SF	96	1	0	0	22	0	1	17.6	17.4	0.3
1980	SF	1795	15	9	100	77	2	4	413.5	81.0	3.4
1981	SF	3565	19	12	193	95	2	2	1188.2	111.3	7.8
1982	SF	2613	17	11	166	118	1	4	692.6	115.9	8.2
1983	SF	3910	26	12	224	284	2	3	1333.0	292.0	10.0
1984	SF	3630	28	10	138	118	2	4	1319.7	125.3	7.9
1985	SF	3653	27	13	246	153	3	5	1075.2	168.3	10.0
1986	SF	2236	8	9	95	38	0	3	634.1	31.9	4.9
1987	SF	3054	31	13	158	141	1	3	958.2	141.8	7.9
1988	SF	2981	18	10	223	132	3	3	897.2	152.3	8.4
1989	SF	3521	26	8	198	227	3	9	1090.2	219.3	9.5
1990	SF	3944	26	16	153	162	1	4	1239.9	161.1	8.6
1992	SF	126	2	0	8	28	0	0	65.0	28.0	0.6
1993	KC	2144	13	7	61	64	0	1	794.0	61.0	5.5
1994	KC	3283	16	9	132	17	0	7	1004.0	7.5	5.5

Hall of Fame? Yes

Pro Bowl Appearances: 8

All-Pro Selections: Consensus - 4, Total - 7 (1981; 1983-1985; 1987; 1989-1990)

Awards: MVP, Super Bowl XVI - 1981; MVP, Super Bowl XIX - 1984; Comeback Player of the Year - 1986 (tie); PFW/PFWA Comeback Player of The Year - 1986 (tie); AP NFL Offensive Player of the Year - 1989; Most Valuable Player (AP) - 1989; Most Valuable Player (Bell) - 1989; PFW/PFWA Offensive Player of the Year - 1989; *Sporting News* NFL Player of the Year - 1989; UPI NFC Offensive Player of the Year - 1989; MVP, Super Bowl XXIV - 1989; Most Valuable Player (AP) - 1990

Warren Moon (29)

Year	Team	PaYds	PaTD	PaInt	PaSkYds	RuYds	RuTD	Fum	APaY	ARuY	Q
1984	HOU	3338	12	14	371	211	1	17	259.1	149.9	2.2
1985	HOU	2709	15	19	366	130	0	12	–41.0	89.5	0.4
1986	HOU	3489	13	26	332	157	2	11	159.9	144.6	2.3
1987	HOU	2806	21	18	198	112	3	8	385.5	116.5	3.6
1988	HOU	2327	17	8	120	88	5	8	559.7	106.8	5.3
1989	HOU	3631	23	14	267	268	4	11	787.6	253.9	7.6
1990	HOU	4689	33	13	252	215	2	18	1141.2	176.3	8.1
1991	HOU	4690	23	21	174	68	2	11	1131.4	67.6	9.1
1992	HOU	2521	18	12	105	147	1	7	564.9	137.6	4.2
1993	HOU	3485	21	21	218	145	1	13	416.0	113.5	3.4
1994	MIN	4264	18	19	235	55	0	9	976.8	40.2	5.5
1995	MIN	4228	33	14	277	82	0	13	1017.3	56.7	6.6
1996	MIN	1610	7	9	122	6	0	7	132.2	–3.2	1.1
1997	SEA	3678	25	16	192	40	1	7	940.3	41.7	6.9
1998	SEA	1632	11	8	140	10	0	8	148.3	–7.3	0.8
1999	KC	20	0	0	0	0	0	0	10.0	0.0	0.1
2000	KC	208	1	1	46	2	0	1	–10.0	0.0	0.0

Hall of Fame? Yes

Pro Bowl Appearances: 9

All-Pro Selections: Consensus - 1, Total - 3 (1988-1990)

Awards: Walter Payton NFL Man of the Year - 1989; AP NFL Offensive Player of the Year - 1990; UPI AFC Offensive Player of the Year - 1990; Pro Bowl MVP - 1997

Earl Morrall (57)

Year	Team	PaYds	PaTD	PaInt	PaSkYds	RuYds	RuTD	Fum	APaY	ARuY	Q
1956	SF	621	1	6	36	10	0	1	45.3	8.1	0.7
1957	PIT	1900	11	12	274	81	2	12	−109.4	41.4	0.0
1958	PIT	275	1	7	17	39	0	0	−119.5	39.0	0.0
1958	DET	188	4	2	–	41	0	1	12.0	34.0	0.6
1959	DET	1102	5	6	228	112	0	7	−82.5	70.2	0.6
1960	DET	423	4	3	–	37	1	3	26.8	26.7	0.7
1961	DET	909	7	9	–	86	0	6	−33.6	58.3	0.3
1962	DET	449	4	4	35	65	1	1	39.8	65.3	1.2
1963	DET	2621	24	14	–	105	1	5	769.2	101.4	8.9
1964	DET	588	4	3	–	70	0	3	101.9	58.2	1.5
1965	NYG	2446	22	12	214	52	0	5	508.8	42.2	5.8
1966	NYG	1105	7	12	152	12	0	3	−101.1	8.6	0.0
1967	NYG	181	3	1	59	11	1	0	11.5	21.0	0.3
1968	BAL	2909	26	17	180	18	1	7	538.3	19.3	5.8
1969	BAL	755	5	7	63	0	0	0	94.5	0.0	1.0
1970	BAL	792	9	4	131	6	0	2	91.5	4.5	0.8
1971	BAL	1210	7	12	89	13	0	3	14.9	9.1	0.3
1972	MIA	1360	11	7	114	67	1	3	267.3	65.7	3.8
1973	MIA	253	0	4	18	9	0	0	−31.5	9.0	0.0
1974	MIA	301	2	3	16	11	0	0	39.5	11.0	0.5
1975	MIA	273	3	2	27	33	0	1	17.6	29.9	0.4
1976	MIA	148	1	1	29	0	0	0	15.0	0.0	0.1

Hall of Fame? No

Pro Bowl Appearances: 2

All-Pro Selections: Consensus - 2, Total - 2 (1968; 1972)

Awards: Most Valuable Player (AP) - 1968; NEA NFL Player of the Year - 1968; PFW/PFWA Offensive Player of the Year - 1968; *Sporting News* NFL Player of the Year - 1968; UPI NFL/NFC Player of the Year - 1968; *Sporting News* AFC Player of the Year - 1972; Comeback Player of the Year - 1972; PFW/PFWA Comeback Player of the Year - 1972

Craig Morton (56)

Year	Team	PaYds	PaTD	PaInt	PaSkYds	RuYds	RuTD	Fum	APaY	ARuY	Q
1965	DAL	173	2	4	68	−8	0	2	−186.4	−13.1	0.0
1966	DAL	225	3	1	8	50	0	0	84.5	50.0	1.5
1967	DAL	978	10	10	125	42	0	5	−118.2	24.2	0.0
1968	DAL	752	4	6	39	28	2	1	108.7	46.3	1.6
1969	DAL	2619	21	15	246	62	1	4	490.9	64.6	5.8
1970	DAL	1819	15	7	166	37	0	1	536.1	34.4	4.8
1971	DAL	1131	7	8	76	9	1	1	205.5	18.0	2.6
1972	DAL	2396	15	21	179	26	2	4	202.5	42.5	2.8
1973	DAL	174	3	1	0	0	0	1	28.2	−1.2	0.4
1974	DAL	12	0	0	0	0	0	0	6.0	0.0	0.1
1974	NYG	1510	9	13	97	5	0	4	90.5	2.5	0.9
1975	NYG	2359	11	16	331	72	0	9	1.8	53.7	0.5
1976	NYG	1865	9	20	285	48	0	7	−275.1	35.6	0.0
1977	DEN	1929	14	8	338	125	4	7	163.0	138.5	3.3
1978	DEN	1802	11	8	238	71	0	6	210.8	58.3	2.9
1979	DEN	2626	16	19	241	13	1	9	146.6	3.4	1.3
1980	DEN	2150	12	13	190	29	1	4	339.7	29.3	2.5
1981	DEN	3195	21	14	394	18	0	2	740.0	16.5	4.6
1982	DEN	193	0	3	19	0	0	1	−67.5	0.0	0.0

Hall of Fame? No

Pro Bowl Appearances: None

All-Pro Selections: Consensus - 0, Total - 1 (1977)

Awards: Sporting News AFC Player of the Year - 1977; UPI AFL/AFC Player of the Year - 1977; Comeback Player of the Year - 1977; PFW/PFWA Comeback Player of the Year - 1977

Joe Namath (47)

Year	Team	PaYds	PaTD	PaInt	PaSkYds	RuYds	RuTD	Fum	APaY	ARuY	Q
1965	NYJ	2220	18	15	–	19	0	6	440.5	13.5	7.2
1966	NYJ	3379	19	27	–	42	2	1	800.0	61.5	8.5
1967	NYJ	4007	26	28	261	14	0	2	813.4	13.1	9.8
1968	NYJ	3147	15	17	112	11	2	1	902.0	30.5	9.9
1969	NYJ	2734	19	17	117	33	2	3	633.4	49.6	8.0
1970	NYJ	1259	5	12	63	–1	0	1	131.7	–1.2	1.1
1971	NYJ	537	5	6	0	–1	0	0	83.5	–1.0	0.9
1972	NYJ	2816	19	21	101	8	0	3	549.1	5.9	6.4
1973	NYJ	966	5	6	97	–2	0	1	161.3	–2.3	2.3
1974	NYJ	2616	20	22	195	1	1	6	207.9	6.1	2.1
1975	NYJ	2286	15	28	253	6	0	4	–170.6	1.6	0.0
1976	NYJ	1090	4	16	150	5	0	3	–264.0	4.0	0.0
1977	LARM	606	3	5	76	5	0	2	–10.3	2.3	0.0

Hall of Fame? Yes

Pro Bowl Appearances: 5

All-Pro Selections: Consensus - 2, Total - 5 (1966-1969; 1972)

Awards: UPI AFL/AFC Rookie of the Year - 1965; AFL All-Star Game Offensive MVP - 1965; AFL All-Star Game Offensive MVP - 1967 (tie); PFW/PFWA Offensive Player of the Year - 1968; UPI AFL/AFC Player of the Year - 1968; MVP, Super Bowl III - 1968; Comeback Player of the Year - 1974; PFW/PFWA Comeback Player of the Year - 1974

Neil O'Donnell (68)

Year	Team	PaYds	PaTD	PaInt	PaSkYds	RuYds	RuTD	Fum	APaY	ARuY	Q
1991	PIT	1963	11	7	214	82	1	11	161.2	68.3	1.7
1992	PIT	2283	13	9	208	5	1	6	461.2	-2.7	2.7
1993	PIT	3208	14	7	331	111	0	5	907.4	101.6	6.5
1994	PIT	2443	13	9	250	80	1	4	572.9	78.6	3.5
1995	PIT	2970	17	7	126	45	0	2	1123.2	40.8	7.2
1996	NYJ	1147	4	7	127	30	0	2	143.8	27.7	1.4
1997	NYJ	2796	17	7	289	36	1	9	610.5	24.5	4.5
1998	CIN	2216	15	4	217	34	0	6	594.1	25.9	3.5
1999	TEN	1382	10	5	63	1	0	5	320.0	-16.0	2.1
2000	TEN	530	2	3	23	-2	0	0	147.0	-2.0	0.7
2001	TEN	496	2	2	58	28	0	1	92.7	25.3	0.9
2002	TEN	24	0	0	0	-3	0	0	12.0	-3.0	0.1
2003	TEN	232	2	1	0	-1	0	0	91.0	-1.0	0.6

Hall of Fame? No

Pro Bowl Appearances: 1

All-Pro Selections: None

Awards: None

Babe Parilli (74)

Year	Team	PaYds	PaTD	PaInt	PaSkYds	RuYds	RuTD	Fum	APaY	ARuY	Q
1952	GB	1416	13	17	–	106	1	4	74.6	97.3	3.0
1953	GB	830	4	19	–	171	4	8	–464.0	151.8	0.1
1956	CLE	409	3	7	63	65	0	4	–205.5	22.0	0.0
1957	GB	669	4	12	–	83	2	3	–162.6	80.1	0.0
1958	GB	1068	10	13	–	15	0	4	–23.2	7.2	0.0
1960	OAK	1003	5	11	106	25	1	3	–67.4	18.4	0.0
1961	BOS	1314	13	9	–	183	5	2	339.9	220.1	5.7
1962	BOS	1988	18	8	–	169	2	6	587.9	165.1	9.8
1963	BOS	2345	13	24	–	126	5	7	144.5	149.0	3.7
1964	BOS	3465	31	27	279	168	2	7	403.8	170.3	9.0
1965	BOS	2597	18	26	–	200	0	8	192.1	166.4	5.7
1966	BOS	2721	20	20	–	42	1	8	462.4	30.1	4.9
1967	BOS	2317	19	24	250	61	0	4	9.3	55.2	0.8
1968	NYJ	401	5	2	23	–2	1	3	25.4	–4.9	0.2
1969	NYJ	138	2	1	0	4	0	0	44.0	4.0	0.6

Hall of Fame? No

Pro Bowl Appearances: None

All-Pro Selections: Consensus - 1, Total - 1 (1964)

Awards: AFL All-Star Game Offensive MVP - 1966

Ace Parker (64)

Year	Team	PaYds	PaTD	PaInt	PaSkYds	RuYds	RuTD	Fum	APaY	ARuY	Q
1937	BKN	514	1	7	–	26	1	–	17.0	36.0	1.0
1938	BKN	865	5	7	–	253	2	–	212.5	273.0	10.0
1939	BKN	977	4	13	–	271	5	–	53.5	321.0	6.4
1940	BKN	817	10	7	–	306	2	–	213.5	326.0	9.2
1941	BKN	642	2	8	–	301	0	–	51.0	301.0	5.1
1945	BOS	123	0	5	–	–49	0	2	–152.7	–78.4	0.0
1946	NY	763	8	3	–	184	3	–	316.5	214.0	6.4

Hall of Fame? Yes

Pro Bowl Appearances: None

All-Pro Selections: Consensus - 2, Total - 5 (1937-1940; 1946)

Awards: Most Valuable Player (Carr) - 1940

Milt Plum (42)

Year	Team	PaYds	PaTD	PaInt	PaSkYds	RuYds	RuTD	Fum	APaY	ARuY	Q
1957	CLE	590	2	5	85	118	0	1	15.2	107.8	2.3
1958	CLE	1619	11	11	145	107	4	2	268.2	134.0	5.5
1959	CLE	1992	14	8	157	20	1	2	555.1	24.2	6.9
1960	CLE	2297	21	5	275	−24	2	2	728.6	−9.1	10.0
1961	CLE	2416	18	10	145	−17	1	9	469.5	−33.5	4.6
1962	DET	2378	15	20	211	170	1	2	282.0	173.7	5.2
1963	DET	339	2	12	–	26	0	0	−240.5	26.0	0.0
1964	DET	2241	18	15	–	28	1	4	531.9	31.6	5.1
1965	DET	1710	12	19	–	37	3	5	62.8	54.2	1.2
1966	DET	943	4	13	–	59	0	2	−37.0	53.0	0.2
1967	DET	925	4	8	–	5	0	4	47.9	−0.4	0.4
1968	LARM	49	1	1	15	3	0	0	−20.5	3.0	0.0
1969	NYG	37	0	0	12	−1	0	1	−29.9	−4.6	0.0

Hall of Fame? No

Pro Bowl Appearances: 2

All-Pro Selections: Consensus - 0, Total - 1 (1960)

Awards: None

Tobin Rote (50)

Year	Team	PaYds	PaTD	PaInt	PaSkYds	RuYds	RuTD	Fum	APaY	ARuY	Q
1950	GB	1231	7	24	–	158	0	9	–510.8	119.3	0.0
1951	GB	1540	15	20	–	523	3	4	22.0	516.5	9.5
1952	GB	1268	13	8	–	313	2	10	128.3	225.6	6.0
1953	GB	1005	5	15	–	180	0	2	–65.1	167.9	1.4
1954	GB	2311	14	18	–	301	8	4	459.4	357.1	10.0
1955	GB	1977	17	19	–	332	5	10	79.7	310.8	8.9
1956	GB	2203	18	15	–	398	11	5	509.4	465.1	10.0
1957	DET	1070	11	10	–	366	1	6	68.0	308.0	7.0
1958	DET	1678	14	10	–	351	3	7	343.6	316.4	9.0
1959	DET	861	5	19	232	156	2	2	–507.3	161.8	0.0
1963	SD	2510	20	17	–	62	2	2	686.2	75.8	9.6
1964	SD	1156	9	15	97	–12	0	6	–224.7	–25.0	0.0
1966	DEN	40	0	1	–	0	0	0	–15.0	0.0	0.0

Hall of Fame? No

Pro Bowl Appearances: 2

All-Pro Selections: Consensus - 1, Total - 3 (1955-1956; 1963)

Awards: None

Frank Ryan (44)

Year	Team	PaYds	PaTD	PaInt	PaSkYds	RuYds	RuTD	Fum	APaY	ARuY	Q
1958	LARM	34	1	3	–	45	0	1	–112.5	34.5	0.0
1959	LARM	709	2	4	–	57	1	5	59.7	31.8	1.1
1960	LARM	816	7	9	–	85	1	1	93.2	89.8	2.8
1961	LARM	1115	5	7	–	139	0	3	242.8	113.7	3.8
1962	CLE	1541	10	7	156	242	1	6	222.2	209.3	4.9
1963	CLE	2026	25	13	179	224	2	6	308.0	200.0	5.2
1964	CLE	2404	25	19	207	217	1	4	309.9	212.1	4.7
1965	CLE	1751	18	13	202	72	0	5	121.8	58.7	1.9
1966	CLE	2974	29	14	223	156	0	5	735.1	139.9	10.0
1967	CLE	2026	20	16	318	57	0	4	85.4	46.6	1.1
1968	CLE	639	7	6	79	64	0	2	–4.4	53.9	0.5
1969	WAS	4	0	0	0	0	0	0	2.0	0.0	0.0
1970	WAS	3	0	0	35	0	0	0	–33.5	0.0	0.0

Hall of Fame? No

Pro Bowl Appearances: 3

All-Pro Selections: Consensus - 0, Total - 1 (1965)

Awards: None

Mark Rypien (72)

Year	Team	PaYds	PaTD	PaInt	PaSkYds	RuYds	RuTD	Fum	APaY	ARuY	Q
1988	WAS	1730	18	13	115	31	1	6	154.4	31.6	1.5
1989	WAS	3768	22	13	108	56	1	14	899.1	37.9	6.8
1990	WAS	2070	16	11	33	4	0	2	620.7	0.3	3.8
1991	WAS	3564	28	11	59	6	1	9	1130.2	3.8	8.6
1992	WAS	3282	13	17	176	50	2	4	785.7	59.3	5.0
1993	WAS	1514	4	10	87	4	3	7	67.3	26.7	0.6
1994	CLE	694	4	3	11	4	0	2	175.1	−0.1	0.9
1995	STL	1448	9	8	60	10	0	1	390.5	8.5	2.5
1996	PHI	76	1	0	0	0	0	0	43.0	0.0	0.4
1997	STL	270	0	2	9	1	0	0	56.0	1.0	0.4
2001	IND	57	0	0	6	0	0	0	22.5	0.0	0.2

Hall of Fame? No

Pro Bowl Appearances: 2

All-Pro Selections: Consensus - 1, Total - 1 (1991)

Awards: UPI NFC Offensive Player of the Year - 1991; MVP, Super Bowl XXVI - 1991

Phil Simms (35)

Year	Team	PaYds	PaTD	PaInt	PaSkYds	RuYds	RuTD	Fum	APaY	ARuY	Q
1979	NYG	1743	13	14	319	166	1	9	−201.1	144.6	0.0
1980	NYG	2321	15	19	233	190	1	6	115.7	181.8	2.0
1981	NYG	2031	11	9	301	42	0	7	188.8	27.7	1.3
1983	NYG	130	0	1	35	0	0	0	−5.0	0.0	0.0
1984	NYG	4044	22	18	434	162	0	8	769.8	140.7	5.0
1985	NYG	3829	22	20	396	132	0	16	329.0	91.5	3.4
1986	NYG	3487	21	22	359	72	1	9	387.3	54.2	3.3
1987	NYG	2230	17	9	225	44	0	4	506.8	37.2	3.9
1988	NYG	3359	21	11	405	152	0	7	730.9	135.6	6.9
1989	NYG	3061	14	14	244	141	1	9	530.7	126.8	4.8
1990	NYG	2284	15	4	104	61	1	7	709.7	54.3	4.7
1991	NYG	993	8	4	79	42	1	4	166.3	43.2	1.6
1992	NYG	912	5	3	67	17	0	0	309.0	17.0	1.9
1993	NYG	3038	15	9	217	31	0	7	799.4	14.2	5.2

Hall of Fame? No

Pro Bowl Appearances: 2

All-Pro Selections: Consensus - 0, Total - 1 (1986)

Awards: Pro Bowl MVP - 1985; NEA NFL Player of the Year - 1986; MVP, Super Bowl XXI - 1986

Ken Stabler (39)

Year	Team	PaYds	PaTD	PaInt	PaSkYds	RuYds	RuTD	Fum	APaY	ARuY	Q
1970	OAK	52	0	1	0	−4	0	1	−44.0	−9.0	0.0
1971	OAK	268	1	4	37	29	2	1	−75.1	46.1	0.0
1972	OAK	524	4	3	75	27	0	2	27.5	21.5	0.6
1973	OAK	1997	14	10	261	101	0	5	270.8	87.7	5.1
1974	OAK	2469	26	12	141	−2	1	3	687.7	3.8	6.9
1975	OAK	2296	16	24	202	−5	0	4	29.0	−8.0	0.2
1976	OAK	2737	27	17	203	−2	1	5	509.9	3.6	4.5
1977	OAK	2176	20	20	141	−3	0	3	228.2	−4.2	2.5
1978	OAK	2944	16	30	347	0	0	9	−201.8	−3.2	0.0
1979	OAK	3615	26	22	284	−4	0	10	495.2	−15.7	4.1
1980	HOU	3202	13	28	264	−22	0	7	150.4	−30.4	0.8
1981	HOU	1988	14	18	254	−3	0	7	−91.4	−11.6	0.0
1982	NO	1343	6	10	106	−4	0	4	87.8	−6.3	0.8
1983	NO	1988	9	18	159	−14	0	4	94.3	−18.3	0.5
1984	NO	339	2	5	40	−1	0	1	−75.0	−1.5	0.0

Hall of Fame? No

Pro Bowl Appearances: 4

All-Pro Selections: Consensus - 2, Total - 3 (1973-1974; 1976)

Awards: AP NFL Offensive Player of the Year - 1974; Most Valuable Player (AP) - 1974; NEA NFL Player of the Year - 1974; *Sporting News* AFC Player of the Year - 1974; UPI AFL/AFC Player of the Year - 1974; Most Valuable Player (Bell) - 1976; PFW/PFWA Offensive Player of the Year - 1976; *Sporting News* AFC Player of the Year - 1976

Bart Starr (19)

Year	Team	PaYds	PaTD	PaInt	PaSkYds	RuYds	RuTD	Fum	APaY	ARuY	Q
1956	GB	325	2	3	–	35	0	0	67.5	35.0	1.1
1957	GB	1489	8	10	–	98	3	4	294.7	107.8	7.5
1958	GB	875	3	12	–	113	1	2	–36.5	112.0	1.0
1959	GB	972	6	7	30	83	0	2	169.5	74.5	2.8
1960	GB	1358	4	8	78	12	0	3	225.7	7.3	3.2
1961	GB	2418	16	16	138	56	1	8	283.5	53.5	3.6
1962	GB	2438	12	9	286	72	1	8	380.0	60.0	5.0
1963	GB	1855	15	10	109	116	0	5	353.2	106.3	4.7
1964	GB	2144	15	4	323	165	3	7	423.9	175.1	5.5
1965	GB	2055	16	9	303	169	1	2	414.3	174.2	6.2
1966	GB	2257	14	3	183	104	2	7	650.2	104.3	8.6
1967	GB	1823	9	17	322	90	0	3	–71.0	80.5	0.1
1968	GB	1617	15	8	261	62	1	2	266.7	67.8	3.5
1969	GB	1161	9	6	217	60	0	4	44.8	53.7	1.0
1970	GB	1645	8	13	252	62	1	6	–74.8	62.3	0.0
1971	GB	286	0	3	64	11	1	1	–63.8	18.8	0.0

Hall of Fame? Yes

Pro Bowl Appearances: 4

All-Pro Selections: Consensus - 1, Total - 4 (1961-1962; 1964; 1966)

Awards: Most Valuable Player (AP) - 1966; NEA NFL Player of the Year - 1966; *Sporting News* NFL Player of the Year - 1966; UPI NFL/NFC Player of the Year - 1966; MVP, Super Bowl I - 1966; Byron "Whizzer" White Award - 1967; MVP, Super Bowl II - 1967

Roger Staubach (10)

Year	Team	PaYds	PaTD	PaInt	PaSkYds	RuYds	RuTD	Fum	APaY	ARuY	Q
1969	DAL	421	1	2	106	60	1	2	−24.3	53.8	0.3
1970	DAL	542	2	8	130	221	0	4	−255.3	187.3	0.0
1971	DAL	1882	15	4	175	343	2	6	496.8	327.2	9.5
1972	DAL	98	0	2	59	45	0	1	−112.9	37.9	0.0
1973	DAL	2428	23	15	269	250	3	5	359.5	255.5	8.7
1974	DAL	2552	11	15	309	320	3	7	246.7	320.9	5.6
1975	DAL	2666	17	16	213	316	4	5	470.1	330.9	7.2
1976	DAL	2715	14	11	215	184	3	4	683.1	198.4	7.7
1977	DAL	2620	18	9	219	171	3	8	582.9	164.1	8.2
1978	DAL	3190	25	16	219	182	1	5	758.2	174.8	10.0
1979	DAL	3586	27	11	240	172	0	8	1005.2	149.8	10.0

Hall of Fame? Yes

Pro Bowl Appearances: 6

All-Pro Selections: Consensus - 3, Total - 5 (1971; 1976-1979)

Awards: Most Valuable Player (Bell) - 1971; *Sporting News* NFC Player of the Year - 1971; MVP, Super Bowl VI - 1971; Walter Payton NFL Man of the Year - 1978; Byron "Whizzer" White Award - 1979

Kordell Stewart (63)

Year	Team	PaYds	PaTD	PaInt	PaSkYds	RuYds	RuTD	Fum	APaY	ARuY	Q
1995	PIT	60	1	0	0	86	1	0	35.0	96.0	2.7
1996	PIT	100	0	2	37	171	5	1	−71.8	203.5	3.8
1997	PIT	3020	21	17	152	476	11	6	666.5	547.5	8.6
1998	PIT	2630	11	18	211	406	2	3	426.4	409.1	4.8
1999	PIT	1464	6	10	131	258	2	4	149.7	253.2	3.1
2000	PIT	1860	11	8	150	436	7	8	297.9	443.1	3.8
2001	PIT	3109	14	11	175	537	5	11	699.0	512.5	8.8
2002	PIT	1155	6	6	46	191	2	4	223.4	179.1	2.3
2003	CHIB	1418	7	12	146	290	3	7	−52.7	270.7	1.4
2004	BAL	0	0	0	0	−1	0	0	0.0	−1.0	0.1

Hall of Fame? Not eligible until 2010

Pro Bowl Appearances: 1

All-Pro Selections: None

Awards: PFW/PFWA Most Improved Player of the Year - 2001

Fran Tarkenton (9)

Year	Team	PaYds	PaTD	PaInt	PaSkYds	RuYds	RuTD	Fum	APaY	ARuY	Q
1961	MIN	1997	18	17	416	308	5	8	−195.3	310.8	1.2
1962	MIN	2595	22	25	450	361	2	5	−97.7	361.2	2.9
1963	MIN	2311	15	15	448	162	1	7	−1.1	150.6	1.5
1964	MIN	2506	22	11	446	330	2	6	321.9	320.1	5.8
1965	MIN	2609	19	11	250	356	1	5	591.6	338.9	9.7
1966	MIN	2561	17	16	322	376	4	8	206.9	372.6	6.6
1967	NYG	3088	29	19	283	306	2	4	596.6	310.4	7.7
1968	NYG	2555	21	12	255	301	3	2	638.3	320.2	10.0
1969	NYG	2918	23	8	289	172	0	7	746.5	150.5	9.3
1970	NYG	2777	19	12	249	236	2	3	705.5	245.0	8.0
1971	NYG	2567	11	21	232	111	3	4	222.3	130.2	4.0
1972	MIN	2651	18	13	203	180	0	3	645.0	172.5	9.4
1973	MIN	2113	15	7	270	202	1	5	440.2	188.3	8.9
1974	MIN	2598	17	12	142	120	2	2	746.3	135.7	8.9
1975	MIN	2994	25	13	245	108	2	1	883.4	126.6	9.1
1976	MIN	2961	17	8	221	45	1	4	913.8	45.7	8.4
1977	MIN	1734	9	14	232	6	0	3	76.1	−0.1	0.8
1978	MIN	3468	25	32	254	−6	1	7	215.8	−6.8	2.2

Hall of Fame? Yes

Pro Bowl Appearances: 9

All-Pro Selections: Consensus - 2, Total - 6 (1970; 1972-1976)

Awards: AP NFL Offensive Player of the Year - 1975; Most Valuable Player (AP) - 1975; Most Valuable Player (Bell) - 1975; NEA NFL Player of the Year - 1975; PFW/PFWA Offensive Player of the Year - 1975; *Sporting News* NFC Player of the Year - 1975; UPI NFL/NFC Player of the Year - 1975

Joe Theismann (36)

Year	Team	PaYds	PaTD	PaInt	PaSkYds	RuYds	RuTD	Fum	APaY	ARuY	Q
1974	WAS	145	1	0	11	12	1	0	66.5	22.0	0.9
1975	WAS	96	1	3	18	34	0	0	−70.0	34.0	0.0
1976	WAS	1036	8	10	172	97	1	2	−37.3	100.3	0.5
1977	WAS	1097	7	9	241	149	1	0	27.5	159.0	2.1
1978	WAS	2593	13	18	391	177	1	8	45.7	161.8	2.2
1979	WAS	2797	20	13	263	181	4	3	672.1	209.4	7.6
1980	WAS	2962	17	16	282	175	3	6	497.5	191.5	4.7
1981	WAS	3568	19	20	259	177	2	7	658.0	179.0	5.0
1982	WAS	2033	13	9	223	150	0	4	399.3	134.2	5.4
1983	WAS	3714	29	11	242	234	1	1	1337.8	241.2	9.7
1984	WAS	3391	24	13	341	314	1	7	769.1	294.4	5.8
1985	WAS	1774	8	16	314	115	2	4	−95.6	124.0	0.2

Hall of Fame? No

Pro Bowl Appearances: 2

All-Pro Selections: Consensus - 2, Total - 3 (1979; 1982-1983)

Awards: Most Valuable Player (Bell) - 1982; Walter Payton NFL Man of the Year - 1982; AP NFL Offensive Player of the Year - 1983; Most Valuable Player (AP) - 1983; NEA NFL Player of the Year - 1983; PFW/PFWA Offensive Player of the Year - 1983; Pro Bowl MVP - 1983

Y.A. Tittle (13)

Year	Team	PaYds	PaTD	PaInt	PaSkYds	RuYds	RuTD	Fum	APaY	ARuY	Q
1948	BAL	2522	16	9	–	157	4	–	1026.0	197.0	10.0
1949	BAL	2209	14	18	–	89	2	–	544.5	109.0	5.1
1950	BAL	1884	8	19	–	77	2	2	241.8	92.2	5.6
1951	SF	808	8	9	–	18	1	3	21.3	15.7	0.6
1952	SF	1407	11	12	–	–11	0	3	224.5	–17.0	3.4
1953	SF	2121	20	16	–	41	6	3	486.7	94.8	7.9
1954	SF	2205	9	9	–	68	4	4	686.4	94.1	9.6
1955	SF	2185	17	28	–	114	0	2	123.4	108.1	5.3
1956	SF	1641	7	12	249	67	4	3	78.4	95.1	1.8
1957	SF	2157	13	15	362	220	6	0	256.5	280.0	10.0
1958	SF	1467	9	15	149	35	2	5	–76.4	35.9	0.0
1959	SF	1331	10	15	–	24	0	7	–73.6	9.4	0.0
1960	SF	694	4	3	–	61	0	2	187.8	55.2	3.4
1961	NYG	2272	17	12	161	85	3	0	640.0	115.0	8.0
1962	NYG	3224	33	20	92	108	2	6	755.4	117.6	10.0
1963	NYG	3145	36	14	205	99	2	5	866.3	110.2	10.0
1964	NYG	1798	10	22	243	–7	1	11	–483.8	–17.2	0.0

Hall of Fame? Yes

Pro Bowl Appearances: 6

All-Pro Selections: Consensus - 3, Total - 4 (1957; 1961-1963)

Awards: UPI NFL/NFC Player of the Year - 1957; NEA NFL Player of the Year - 1961; *Sporting News* NFL Player of the Year - 1962; UPI NFL/NFC Player of the Year - 1962; Most Valuable Player (AP) - 1963; NEA NFL Player of the Year - 1963 (tie); *Sporting News* NFL Player of the Year - 1963

Johnny Unitas (5)

Year	Team	PaYds	PaTD	PaInt	PaSkYds	RuYds	RuTD	Fum	APaY	ARuY	Q
1956	BAL	1498	9	10	202	155	1	4	102.4	145.3	2.5
1957	BAL	2550	24	17	212	171	1	7	342.3	146.7	9.1
1958	BAL	2007	19	7	120	139	3	5	555.8	146.7	9.6
1959	BAL	2899	32	14	185	145	2	6	712.1	147.4	10.0
1960	BAL	3099	25	24	190	195	0	8	352.3	167.2	7.2
1961	BAL	2990	16	24	204	190	2	9	212.0	169.0	4.1
1962	BAL	2967	23	23	255	137	0	5	361.3	114.2	5.4
1963	BAL	3481	20	12	298	224	0	13	651.5	175.0	8.5
1964	BAL	2824	19	6	254	162	2	6	826.4	158.6	9.0
1965	BAL	2530	23	12	221	68	1	7	473.5	63.5	5.6
1966	BAL	2748	22	24	146	44	1	5	308.3	43.7	4.0
1967	BAL	3428	20	16	198	89	0	4	903.3	81.7	8.4
1968	BAL	139	2	4	15	−1	0	3	−185.8	−10.7	0.0
1969	BAL	2342	12	20	93	23	0	2	360.5	20.5	4.0
1970	BAL	2213	14	18	158	16	0	2	310.6	13.9	2.7
1971	BAL	942	3	9	129	5	0	3	−72.6	−0.4	0.0
1972	BAL	1111	4	6	114	15	0	3	133.6	12.9	1.7
1973	SD	471	3	7	96	0	0	3	−210.5	0.0	0.0

Hall of Fame? Yes

Pro Bowl Appearances: 10

All-Pro Selections: Consensus - 5, Total - 9 (1957-1960; 1963-1965; 1967; 1970)

Awards: NEA NFL Player of the Year - 1957; Most Valuable Player (Bell) - 1959; *Sporting News* NFL Player of the Year - 1959; UPI NFL/NFC Player of the Year - 1959; Most Valuable Player (AP) - 1964; Most Valuable Player (Bell) - 1964; *Sporting News* NFL Player of the Year - 1964; UPI NFL/NFC Player of the Year - 1964; Most Valuable Player (AP) - 1967; Most Valuable Player (Bell) - 1967; NEA NFL Player of the Year - 1967; *Sporting News* NFL Player of the Year - 1967; UPI NFL/NFC Player of the Year - 1967; Walter Payton NFL Man of the Year - 1970

Norm Van Brocklin (14)

Year	Team	PaYds	PaTD	PaInt	PaSkYds	RuYds	RuTD	Fum	APaY	ARuY	Q
1949	LARM	601	6	2	–	–1	0	2	188.0	–6.0	2.6
1950	LARM	2061	18	14	–	22	1	6	414.6	18.1	7.3
1951	LARM	1725	13	11	–	2	2	3	449.0	18.6	8.2
1952	LARM	1736	14	17	–	–10	0	5	172.9	–15.8	2.5
1953	LARM	2393	19	14	–	11	0	3	704.6	8.3	9.6
1954	LARM	2637	13	21	–	–10	0	3	547.9	–12.3	6.6
1955	LARM	1890	8	15	–	24	0	3	364.8	20.2	8.8
1956	LARM	966	7	12	–	1	1	2	41.6	9.2	2.0
1957	LARM	2105	20	21	–	–4	4	4	288.6	31.1	6.0
1958	PHI	2409	15	20	46	5	1	3	430.6	12.8	6.1
1959	PHI	2617	16	14	72	13	2	4	691.8	28.6	8.4
1960	PHI	2471	24	17	96	–13	0	7	440.5	–21.7	5.8

Hall of Fame? Yes

Pro Bowl Appearances: 9

All-Pro Selections: Consensus - 1, Total - 4 (1952; 1954-1955; 1960)

Awards: Most Valuable Player (AP) - 1960 (tie); Most Valuable Player (Bell) - 1960; NEA NFL Player of the Year - 1960; *Sporting News* NFL Player of the Year - 1960; UPI NFL/NFC Player of the Year - 1960

Billy Wade (55)

Year	Team	PaYds	PaTD	PaInt	PaSkYds	RuYds	RuTD	Fum	APaY	ARuY	Q
1954	LARM	509	2	1	–	190	1	5	93.9	135.6	2.8
1955	LARM	316	1	3	–	43	0	4	–80.5	21.5	0.0
1956	LARM	1461	10	13	–	93	3	4	185.9	102.6	3.0
1957	LARM	116	1	1	–	5	0	0	28.0	5.0	0.6
1958	LARM	2875	18	22	–	90	2	14	258.9	48.6	4.2
1959	LARM	2001	12	17	–	95	2	6	246.5	94.0	4.0
1960	LARM	1294	12	11	–	171	2	5	147.0	166.0	4.4
1961	CHIB	2258	22	13	–	255	2	3	682.3	256.7	10.0
1962	CHIB	3172	18	24	–	146	5	7	580.8	171.2	8.6
1963	CHIB	2301	15	12	–	132	6	5	627.9	169.6	8.2
1964	CHIB	1944	13	14	157	96	1	2	315.1	100.9	3.8
1965	CHIB	204	0	2	40	18	0	2	–80.2	10.2	0.0
1966	CHIB	79	0	1	0	0	0	0	4.5	0.0	0.1

Hall of Fame? No

Pro Bowl Appearances: None

All-Pro Selections: Consensus - 0, Total - 2 (1962-1963)

Awards: None

Kurt Warner (70)

Year	Team	PaYds	PaTD	PaInt	PaSkYds	RuYds	RuTD	Fum	APaY	ARuY	Q
1998	STL	39	0	0	0	0	0	0	19.5	0.0	0.1
1999	STL	4353	41	13	201	92	1	9	1380.5	87.0	10.0
2000	STL	3429	21	18	115	17	0	4	922.0	9.5	4.7
2001	STL	4830	36	22	233	60	0	10	1210.3	41.7	9.1
2002	STL	1431	3	11	130	33	0	8	−94.2	22.7	0.0
2003	STL	365	1	1	38	0	0	6	−122.2	−3.3	0.0
2004	NYG	2054	6	4	196	30	1	12	260.0	21.0	1.4
2005	ARI	2713	11	9	158	28	0	9	590.7	16.6	4.2
2006	ARI	1377	6	5	104	3	0	10	66.2	−23.7	0.2
2007	ARI	3417	27	17	140	15	1	12	645.2	8.3	3.1

Hall of Fame? Not eligible (active)

Pro Bowl Appearances: 3

All-Pro Selections: Consensus - 2, Total - 2 (1999; 2001)

Awards: Most Valuable Player (AP) - 1999; Most Valuable Player (Bell) - 1999; PFW/PFWA Offensive Player of the Year - 1999; *Sporting News* NFL Player of the Year - 1999; MVP, Super Bowl XXXIV - 1999; Most Valuable Player (AP) - 2001

Bob Waterfield (59)

Year	Team	PaYds	PaTD	PaInt	PaSkYds	RuYds	RuTD	Fum	APaY	ARuY	Q
1945	CLE	1609	14	17	–	18	5	9	48.9	43.7	1.8
1946	LARM	1747	17	17	–	–60	1	6	192.8	–60.9	10.0
1947	LARM	1210	8	18	–	6	1	2	–38.3	15.3	3.2
1948	LARM	1354	14	18	–	12	0	5	–9.3	7.1	2.4
1949	LARM	2168	17	24	–	–4	1	4	213.8	4.1	3.2
1950	LARM	1540	11	13	–	14	1	4	271.2	20.3	4.9
1951	LARM	1566	13	10	–	49	3	2	442.8	76.2	9.1
1952	LARM	655	3	11	–	–14	1	4	–124.8	–10.8	1.8

Hall of Fame? Yes

Pro Bowl Appearances: 2

All-Pro Selections: Consensus - 3, Total - 5 (1945-1946; 1949-1951)

Awards: Most Valuable Player (Carr) - 1945

Danny White (58)

Year	Team	PaYds	PaTD	PaInt	PaSkYds	RuYds	RuTD	Fum	APaY	ARuY	Q
1976	DAL	213	2	2	15	17	0	0	31.5	17.0	0.4
1977	DAL	35	0	1	15	−2	0	0	−32.5	−2.0	2.0
1978	DAL	215	0	1	10	7	0	2	38.4	3.6	1.6
1979	DAL	267	1	2	46	25	0	1	8.2	24.7	2.3
1980	DAL	3287	28	25	252	114	1	8	392.6	108.7	3.4
1981	DAL	3098	22	13	234	104	0	14	531.8	64.4	3.6
1982	DAL	2079	16	12	264	91	0	10	101.8	70.1	1.7
1983	DAL	3980	29	23	314	31	4	10	652.4	59.5	4.5
1984	DAL	1580	11	11	178	21	0	2	222.5	19.6	1.3
1985	DAL	3157	21	17	257	44	1	6	602.9	43.5	5.3
1986	DAL	1157	12	5	98	16	1	6	136.7	14.8	1.1
1987	DAL	2617	12	17	353	14	1	9	69.2	15.3	0.6
1988	DAL	274	1	3	47	0	0	0	−10.0	0.0	0.0

Hall of Fame? No

Pro Bowl Appearances: 1

All-Pro Selections: Consensus - 0, Total - 3 (1979; 1981-1982)

Awards: None

Steve Young (7)

Year	Team	PaYds	PaTD	PaInt	PaSkYds	RuYds	RuTD	Fum	APaY	ARuY	Q
1985	TB	935	3	8	158	233	1	4	−83.3	210.8	1.0
1986	TB	2282	8	13	326	425	5	11	27.3	407.7	3.2
1987	SF	570	10	0	25	190	1	0	310.0	200.0	3.6
1988	SF	680	3	3	75	184	1	5	13.3	155.7	1.4
1989	SF	1001	8	3	84	126	2	2	292.9	124.6	3.0
1990	SF	427	2	0	41	159	0	1	149.6	151.9	1.9
1991	SF	2517	17	8	79	415	4	3	886.6	432.9	10.0
1992	SF	3465	25	7	152	537	4	9	1154.5	523.0	10.0
1993	SF	4023	29	16	160	407	2	8	1156.8	387.9	10.0
1994	SF	3969	35	10	163	293	7	4	1503.4	346.1	10.0
1995	SF	3200	20	11	115	250	3	3	1091.5	268.5	8.4
1996	SF	2410	14	6	160	310	4	3	800.5	334.5	9.3
1997	SF	3029	19	6	220	199	3	4	1037.6	210.9	8.8
1998	SF	4170	36	12	234	454	6	9	1290.7	474.3	10.0
1999	SF	446	3	4	63	57	0	2	−36.5	48.5	0.1

Hall of Fame? Yes

Pro Bowl Appearances: None

All-Pro Selections: Consensus - 4, Total - 7 (1992-1998)

Awards: AP NFL Offensive Player of the Year - 1992; Most Valuable Player (AP) - 1992; Most Valuable Player (Bell) - 1992; PFW/PFWA Offensive Player of the Year - 1992; *Sporting News* NFL Player of the Year - 1992; UPI NFC Offensive Player of the Year - 1992; Most Valuable Player (AP) - 1994; Most Valuable Player (Bell) - 1994; PFW/PFWA Offensive Player of the Year - 1994; *Sporting News* NFL Player of the Year - 1994; UPI NFC Offensive Player of the Year - 1994; MVP, Super Bowl XXIX - 1994

Running Backs

Shaun Alexander (36)

Year	Team	RuYds	RuTD	ReYds	ReTD	Fum	ARuY	AReY	ASptY	Q
2000	SEA	313	2	41	0	2	258.8	14.7	0.0	1.4
2001	SEA	1318	14	343	2	4	1317.9	161.6	0.0	8.2
2002	SEA	1175	16	460	2	3	1235.0	220.0	0.0	6.8
2003	SEA	1435	14	295	2	4	1433.3	139.2	0.0	7.5
2004	SEA	1696	16	170	4	5	1668.2	92.8	0.0	9.4
2005	SEA	1880	27	78	1	5	1957.8	36.2	0.0	9.1
2006	SEA	896	7	48	0	6	736.9	13.1	0.0	3.3
2007	SEA	716	4	76	1	2	681.1	37.9	0.0	3.8

Hall of Fame? Not eligible (active)

Pro Bowl Appearances: 3

All-Pro Selections: Consensus - 2, Total - 2 (2004-2005)

Awards: AP NFL Offensive Player of the Year - 2005; Most Valuable Player (AP) - 2005; Most Valuable Player (Bell) - 2005; PFW/PFWA Offensive Player of the Year - 2005; *Sporting News* NFL Player of the Year - 2005

Marcus Allen (16)

Year	Team	RuYds	RuTD	ReYds	ReTD	Fum	ARuY	AReY	ASptY	Q
1982	LARI	697	11	401	3	5	648.6	177.9	0.0	10.0
1983	LARI	1014	9	590	2	14	671.0	194.3	0.0	5.2
1984	LARI	1168	13	758	5	8	1042.2	344.5	0.0	7.9
1985	LARI	1759	11	555	3	3	1767.4	274.6	0.0	10.0
1986	LARI	759	5	453	2	7	579.7	185.8	0.0	4.9
1987	LARI	754	5	410	0	3	709.5	180.9	0.0	7.3
1988	LARI	831	7	303	1	5	729.5	130.3	0.0	4.8
1989	LARI	293	2	191	0	2	251.0	77.5	0.0	2.3
1990	LARI	682	12	189	1	1	765.3	96.4	0.0	5.4
1991	LARI	287	2	131	0	1	275.5	58.0	0.0	2.1
1992	LARI	301	2	277	1	1	292.8	131.7	0.0	2.2
1993	KC	764	12	238	3	4	746.7	111.3	0.0	5.3
1994	KC	709	7	349	0	3	680.8	152.7	0.0	4.0
1995	KC	890	5	210	0	2	869.2	95.8	0.0	5.0
1996	KC	830	9	270	0	2	849.6	125.8	0.0	6.0
1997	KC	505	11	86	0	4	470.2	30.2	0.0	2.3

Hall of Fame? Yes

Pro Bowl Appearances: 6

All-Pro Selections: Consensus - 4, Total - 5 (1982; 1984-1986; 1993)

Awards: AP NFL Offensive Rookie of the Year - 1982; NEA NFL Rookie of the Year - 1982; PFW/PFWA Offensive Rookie of the Year - 1982; *Sporting News* NFL Rookie of the Year - 1982; UPI AFL/AFC Rookie of the Year - 1982; MVP, Super Bowl XVIII - 1983; AP NFL Offensive Player of the Year - 1985; Most Valuable Player (AP) - 1985; *Sporting News* NFL Player of the Year - 1985; UPI AFC Offensive Player of the Year - 1985; Comeback Player of the Year - 1993; PFW/PFWA Comeback Player of the Year - 1993

Terry Allen (70)

Year	Team	RuYds	RuTD	ReYds	ReTD	Fum	ARuY	AReY	ASptY	Q
1991	MIN	563	2	49	1	4	431.8	21.9	–7.3	2.7
1992	MIN	1201	13	478	2	9	1027.0	193.0	0.0	6.4
1994	MIN	1031	8	148	0	3	998.5	66.5	0.0	5.1
1995	WAS	1309	10	232	1	6	1189.2	100.8	0.0	6.7
1996	WAS	1353	21	194	0	4	1416.5	83.5	0.0	9.2
1997	WAS	724	4	172	1	2	691.0	84.0	0.0	3.5
1998	WAS	700	2	128	0	4	576.5	47.5	0.0	2.8
1999	NE	896	8	125	1	8	672.7	50.8	0.0	3.8
2000	NO	179	2	7	0	0	199.0	3.5	6.0	1.0
2001	BAL	658	3	68	0	1	651.7	30.3	0.0	3.8

Hall of Fame? No

Pro Bowl Appearances: 1

All-Pro Selections: Consensus - 1, Total - 3 (1994-1996)

Awards: None

Neal Anderson (53)

Year	Team	RuYds	RuTD	ReYds	ReTD	Fum	ARuY	AReY	ASptY	Q
1986	CHIB	146	0	80	1	1	113.4	41.3	–57.7	1.0
1987	CHIB	586	3	467	3	2	557.4	227.1	0.0	6.4
1988	CHIB	1106	12	371	0	8	950.3	142.3	0.0	6.1
1989	CHIB	1275	11	434	4	5	1215.9	206.1	0.0	10.0
1990	CHIB	1078	10	484	3	2	1109.1	245.9	0.0	8.9
1991	CHIB	747	6	368	3	5	644.2	162.6	0.0	4.8
1992	CHIB	582	5	399	6	6	442.9	178.6	0.0	3.3
1993	CHIB	646	4	160	0	2	616.9	69.4	0.0	4.2

Hall of Fame? No

Pro Bowl Appearances: 4

All-Pro Selections: Consensus - 2, Total - 4 (1986; 1988-1990)

Awards: None

Ottis Anderson (19)

Year	Team	RuYds	RuTD	ReYds	ReTD	Fum	ARuY	AReY	ASptY	Q
1979	STL	1605	8	308	2	10	1330.0	120.0	0.0	8.7
1980	STL	1352	9	308	0	5	1263.4	132.6	0.0	7.1
1981	STL	1376	9	387	0	13	1016.0	123.5	0.0	7.5
1982	STL	587	3	106	0	2	544.0	46.0	0.0	7.0
1983	STL	1270	5	459	1	10	981.7	172.8	0.0	6.7
1984	STL	1174	6	611	2	8	976.4	253.1	0.0	6.9
1985	STL	479	4	225	0	3	418.7	92.8	0.0	2.5
1986	STL	156	2	91	0	2	109.1	32.4	0.0	0.9
1986	NYG	81	1	46	0	0	91.0	23.0	0.0	0.7
1987	NYG	6	0	16	0	0	6.0	8.0	0.0	0.1
1988	NYG	208	8	57	0	0	288.0	28.5	0.0	1.8
1989	NYG	1023	14	268	0	2	1089.3	127.7	0.0	8.6
1990	NYG	784	11	139	0	1	857.0	66.5	0.0	6.0
1991	NYG	141	1	41	0	0	151.0	20.5	0.0	1.0
1992	NYG	31	0	0	0	0	31.0	0.0	0.0	0.2

Hall of Fame? No

Pro Bowl Appearances: 2

All-Pro Selections: Consensus - 2, Total - 2 (1979-1980)

Awards: AP NFL Offensive Rookie of the Year - 1979; NEA NFL Rookie of the Year - 1979; PFW/PFWA Offensive Rookie of the Year - 1979; *Sporting News* NFC Rookie of the Year - 1979; UPI NFL/NFC Rookie of the Year - 1979; *Sporting News* NFC Player of the Year - 1979; UPI NFL/NFC Player of the Year - 1979; Comeback Player of the Year - 1989; PFW/PFWA Comeback Player of the Year - 1989; MVP, Super Bowl XXV - 1990

William Andrews (46)

Year	Team	RuYds	RuTD	ReYds	ReTD	Fum	ARuY	AReY	ASptY	Q
1979	ATL	1023	3	309	2	5	881.1	136.4	0.0	6.1
1980	ATL	1308	4	456	1	6	1146.7	194.3	0.0	6.8
1981	ATL	1301	10	735	2	12	1026.1	272.4	0.0	8.6
1982	ATL	573	5	503	2	1	592.5	252.3	0.0	10.0
1983	ATL	1567	7	609	4	6	1433.8	288.3	0.0	10.0
1986	ATL	214	1	35	0	0	224.0	17.5	−9.0	1.5

Hall of Fame? No

Pro Bowl Appearances: 4

All-Pro Selections: Consensus - 2, Total - 4 (1980-1983)

Awards: None

Tiki Barber (23)

Year	Team	RuYds	RuTD	ReYds	ReTD	Fum	ARuY	AReY	ASptY	Q
1997	NYG	511	3	299	1	3	445.0	130.5	0.0	2.6
1998	NYG	166	0	348	3	1	146.7	173.4	−35.2	1.4
1999	NYG	258	0	609	2	5	195.1	247.5	471.9	2.3
2000	NYG	1006	8	719	1	9	862.4	291.0	277.0	5.8
2001	NYG	865	4	577	0	8	720.6	208.5	282.4	5.1
2002	NYG	1387	11	597	0	9	1205.2	232.3	3.1	6.7
2003	NYG	1216	2	461	1	9	947.6	163.9	0.0	5.3
2004	NYG	1518	13	578	2	5	1475.8	271.2	0.0	9.3
2005	NYG	1860	9	530	2	1	1915.3	269.8	0.0	10.0
2006	NYG	1662	5	465	0	3	1610.1	214.4	0.0	7.9

Hall of Fame? Not eligible until 2011

Pro Bowl Appearances: 2

All-Pro Selections: Consensus - 3, Total - 3 (2002; 2004-2005)

Awards: None

Cliff Battles (37)

Year	Team	RuYds	RuTD	ReYds	ReTD	Fum	ARuY	AReY	ASptY	Q
1932	BOS	576	3	60	1	–	606.0	35.0	0.0	9.7
1933	BOS	737	3	185	0	–	767.0	92.5	10.0	10.0
1934	BOS	480	6	95	1	–	540.0	52.5	0.0	5.3
1935	BOS	230	1	22	0	–	240.0	11.0	10.0	4.0
1936	BOS	614	5	103	1	–	664.0	56.5	10.0	7.2
1937	WAS	874	5	81	1	–	924.0	45.5	0.0	10.0

Hall of Fame? Yes

Pro Bowl Appearances: None

All-Pro Selections: Consensus - 3, Total - 6 (1932-1937)

Awards: None

Jerome Bettis (24)

Year	Team	RuYds	RuTD	ReYds	ReTD	Fum	ARuY	AReY	ASptY	Q
1993	LARM	1429	7	244	0	4	1352.0	109.0	0.0	9.0
1994	LARM	1025	3	293	1	5	872.7	133.8	0.0	4.8
1995	STL	637	3	106	0	4	521.3	38.7	0.0	2.9
1996	PIT	1431	11	122	0	7	1279.0	43.0	0.0	8.1
1997	PIT	1665	7	110	2	6	1504.2	55.8	0.0	7.1
1998	PIT	1185	3	90	0	2	1138.9	41.1	0.0	5.2
1999	PIT	1091	7	110	0	2	1086.5	49.8	0.0	6.0
2000	PIT	1341	8	97	0	1	1382.6	47.1	0.0	7.0
2001	PIT	1072	4	48	0	3	997.1	19.9	0.0	5.7
2002	PIT	666	9	57	0	1	717.4	27.1	0.0	3.5
2003	PIT	811	7	86	0	5	691.0	33.0	0.0	3.5
2004	PIT	941	13	46	0	1	1032.1	22.1	0.0	5.7
2005	PIT	368	9	40	0	0	458.0	20.0	0.0	2.2

Hall of Fame? Not eligible until 2010

Pro Bowl Appearances: 6

All-Pro Selections: Consensus - 3, Total - 3 (1993; 1996-1997)

Awards: AP NFL Offensive Rookie of the Year - 1993; PFW/PFWA Offensive Rookie of the Year - 1993; *Sporting News* NFL Rookie of the Year - 1993; UPI NFL/NFC Rookie of the Year - 1993; Comeback Player of the Year - 1996; PFW/PFWA Comeback Player of the Year - 1996; Walter Payton NFL Man of the Year - 2001

James Brooks (41)

Year	Team	RuYds	RuTD	ReYds	ReTD	Fum	ARuY	AReY	ASptY	Q
1981	SD	525	3	329	3	7	418.1	121.7	353.6	3.6
1982	SD	430	6	66	0	4	396.6	19.0	174.4	4.9
1983	SD	516	3	215	0	8	348.7	68.7	20.1	2.4
1984	CIN	396	2	268	2	4	301.6	106.2	−3.8	2.3
1985	CIN	929	7	576	5	7	784.8	251.6	−25.3	5.1
1986	CIN	1087	5	686	4	2	1073.9	346.4	0.0	9.1
1987	CIN	290	1	272	2	0	300.0	146.0	2.0	3.6
1988	CIN	931	8	287	6	1	976.7	168.0	−26.2	6.4
1989	CIN	1239	7	306	2	9	1000.6	111.4	0.0	7.8
1990	CIN	1004	5	269	4	3	948.1	140.4	0.0	7.1
1991	CIN	571	2	348	2	5	441.2	144.6	−40.8	3.5
1992	CLE	38	0	−1	0	0	38.0	−0.5	0.0	0.2
1992	TB	6	0	0	0	1	−19.0	0.0	−26.0	0.0

Hall of Fame? No

Pro Bowl Appearances: 4

All-Pro Selections: Consensus - 1, Total - 4 (1986; 1988-1990)

Awards: None

Jim Brown (1)

Year	Team	RuYds	RuTD	ReYds	ReTD	Fum	ARuY	AReY	ASptY	Q
1957	CLE	942	9	55	1	7	779.5	12.5	8.5	9.8
1958	CLE	1527	17	138	1	5	1510.8	62.4	11.8	10.0
1959	CLE	1329	14	190	0	2	1396.0	89.0	7.0	10.0
1960	CLE	1257	9	204	2	9	1016.2	82.8	0.0	10.0
1961	CLE	1408	8	459	2	6	1282.4	208.5	8.7	10.0
1962	CLE	996	13	517	5	9	829.2	222.9	0.0	7.0
1963	CLE	1863	12	268	3	7	1728.4	128.0	0.0	10.0
1964	CLE	1446	7	340	2	6	1304.0	152.7	0.0	10.0
1965	CLE	1544	17	328	4	6	1500.6	158.9	0.0	10.0

Hall of Fame? Yes

Pro Bowl Appearances: 9

All-Pro Selections: Consensus - 8, Total - 9 (1957-1965)

Awards: Sporting News NFL Rookie of the Year - 1957; UPI NFL/NFC Rookie of the Year - 1957; Most Valuable Player (AP) - 1957; *Sporting News* NFL Player of the Year - 1957; NEA NFL Player of the Year - 1958; *Sporting News* NFL Player of the Year - 1958; UPI NFL/NFC Player of the Year - 1958; Most Valuable Player (Bell) - 1963; NEA NFL Player of the Year - 1963 (tie); UPI NFL/NFC Player of the Year - 1963; Most Valuable Player (AP) - 1965; NEA NFL Player of the Year - 1965; *Sporting News* NFL Player of the Year - 1965; UPI NFL/NFC Player of the Year - 1965

Larry Brown (54)

Year	Team	RuYds	RuTD	ReYds	ReTD	Fum	ARuY	AReY	ASptY	Q
1969	WAS	888	4	302	0	6	722.6	116.4	0.0	7.3
1970	WAS	1125	5	341	2	6	967.4	148.1	0.0	9.3
1971	WAS	948	4	176	2	6	762.3	83.7	0.0	7.2
1972	WAS	1216	8	473	4	9	972.3	220.2	0.0	8.5
1973	WAS	860	8	482	6	7	695.8	235.2	0.0	5.0
1974	WAS	430	3	388	4	2	395.1	199.3	0.0	4.0
1975	WAS	352	3	225	2	2	318.4	106.1	0.0	2.2
1976	WAS	56	0	98	0	2	12.8	12.2	0.0	0.2

Hall of Fame? No

Pro Bowl Appearances: None

All-Pro Selections: Consensus - 3, Total - 3 (1970-1972)

Awards: AP NFL Offensive Player of the Year - 1972; Most Valuable Player (AP) - 1972; Most Valuable Player (Bell) - 1972; NEA NFL Player of the Year - 1972; PFW/PFWA Offensive Player of the Year - 1972; *Sporting News* NFC Player of the Year - 1972; UPI NFL/NFC Player of the Year - 1972

Earnest Byner (49)

Year	Team	RuYds	RuTD	ReYds	ReTD	Fum	ARuY	AReY	ASptY	Q
1984	CLE	426	2	118	0	3	363.7	46.4	−50.1	2.3
1985	CLE	1002	8	460	2	5	913.1	208.9	0.0	5.5
1986	CLE	277	2	328	2	1	268.3	162.7	0.0	2.8
1987	CLE	432	8	552	2	5	379.1	220.2	−19.3	4.9
1988	CLE	576	3	576	2	5	460.6	243.4	0.0	3.9
1989	WAS	580	7	458	2	2	593.3	216.1	0.0	5.7
1990	WAS	1219	6	279	1	2	1207.0	137.0	0.0	8.9
1991	WAS	1048	5	308	0	3	992.6	140.9	0.0	6.9
1992	WAS	998	6	338	1	1	1023.5	168.9	0.0	6.4
1993	WAS	105	1	194	0	0	115.0	97.0	0.0	1.3
1994	CLE	219	2	102	0	0	239.0	51.0	0.0	1.4
1995	CLE	432	2	494	2	1	426.6	243.5	−3.1	3.5
1996	BAL	634	4	270	1	1	641.0	133.8	−19.8	4.7
1997	BAL	313	0	128	0	2	249.6	48.2	−20.8	1.3

Hall of Fame? No

Pro Bowl Appearances: 2

All-Pro Selections: Consensus - 0, Total - 3 (1987; 1990-1991)

Awards: None

Earl Campbell (21)

Year	Team	RuYds	RuTD	ReYds	ReTD	Fum	ARuY	AReY	ASptY	Q
1978	HOU	1450	13	48	0	9	1233.8	10.2	0.0	8.1
1979	HOU	1697	19	94	0	8	1580.3	33.7	0.0	9.7
1980	HOU	1934	13	47	0	4	1909.4	18.9	0.0	10.0
1981	HOU	1376	10	156	0	10	1112.3	41.7	0.0	7.6
1982	HOU	538	2	130	0	2	486.6	56.8	0.0	6.0
1983	HOU	1301	12	216	0	4	1269.9	99.1	0.0	8.0
1984	HOU	278	4	27	0	2	240.4	11.1	0.0	1.4
1984	NO	190	0	0	0	0	190.0	0.0	0.0	1.1
1985	NO	643	1	88	0	4	498.9	38.1	0.0	2.6

Hall of Fame? Yes

Pro Bowl Appearances: 5

All-Pro Selections: Consensus - 3, Total - 4 (1978-1981)

Awards: AP NFL Offensive Rookie of the Year - 1978; NEA NFL Rookie of the Year - 1978; PFW/PFWA Offensive Rookie of the Year - 1978; *Sporting News* AFC Rookie of the Year - 1978; UPI AFL/AFC Rookie of the Year - 1978; AP NFL Offensive Player of the Year - 1978; NEA NFL Player of the Year - 1978; PFW/PFWA Offensive Player of the Year - 1978; *Sporting News* AFC Player of the Year - 1978; UPI AFL/AFC Player of the Year - 1978; AP NFL Offensive Player of the Year - 1979; Most Valuable Player (AP) - 1979; Most Valuable Player (Bell) - 1979; NEA NFL Player of the Year - 1979; PFW/PFWA Offensive Player of the Year - 1979; AP NFL Offensive Player of the Year - 1980; NEA NFL Player of the Year - 1980

Tony Canadeo (65)

Year	Team	RuYds	RuTD	ReYds	ReTD	Fum	ARuY	AReY	ASptY	Q
1941	GB	137	3	0	0	–	167.0	0.0	56.0	2.7
1942	GB	272	3	66	0	–	302.0	33.0	93.0	4.5
1943	GB	489	3	31	2	–	519.0	25.5	135.0	7.2
1944	GB	149	0	12	0	–	149.0	6.0	–4.0	2.6
1946	GB	476	0	25	0	3	386.2	11.0	110.2	7.3
1947	GB	464	2	0	0	0	484.0	0.0	123.0	4.9
1948	GB	589	4	81	0	5	469.3	28.8	24.1	5.8
1949	GB	1052	4	–2	0	6	857.6	–4.4	–22.3	7.2
1950	GB	247	4	54	0	4	167.0	14.1	131.9	2.5
1951	GB	131	1	226	2	2	87.0	101.0	17.0	2.4
1952	GB	191	2	86	1	4	77.7	29.5	19.8	1.2

Hall of Fame? Yes

Pro Bowl Appearances: None

All-Pro Selections: Consensus - 2, Total - 4 (1943; 1947-1949)

Awards: None

Rick Casares (51)

Year	Team	RuYds	RuTD	ReYds	ReTD	Fum	ARuY	AReY	ASptY	Q
1955	CHIB	672	4	136	1	3	607.8	59.7	0.0	6.5
1956	CHIB	1126	12	203	2	5	1068.7	94.1	32.7	10.0
1957	CHIB	700	6	225	0	2	690.3	104.0	−20.3	10.0
1958	CHIB	651	2	290	1	5	505.0	119.8	0.0	4.0
1959	CHIB	699	10	273	2	7	560.7	110.2	0.0	4.3
1960	CHIB	566	5	64	0	5	426.7	22.5	0.0	4.1
1961	CHIB	588	8	69	0	1	630.2	32.3	0.0	4.4
1962	CHIB	255	2	71	1	4	137.1	22.1	0.0	1.2
1963	CHIB	277	0	94	1	2	216.5	34.3	−23.9	1.4
1964	CHIB	123	0	113	2	1	94.4	55.1	0.0	1.0
1965	WAS	5	0	5	0	0	5.0	2.5	0.0	0.0
1966	MIA	135	0	45	1	0	135.0	27.5	0.0	1.2

Hall of Fame? No

Pro Bowl Appearances: 5

All-Pro Selections: Consensus - 1, Total - 4 (1955-1958)

Awards: None

Roger Craig (30)

Year	Team	RuYds	RuTD	ReYds	ReTD	Fum	ARuY	AReY	ASptY	Q
1983	SF	725	8	427	4	6	616.4	182.1	0.0	4.6
1984	SF	649	7	675	3	3	636.7	314.8	0.0	5.4
1985	SF	1050	9	1016	6	5	1000.1	477.9	0.0	7.2
1986	SF	830	7	624	0	4	785.5	266.5	0.0	6.7
1987	SF	815	3	492	1	5	692.0	204.0	0.0	7.3
1988	SF	1502	9	534	1	8	1336.3	209.3	−9.6	8.6
1989	SF	1054	6	473	1	4	978.5	217.0	0.0	8.4
1990	SF	439	1	201	0	2	381.0	88.5	0.0	3.1
1991	LARI	590	1	136	0	2	527.6	60.4	0.0	3.5
1992	MIN	416	4	164	0	2	389.9	68.1	0.0	2.4
1993	MIN	119	1	169	1	1	102.8	76.4	−9.7	1.1

Hall of Fame? No

Pro Bowl Appearances: 4

All-Pro Selections: Consensus - 2, Total - 4 (1985; 1987-1989)

Awards: AP NFL Offensive Player of the Year - 1988; NEA NFL Player of the Year - 1988; UPI NFC Offensive Player of the Year - 1988

Larry Csonka (25)

Year	Team	RuYds	RuTD	ReYds	ReTD	Fum	ARuY	AReY	ASptY	Q
1968	MIA	540	6	118	1	3	488.9	55.1	0.0	5.4
1969	MIA	566	2	183	1	1	551.5	91.0	0.0	6.9
1970	MIA	874	6	94	0	3	820.5	40.5	0.0	7.2
1971	MIA	1051	7	113	1	0	1121.0	61.5	0.0	10.0
1972	MIA	1117	6	48	0	2	1098.8	22.2	0.0	8.0
1973	MIA	1003	5	22	0	3	936.7	7.3	0.0	5.0
1974	MIA	749	9	35	0	2	761.7	14.8	0.0	5.2
1976	NYG	569	4	39	0	2	531.9	16.6	0.0	3.7
1977	NYG	464	1	20	0	0	474.0	10.0	0.0	2.8
1978	NYG	311	6	73	0	1	333.9	33.6	0.0	2.4
1979	MIA	837	12	75	1	4	807.8	31.7	0.0	5.0

Hall of Fame? Yes

Pro Bowl Appearances: 5

All-Pro Selections: Consensus - 3, Total - 4 (1970-1973)

Awards: MVP, Super Bowl VIII - 1973; Comeback Player of the Year - 1979; PFW/PFWA Comeback Player of the Year - 1979

Clem Daniels (44)

Year	Team	RuYds	RuTD	ReYds	ReTD	Fum	ARuY	AReY	ASptY	Q
1960	DTX	-2	0	0	0	1	-5.1	0.0	14.1	0.0
1961	OAK	154	2	150	0	3	114.0	49.8	15.2	1.4
1962	OAK	766	7	318	1	8	590.7	127.4	13.4	5.3
1963	OAK	1099	3	685	5	8	849.5	328.3	0.0	10.0
1964	OAK	824	2	696	6	9	557.0	308.3	10.3	7.4
1965	OAK	884	5	568	7	6	729.5	285.4	0.0	8.8
1966	OAK	801	7	652	3	7	639.7	295.7	0.0	6.7
1967	OAK	575	4	222	2	2	544.3	112.3	0.0	4.9
1968	SF	37	0	23	0	0	37.0	11.5	6.0	0.4

Hall of Fame? No

Pro Bowl Appearances: 4

All-Pro Selections: Consensus - 2, Total - 4 (1963-1966)

Awards: None

Terrell Davis (59)

Year	Team	RuYds	RuTD	ReYds	ReTD	Fum	ARuY	AReY	ASptY	Q
1995	DEN	1117	7	367	1	5	1021.3	154.2	0.0	6.1
1996	DEN	1538	13	310	2	5	1486.9	146.1	0.0	10.0
1997	DEN	1750	15	287	0	4	1756.4	127.1	0.0	8.5
1998	DEN	2008	21	217	2	2	2142.8	113.7	0.0	10.0
1999	DEN	211	2	26	0	1	192.7	11.3	0.0	1.1
2000	DEN	282	2	4	0	1	263.0	1.0	0.0	1.3
2001	DEN	701	0	69	0	2	626.4	29.1	0.0	3.6

Hall of Fame? No

Pro Bowl Appearances: 3

All-Pro Selections: Consensus - 3, Total - 4 (1995-1998)

Awards: AP NFL Offensive Player of the Year - 1996; UPI AFC Offensive Player of the Year - 1996; MVP, Super Bowl XXXII - 1997; AP NFL Offensive Player of the Year - 1998; Most Valuable Player (AP) - 1998; PFW/PFWA Offensive Player of the Year - 1998; *Sporting News* NFL Player of the Year - 1998

Eric Dickerson (5)

Year	Team	RuYds	RuTD	ReYds	ReTD	Fum	ARuY	AReY	ASptY	Q
1983	LARM	1808	18	404	2	13	1528.1	151.9	0.0	9.8
1984	LARM	2105	14	139	0	14	1715.7	40.2	0.0	9.7
1985	LARM	1234	12	126	0	10	979.6	37.4	0.0	5.0
1986	LARM	1821	11	205	0	12	1481.1	73.5	0.0	10.0
1987	LARM	277	1	38	0	2	213.2	12.8	0.0	1.8
1987	IND	1011	5	133	0	5	872.0	55.5	0.0	7.6
1988	IND	1659	14	377	1	5	1616.0	176.5	0.0	10.0
1989	IND	1311	7	211	1	10	1016.9	75.7	0.0	7.6
1990	IND	677	4	92	0	0	717.0	46.0	0.0	5.0
1991	IND	536	2	269	1	6	363.3	92.2	0.0	2.7
1992	LARI	729	2	85	1	1	711.8	44.7	0.0	4.0
1993	ATL	91	0	58	0	0	91.0	29.0	0.0	0.7

Hall of Fame? Yes

Pro Bowl Appearances: 6

All-Pro Selections: Consensus - 5, Total - 5 (1983-1984; 1986-1988)

Awards: AP NFL Offensive Rookie of the Year - 1983; NEA NFL Rookie of the Year - 1983; PFW/PFWA Offensive Rookie of the Year - 1983; UPI NFL/NFC Rookie of the Year - 1983; *Sporting News* NFL Player of the Year - 1983; UPI NFC Offensive Player of the Year - 1983; UPI NFC Offensive Player of the Year - 1984; AP NFL Offensive Player of the Year - 1986; UPI NFC Offensive Player of the Year - 1986

Corey Dillon (34)

Year	Team	RuYds	RuTD	ReYds	ReTD	Fum	ARuY	AReY	ASptY	Q
1997	CIN	1129	10	259	0	1	1194.0	125.4	61.1	6.0
1998	CIN	1130	4	178	1	2	1097.7	86.3	0.0	5.2
1999	CIN	1200	5	290	1	3	1143.0	137.4	−16.4	6.7
2000	CIN	1435	7	158	0	4	1353.6	70.4	0.0	7.1
2001	CIN	1315	10	228	3	5	1233.7	110.9	0.0	7.2
2002	CIN	1311	7	298	0	5	1205.1	124.9	0.0	6.2
2003	CIN	541	2	71	0	0	561.0	35.5	0.0	2.8
2004	NE	1635	12	103	1	5	1563.3	48.2	0.0	8.6
2005	NE	733	12	181	1	1	816.8	91.7	0.0	4.2
2006	NE	812	13	147	0	2	867.6	67.9	0.0	4.1

Hall of Fame? Not eligible until 2011

Pro Bowl Appearances: 4

All-Pro Selections: None

Awards: None

Tony Dorsett (20)

Year	Team	RuYds	RuTD	ReYds	ReTD	Fum	ARuY	AReY	ASptY	Q
1977	DAL	1007	12	273	1	7	882.3	107.4	0.0	5.9
1978	DAL	1325	7	378	2	12	970.6	144.9	0.0	7.2
1979	DAL	1107	6	375	1	9	861.9	137.6	0.0	6.0
1980	DAL	1185	11	263	0	8	1010.8	96.7	0.0	5.6
1981	DAL	1646	4	325	2	10	1320.2	138.3	0.0	9.6
1982	DAL	745	5	179	0	6	584.7	61.0	0.0	7.6
1983	DAL	1321	8	287	1	5	1225.8	124.3	0.0	7.8
1984	DAL	1189	6	459	1	12	839.5	165.3	0.0	5.5
1985	DAL	1307	7	449	3	7	1133.7	202.8	0.0	6.5
1986	DAL	748	5	267	1	5	621.9	114.6	0.0	4.7
1987	DAL	456	1	177	1	3	361.3	78.2	0.0	3.6
1988	DEN	703	5	122	0	6	534.7	41.7	0.0	3.2

Hall of Fame? Yes

Pro Bowl Appearances: 4

All-Pro Selections: Consensus - 2, Total - 5 (1977-1978; 1981-1983)

Awards: AP NFL Offensive Rookie of the Year - 1977; NEA NFL Rookie of the Year - 1977; PFW/PFWA Offensive Rookie of the Year - 1977; *Sporting News* NFC Rookie of the Year - 1977; UPI NFL/NFC Rookie of the Year - 1977; UPI NFL/NFC Player of the Year - 1981

Paddy Driscoll (50)

Year	Team	RuYds	RuTD	ReYds	ReTD	Fum	ARuY	AReY	ASptY	Q
1920	DEC	–	0	–	–	–	0.0	0.0	0.0	0.0
1920	CHIC	–	2	–	–	–	20.0	0.0	0.0	10.0
1921	CHIC	–	2	–	–	–	20.0	0.0	10.0	5.6
1922	CHIC	–	1	–	1	–	10.0	5.0	0.0	4.0
1923	CHIC	–	0	–	0	–	0.0	0.0	0.0	0.0
1924	CHIC	–	2	–	0	–	0.0	0.0	0.0	0.0
1925	CHIC	–	3	–	0	–	0.0	0.0	0.0	0.0
1926	CHIB	–	4	–	1	–	0.0	0.0	0.0	0.0
1927	CHIB	–	5	–	0	–	50.0	0.0	0.0	10.0
1928	CHIB	–	2	–	0	–	20.0	0.0	0.0	10.0
1929	CHIB	–	1	–	0	–	10.0	0.0	0.0	2.2

Hall of Fame? Yes

Pro Bowl Appearances: None

All-Pro Selections: Consensus - 7, Total - 8 (1920; 1922-1928)

Awards: None

Warrick Dunn (60)

Year	Team	RuYds	RuTD	ReYds	ReTD	Fum	ARuY	AReY	ASptY	Q
1997	TB	978	4	462	3	4	887.2	223.2	50.6	5.0
1998	TB	1026	2	344	0	1	1012.2	165.9	4.9	5.2
1999	TB	616	0	589	2	3	528.4	275.7	-7.6	4.2
2000	TB	1133	8	422	1	1	1179.0	210.0	0.0	7.0
2001	TB	447	3	557	3	2	421.1	269.4	0.0	3.8
2002	ATL	927	7	377	2	4	865.6	169.9	0.0	4.8
2003	ATL	672	3	336	2	2	640.7	159.8	0.0	3.8
2004	ATL	1106	9	294	0	3	1087.8	135.2	0.0	6.5
2005	ATL	1416	3	220	1	3	1337.3	103.7	0.0	6.6
2006	ATL	1140	4	170	1	1	1142.9	87.1	0.0	5.3
2007	ATL	720	4	238	0	2	691.2	107.8	0.0	4.2

Hall of Fame? Not eligible (active)

Pro Bowl Appearances: 3

All-Pro Selections: None

Awards: AP NFL Offensive Rookie of the Year - 1997; PFW/PFWA Offensive Rookie of the Year - 1997; *Sporting News* NFL Rookie of the Year - 1997; Walter Payton NFL Man of the Year - 2004

Marshall Faulk (9)

Year	Team	RuYds	RuTD	ReYds	ReTD	Fum	ARuY	AReY	ASptY	Q
1994	IND	1282	11	522	1	5	1220.4	237.6	0.0	6.9
1995	IND	1078	11	475	3	8	919.9	200.6	0.0	5.8
1996	IND	587	7	428	0	2	594.6	196.4	0.0	4.8
1997	IND	1054	7	471	1	5	954.2	210.3	0.0	5.3
1998	IND	1319	6	908	4	3	1284.2	448.8	0.0	7.7
1999	STL	1381	7	1048	5	2	1391.6	528.6	0.0	10.0
2000	STL	1359	18	830	8	0	1539.0	455.0	−2.0	10.0
2001	STL	1382	12	765	9	3	1411.3	398.5	0.0	10.0
2002	STL	953	8	537	2	4	916.8	234.7	0.0	5.4
2003	STL	818	10	290	1	0	918.0	150.0	0.0	5.1
2004	STL	774	3	310	1	2	740.6	143.7	−20.3	4.7
2005	STL	292	0	291	1	2	244.3	118.2	0.0	1.7
2006	STL	0	0	0	0	0	0.0	0.0	0.0	0.0

Hall of Fame? Not eligible until 2011

Pro Bowl Appearances: 7

All-Pro Selections: Consensus - 5, Total - 6 (1994-1995; 1998-2001)

Awards: AP NFL Offensive Rookie of the Year - 1994; PFW/PFWA Offensive Rookie of the Year - 1994; *Sporting News* NFL Rookie of the Year - 1994; UPI AFL/AFC Rookie of the Year - 1994; Pro Bowl MVP - 1994; AP NFL Offensive Player of the Year - 1999; AP NFL Offensive Player of the Year - 2000; Most Valuable Player (AP) - 2000; PFW/PFWA Offensive Player of the Year - 2000; *Sporting News* NFL Player of the Year - 2000; AP NFL Offensive Player of the Year - 2001; Most Valuable Player (Bell) - 2001; PFW/PFWA Offensive Player of the Year - 2001; *Sporting News* NFL Player of the Year - 2001

Mike Garrett (63)

Year	Team	RuYds	RuTD	ReYds	ReTD	Fum	ARuY	AReY	ASptY	Q
1966	KC	801	6	175	1	5	709.5	77.0	160.0	5.9
1967	KC	1087	9	261	1	6	981.7	97.4	18.7	7.9
1968	KC	564	3	359	3	6	397.2	154.9	1.6	5.1
1969	KC	732	6	432	2	4	669.8	194.7	21.5	9.2
1970	KC	62	0	4	0	1	32.0	−3.7	25.7	0.2
1970	SD	146	1	127	1	3	59.2	47.4	0.0	0.8
1971	SD	591	4	283	3	6	449.4	103.3	−1.9	4.9
1972	SD	1031	6	245	1	8	809.3	95.4	6.9	6.3
1973	SD	467	0	124	1	6	256.5	39.3	0.0	1.6

Hall of Fame? No

Pro Bowl Appearances: None

All-Pro Selections: Consensus - 1, Total - 3 (1966-1967; 1969)

Awards: None

Eddie George (31)

Year	Team	RuYds	RuTD	ReYds	ReTD	Fum	ARuY	AReY	ASptY	Q
1996	HOU	1368	8	182	0	3	1335.7	83.3	0.0	8.7
1997	TEN	1399	6	44	1	4	1302.1	23.9	0.0	6.0
1998	TEN	1294	5	310	1	7	1090.9	133.1	0.0	5.4
1999	TEN	1304	9	458	4	5	1219.6	223.4	0.0	7.5
2000	TEN	1509	14	453	2	5	1471.1	214.4	0.0	8.5
2001	TEN	939	5	279	0	8	702.6	105.9	0.0	4.5
2002	TEN	1165	12	255	2	1	1248.8	133.7	0.0	6.5
2003	TEN	1031	5	163	0	1	1043.6	78.9	0.0	5.4
2004	DAL	432	4	83	0	3	359.7	33.8	0.0	2.1

Hall of Fame? Not eligible until 2009

Pro Bowl Appearances: 4

All-Pro Selections: Consensus - 2, Total - 3 (1996; 1999-2000)

Awards: AP NFL Offensive Rookie of the Year - 1996; PFW/PFWA Offensive Rookie of the Year - 1996; *Sporting News* NFL Rookie of the Year - 1996

Frank Gifford (64)

Year	Team	RuYds	RuTD	ReYds	ReTD	Fum	ARuY	AReY	ASptY	Q
1952	NYG	116	0	36	0	3	24.8	6.0	35.0	0.5
1953	NYG	157	2	292	4	2	140.6	152.9	151.9	0.0
1954	NYG	368	2	154	1	7	197.5	41.6	−5.0	2.7
1955	NYG	351	3	437	4	5	248.7	187.7	6.3	4.8
1956	NYG	819	5	603	4	5	728.3	276.4	0.0	8.8
1957	NYG	528	5	588	4	9	310.5	233.3	0.0	7.6
1958	NYG	468	8	330	2	3	458.4	152.4	0.0	4.0
1959	NYG	540	3	768	4	5	436.7	351.2	0.0	5.3
1960	NYG	232	4	344	3	6	99.3	133.2	0.0	1.8
1962	NYG	18	1	796	7	1	26.1	396.7	0.0	6.8
1963	NYG	10	0	657	7	2	3.0	290.5	0.0	1.6
1964	NYG	2	1	429	3	0	12.0	229.5	0.0	1.8

Hall of Fame? Yes

Pro Bowl Appearances: 7

All-Pro Selections: Consensus - 3, Total - 6 (1953; 1955-1959)

Awards: NEA NFL Player of the Year - 1956; *Sporting News* NFL Player of the Year - 1956; UPI NFL/NFC Player of the Year - 1956; Pete Rozelle Radio-Television Award - 1995

Ahman Green (45)

Year	Team	RuYds	RuTD	ReYds	ReTD	Fum	ARuY	AReY	ASptY	Q
1998	SEA	209	1	2	0	1	197.5	–0.8	63.4	0.9
1999	SEA	120	0	0	0	2	86.5	0.0	51.5	0.5
2000	GB	1175	10	559	3	6	1087.7	242.5	0.0	6.7
2001	GB	1387	9	594	2	5	1310.9	273.1	0.0	8.8
2002	GB	1240	7	393	2	4	1176.6	179.9	0.0	6.4
2003	GB	1883	15	367	5	7	1787.6	173.9	0.0	9.4
2004	GB	1163	7	275	1	7	991.3	105.2	0.0	5.9
2005	GB	255	0	147	0	1	222.9	65.6	0.0	1.3
2006	GB	1059	5	373	1	4	972.6	167.9	0.0	5.0
2007	HOU	260	2	123	0	0	280.0	61.5	0.0	1.8

Hall of Fame? Not eligible (active)

Pro Bowl Appearances: 4

All-Pro Selections: Consensus - 2, Total - 2 (2001; 2003)

Awards: None

Franco Harris (29)

Year	Team	RuYds	RuTD	ReYds	ReTD	Fum	ARuY	AReY	ASptY	Q
1972	PIT	1055	10	180	1	7	912.4	67.9	12.7	7.0
1973	PIT	698	3	69	0	8	425.7	18.4	1.4	2.4
1974	PIT	1006	5	200	1	9	731.8	69.2	0.0	5.4
1975	PIT	1246	10	214	1	9	1021.9	77.4	5.8	5.7
1976	PIT	1128	14	151	0	8	971.6	51.9	0.0	6.9
1977	PIT	1162	11	62	0	10	886.1	16.9	0.0	5.3
1978	PIT	1082	8	144	0	4	1013.1	61.4	0.0	7.0
1979	PIT	1186	11	291	1	11	908.3	98.2	0.0	6.0
1980	PIT	789	4	196	2	7	584.3	72.7	0.0	3.4
1981	PIT	987	8	250	1	6	858.8	98.2	0.0	6.3
1982	PIT	604	2	249	0	1	591.3	117.2	0.0	8.4
1983	PIT	1007	5	278	2	10	700.5	105.5	0.0	4.7
1984	SEA	170	0	3	0	0	170.0	1.5	0.0	1.0

Hall of Fame? Yes

Pro Bowl Appearances: 9

All-Pro Selections: Consensus - 2, Total - 7 (1972; 1974-1979)

Awards: AP NFL Offensive Rookie of the Year - 1972; NEA AFC Rookie of the Year - 1972; PFW/PFWA Offensive Rookie of the Year - 1972; *Sporting News* AFC Rookie of the Year - 1972; UPI AFL/AFC Rookie of the Year - 1972; MVP, Super Bowl IX - 1974; Walter Payton NFL Man of the Year - 1976; Byron "Whizzer" White Award - 1982

Abner Haynes (47)

Year	Team	RuYds	RuTD	ReYds	ReTD	Fum	ARuY	AReY	ASptY	Q
1960	DAL	875	9	576	3	9	735.8	222.2	220.5	8.8
1961	DAL	841	9	558	3	11	602.8	231.7	266.5	7.4
1962	DAL	1049	13	573	6	4	1051.3	294.0	116.8	10.0
1963	KC	352	4	470	2	6	235.7	192.9	105.6	3.7
1964	KC	697	4	562	3	0	737.0	296.0	49.0	10.0
1965	DEN	166	3	216	2	5	125.3	73.2	269.2	1.6
1966	DEN	304	2	480	1	11	34.4	141.7	125.3	0.8
1967	MIA	274	2	100	0	6	162.2	12.4	−29.6	1.3
1967	NYJ	72	0	0	0	0	72.0	0.0	45.0	0.5

Hall of Fame? No

Pro Bowl Appearances: 3

All-Pro Selections: Consensus - 3, Total - 4 (1960-1962; 1964)

Awards: UPI AFL/AFC Rookie of the Year - 1960; UPI AFL/AFC Player of the Year - 1960

Clarke Hinkle (39)

Year	Team	RuYds	RuTD	ReYds	ReTD	Fum	ARuY	AReY	ASptY	Q
1932	GB	331	3	–	–	–	361.0	0.0	0.0	5.9
1933	GB	413	2	38	0	–	433.0	19.0	0.0	5.3
1934	GB	359	1	113	1	–	369.0	61.5	0.0	3.6
1935	GB	273	2	–4	0	–	293.0	–2.0	0.0	4.4
1936	GB	476	5	0	0	–	526.0	0.0	0.0	6.0
1937	GB	552	5	116	2	–	602.0	68.0	0.0	7.4
1938	GB	299	3	98	4	–	329.0	69.0	0.0	7.5
1939	GB	381	5	70	0	–	431.0	35.0	0.0	5.5
1940	GB	383	2	28	1	–	403.0	19.0	0.0	6.3
1941	GB	393	5	78	1	–	443.0	44.0	39.0	6.4

Hall of Fame? Yes

Pro Bowl Appearances: 3

All-Pro Selections: Consensus - 3, Total - 10 (1932-1941)

Awards: None

Bob Hoernschemeyer (33)

Year	Team	RuYds	RuTD	ReYds	ReTD	Fum	ARuY	AReY	ASptY	Q
1946	CHI	375	0	11	0	–	375.0	5.5	186.0	8.3
1947	CHI	2	0	4	0	–	2.0	2.0	–9.0	0.4
1947	BKN	702	5	0	0	–	752.0	0.0	19.0	4.3
1948	BKN	574	3	173	3	–	604.0	101.5	21.0	4.8
1949	CHI	456	2	0	0	–	476.0	0.0	97.0	6.9
1950	DET	471	1	78	1	1	447.4	40.8	0.0	6.5
1951	DET	678	2	263	3	3	601.4	129.7	30.3	9.9
1952	DET	457	4	139	0	3	397.6	53.6	2.1	4.9
1953	DET	482	7	282	2	3	458.8	129.8	–10.9	6.1
1954	DET	242	2	153	1	3	171.8	62.3	–10.8	2.4
1955	DET	109	1	36	0	1	85.5	13.3	0.0	0.8

Hall of Fame? No

Pro Bowl Appearances: 2

All-Pro Selections: Consensus - 0, Total - 5 (1946; 1949; 1951-1953)

Awards: None

Priest Holmes (38)

Year	Team	RuYds	RuTD	ReYds	ReTD	Fum	ARuY	AReY	ASptY	Q
1997	BAL	0	0	0	0	0	0.0	0.0	−6.0	0.0
1998	BAL	1008	7	260	0	3	977.8	111.5	−10.9	4.7
1999	BAL	506	1	104	1	0	516.0	57.0	0.0	3.0
2000	BAL	588	2	221	0	2	543.5	95.4	−13.5	3.2
2001	KC	1555	8	614	2	4	1500.5	291.5	0.0	9.9
2002	KC	1615	21	672	3	1	1792.4	343.7	0.0	10.0
2003	KC	1420	27	690	0	1	1657.6	337.5	0.0	9.5
2004	KC	892	14	187	1	4	886.1	84.4	0.0	5.2
2005	KC	451	6	197	1	1	477.0	97.5	0.0	2.6
2006	KC	0	0	0	0	0	0.0	0.0	0.0	0.0
2007	KC	137	0	17	0	0	137.0	8.5	0.0	0.8

Hall of Fame? Not eligible (active)

Pro Bowl Appearances: 3

All-Pro Selections: Consensus - 3, Total - 3 (2001-2003)

Awards: AP NFL Offensive Player of the Year - 2002

Cecil Isbell (42)

Year	Team	RuYds	RuTD	ReYds	ReTD	Fum	ARuY	AReY	ASptY	Q
1938	GB	445	2	104	0	–	465.0	52.0	0.0	10.0
1939	GB	407	2	71	0	–	427.0	35.5	0.0	8.2
1940	GB	270	4	0	0	–	310.0	0.0	0.0	6.7
1941	GB	317	1	–1	0	–	327.0	–0.5	11.0	10.0
1942	GB	83	1	0	0	–	93.0	0.0	–3.0	9.0

Hall of Fame? No

Pro Bowl Appearances: 4

All-Pro Selections: Consensus - 2, Total - 5 (1938-1942)

Awards: None

Edgerrin James (15)

Year	Team	RuYds	RuTD	ReYds	ReTD	Fum	ARuY	AReY	ASptY	Q
1999	IND	1553	13	586	4	8	1409.0	267.0	0.0	8.7
2000	IND	1709	13	594	5	5	1667.0	294.0	0.0	9.8
2001	IND	662	3	193	0	3	588.5	80.0	0.0	3.7
2002	IND	989	2	354	1	4	877.9	153.1	0.0	4.8
2003	IND	1259	11	292	0	5	1197.3	117.7	0.0	6.3
2004	IND	1548	9	483	0	6	1429.8	209.7	0.0	8.8
2005	IND	1506	13	337	1	2	1564.7	164.8	0.0	7.9
2006	ARI	1159	6	217	0	3	1111.2	96.3	0.0	5.2
2007	ARI	1222	7	204	0	5	1105.8	88.2	0.0	6.3

Hall of Fame? Not eligible (active)

Pro Bowl Appearances: 4

All-Pro Selections: Consensus - 3, Total - 4 (1999-2000; 2004-2005)

Awards: AP NFL Offensive Rookie of the Year - 1999; PFW/PFWA Offensive Rookie of the Year - 1999; *Sporting News* NFL Rookie of the Year - 1999

John Henry Johnson (75)

Year	Team	RuYds	RuTD	ReYds	ReTD	Fum	ARuY	AReY	ASptY	Q
1954	SF	681	9	183	0	5	610.8	56.7	−17.5	6.6
1955	SF	69	1	6	0	0	79.0	3.0	6.0	0.8
1956	SF	301	2	90	0	1	285.0	41.4	2.6	2.9
1957	DET	621	5	141	0	9	359.3	22.2	0.0	4.7
1958	DET	254	0	60	0	3	147.3	16.7	0.0	1.0
1959	DET	270	2	34	1	4	142.6	9.4	0.0	1.0
1960	PIT	621	2	112	1	5	460.8	42.7	0.0	4.7
1961	PIT	787	6	262	1	7	598.5	108.0	−10.2	4.4
1962	PIT	1141	7	226	2	5	1033.6	100.4	0.0	7.5
1963	PIT	773	4	145	1	5	633.3	57.2	0.0	3.7
1964	PIT	1048	7	69	1	4	968.8	28.7	0.0	6.8
1965	PIT	11	0	0	0	0	11.0	0.0	0.0	0.1
1966	HOU	226	3	150	0	0	256.0	75.0	0.0	2.5

Hall of Fame? Yes

Pro Bowl Appearances: 4

All-Pro Selections: Consensus - 0, Total - 2 (1954; 1962)

Awards: None

Pete Johnson (73)

Year	Team	RuYds	RuTD	ReYds	ReTD	Fum	ARuY	AReY	ASptY	Q
1977	CIN	585	4	49	0	1	586.5	23.2	−9.3	3.6
1978	CIN	762	7	236	0	4	695.5	94.5	0.0	5.1
1979	CIN	865	14	154	1	6	786.6	60.4	0.0	5.1
1980	CIN	747	6	172	1	2	735.1	82.9	0.0	4.2
1981	CIN	1077	12	320	4	4	1060.0	157.0	0.0	8.0
1982	CIN	622	7	267	0	1	658.6	126.9	0.0	9.3
1983	CIN	763	14	129	0	2	828.3	59.2	0.0	5.2
1984	MIA	159	9	0	0	1	209.0	0.0	0.0	1.2
1984	SD	46	3	7	0	0	76.0	3.5	0.0	0.4

Hall of Fame? No

Pro Bowl Appearances: None

All-Pro Selections: Consensus - 0, Total - 1 (1981)

Awards: None

Leroy Kelly (13)

Year	Team	RuYds	RuTD	ReYds	ReTD	Fum	ARuY	AReY	ASptY	Q
1964	CLE	12	0	0	0	0	12.0	0.0	283.0	0.1
1965	CLE	139	0	122	0	3	91.3	49.4	365.4	0.8
1966	CLE	1141	15	366	1	1	1261.1	183.4	121.6	9.8
1967	CLE	1205	11	282	2	7	1083.3	131.3	72.3	10.0
1968	CLE	1239	16	297	4	6	1183.3	149.4	-2.7	10.0
1969	CLE	817	9	267	1	1	872.9	135.0	12.4	9.0
1970	CLE	656	6	311	2	3	609.4	153.1	14.0	6.4
1971	CLE	865	10	252	2	7	745.1	112.5	250.1	7.3
1972	CLE	811	4	204	1	4	711.5	92.7	35.0	5.7
1973	CLE	389	3	180	0	3	312.0	77.8	6.2	2.1

Hall of Fame? Yes

Pro Bowl Appearances: 6

All-Pro Selections: Consensus - 3, Total - 5 (1966-1969; 1971)

Awards: Most Valuable Player (Bell) - 1968

Tuffy Leemans (17)

Year	Team	RuYds	RuTD	ReYds	ReTD	Fum	ARuY	AReY	ASptY	Q
1936	NYG	830	2	22	0	–	850.0	11.0	0.0	9.0
1937	NYG	429	0	157	1	–	429.0	83.5	0.0	9.5
1938	NYG	463	4	68	0	–	503.0	34.0	0.0	8.8
1939	NYG	429	3	185	2	–	459.0	102.5	0.0	10.0
1940	NYG	474	1	0	0	–	484.0	0.0	0.0	7.0
1941	NYG	332	4	0	0	–	372.0	0.0	158.0	6.0
1942	NYG	116	3	–10	0	–	146.0	–5.0	26.0	3.9
1943	NYG	69	0	0	0	–	69.0	0.0	55.0	1.2

Hall of Fame? Yes

Pro Bowl Appearances: None

All-Pro Selections: Consensus - 2, Total - 7 (1936-1942)

Awards: None

Jamal Lewis (58)

Year	Team	RuYds	RuTD	ReYds	ReTD	Fum	ARuY	AReY	ASptY	Q
2000	BAL	1364	6	296	0	6	1203.3	128.7	0.0	6.7
2002	BAL	1327	6	442	1	8	1109.4	183.6	0.0	6.1
2003	BAL	2066	14	205	0	8	1906.1	82.4	0.0	9.5
2004	BAL	1006	7	116	0	2	999.3	54.7	0.0	5.6
2005	BAL	906	3	191	1	5	757.3	79.2	0.0	3.8
2006	BAL	1132	9	115	0	4	1070.7	48.8	0.0	4.9
2007	CLE	1304	9	248	2	4	1248.6	119.4	0.0	7.2

Hall of Fame? Not eligible (active)

Pro Bowl Appearances: 1

All-Pro Selections: Consensus - 1, Total - 1 (2003)

Awards: AP NFL Offensive Player of the Year - 2003; PFW/PFWA Offensive Player of the Year - 2003

Floyd Little (28)

Year	Team	RuYds	RuTD	ReYds	ReTD	Fum	ARuY	AReY	ASptY	Q
1967	DEN	381	1	11	0	3	310.6	1.2	486.7	2.3
1968	DEN	584	3	331	1	6	451.9	151.0	343.6	5.9
1969	DEN	729	6	218	1	2	723.7	105.5	85.6	8.9
1970	DEN	901	3	161	0	6	738.1	64.8	164.4	6.6
1971	DEN	1133	6	255	0	4	1050.1	114.4	55.5	9.8
1972	DEN	859	9	367	4	4	815.6	186.2	44.0	7.3
1973	DEN	979	12	423	1	3	995.9	200.0	6.6	6.4
1974	DEN	312	1	344	0	2	263.1	157.4	38.5	2.8
1975	DEN	445	2	308	2	2	406.2	150.4	–20.5	2.9

Hall of Fame? No

Pro Bowl Appearances: 5

All-Pro Selections: Consensus - 3, Total - 5 (1969-1973)

Awards: Byron "Whizzer" White Award - 1974

Paul Lowe (43)

Year	Team	RuYds	RuTD	ReYds	ReTD	Fum	ARuY	AReY	ASptY	Q
1960	LAC	855	9	377	2	2	888.0	188.9	38.9	10.0
1961	SD	767	9	103	0	6	654.1	31.8	27.2	6.3
1963	SD	1010	8	191	2	7	856.2	71.2	25.4	8.0
1964	SD	496	3	182	2	2	454.8	93.3	0.0	4.7
1965	SD	1121	6	126	1	2	1107.9	62.4	0.0	10.0
1966	SD	643	3	41	0	3	568.7	11.9	22.0	4.4
1967	SD	71	1	25	0	0	81.0	12.5	–15.0	0.8
1968	SD	9	0	0	0	0	9.0	0.0	0.0	0.1
1968	KC	–10	0	0	0	0	–10.0	0.0	0.0	0.0
1969	KC	33	0	0	0	1	6.3	0.0	2.7	0.1

Hall of Fame? No

Pro Bowl Appearances: 2

All-Pro Selections: Consensus - 2, Total - 4 (1960-1961; 1963; 1965)

Awards: UPI AFL/AFC Player of the Year - 1965

Curtis Martin (7)

Year	Team	RuYds	RuTD	ReYds	ReTD	Fum	ARuY	AReY	ASptY	Q
1995	NE	1487	14	261	1	5	1442.1	120.4	0.0	8.1
1996	NE	1152	14	333	3	4	1152.3	161.2	0.0	8.0
1997	NE	1160	4	296	1	3	1095.6	137.4	0.0	5.6
1998	NYJ	1287	8	365	1	5	1187.9	166.6	0.0	6.0
1999	NYJ	1464	5	259	0	2	1442.7	120.8	0.0	8.1
2000	NYJ	1204	9	508	2	2	1228.7	249.5	0.0	7.5
2001	NYJ	1513	10	320	0	2	1544.2	149.0	0.0	9.4
2002	NYJ	1094	7	362	0	0	1164.0	181.0	0.0	6.3
2003	NYJ	1308	2	262	0	2	1257.2	121.8	0.0	6.6
2004	NYJ	1697	12	245	2	2	1745.0	124.5	0.0	10.0
2005	NYJ	735	5	118	0	2	712.9	51.1	0.0	3.5
2006	NYJ	0	0	0	0	0	0.0	0.0	0.0	0.0

Hall of Fame? Not eligible until 2011

Pro Bowl Appearances: 5

All-Pro Selections: Consensus - 3, Total - 5 (1995-1996; 1999; 2001; 2004)

Awards: AP NFL Offensive Rookie of the Year - 1995; PFW/PFWA Offensive Rookie of the Year - 1995; *Sporting News* NFL Rookie of the Year - 1995; UPI AFL/AFC Rookie of the Year - 1995

Tom Matte (71)

Year	Team	RuYds	RuTD	ReYds	ReTD	Fum	ARuY	AReY	ASptY	Q
1961	BAL	54	0	8	0	0	54.0	4.0	10.0	0.4
1962	BAL	226	2	81	1	2	197.5	40.3	55.3	1.8
1963	BAL	541	4	466	1	2	528.3	219.0	4.7	4.1
1964	BAL	215	1	169	0	0	225.0	84.5	11.0	2.3
1965	BAL	235	1	131	0	2	188.1	55.6	44.4	1.2
1966	BAL	381	0	307	3	2	322.2	152.8	−8.4	3.0
1967	BAL	636	9	496	3	1	694.7	255.6	−6.2	7.9
1968	BAL	662	9	275	1	2	682.3	133.0	1.6	6.0
1969	BAL	909	11	513	2	4	885.2	242.0	0.0	10.0
1970	BAL	43	0	2	0	0	43.0	1.0	0.0	0.4
1971	BAL	607	8	239	0	4	552.0	96.9	−20.8	5.4
1972	BAL	137	0	182	1	2	80.8	72.2	0.0	1.1

Hall of Fame? No

Pro Bowl Appearances: 2

All-Pro Selections: Consensus - 0, Total - 1 (1969)

Awards: None

Hugh McElhenny (56)

Year	Team	RuYds	RuTD	ReYds	ReTD	Fum	ARuY	AReY	ASptY	Q
1952	SF	684	6	367	3	5	623.0	166.4	283.1	9.1
1953	SF	503	3	474	2	6	379.4	205.9	130.9	6.4
1954	SF	515	6	162	0	4	458.6	66.5	98.9	5.2
1955	SF	327	4	203	2	3	274.7	100.2	2.6	3.7
1956	SF	916	8	193	0	4	867.3	85.4	58.5	8.1
1957	SF	478	1	458	2	8	268.9	159.5	19.5	5.2
1958	SF	451	6	366	2	10	248.2	120.9	23.5	2.3
1959	SF	67	1	329	3	1	59.0	157.5	0.0	1.5
1960	SF	347	0	114	1	2	277.3	51.7	0.0	3.0
1961	MIN	570	3	283	3	8	379.3	88.5	154.6	3.1
1962	MIN	200	0	191	0	3	125.0	71.5	42.0	1.3
1963	NYG	175	0	91	2	3	100.0	40.5	60.0	0.8
1964	DET	48	0	16	0	0	48.0	8.0	12.0	0.4

Hall of Fame? Yes

Pro Bowl Appearances: 6

All-Pro Selections: Consensus - 2, Total - 5 (1952-1954; 1956-1957)

Awards: None

Freeman McNeil (61)

Year	Team	RuYds	RuTD	ReYds	ReTD	Fum	ARuY	AReY	ASptY	Q
1981	NYJ	623	2	171	1	5	466.2	67.3	0.0	3.5
1982	NYJ	786	6	187	1	7	592.8	71.7	0.0	7.9
1983	NYJ	654	1	172	3	4	523.3	82.5	0.0	3.6
1984	NYJ	1070	5	294	1	4	975.7	136.3	0.0	6.3
1985	NYJ	1331	3	427	2	9	1042.2	182.3	0.0	6.0
1986	NYJ	856	5	410	1	8	645.6	150.4	0.0	5.1
1987	NYJ	530	0	262	1	1	496.6	129.4	0.0	5.1
1988	NYJ	944	6	288	1	3	900.1	132.9	0.0	5.8
1989	NYJ	352	2	310	1	1	343.2	148.8	0.0	3.5
1990	NYJ	458	6	230	0	1	483.6	109.4	0.0	3.9
1991	NYJ	300	2	56	0	1	284.8	23.2	0.0	1.8
1992	NYJ	170	0	154	0	1	140.8	66.2	0.0	1.1

Hall of Fame? No

Pro Bowl Appearances: 3

All-Pro Selections: Consensus - 2, Total - 3 (1982; 1984-1985)

Awards: None

Lydell Mitchell (52)

Year	Team	RuYds	RuTD	ReYds	ReTD	Fum	ARuY	AReY	ASptY	Q
1972	BAL	215	1	147	1	3	139.3	44.2	0.0	1.3
1973	BAL	963	2	113	0	2	908.0	51.5	0.0	5.1
1974	BAL	757	5	544	2	6	627.4	221.6	0.0	5.7
1975	BAL	1193	11	544	4	5	1137.4	257.6	0.0	7.2
1976	BAL	1200	5	555	3	4	1117.5	265.0	0.0	9.4
1977	BAL	1159	3	620	4	5	1027.2	291.8	0.0	7.8
1978	SD	820	3	500	2	2	786.8	243.2	0.0	6.7
1979	SD	211	0	159	1	2	150.3	66.2	–6.0	1.3
1980	LARM	16	0	21	0	0	16.0	10.5	0.0	0.1

Hall of Fame? No

Pro Bowl Appearances: 3

All-Pro Selections: Consensus - 2, Total - 3 (1975-1977)

Awards: None

Wilbert Montgomery (48)

Year	Team	RuYds	RuTD	ReYds	ReTD	Fum	ARuY	AReY	ASptY	Q
1977	PHI	183	2	18	0	4	101.6	2.2	117.2	0.6
1978	PHI	1220	9	195	1	6	1102.1	75.2	29.2	7.6
1979	PHI	1512	9	494	5	14	1103.9	211.6	−15.5	7.9
1980	PHI	778	8	407	2	3	763.5	189.0	2.5	4.9
1981	PHI	1402	8	521	2	6	1277.1	235.4	0.0	10.0
1982	PHI	515	7	258	2	3	483.7	121.2	−8.9	7.2
1983	PHI	139	0	53	0	1	108.5	17.0	0.0	0.7
1984	PHI	789	2	501	0	5	656.7	205.0	0.0	4.8
1985	DET	251	0	55	0	0	251.0	27.5	0.0	1.4

Hall of Fame? No

Pro Bowl Appearances: 2

All-Pro Selections: Consensus - 1, Total - 2 (1978-1979)

Awards: None

Lenny Moore (18)

Year	Team	RuYds	RuTD	ReYds	ReTD	Fum	ARuY	AReY	ASptY	Q
1956	BAL	649	8	102	1	5	584.5	37.5	–63.3	5.2
1957	BAL	488	3	687	7	6	353.5	311.4	93.0	8.2
1958	BAL	598	7	938	7	5	549.2	431.5	13.3	6.2
1959	BAL	422	2	846	6	4	338.3	400.0	0.0	10.0
1960	BAL	374	4	936	9	3	334.9	473.9	2.1	10.0
1961	BAL	648	7	728	8	1	692.3	390.3	0.0	6.9
1962	BAL	470	2	215	2	1	455.8	111.7	0.0	3.7
1963	BAL	136	2	288	2	2	113.6	121.1	2.3	3.7
1964	BAL	584	16	472	3	8	461.8	213.2	0.0	4.6
1965	BAL	464	5	414	3	3	414.3	201.8	0.0	3.7
1966	BAL	209	3	260	0	2	190.1	113.7	79.0	2.0
1967	BAL	132	4	153	0	1	148.3	69.2	63.0	1.8

Hall of Fame? Yes

Pro Bowl Appearances: 7

All-Pro Selections: Consensus - 5, Total - 7 (1956-1961; 1964)

Awards: UPI NFL/NFC Rookie of the Year - 1956; NEA NFL Player of the Year - 1964

Marion Motley (26)

Year	Team	RuYds	RuTD	ReYds	ReTD	Fum	ARuY	AReY	ASptY	Q
1946	CLE	601	5	188	1	–	651.0	99.0	–7.0	9.1
1947	CLE	889	8	73	1	–	969.0	41.5	62.0	5.6
1948	CLE	964	5	192	2	–	1014.0	106.0	57.0	8.3
1949	CLE	570	8	191	0	–	650.0	95.5	22.0	7.8
1950	CLE	810	3	151	1	5	654.6	65.9	0.0	10.0
1951	CLE	273	1	52	0	1	248.6	20.4	0.0	3.5
1952	CLE	444	1	213	2	2	385.8	108.0	26.0	5.7
1953	CLE	161	0	47	0	1	129.8	17.6	–2.9	1.6
1955	PIT	8	0	0	0	0	8.0	0.0	0.0	0.1

Hall of Fame? Yes

Pro Bowl Appearances: 1

All-Pro Selections: Consensus - 4, Total - 5 (1946-1950)

Awards: None

Chuck Muncie (69)

Year	Team	RuYds	RuTD	ReYds	ReTD	Fum	ARuY	AReY	ASptY	Q
1976	NO	659	2	272	0	6	483.6	95.3	5.1	3.9
1977	NO	811	6	248	1	3	762.8	117.7	−1.5	5.2
1978	NO	557	7	233	0	7	387.4	77.6	0.0	3.0
1979	NO	1198	11	308	0	8	1036.0	108.3	0.0	7.0
1980	NO	168	2	25	0	1	154.0	6.5	0.0	0.8
1980	SD	659	4	234	0	10	390.4	62.1	−12.6	2.3
1981	SD	1144	19	362	0	9	1027.7	128.5	0.0	7.7
1982	SD	569	8	207	1	4	516.0	84.4	0.0	7.7
1983	SD	886	12	396	1	8	734.5	154.5	0.0	5.2
1984	SD	51	0	38	0	1	19.9	10.1	0.0	0.2

Hall of Fame? No

Pro Bowl Appearances: 3

All-Pro Selections: Consensus - 1, Total - 3 (1979; 1981-1982)

Awards: Pro Bowl MVP - 1979

Jim Nance (55)

Year	Team	RuYds	RuTD	ReYds	ReTD	Fum	ARuY	AReY	ASptY	Q
1965	BOS	321	5	83	0	2	301.1	33.9	−6.5	2.8
1966	BOS	1458	11	103	0	7	1295.3	44.2	0.0	10.0
1967	BOS	1216	7	196	1	10	916.2	72.8	0.0	7.2
1968	BOS	593	4	51	0	2	558.9	19.6	0.0	5.7
1969	BOS	750	6	168	0	1	775.2	78.8	0.0	9.1
1970	BOS	522	7	148	0	6	388.5	37.5	0.0	3.6
1971	NE	463	5	95	0	2	442.8	37.7	0.0	4.1
1973	NYJ	78	0	26	0	1	45.3	5.7	0.0	0.3

Hall of Fame? No

Pro Bowl Appearances: 2

All-Pro Selections: Consensus - 2, Total - 3 (1966-1967; 1969)

Awards: UPI AFL/AFC Player of the Year - 1966

Walter Payton (3)

Year	Team	RuYds	RuTD	ReYds	ReTD	Fum	ARuY	AReY	ASptY	Q
1975	CHIB	679	7	213	0	9	461.0	58.0	143.4	2.5
1976	CHIB	1390	13	149	0	10	1139.6	56.2	−21.2	8.1
1977	CHIB	1852	14	269	2	11	1586.7	112.2	52.6	10.0
1978	CHIB	1395	11	480	0	5	1331.1	213.9	0.0	10.0
1979	CHIB	1610	14	313	2	7	1492.3	144.9	0.0	10.0
1980	CHIB	1460	6	367	1	5	1346.8	163.4	0.0	7.7
1981	CHIB	1222	6	379	2	9	962.5	160.9	0.0	7.4
1982	CHIB	596	1	311	0	3	509.0	134.5	0.0	7.9
1983	CHIB	1421	6	607	2	5	1312.6	285.1	0.0	9.2
1984	CHIB	1684	11	368	0	5	1618.4	163.3	0.0	10.0
1985	CHIB	1551	9	483	2	6	1435.3	220.4	0.0	8.3
1986	CHIB	1333	8	382	3	6	1200.2	181.5	0.0	8.6
1987	CHIB	533	4	217	1	5	410.8	76.8	0.0	3.7

Hall of Fame? Yes

Pro Bowl Appearances: 9

All-Pro Selections: Consensus - 8, Total - 9 (1976-1980; 1983-1986)

Awards: Sporting News NFC Player of the Year - 1976; AP NFL Offensive Player of the Year - 1977; Most Valuable Player (AP) - 1977; NEA NFL Player of the Year - 1977; PFW/PFWA Offensive Player of the Year - 1977; *Sporting News* NFC Player of the Year - 1977; UPI NFL/NFC Player of the Year - 1977; Pro Bowl MVP - 1977; Walter Payton NFL Man of the Year - 1977; Most Valuable Player (Bell) - 1985; NEA NFL Player of the Year - 1985; UPI NFC Offensive Player of the Year - 1985

Don Perkins (68)

Year	Team	RuYds	RuTD	ReYds	ReTD	Fum	ARuY	AReY	ASptY	Q
1961	DAL	815	4	298	1	5	699.4	129.1	−8.5	5.5
1962	DAL	945	7	104	0	2	939.4	47.6	0.0	6.5
1963	DAL	614	7	84	0	0	684.0	42.0	0.0	3.9
1964	DAL	768	6	155	0	4	680.7	64.8	0.0	5.1
1965	DAL	690	0	142	0	2	615.9	65.1	0.0	4.0
1966	DAL	726	8	231	0	1	770.4	111.1	0.0	6.0
1967	DAL	823	6	116	0	1	846.3	54.7	0.0	7.4
1968	DAL	836	4	180	2	3	765.8	90.2	0.0	6.3

Hall of Fame? No

Pro Bowl Appearances: None

All-Pro Selections: Consensus - 0, Total - 4 (1961-1962; 1967-1968)

Awards: None

Joe Perry (11)

Year	Team	RuYds	RuTD	ReYds	ReTD	Fum	ARuY	AReY	ASptY	Q
1948	SF	562	10	79	1	–	662.0	44.5	75.0	5.2
1949	SF	783	8	146	3	–	863.0	88.0	57.0	10.0
1950	SF	647	5	69	1	11	330.8	1.1	–52.4	4.6
1951	SF	677	3	167	1	5	532.6	65.4	10.7	8.0
1952	SF	725	8	81	0	6	588.3	19.9	0.0	7.0
1953	SF	1018	10	191	3	8	834.9	82.5	–21.9	10.0
1954	SF	1049	8	203	0	6	931.3	71.8	0.0	10.0
1955	SF	701	2	55	1	6	509.5	6.7	0.0	5.1
1956	SF	520	3	104	0	3	446.2	35.8	0.0	4.3
1957	SF	454	3	130	0	3	381.0	49.1	0.0	5.3
1958	SF	758	4	218	1	3	696.6	95.4	0.0	5.0
1959	SF	602	3	53	0	6	411.1	7.4	0.0	2.8
1960	SF	95	1	–3	0	2	31.2	–7.7	0.0	0.2
1961	BAL	675	3	322	1	3	605.2	145.8	0.0	5.0
1962	BAL	359	0	194	0	3	261.8	74.2	0.0	2.2
1963	SF	98	0	12	0	1	64.9	0.5	0.0	0.3

Hall of Fame? Yes

Pro Bowl Appearances: 3

All-Pro Selections: Consensus - 3, Total - 4 (1949; 1953-1954; 1958)

Awards: UPI NFL/NFC Player of the Year - 1954

Clinton Portis (66)

Year	Team	RuYds	RuTD	ReYds	ReTD	Fum	ARuY	AReY	ASptY	Q
2002	DEN	1508	15	364	2	5	1479.6	170.4	0.0	7.7
2003	DEN	1591	14	314	0	3	1624.9	143.1	0.0	8.4
2004	WAS	1315	5	235	2	5	1186.8	106.7	0.0	7.0
2005	WAS	1516	11	216	0	3	1516.0	98.6	0.0	7.4
2006	WAS	523	7	170	0	0	593.0	85.0	0.0	2.9
2007	WAS	1262	11	389	0	6	1163.4	164.3	0.0	7.1

Hall of Fame? No

Pro Bowl Appearances: 1

All-Pro Selections: None

Awards: AP NFL Offensive Rookie of the Year - 2002; PFW/PFWA Offensive Rookie of the Year - 2002; *Sporting News* NFL Rookie of the Year - 2002

Mike Pruitt (62)

Year	Team	RuYds	RuTD	ReYds	ReTD	Fum	ARuY	AReY	ASptY	Q
1976	CLE	138	0	26	0	4	11.9	–6.4	–28.5	0.0
1977	CLE	205	1	12	0	1	181.4	3.9	6.7	1.1
1978	CLE	560	5	112	0	3	505.5	40.5	0.0	3.5
1979	CLE	1294	9	372	2	6	1176.3	163.7	0.0	8.0
1980	CLE	1034	6	471	0	9	806.7	162.8	0.0	4.9
1981	CLE	1103	7	442	1	5	1013.6	185.4	0.0	7.9
1982	CLE	516	3	140	0	4	407.3	48.7	0.0	5.4
1983	CLE	1184	10	157	2	4	1138.9	73.6	0.0	7.0
1984	CLE	506	6	29	0	1	527.2	13.3	0.0	3.0
1985	BUF	24	0	0	0	0	24.0	0.0	0.0	0.1
1985	KC	366	2	43	0	0	386.0	21.5	0.0	2.0
1986	KC	448	2	56	0	0	468.0	28.0	0.0	3.2

Hall of Fame? No

Pro Bowl Appearances: 2

All-Pro Selections: Consensus - 1, Total - 3 (1979-1980; 1983)

Awards: None

John Riggins (32)

Year	Team	RuYds	RuTD	ReYds	ReTD	Fum	ARuY	AReY	ASptY	Q
1971	NYJ	769	1	231	2	6	579.0	85.5	0.0	5.6
1972	NYJ	944	7	230	1	2	941.4	112.6	0.0	7.5
1973	NYJ	482	4	158	0	6	317.2	43.8	0.0	1.9
1974	NYJ	680	5	180	2	3	622.1	87.9	0.0	4.8
1975	NYJ	1005	8	363	1	5	907.4	164.1	0.0	5.5
1976	WAS	572	3	172	1	6	389.5	63.5	0.0	3.1
1977	WAS	203	0	95	2	0	203.0	57.5	0.0	1.5
1978	WAS	1014	5	299	0	7	815.1	118.4	0.0	6.0
1979	WAS	1153	9	163	3	5	1062.4	77.1	0.0	6.8
1981	WAS	714	13	59	0	1	805.2	28.3	0.0	5.5
1982	WAS	553	3	50	0	2	507.3	20.7	0.0	6.2
1983	WAS	1347	24	29	0	5	1390.1	11.9	0.0	8.1
1984	WAS	1239	14	43	0	7	1104.9	15.6	0.0	6.3
1985	WAS	677	8	18	0	3	641.6	5.1	0.0	3.2

Hall of Fame? Yes

Pro Bowl Appearances: 1

All-Pro Selections: Consensus - 1, Total - 2 (1975; 1983)

Awards: Comeback Player of the Year - 1978; MVP, Super Bowl XVII - 1982; Most Valuable Player (Bell) - 1983

Gerald Riggs (40)

Year	Team	RuYds	RuTD	ReYds	ReTD	Fum	ARuY	AReY	ASptY	Q
1982	ATL	299	5	185	0	1	318.1	83.4	0.0	4.7
1983	ATL	437	8	149	0	7	308.0	39.0	−45.5	2.0
1984	ATL	1486	13	277	0	11	1222.8	91.7	0.0	7.4
1985	ATL	1719	10	267	0	0	1819.0	133.5	0.0	9.5
1986	ATL	1327	9	136	0	6	1193.3	52.3	0.0	8.0
1987	ATL	875	2	199	0	4	752.5	82.0	0.0	6.8
1988	ATL	488	1	171	0	3	397.6	65.9	0.0	2.6
1989	WAS	834	4	67	0	3	758.0	29.5	0.0	5.5
1990	WAS	475	6	60	0	2	459.3	25.7	0.0	3.2
1991	WAS	248	11	5	0	1	318.5	2.0	0.0	1.9

Hall of Fame? No

Pro Bowl Appearances: 3

All-Pro Selections: Consensus - 1, Total - 2 (1984-1985)

Awards: None

Barry Sanders (2)

Year	Team	RuYds	RuTD	ReYds	ReTD	Fum	ARuY	AReY	ASptY	Q
1989	DET	1470	14	282	0	10	1247.5	109.9	11.5	9.5
1990	DET	1304	13	480	3	4	1293.8	235.2	0.0	10.0
1991	DET	1548	16	307	1	5	1529.4	137.1	0.0	10.0
1992	DET	1352	9	225	1	6	1223.1	97.1	0.0	6.9
1993	DET	1115	3	205	0	3	1040.5	87.0	0.0	6.9
1994	DET	1883	7	283	1	0	1953.0	146.5	0.0	10.0
1995	DET	1500	11	398	1	3	1506.5	188.2	0.0	8.8
1996	DET	1553	11	147	0	4	1515.0	61.9	0.0	9.4
1997	DET	2053	11	305	3	3	2053.8	156.7	0.0	10.0
1998	DET	1491	4	289	0	3	1422.7	132.8	0.0	6.9

Hall of Fame? Yes

Pro Bowl Appearances: 10

All-Pro Selections: Consensus - 8, Total - 10 (1989-1998)

Awards: AP NFL Offensive Rookie of the Year - 1989; NEA NFL Rookie of the Year - 1989; PFW/PFWA Offensive Rookie of the Year - 1989; *Sporting News* NFL Rookie of the Year - 1989; UPI NFL/NFC Rookie of the Year - 1989; Most Valuable Player (Bell) - 1991; AP NFL Offensive Player of the Year - 1997; Most Valuable Player (AP) - 1997 (tie); Most Valuable Player (Bell) - 1997; PFW/PFWA Offensive Player of the Year - 1997; *Sporting News* NFL Player of the Year - 1997

O.J. Simpson (12)

Year	Team	RuYds	RuTD	ReYds	ReTD	Fum	ARuY	AReY	ASptY	Q
1969	BUF	697	2	343	3	6	529.8	155.5	87.3	7.3
1970	BUF	488	5	139	0	6	330.8	52.2	190.9	3.2
1971	BUF	742	5	162	0	5	617.7	61.0	23.2	5.7
1972	BUF	1251	6	198	0	8	1027.0	72.7	0.0	8.1
1973	BUF	2003	12	70	0	7	1849.6	30.1	0.0	10.0
1974	BUF	1125	3	189	1	7	890.7	84.8	0.0	6.6
1975	BUF	1817	16	426	7	7	1719.0	226.0	0.0	10.0
1976	BUF	1503	8	259	1	6	1359.9	117.6	0.0	10.0
1977	BUF	557	0	138	0	2	486.5	60.0	0.0	3.2
1978	SF	593	1	172	2	5	426.1	72.9	0.0	3.2
1979	SF	460	3	46	0	3	376.6	16.4	0.0	2.4

Hall of Fame? Yes

Pro Bowl Appearances: 6

All-Pro Selections: Consensus - 5, Total - 5 (1972-1976)

Awards: UPI AFL/AFC Player of the Year - 1972; Pro Bowl MVP - 1972; AP NFL Offensive Player of the Year - 1973; Most Valuable Player (AP) - 1973; Most Valuable Player (Bell) - 1973; NEA NFL Player of the Year - 1973; PFW/PFWA Offensive Player of the Year - 1973; *Sporting News* AFC Player of the Year - 1973; UPI AFL/AFC Player of the Year - 1973; *Sporting News* AFC Player of the Year - 1975; UPI AFL/AFC Player of the Year - 1975

Emmitt Smith (4)

Year	Team	RuYds	RuTD	ReYds	ReTD	Fum	ARuY	AReY	ASptY	Q
1990	DAL	937	11	228	0	7	792.4	88.6	0.0	5.8
1991	DAL	1563	12	258	1	8	1400.9	96.1	0.0	9.0
1992	DAL	1713	18	335	1	4	1754.9	150.6	0.0	10.0
1993	DAL	1486	9	414	1	4	1442.8	185.2	0.0	10.0
1994	DAL	1484	21	341	1	1	1658.8	170.7	0.0	8.7
1995	DAL	1773	25	375	0	7	1782.5	148.0	0.0	10.0
1996	DAL	1204	12	249	3	5	1149.1	114.4	0.0	7.7
1997	DAL	1074	4	234	0	1	1079.3	111.7	0.0	5.4
1998	DAL	1332	13	175	2	3	1351.4	88.1	0.0	6.4
1999	DAL	1397	11	119	2	5	1322.2	54.3	0.0	7.2
2000	DAL	1203	9	79	0	6	1061.7	30.8	0.0	5.5
2001	DAL	1021	3	116	0	1	1013.4	55.6	0.0	5.9
2002	DAL	975	5	89	0	3	912.1	37.4	0.0	4.4
2003	ARI	256	2	107	0	2	206.8	42.7	0.0	1.2
2004	ARI	937	9	105	0	4	876.0	44.0	0.0	5.0

Hall of Fame? Not eligible until 2009

Pro Bowl Appearances: 8

All-Pro Selections: Consensus - 5, Total - 6 (1991-1996)

Awards: AP NFL Offensive Rookie of the Year - 1990; PFW/PFWA Offensive Rookie of the Year - 1990; Most Valuable Player (AP) - 1993; Most Valuable Player (Bell) - 1993; PFW/PFWA Offensive Player of the Year - 1993; *Sporting News* NFL Player of the Year - 1993; UPI NFC Offensive Player of the Year - 1993; MVP, Super Bowl XXVIII - 1993

Matt Snell (67)

Year	Team	RuYds	RuTD	ReYds	ReTD	Fum	ARuY	AReY	ASptY	Q
1964	NYJ	948	5	393	1	0	998.0	201.5	18.0	10.0
1965	NYJ	763	4	264	0	3	705.0	110.0	0.0	6.7
1966	NYJ	644	4	346	4	3	589.9	167.6	0.0	5.7
1967	NYJ	207	0	54	0	2	139.2	14.8	0.0	1.1
1968	NYJ	747	6	105	1	2	735.0	51.1	−33.2	7.9
1969	NYJ	695	4	187	1	5	555.7	77.8	0.0	6.8
1970	NYJ	281	1	26	0	2	213.4	10.6	0.0	1.9
1971	NYJ	0	0	0	0	0	0.0	0.0	0.0	0.0
1972	NYJ	0	0	0	0	0	0.0	0.0	−6.0	0.0

Hall of Fame? No

Pro Bowl Appearances: 3

All-Pro Selections: Consensus - 1, Total - 4 (1964-1965; 1968-1969)

Awards: UPI AFL/AFC Rookie of the Year - 1964

Fred Taylor (35)

Year	Team	RuYds	RuTD	ReYds	ReTD	Fum	ARuY	AReY	ASptY	Q
1998	JAC	1223	14	421	3	3	1260.1	208.4	0.0	6.5
1999	JAC	732	6	83	0	0	792.0	41.5	0.0	4.3
2000	JAC	1399	12	240	2	4	1376.6	112.4	0.0	7.5
2001	JAC	116	0	13	0	1	78.5	4.0	0.0	0.5
2002	JAC	1314	8	408	0	3	1291.5	186.5	0.0	6.9
2003	JAC	1572	6	370	1	6	1421.3	160.7	0.0	7.6
2004	JAC	1224	2	345	1	3	1138.6	162.9	0.0	7.0
2005	JAC	787	3	83	0	0	817.0	41.5	0.0	3.9
2006	JAC	1146	5	242	1	3	1086.9	115.1	0.0	5.2
2007	JAC	1202	5	58	0	2	1175.1	25.9	0.0	6.4

Hall of Fame? Not eligible (active)

Pro Bowl Appearances: 1

All-Pro Selections: None

Awards: None

Jimmy Taylor (14)

Year	Team	RuYds	RuTD	ReYds	ReTD	Fum	ARuY	AReY	ASptY	Q
1958	GB	247	1	72	1	1	224.0	38.5	40.6	1.7
1959	GB	452	6	71	2	2	437.6	39.9	0.0	3.2
1960	GB	1101	11	121	0	5	1023.2	48.3	0.0	9.7
1961	GB	1307	15	175	1	2	1384.5	85.0	0.0	9.7
1962	GB	1474	19	106	0	5	1479.0	38.0	0.0	10.0
1963	GB	1018	9	68	1	5	918.7	29.1	0.0	5.1
1964	GB	1169	12	354	3	6	1082.4	158.6	0.0	8.5
1965	GB	734	4	207	0	3	664.6	92.9	0.0	4.5
1966	GB	705	4	331	2	4	611.8	148.7	0.0	5.2
1967	NO	390	2	251	0	1	379.0	116.5	0.0	4.1

Hall of Fame? Yes

Pro Bowl Appearances: 5

All-Pro Selections: Consensus - 1, Total - 6 (1960-1964; 1966)

Awards: Most Valuable Player (AP) - 1962; NEA NFL Player of the Year - 1962

Thurman Thomas (6)

Year	Team	RuYds	RuTD	ReYds	ReTD	Fum	ARuY	AReY	ASptY	Q
1988	BUF	881	2	208	0	9	569.8	75.2	0.0	3.6
1989	BUF	1244	6	669	6	7	1070.9	317.6	0.0	9.8
1990	BUF	1297	11	532	2	6	1203.8	239.3	0.0	9.4
1991	BUF	1407	7	631	5	5	1312.4	305.1	0.0	9.7
1992	BUF	1487	9	626	3	6	1374.6	290.4	0.0	8.7
1993	BUF	1315	6	387	0	6	1164.1	165.0	0.0	8.2
1994	BUF	1093	7	349	2	1	1128.9	178.6	0.0	6.2
1995	BUF	1005	6	220	2	6	846.3	98.7	0.0	4.9
1996	BUF	1033	8	254	0	1	1076.4	123.6	0.0	7.3
1997	BUF	643	1	208	0	2	586.0	91.0	0.0	3.1
1998	BUF	381	2	220	1	0	401.0	115.0	0.0	2.3
1999	BUF	152	0	37	1	0	152.0	23.5	0.0	0.9
2000	MIA	136	0	117	1	1	111.1	49.3	0.0	0.8

Hall of Fame? Yes

Pro Bowl Appearances: 5

All-Pro Selections: Consensus - 5, Total - 6 (1989-1994)

Awards: AP NFL Offensive Player of the Year - 1991; Most Valuable Player (AP) - 1991; PFW/PFWA Offensive Player of the Year - 1991; *Sporting News* NFL Player of the Year - 1991; UPI AFC Offensive Player of the Year - 1991

LaDainian Tomlinson (10)

Year	Team	RuYds	RuTD	ReYds	ReTD	Fum	ARuY	AReY	ASptY	Q
2001	SD	1236	10	367	0	8	1063.4	136.1	0.0	6.6
2002	SD	1683	14	489	1	3	1724.0	228.5	0.0	9.1
2003	SD	1645	13	725	4	2	1714.5	363.2	0.0	10.0
2004	SD	1335	17	441	1	6	1299.0	193.3	0.0	8.1
2005	SD	1462	18	370	2	3	1538.8	179.5	0.0	8.0
2006	SD	1815	28	508	3	2	2026.6	258.0	0.0	10.0
2007	SD	1474	15	475	3	0	1624.0	252.5	0.0	10.0

Hall of Fame? Not eligible (active)

Pro Bowl Appearances: 5

All-Pro Selections: Consensus - 4, Total - 6 (2002-2007)

Awards: AP NFL Offensive Player of the Year - 2006; Most Valuable Player (AP) - 2006

Steve Van Buren (8)

Year	Team	RuYds	RuTD	ReYds	ReTD	Fum	ARuY	AReY	ASptY	Q
1944	PHI	444	5	0	0	–	494.0	0.0	356.0	6.4
1945	PHI	832	15	123	2	7	763.2	56.2	235.7	10.0
1946	PHI	529	5	75	0	8	313.9	23.8	161.4	6.9
1947	PHI	1008	13	79	0	4	992.7	33.5	123.3	10.0
1948	PHI	945	10	96	0	6	831.5	37.4	–2.9	10.0
1949	PHI	1146	11	88	1	3	1142.9	47.3	42.8	10.0
1950	PHI	629	4	34	0	3	553.3	15.8	6.9	7.9
1951	PHI	327	6	28	0	3	271.1	9.9	0.0	3.6

Hall of Fame? Yes

Pro Bowl Appearances: None

All-Pro Selections: Consensus - 6, Total - 7 (1944-1950)

Awards: None

Herschel Walker (27)

Year	Team	RuYds	RuTD	ReYds	ReTD	Fum	ARuY	AReY	ASptY	Q
1986	DAL	737	12	837	2	5	724.0	361.5	0.0	6.9
1987	DAL	891	7	715	1	4	836.7	326.8	0.0	9.5
1988	DAL	1514	5	505	2	6	1354.7	231.8	0.0	8.9
1989	DAL	246	2	261	1	2	203.1	118.4	0.0	2.3
1989	MIN	669	5	162	1	5	550.0	68.0	111.0	4.3
1990	MIN	770	5	315	4	4	708.9	156.4	59.4	5.7
1991	MIN	825	10	204	0	2	857.9	90.8	−18.7	5.7
1992	PHI	1070	8	278	2	6	942.6	119.5	6.7	5.6
1993	PHI	746	1	610	3	3	676.0	285.5	−41.1	5.9
1994	PHI	528	5	500	2	4	479.7	216.5	152.7	3.3
1995	NYG	126	0	234	1	0	126.0	122.0	61.0	1.3
1996	DAL	83	1	89	0	0	93.0	44.5	239.0	0.8
1997	DAL	20	0	149	2	0	20.0	84.5	167.0	0.5

Hall of Fame? No

Pro Bowl Appearances: 2

All-Pro Selections: Consensus - 2, Total - 2 (1987-1988)

Awards: None

Curt Warner (57)

Year	Team	RuYds	RuTD	ReYds	ReTD	Fum	ARuY	AReY	ASptY	Q
1983	SEA	1449	13	325	1	6	1365.7	140.8	0.0	8.8
1984	SEA	40	0	19	0	0	40.0	9.5	0.0	0.3
1985	SEA	1094	8	307	1	8	898.5	114.0	0.0	4.9
1986	SEA	1481	13	342	0	6	1398.3	143.7	0.0	9.8
1987	SEA	985	8	167	2	4	915.8	82.7	0.0	8.1
1988	SEA	1025	10	154	2	5	940.3	71.7	0.0	5.6
1989	SEA	631	3	153	1	7	410.7	51.8	0.0	3.3
1990	LARM	139	1	0	0	1	109.0	0.0	0.0	0.7

Hall of Fame? No

Pro Bowl Appearances: 3

All-Pro Selections: Consensus - 3, Total - 4 (1983; 1985-1987)

Awards: UPI AFL/AFC Rookie of the Year - 1983; UPI AFC Offensive Player of the Year - 1983; UPI AFC Offensive Player of the Year - 1986

Chris Warren (72)

Year	Team	RuYds	RuTD	ReYds	ReTD	Fum	ARuY	AReY	ASptY	Q
1990	SEA	11	1	0	0	3	11.1	0.0	176.9	0.1
1991	SEA	13	0	9	0	3	−0.3	2.1	295.8	0.0
1992	SEA	1017	3	134	0	2	992.3	63.1	194.7	5.5
1993	SEA	1072	7	99	0	3	1028.3	43.3	0.0	6.6
1994	SEA	1545	9	323	2	5	1456.9	149.6	0.0	7.7
1995	SEA	1346	15	247	1	5	1316.3	108.2	0.0	7.4
1996	SEA	855	5	273	0	3	804.8	116.7	0.0	5.6
1997	SEA	847	4	257	0	2	821.7	113.8	0.0	4.2
1998	DAL	291	4	66	1	0	331.0	38.0	1.0	1.6
1999	DAL	403	2	224	0	4	303.9	71.1	0.0	2.0
2000	DAL	254	2	302	1	1	247.8	142.2	0.0	2.0
2000	PHI	42	0	1	0	2	−33.0	−4.5	0.0	0.0

Hall of Fame? No

Pro Bowl Appearances: 3

All-Pro Selections: Consensus - 2, Total - 2 (1994-1995)

Awards: None

Ricky Watters (22)

Year	Team	RuYds	RuTD	ReYds	ReTD	Fum	ARuY	AReY	ASptY	Q
1992	SF	1013	9	405	2	2	1037.1	198.7	0.0	6.5
1993	SF	950	10	326	1	5	875.9	142.1	0.0	6.3
1994	SF	877	6	719	5	8	686.2	315.3	0.0	4.8
1995	PHI	1273	11	434	1	6	1180.3	184.7	0.0	7.1
1996	PHI	1411	13	444	0	5	1366.2	196.8	0.0	9.6
1997	PHI	1110	7	440	0	3	1077.3	202.7	0.0	5.8
1998	SEA	1239	9	373	0	4	1191.8	164.1	0.0	6.0
1999	SEA	1210	5	387	2	4	1117.5	186.0	0.0	6.8
2000	SEA	1242	7	613	2	5	1149.0	279.5	0.0	7.2
2001	SEA	318	1	107	0	1	293.3	48.2	0.0	1.9

Hall of Fame? No

Pro Bowl Appearances: 5

All-Pro Selections: Consensus - 0, Total - 3 (1994-1996)

Awards: None

Ken Willard (74)

Year	Team	RuYds	RuTD	ReYds	ReTD	Fum	ARuY	AReY	ASptY	Q
1965	SF	778	5	253	4	7	589.6	106.1	0.0	3.9
1966	SF	763	5	351	2	7	583.5	135.0	0.0	4.9
1967	SF	510	5	242	1	1	524.8	121.2	0.0	5.3
1968	SF	967	7	232	0	4	898.9	94.1	0.0	7.3
1969	SF	557	7	326	3	6	428.7	136.3	0.0	4.9
1970	SF	789	7	259	3	3	752.9	130.6	0.0	7.4
1971	SF	855	4	202	1	8	610.6	70.4	0.0	5.8
1972	SF	345	4	131	1	3	288.2	47.3	0.0	2.4
1973	SF	366	1	160	1	2	313.4	68.4	−20.8	2.0
1974	STL	175	0	28	1	0	175.0	19.0	0.0	1.3

Hall of Fame? No

Pro Bowl Appearances: 4

All-Pro Selections: Consensus - 0, Total - 2 (1965; 1968)

Awards: None

Wide Receivers

Lance Alworth (7)

Year	Team	ReYds	ReTD	RuYds	RuTD	Fum	AReY	ARuY	ASptY	Q
1962	SD	226	3	17	0	0	128.0	17.0	0.0	2.6
1963	SD	1205	11	14	0	0	657.5	14.0	136.0	9.2
1964	SD	1235	13	60	2	3	594.3	75.7	163.0	6.4
1965	SD	1602	14	−12	0	2	794.3	−15.3	0.0	10.0
1966	SD	1383	13	10	0	0	756.5	10.0	0.0	10.0
1967	SD	1010	9	5	0	0	550.0	5.0	0.0	7.4
1968	SD	1312	10	18	0	0	706.0	18.0	0.0	10.0
1969	SD	1003	4	25	0	0	521.5	25.0	0.0	9.0
1970	SD	608	4	0	0	0	324.0	0.0	0.0	5.3
1971	DAL	487	2	−10	0	0	253.5	−10.0	0.0	3.9
1972	DAL	195	2	2	0	0	107.5	2.0	0.0	2.0

Hall of Fame? Yes

Pro Bowl Appearances: 7

All-Pro Selections: Consensus - 7, Total - 7 (1963-1969)

Awards: UPI AFL/AFC Player of the Year - 1963

Raymond Berry (18)

Year	Team	ReYds	ReTD	RuYds	RuTD	Fum	AReY	ARuY	ASptY	Q
1955	BAL	205	0	0	0	0	102.5	0.0	−13.0	1.8
1956	BAL	601	2	0	0	0	310.5	0.0	0.0	4.7
1957	BAL	800	6	0	0	0	430.0	0.0	0.0	10.0
1958	BAL	794	9	0	0	0	442.0	0.0	0.0	7.8
1959	BAL	959	14	0	0	0	549.5	0.0	0.0	7.3
1960	BAL	1298	10	0	0	0	699.0	0.0	0.0	8.7
1961	BAL	873	0	0	0	0	436.5	0.0	0.0	7.5
1962	BAL	687	3	0	0	1	318.5	0.0	0.0	5.1
1963	BAL	703	3	0	0	0	366.5	0.0	0.0	5.8
1964	BAL	663	6	0	0	0	361.5	0.0	0.0	5.9
1965	BAL	739	7	0	0	0	404.5	0.0	0.0	5.8
1966	BAL	786	7	0	0	0	428.0	0.0	0.0	6.2
1967	BAL	167	1	0	0	0	88.5	0.0	0.0	1.3

Hall of Fame? Yes

Pro Bowl Appearances: 5

All-Pro Selections: Consensus - 3, Total - 6 (1957-1961; 1965)

Awards: UPI AFL/AFC Coach of the Year - 1985

Fred Biletnikoff (39)

Year	Team	ReYds	ReTD	RuYds	RuTD	Fum	AReY	ARuY	ASptY	Q
1965	OAK	331	0	0	0	0	165.5	0.0	0.0	2.1
1966	OAK	272	3	0	0	2	71.0	0.0	0.0	0.9
1967	OAK	876	5	0	0	1	423.0	0.0	0.0	5.7
1968	OAK	1037	6	0	0	0	548.5	0.0	0.0	7.6
1969	OAK	837	12	0	0	1	438.5	0.0	0.0	7.3
1970	OAK	768	7	0	0	0	419.0	0.0	0.0	6.9
1971	OAK	929	9	0	0	1	469.5	0.0	0.0	7.5
1972	OAK	802	7	0	0	0	436.0	0.0	0.0	8.1
1973	OAK	660	4	0	0	0	350.0	0.0	0.0	6.5
1974	OAK	593	7	0	0	0	331.5	0.0	0.0	5.8
1975	OAK	587	2	0	0	0	303.5	0.0	0.0	5.7
1976	OAK	551	7	0	0	0	310.5	0.0	0.0	4.9
1977	OAK	446	5	0	0	1	208.0	0.0	0.0	3.8
1978	OAK	285	2	0	0	0	152.5	0.0	0.0	2.4

Hall of Fame? Yes

Pro Bowl Appearances: 6

All-Pro Selections: Consensus - 2, Total - 6 (1969-1974)

Awards: MVP, Super Bowl XI - 1976

Cliff Branch (17)

Year	Team	ReYds	ReTD	RuYds	RuTD	Fum	AReY	ARuY	ASptY	Q
1972	OAK	41	0	5	0	2	12.5	2.3	–37.3	0.3
1973	OAK	290	3	0	0	0	160.0	0.0	0.0	3.0
1974	OAK	1092	13	0	0	1	571.0	0.0	0.0	10.0
1975	OAK	893	9	18	0	0	491.5	18.0	0.0	9.6
1976	OAK	1111	12	12	0	0	615.5	12.0	0.0	10.0
1977	OAK	540	6	0	0	0	300.0	0.0	0.0	5.5
1978	OAK	709	1	0	0	2	279.5	0.0	0.0	4.5
1979	OAK	844	6	4	0	1	412.7	3.3	0.0	6.3
1980	OAK	858	7	1	0	0	464.0	1.0	0.0	6.2
1981	OAK	635	1	0	0	0	322.5	0.0	0.0	4.7
1982	LARI	575	4	10	0	0	307.5	10.0	0.0	5.4
1983	LARI	696	5	20	0	0	373.0	20.0	0.0	5.4
1984	LARI	401	0	0	0	0	200.5	0.0	0.0	2.5
1985	LARI	0	0	0	0	0	0.0	0.0	0.0	0.0

Hall of Fame? No

Pro Bowl Appearances: 4

All-Pro Selections: Consensus - 3, Total - 4 (1974-1977)

Awards: None

Tim Brown (15)

Year	Team	ReYds	ReTD	RuYds	RuTD	Fum	AReY	ARuY	ASptY	Q
1988	LARI	725	5	50	1	5	332.7	42.2	604.6	5.3
1989	LARI	8	0	0	0	1	−1.0	0.0	11.0	0.0
1990	LARI	265	3	0	0	3	111.5	0.0	211.0	1.4
1991	LARI	554	5	16	0	1	284.2	13.5	329.2	4.1
1992	LARI	693	7	−4	0	6	274.6	−10.5	230.5	3.6
1993	LARI	1180	7	7	0	1	602.5	6.4	458.1	7.8
1994	LARI	1309	9	0	0	3	624.8	0.0	441.7	7.0
1995	OAK	1342	10	0	0	0	721.0	0.0	364.0	7.6
1996	OAK	1104	9	35	0	3	525.0	30.2	232.8	7.4
1997	OAK	1408	5	19	0	1	691.2	17.2	−13.4	8.5
1998	OAK	1012	9	−7	0	3	438.0	−8.4	17.4	5.5
1999	OAK	1344	6	4	0	0	702.0	4.0	0.0	8.7
2000	OAK	1128	11	12	0	0	619.0	12.0	0.0	6.9
2001	OAK	1165	9	39	0	1	597.7	37.7	112.1	7.6
2002	OAK	930	2	19	0	3	389.7	12.7	26.6	4.3
2003	OAK	567	2	0	0	0	293.5	0.0	0.0	3.3
2004	TB	200	1	0	0	2	59.3	0.0	13.7	0.8

Hall of Fame? Not eligible until 2009

Pro Bowl Appearances: 9

All-Pro Selections: Consensus - 5, Total - 7 (1988; 1991; 1993-1997)

Awards: None

Isaac Bruce (14)

Year	Team	ReYds	ReTD	RuYds	RuTD	Fum	AReY	ARuY	ASptY	Q
1994	LARM	272	3	2	0	0	151.0	2.0	0.0	1.7
1995	STL	1781	13	17	0	2	877.5	15.0	52.0	9.4
1996	STL	1338	7	4	0	1	665.4	3.5	0.0	8.5
1997	STL	815	5	0	0	1	392.5	0.0	0.0	4.7
1998	STL	457	1	30	0	0	233.5	30.0	0.0	3.3
1999	STL	1165	12	32	0	0	642.5	32.0	0.0	8.3
2000	STL	1471	9	11	0	1	741.0	10.5	0.0	8.3
2001	STL	1106	6	23	0	4	432.4	13.6	0.0	5.3
2002	STL	1075	7	18	0	2	495.4	15.1	0.0	5.5
2003	STL	981	5	17	0	0	515.5	17.0	0.0	6.4
2004	STL	1292	6	0	0	5	480.4	0.0	0.0	6.3
2005	STL	525	3	0	0	0	277.5	0.0	0.0	3.4
2006	STL	1098	3	0	0	0	564.0	0.0	0.0	7.9
2007	STL	733	4	−4	0	0	386.5	−4.0	0.0	4.4

Hall of Fame? Not eligible (active)

Pro Bowl Appearances: 4

All-Pro Selections: Consensus - 1, Total - 3 (1995-1996; 1999)

Awards: None

Harold Carmichael (37)

Year	Team	ReYds	ReTD	RuYds	RuTD	Fum	AReY	ARuY	ASptY	Q
1971	PHI	288	0	0	0	2	64.0	0.0	0.0	1.0
1972	PHI	276	2	0	0	1	108.0	0.0	0.0	3.1
1973	PHI	1116	9	42	0	3	488.1	36.9	0.0	9.7
1974	PHI	649	8	–6	0	1	326.5	–7.4	0.0	5.6
1975	PHI	639	7	6	0	2	276.1	4.4	0.0	5.3
1976	PHI	503	5	0	0	0	276.5	0.0	0.0	4.4
1977	PHI	665	7	0	0	0	367.5	0.0	0.0	6.8
1978	PHI	1072	8	21	0	1	536.7	20.3	0.0	8.9
1979	PHI	872	11	0	0	0	491.0	0.0	0.0	7.4
1980	PHI	815	9	0	0	1	412.5	0.0	0.0	5.5
1981	PHI	1028	6	1	0	3	425.9	–0.9	0.0	6.1
1982	PHI	540	4	0	0	3	170.0	0.0	0.0	2.9
1983	PHI	515	3	0	0	0	272.5	0.0	0.0	4.1
1984	DAL	7	0	0	0	0	3.5	0.0	0.0	0.0

Hall of Fame? No

Pro Bowl Appearances: 4

All-Pro Selections: Consensus - 3, Total - 6 (1973-1974; 1977-1980)

Awards: Walter Payton NFL Man of the Year - 1980

Cris Carter (25)

Year	Team	ReYds	ReTD	RuYds	RuTD	Fum	AReY	ARuY	ASptY	Q
1987	PHI	84	2	0	0	0	52.0	0.0	1.0	0.8
1988	PHI	761	6	1	0	0	410.5	1.0	0.0	5.8
1989	PHI	605	11	16	0	1	319.2	14.3	0.0	3.9
1990	MIN	413	3	6	0	0	221.5	6.0	0.0	2.9
1991	MIN	962	5	0	0	1	466.0	0.0	0.0	6.5
1992	MIN	681	6	15	0	1	333.9	11.6	0.0	4.8
1993	MIN	1071	9	0	0	0	580.5	0.0	0.0	7.4
1994	MIN	1256	7	0	0	4	503.0	0.0	0.0	5.7
1995	MIN	1371	17	0	0	0	770.5	0.0	0.0	8.1
1996	MIN	1163	10	0	0	1	591.9	0.0	−17.4	7.9
1997	MIN	1069	13	0	0	3	479.5	0.0	0.0	5.8
1998	MIN	1011	12	−1	0	0	565.5	−1.0	0.0	7.2
1999	MIN	1241	13	0	0	0	685.5	0.0	0.0	8.4
2000	MIN	1274	9	0	0	3	562.0	0.0	0.0	6.2
2001	MIN	871	6	4	0	2	386.6	2.9	0.0	4.6
2002	MIA	66	1	0	0	1	−2.0	0.0	0.0	0.0

Hall of Fame? No

Pro Bowl Appearances: 8

All-Pro Selections: Consensus - 2, Total - 4 (1994-1996; 1999)

Awards: Byron "Whizzer" White Award - 1999; Walter Payton NFL Man of the Year - 1999

Wes Chandler (34)

Year	Team	ReYds	ReTD	RuYds	RuTD	Fum	AReY	ARuY	ASptY	Q
1978	NO	472	2	10	0	1	233.6	9.3	326.1	3.9
1979	NO	1069	6	0	0	0	564.5	0.0	9.0	8.5
1980	NO	975	6	9	0	2	454.1	8.0	22.3	6.3
1981	SD	857	5	–1	0	1	425.8	–3.7	35.5	6.1
1981	NO	285	1	0	0	0	147.5	0.0	0.0	2.1
1982	SD	1032	9	32	0	0	561.0	32.0	0.0	10.0
1983	SD	845	5	25	0	3	354.7	21.8	3.6	5.1
1984	SD	708	6	0	0	0	384.0	0.0	0.0	4.9
1985	SD	1199	10	9	0	1	610.1	8.4	0.0	9.2
1986	SD	874	4	0	0	2	388.1	0.0	–0.9	4.5
1987	SD	617	2	0	0	1	278.5	0.0	0.0	4.4
1988	SF	33	0	0	0	0	16.5	0.0	28.0	0.2

Hall of Fame? No

Pro Bowl Appearances: 4

All-Pro Selections: Consensus - 1, Total - 2 (1979; 1982)

Awards: None

Gary Clark (20)

Year	Team	ReYds	ReTD	RuYds	RuTD	Fum	AReY	ARuY	ASptY	Q
1985	WAS	926	5	10	0	0	488.0	10.0	0.0	7.4
1986	WAS	1265	7	0	0	1	629.6	0.0	11.9	7.2
1987	WAS	1066	7	0	0	3	450.1	−2.1	0.0	7.1
1988	WAS	892	7	6	0	2	415.4	3.8	35.8	5.9
1989	WAS	1229	9	19	0	1	620.5	18.0	0.0	7.4
1990	WAS	1112	8	1	0	0	596.0	1.0	0.0	7.7
1991	WAS	1340	10	0	0	0	720.0	0.0	0.0	10.0
1992	WAS	912	5	18	0	1	442.2	16.8	0.0	6.3
1993	PHX	818	4	0	0	1	389.0	0.0	0.0	5.0
1994	ARI	771	1	0	0	0	390.5	0.0	0.0	4.4
1995	MIA	525	2	0	0	0	272.5	0.0	0.0	2.9

Hall of Fame? No

Pro Bowl Appearances: 4

All-Pro Selections: Consensus - 2, Total - 4 (1986-1987; 1990-1991)

Awards: None

Mark Clayton (33)

Year	Team	ReYds	ReTD	RuYds	RuTD	Fum	AReY	ARuY	ASptY	Q
1983	MIA	114	1	9	0	3	50.4	5.1	304.4	1.1
1984	MIA	1389	18	35	0	2	718.9	32.3	43.2	9.1
1985	MIA	996	4	10	0	2	442.3	8.9	11.8	6.6
1986	MIA	1150	10	33	0	1	586.9	31.7	−0.6	7.1
1987	MIA	776	7	8	0	0	423.0	8.0	0.0	6.8
1988	MIA	1129	14	4	0	0	634.5	4.0	0.0	9.0
1989	MIA	1011	9	9	0	1	512.3	7.2	0.0	6.0
1990	MIA	406	3	0	0	1	178.0	0.0	0.0	2.3
1991	MIA	1053	12	0	0	0	586.5	0.0	0.0	8.1
1992	MIA	619	3	0	0	1	284.5	0.0	0.0	3.9
1993	GB	331	3	0	0	0	180.5	0.0	0.0	2.3

Hall of Fame? No

Pro Bowl Appearances: None

All-Pro Selections: Consensus - 1, Total - 3 (1984-1985; 1988)

Awards: None

Henry Ellard (21)

Year	Team	ReYds	ReTD	RuYds	RuTD	Fum	AReY	ARuY	ASptY	Q
1983	LARM	268	0	7	0	2	110.3	2.6	189.1	1.5
1984	LARM	622	6	−5	0	4	265.4	−11.7	329.2	3.2
1985	LARM	811	5	8	0	5	325.6	2.2	421.7	4.9
1986	LARM	447	4	−15	0	3	175.5	−17.0	75.0	1.8
1987	LARM	799	3	4	0	3	331.8	2.4	59.3	5.3
1988	LARM	1414	10	7	0	3	660.6	5.9	96.6	9.4
1989	LARM	1382	8	10	0	0	731.0	10.0	20.0	8.6
1990	LARM	1294	4	21	0	4	515.0	17.0	11.0	6.9
1991	LARM	1052	3	0	0	1	501.0	0.0	0.0	7.0
1992	LARM	727	3	0	0	0	378.5	0.0	0.0	5.2
1993	LARM	945	2	18	0	0	482.5	18.0	18.0	6.4
1994	WAS	1397	6	−5	0	1	689.0	−5.5	0.0	7.7
1995	WAS	1005	5	0	0	1	487.5	0.0	0.0	5.1
1996	WAS	1014	2	0	0	0	517.0	0.0	0.0	6.9
1997	WAS	485	4	0	0	0	262.5	0.0	0.0	3.2
1998	WAS	29	0	0	0	0	14.5	0.0	0.0	0.2
1998	NE	86	0	0	0	0	43.0	0.0	0.0	0.5

Hall of Fame? No

Pro Bowl Appearances: 3

All-Pro Selections: Consensus - 1, Total - 4 (1984-1985; 1988-1989)

Awards: None

Joey Galloway (31)

Year	Team	ReYds	ReTD	RuYds	RuTD	Fum	AReY	ARuY	ASptY	Q
1995	SEA	1039	7	154	1	1	533.6	160.6	344.4	7.3
1996	SEA	987	7	127	0	2	478.9	114.0	150.6	7.9
1997	SEA	1049	12	72	0	1	549.4	67.6	0.0	7.2
1998	SEA	1047	10	26	0	1	548.5	22.5	259.5	7.3
1999	SEA	335	1	–1	0	0	172.5	–1.0	54.0	2.1
2000	DAL	62	1	0	0	0	36.0	0.0	2.0	0.4
2001	DAL	699	3	32	0	1	328.0	29.9	5.3	4.2
2002	DAL	908	6	31	0	2	428.5	27.4	160.1	4.9
2003	DAL	672	2	22	0	1	326.3	19.7	138.0	3.9
2004	TB	416	5	19	0	3	170.1	15.2	98.7	2.5
2005	TB	1287	10	4	0	0	693.5	4.0	0.0	8.5
2006	TB	1057	7	9	0	0	563.5	9.0	3.0	8.0
2007	TB	1014	6	1	0	0	537.0	1.0	14.0	6.2

Hall of Fame? Not eligible (active)

Pro Bowl Appearances: None

All-Pro Selections: None

Awards: None

Gary Garrison (38)

Year	Team	ReYds	ReTD	RuYds	RuTD	Fum	AReY	ARuY	ASptY	Q
1966	SD	642	4	–3	0	0	341.0	–3.0	0.0	4.4
1967	SD	772	2	1	0	0	396.0	1.0	0.0	5.3
1968	SD	1103	10	0	0	1	561.5	0.0	0.0	7.8
1969	SD	804	7	0	0	1	397.0	0.0	0.0	6.6
1970	SD	1006	12	7	0	0	563.0	7.0	0.0	9.3
1971	SD	889	6	0	0	0	474.5	0.0	0.0	7.6
1972	SD	744	7	–6	0	0	407.0	–6.0	0.0	7.4
1973	SD	292	2	0	0	0	156.0	0.0	0.0	2.9
1974	SD	785	5	0	0	1	377.5	0.0	0.0	6.6
1975	SD	438	2	30	0	0	229.0	30.0	0.0	4.9
1976	SD	58	1	0	0	0	34.0	0.0	0.0	0.5
1977	HOU	5	0	0	0	0	2.5	0.0	0.0	0.0

Hall of Fame? No

Pro Bowl Appearances: 4

All-Pro Selections: Consensus - 0, Total - 4 (1968; 1970-1972)

Awards: None

John Gilliam (32)

Year	Team	ReYds	ReTD	RuYds	RuTD	Fum	AReY	ARuY	ASptY	Q
1967	NO	264	1	41	0	2	106.7	31.3	144.0	1.1
1968	NO	284	0	36	0	0	142.0	36.0	88.0	3.0
1969	STL	997	9	−4	0	1	511.0	−4.6	122.1	6.4
1970	STL	952	5	68	1	3	402.8	67.1	−3.9	7.7
1971	STL	837	3	16	0	2	358.8	12.4	19.2	5.9
1972	MIN	1035	7	14	0	2	498.0	4.7	72.8	9.3
1973	MIN	907	8	71	1	1	464.0	77.5	−33.0	10.0
1974	MIN	578	5	16	0	0	314.0	16.0	26.0	5.8
1975	MIN	777	7	35	0	1	385.8	32.7	0.0	7.9
1976	ATL	292	2	0	0	0	156.0	0.0	0.0	2.5
1977	NO	133	1	0	0	0	71.5	0.0	0.0	1.3
1977	CHIB	0	0	0	0	0	0.0	0.0	0.0	0.0

Hall of Fame? No

Pro Bowl Appearances: 4

All-Pro Selections: Consensus - 1, Total - 3 (1972-1973; 1975)

Awards: None

Marvin Harrison (3)

Year	Team	ReYds	ReTD	RuYds	RuTD	Fum	AReY	ARuY	ASptY	Q
1996	IND	836	8	15	0	1	430.8	13.7	165.5	5.9
1997	IND	866	6	–7	0	2	386.2	–9.1	–1.1	4.5
1998	IND	776	7	0	0	0	423.0	0.0	0.0	5.4
1999	IND	1663	12	4	0	2	812.2	3.3	0.0	10.0
2000	IND	1413	14	0	0	2	696.5	0.0	0.0	7.7
2001	IND	1524	15	3	0	0	837.0	3.0	0.0	10.0
2002	IND	1722	11	10	0	0	916.0	10.0	0.0	10.0
2003	IND	1272	10	3	0	2	607.7	2.2	–0.8	6.9
2004	IND	1113	15	0	0	1	591.5	0.0	0.0	7.8
2005	IND	1146	12	0	0	0	633.0	0.0	10.0	7.8
2006	IND	1366	12	0	0	1	703.0	0.0	0.0	9.8
2007	IND	247	1	0	0	0	128.5	0.0	0.0	1.5

Hall of Fame? Not eligible (active)

Pro Bowl Appearances: 8

All-Pro Selections: Consensus - 8, Total - 8 (1999-2006)

Awards: None

Drew Hill (36)

Year	Team	ReYds	ReTD	RuYds	RuTD	Fum	AReY	ARuY	ASptY	Q
1979	LARM	94	1	0	0	2	44.9	0.0	−69.9	0.7
1980	LARM	416	2	4	0	2	193.9	2.7	−24.6	2.6
1981	LARM	355	3	14	0	1	184.4	13.5	−39.4	2.9
1982	LARM	92	0	0	0	0	46.0	0.0	2.0	0.8
1984	LARM	390	4	0	0	0	215.0	0.0	23.0	2.7
1985	HOU	1169	9	0	0	0	629.5	0.0	2.0	9.3
1986	HOU	1112	5	0	0	0	581.0	0.0	0.0	6.7
1987	HOU	989	6	0	0	1	485.3	0.0	0.0	7.7
1988	HOU	1141	10	0	0	0	620.5	0.0	0.0	8.8
1989	HOU	938	8	0	0	1	469.0	0.0	0.0	5.5
1990	HOU	1019	5	0	0	0	534.5	0.0	0.0	6.9
1991	HOU	1109	4	1	0	2	495.4	0.1	0.0	6.9
1992	ATL	623	3	0	0	1	286.5	0.0	0.0	4.0
1993	ATL	384	0	0	0	0	192.0	0.0	0.0	2.4

Hall of Fame? No

Pro Bowl Appearances: 2

All-Pro Selections: Consensus - 0, Total - 2 (1988; 1990)

Awards: None

Torry Holt (12)

Year	Team	ReYds	ReTD	RuYds	RuTD	Fum	AReY	ARuY	ASptY	Q
1999	STL	788	6	25	0	4	285.3	17.0	1.7	3.7
2000	STL	1635	6	7	0	2	769.4	5.1	0.0	8.5
2001	STL	1363	7	0	0	2	638.4	−1.9	0.0	7.6
2002	STL	1302	4	18	0	1	631.9	17.1	0.0	7.0
2003	STL	1696	12	5	0	1	868.3	4.7	0.0	9.9
2004	STL	1372	10	0	0	3	616.0	0.0	0.0	8.2
2005	STL	1331	9	2	0	2	631.3	1.2	0.0	7.7
2006	STL	1188	10	0	0	2	564.0	0.0	0.0	7.9
2007	STL	1189	7	0	0	2	549.5	0.0	0.0	6.4

Hall of Fame? Not eligible (active)

Pro Bowl Appearances: 7

All-Pro Selections: Consensus - 1, Total - 2 (2003; 2006)

Awards: None

Billy Howton (19)

Year	Team	ReYds	ReTD	RuYds	RuTD	Fum	AReY	ARuY	ASptY	Q
1952	GB	1231	13	0	0	1	640.5	0.0	0.0	10.0
1953	GB	463	4	0	0	1	211.5	0.0	0.0	3.7
1954	GB	768	2	0	0	0	394.0	0.0	0.0	6.3
1955	GB	697	5	0	0	2	293.5	0.0	0.0	5.2
1956	GB	1188	12	0	0	0	654.0	0.0	0.0	10.0
1957	GB	727	5	20	0	1	352.3	16.2	0.0	8.6
1958	GB	507	2	0	0	0	263.5	0.0	0.0	4.6
1959	CLE	510	1	0	0	0	260.0	0.0	0.0	3.5
1960	DAL	363	4	0	0	0	201.5	0.0	0.0	2.5
1961	DAL	785	4	9	0	1	373.2	8.3	0.0	6.5
1962	DAL	706	6	0	0	0	383.0	0.0	0.0	6.1
1963	DAL	514	3	0	0	0	272.0	0.0	0.0	4.3

Hall of Fame? No

Pro Bowl Appearances: 4

All-Pro Selections: Consensus - 3, Total - 5 (1952; 1955-1957; 1959)

Awards: None

Don Hutson (2)

Year	Team	ReYds	ReTD	RuYds	RuTD	Fum	AReY	ARuY	ASptY	Q
1935	GB	420	6	22	0	–	240.0	22.0	0.0	10.0
1936	GB	536	8	–3	0	–	308.0	–3.0	0.0	10.0
1937	GB	552	7	26	0	–	311.0	26.0	0.0	8.3
1938	GB	548	9	–1	0	–	319.0	–1.0	0.0	10.0
1939	GB	846	6	26	0	–	453.0	26.0	0.0	10.0
1940	GB	664	7	0	0	–	367.0	0.0	0.0	9.9
1941	GB	738	10	22	2	–	419.0	42.0	–12.0	10.0
1942	GB	1211	17	4	0	–	690.5	4.0	0.0	10.0
1943	GB	776	11	41	0	–	443.0	41.0	0.0	10.0
1944	GB	866	9	87	0	–	478.0	87.0	0.0	10.0
1945	GB	834	9	60	1	1	442.8	66.7	–44.6	10.0

Hall of Fame? Yes

Pro Bowl Appearances: 4

All-Pro Selections: Consensus - 10, Total - 11 (1935-1945)

Awards: Most Valuable Player (Carr) - 1941; Most Valuable Player (Carr) - 1942

Michael Irvin (10)

Year	Team	ReYds	ReTD	RuYds	RuTD	Fum	AReY	ARuY	ASptY	Q
1988	DAL	654	5	2	0	0	352.0	2.0	0.0	5.0
1989	DAL	378	2	6	0	0	199.0	6.0	0.0	2.4
1990	DAL	413	5	0	0	0	231.5	0.0	0.0	3.0
1991	DAL	1523	8	0	0	3	681.5	0.0	0.0	9.5
1992	DAL	1396	7	−9	0	1	693.5	−9.5	0.0	9.5
1993	DAL	1330	7	6	0	0	700.0	6.0	0.0	9.0
1994	DAL	1241	6	0	0	0	650.5	0.0	0.0	7.3
1995	DAL	1603	10	0	0	1	811.5	0.0	0.0	8.5
1996	DAL	962	2	0	0	1	451.0	0.0	0.0	6.0
1997	DAL	1180	9	0	0	0	635.0	0.0	0.0	7.6
1998	DAL	1057	1	1	0	1	494.0	0.5	0.0	6.3
1999	DAL	167	3	0	0	0	98.5	0.0	0.0	1.2

Hall of Fame? Yes

Pro Bowl Appearances: 5

All-Pro Selections: Consensus - 1, Total - 3 (1991-1993)

Awards: Pro Bowl MVP - 1991

Harold Jackson (11)

Year	Team	ReYds	ReTD	RuYds	RuTD	Fum	AReY	ARuY	ASptY	Q
1968	LARM	0	0	0	0	0	0.0	0.0	0.0	0.0
1969	PHI	1116	9	10	0	0	603.0	10.0	0.0	7.8
1970	PHI	613	5	−5	0	0	331.5	−5.0	0.0	5.4
1971	PHI	716	3	41	0	1	338.2	37.3	6.5	6.0
1972	PHI	1048	4	76	0	2	474.1	65.9	0.0	10.0
1973	LARM	874	13	−8	0	0	502.0	−8.0	0.0	9.1
1974	LARM	514	5	4	0	0	282.0	4.0	0.0	5.0
1975	LARM	786	7	0	0	1	388.0	0.0	0.0	7.3
1976	LARM	751	5	15	0	1	361.5	14.0	0.0	6.0
1977	LARM	666	6	6	0	0	363.0	6.0	0.0	6.8
1978	NE	743	6	7	0	0	401.5	7.0	0.0	6.5
1979	NE	1013	7	12	0	0	541.5	12.0	0.0	8.3
1980	NE	737	5	37	0	0	393.5	37.0	0.0	6.0
1981	NE	669	0	−14	0	1	297.4	−15.9	0.0	4.0
1982	MIN	0	0	0	0	0	0.0	0.0	0.0	0.0
1983	SEA	126	1	0	0	1	28.0	0.0	0.0	0.4

Hall of Fame? No

Pro Bowl Appearances: 5

All-Pro Selections: Consensus - 3, Total - 4 (1972-1973; 1976-1977)

Awards: None

Chad Johnson (35)

Year	Team	ReYds	ReTD	RuYds	RuTD	Fum	AReY	ARuY	ASptY	Q
2001	CIN	329	1	0	0	0	169.5	0.0	0.0	2.0
2002	CIN	1166	5	0	0	0	608.0	0.0	0.0	6.6
2003	CIN	1355	10	0	0	0	727.5	0.0	0.0	8.3
2004	CIN	1274	9	39	0	1	643.6	37.4	0.0	9.0
2005	CIN	1432	9	33	0	1	723.0	31.0	0.0	9.2
2006	CIN	1369	7	24	0	1	682.1	21.4	0.0	9.8
2007	CIN	1440	8	47	0	2	684.8	42.2	0.0	8.4

Hall of Fame? Not eligible (active)

Pro Bowl Appearances: 4

All-Pro Selections: Consensus - 4, Total - 4 (2003-2006)

Awards: None

Charlie Joiner (40)

Year	Team	ReYds	ReTD	RuYds	RuTD	Fum	AReY	ARuY	ASptY	Q
1969	HOU	77	0	0	0	0	38.5	0.0	13.0	0.6
1970	HOU	416	3	0	0	0	223.0	0.0	0.0	3.7
1971	HOU	681	7	0	0	1	336.8	0.0	3.8	5.4
1972	HOU	306	2	12	0	1	127.4	7.6	0.0	2.5
1972	CIN	133	0	2	0	1	43.6	−0.9	−26.3	0.8
1973	CIN	214	0	0	0	1	67.0	0.0	0.0	1.2
1974	CIN	390	1	20	0	3	97.1	2.9	0.0	1.8
1975	CIN	726	5	0	0	1	348.0	0.0	0.0	6.5
1976	SD	1056	7	0	0	0	563.0	0.0	0.0	9.0
1977	SD	542	6	0	0	1	262.1	0.0	−13.1	4.8
1978	SD	607	1	0	0	2	228.5	0.0	0.0	3.7
1979	SD	1008	4	−12	0	1	484.5	−12.5	0.0	7.1
1980	SD	1132	4	0	0	3	466.0	0.0	0.0	6.2
1981	SD	1188	7	0	0	2	549.0	0.0	0.0	7.9
1982	SD	545	0	0	0	1	232.5	0.0	0.0	3.9
1983	SD	960	3	0	0	2	415.0	0.0	0.0	5.7
1984	SD	793	6	0	0	0	426.5	0.0	0.0	5.4
1985	SD	932	7	0	0	1	461.0	0.0	0.0	6.8
1986	SD	440	2	0	0	0	230.0	0.0	0.0	2.6

Hall of Fame? Yes

Pro Bowl Appearances: 3

All-Pro Selections: Consensus - 0, Total - 2 (1976; 1980)

Awards: None

Steve Largent (4)

Year	Team	ReYds	ReTD	RuYds	RuTD	Fum	AReY	ARuY	ASptY	Q
1976	SEA	705	4	−14	0	2	311.7	−18.5	18.5	4.7
1977	SEA	643	10	0	0	0	371.5	0.0	32.0	6.9
1978	SEA	1168	8	0	0	0	624.0	0.0	0.0	10.0
1979	SEA	1237	9	0	0	0	663.5	0.0	0.0	10.0
1980	SEA	1064	6	2	0	1	522.6	1.4	0.0	7.0
1981	SEA	1224	9	47	1	2	583.8	51.1	0.0	9.1
1982	SEA	493	3	8	0	0	261.5	8.0	0.0	4.5
1983	SEA	1074	11	0	0	3	473.6	0.0	0.0	6.5
1984	SEA	1164	12	10	0	1	603.1	8.9	0.0	7.8
1985	SEA	1287	6	0	0	0	673.5	0.0	0.0	10.0
1986	SEA	1070	9	0	0	3	461.7	0.0	0.0	5.4
1987	SEA	912	8	33	0	2	421.2	30.4	0.0	7.1
1988	SEA	645	2	−3	0	3	215.5	−6.0	0.0	3.0
1989	SEA	403	3	0	0	0	216.5	0.0	0.0	2.5

Hall of Fame? Yes

Pro Bowl Appearances: 7

All-Pro Selections: Consensus - 3, Total - 8 (1978-1979; 1981; 1983-1987)

Awards: Walter Payton NFL Man of the Year - 1988

James Lofton (5)

Year	Team	ReYds	ReTD	RuYds	RuTD	Fum	AReY	ARuY	ASptY	Q
1978	GB	818	6	13	0	2	368.2	8.4	−21.5	6.0
1979	GB	968	4	−1	0	5	311.1	−4.6	0.0	4.6
1980	GB	1226	4	0	0	0	633.0	0.0	0.0	8.4
1981	GB	1294	8	0	0	0	687.0	0.0	0.0	9.9
1982	GB	696	4	101	1	0	368.0	111.0	0.0	8.4
1983	GB	1300	8	36	0	0	690.0	36.0	0.0	10.0
1984	GB	1361	7	82	0	1	681.1	76.4	0.0	9.6
1985	GB	1153	4	14	0	3	483.1	7.4	0.0	7.3
1986	GB	840	4	0	0	3	321.8	0.0	0.0	3.7
1987	LARI	880	5	1	0	0	465.0	1.0	0.0	7.4
1988	LARI	549	0	0	0	0	274.5	0.0	0.0	3.9
1989	BUF	166	3	0	0	0	98.0	0.0	0.0	1.1
1990	BUF	712	4	0	0	0	376.0	0.0	0.0	4.8
1991	BUF	1072	8	0	0	2	496.0	0.0	0.0	6.9
1992	BUF	786	6	0	0	0	423.0	0.0	0.0	5.8
1993	PHI	167	0	0	0	0	83.5	0.0	0.0	1.1
1993	LARM	16	0	0	0	0	8.0	0.0	0.0	0.1

Hall of Fame? Yes

Pro Bowl Appearances: 8

All-Pro Selections: Consensus - 4, Total - 6 (1980-1985)

Awards: None

Don Maynard (8)

Year	Team	ReYds	ReTD	RuYds	RuTD	Fum	AReY	ARuY	ASptY	Q
1958	NYG	84	0	45	0	3	30.5	17.3	100.2	0.3
1960	NYT	1265	6	0	0	0	662.5	0.0	−1.0	9.2
1961	NYT	629	8	0	0	1	315.4	0.0	8.1	3.4
1962	NYT	1041	8	0	0	0	560.5	0.0	0.0	9.9
1963	NYJ	780	9	6	0	0	435.0	6.0	6.0	6.0
1964	NYJ	847	8	3	0	1	425.9	0.6	0.0	4.1
1965	NYJ	1218	14	2	0	1	639.6	1.4	0.0	8.2
1966	NYJ	840	5	0	0	0	445.0	0.0	0.0	5.8
1967	NYJ	1434	10	18	0	1	729.1	15.9	0.0	10.0
1968	NYJ	1297	10	0	0	0	698.5	0.0	0.0	9.6
1969	NYJ	938	6	−6	0	0	499.0	−6.0	0.0	8.2
1970	NYJ	525	0	0	0	1	222.5	0.0	0.0	3.6
1971	NYJ	408	2	2	0	0	214.0	2.0	0.0	3.5
1972	NYJ	510	2	0	0	0	265.0	0.0	0.0	4.9
1973	STL	18	0	0	0	0	9.0	0.0	0.0	0.2

Hall of Fame? Yes

Pro Bowl Appearances: 4

All-Pro Selections: Consensus - 0, Total - 5 (1960; 1965; 1967-1969)

Awards: AFL All-Star Game Offensive MVP - 1967 (tie)

Art Monk (23)

Year	Team	ReYds	ReTD	RuYds	RuTD	Fum	AReY	ARuY	ASptY	Q
1980	WAS	797	3	0	0	0	413.5	0.0	−10.0	5.5
1981	WAS	894	6	−5	0	0	477.0	−5.0	0.0	6.8
1982	WAS	447	1	21	0	3	128.5	1.0	0.0	2.2
1983	WAS	746	5	−19	0	0	398.0	−19.0	0.0	5.5
1984	WAS	1372	7	18	0	1	681.7	17.3	0.0	8.9
1985	WAS	1226	2	51	0	2	548.7	45.3	0.0	8.8
1986	WAS	1068	4	27	0	2	478.2	22.8	0.0	5.8
1987	WAS	483	6	63	0	0	271.5	63.0	0.0	5.3
1988	WAS	946	5	46	0	0	498.0	46.0	0.0	7.7
1989	WAS	1186	8	8	0	2	555.7	5.3	0.0	6.5
1990	WAS	770	5	59	0	0	410.0	59.0	0.0	6.0
1991	WAS	1049	8	19	0	2	493.5	10.0	0.0	7.0
1992	WAS	644	3	45	0	1	301.6	40.4	0.0	4.7
1993	WAS	398	2	−1	0	0	209.0	−1.0	0.0	2.6
1994	NYJ	581	3	0	0	0	305.5	0.0	0.0	3.4
1995	PHI	114	0	0	0	0	57.0	0.0	0.0	0.6

Hall of Fame? Yes

Pro Bowl Appearances: 3

All-Pro Selections: Consensus - 2, Total - 3 (1984-1986)

Awards: None

Randy Moss (6)

Year	Team	ReYds	ReTD	RuYds	RuTD	Fum	AReY	ARuY	ASptY	Q
1998	MIN	1313	17	4	0	2	665.9	2.9	–3.3	8.5
1999	MIN	1413	11	43	0	3	670.9	38.5	148.2	8.9
2000	MIN	1437	15	5	0	2	716.5	2.0	0.0	7.9
2001	MIN	1233	10	38	0	0	666.5	38.0	0.0	8.6
2002	MIN	1347	7	51	0	1	671.9	48.9	–9.3	7.9
2003	MIN	1632	17	18	0	1	863.7	16.0	1.7	10.0
2004	MIN	767	13	0	0	1	410.8	0.0	–0.8	5.2
2005	OAK	1005	8	0	0	0	542.5	0.0	0.0	6.6
2006	OAK	553	3	0	0	0	291.5	0.0	0.0	4.1
2007	NE	1493	23	0	0	0	861.5	0.0	0.0	10.0

Hall of Fame? Not eligible (active)

Pro Bowl Appearances: 5

All-Pro Selections: Consensus - 5, Total - 5 (1998; 2000; 2002-2003; 2007)

Awards: AP NFL Offensive Rookie of the Year - 1998; PFW/PFWA Offensive Rookie of the Year - 1998; *Sporting News* NFL Rookie of the Year - 1998; Pro Bowl MVP - 1999

Terrell Owens (9)

Year	Team	ReYds	ReTD	RuYds	RuTD	Fum	AReY	ARuY	ASptY	Q
1996	SF	520	4	0	0	1	243.2	0.0	−16.2	3.2
1997	SF	936	8	0	0	1	469.3	0.0	−10.3	5.6
1998	SF	1097	14	53	1	1	580.8	60.7	0.0	8.2
1999	SF	754	4	0	0	1	357.0	0.0	0.0	4.4
2000	SF	1451	13	11	0	3	674.1	7.4	0.0	7.5
2001	SF	1412	16	21	0	0	786.0	21.0	0.0	9.6
2002	SF	1300	13	79	1	0	715.0	89.0	0.0	8.7
2003	SF	1102	9	−2	0	0	596.0	−2.0	0.0	6.8
2004	PHI	1200	14	−5	0	2	593.0	−8.0	0.0	7.8
2005	PHI	763	6	2	0	0	411.5	2.0	0.0	5.1
2006	DAL	1180	13	0	0	0	655.0	0.0	0.0	9.2
2007	DAL	1355	15	5	0	0	752.5	5.0	0.0	8.8

Hall of Fame? Not eligible (active)

Pro Bowl Appearances: 6

All-Pro Selections: Consensus - 5, Total - 5 (2000-2002; 2004; 2007)

Awards: None

Drew Pearson (24)

Year	Team	ReYds	ReTD	RuYds	RuTD	Fum	AReY	ARuY	ASptY	Q
1973	DAL	388	2	0	0	1	175.6	0.0	16.4	3.2
1974	DAL	1087	2	6	0	1	515.9	4.2	0.0	9.6
1975	DAL	822	8	11	0	1	411.9	10.1	0.0	7.9
1976	DAL	806	6	20	0	1	395.0	18.7	0.0	7.0
1977	DAL	870	2	22	0	0	445.0	22.0	0.0	8.6
1978	DAL	714	3	29	0	0	372.0	29.0	0.0	6.4
1979	DAL	1026	8	27	0	0	553.0	27.0	0.0	8.7
1980	DAL	568	6	30	0	0	314.0	30.0	0.0	4.6
1981	DAL	614	3	31	0	4	180.6	19.8	0.0	3.4
1982	DAL	382	3	0	0	0	206.0	0.0	0.0	3.1
1983	DAL	545	5	13	0	1	259.9	11.4	0.0	3.2

Hall of Fame? No

Pro Bowl Appearances: 3

All-Pro Selections: Consensus - 3, Total - 5 (1974-1978)

Awards: None

Art Powell (26)

Year	Team	ReYds	ReTD	RuYds	RuTD	Fum	AReY	ARuY	ASptY	Q
1959	PHI	0	0	0	0	2	0.0	0.0	153.0	0.0
1960	NYT	1167	14	0	0	0	653.5	0.0	23.0	9.0
1961	NYT	881	5	0	0	1	425.5	0.0	0.0	4.6
1962	NYT	1130	8	0	0	1	565.0	0.0	0.0	10.0
1963	OAK	1304	16	0	0	0	732.0	0.0	0.0	10.0
1964	OAK	1361	11	0	0	0	735.5	0.0	0.0	7.1
1965	OAK	800	12	0	0	0	460.0	0.0	0.0	5.9
1966	OAK	1026	11	0	0	0	568.0	0.0	0.0	7.4
1967	BUF	346	4	0	0	0	193.0	0.0	0.0	2.6
1968	MIN	31	0	0	0	0	15.5	0.0	0.0	0.3

Hall of Fame? No

Pro Bowl Appearances: 4

All-Pro Selections: Consensus - 2, Total - 6 (1960; 1962-1966)

Awards: None

Andre Reed (30)

Year	Team	ReYds	ReTD	RuYds	RuTD	Fum	AReY	ARuY	ASptY	Q
1986	BUF	739	7	-8	0	2	328.8	-12.3	0.0	3.6
1987	BUF	752	5	1	0	0	401.0	1.0	0.0	6.4
1988	BUF	968	6	64	0	1	477.1	60.9	0.0	7.6
1989	BUF	1312	9	31	0	4	544.6	27.4	0.0	6.7
1990	BUF	945	8	23	0	1	474.1	21.4	0.0	6.4
1991	BUF	1113	10	136	0	1	571.7	130.8	0.0	9.8
1992	BUF	913	3	65	0	4	329.0	47.5	0.0	5.2
1993	BUF	854	6	21	0	3	354.7	3.3	0.0	4.6
1994	BUF	1303	8	87	0	3	584.6	75.1	0.0	7.6
1995	BUF	312	3	48	0	2	109.1	29.9	0.0	1.5
1996	BUF	1036	6	22	0	1	512.3	17.7	0.0	7.0
1997	BUF	880	5	11	0	1	427.5	9.1	0.0	5.0
1998	BUF	795	5	0	0	0	422.5	0.0	0.0	5.4
1999	BUF	536	1	0	0	0	273.0	0.0	0.0	3.3
2000	WAS	103	1	0	0	0	56.5	0.0	0.0	0.6

Hall of Fame? No

Pro Bowl Appearances: None

All-Pro Selections: Consensus - 4, Total - 4 (1989-1991; 1994)

Awards: None

Jerry Rice (1)

Year	Team	ReYds	ReTD	RuYds	RuTD	Fum	AReY	ARuY	ASptY	Q
1985	SF	927	3	26	1	1	443.5	31.7	−14.7	7.1
1986	SF	1570	15	72	1	2	789.8	73.8	0.0	10.0
1987	SF	1078	22	51	1	2	577.8	52.2	0.0	10.0
1988	SF	1306	9	107	1	2	634.0	104.0	0.0	10.0
1989	SF	1483	17	33	0	0	826.5	33.0	0.0	10.0
1990	SF	1502	13	0	0	1	776.8	−0.8	0.0	10.0
1991	SF	1206	14	2	0	1	633.5	1.5	0.0	8.8
1992	SF	1201	10	58	1	2	578.2	60.3	0.0	8.8
1993	SF	1503	15	69	1	3	710.1	75.4	0.0	10.0
1994	SF	1499	13	93	2	1	776.9	110.6	0.0	10.0
1995	SF	1848	15	36	1	3	884.6	41.3	0.0	10.0
1996	SF	1254	8	77	1	0	667.0	87.0	0.0	10.0
1997	SF	78	1	−10	0	0	44.0	−10.0	0.0	0.4
1998	SF	1157	9	0	0	2	543.5	0.0	0.0	6.9
1999	SF	830	5	13	0	0	440.0	13.0	0.0	5.6
2000	SF	805	7	−2	0	3	320.6	−3.6	0.0	3.5
2001	OAK	1139	9	0	0	1	574.5	0.0	0.0	6.8
2002	OAK	1211	7	20	0	1	601.8	18.7	0.0	6.7
2003	OAK	869	2	0	0	2	365.8	0.0	0.0	4.1
2004	OAK	67	0	0	0	0	33.5	0.0	0.0	0.4
2004	SEA	362	3	0	0	0	196.0	0.0	0.0	2.6

Hall of Fame? Not eligible until 2009

Pro Bowl Appearances: 12

All-Pro Selections: Consensus - 11, Total - 12 (1986-1996; 2002)

Awards: UPI NFL/NFC Rookie of the Year - 1985; PFW/PFWA Offensive Player of the Year - 1986; AP NFL Offensive Player of the Year - 1987; Most Valuable Player (Bell) - 1987; NEA NFL Player of the Year - 1987; PFW/PFWA Offensive Player of the Year - 1987; *Sporting News* NFL Player of the Year - 1987; UPI NFC Offensive Player of the Year - 1987; MVP, Super Bowl XXIII - 1988; *Sporting News* NFL Player of the Year - 1990; AP NFL Offensive Player of the Year - 1993; Pro Bowl MVP - 1995

Del Shofner (27)

Year	Team	ReYds	ReTD	RuYds	RuTD	Fum	AReY	ARuY	ASptY	Q
1957	LARM	0	0	0	0	0	0.0	0.0	0.0	0.0
1958	LARM	1097	8	0	0	1	568.3	0.0	0.0	10.0
1959	LARM	936	7	6	0	0	503.0	6.0	0.0	6.8
1960	LARM	122	1	−15	0	0	66.0	−15.0	0.0	2.1
1961	NYG	1125	11	6	0	1	578.1	5.4	0.0	10.0
1962	NYG	1133	12	4	0	0	626.5	4.0	0.0	10.0
1963	NYG	1181	9	0	0	0	635.5	0.0	0.0	10.0
1964	NYG	323	0	0	0	0	161.5	0.0	0.0	2.6
1965	NYG	388	2	0	0	0	204.0	0.0	0.0	2.9
1966	NYG	19	0	0	0	0	9.5	0.0	0.0	0.1
1967	NYG	146	1	0	0	0	78.0	0.0	0.0	1.1

Hall of Fame? No

Pro Bowl Appearances: 5

All-Pro Selections: Consensus - 5, Total - 5 (1958-1959; 1961-1963)

Awards: None

Jimmy Smith (13)

Year	Team	ReYds	ReTD	RuYds	RuTD	Fum	AReY	ARuY	ASptY	Q
1992	DAL	0	0	0	0	0	0.0	0.0	0.0	0.0
1995	JAC	288	3	0	0	2	120.7	0.0	28.3	1.3
1996	JAC	1244	7	0	0	1	617.9	0.0	8.1	8.2
1997	JAC	1324	4	0	0	1	642.0	0.0	0.0	7.7
1998	JAC	1182	8	0	0	2	551.0	0.0	0.0	7.0
1999	JAC	1636	6	0	0	1	808.0	0.0	0.0	9.9
2000	JAC	1213	8	0	0	1	606.5	0.0	0.0	6.7
2001	JAC	1373	8	–3	0	1	686.9	–3.4	0.0	8.1
2002	JAC	1027	7	2	0	0	548.5	2.0	0.0	5.9
2003	JAC	805	4	0	0	1	382.5	0.0	0.0	4.4
2004	JAC	1172	6	0	0	2	536.0	0.0	0.0	7.1
2005	JAC	1023	6	0	0	0	541.5	0.0	0.0	6.6

Hall of Fame? Not eligible until 2010

Pro Bowl Appearances: None

All-Pro Selections: Consensus - 1, Total - 2 (1998-1999)

Awards: None

Rod Smith (16)

Year	Team	ReYds	ReTD	RuYds	RuTD	Fum	AReY	ARuY	ASptY	Q
1995	DEN	152	1	0	0	0	81.0	0.0	−26.0	0.9
1996	DEN	237	2	1	0	1	117.1	0.3	264.1	1.6
1997	DEN	1180	12	16	0	3	539.5	8.1	10.4	6.6
1998	DEN	1222	6	63	0	0	641.0	63.0	0.0	9.0
1999	DEN	1020	4	0	0	1	491.0	0.0	−10.5	6.0
2000	DEN	1602	8	99	1	1	803.3	106.7	0.0	10.0
2001	DEN	1343	11	27	0	1	687.5	26.0	0.0	8.5
2002	DEN	1027	5	9	0	1	501.4	6.5	0.0	5.5
2003	DEN	845	3	98	0	0	437.5	98.0	137.0	6.5
2004	DEN	1144	7	33	0	4	496.1	26.0	180.9	6.9
2005	DEN	1105	6	7	0	2	505.2	6.1	0.0	6.1
2006	DEN	512	3	-5	0	2	231.0	-5.0	2.0	2.6

Hall of Fame? Not eligible until 2011

Pro Bowl Appearances: 3

All-Pro Selections: Consensus - 2, Total - 2 (2000-2001)

Awards: None

Charley Taylor (29)

Year	Team	ReYds	ReTD	RuYds	RuTD	Fum	AReY	ARuY	ASptY	Q
1964	WAS	814	5	755	5	7	375.6	593.1	−1.1	6.5
1965	WAS	577	3	402	3	10	219.3	126.7	−7.1	2.2
1966	WAS	1119	12	262	3	6	518.4	169.9	84.2	10.0
1967	WAS	990	9	0	0	3	424.9	0.0	−4.9	6.1
1968	WAS	650	5	−3	0	1	311.6	−4.6	0.0	5.2
1969	WAS	883	8	24	0	1	443.1	22.4	0.0	5.9
1970	WAS	593	8	17	0	1	297.4	16.1	0.0	5.1
1971	WAS	370	4	0	0	0	205.0	0.0	0.0	0.0
1972	WAS	673	7	39	0	1	333.8	36.7	0.0	6.9
1973	WAS	801	7	−7	0	1	396.2	−7.7	0.0	7.2
1974	WAS	738	5	−1	0	0	394.0	−1.0	0.0	6.9
1975	WAS	744	6	0	0	0	402.0	0.0	0.0	7.6
1977	WAS	158	0	0	0	0	79.0	0.0	0.0	1.5

Hall of Fame? Yes

Pro Bowl Appearances: 8

All-Pro Selections: Consensus - 1, Total - 10 (1964; 1966-1970; 1972-1975)

Awards: NEA NFL Rookie of the Year - 1964; *Sporting News* NFL Rookie of the Year - 1964; UPI NFL/NFC Rookie of the Year - 1964

Paul Warfield (22)

Year	Team	ReYds	ReTD	RuYds	RuTD	Fum	AReY	ARuY	ASptY	Q
1964	CLE	920	9	0	0	0	505.0	0.0	−16.0	8.3
1965	CLE	30	0	0	0	0	15.0	0.0	0.0	0.2
1966	CLE	741	5	0	0	0	395.5	0.0	0.0	5.7
1967	CLE	702	8	10	0	0	391.0	10.0	0.0	5.7
1968	CLE	1067	12	0	0	0	593.5	0.0	0.0	10.0
1969	CLE	886	10	23	0	0	493.0	23.0	0.0	6.6
1970	MIA	703	6	13	0	0	381.5	13.0	0.0	6.5
1971	MIA	996	11	115	0	3	453.8	94.2	0.0	8.8
1972	MIA	606	3	23	0	1	282.8	18.2	0.0	5.6
1973	MIA	514	11	15	0	1	273.3	13.7	0.0	5.3
1974	MIA	536	2	0	0	0	278.0	0.0	0.0	4.9
1976	CLE	613	6	3	0	3	219.6	−0.1	0.0	3.5
1977	CLE	251	2	2	0	0	135.5	2.0	0.0	2.5

Hall of Fame? Yes

Pro Bowl Appearances: 8

All-Pro Selections: Consensus - 5, Total - 8 (1964; 1968-1974)

Awards: None

Gene Washington (28)

Year	Team	ReYds	ReTD	RuYds	RuTD	Fum	AReY	ARuY	ASptY	Q
1969	SF	711	3	−4	0	0	370.5	−4.0	0.0	4.7
1970	SF	1100	12	0	0	0	610.0	0.0	0.0	10.0
1971	SF	884	4	0	0	0	462.0	0.0	0.0	7.4
1972	SF	918	12	0	0	0	519.0	0.0	0.0	9.6
1973	SF	606	2	0	0	1	273.0	0.0	0.0	5.0
1974	SF	615	6	4	0	0	337.5	4.0	0.0	6.0
1975	SF	735	9	−4	0	1	374.2	−4.9	0.0	6.9
1976	SF	457	6	3	0	0	258.5	3.0	0.0	4.2
1977	SF	638	5	0	0	0	344.0	0.0	0.0	6.4
1979	DET	192	1	24	0	0	101.0	24.0	0.0	1.9

Hall of Fame? No

Pro Bowl Appearances: None

All-Pro Selections: None

Awards: None

Tight Ends

Mark Bavaro (19)

Year	Team	ReYds	ReTD	RuYds	RuTD	Fum	AReY	ARuY	ASptY	Q
1985	NYG	511	4	0	0	0	275.5	0.0	0.0	5.3
1986	NYG	1001	4	0	0	3	400.5	0.0	0.0	6.9
1987	NYG	867	8	0	0	2	394.9	0.0	−5.4	10.0
1988	NYG	672	4	0	0	1	316.0	0.0	0.0	8.2
1989	NYG	278	3	0	0	0	154.0	0.0	0.0	3.7
1990	NYG	393	5	0	0	0	221.5	0.0	0.0	6.8
1992	CLE	315	2	0	0	0	167.5	0.0	0.0	4.9
1993	PHI	481	6	0	0	0	270.5	0.0	0.0	5.4
1994	PHI	215	3	0	0	0	122.5	0.0	0.0	2.3

Hall of Fame? No

Pro Bowl Appearances: 2

All-Pro Selections: Consensus - 2, Total - 2 (1986-1987)

Awards: None

Billy Cannon (25)

Year	Team	ReYds	ReTD	RuYds	RuTD	Fum	AReY	ARuY	ASptY	Q
1960	HOU	187	5	644	1	3	108.6	553.8	204.1	6.1
1961	HOU	586	9	948	6	5	306.7	862.5	129.4	10.0
1962	HOU	451	6	474	7	5	223.5	397.0	64.0	4.8
1963	HOU	39	0	45	0	2	0.5	−4.5	−8.6	0.0
1964	OAK	454	5	338	3	5	201.7	246.9	69.4	3.9
1965	OAK	127	0	0	0	0	63.5	0.0	0.0	2.1
1966	OAK	436	2	0	0	0	228.0	0.0	12.0	6.0
1967	OAK	629	10	0	0	1	324.5	0.0	0.0	8.3
1968	OAK	360	6	0	0	0	210.0	0.0	0.0	5.3
1969	OAK	262	2	0	0	0	141.0	0.0	0.0	3.7
1970	KC	125	2	6	0	0	72.5	6.0	0.0	1.9

Hall of Fame? No

Pro Bowl Appearances: None

All-Pro Selections: Consensus - 2, Total - 4 (1960-1961; 1967-1968)

Awards: None

Dave Casper (11)

Year	Team	ReYds	ReTD	RuYds	RuTD	Fum	AReY	ARuY	ASptY	Q
1974	OAK	26	3	0	0	0	28.0	0.0	0.0	0.7
1975	OAK	71	1	0	0	0	40.5	0.0	0.0	0.9
1976	OAK	691	10	5	0	0	395.5	5.0	0.0	8.8
1977	OAK	584	6	0	0	1	282.0	0.0	0.0	8.8
1978	OAK	852	9	5	0	1	432.3	4.4	0.0	10.0
1979	OAK	771	3	0	0	1	360.5	0.0	0.0	8.2
1980	OAK	270	1	0	0	1	100.0	0.0	0.0	1.6
1980	HOU	526	3	8	0	2	202.4	3.6	0.0	3.4
1981	HOU	572	8	0	0	0	326.0	0.0	0.0	5.9
1982	HOU	573	6	9	0	1	278.6	6.9	0.0	8.1
1983	HOU	79	0	0	0	0	39.5	0.0	0.0	0.6
1983	MIN	172	0	0	0	0	86.0	0.0	0.0	1.3
1984	LARI	29	2	0	0	0	24.5	0.0	0.0	0.5

Hall of Fame? Yes

Pro Bowl Appearances: 5

All-Pro Selections: Consensus - 4, Total - 4 (1976-1979)

Awards: None

Raymond Chester (15)

Year	Team	ReYds	ReTD	RuYds	RuTD	Fum	AReY	ARuY	ASptY	Q
1970	OAK	556	7	0	0	1	273.0	0.0	0.0	6.7
1971	OAK	442	7	5	0	0	256.0	5.0	0.0	7.6
1972	OAK	576	8	3	0	0	328.0	3.0	0.0	9.4
1973	BAL	181	1	1	0	1	57.6	−1.1	0.0	1.2
1974	BAL	461	1	0	0	3	115.5	0.0	0.0	3.1
1975	BAL	457	3	0	0	1	203.5	0.0	0.0	4.7
1976	BAL	467	3	0	0	0	248.5	0.0	0.0	5.5
1977	BAL	556	3	0	0	1	253.0	0.0	0.0	7.9
1978	OAK	146	2	0	0	0	83.0	0.0	−13.0	1.9
1979	OAK	712	8	0	0	0	396.0	0.0	0.0	9.0
1980	OAK	366	4	0	0	1	163.0	0.0	0.0	2.7
1981	OAK	93	1	0	0	0	51.5	0.0	0.0	0.9

Hall of Fame? No

Pro Bowl Appearances: 4

All-Pro Selections: Consensus - 1, Total - 4 (1970-1972; 1979)

Awards: NEA NFL Rookie of the Year - 1970

Todd Christensen (8)

Year	Team	ReYds	ReTD	RuYds	RuTD	Fum	AReY	ARuY	ASptY	Q
1979	OAK	0	0	0	0	0	0.0	0.0	0.0	0.0
1979	NYG	0	0	0	0	0	0.0	0.0	0.0	0.0
1980	OAK	0	0	0	0	0	0.0	0.0	−10.0	0.0
1981	OAK	115	2	0	0	0	67.5	0.0	−26.0	1.2
1982	LARI	510	4	−6	0	3	157.8	−8.8	0.0	4.3
1983	LARI	1247	12	0	0	1	643.5	0.0	0.0	10.0
1984	LARI	1007	7	0	0	1	498.5	0.0	0.0	9.5
1985	LARI	987	6	0	0	0	523.5	0.0	0.0	10.0
1986	LARI	1153	8	0	0	1	576.5	0.0	0.0	10.0
1987	LARI	663	2	0	0	0	341.5	0.0	0.0	8.6
1988	LARI	190	0	0	0	0	95.0	0.0	0.0	2.5

Hall of Fame? No

Pro Bowl Appearances: 5

All-Pro Selections: Consensus - 4, Total - 5 (1983-1987)

Awards: None

Ben Coates (13)

Year	Team	ReYds	ReTD	RuYds	RuTD	Fum	AReY	ARuY	ASptY	Q
1991	NE	95	1	−6	0	0	52.5	−6.0	−14.0	1.4
1992	NE	171	3	2	0	1	62.4	0.1	0.0	1.8
1993	NE	659	8	0	0	0	369.5	0.0	0.0	7.3
1994	NE	1174	7	0	0	2	542.8	−0.8	0.0	10.0
1995	NE	915	6	0	0	4	327.5	0.0	0.0	8.7
1996	NE	682	9	0	0	1	346.0	0.0	0.0	6.4
1997	NE	737	8	0	0	0	408.5	0.0	0.0	7.7
1998	NE	668	6	0	0	0	364.0	0.0	0.0	8.4
1999	NE	370	2	0	0	0	195.0	0.0	0.0	4.5
2000	BAL	84	0	0	0	0	42.0	0.0	0.0	0.6

Hall of Fame? No

Pro Bowl Appearances: 5

All-Pro Selections: Consensus - 2, Total - 4 (1994-1996; 1998)

Awards: None

Mike Ditka (7)

Year	Team	ReYds	ReTD	RuYds	RuTD	Fum	AReY	ARuY	ASptY	Q
1961	CHIB	1076	12	0	0	2	518.0	0.0	0.0	10.0
1962	CHIB	904	5	0	0	4	317.0	0.0	0.0	10.0
1963	CHIB	794	8	0	0	0	437.0	0.0	0.0	10.0
1964	CHIB	897	5	0	0	2	393.5	0.0	0.0	10.0
1965	CHIB	454	2	0	0	1	197.0	0.0	0.0	3.1
1966	CHIB	378	2	0	0	0	199.0	0.0	0.0	4.4
1967	PHI	274	2	0	0	0	147.0	0.0	0.0	2.5
1968	PHI	111	2	0	0	0	65.5	0.0	0.0	1.1
1969	DAL	268	3	0	0	0	149.0	0.0	0.0	3.8
1970	DAL	98	0	0	0	0	49.0	0.0	0.0	1.2
1971	DAL	360	1	2	0	0	185.0	2.0	−30.0	5.5
1972	DAL	198	1	0	0	0	104.0	0.0	0.0	3.0

Hall of Fame? Yes

Pro Bowl Appearances: 5

All-Pro Selections: Consensus - 3, Total - 6 (1961-1966)

Awards: Sporting News NFL Rookie of the Year - 1961; UPI NFL/NFC Rookie of the Year - 1961; AP NFL Coach of the Year - 1985; *Sporting News* NFL Coach of the Year - 1985; UPI NFL/NFC Coach of the Year - 1985; AP NFL Coach of the Year - 1988; PFW/PFWA Coach of the Year - 1988; UPI NFL/NFC Coach of the Year - 1988

Tony Gonzalez (1)

Year	Team	ReYds	ReTD	RuYds	RuTD	Fum	AReY	ARuY	ASptY	Q
1997	KC	368	2	0	0	0	194.0	0.0	0.0	3.7
1998	KC	621	2	0	0	3	200.5	0.0	0.0	4.6
1999	KC	849	11	0	0	2	399.5	0.0	0.0	9.3
2000	KC	1203	9	0	0	0	646.5	0.0	0.0	10.0
2001	KC	917	6	9	0	0	488.5	9.0	0.0	10.0
2002	KC	773	7	0	0	0	421.5	0.0	0.0	8.7
2003	KC	916	10	0	0	0	508.0	0.0	0.0	10.0
2004	KC	1258	7	5	0	0	664.0	5.0	0.0	10.0
2005	KC	905	2	0	0	0	462.5	0.0	0.0	7.7
2006	KC	900	5	0	0	1	435.0	0.0	0.0	8.6

Hall of Fame? Not eligible (active)

Pro Bowl Appearances: 8

All-Pro Selections: Consensus - 5, Total - 9 (1999-2007)

Awards: None

Keith Jackson (14)

Year	Team	ReYds	ReTD	RuYds	RuTD	Fum	AReY	ARuY	ASptY	Q
1988	PHI	869	6	0	0	3	344.5	0.0	0.0	8.9
1989	PHI	648	3	0	0	1	299.0	0.0	0.0	7.2
1990	PHI	670	6	0	0	1	325.0	0.0	0.0	10.0
1991	PHI	569	5	0	0	2	229.5	0.0	0.0	6.8
1992	MIA	594	5	0	0	2	242.0	0.0	0.0	7.0
1993	MIA	613	6	0	0	2	256.5	0.0	0.0	5.1
1994	MIA	673	7	0	0	2	291.5	0.0	0.0	5.4
1995	GB	142	1	0	0	0	76.0	0.0	0.0	2.0
1996	GB	505	10	0	0	0	302.5	0.0	0.0	5.6

Hall of Fame? No

Pro Bowl Appearances: 5

All-Pro Selections: Consensus - 4, Total - 5 (1988-1990; 1992; 1996)

Awards: Sporting News NFL Rookie of the Year - 1988; UPI NFL/NFC Rookie of the Year - 1988

Brent Jones (21)

Year	Team	ReYds	ReTD	RuYds	RuTD	Fum	AReY	ARuY	ASptY	Q
1987	SF	35	0	0	0	0	17.5	0.0	0.0	0.4
1988	SF	57	2	0	0	0	38.5	0.0	0.0	1.0
1989	SF	500	4	0	0	0	270.0	0.0	0.0	6.5
1990	SF	747	5	0	0	2	318.5	0.0	0.0	9.8
1991	SF	417	0	0	0	2	128.5	0.0	0.0	3.8
1992	SF	628	4	0	0	1	294.0	0.0	0.0	8.5
1993	SF	735	3	0	0	2	302.5	0.0	0.0	6.0
1994	SF	670	9	0	0	1	340.0	0.0	0.0	6.3
1995	SF	595	3	0	0	3	192.5	0.0	0.0	5.1
1996	SF	428	1	0	0	0	219.0	0.0	0.0	4.0
1997	SF	383	2	0	0	1	161.5	0.0	0.0	3.1

Hall of Fame? No

Pro Bowl Appearances: 4

All-Pro Selections: Consensus - 2, Total - 3 (1992-1994)

Awards: None

Steve Jordan (17)

Year	Team	ReYds	ReTD	RuYds	RuTD	Fum	AReY	ARuY	ASptY	Q
1982	MIN	42	0	0	0	0	21.0	0.0	0.0	0.6
1983	MIN	212	2	0	0	0	116.0	0.0	0.0	1.8
1984	MIN	414	2	4	1	0	217.0	14.0	0.0	4.4
1985	MIN	795	0	0	0	2	317.5	0.0	0.0	6.1
1986	MIN	859	6	0	0	0	459.5	0.0	0.0	8.0
1987	MIN	490	2	0	0	1	215.0	0.0	0.0	5.4
1988	MIN	756	5	0	0	2	323.0	0.0	0.0	8.3
1989	MIN	506	3	0	0	1	228.0	0.0	0.0	5.5
1990	MIN	636	3	0	0	3	215.6	0.0	−25.6	6.6
1991	MIN	638	2	0	0	2	249.0	0.0	0.0	7.3
1992	MIN	394	2	0	0	0	207.0	0.0	0.0	6.0
1993	MIN	542	1	0	0	0	276.0	0.0	0.0	5.5
1994	MIN	23	0	0	0	0	11.5	0.0	0.0	0.2

Hall of Fame? No

Pro Bowl Appearances: None

All-Pro Selections: Consensus - 0, Total - 3 (1986-1987; 1989)

Awards: None

John Mackey (23)

Year	Team	ReYds	ReTD	RuYds	RuTD	Fum	AReY	ARuY	ASptY	Q
1963	BAL	726	7	3	0	2	335.8	1.2	75.0	7.7
1964	BAL	406	2	–1	0	1	174.7	–2.7	0.0	4.4
1965	BAL	814	7	7	0	2	364.0	5.0	0.0	5.7
1966	BAL	829	9	–6	0	0	459.5	–6.0	0.0	10.0
1967	BAL	686	3	0	0	1	318.0	0.0	0.0	5.5
1968	BAL	644	5	103	0	1	314.3	95.7	0.0	6.9
1969	BAL	443	2	3	0	1	193.7	0.8	0.0	4.9
1970	BAL	435	3	0	0	1	192.5	0.0	0.0	4.7
1971	BAL	143	0	18	0	1	40.1	9.4	0.0	1.4
1972	SD	110	0	0	0	1	15.0	0.0	0.0	0.4

Hall of Fame? Yes

Pro Bowl Appearances: 5

All-Pro Selections: Consensus - 3, Total - 3 (1966-1968)

Awards: None

Jim Mitchell (22)

Year	Team	ReYds	ReTD	RuYds	RuTD	Fum	AReY	ARuY	ASptY	Q
1969	ATL	339	4	77	0	1	156.9	69.6	0.0	5.7
1970	ATL	650	6	23	1	0	355.0	33.0	0.0	9.5
1971	ATL	593	5	25	0	3	214.5	12.0	0.0	6.6
1972	ATL	470	4	19	0	0	255.0	19.0	0.0	7.8
1973	ATL	420	0	34	0	0	210.0	34.0	0.0	5.0
1974	ATL	479	1	21	0	1	208.1	17.4	0.0	6.0
1975	ATL	536	4	0	0	0	288.0	0.0	0.0	6.7
1976	ATL	209	0	−6	0	0	104.5	−6.0	0.0	2.2
1977	ATL	178	0	−6	0	0	89.0	−6.0	0.0	2.6
1978	ATL	366	2	0	0	2	115.4	0.0	−8.4	2.6
1979	ATL	118	2	0	0	0	69.0	0.0	0.0	1.6

Hall of Fame? No

Pro Bowl Appearances: None

All-Pro Selections: Consensus - 0, Total - 1 (1972)

Awards: None

Ozzie Newsome (3)

Year	Team	ReYds	ReTD	RuYds	RuTD	Fum	AReY	ARuY	ASptY	Q
1978	CLE	589	2	96	2	1	276.4	106.4	26.8	8.8
1979	CLE	781	9	6	0	0	435.5	6.0	0.0	10.0
1980	CLE	594	3	13	0	2	235.0	10.0	0.0	4.0
1981	CLE	1002	6	20	0	0	531.0	20.0	0.0	10.0
1982	CLE	633	3	0	0	0	331.5	0.0	0.0	9.5
1983	CLE	970	6	0	0	0	515.0	0.0	0.0	8.0
1984	CLE	1001	5	0	0	0	525.5	0.0	0.0	10.0
1985	CLE	711	5	0	0	0	380.5	0.0	0.0	7.3
1986	CLE	417	3	0	0	0	223.5	0.0	0.0	3.9
1987	CLE	375	0	0	0	0	187.5	0.0	0.0	4.7
1988	CLE	343	2	0	0	0	181.5	0.0	0.0	4.7
1989	CLE	324	1	0	0	0	167.0	0.0	0.0	4.0
1990	CLE	240	2	0	0	0	130.0	0.0	0.0	4.0

Hall of Fame? Yes

Pro Bowl Appearances: 3

All-Pro Selections: Consensus - 4, Total - 7 (1979-1985)

Awards: Byron "Whizzer" White Award - 1990

Jay Novacek (12)

Year	Team	ReYds	ReTD	RuYds	RuTD	Fum	AReY	ARuY	ASptY	Q
1985	STL	4	0	0	0	0	2.0	0.0	0.0	0.0
1986	STL	2	0	0	0	0	1.0	0.0	0.0	0.0
1987	STL	254	3	0	0	1	102.0	0.0	0.0	2.6
1988	PHX	569	4	10	0	0	304.5	10.0	0.0	8.1
1989	PHX	225	1	0	0	0	117.5	0.0	0.0	2.8
1990	DAL	657	4	0	0	1	308.5	0.0	0.0	9.5
1991	DAL	664	4	0	0	3	232.0	0.0	0.0	6.8
1992	DAL	630	6	0	0	0	345.0	0.0	0.0	10.0
1993	DAL	445	1	2	1	3	112.7	9.4	−23.6	2.4
1994	DAL	475	2	0	0	0	247.5	0.0	0.0	4.6
1995	DAL	705	5	0	0	1	337.5	0.0	0.0	9.0

Hall of Fame? No

Pro Bowl Appearances: 5

All-Pro Selections: Consensus - 2, Total - 5 (1990-1992; 1994-1995)

Awards: None

Riley Odoms (10)

Year	Team	ReYds	ReTD	RuYds	RuTD	Fum	AReY	ARuY	ASptY	Q
1972	DEN	320	1	72	0	1	132.7	64.3	0.0	5.6
1973	DEN	629	7	53	0	1	313.7	48.8	0.0	7.4
1974	DEN	639	6	25	0	0	349.5	25.0	0.0	10.0
1975	DEN	544	3	27	0	2	215.9	18.1	0.0	5.4
1976	DEN	477	3	36	2	0	253.5	56.0	0.0	6.8
1977	DEN	429	3	0	0	1	189.5	0.0	0.0	5.9
1978	DEN	829	6	5	0	2	367.4	2.1	0.0	8.5
1979	DEN	638	1	−7	0	0	324.0	−7.0	0.0	7.2
1980	DEN	590	6	0	0	0	325.0	0.0	0.0	5.3
1981	DEN	516	5	0	0	1	243.0	0.0	0.0	4.4
1982	DEN	82	0	0	0	0	41.0	0.0	0.0	1.2
1983	DEN	62	0	0	0	0	31.0	0.0	0.0	0.5

Hall of Fame? No

Pro Bowl Appearances: 4

All-Pro Selections: Consensus - 3, Total - 5 (1973-1977)

Awards: None

Pete Retzlaff (5)

Year	Team	ReYds	ReTD	RuYds	RuTD	Fum	AReY	ARuY	ASptY	Q
1956	PHI	159	0	0	0	0	79.5	0.0	0.0	1.2
1957	PHI	120	0	0	0	0	60.0	0.0	0.0	0.0
1958	PHI	766	2	−4	0	0	393.0	−4.0	0.0	6.8
1959	PHI	595	1	−11	0	1	264.7	−13.2	0.0	3.3
1960	PHI	826	5	3	0	1	399.7	1.3	0.0	5.0
1961	PHI	769	8	8	0	0	424.5	8.0	0.0	7.4
1962	PHI	584	3	0	0	0	307.0	0.0	0.0	9.7
1963	PHI	895	4	0	0	2	387.5	0.0	0.0	8.9
1964	PHI	855	8	0	0	0	467.5	0.0	0.0	7.7
1965	PHI	1190	10	0	0	0	645.0	0.0	0.0	10.0
1966	PHI	653	6	0	0	0	356.5	0.0	0.0	5.2

Hall of Fame? No

Pro Bowl Appearances: 5

All-Pro Selections: Consensus - 1, Total - 5 (1958; 1963-1966)

Awards: Most Valuable Player (Bell) - 1965

Charlie Sanders (20)

Year	Team	ReYds	ReTD	RuYds	RuTD	Fum	AReY	ARuY	ASptY	Q
1968	DET	533	1	3	0	2	195.3	−0.8	0.0	3.3
1969	DET	656	3	−8	0	0	343.0	−8.0	0.0	8.5
1970	DET	544	6	0	0	0	302.0	0.0	0.0	7.4
1971	DET	502	5	0	0	0	276.0	0.0	0.0	8.1
1972	DET	416	2	0	0	1	178.0	0.0	0.0	5.1
1973	DET	433	2	−1	0	1	187.9	−2.4	0.0	3.8
1974	DET	532	3	0	0	1	241.0	0.0	0.0	6.4
1975	DET	486	3	0	0	1	218.0	0.0	0.0	5.1
1976	DET	545	5	0	0	0	297.5	0.0	0.0	6.6
1977	DET	170	1	0	0	0	90.0	0.0	0.0	2.8

Hall of Fame? Yes

Pro Bowl Appearances: 7

All-Pro Selections: Consensus - 2, Total - 6 (1969-1971; 1974-1976)

Awards: None

Shannon Sharpe (2)

Year	Team	ReYds	ReTD	RuYds	RuTD	Fum	AReY	ARuY	ASptY	Q
1990	DEN	99	1	0	0	1	14.5	0.0	0.0	0.2
1991	DEN	322	1	15	0	0	166.0	15.0	0.0	2.5
1992	DEN	640	2	−6	0	1	291.5	−7.5	0.0	8.2
1993	DEN	995	9	0	0	1	503.0	0.0	−20.5	10.0
1994	DEN	1010	4	0	0	1	485.0	0.0	0.0	8.9
1995	DEN	756	4	0	0	1	358.0	0.0	0.0	9.6
1996	DEN	1062	10	0	0	1	541.0	0.0	0.0	10.0
1997	DEN	1107	3	0	0	1	528.5	0.0	0.0	10.0
1998	DEN	768	10	0	0	0	434.0	0.0	0.0	10.0
1999	DEN	224	0	0	0	0	112.0	0.0	0.0	2.6
2000	BAL	810	5	0	0	0	430.0	0.0	0.0	6.7
2001	BAL	811	2	0	0	1	375.5	0.0	0.0	7.3
2002	DEN	686	3	0	0	0	358.0	0.0	0.0	7.4
2003	DEN	770	8	0	0	0	425.0	0.0	0.0	8.4

Hall of Fame? Not eligible until 2009

Pro Bowl Appearances: 8

All-Pro Selections: Consensus - 4, Total - 6 (1993-1998)

Awards: None

Jackie Smith (4)

Year	Team	ReYds	ReTD	RuYds	RuTD	Fum	AReY	ARuY	ASptY	Q
1963	STL	445	2	0	0	2	152.5	0.0	0.0	3.5
1964	STL	657	4	0	0	2	305.8	0.0	0.0	7.8
1965	STL	648	2	0	0	0	334.0	0.0	0.0	5.2
1966	STL	810	3	8	0	1	400.6	7.6	0.0	9.0
1967	STL	1205	9	86	0	3	545.7	69.6	0.0	10.0
1968	STL	789	2	163	3	0	404.5	193.0	0.0	10.0
1969	STL	561	1	0	0	1	248.9	−3.4	0.0	6.2
1970	STL	687	4	43	0	0	363.5	43.0	0.0	10.0
1971	STL	379	4	10	0	0	209.5	10.0	0.0	6.4
1972	STL	407	2	31	0	0	213.5	31.0	0.0	7.0
1973	STL	600	1	−14	0	1	266.0	−15.0	0.0	5.1
1974	STL	413	3	0	0	1	181.5	0.0	0.0	4.8
1975	STL	246	2	0	0	0	133.0	0.0	5.0	3.1
1976	STL	22	0	0	0	0	11.0	0.0	3.0	0.2
1977	STL	49	1	0	0	1	−3.8	0.0	−11.7	0.0
1978	DAL	0	0	0	0	0	0.0	0.0	0.0	0.0

Hall of Fame? Yes

Pro Bowl Appearances: 5

All-Pro Selections: Consensus - 0, Total - 5 (1966-1970)

Awards: None

Jerry Smith (9)

Year	Team	ReYds	ReTD	RuYds	RuTD	Fum	AReY	ARuY	ASptY	Q
1965	WAS	257	2	0	0	0	138.5	0.0	0.0	2.1
1966	WAS	686	6	0	0	0	373.0	0.0	0.0	8.2
1967	WAS	849	12	0	0	2	404.5	0.0	0.0	7.0
1968	WAS	626	6	0	0	0	343.0	0.0	0.0	5.7
1969	WAS	682	9	8	0	0	386.0	8.0	0.0	10.0
1970	WAS	575	9	29	0	0	332.5	29.0	0.0	8.9
1971	WAS	227	1	5	0	1	80.9	2.6	0.0	2.4
1972	WAS	353	7	9	0	0	211.5	9.0	0.0	6.3
1973	WAS	215	0	0	0	1	69.5	0.0	−2.0	1.4
1974	WAS	554	3	5	0	1	252.9	4.1	0.0	6.9
1975	WAS	391	3	0	0	0	210.5	0.0	0.0	4.9
1976	WAS	75	2	0	0	0	47.5	0.0	0.0	1.0
1977	WAS	6	0	0	0	0	3.0	0.0	0.0	0.1

Hall of Fame? No

Pro Bowl Appearances: None

All-Pro Selections: Consensus - 1, Total - 2 (1967; 1969)

Awards: None

Bob Trumpy (18)

Year	Team	ReYds	ReTD	RuYds	RuTD	Fum	AReY	ARuY	ASptY	Q
1968	CIN	639	3	−1	0	1	295.6	−2.1	0.0	7.4
1969	CIN	835	9	0	0	2	382.5	0.0	0.0	10.0
1970	CIN	480	2	0	0	1	210.0	0.0	0.0	5.2
1971	CIN	531	3	0	0	0	280.5	0.0	0.0	8.2
1972	CIN	500	2	0	0	0	260.0	0.0	0.0	7.4
1973	CIN	435	5	0	0	0	242.5	0.0	0.0	4.9
1974	CIN	330	2	0	0	0	175.0	0.0	0.0	4.7
1975	CIN	276	1	0	0	1	103.0	0.0	0.0	2.4
1976	CIN	323	7	0	0	1	156.5	0.0	0.0	3.4
1977	CIN	251	1	0	0	1	90.5	0.0	0.0	2.8

Hall of Fame? No

Pro Bowl Appearances: 4

All-Pro Selections: Consensus - 2, Total - 2 (1969-1970)

Awards: None

Wesley Walls (16)

Year	Team	ReYds	ReTD	RuYds	RuTD	Fum	AReY	ARuY	ASptY	Q
1989	SF	16	1	0	0	1	–27.0	0.0	0.0	0.0
1990	SF	27	0	0	0	0	13.5	0.0	–4.0	0.4
1991	SF	24	0	0	0	0	12.0	0.0	0.0	0.4
1993	SF	0	0	0	0	0	0.0	0.0	0.0	0.0
1994	NO	406	4	0	0	0	223.0	0.0	0.0	4.1
1995	NO	694	4	0	0	1	327.7	0.0	–14.7	8.8
1996	CAR	713	10	0	0	0	406.5	0.0	0.0	7.5
1997	CAR	746	6	0	0	0	403.0	0.0	0.0	7.6
1998	CAR	506	5	0	0	0	278.0	0.0	0.0	6.4
1999	CAR	822	12	0	0	1	431.0	0.0	0.0	10.0
2000	CAR	422	2	0	0	0	221.0	0.0	0.0	3.4
2001	CAR	452	5	0	0	0	251.0	0.0	0.0	4.9
2002	CAR	241	4	0	0	0	140.5	0.0	0.0	2.9
2003	GB	222	1	0	0	0	116.0	0.0	0.0	2.3

Hall of Fame? Not eligible until 2009

Pro Bowl Appearances: 5

All-Pro Selections: Consensus - 4, Total - 4 (1996-1997; 1999; 2001)

Awards: None

Kellen Winslow (6)

Year	Team	ReYds	ReTD	RuYds	RuTD	Fum	AReY	ARuY	ASptY	Q
1979	SD	255	2	0	0	1	97.5	0.0	0.0	2.2
1980	SD	1290	9	0	0	2	610.0	0.0	0.0	10.0
1981	SD	1075	10	0	0	2	509.3	0.0	0.0	9.2
1982	SD	721	6	0	0	1	351.2	0.0	0.0	10.0
1983	SD	1172	8	0	0	3	506.0	0.0	0.0	7.9
1984	SD	663	2	0	0	1	301.5	0.0	0.0	5.7
1985	SD	318	0	0	0	0	159.0	0.0	0.0	3.0
1986	SD	728	5	0	0	0	389.0	0.0	−29.0	6.7
1987	SD	519	3	0	0	1	234.5	0.0	0.0	5.9

Hall of Fame? Yes

Pro Bowl Appearances: None

All-Pro Selections: Consensus - 4, Total - 4 (1980-1982; 1987)

Awards: Pro Bowl MVP - 1981 (tie)

Frank Wycheck (24)

Year	Team	ReYds	ReTD	RuYds	RuTD	Fum	AReY	ARuY	ASptY	Q
1993	WAS	113	0	0	0	1	16.5	0.0	0.0	0.3
1994	WAS	55	1	0	0	0	32.5	0.0	4.0	0.2
1995	HOU	471	1	1	1	0	240.5	11.0	0.0	6.7
1996	HOU	511	6	3	0	2	211.1	0.2	−37.8	3.9
1997	TEN	748	4	0	0	0	394.0	0.0	−17.0	7.5
1998	TEN	768	2	0	0	2	315.1	0.0	−11.1	7.3
1999	TEN	641	2	0	0	0	330.5	0.0	0.0	8.5
2000	TEN	636	4	0	0	2	260.2	0.0	0.0	4.5
2001	TEN	672	4	1	0	0	356.0	1.0	0.0	7.1
2002	TEN	346	2	0	0	1	144.9	0.0	0.0	3.1
2003	TEN	165	2	0	0	0	92.5	0.0	0.0	1.8

Hall of Fame? Not eligible until 2009

Pro Bowl Appearances: 3

All-Pro Selections: Consensus - 0, Total - 1 (2000)

Awards: None

ALL-TIME LEADERS:
Overall Rankings by Position

Quarterbacks								
Rk	Player	Score	Q5	Q10	Q15	NetW	AY	Career
1	Montana, Joe	212.08	46.5	37.3	14.7	81	14436.5	1979-1994
2	Marino, Dan	199.95	46.6	37.8	29.8	53	17785.5	1983-1999
3	Elway, John	194.93	44.6	34.1	17.4	68	13900.7	1983-1998
4	Favre, Brett	190.33	42.9	29.5	23.1	66	16102.0	1991-2007
5	Unitas, Johnny	187.58	46.2	30.7	14.9	65	8212.0	1956-1973
6	Graham, Otto	187.13	49.5	19.9	0.0	88	6272.0	1946-1955
7	Young, Steve	174.03	50.0	33.3	7.4	50	13872.0	1985-1999
8	Manning, Peyton	169.63	57.5	26.7	0.0	50	14571.0	1998-2007
9	Tarkenton, Fran	159.13	47.5	41.9	21.5	14	11322.5	1961-1978
10	Staubach, Roger	149.60	46.4	20.8	0.0	54	6546.5	1969-1979
11	Dawson, Len	141.28	48.1	23.3	2.0	38	5989.0	1957-1975
12	Layne, Bobby	133.70	43.9	28.2	6.6	26	5389.7	1948-1962
13	Tittle, Y.A.	132.48	49.6	31.9	9.2	9	7606.0	1948-1964
14	Van Brocklin, Norm	131.83	42.3	27.1	4.5	30	4970.2	1949-1960
15	McNair, Steve	128.38	40.5	26.1	1.0	34	10792.1	1995-2007
16	Anderson, Ken	127.08	48.2	26.7	6.4	15	9269.0	1971-1986
17	Baugh, Sammy	126.85	44.6	21.4	6.2	27	4369.9	1937-1952
18	Brady, Tom	126.83	41.8	3.3	0.0	60	7967.3	2000-2007
19	Starr, Bart	125.65	32.8	17.8	3.2	51	4678.5	1956-1971
20	Luckman, Sid	124.03	39.5	12.3	0.4	49	2699.2	1939-1950
21	Kelly, Jim	121.78	33.6	22.7	2.0	41	8465.5	1986-1996

22	Lamonica, Daryle	120.03	42.1	7.1	0.0	48	4343.0	1963-1974
23	Gabriel, Roman	117.23	41.7	20.7	7.8	21	6710.5	1962-1977
24	Cunningham, Randall	113.58	41.0	15.1	2.2	31	8965.7	1985-2001
25	Bradshaw, Terry	109.65	26.5	12.4	1.4	53	4412.7	1970-1983
26	McNabb, Donovan	107.25	37.5	10.4	0.0	38	9521.0	1999-2007
27	Aikman, Troy	106.35	35.3	23.2	2.4	22	9389.5	1989-2000
28	Hadl, John	103.83	43.8	22.9	1.5	8	5701.3	1962-1977
29	Moon, Warren	102.75	38.3	22.0	6.8	11	10073.5	1984-2000
30	Conerly, Charley	102.60	32.9	15.8	2.5	31	3868.4	1948-1961
31	Brodie, John	99.78	42.6	22.3	8.0	0	6976.0	1957-1973
32	Brunell, Mark	99.15	39.3	26.8	0.7	6	10359.0	1994-2007
33	Gannon, Rich	95.15	44.0	12.6	3.4	10	9466.0	1987-2004
34	Jurgensen, Sonny	94.33	45.2	24.5	5.9	-10	7514.5	1957-1974
35	Simms, Phil	93.93	26.6	14.5	2.9	33	6470.0	1979-1993
36	Theismann, Joe	92.45	33.5	10.4	0.2	29	6157.4	1974-1985
37	Clark, Dutch	91.63	50.0	6.9	0.0	8	3246.0	1931-1938
38	McMahon, Jim	90.15	25.2	15.8	0.6	32	5760.6	1982-1996
39	Stabler, Ken	88.28	23.1	2.9	0.0	50	2614.5	1970-1984
40	Johnson, Brad	85.58	34.3	15.7	0.5	14	7700.0	1994-2007
41	Griese, Bob	85.40	20.1	13.0	4.0	35	3589.5	1967-1980
42	Plum, Milt	84.93	32.7	8.7	0.0	25	3469.3	1957-1969
43	Albert, Frankie	82.30	33.7	8.6	0.0	21	3930.4	1946-1952
44	Ryan, Frank	82.15	28.6	7.4	0.0	30	3352.0	1958-1970
45	Brown, Ed	81.05	33.0	11.0	1.8	16	3626.1	1954-1965
46	Bledsoe, Drew	79.45	34.0	19.0	4.7	0	9155.1	1993-2006
47	Namath, Joe	79.10	43.4	12.8	0.0	-2	4898.5	1965-1977
48	Hasselbeck, Matt	77.93	34.7	3.1	0.0	22	7004.5	1998-2007
49	Kilmer, Billy	76.95	25.5	14.0	2.2	19	3902.7	1961-1978
50	Rote, Tobin	74.28	48.1	23.3	0.0	-27	4997.4	1950-1966
51	Green, Trent	73.13	38.5	9.1	0.0	4	8012.5	1997-2007
52	Kemp, Jack	73.05	27.7	3.6	0.0	27	2547.0	1957-1969
53	Hart, Jim	72.85	34.1	13.6	5.7	-1	5410.0	1966-1984
54	Fouts, Dan	72.60	37.0	20.4	6.6	-15	8421.0	1973-1987
55	Wade, Billy	71.95	35.4	14.2	0.1	1	4426.0	1954-1966
56	Morton, Craig	70.05	21.4	11.0	3.2	21	3911.5	1965-1982
57	Morrall, Earl	69.60	25.8	4.4	2.4	23	3174.6	1956-1976
58	White, Danny	69.28	19.1	7.7	1.0	30	3764.1	1976-1988

59	Waterfield, Bob	69.10	30.4	6.0	0.0	16	1777.0	1945-1952
60	Kosar, Bernie	68.88	37.0	5.5	0.5	6	5937.0	1985-1996
61	Blanda, George	67.05	33.6	13.4	3.9	−4	3890.9	1949-1975
62	Grogan, Steve	67.05	24.9	12.0	2.7	12	4701.5	1975-1990
63	Stewart, Kordell	66.70	29.8	9.6	0.0	10	5641.2	1995-2005
64	Parker, Ace	65.90	37.1	1.0	0.0	9	2454.0	1937-1946
65	Lujack, Johnny	65.90	34.6	0.0	0.0	14	2180.7	1948-1951
66	Jones, Bert	63.28	39.1	6.9	0.0	−4	5287.5	1973-1982
67	Brees, Drew	63.20	32.3	2.2	0.0	12	6356.0	2001-2007
68	O'Donnell, Neil	62.20	25.2	8.8	1.4	12	5605.0	1991-2003
69	Harbaugh, Jim	61.78	29.9	15.7	3.3	−6	7365.0	1987-2000
70	Warner, Kurt	61.03	31.1	0.3	0.0	14	5056.9	1998-2007
71	Garcia, Jeff	61.00	41.0	6.0	0.0	−8	8012.5	1999-2007
72	Rypien, Mark	59.00	26.7	3.8	0.2	14	4513.5	1988-2001
73	Esiason, Boomer	58.18	38.6	19.5	2.9	−27	8394.3	1984-1997
74	Parilli, Babe	58.13	35.1	8.3	0.1	−5	3359.6	1952-1969
75	Krieg, Dave	57.95	19.3	11.2	4.0	11	5068.5	1980-1998
76	Hebert, Bobby	56.85	24.4	9.0	0.0	9	4708.0	1985-1996
77	Schroeder, Jay	55.78	18.6	5.5	0.0	21	3475.8	1985-1994
78	Plummer, Jake	54.95	34.3	9.2	0.0	-8	7086.6	1997-2006
79	Grbac, Elvis	54.90	24.6	3.2	0.0	14	4381.5	1994-2001
80	Flutie, Doug	52.70	27.0	4.8	0.2	6	5014.0	1986-2005
81	Sipe, Brian	52.53	27.6	4.9	0.0	5	4300.3	1974-1983
82	Everett, Jim	52.33	40.3	16.3	0.5	−29	8510.0	1986-1997
83	Landry, Greg	52.18	32.8	7.1	0.1	−6	3856.5	1968-1984
84	Meredith, Don	51.90	27.6	1.2	0.0	9	2698.0	1960-1968
85	Wilson, Wade	51.38	22.9	4.5	0.4	11	3978.9	1981-1998
86	Roethlisberger, Ben	50.85	17.9	0.0	0.0	24	3272.9	2004-2007
87	Thompson, Tommy	50.40	27.1	0.6	0.0	9	1543.5	1940-1950
88	Culpepper, Daunte	50.38	33.0	2.3	0.0	−2	6282.9	1999-2007
89	Vick, Michael	50.35	28.9	0.0	0.0	7	5005.1	2001-2006
90	Humphries, Stan	48.75	21.0	2.6	0.0	14	3726.0	1989-1997
91	Fiedler, Jay	47.53	19.6	0.1	0.0	18	3165.5	1998-2005
92	Hostetler, Jeff	46.28	27.1	4.5	0.0	0	4719.5	1985-1997
93	Jaworski, Ron	45.20	24.2	8.8	0.9	−3	4680.0	1974-1989
94	O'Brien, Ken	44.53	26.1	7.5	0.0	−4	4630.9	1984-1993
95	Collins, Kerry	43.70	26.9	9.8	1.1	−10	6020.0	1995-2007

96	Testaverde, Vinny	42.98	31.4	17.9	10.5	−37	9284.5	1987-2007
97	Plunkett, Jim	41.90	18.3	7.4	0.2	5	2813.5	1971-1986
98	Williams, Doug	41.90	28.1	4.6	0.0	−6	4404.0	1978-1989
99	Nelsen, Bill	41.83	22.8	0.5	0.0	7	2241.5	1963-1972
100	Masterson, Bernie	40.53	12.1	0.3	0.0	22	684.5	1934-1940

Running Backs

Rk	Player	Score	Q3	Q6	Q9	AY	Career
1	Brown, Jim	235.20	30.0	60.0	86.8	12555.0	1957-1965
2	Sanders, Barry	225.88	30.0	58.9	81.5	16117.8	1989-1998
3	Payton, Walter	225.40	30.0	57.8	82.1	16926.1	1975-1987
4	Smith, Emmitt	211.60	30.0	55.4	74.9	19237.4	1990-2004
5	Dickerson, Eric	201.23	29.8	54.7	68.7	12108.9	1983-1993
6	Thomas, Thurman	196.98	28.9	53.1	67.8	13066.1	1988-2000
7	Martin, Curtis	196.38	27.5	51.1	70.0	15579.5	1995-2006
8	Van Buren, Steve	195.70	30.0	54.8	64.8	6522.4	1944-1951
9	Faulk, Marshall	192.30	30.0	50.4	66.2	15434.5	1994-2005
10	Tomlinson, LaDainian	191.70	30.0	55.2	61.8	12703.1	2001-2007
11	Perry, Joe	191.28	30.0	50.3	65.6	9031.9	1948-1963
12	Simpson, O.J.	191.15	30.0	52.0	64.1	10895.9	1969-1979
13	Kelly, Leroy	187.08	29.8	52.5	61.1	9162.8	1964-1973
14	Taylor, Jim	179.65	29.4	48.2	60.0	9030.1	1958-1967
15	James, Edgerrin	179.30	27.3	47.8	61.5	12422.0	1999-2007
16	Allen, Marcus	179.30	27.9	46.6	62.1	13787.7	1982-1997
17	Leemans, Tuffy	174.48	28.5	50.3	55.4	3944.0	1936-1943
18	Moore, Lenny	174.08	28.2	46.5	58.5	7628.0	1956-1967
19	Anderson, Ottis	173.55	24.8	45.8	61.0	10398.9	1979-1992
20	Dorsett, Tony	173.43	25.0	44.7	61.7	11741.4	1977-1988
21	Campbell, Earl	171.30	27.8	49.4	54.5	8828.4	1978-1985
22	Watters, Ricky	168.43	23.9	43.5	60.1	11897.5	1992-2001
23	Barber, Tiki	165.95	27.2	45.0	55.0	12725.5	1997-2006
24	Bettis, Jerome	165.73	24.2	42.9	58.6	13683.1	1993-2005
25	Csonka, Larry	163.18	25.2	42.7	56.4	8311.0	1968-1979
26	Motley, Marion	163.08	27.4	46.5	51.7	5420.5	1946-1955
27	Walker, Herschel	162.25	25.3	42.6	55.8	10534.3	1986-1997
28	Little, Floyd	161.48	26.0	44.9	52.9	8104.6	1967-1975

29	Harris, Franco	161.40	22.4	41.6	58.0	10651.6	1972-1984
30	Craig, Roger	161.00	24.3	43.6	54.8	9592.5	1983-1993
31	George, Eddie	159.85	24.7	42.6	54.6	10804.5	1996-2004
32	Riggins, John	159.78	22.4	40.9	57.5	11177.0	1971-1985
33	Hoernschemeyer, Bob	159.50	25.1	42.6	54.1	5614.2	1946-1955
34	Dillon, Corey	158.10	22.9	41.8	55.3	11943.6	1997-2006
35	Taylor, Fred	157.43	22.1	41.9	55.3	11496.5	1998-2007
36	Alexander, Shaun	156.95	26.7	44.8	49.5	10004.5	2000-2007
37	Battles, Cliff	156.75	29.7	46.2	46.2	3839.0	1932-1937
38	Holmes, Priest	155.88	29.4	42.5	48.9	9848.9	1997-2007
39	Hinkle, Clarke	152.73	21.3	39.5	54.7	4525.5	1932-1941
40	Riggs, Gerald	151.83	24.9	41.9	49.7	8105.9	1982-1991
41	Brooks, James	151.15	24.0	40.4	51.1	9068.4	1981-1992
42	Isbell, Cecil	149.73	29.0	43.9	43.9	3174.5	1938-1942
43	Lowe, Paul	148.85	28.0	43.4	44.4	5306.5	1960-1969
44	Daniels, Clem	147.43	26.2	43.1	44.9	5655.4	1960-1968
45	Green, Ahman	146.95	24.9	42.2	46.2	9510.7	1998-2007
46	Andrews, William	146.85	28.6	43.0	43.0	6453.6	1979-1986
47	Haynes, Abner	146.83	28.8	41.5	44.1	6319.5	1960-1967
48	Montgomery, Wilbert	146.15	25.5	42.4	45.1	7043.9	1977-1985
49	Byner, Earnest	145.68	22.2	38.3	50.4	9934.5	1984-1997
50	Driscoll, Paddy	144.95	30.0	41.8	41.8	195.0	1920-1929
51	Casares, Rick	144.48	26.5	39.3	45.9	5699.2	1955-1966
52	Mitchell, Lydell	143.68	24.4	41.9	44.6	7355.5	1972-1980
53	Anderson, Neal	142.85	25.3	40.4	44.7	6863.5	1986-1993
54	Brown, Larry	142.28	25.1	41.3	43.7	5975.5	1969-1976
55	Nance, Jim	140.13	26.3	39.7	42.8	5047.0	1965-1973
56	McElhenny, Hugh	139.88	23.6	37.7	46.1	6273.1	1952-1964
57	Warner, Curt	139.58	26.7	40.5	41.5	6692.5	1983-1990
58	Lewis, Jamal	139.10	23.4	40.0	43.8	8991.5	2000-2007
59	Davis, Terrell	138.78	28.5	39.5	40.6	8072.0	1995-2001
60	Dunn, Warrick	137.80	20.1	35.6	48.8	11745.5	1997-2007
61	McNeil, Freeman	136.25	20.2	36.2	47.2	8201.9	1981-1992
62	Pruitt, Mike	136.13	22.9	36.7	44.9	7360.0	1976-1986
63	Garrett, Mike	135.38	23.4	39.3	41.9	5373.1	1966-1973
64	Gifford, Frank	135.23	23.2	37.3	43.6	5502.3	1952-1964

65	Canadeo, Tony	134.88	21.7	36.9	44.7	4762.6	1941-1952
66	Portis, Clinton	134.88	23.5	40.5	40.5	8365.5	2002-2007
67	Snell, Matt	133.60	24.7	39.0	40.1	4525.5	1964-1972
68	Perkins, Don	133.25	20.2	36.8	44.7	6598.1	1961-1968
69	Muncie, Chuck	132.48	22.4	36.7	42.8	6423.4	1976-1984
70	Allen, Terry	132.05	22.3	35.0	44.0	8534.4	1991-2001
71	Matte, Tom	131.95	23.9	36.4	41.7	5921.5	1961-1972
72	Warren, Chris	131.85	21.7	37.0	42.6	8792.7	1990-2000
73	Johnson, Pete	131.78	22.5	36.9	42.1	6233.9	1977-1984
74	Willard, Ken	130.85	20.5	35.6	43.9	6036.9	1965-1974
75	Johnson, John Henry	129.98	20.9	34.7	43.8	6109.5	1954-1966
76	Kiick, Jim	129.73	24.1	37.1	39.5	4635.9	1968-1977
77	Van Eeghen, Mark	129.73	21.6	36.1	42.0	6804.5	1974-1983
78	Harder, Pat	129.70	23.9	37.0	39.7	3081.8	1946-1953
79	Strzykalski, Johnny	129.70	24.3	38.0	38.6	4557.0	1946-1952
80	Hill, Calvin	129.30	21.4	35.8	42.1	6455.6	1969-1981
81	Hampton, Rodney	128.83	20.8	37.1	41.1	7275.5	1990-1997
82	Towler, Dan	128.68	28.3	36.5	36.5	3106.5	1950-1955
83	Davis, Stephen	128.28	22.2	35.9	40.8	8471.1	1996-2006
84	Ameche, Alan	127.43	24.3	37.5	37.5	4289.4	1955-1960
85	Farkas, Andy	127.40	24.8	36.6	37.9	3869.1	1938-1945
86	Jones, Dub	127.13	25.2	35.7	38.2	3494.9	1946-1955
87	Granger, Hoyle	126.95	29.2	35.0	36.0	4102.4	1966-1972
88	Rogers, George	126.58	21.3	36.1	40.1	6100.0	1981-1987
89	Garner, Charlie	125.33	21.3	33.9	41.1	8681.5	1994-2004
90	Dixon, Hewritt	125.23	21.0	35.5	39.9	3625.6	1963-1970
91	Hearst, Garrison	125.03	20.9	34.7	40.5	8206.4	1993-2004
92	Mutryn, Chet	123.85	25.4	35.8	35.8	5097.3	1946-1950
93	Matson, Ollie	123.00	22.3	33.4	39.3	6269.0	1952-1966
94	Dudley, Bill	122.98	23.9	34.5	37.3	4451.1	1942-1953
95	Williams, John L.	122.40	18.5	33.2	41.6	6809.0	1986-1995
96	Webster, Alex	122.30	19.6	34.4	39.8	5092.5	1955-1964
97	Price, Eddie	122.23	25.7	35.1	35.1	2969.0	1950-1955
98	Sayers, Gale	121.23	24.0	35.3	35.4	6103.9	1965-1971
99	Wilder, James	121.05	20.0	32.6	40.2	6431.9	1981-1990
100	Foreman, Chuck	120.33	21.0	35.3	36.8	6086.9	1973-1980

Wide Receivers

Rk	Player	Score	Q3	Q6	Q9	AY	Career
1	Rice, Jerry	240.00	30.0	60.0	90.0	12103.6	1985-2004
2	Hutson, Don	240.00	30.0	60.0	90.0	4736.0	1935-1945
3	Harrison, Marvin	213.10	30.0	55.4	75.9	7188.5	1996-2007
4	Largent, Steve	209.10	30.0	54.0	74.4	6485.5	1976-1989
5	Lofton, James	207.48	29.5	53.7	73.9	7015.9	1978-1993
6	Moss, Randy	206.68	28.9	53.9	73.6	6532.1	1998-2007
7	Alworth, Lance	206.30	30.0	55.6	71.2	5527.6	1962-1972
8	Maynard, Don	206.08	29.5	55.1	71.8	6188.7	1958-1973
9	Owens, Terrell	201.28	27.6	52.3	72.2	7008.5	1996-2007
10	Irvin, Michael	195.30	28.0	51.4	68.7	6003.0	1988-1999
11	Jackson, Harold	190.73	27.4	49.3	67.8	5486.0	1968-1983
12	Holt, Torry	189.20	26.6	49.8	66.9	5597.3	1999-2007
13	Smith, Jimmy	187.00	26.2	48.0	67.2	6040.1	1992-2005
14	Bruce, Isaac	186.05	26.2	48.8	65.9	6990.0	1994-2007
15	Brown, Tim	185.00	25.0	47.6	67.0	7422.7	1988-2004
16	Smith, Rod	184.53	27.5	47.5	65.1	5670.6	1995-2006
17	Branch, Cliff	183.75	29.6	47.6	63.1	4576.8	1972-1985
18	Berry, Raymond	183.38	26.5	47.5	65.0	4937.5	1955-1967
19	Howton, Billy	180.38	28.6	47.5	61.6	4323.5	1952-1963
20	Clark, Gary	179.60	25.1	46.8	64.0	5461.3	1985-1995
21	Ellard, Henry	178.93	25.7	46.5	63.4	6514.6	1983-1998
22	Warfield, Paul	178.23	27.1	45.9	62.5	4591.5	1964-1977
23	Monk, Art	177.03	25.4	45.7	63.0	6535.5	1980-1995
24	Pearson, Drew	176.25	26.9	48.2	59.4	4032.6	1973-1983
25	Carter, Cris	176.23	24.4	45.5	63.3	6960.9	1987-2002
26	Powell, Art	176.10	29.0	49.4	56.9	4348.0	1959-1968
27	Shofner, Del	175.38	30.0	49.7	55.5	3430.4	1957-1967
28	Washington, Gene	175.18	27.0	46.3	60.2	3670.9	1969-1979
29	Taylor, Charley	174.63	24.8	45.1	62.3	5352.4	1964-1977
30	Reed, Andre	174.53	25.0	45.1	62.1	6547.1	1985-2000
31	Galloway, Joey	174.40	24.4	46.2	61.5	5819.0	1995-2007
32	Gilliam, John	173.95	27.2	47.2	58.5	3683.7	1967-1977
33	Clayton, Mark	172.93	26.2	46.7	58.9	4678.1	1983-1993
34	Chandler, Wes	172.70	27.7	45.2	59.0	4498.0	1978-1988
35	Johnson, Chad	172.08	28.0	51.3	53.3	4370.5	2001-2007

36	Hill, Drew	171.73	25.8	46.3	58.7	4993.4	1979-1993
37	Carmichael, Harold	171.18	26.0	44.5	59.7	4298.9	1971-1984
38	Garrison, Gary	171.18	24.7	45.3	59.9	3968.0	1966-1977
39	Biletnikoff, Fred	169.73	23.2	43.9	61.1	4627.0	1965-1978
40	Joiner, Charlie	168.38	24.0	43.5	60.0	5596.6	1969-1986
41	Moore, Herman	168.38	26.3	46.7	55.8	4697.0	1991-2002
42	Morgan, Stanley	168.15	25.3	43.6	58.9	5331.5	1977-1990
43	Sharpe, Sterling	166.75	27.2	48.4	52.7	4131.4	1988-1994
44	Mitchell, Bobby	165.93	25.5	44.9	56.2	6180.6	1958-1968
45	Speedie, Mac	165.23	28.7	47.9	51.1	2926.0	1946-1952
46	Hill, Tony	165.15	24.2	43.4	57.8	4085.6	1977-1986
47	Fryar, Irving	165.00	23.9	42.8	58.4	6614.1	1984-2000
48	Gray, Mel	164.93	24.9	43.5	57.1	3615.8	1971-1982
49	Parks, Dave	163.30	27.4	45.6	52.6	2859.5	1964-1973
50	Taylor, Otis	163.20	26.2	43.6	55.0	3774.0	1965-1975
51	Duper, Mark	162.90	24.8	42.8	56.4	4559.5	1982-1992
52	Hayes, Bob	162.35	23.8	45.2	54.7	3629.4	1965-1975
53	Ward, Hines	160.68	23.7	43.1	55.4	4775.7	1998-2007
54	Benton, Jim	160.50	27.2	42.8	53.2	2489.5	1938-1947
55	Stallworth, John	160.45	24.3	43.4	54.6	4197.5	1974-1987
56	Carter, Anthony	159.78	23.6	42.1	55.7	4187.9	1985-1995
57	Johnson, Keyshawn	159.60	22.9	41.2	56.8	5277.5	1996-2006
58	Moulds, Eric	159.10	23.8	42.0	55.2	5097.5	1996-2007
59	Miller, Anthony	158.70	23.3	41.6	55.6	4774.3	1988-1997
60	Orr, Jimmy	158.50	24.1	42.0	54.6	4119.5	1958-1970
61	Rison, Andre	157.60	22.6	42.6	54.5	5074.6	1989-2000
62	Lavelli, Dante	157.40	24.5	41.4	54.1	3417.0	1946-1956
63	Moore, Rob	157.28	23.6	41.3	54.7	4718.5	1990-1999
64	Green, Roy	157.18	26.7	42.1	51.9	4420.9	1979-1992
65	Moore, Nat	157.03	24.4	41.3	54.0	4101.9	1974-1986
66	Wilson, Billy	156.35	24.9	43.6	51.3	3036.0	1951-1960
67	Caster, Rich	156.13	27.5	42.3	50.5	2703.2	1970-1982
68	Horn, Joe	155.30	25.1	42.6	51.3	4398.4	1996-2007
69	Hirsch, Elroy	154.25	23.5	39.8	54.0	4280.5	1946-1957
70	McCardell, Keenan	153.13	21.2	39.9	54.7	5647.0	1992-2007
71	Burrough, Ken	152.53	23.8	39.5	52.9	3411.2	1970-1981
72	Glenn, Terry	152.15	23.3	40.8	51.9	4500.5	1996-2007

		Score	Q3	Q6	Q9	AY	Career
73	Givins, Ernest	152.08	22.4	40.5	52.7	4152.9	1986-1995
74	Jefferson, John	150.18	28.2	43.1	45.4	3113.0	1978-1985
75	Curtis, Isaac	149.75	23.7	39.4	51.2	3491.5	1973-1984

Tight Ends

Rk	Player	Score	Q3	Q6	Q9	AY	Career
1	Gonzalez, Tony	230.58	30.0	59.3	84.3	5065.0	1997-2007
2	Sharpe, Shannon	226.88	30.0	58.5	82.5	5029.5	1990-2003
3	Newsome, Ozzie	209.88	30.0	56.3	73.0	4262.3	1978-1990
4	Smith, Jackie	204.65	30.0	53.8	71.6	4065.2	1963-1978
5	Retzlaff, Pete	187.73	28.6	50.5	64.0	3777.0	1956-1966
6	Winslow, Kellen	182.23	29.2	49.7	60.6	3155.5	1979-1987
7	Ditka, Mike	182.08	30.0	49.9	59.8	2763.0	1961-1972
8	Christensen, Todd	179.65	30.0	52.4	56.1	2888.0	1979-1988
9	Smith, Jerry	176.68	27.1	47.3	60.3	2906.0	1965-1977
10	Odoms, Riley	176.30	25.9	45.8	62.1	2993.5	1972-1983
11	Casper, Dave	174.00	27.6	49.8	56.1	2615.1	1974-1984
12	Novacek, Jay	172.20	28.5	48.0	55.8	2129.6	1985-1995
13	Coates, Ben	172.03	27.1	48.5	56.2	2703.5	1991-2000
14	Jackson, Keith	169.98	26.1	45.5	58.0	2366.5	1988-1996
15	Chester, Raymond	168.83	26.3	46.1	56.6	2435.5	1970-1981
16	Walls, Wesley	166.30	26.4	45.2	55.6	2796.2	1989-2003
17	Jordan, Steve	164.53	23.6	42.3	58.7	2870.1	1982-1994
18	Trumpy, Bob	160.48	25.6	43.1	54.0	2194.0	1968-1977
19	Bavaro, Mark	158.60	25.1	42.6	53.5	2322.9	1985-1994
20	Sanders, Charlie	158.08	24.0	42.1	54.3	2317.5	1968-1977
21	Jones, Brent	157.20	24.8	42.2	53.1	2282.5	1987-1997
22	Mitchell, Jim	155.63	24.0	42.3	52.5	2238.4	1969-1979
23	Mackey, John	152.28	24.6	40.7	51.2	2511.0	1963-1972
24	Wycheck, Frank	150.90	23.3	41.6	50.4	2485.9	1993-2003
25	Cannon, Billy	150.33	24.4	40.5	50.2	3922.8	1960-1970
26	Tucker, Bob	150.25	23.6	40.0	51.1	2181.5	1970-1980
27	Holman, Rodney	149.40	24.5	39.8	50.1	2207.8	1982-1995
28	Shuler, Mickey	143.98	25.6	39.5	46.0	2384.6	1978-1991
29	Frazier, Willie	141.43	29.1	38.5	42.8	1597.5	1964-1975
30	Gates, Antonio	139.35	28.8	40.2	40.2	2356.0	2003-2007
31	Whalen, Jim	139.25	25.1	40.2	42.6	1597.5	1965-1971

32	Morin, Milt	138.70	21.7	39.0	45.5	1946.1	1966-1975
33	Kocourek, Dave	136.90	24.8	38.8	42.4	2085.0	1960-1968
34	Childs, Henry	135.48	28.1	38.5	39.5	1702.5	1974-1984
35	Carpenter, Preston	134.90	19.5	35.8	47.1	2814.3	1956-1967
36	Young, Charle	134.33	24.4	35.5	43.7	2298.0	1973-1985
37	Green, Eric	132.78	21.7	37.5	42.8	1856.1	1990-1999
38	Harris, Jackie	129.15	22.2	34.2	42.8	2131.0	1990-2001
39	Francis, Russ	129.05	19.9	34.4	44.1	2465.5	1975-1988
40	Kwalick, Ted	125.28	27.9	35.3	35.5	1377.7	1969-1977
41	Heap, Todd	124.93	24.8	35.7	37.0	1982.5	2001-2007
42	Arbanas, Fred	123.90	22.3	34.6	38.9	1575.5	1962-1970
43	Barkum, Jerome	123.38	18.7	33.1	42.2	2433.9	1972-1983
44	Giles, Jimmie	122.60	20.5	32.6	40.9	2390.9	1977-1989
45	Crumpler, Alge	122.48	21.2	35.3	38.1	2125.3	2001-2007
46	Shockey, Jeremy	122.35	21.7	36.6	36.6	2055.0	2002-2007
47	Jones, Freddie	122.30	19.8	33.4	40.5	2066.0	1997-2004
48	Cosbie, Doug	120.00	20.5	34.0	38.0	1850.8	1979-1988
49	Coffman, Paul	118.35	18.7	33.4	38.6	2025.1	1978-1988
50	McGee, Tony	117.00	17.6	30.8	40.6	2029.5	1993-2003

Offensive Linemen

Rk	Player	Score	Q3	Q6	Q9	GmBonus	AllPro	Career
1	Otto, Jim	335.86	28.1	50.4	66.4	20.0	13/12	1960-1974
2	Matthews, Bruce	328.95	25.1	42.8	57.8	48.7	12/11	1983-2001
3	Hickerson, Gene	302.43	30.0	60.0	86.7	17.3	7/3	1958-1973
4	Slater, Jackie	299.04	28.9	53.1	68.3	36.3	7/6	1976-1995
5	Upshaw, Gene	295.01	26.9	47.1	61.3	22.3	11/8	1967-1981
6	Hannah, John	291.77	27.2	46.7	60.1	11.0	11/10	1973-1985
7	Shields, Will	285.70	26.1	48.7	66.0	24.7	9/6	1993-2006
8	McDaniel, Randall	284.25	25.2	39.9	53.4	24.0	11/10	1988-2001
9	Ringo, Jim	281.98	28.6	51.5	67.8	12.3	9/6	1953-1967
10	Mack, Tom	279.88	25.6	45.8	60.5	11.3	11/8	1966-1978
11	Mix, Ron	279.00	30.0	51.1	63.4	0.0	9/9	1960-1971
12	Munoz, Anthony	275.11	23.2	39.6	54.1	11.3	11/11	1980-1992
13	Groza, Lou	272.73	29.3	51.3	65.3	11.3	8/6	1946-1967
14	Gregg, Forrest	272.50	28.6	50.8	64.3	14.0	9/5	1956-1971

15	Schafrath, Dick	270.56	30.0	60.0	84.6	8.7	4/2	1959-1971
16	Roaf, Willie	270.01	23.6	42.7	56.7	13.0	10/9	1993-2005
17	Tyrer, Jim	268.61	24.0	42.2	58.1	14.7	10/8	1961-1974
18	Brown, Lomas	263.82	23.4	42.6	59.0	38.7	7/5	1985-2002
19	Banducci, Bruno	262.51	30.0	53.9	70.1	0.0	7/5	1944-1954
20	Webster, Mike	259.44	21.5	37.6	52.9	31.7	10/6	1974-1990
21	Little, Larry	259.20	27.8	48.7	63.0	11.0	7/6	1967-1980
22	Sweeney, Walt	254.73	30.0	51.3	66.6	10.7	6/4	1963-1975
23	Allen, Larry	254.11	26.5	44.0	56.4	18.0	7/7	1994-2007
24	Foster, Roy	253.24	30.0	60.0	78.9	5.0	4/1	1982-1993
25	DeLamielleure, Joe	253.03	24.4	44.3	57.8	11.7	9/6	1973-1985
26	Mawae, Kevin	252.66	26.5	46.4	62.1	20.0	6/5	1994-2007
27	Putnam, Duane	252.20	29.0	54.1	73.8	0.0	6/3	1952-1962
28	Dierdorf, Dan	250.09	29.8	51.5	65.1	3.3	6/5	1971-1983
29	Zimmerman, Gary	246.66	26.4	42.7	53.7	11.3	9/6	1986-1997
30	Nalen, Tom	245.40	28.3	53.4	73.8	14.7	3/2	1994-2007
31	Hill, Winston	244.58	27.8	47.2	61.2	16.0	8/2	1963-1977
32	Webb, Richmond	243.91	29.2	49.2	64.6	11.3	5/4	1990-2002
33	Brown, Ray	239.95	28.4	50.5	67.4	37.3	1/1	1986-2005
34	Brown, Bob	239.35	24.5	44.1	56.5	0.0	9/6	1964-1973
35	Newton, Nate	239.09	29.6	50.7	63.4	16.0	5/2	1986-1999
36	Langer, Jim	238.07	27.8	49.1	62.4	0.3	6/5	1970-1981
37	Wisniewski, Steve	237.65	21.7	36.4	47.8	18.7	8/8	1989-2001
38	Banks, Tom	236.45	29.8	51.5	64.9	0.0	5/4	1971-1980
39	Young, Bob	234.98	29.8	53.1	69.8	9.0	3/2	1968-1981
40	Iman, Ken	234.83	30.0	56.2	76.6	14.7	1/0	1960-1974
41	Rohde, Len	234.71	29.5	53.9	75.7	19.3	1/0	1960-1974
42	White, Ed	234.58	28.5	45.5	55.9	30.3	5/2	1969-1985
43	McMillan, Ernie	233.66	28.5	48.1	60.9	13.7	7/1	1961-1975
44	St. Clair, Bob	232.50	28.4	48.6	62.2	0.0	9/1	1953-1963
45	Kramer, Jerry	231.99	28.6	50.8	59.9	0.0	7/3	1958-1968
46	Wooten, John	230.47	30.0	57.9	78.7	0.0	2/	1959-1968
47	Dobler, Conrad	229.36	29.8	55.3	70.3	0.0	4/1	1972-1981
48	Munchak, Mike	229.05	23.9	38.0	46.5	3.0	10/7	1982-1993
49	Stephenson, Dwight	229.03	30.0	53.3	54.9	0.0	5/5	1980-1987
50	Shell, Art	228.57	22.3	38.0	49.8	19.0	7/6	1968-1982

Defensive Linemen

Rk	Player	Score	Q3	Q6	Q9	GmBonus	AllPro	Career
1	Smith, Bruce	367.83	29.3	55.9	77.1	43.0	12/10	1985-2003
2	White, Reggie	362.13	28.6	54.0	75.8	27.3	13/12	1985-2000
3	Olsen, Merlin	346.71	29.8	57.5	83.8	19.3	13/7	1962-1976
4	Lilly, Bob	334.53	30.0	57.6	84.8	15.3	10/8	1961-1974
5	Greene, Joe	313.73	29.7	55.4	76.3	10.3	11/7	1969-1981
6	White, Randy	312.99	28.1	52.1	73.4	19.7	9/9	1975-1988
7	Page, Alan	305.59	27.2	49.9	68.9	22.7	11/7	1967-1981
8	Youngblood, Jack	299.38	28.0	53.6	74.7	17.3	9/6	1971-1984
9	Jones, Deacon	299.06	29.1	55.7	78.0	13.3	8/6	1961-1974
10	Robustelli, Andy	293.73	30.0	55.9	73.9	8.0	11/4	1951-1964
11	Doleman, Chris	288.26	29.2	54.3	75.9	27.3	6/4	1985-1999
12	Hampton, Dan	281.38	30.0	56.2	79.2	2.3	6/6	1979-1990
13	Eller, Carl	280.23	27.2	46.1	63.6	25.0	9/6	1964-1979
14	Long, Howie	276.37	29.6	56.2	77.9	9.7	6/4	1981-1993
15	Jones, Ed	275.52	28.3	54.0	76.7	24.7	5/3	1974-1989
16	Karras, Alex	273.79	29.9	54.9	74.4	3.7	9/3	1958-1970
17	Strahan, Michael	270.43	27.2	50.3	68.9	22.0	6/5	1993-2007
18	McDole, Ron	270.28	30.0	55.7	77.1	30.0	5/0	1961-1978
19	McMichael, Steve	267.33	30.0	57.1	73.3	21.0	5/2	1980-1994
20	Marchetti, Gino	266.05	28.1	49.4	60.8	0.0	10/7	1953-1966
21	Atkins, Doug	265.46	29.6	50.5	65.6	14.3	10/2	1953-1969
22	Dent, Richard	262.34	27.8	52.3	71.0	17.7	5/4	1983-1997
23	Buchanan, Buck	261.43	28.5	49.8	66.9	10.3	8/4	1963-1975
24	Grier, Rosey	260.88	30.0	57.3	79.5	0.0	7/1	1955-1966
25	Greenwood, L.C.	259.77	28.4	54.0	74.8	6.7	6/3	1969-1981
26	Bethea, Elvin	258.48	27.4	49.7	69.3	20.0	8/1	1968-1983
27	Katcavage, Jim	257.28	30.0	55.9	71.6	5.0	6/3	1956-1968
28	Alzado, Lyle	256.33	28.7	52.8	74.2	15.3	5/2	1971-1985
29	Brown, Roger	254.55	30.0	57.2	78.7	0.0	6/1	1960-1969
30	Fuller, William	252.04	29.3	53.9	73.8	14.7	4/2	1986-1998
31	Randle, John	250.58	24.2	42.3	57.0	23.0	7/6	1990-2003
32	Taylor, Jason	248.73	27.8	51.0	69.9	7.3	5/4	1997-2007
33	Brooks, Larry	247.80	28.0	53.6	75.2	0.0	6/2	1972-1982
34	Washington, Ted	245.89	26.8	49.3	69.2	28.7	3/2	1991-2007
35	Marshall, Jim	245.70	27.2	47.6	66.0	40.0	4/0	1961-1979

36	Simmons, Clyde	245.64	27.8	51.7	69.7	28.7	3/1	1986-2000
37	Pugh, Jethro	244.63	30.0	57.5	84.5	11.0	1/0	1965-1978
38	Martin, Harvey	244.59	28.3	55.1	76.5	2.7	4/2	1973-1983
39	Jordan, Henry	244.38	26.5	48.0	65.7	4.3	7/4	1957-1969
40	Andrie, George	243.50	30.0	57.6	81.0	0.0	4/0	1962-1972
41	Mays, Jerry	241.10	28.5	47.8	61.9	0.0	9/3	1961-1970
42	Antwine, Houston	239.11	30.0	52.7	68.6	0.3	6/2	1961-1972
43	Childress, Ray	237.18	27.9	46.4	61.3	4.3	6/5	1985-1996
44	Young, Bryant	237.08	26.2	48.8	63.7	19.3	4/3	1994-2007
45	Bacon, Coy	236.78	28.7	52.9	71.3	10.0	4/1	1968-1981
46	Thomas, Henry	234.78	28.2	52.1	70.3	21.0	3/0	1987-2000
47	White, Dwight	234.75	29.7	54.4	74.7	0.0	4/1	1971-1980
48	Humphrey, Claude	234.45	23.6	40.6	55.4	7.0	8/6	1968-1981
49	Sapp, Warren	232.93	21.8	41.3	59.0	16.0	6/5	1995-2007
50	Davis, Willie	232.80	26.5	48.0	64.2	0.0	6/4	1958-1969

Linebackers

Rk	Player	Score	Q3	Q6	Q9	GmBonus	AllPro	Career
1	Seau, Junior	346.62	29.2	56.8	80.5	35.7	10/8	1990-2007
2	Singletary, Mike	318.12	30.0	56.8	78.3	9.7	9/9	1981-1992
3	Taylor, Lawrence	314.26	28.1	52.5	72.8	11.3	10/10	1981-1993
4	Ham, Jack	304.33	29.7	56.5	80.0	4.0	9/7	1971-1982
5	Hendricks, Ted	301.04	28.9	51.9	70.4	21.7	11/5	1969-1983
6	Brooks, Derrick	291.41	25.8	46.3	65.6	19.3	9/9	1995-2007
7	Howley, Chuck	288.63	29.3	56.7	82.3	10.0	7/4	1958-1973
8	Lambert, Jack	285.03	29.2	52.9	69.8	0.0	9/8	1974-1984
9	Jackson, Rickey	285.02	26.9	51.2	72.3	25.7	7/5	1981-1995
10	Carson, Harry	284.47	27.8	53.2	75.0	7.7	7/7	1976-1988
11	Lewis, Ray	282.95	29.3	54.6	77.6	4.0	7/6	1996-2007
12	Schmidt, Joe	281.21	28.8	51.5	67.8	1.3	10/7	1953-1965
13	Buoniconti, Nick	280.23	28.7	51.7	70.6	11.0	10/4	1962-1976
14	Huff, Sam	278.58	30.0	58.5	76.3	6.0	8/3	1956-1969
15	Bell, Bobby	277.10	28.5	49.8	66.9	6.0	9/7	1963-1974
16	Walker, Wayne	272.24	29.9	55.9	77.2	16.7	5/3	1958-1972
17	Jordan, Lee Roy	271.20	30.0	57.6	84.8	12.0	5/1	1963-1976
18	Grantham, Larry	265.88	26.5	47.4	61.2	8.3	11/5	1960-1972
19	Robertson, Isiah	261.33	27.4	51.7	72.2	6.0	7/4	1971-1982

20	Bennett, Cornelius	260.04	29.2	53.5	70.2	18.7	6/2	1987-2000
21	George, Bill	259.53	28.7	49.3	62.8	0.0	8/7	1955-1966
22	Hanburger, Chris	255.66	25.7	45.9	63.5	12.3	8/5	1965-1978
23	Nitschke, Ray	254.83	28.5	51.1	68.3	15.0	7/2	1958-1972
24	Thomas, Derrick	253.56	27.9	47.5	63.3	6.3	8/5	1989-1999
25	Bednarik, Chuck	251.60	25.8	47.8	60.7	0.0	8/7	1950-1962
26	Russell, Andy	251.38	28.5	52.3	71.0	6.0	7/2	1963-1976
27	Martin, Rod	249.70	29.3	54.8	74.6	5.0	5/2	1977-1988
28	Pardee, Jack	249.56	29.8	55.5	76.7	15.3	2/2	1957-1972
29	Thomas, Zach	248.93	27.8	51.5	70.5	6.0	7/2	1996-2007
30	O'Neal, Leslie	247.63	28.8	49.8	67.5	15.3	5/3	1986-1999
31	Joyner, Seth	246.53	27.8	51.7	69.4	15.0	5/2	1986-1998
32	Marshall, Wilber	246.14	29.4	53.7	73.3	9.7	4/2	1984-1995
33	Baughan, Maxie	244.15	29.1	52.8	72.7	0.0	7/1	1960-1974
34	Brazile, Robert	240.75	25.7	46.2	58.2	0.0	8/6	1975-1984
35	Van Pelt, Brad	239.21	27.3	51.1	67.8	11.3	5/2	1973-1986
36	Millen, Matt	238.95	29.7	56.0	79.5	10.0	2/0	1980-1991
37	Nelson, Steve	237.60	27.7	50.0	69.6	8.0	5/2	1974-1987
38	Edwards, Dave	236.06	29.3	56.7	83.7	10.3	0/0	1963-1975
39	Lanier, Willie	234.95	25.6	43.8	56.4	0.0	8/6	1967-1977
40	Matthews, Clay	234.87	25.0	44.2	61.3	42.7	3/1	1978-1996
41	Lewis, D.D.	233.69	29.1	56.3	81.7	11.7	0/0	1968-1981
42	Robinson, Dave	232.63	29.6	53.1	71.1	0.0	4/2	1963-1974
43	Swilling, Pat	232.09	24.8	45.5	62.5	11.7	6/3	1986-1998
44	Reynolds, Jack	230.95	28.0	53.6	73.3	16.0	2/0	1970-1984
45	Lloyd, Greg	230.90	29.2	54.2	69.3	0.0	3/3	1988-1998
46	Gradishar, Randy	230.70	22.5	41.8	57.3	0.0	8/6	1974-1983
47	Robinson, Jerry	229.83	26.7	49.8	69.7	11.3	3/2	1979-1991
48	Romanowski, Bill	229.20	27.8	50.0	68.6	31.0	1/0	1988-2003
49	Addison, Tom	228.68	30.0	52.7	65.2	0.0	5/2	1960-1967
50	Butkus, Dick	227.83	23.2	41.1	55.5	0.0	8/6	1965-1973

Defensive Backs

Rk	Player	Score	Q3	Q6	Q9	GmBonus	AllPro	Career
1	Woodson, Rod	364.77	30.0	57.8	81.9	39.7	11/9	1987-2003
2	Sanders, Deion	333.23	22.8	39.5	52.7	37.0	15/14	1989-2005
3	Krause, Paul	326.38	30.0	58.4	82.7	24.3	9/6	1964-1979

4	Brown, Willie	320.51	29.1	54.9	76.3	18.3	11/7	1963-1978
5	Houston, Ken	316.74	28.5	53.3	75.3	13.7	12/7	1967-1980
6	Wood, Willie	306.38	30.0	57.2	79.7	5.3	10/6	1960-1971
7	Blount, Mel	294.32	30.0	58.8	86.1	16.7	6/3	1970-1983
8	Robinson, Johnny	290.17	29.7	57.0	79.7	4.7	8/5	1960-1971
9	Adderley, Herb	289.09	30.0	58.1	81.2	4.7	8/4	1961-1972
10	Lake, Carnell	279.37	29.6	53.8	73.9	11.7	7/5	1989-2001
11	Lane, Dick	279.36	29.7	55.7	71.8	2.3	10/4	1952-1965
12	Lott, Ronnie	277.15	24.3	46.4	63.9	14.0	9/8	1981-1994
13	Tunnell, Emlen	271.98	28.7	53.2	74.3	5.3	8/4	1948-1961
14	Grayson, Dave	271.78	29.1	55.3	75.7	0.0	7/5	1961-1970
15	Allen, Eric	271.66	28.7	52.9	73.0	22.3	6/3	1988-2001
16	Lary, Yale	270.50	28.0	52.2	71.5	0.0	9/5	1952-1964
17	Green, Darrell	268.16	25.6	47.7	66.4	48.3	4/3	1983-2002
18	Lynch, John	260.68	28.9	52.1	71.1	25.0	4/3	1993-2007
19	McDonald, Tim	259.67	27.5	49.4	64.5	13.7	8/4	1987-1999
20	Thomas, Emmitt	259.66	29.2	53.1	72.5	10.3	6/3	1966-1978
21	Fischer, Pat	255.95	28.9	51.4	71.2	21.0	6/1	1961-1977
22	Shell, Donnie	253.48	29.2	50.9	69.1	17.0	5/3	1974-1987
23	Wright, Louis	252.89	26.7	49.1	66.1	5.7	8/4	1975-1986
24	Lahr, Warren	252.78	29.2	56.3	78.8	0.0	6/1	1949-1959
25	Parrish, Lemar	251.48	27.4	51.0	70.0	5.3	8/2	1970-1982
26	Fencik, Gary	251.27	28.9	52.2	68.3	4.7	6/4	1976-1987
27	Renfro, Mel	251.18	23.5	42.9	60.7	8.0	10/5	1964-1977
28	Haynes, Mike	250.08	22.9	41.9	57.2	9.0	8/8	1976-1989
29	Patton, Jimmy	249.40	27.6	49.6	69.2	1.0	6/5	1955-1966
30	Barnes, Erich	247.72	28.6	51.8	69.8	9.7	7/1	1958-1971
31	Barber, Ronde	246.84	28.6	52.9	72.3	3.7	5/3	1997-2007
32	Robinson, Eugene	243.41	28.8	50.7	68.6	33.3	2/1	1985-2000
33	Butler, Le Roy	243.36	28.8	49.9	67.9	10.3	4/4	1990-2001
34	Johnson, Jimmy	239.79	21.4	39.7	55.4	20.7	9/4	1961-1976
35	Petitbon, Richie	239.49	29.3	53.3	72.6	9.7	5/0	1959-1972
36	Wehrli, Roger	239.46	22.4	41.3	57.4	14.3	7/6	1969-1982
37	Scott, Jake	238.93	27.2	50.7	68.9	0.0	5/4	1970-1978
38	Riley, Ken	236.63	25.8	48.7	67.3	19.0	4/2	1969-1983
39	Lewis, Albert	233.33	23.4	43.1	60.7	25.0	5/3	1983-1998
40	Sample, Johnny	232.15	28.3	52.8	71.9	0.0	5/1	1958-1968

41	Williams, Aeneas	232.03	23.9	42.2	56.7	20.3	5/5	1991-2004
42	Christiansen, Jack	230.05	28.0	49.0	57.2	0.0	6/5	1951-1958
43	Meador, Eddie	230.01	27.8	47.9	62.0	4.3	9/0	1959-1970
44	Atwater, Steve	229.99	25.6	45.3	61.4	5.7	6/4	1989-1999
45	Cherry, Deron	229.95	26.3	47.0	56.6	0.0	7/5	1981-1991
46	Wilson, Larry	229.76	21.8	40.5	54.0	6.3	8/6	1960-1972
47	Thompson, Billy	229.37	26.1	48.4	65.4	9.7	5/2	1969-1981
48	Woodson, Darren	229.33	26.2	48.8	65.2	9.3	4/3	1992-2003
49	Barney, Lem	229.33	27.5	48.3	64.3	0.0	7/2	1967-1977
50	Wagner, Mike	228.73	29.6	55.3	70.0	0.0	4/1	1971-1980

Kickers

Rk	Player	Score	Q3	Q6	Q9	Career
1	Groza, Lou	223.95	30.0	60.0	79.3	1948-1967
2	Stover, Matt	212.95	29.2	55.2	76.5	1991-2007
3	Andersen, Morten	209.33	30.0	54.3	74.3	1982-2007
4	Carney, John	202.18	28.9	52.7	71.6	1988-2007
5	Anderson, Gary	199.25	28.6	51.2	71.1	1982-2004
6	Stenerud, Jan	198.33	30.0	53.3	67.8	1967-1985
7	Lowery, Nick	194.18	26.8	50.5	69.5	1978-1996
8	Elam, Jason	189.13	27.2	49.5	66.7	1993-2007
9	Bakken, Jim	187.98	29.0	51.1	63.4	1962-1978
10	Wilkins, Jeff	184.55	28.7	48.6	63.4	1995-2007
11	Cockroft, Don	179.15	30.0	51.4	56.6	1968-1980
12	Hanson, Jason	177.15	24.5	45.2	64.1	1992-2007
13	Vinatieri, Adam	176.35	26.9	45.4	61.8	1996-2007
14	Vanderjagt, Mike	173.38	27.9	46.9	57.9	1998-2006
15	Yepremian, Garo	172.25	29.6	45.6	57.1	1966-1981
16	Del Greco, Al	170.78	25.8	45.3	58.9	1984-2000
17	Murray, Eddie	170.60	25.5	44.2	59.9	1980-2000
18	Johnson, Norm	169.00	26.2	43.2	59.2	1982-1999
19	Stoyanovich, Pete	168.95	26.8	44.0	58.1	1989-2000
20	Layne, Bobby	168.33	26.8	44.1	57.6	1948-1961
21	Kasay, John	168.13	23.1	42.7	61.1	1991-2007
22	Turner, Jim	160.10	25.1	42.0	55.0	1964-1979
23	Longwell, Ryan	159.53	23.0	41.3	56.6	1997-2007

| 24 | Cox, Fred | 157.60 | 26.1 | 43.4 | 51.5 | 1963-1977 |
| 25 | Blanda, George | 153.85 | 29.4 | 42.2 | 47.8 | 1949-1975 |

Punters

Rk	Player	Score	Q3	Q6	Q9	Career
1	Jennings, Dave	215.95	30.0	57.8	75.8	1974-1987
2	Wilson, Jerrel	215.15	29.8	54.8	77.9	1963-1978
3	Walden, Bobby	215.13	30.0	57.5	75.5	1964-1977
4	Green, Bobby Joe	214.95	29.8	56.2	76.6	1960-1973
5	Stark, Rohn	213.93	30.0	55.7	76.2	1982-1997
6	Landeta, Sean	213.18	28.5	54.5	77.7	1985-2005
7	Maguire, Paul	212.50	30.0	56.6	74.5	1960-1970
8	Camarillo, Rich	210.30	29.2	54.4	75.4	1981-1995
9	Baugh, Sammy	206.23	30.0	57.7	69.4	1937-1952
10	Bennett, Darren	204.73	29.3	53.7	72.2	1995-2005
11	Tuten, Rick	196.90	29.8	54.0	66.4	1989-1999
12	Guy, Ray	196.58	29.2	51.1	69.0	1973-1986
13	Gardocki, Chris	192.23	28.1	49.7	68.0	1992-2006
14	Davis, Tommy	191.98	28.3	50.9	66.7	1959-1969
15	Arnold, Jim	191.58	28.4	51.1	66.2	1983-1994
16	Maynard, Brad	190.18	27.8	50.1	66.5	1997-2007
17	Baker, Sam	189.23	27.0	50.1	66.4	1953-1968
18	Sauerbrun, Todd	184.83	27.5	48.1	64.8	1995-2006
19	Chandler, Don	184.25	30.0	49.0	62.0	1956-1966
20	Royals, Mark	183.33	26.6	48.7	63.9	1987-2003
21	Roby, Reggie	181.03	25.7	45.9	65.3	1983-1998
22	Horan, Mike	179.18	25.0	46.3	64.2	1984-1999
23	Van Brocklin, Norm	178.30	27.4	47.4	61.1	1949-1960
24	Feagles, Jeff	177.08	22.6	44.5	65.9	1988-2007
25	Tupa, Tom	176.20	25.8	45.8	62.1	1989-2004

Return Specialists

Rk	Player	Score	Q3	Q6	Q9	AY-KR	AY-PR	Career
1	Mitchell, Brian	196.93	28.0	52.1	69.2	1313.6	4300.9	1990-2003
2	Johnson, Billy	186.15	30.0	53.6	59.4	384.3	3016.9	1974-1988
3	Woodson, Abe	176.08	30.0	51.9	54.2	1407.6	704.0	1958-1965

4	Sikahema, Vai	168.19	30.0	47.9	52.2	32.6	2868.6	1986-1993
5	Duncan, Speedy	164.13	27.1	47.3	52.0	471.1	1668.9	1964-1974
6	Meggett, Dave	164.03	27.3	44.1	54.4	218.6	3205.3	1989-1998
7	Milburn, Glyn	162.43	25.1	45.3	53.8	1358.3	2551.4	1993-2001
8	Haymond, Alvin	162.08	30.0	44.7	50.8	782.4	1527.6	1965-1973
9	Upchurch, Rick	159.23	25.8	45.4	51.2	284.0	2592.3	1975-1983
10	Tunnell, Emlen	155.58	28.0	43.3	48.9	228.7	1932.0	1948-1959
11	Hall, Dante	154.60	26.9	44.1	48.4	1312.3	1976.4	2000-2007
12	Gray, Mel	151.33	24.3	40.4	51.0	1282.4	2181.1	1986-1997
13	McAfee, George	147.78	25.8	43.4	45.2	146.0	1307.8	1940-1950
14	Nelms, Mike	144.94	27.5	42.7	42.7	507.1	1808.9	1980-1984
15	Carmichael, Al	143.90	23.7	41.4	45.6	778.5	705.8	1953-1960
16	Brown, Tim	143.24	23.4	38.8	47.6	191.7	2847.5	1988-2004
17	Smith, J.T.	142.04	26.2	40.5	43.5	−42.1	2558.1	1978-1990
18	Lewis, Jermaine	141.16	24.4	39.5	44.9	152.5	3018.7	1996-2004
19	Farkas, Andy	140.81	29.9	40.3	40.3	238.2	738.9	1939-1945
20	Howard, Desmond	134.56	24.2	37.2	42.6	563.4	2739.2	1992-2002
21	Lewis, Woodley	131.78	27.8	37.4	38.2	478.2	903.7	1950-1958
22	Rossum, Allen	130.38	21.0	34.9	43.8	807.6	2273.7	1998-2007
23	Smith, Ron	128.47	22.5	35.7	40.9	701.3	1096.7	1966-1974
24	Todd, Dick	127.26	27.5	35.7	36.7	17.3	580.2	1939-1948
25	Arnett, Jon	126.52	21.7	35.8	40.0	505.3	854.3	1957-1966

Yearly Adjusted-Yards Leaders

Quarterbacks

Year	AY	Player
2007	2123.0	Tom Brady (NE)
2006	1948.5	Peyton Manning (Ind)
2005	1446.0	Tom Brady (NE)
2004	1996.5	Daunte Culpepper (Min)
2003	1606.5	Peyton Manning (Ind)
2002	1736.5	Rich Gannon (Oak)
2001	1373.0	Steve McNair (Ten)
2000	1963.0	Jeff Garcia (SF)
1999	1467.5	Kurt Warner (StL)
1998	1765.0	Steve Young (SF)
1997	1413.5	Mark Brunell (Jac)
1996	1221.0	Jeff Blake (Cin)
1995	1615.5	Brett Favre (GB)
1994	1849.5	Steve Young (SF)
1993	1544.5	Steve Young (SF)
1992	1677.5	Steve Young (SF)
1991	1319.5	Steve Young (SF)
1990	1629.0	Randall Cunningham (Phi)
1989	1372.0	Jim Everett (LaRm)
1988	1249.4	Boomer Esiason (Cin)
1987	1400.2	John Elway (Den)
1986	1346.0	Dan Marino (Mia)
1985	1243.5	Joe Montana (SF)
1984	1820.0	Dan Marino (Mia)
1983	1625.0	Joe Montana (SF)
1982	985.5	Dan Fouts (SD)
1981	1662.0	Ken Anderson (Cin)
1980	1454.0	Brian Sipe (Cle)
1979	1158.5	Jim Zorn (Sea)
1978	933.0	Roger Staubach (Dal)
1977	908.0	Bert Jones (Bal)
1976	1147.0	Bert Jones (Bal)
1975	1105.5	Ken Anderson (Cin)
1974	995.5	Ken Anderson (Cin)
1973	705.5	Roman Gabriel (Phi)
1972	873.0	Greg Landry (Det)
1971	871.5	Greg Landry (Det)
1970	1182.5	John Brodie (SF)
1969	963.5	Roman Gabriel (Larm)
1969a	852.0	Daryle Lamonica (Oak)
1968	958.5	Fran Tarkenton (NYG)
1968a	946.5	Daryle Lamonica (Oak)
1967	1177.5	Sonny Jurgensen (Was)
1967a	839.5	John Hadl (SD)
1966	875.0	Frank Ryan (Cle)
1966a	1010.5	Len Dawson (KC)

Year	AY	Player
1965	955.0	John Brodie (SF)
1965a	628.0	Len Dawson (KC)
1964	1099.0	Sonny Jurgensen (Was)
1964a	635.5	Cotton Davidson (Oak)
1963	976.5	Y. A. Tittle (NYG)
1963a	791.5	Len Dawson (KC)
1962	873.0	Y. A. Tittle (NYG)
1962a	771.5	Len Dawson (Dal)
1961	939.0	Billy Wade (ChiB)
1961a	982.7	George Blanda (Hou)
1960	719.5	Milt Plum (Cle)
1960a	403.0	Butch Songin (Bos)
1959	859.5	Johnny Unitas (Bal)
1958	731.5	Bobby Layne (Pit)
1957	536.5	Y. A. Tittle (SF)
1956	974.5	Tobin Rote (GB)
1955	439.5	Ed Brown (ChiB)
1954	816.5	Tobin Rote (GB)
1953	739.0	Otto Graham (Cle)
1952	616.5	Bobby Layne (Det)
1951	572.3	Johnny Lujack (ChiB)
1950	594.4	Johnny Lujack (ChiB)
1949	688.4	Johnny Lujack (ChiB)
1949a	1274.5	Otto Graham (Cle)
1948	704.5	Tommy Thompson (Phi)
1948a	1223.0	Y.A. Tittle (Bal)
1947	586.7	Sammy Baugh (Was)
1947a	1198.5	Otto Graham (Cle)
1946	189.0	Bob Waterfield (LaRm)
1946a	712.0	Otto Graham (Cle)
1945	508.2	Sammy Baugh (Was)
1944	400.5	Bob Davis (Bos)
1943	787.0	Sid Luckman (ChiB)
1942	235.5	Ray Hare (Was)
1941	453.5	Sid Luckman (ChiB)
1940	402.0	Whizzer White (Det)
1939	590.5	Tuffy Leemans (NYG)

Year	AY	Player
1938	500.0	Ace Parker (Bkn)
1937	540.5	Dutch Clark (Det)
1936	744.0	Dutch Clark (Det)
1935	475.5	Dutch Clark (Det)
1934	965.5	Dutch Clark (Det)
1933	585.5	Glenn Presnell (Por)
1932	613.0	Bob Campiglio (SI)
1931	95.0	Dutch Clark (Por)
1930	60.0	Red Dunn (GB)
1929	25.0	Red Dunn (GB)
1928	60.0	Joey Sternaman (ChiB)
1927	20.0	Red Dunn (GB)/Joey Sternaman (ChiB)
1926	40.0	Tut Imlay (LAA)
1926a	35.0	Joey Sternaman (ChiBu)
1925	15.0	Paul Hogan (Can)/Jimmy Robertson (Akr)
1924	50.0	Red Dunn (Mil)/Joey Sternaman (ChiB)
1923	50.0	Sonny Winters (Col)
1922	75.0	Jimmy Conzelman (RI)
1921	45.0	Benny Boynton (Roc)
1920	20.0	Paddy Driscoll (ChiC)

Running Backs

Year	AY	Player
2007	1890.0	LaDainian Tomlinson (SD)
2006	2304.0	LaDainian Tomlinson (SD)
2005	2185.0	Tiki Barber (NYG)
2004	1869.5	Curtis Martin (NYJ)
2003	2093.0	LaDainian Tomlinson (SD)
2002	2136.0	Priest Holmes (KC)
2001	1809.5	Marshall Faulk (StL)
2000	1994.0	Marshall Faulk (StL)
1999	1920.0	Marshall Faulk (StL)
1998	2256.5	Terrell Davis (Den)
1997	2210.5	Barry Sanders (Det)
1996	1633.0	Terrell Davis (Den)

1995	1930.5	Emmitt Smith (Dal)
1994	2099.5	Barry Sanders (Det)
1993	1628.0	Emmitt Smith (Dal)
1992	1905.5	Emmitt Smith (Dal)
1991	1666.5	Barry Sanders (Det)
1990	1529.0	Barry Sanders (Det)
1989	1422.0	Neal Anderson (ChiB)
1988	1792.5	Eric Dickerson (Ind)
1987	1227.2	Charles White (LaRm)
1986	1566.0	Eric Dickerson (LaRm)
1985	2049.5	Marcus Allen (LaRd)
1984	1776.5	Walter Payton (ChiB)
1983	1721.5	William Andrews (Atl)
1982	846.0	Marcus Allen (LaRd)
1981	1512.5	Wilbert Montgomery (Phi)
1980	1961.0	Earl Campbell (Hou)
1979	1668.5	Walter Payton (ChiB)
1978	1545.0	Walter Payton (ChiB)
1977	1698.9	Walter Payton (ChiB)
1976	1477.5	O.J. Simpson (Buf)
1975	1945.0	O.J. Simpson (Buf)
1974	1486.6	Otis Armstrong (Den)
1973	1876.5	O.J. Simpson (Buf)
1972	1402.5	Ron Johnson (NYG)
1971	1182.5	Larry Csonka (Mia)
1970	1199.5	Mac Arthur Lane (StL)
1969	1148.5	Tom Matte (Bal)
1969a	934.8	Dickie Post (SD)
1968	1351.2	Leroy Kelly (Cle)
1968a	1014.4	Paul Robinson (Cin)
1967	1213.6	Leroy Kelly (Cle)
1967a	1379.0	Hoyle Granger (Hou)
1966	1468.9	Gale Sayers (ChiB)
1966a	1339.5	Jim Nance (Bos)
1965	1682.5	Jim Brown (Cle)
1965a	1209.5	Paul Lowe (SD)
1964	1467.5	Jim Brown (Cle)

1964a	1164.5	Matt Snell (NYJ)
1963	1844.0	Jim Brown (Cle)
1963a	1181.5	Clem Daniels (Oak)
1962	1517.0	Jimmy Taylor (GB)
1962a	1344.7	Abner Haynes (Dal)
1961	1512.3	Jim Brown (Cle)
1961a	1130.6	Billy Cannon (Hou)
1960	1099.0	Jim Brown (Cle)
1960a	1087.6	Paul Lowe (LAC)
1959	1485.0	Jim Brown (Cle)
1958	1573.2	Jim Brown (Cle)
1957	809.5	Rick Casares (ChiB)
1956	1125.5	Rick Casares (ChiB)
1955	1003.5	Alan Ameche (Bal)
1954	1018.9	Joe Perry (SF)
1953	922.9	Joe Perry (SF)
1952	869.9	Dan Towler (LaRm)
1951	770.5	Eddie Price (NYG)
1950	720.5	Marion Motley (Cle)
1949	1190.2	Steve Van Buren (Phi)
1949a	951.0	Joe Perry (SF)
1948	867.9	Steve Van Buren (Phi)
1948a	1355.5	Chet Mutryn (Buf)
1947	1026.2	Steve Van Buren (Phi)
1947a	1814.5	Spec Sanders (NYT)
1946	507.8	Pat Harder (Chic)
1946a	824.0	Spec Sanders (NYY)
1945	817.9	Steve Van Buren (Phi)
1944	772.5	Bill Paschal (NYG)
1943	843.5	Harry Clark (ChiB)
1942	812.0	Bill Dudley (Pit)
1941	756.0	Cecil Isbell (GB)
1940	672.5	Dick Todd (Was)
1939	840.5	Andy Farkas (Was)
1938	531.5	Cecil Isbell (GB)
1937	935.5	Cliff Battles (Was)
1936	887.0	Ace Gutowsky (Det)

Year	AY	Player
1935	655.0	Ernie Caddel (Det)
1934	1131.5	Beattie Feathers (ChiB)
1933	787.0	Cliff Battles (Bos)
1932	626.5	Bronko Nagurski (ChiB)
1931	105.0	Ernie Nevers (ChiC)
1930	95.0	Verne Lewellen (GB)
1929	90.0	Verne Lewellen (GB)
1928	35.0	Paddy Driscoll (ChiB)/Bill Senn (ChiB)
1927	65.0	Paddy Driscoll (ChiB)/ Ernie Nevers (Dul)
1926	90.0	Ernie Nevers (Dul)
1926a	65.0	Eddie Tryon (NYY)
1925	50.0	Barney Wentz (Pot)
1924	30.0	Hank Gillo (Rac)/Ed Sternaman (ChiB)
1923	35.0	Curly Lambeau (GB)
1922	50.0	Hal Lauer (RI)/Ed Shaw (Can)
1921	50.0	Carl Cramer (Akr)
1920	35.0	Frank Bacon (Day)

Wide Receivers

Year	AY	Player
2007	861.5	Randy Moss (NE)
2006	715.0	Javon Walker (Den)
2005	816.6	Steve Smith (Car)
2005	816.6	Steve Smith (Car)
2004	754.5	Joe Horn (NO)
2003	879.3	Randy Moss (Min)
2002	926.0	Marvin Harrison (Ind)
2001	840.0	Marvin Harrison (Ind)
2000	910.0	Rod Smith (Den)
1999	815.5	Marvin Harrison (Ind)
1998	787.0	Antonio Freeman (GB)
1997	832.0	Rob Moore (Ari)
1996	754.0	Jerry Rice (SF)
1995	950.5	Jerry Rice (SF)
1994	887.5	Jerry Rice (SF)

Year	AY	Player
1993	785.5	Jerry Rice (SF)
1992	723.5	Sterling Sharpe (GB)
1991	720.0	Gary Clark (Was)
1990	776.0	Jerry Rice (SF)
1989	859.5	Jerry Rice (SF)
1988	707.0	Jerry Rice (SF)
1987	630.0	Jerry Rice (SF)
1986	870.0	Jerry Rice (SF)
1985	673.5	Steve Largent (Sea)
1984	788.5	Roy Green (StL)
1983	729.5	Mike Quick (Phi)
1982	593.0	Wes Chandler (SD)
1981	693.0	Steve Watson (Den)
1980	751.0	John Jefferson (SD)
1979	663.5	Steve Largent (Sea)
1978	624.0	Steve Largent (Sea)
1977	541.5	Nat Moore (Mia)
1976	627.5	Cliff Branch (Oak)
1975	531.5	Ken Burrough (Hou)
1974	571.0	Cliff Branch (Oak)
1973	541.5	John Gilliam (Min)
1972	540.0	Harold Jackson (Phi)
1971	625.0	Otis Taylor (KC)
1970	610.0	Gene Washington (SF)
1969	785.5	Joe Morrison (NYG)
1969a	604.0	Warren Wells (Oak)
1968	593.5	Paul Warfield (Cle)
1968a	724.0	Lance Alworth (SD)
1967	700.9	Homer Jones (NYG)
1967a	745.0	Don Maynard (NYJ)
1966	688.3	Charley Taylor (Was)
1966a	766.5	Lance Alworth (SD)
1965	692.0	Dave Parks (SF)
1965a	779.0	Lance Alworth (SD)
1964	610.0	Johnny Morris (ChiB)
1964a	1033.0	Abner Haynes (KC)
1963	635.5	Del Shofner (NYG)

1963a	732.0	Art Powell (Oak)
1962	630.5	Del Shofner (NYG)
1962a	565.0	Art Powell (NYT)
1961	583.5	Del Shofner (NYG)
1961a	933.0	Charley Hennigan (Hou)
1960	807.9	Lenny Moore (Bal)
1960a	723.0	Bill Groman (Hou)
1959	752.5	Lenny Moore (Bal)
1958	567.9	Del Shofner (LaRm)
1957	430.0	Raymond Berry (Bal)
1956	654.0	Billy Howton (GB)
1955	567.5	Dave Middleton (Det)
1954	622.0	Harlon Hill (ChiB)
1953	574.5	Pete Pihos (Phi)
1952	640.5	Billy Howton (GB)
1951	835.5	Elroy Hirsch (LaRm)
1950	559.5	Cloyce Box (Det)
1949	548.5	Tom Fears (LaRm)
1949a	549.0	Mac Speedie (Cle)
1948	601.5	Mal Kutner (ChiC)
1948a	498.0	Al Baldwin (Buf)
1947	474.0	Ken Kavanaugh (ChiB)
1947a	596.0	Mac Speedie (Cle)
1946	480.5	Jim Benton (LaRm)
1946a	475.5	Dante Lavelli (Cle)
1945	509.6	Don Hutson (GB)
1944	565.0	Don Hutson (GB)
1943	473.0	Don Hutson (GB)
1942	694.5	Don Hutson (GB)
1941	461.0	Don Hutson (GB)
1940	369.5	Don Looney (Phi)
1939	479.0	Don Hutson (GB)
1938	318.0	Don Hutson (GB)
1937	364.5	Gaynell Tinsley (ChiC)
1936	305.0	Don Hutson (GB)
1935	262.0	Don Hutson (GB)
1934	142.0	Harry Ebding (Det)

1933	201.5	Paul Moss (Pit)
1932	216.5	Ray Flaherty (NYG)

Tight Ends

Year	AY	Player
2007	611.0	Tony Gonzalez (KC)
2006	507.0	Antonio Gates (SD)
2005	600.5	Antonio Gates (SD)
2004	669.0	Tony Gonzalez (KC)
2003	508.0	Tony Gonzalez (KC)
2002	486.0	Todd Heap (Bal)
2001	517.5	Tony Gonzalez (KC)
2000	646.5	Tony Gonzalez (KC)
1999	431.0	Wesley Walls (Car)
1998	434.0	Shannon Sharpe (Den)
1997	528.5	Shannon Sharpe (Den)
1996	541.0	Shannon Sharpe (Den)
1995	374.5	Mark Chmura (GB)
1994	542.0	Ben Coates (NE)
1993	503.0	Shannon Sharpe (Den)
1992	345.0	Jay Novacek (Dal)
1991	339.0	Marv Cook (NE)
1990	325.0	Keith Jackson (Phi)
1989	413.0	Rodney Holman (Cin)
1988	387.5	Mickey Shuler (NYJ)
1987	394.9	Mark Bavaro (NYG)
1986	576.5	Todd Christensen (LaRd)
1985	523.5	Todd Christensen (LaRd)
1984	525.5	Ozzie Newsome (Cle)
1983	643.5	Todd Christensen (LaRd)
1982	350.5	Kellen Winslow (SD)
1981	551.0	Ozzie Newsome (Cle)
1980	610.0	Kellen Winslow (SD)
1979	441.5	Ozzie Newsome (Cle)
1978	436.0	Dave Casper (Oak)
1977	319.0	Walter White (KC)
1976	454.0	Walter White (KC)

1975	430.0	Rich Caster (NYJ)
1974	374.5	Riley Odoms (Den)
1973	491.0	Charle Young (Phi)
1972	351.5	Ted Kwalick (SF)
1971	341.7	Ted Kwalick (SF)
1970	406.5	Jackie Smith (StL)
1969	394.0	Jerry Smith (Was)
1969a	382.5	Bob Trumpy (Cin)
1968	597.5	Jackie Smith (StL)
1968a	394.0	Jim Whalen (Bos)
1967	578.5	Jackie Smith (StL)
1967a	391.0	Willie Frazier (SD)
1966	453.5	John Mackey (Bal)
1966a	377.5	Al Denson (Den)
1965	645.0	Pete Retzlaff (Phi)
1965a	300.5	Willie Frazier (Hou)
1964	393.5	Mike Ditka (ChiB)
1964a	383.0	Fred Arbanas (KC)
1963	437.0	Mike Ditka (ChiB)
1963a	290.0	Bob Mc Leod (Hou)
1962	317.0	Mike Ditka (ChiB)
1962a	364.0	Dave Kocourek (SD)
1961	518.0	Mike Ditka (ChiB)
1961a	260.5	Doug Asad (Oak)
1960	427.0	Willard Dewveall (ChiB)
1960a	212.0	Gene Prebola (Oak)

Kickers

Year	AY	Player
2007	580	Rob Bironas (Ten)
2006	520	Robbie Gould (ChiB)
2005	740	Neil Rackers (Ari)
2004	560	Adam Vinatieri (NE)
2003	740	Mike Vanderjagt (Ind)
2002	500	John Carney (No)
2001	470	Jason Elam (Den)
2000	580	Matt Stover (Bal)

1999	570	Olindo Mare (Mia)
1998	700	Gary Anderson (Min)
1997	640	Jeff Wilkins (StL)
1996	600	Cary Blanchard (Ind)
1995	510	Chris Boniol (Dal)
1994	560	John Carney (SD)
1993	500	Gary Anderson (Pit)
1992	430	Morten Andersen (NO)
1991	440	Pete Stoyanovich (Mia)
1990	590	Nick Lowery (KC)
1989	380	Rich Karlis (Min)
1988	490	Scott Norwood (Buf)
1987	390	Dean Biasucci (Ind)
1986	400	Morten Andersen (NO)
1985	500	Morten Andersen (NO)
1984	390	Paul Mc Fadden (Phi)
1983	490	Ali Haji-Sheikh (NYG)
1982	370	Mark Moseley (Was)
1981	380	Jan Stenerud (GB)
1980	280	John Smith (NE)/Fred Steinfort (Den)
1979	300	Toni Fritsch (Hou)
1978	260	Garo Yepremian (Mia)
1977	160	Rolf Benirschke (SD) /Don Cockroft (Cle)/Errol Mann (Oak)
1976	210	Efren Herrera (Dal)/Rich Szaro (NO)
1975	270	Tom Dempsey (LaRm)
1974	220	Don Cockroft (Cle)
1973	310	Bruce Gossett (SF)
1972	290	Don Cockroft (Cle)
1971	200	Garo Yepremian (Mia)
1970	240	Jan Stenerud (KC)
1969	190	Fred Cox (Min)
1969a	300	Jan Stenerud (KC)
1968	180	Don Cockroft (Cle)
1968a	320	Jim Turner (NYJ)
1967	180	Jim Bakken (StL)

1967a	100	George Blanda (Oak)
1966	150	Sam Baker (Phi)
1966a	220	Mike Mercer (KC)
1965	120	Jim Bakken (StL)
1965a	40	Gino Cappelletti (Bos)
1964	180	Bruce Gossett (LaRm)
1964a	80	Gino Cappelletti (Bos)
1963	60	Lou Groza (Cle)
1963a	10	George Blair (SD)
1962	120	Jerry Kramer (GB)
1962a	250	George Blair (SD)
1961	110	Lou Groza (Cle)
1961a	20	George Blanda (Hou)
1960	100	Bobby Walston (Phi)
1960a	60	Gene Mingo (Den)
1959	130	Pat Summerall (NYG)
1958	80	Gerry Perry (Det)
1957	90	Fred Cone (GB)
1956	150	Bobby Layne (Det)
1955	80	Fred Cone (GB)
1954	80	Lou Groza (Cle)
1953	370	Lou Groza (Cle)
1952	20	Fred Cone (GB)
1951	120	Ray Poole (NYG)
1950	80	Lou Groza (Cle)
1949a	-30	Bob Nelson (La)
1949	70	Vinnie Yablonski (ChiC)
1948a	10	Joe Vetrano (SF)
1948	40	Dick Poillon (Was)
1947	50	Pat Harder (ChiC)
1946	30	Jack Helms (Det)
1945	80	Ben Agajanian (Pit)
1944	20	Tommy Colella (Cle)
1943	20	Frank Kinard (Bkn)
1942	50	Frank Maznicki (ChiB)
1941	50	Andy Marefos (NYG)
1940	40	Phil Martinovich (ChiB)

1939	50	Chuck Hanneman (Det)
1938	50	Regis Monahan (Det)

Punters

Year	AY	Player
2007	646.5	Andy Lee (SF)
2006	561.5	Jason Baker (Car)
2005	508.0	Nick Harris (Det)
2004	549.0	Brad Maynard (ChiB)
2003	576.5	Shane Lechler (Oak)
2002	550.0	Todd Sauerbrun (Car)
2001	554.5	Todd Sauerbrun (Car)
2000	644.5	Chris Gardocki (Cle)
1999	497.5	Darren Bennett (SD)
1998	600.5	Brad Maynard (NYG)
1997	547.0	Leo Araguz (Oak)
1996	516.0	Darren Bennett (SD)
1995	440.0	Rick Tuten (Sea)
1994	462.5	Rich Camarillo (Hou)
1993	443.0	Mark Royals (Pit)
1992	555.0	Rick Tuten (Sea)
1991	418.0	Jeff Gossett (LaRd)
1990	357.0	Rohn Stark (Ind)
1989	364.0	Rich Camarillo (Phx)
1988	397.5	Jim Arnold (Det)
1987	262.5	Dale Hatcher (LaRm)
1986	446.0	Rohn Stark (Ind)
1985	425.5	Dale Hatcher (LaRm)
1984	511.5	Rohn Stark (Ind)
1983	479.5	Rohn Stark (Bal)
1982	245.5	Luke Prestridge (Den)
1981	382.5	Ray Guy (Oak)
1980	410.5	Dave Jennings (NYG)
1979	407.5	Dave Jennings (NYG)
1978	392.0	Pat Mc Inally (Cin)
1977	302.0	John James (Atl)
1976	379.0	John James (Atl)

1975	299.5	Ray Guy (Oak)
1974	312.0	Tom Blanchard (NO)
1973	388.5	Jerrel Wilson (KC)
1972	292.5	Jerrel Wilson (KC)
1971	345.0	Bobby Walden (Pit)
1970	384.0	Bobby Walden (Pit)
1969	279.5	Bobby Walden (Pit)
1969a	402.0	Dennis Partee (SD)
1968	289.5	Billy Lothridge (Atl)
1968a	425.0	Paul Maguire (Buf)
1967	321.0	Bobby Walden (Min)
1967a	486.5	Bob Scarpitto (Den)
1966	279.0	Bobby Joe Green (ChiB)
1966a	360.0	Bob Scarpitto (Den)
1965	361.5	Frank Lambert (Pit)
1965a	370.0	Curley Johnson (NYJ)
1964	490.5	Bobby Walden (Min)
1964a	366.0	Paul Maguire (Buf)
1963	421.5	Danny Villanueva (LaRm)
1963a	282.5	Jim Fraser (Den)
1962	355.0	Danny Villanueva
1962a	317.0	Paul Maguire (Buf)
1961	438.0	Bobby Joe Green (Pit)
1961a	371.5	Billy Atkins (Buf)
1960	283.5	Tommy Davis (SF)
1960a	176.5	Billy Atkins (Buf)
1959	320.0	Don Chandler (NYG)
1958	292.0	Don Chandler (NYG)
1957	286.5	Don Chandler (NYG)
1956	239.5	Dick Deschaine (GB)
1955	288.0	Norm Van Brocklin (LaRm)
1954	271.0	Pat Brady (Pit)
1953	476.0	Pat Brady (Pit)
1952	316.5	Pat Brady (Pit)
1951	303.0	Horace Gillom (Cle)
1950	237.5	Fred Morrison (ChiB)
1949	257.5	Mike Boyda (NYB)

1949a	205.0	Frankie Albert (SF)
1948	369.5	Joe Muha (Phi)
1948a	380.5	Glenn Dobbs (LAD)
1947	224.0	Joe Muha (Phi)
1947a	272.0	Mickey Colmer (Bkn)
1946	215.0	Roy McKay (GB)
1946a	448.0	Glenn Dobbs (Bkn)
1945	137.0	Sammy Baugh (Was)
1944	135.0	Frankie Sinkwich (Det)
1943	175.0	Sammy Baugh (Was)
1942	215.0	Sammy Baugh (Was)
1941	206.0	Sammy Baugh (Was)
1940	254.5	Sammy Baugh (Was)
1939	169.5	Parker Hall (Cle)

Return Specialists

Year	AY	Player
2007	885.6	Josh Cribbs (Cle)
2006	518.0	Chris Carr (Oak)
2005	519.0	B.J. Sams (Bal)
2004	628.0	Eddie Drummond (Det)
2003	773.6	Dante Hall (KC)
2002	838.7	Michael Lewis (NO)
2001	647.8	Jermaine Lewis (Bal)
2000	938.7	Derrick Mason (Ten)
1999	533.0	Tamarick Vanover (KC)
1998	676.5	Reggie Barlow (Jac)
1997	711.6	Eric Guliford (NO)
1996	854.5	Desmond Howard (GB)
1995	770.9	Tamarick Vanover (KC)
1994	706.7	Brian Mitchell (Was)
1993	686.0	Tyrone Hughes (NO)
1992	521.0	Vai Sikahema (Phi)
1991	491.5	Mel Gray (Det)
1990	482.4	Dave Meggett (NYG)
1989	477.0	Gerald Mc Neil (Cle)
1988	604.6	Tim Brown (LaRd)

Year	Avg	Player		Year	Avg	Player
1987	641.0	Vai Sikahema (StL)		1963a	442.0	Bobby Jancik (Hou)
1986	586.0	Vai Sikahema (StL)		1962	526.0	Abe Woodson (SF)
1985	539.0	Fulton Walker (LaRd)		1962a	370.0	Bobby Jancik (Hou)
1984	511.0	Dana McLemore (SF)		1961	365.0	Johnny Sample (Pit)
1983	437.5	Billy Johnson (Atl)		1961a	398.8	Dick Christy (NYT)
1982	317.0	Leon Bright (NYG)		1960	296.7	Abe Woodson (SF)
1981	791.0	Mike Nelms (Was)		1960a	246.8	Ken Hall (Hou)
1980	580.6	J. T. Smith (KC)		1959	279.0	Johnny Morris (ChiB)
1979	551.2	J. T. Smith (KC)		1958	259.1	Bobby Mitchell (Cle)
1978	510.9	Rick Upchurch (Den)		1957	280.7	Woodley Lewis (ChiC)
1977	641.7	Billy Johnson (Hou)		1956	367.3	Joe Arenas (SF)
1976	634.0	Eddie Brown (Was)		1955	388.6	Joe Scudero (Was)
1975	662.4	Billy Johnson (Hou)		1954	346.5	Veryl Switzer (GB)
1974	588.2	Billy Johnson (Hou)		1953	389.3	Woodley Lewis (LaRm)
1973	426.7	Mack Herron (NE)		1952	441.2	Ray Mathews (Pit)
1972	377.0	Ron Smith (ChiB)		1951	556.0	Emlen Tunnell (NYG)
1971	293.0	Dave Hampton (GB)		1950	542.2	Billy Joe Grimes (GB)
1970	508.0	Alvin Haymond (LaRm)		1949	355.5	Vitamin Smith (LaRm)
1969	370.0	Alvin Haymond (LaRm)		1949a	378.0	Jim Cason (SF)
1969a	346.6	Jerry LeVias (Hou)		1948	433.3	Jerry Davis (ChiC)
1968	605.3	Chuck Latourette (StL)		1948a	388.0	Herman Wedemeyer (LAD)
1968a	392.0	George Atkinson (Oak)		1947	468.2	Eddie Saenz (Was)
1967	406.6	Travis Williams (GB)		1947a	468.0	Chet Mutryn (Buf)
1967a	595.0	Rodger Bird (Oak)		1946	346.6	Bill Dudley (Pit)
1966	311.6	Gale Sayers (ChiB)		1946a	448.0	Chuck Fenenbock (LAD)
1966a	333.0	Rodger Bird (Oak)		1945	311.1	Steve Bagarus (Was)
1965	577.0	Alvin Haymond (Bal)		1944	356.0	Steve Van Buren (Phi)
1965a	496.0	Speedy Duncan (SD)		1943	267.0	Andy Farkas (Was)
1964	485.0	Mel Renfro (Dal)		1942	359.0	Bill Dudley (Pit)
1964a	339.0	Claude Gibson (Oak)		1941	327.0	Whizzer White (Det)
1963	400.0	Abe Woodson (SF)				

Reference Sources

A BOOK LIKE THIS can't spring from one person's head. In writing it, I relied on a wide array of source materials to inform my research. I've always felt that a robust bibliography was crucial to a work of nonfiction, not only to identify and provide credit to the sources that informed the author's research but also to provide the reader with a roadmap for his or her own further exploration. If my chapter on players from the two-way era piqued your interest, for example, my bibliography would point you toward the books that I thought were most relevant and helpful on that particular subject.

A traditional bibliography seems insufficient to document the sources that I consulted in writing this book, so I'd like to preface the traditional bibliography with some comments on nontraditional sources.

One of the great things about doing football research is the long tradition of coaches using game film to study the play of their own teams as well as their opponents. That practice has left us with a rich archive of game footage, and I was able to tap into a number of private collections to watch games from as far back as 1951. The folks at NFL Films have also provided a treasure trove with their exhaustive footage dating back to 1962.

During my college days I spent hours and hours poring through newspaper microfilm in my job as a research assistant. That process has been made much easier with the advent of the Internet. Not only can I look up box scores from home in my pajamas, but I can also conduct complex searches that aren't possible when manually churning through traditional paper pages.

I made liberal use of the ProQuest historical newspaper database to access thousands of articles from the *New York Times*, *Washington Post*, *Los Angeles Times*, *Boston Globe*, *Chicago Tribune*, *Atlanta Journal-Constitution*, and other papers. I took advantage of the online archives for newspapers in every current and former NFL and AFL city. To a lesser extent, I used the online archives of *Sporting News* and *Time* magazines.

The Professional Football Researchers Association has published a number of books that document otherwise overlooked areas of football history. I also read dozens and dozens of issues of The Coffin Corner, the PFRA's official newsletter-magazine.

Hub Arkush, publisher of *Pro Football Weekly*, granted access to content from his archives.

In my efforts to collect play-by-play accounts for NFL games, a handful of teams provided access to their historical archives. I consulted hundreds of team media guides from my personal collection.

For the sake of simplicity, I chose to omit annuals from the bibliography, but I relied on three of them heavily.

- The NFL has published an official record book each year since 1941. The name has changed over the years, and the quality and quantity of content wasn't so great in the early years, but it is an indispensable resource.
- The *Sporting News* Football Register from 1973 to 2006, and the Football Guide from 1965 to 2006.
- Joel Buschbaum's *Draft Preview*, published from 1978 to 2002.

I have what I believe might be the largest private collection of sports encyclopedias in North America. It includes nearly one hundred different football encyclopedias, some of which are groundbreaking and some of which are forgettable. Some are collections of photographs, some are full of colorful stories, and some are nothing but pages and pages of statistics. When it comes to authoritative sources, there have been five major pro football encyclopedias, four of which have published multiple editions. Rather than list each individual edition separately, I'll acknowledge them here as a series.

- *The Official Encyclopedia of Football*. Sixteen editions published between 1952 and 1979. Originally edited by Roger Treat.
- *The Sports Encyclopedia: Pro Football*. Seventeen editions published between 1974 and 1998. Originally edited by David Neft, Roland Johnson, Richard Cohen, and Jordan Deutsch. This series had a handful of spin-offs that appeared under different titles, including *The Complete All-Time Pro Football Register* (1976), *Pro Football: The Early Years* (1978), and *The Football Encyclopedia* (1994).
- *The Pro Football Encyclopedia*. One edition was published, and it was edited by Tod Maher and Bob Gill.
- *Total Football*. Two editions published in 1997 and 1999. It was edited by Bob Carroll, Michael Gershman, David Neft, and John Thorn.
- *The ESPN Pro Football Encyclopedia*. Two editions published in 2006 and 2007. Edited by Pete Palmer, Ken Pullis, Sean Lahman, Matthew Silverman, and Gary Gillette.

Other encyclopedias that I used as sources for this book appear in the bibliography that follows.

Bibliography

Game Plans for Success: Winning Strategies for Business and Life from Ten Top NFL Head Coaches. Little Brown and Company, 1995.

The First Fifty Years. National Football League, 1974.

The Gladiators. Prentice-Hall, 1973.

The NFL Century: The Complete Story of the National Football League, 1920-2000. Smithmark Publishers, 1999.

Adler, Brad. 2003. *Coaching Matters: Leadership and Tactics of the NFL's Ten Greatest Coaches*. Potomac Books.

Allen, George. 1982. *Football's Greatest Players*. Bobbs–Merrill Company.

———. 1982. *Merry Christmas —You're Fired!* Simon and Schuster.

———. 1990. *Strategies for Winning*. McGraw Hill.

Allen, Maury. 1969. *Greatest Pro Quarterbacks*. Scholastic.

Alzado, Lyle, with Zimmerman, Paul. 1978. *Mile High*. Atheneum.

Anderson, Dave. 1965. *Great Quarterbacks of the NFL*. Random House.

———. 1967. *Great Defensive Players of the NFL*. Random House.

———. 1969. *Countdown to Super Bowl*. New American Library.

Ashe, Arthur. 1993. *A Hard Road To Glory: A History Of The African American Athlete: Football (Hard Road to Glory)*. Amistad.

Asinof, Elliot. 1968. *Seven Days to Sunday*. Simon and Schuster.

Bayless, Skip. 1990. *God's Coach: The Hymns, Hype, and Hypocrisy of Tom Landry's Cowboys.* Simon and Schuster.

———. 1994. *The Boys: Jones vs. Johnson.* Pocket Books.

Beer, Tom. 1974. *Sunday's Fools.* Houghton Mifflin.

Benedict, Jeff, and Yaeger, Don. 1998. *Pros and Cons: The Criminals Who Play in the NFL.* Warner Books.

Bengston, Phil. 1969. *Packer Dynasty.* Doubleday.

Bennett, Tom. 1976. *Pro Style.* Prentice-Hall.

Bissinger, H. G. 1990. *Friday Night Lights: A Town, a Team, and a Dream.* Addison.

Blinn, William. 1972. *Brian's Song.* Bantam Books.

Blount Jr, Roy. 1980. *About Three Bricks Shy of a Load.* Random House.

Bosworth, Brian, and Reilly, Rick. 1988. *The Boz: Confessions of a Modern Anti Hero.* Doubleday.

Bowden, Mark. 1994. *Bringing the Heat.* Knopf.

Boyd, Denny, and Scrivener, Brian. 1997. *Legends of Autumn: The Glory Years of Canadian Football.* Greystone Books.

Bradshaw, Terry. 2001. *It's Only a Game.* Atria.

Bradshaw, Terry, and Diles, David. 1979. *Terry Bradshaw: Man of Steel.* Zondervan.

Bradshaw, Terry, with Fisher, Davis. 2003. *Keep it Simple.* Pocket Books.

Brenner, Richard. 1989. *The Complete Super Bowl Story.* Lerner.

Brodie, John, and Houston, James. 1974. *Open Field.* Houghton Mifflin.

Brown, Chad. 2000. *Inside the Meat Grinder.* St. Martin's Press.

Brown, Jim. 1989. *Out of Bounds.* Kensington Publishing.

Brown, Paul. 1981. *PB: The Paul Brown Story.* New American Library.

Burt, Jim. 1987. *Hard Nose.* Harcourt.

Butkus, Dick, and Billings, Robert. 1972. *Stop Action.* E. P. Dutton.

Byrd, Dennis. 1993. *Rise and Walk.* Harper Collins.

Byrne, Jim. 1987. *The One-Dollar League.* Prentice-Hall.

Cafardo, Nick. 2002. *The Impossible Team: The Worst to First Patriot's Super Bowl Season.* Triumph Books.

Cameron, Steve. 1997. *Brett Favre.* Masters Press.

Carroll, Bob. 1989. *100 Greatest Runningbacks.* Crescent.

———. 1990. *Bulldogs on Sunday: 1919.* Professional Football Researchers Association.

———. 1990. *Bulldogs on Sunday: 1920.* Professional Football Researchers Association.

———. 1993. *When the Grass Was Real.* Simon and Schuster.

Carroll, Bob; Gershman, Michael; Neft, David; and Thorn, John. 1998. *Total Super Bowl.* Harper Perennial.

Carroll, Bob; Palmer, Pete; and Thorn, John. 1988. *The Hidden Game of Football.* Warner Books.

———. 1998. *The Hidden Game of Football: The Next Edition.* Total Sports Publishing.

Carroll, John. 2004. *Red Grange and the Rise of Football.* University of Illinois Press.

Carson, Harry, and Smith, James. 1987. *Point of Attack: The Defense Strikes Back.* McGraw Hill.

Carucci, Vic. 1991. *The Buffalo Bills and the Almost Dream Season.* Simon and Schuster.

Chass, Murray. 1973. *Power Football.* E.P. Dutton.

Chastain, Bill. 2005. *Steel Dynasty: The Team That Changed the NFL.* Triumph Books.

Chrebet, Wayne. 1999. *Every Down, Every Distance.* Doubleday.

Claassen, Harold. 1963. *The History Of Professional Football.* Prentice-Hall.

Claerbaut, Davis. 2004. *Bart Starr: When Leadership Mattered*. Taylor Trade Publishing.

Clary, Jack. 1976. *Thirty Years of Pro Football's Great Moments*. Rutledge Books.

Coenen, Craig. 2005. *From Sandlots to the Super Bowl: The National Football League, 1920–1967*. University of Tennessee Press.

Cohen, Richard M., and Deutsch, Jordan A. 1979. *The Scrapbook History of Pro Football, 1893-1979*. Bobbs–Merrill Company.

Connor, Dick. 1974. *Denver Broncos*. Prentice-Hall.

Courson, Steve. 1991. *False Glory*. Borders Press.

Crawford, Bill. 2004. *All-American: The Rise and Fall of Jim Thorpe*. Wiley and Sons.

Cunningham, Randall. 1993. *I'm Still Scrambling*. Doubleday.

Curtis, Mike, with Gilbert, Bill. 1972. *Keep Off My Turf*. Lippincott.

Daley, Arthur. 1968. *Pro Football's Hall of Fame*. Grosset and Dunlap.

Daly, Dan, and O'Donnell, Bob 1990. *The Pro Football Chronicle: The Complete (Well, Almost) Record of the Best Players, the Greatest Photos, the Hardest Hits*. MacMillan.

Danzig, Allison. 1971. *Oh, How They Played the Game*. MacMillan.

Daugherty, Paul. 1999. *Fair Game*. Orange Frazer Press.

Davis, Jeff. 2004. *Papa Bear: The Life and Legacy of George Halas*. McGraw Hill.

Davis, Mac. 1974. *100 Greatest Football Heroes*. Putnam.

DeLuca, Sam. 1972. *The Football Playbook*. Jonathan David Publishers.

———. 1978. *The Football Handbook*. Jonathan David Publishers.

Dent, Jim. 2004. *Monster of the Midway: Bronko Nagurski, the 1943 Chicago Bears, and the Greatest Comeback Ever*. St. Martin's Press.

Devaney, John. 1966. *The Pro Quarterbacks*. Putnam.

———. 1988. *Bo Jackson*. Walker and Company.

Dickey, Glenn. 1991. *Just Win Baby*. Harcourt.

Dienhart, Tom. 1995. *The Sporting News Complete Super Bowl Book*. Sporting News Publishing.

Ditka, Mike. 1987. *Ditka*. Bonus Books.

Dobler, Conrad. 1989. *They Call Me Dirty*. Jove.

Donovan, Art, and Drury, Bob. 1987. *Fatso: Football When Men Were Really Men*. William Morrow.

Dowling, Tom. 1970. *Coach: A Season with Lombardi*. W. W. Norton.

Dunnavant, Keith. 2004. *The Fifty-Year Seduction: How Television Manipulated College Football, from the Birth of the Modern NCAA to the Creation of the BCS*. Thomas Dunne Books.

Epstein, Eddie. 2003. *Dominance: The Best Seasons of Pro Football's Greatest Teams*. Potomac Books.

Eskenazi, Gerald. 1987. *They Were Giants in Those Days*. Simon and Schuster.

———. 1998. *Gang Green*. Simon and Schuster.

Falgoux, Woody. 2001. *One Dream: The NFL*. Gale Group.

Flutie, Doug. 1999. *Flutie*. Sports Masters.

Flynn, George. 1976. *Vince Lombardi Scrapbook*. Grosset and Dunlap.

———. 1988. *Great Moments in Football*. Gallery Books.

Fox, Larry. 1975. *Mean Joe Greene and the Steeler Front Four*. Dodd Mead.

Freeman, Denne, and Aron, Jaime. 2001. *I Remember Tom Landry*. Sports Publishing.

Freeman, Mike. 2004. *Bloody Sundays: Inside the Rough-and-Tumble World of the NFL*. Harper Collins.

Fuoss, Donald. 1959. *The Complete Kicking Game*. Prentice-Hall.

Gabriel, Roman, with Oates, Bob. 1970. *Player of the Year*. World Publishing.

Gay, Timothy. 2005. *The Physics of Football*. Harper Collins.

Gelman, Steve. 1968. *Pro Football Heroes*. Scholastic.

Gildea, William. 1972. *The Future is Now: George Allen, Football's Most Controversial Coach*. Houghton Mifflin.

Gill, Bob, and Maher, Tod. 1989. *The Outsiders: The Three American Football Leagues of 1936–1941*. Professional Football Researchers Association.

Gilma, Kay Iselin. 1975. *Inside the Pressure Cooker*. Berkley Publishing.

Grange, Red, with Martin, Ira. 1953. *The Red Grange Story*. Putnam.

Green, Jerry. 1973. *Detroit Lions*. MacMillan.

Green, Tim. 1996. *The Dark Side of the Game*. Warner Books.

Grier, Rosey. 1986. *Rosey: The Gentle Giant*. Harrison House.

Griese, Bob, and Griese, Brian. 2000. *Undefeated*. Nelson Books.

Griffith, Corinne. 1947. *My Life With the Redskins*. A. S. Barnes.

Gruden, Jon, with Carucci, Vic. 2003. *Do You Love Football: Winning with Heart, Passion, & Not Much Sleep*. Harper Collins.

Gruver, Ed. 2005. *Ice Bowl: The Cold Truth about Football's Most Unforgettable Game*. McBooks Press.

Gutman, Bill. 2000. *Parcells: A Biography*. Carroll and Graf.

Haden, Pat, and Kaiser, Robert. 1977. *My Rookie Season with the LA Rams*. William Morrow.

Hahn, James, and Hahn, Lynn. 1981. *Sayers*. Crestwood House.

Halas, George, with Morgan, Gwen, and Veysey, Arthur. 1979. *Halas By Halas*. McGraw Hill.

Halberstam, David. 2005. *The Education of a Coach*. Hyperion.

Harris, David. 1986. *The League: The Rise and Decline of the NFL*. Bantam Books.

Heisman, John. 2000. *Principles of Football*. Hill Street Press.

Henderson, Thomas. 1987. *Out of Control: Confessions of an NFL Casualty*. Pocket Books.

———. 2004. *In Control*. Sports Publishing.

Hersch, Hank. 1998. *Greatest Football Games of All Time*. Time-Life Books.

Herskowitz, Mickey. 1990. *The Quarterbacks*. Harper Collins.

Hession, Joseph, and Cassady, Steve. 1987. *Raiders: From Oakland to LA*. Foghorn Press.

Hickok, Ralph. 1995. *A Who's Who of Sports Champions: Their Stories and Records*. Houghton Mifflin.

Higdon, Hal. 1968. *Pro Football USA*. Putnam.

Hogrogian, John. 1995. *All-Pros: The First 40 Years*. Professional Football Researchers Association.

Hollander, Zander. 1983. *Great Quarterbacks of the NFL*. Random House.

Holley, Michael. 2005. *Patriot Reign: Bill Belichick, the Coaches, and the Players Who Built a Champion*. Harper Collins.

Holovak, Mike. 1967. *Violence Every Sunday*. Coward–McCann.

Hornung, Paul. 2004. *Golden Boy*. Simon and Schuster.

Hornung, Paul, and Reed, Billy. 2006. *Lombardi and Me*. Triumph Books.

Hornung, Paul, and Silverman, Al. 1965. *Football and the Single Man*. Doubleday.

Huff, Sam. 1989. *Tough Stuff*. St. Martin's Press.

Huizenga, Rob. 1995. *You're OK, It's Just A Bruise: A Doctor's Sideline Secrets About Pro Football's Most Outrageous Team*. St. Martin's Press.

Izenberg, Jerry. 1990. *No Medals for Trying*. Mac-Millan.

Jackson, Tom. 1987. *Blitz*. Contemporary Books.

James, Bill. 2001. *The New Bill James Historical Baseball Abstract*. Free Press.

Jarrett, William. 1992. *Timetables of Sports History: Football*. Facts on File.

Jenkins, Sally. 1996. *Men Will Be Boys*. Doubleday.

Johnson, Jimmy. 1993. *Turning the Thing Around*. Hyperion.

Karras, Alex, with Gluck, Herb. 1977. *Even Big Guys Cry*. Holt, Rinehart, and Winston.

Keim, John. 1999. *Legends by the Lake: The Cleveland Browns at Municipal Stadium*. University of Akron Press.

Kelly, Jim, and Carrucci, Vic. 1992. *Armed and Dangerous*. Doubleday.

Ketayien, Armen. 1992. *Ditka: Monster of the Midway*. Simon and Schuster.

King, Joe. 1958. *Inside Pro Football*. Prentice-Hall.

King, Peter. 1993. *Inside the Helmet*. Simon and Schuster.

———. 1997. *Football: A History of the Professional Game*. Time-Life Books.

Klawitter, John. 1996. *Headslap: The Life and Times of Deacon Jones*. Prometheus Books.

Klein, Dave. 1976. *The Game of Their Lives*. Signet.

Klobuchar, Jim, and Tarkenton, Fran. 1976. *Tarkenton*. Harper and Row.

Knox, Chuck. 1988. *Hard Knox*. Harcourt.

Kopay, David, and Young, Perry Deane. 1977. *The David Kopay Story*. Arbor House.

Koppett, Leonard. 1974. *The New York Times at the Super Bowl*. Quadrangle.

Korch, Rick. 1993. *The Truly Great: The 200 Best Pro Football Players of All Time*. Taylor Publishing.

Kramer, Jerry. 1969. *Farewell to Football*. World Publishing.

———. 1985. *Distant Replay*. Putnam.

Kramer, Jerry, with Schaap, Dick. 1968. *Instant Replay*. World Publishing.

Kriegel, Mark. 2004. *Namath: A Biography*. Viking.

Lahman, Sean, and Greanier, Todd. 2002. *Pro Football Prospectus: 2002*. Potomac Books.

———. 2003. *Pro Football Prospectus: 2003*. Potomac Books.

———. 2004. *Pro Football Forecast 2004*. Potomac Books.

Lamb, Kevin. 1987. *Quarterbacks, Nickelbacks and Other Loose Change: A Fan's Guide to the Changing Game of Pro Football*. Book Sales.

LaMonte, Bob, with Shook, Robert L. 2005. *Winning the NFL Way: Leadership Lessons from Football's Top Head Coaches*. Harper Collins.

Landry, Tom. 1990. *Landry*. Zondervan.

Landry, Tom, with Lewis, Gregg. 1990. *Tom Landry*. Zondervan.

Latimer, Clay. 2002. *John Elway: Armed and Dangerous*. Addax.

Lazenby, Roland. 1988. *100 Greatest Quarterbacks*. Crescent.

Lea, Bud. 2002. *Magnificent Seven: The Championship Games that Built the Lombardi Dynasty*. Triumph Books.

Leuthner, Stuart. 1988. *Iron Men*. Doubleday.

Levy, Marv. 2004. *Where Else Would You Rather Be?* Sports Publishing.

Libby, Bill. 1970. *Life in the Pit: The Deacon Jones Story*. Doubleday.

Lomax, Neil. 1986. *Third and Long*. Fleming H. Revell Company.

Lombardi, Vince. 1968. *Run to Daylight*. Tempo Books.

Lombardi, Vince, and George, Ed. 1973. *Vince Lombardi on Football (Vols. I & II)*. NY Graphic Society.

Lott, Ronnie. 1991. *Total Impact*. Doubleday.

Lowry, Phillip. 1990. *Green Gridirons*. Professional Football Researchers Association.

Lyons, Bill, and Zordich, Cynthia. 1999. *When the Clock Runs Out: 20 NFL Greats Share Their Stories of Hardship and Triumph*. Triumph Books.

MacCambridge, Michael. 2004. *America's Game: The Epic Story of How Pro Football Captured a Nation*. Random House.

Mackey, John. 2003. *Blazing Trails*. Triumph Books.

Madden, John. 1984. *Hey, Wait a Minute (I Wrote a Book!)*. Villard.

———. 1986. *One Knee Equals Two Feet*. Villard.

———. 1996. *All Madden: Hey, I'm Talking Pro Football!* Harper Collins.

Maher, Tod. 1986. *The All-Time United States Football League Register*. Professional Football Researchers Association.

———. 1990. *Wiffle: The World Football League Chronicle*. Professional Football Researchers Association.

Maiorana, Sal. 1994. *Relentless*. Quality Sports Publications.

———. 2003. *If You Can't Join 'Em, Beat 'Em*. Authorhouse.

Mandelbaum, Michael. 2005. *The Meaning of Sports: Why Americans Watch Baseball, Football, and Basketball and What They See When They Do*. Public Affairs.

Mandell, Arnold. 1976. *The Nightmare Season*. Random House.

Manning, Archie, and Manning, Peyton. 2001. *Manning*. Harper Entertainment.

Maraniss, David. 1999. *When Pride Still Mattered: A Life of Vince Lombardi*. Simon and Schuster.

March, Harry A., Dr. 1934. *Pro Football: Its Ups and Downs A Light-hearted History of the Post Graduate Game*. J. B. Lyon Company.

Markbreit, Jerry. 1972. *The Armchair Referee*. Doubleday.

———. 1988. *Born to Referee*. William Morrow.

———. 2001. *Last Call*. Sport Masters.

Maule, Tex. 1963. *The Game: Football*. Random House.

McClellan, Keith. 1998. *The Sunday Game: At the Dawn of Professional Football (Ohio History and Culture)*. University of Akron Press.

McCullough, Bob. 2002. *My Greatest Day in Football*. St. Martin's Press.

McDonnel, Chris. 2004. *The Football Game I'll Never Forget*. Firefly Books.

McGuff, Joe. 1970. *Winning It All: The Chiefs of the AFL*. Doubleday.

McMahon, Jim. 1987. *McMahon*. Warner Books.

Meggyesey, Dave. 2005. *Out of Their League*. University of Nebraska Press.

Mendell, Ronald L. 1974. *Who's Who in Football*. Arlington House.

Merchant, Larry. 1970. *And Every Day You Take a Bite*. Dell Publishing.

Meserole, Mike. 1999. *20th Century Sports: Images of Greatness*. Total Sports Publishing.

Michael, Paul. 1972. *Professional Football's Greatest Games*. Prentice-Hall.

Miller, Jeff. 2004. *Going Long: The Wild Ten Year Saga of the Renegade American Football League in the Words of Those Who Lived It*. McGraw Hill.

Montana, Joe. 1986. *Audibles*. William Morrow.

Morgan, John. 1997. *Glory for Sale: Inside the Browns' Move to Baltimore & the New NFL*. Bancroft Press.

Morris, Jeannie. 1971. *Brian Piccolo: A Short Season*. Rand McNally.

Morris, Willie. 1992. *The Courting of Marcus DuPree*. University Press of Mississippi.

Mullin, John. 2005. *The Rise and Self-Destruction of the Greatest Football Team in History: The Chicago Bears and Super Bowl XX*. Triumph Books.

Nash, Bruce, and Zullo, Allan. 1990. *Football Hall of Shame*. Pocket Books.

———. 1991. *Football Hall of Shame 2*. Simon and Schuster.

New York Daily News. 1999. *New York Giants: 75 Years of Memories*. Sports Publishing.

Nitschke, Ray. 1998. *Mean on Sunday*. Prairie Oak Press.

O'Brien, Michael. 1987. *Vince*. William Morrow.

Olderman, Murray. 1967. *The Pro Quarterback*. Prentice-Hall.

———. 1980. *The Defenders*. Book Sales.

Paolantonio, Sal, and Frank, Reuben. 2007. *The Paolantonio Report: The Most Overrated and Underrated Players, Teams, Coaches, and Moments in NFL History*. Triumph Books.

Parcells, Bill, with Lupica, Mike. 1987. *Parcells*. Bonus Books.

Parcells, Bill, with McDonough, Will. 2000. *The Final Season*. Harper Collins.

Patton, Phil. 1984. *Razzle Dazzle: The Curious Marriage of Television and Professional Football*. Dial Press.

Paul, William Henry. 1974. *The Gray-Flannel Pigskin*. Lippincott.

Payton, Walter, with Yaeger, Don. 2001. *Never Die Easy*. Random House.

Peterson, Robert W. 1996. *Pigskin: The Early Years of Pro Football*. Oxford University Press.

Phillips, Donald. 2001. *Run to Win: Vince Lombardi on Coaching and Leadership*. St. Martin's Press.

Piascik, Andy. 2007. *The Best Show in Football*. Taylor Trade Publishing.

Plimpton, George. 1965. *Paper Lion*. Harper and Row.

———. 1967. *The Paper Lion*. Pocket Books.

———. 1973. *Mad Ducks & Bears*. Random House.

———. 1977. *One More July*. Harper Collins.

———. 2005. *On Sports*. Lyons Press.

Pluto, Terry. 2003. *Browns Town 1964*. Gray and Company.

Powel, Hartford. 1976. *Walter Camp*. Books for Libraries Press.

Quirk, James, and Fort, Rodney. 1997. *Pay Dirt: The Business of Professional Team Sports*. Princeton University Press.

Ralbovsky, Marty. 1976. *The Namath Effect*. Prentice-Hall.

Rand, Jonathan. 2003. *Riddell Presents: The Gridiron's Greatest Linebackers*. Sports Publishing.

———. 2004. *Riddell Presents the Gridiron's Greatest Quarterbacks*. Sports Publishing.

Rathet, Mike, and Smith, Don R. 1984. *Their Deeds and Dogged Faith*. Rutledge Books.

Ratterman, George. 1962. *Confessions of a Gypsy Quarterback*. Coward–McCann.

Reeths, Paul. 1999. *The United States Football League Chronicle*. Professional Football Researchers Association.

Reeves, Dan, and Connor, Dick. 1988. *Reeves*. Bonus Books.

Richardson, Steve. 1999. *Ricky Williams: Dreadlocks to Ditka*. Sports Publishing.

Richler, Ed. 1966. *Making of a Pro Quarterback.* Grosset and Dunlap.

Riffenburgh, Beau. 1984. *Running Wild: A Pictorial Tribute to the NFL's Greatest Runners.* NFL Properties.

———. 1986. *The NFL Encyclopedia.* E. P. Dutton.

———. 1989. *The Great Ones: NFL Quarterbacks from Baugh to Montana.* Viking.

Roberts, Howard. 1947. *Chicago Bears.* Putnam.

———. 1953. *The Story of Pro Football.* Rand McNally.

Robowsky, Mark. 1991. *Slick.* MacMillan.

Rosenthal, Harold. 1970. *American Football League Official History, 1960–1969.* Sporting News Publishing.

———. 1981. *Fifty Faces of Football.* Simon and Schuster.

Rosentraub, Mark S. 1999. *Major League Losers: The Real Cost of Sports and Who's Paying For It.* Basic Books

Ross, Charles K. 2001. *Outside the Lines: African Americans and the Integration of the National Football League.* NYU Press.

Ryczek, Bill. 2000. *Crash of the Titans.* Total Sports Publishing.

Sablijzk, Mark, and Greenberg, Martin. 1986. *Who's Who in the Super Bowls.* Dembner Books.

Sahadi, Lou. 1969. *The Long Pass.* World Publishing.

———. 2004. *Johnny Unitas: America's Quarterback.* Triumph Books.

Sanders, Barry, with McCormick, Mark E. 2003. *Now You See Him . . . The Barry Sanders Story.* Emmis.

Sayers, Gale, with Silverman, Al. 1970. *I Am Third.* Viking.

Schaaf, Phil. 2003. *Sports, Inc: 100 Years of Sports Business.* Prometheus Books.

Schoor, Gene. 1958. *Red Grange.* J. Messner.

———. 1977. *Bart Starr.* Doubleday.

Schwarz, Alan. 2004. *The Numbers Game.* Thomas Dunne Books.

Shapiro, Milton. 1971. *The Pro Quarterbacks.* J. Messner.

Shropshire, Mike. 2004. *When the Tuna Went Down to Texas.* William Morrow.

Shula, Don, and Blanchard, Ken. 1995. *Everyone's a Coach.* Harper Business.

Shula, Don, with Sahadi, Lou. 1973. *The Winning Edge.* E. P. Dutton.

Simms, Phil, and McConkey, Phil. 1987. *Simms to McConkey.* Crown.

Simms, Phil, and Carucci, Vic. 2004. *Sunday Morning Quarterback.* Harper Collins.

Singletary, Mike. 1991. *Singletary on Singletary.* Thomas Nelson. Inc.

Smerlas, Fred. 1990. *By a Nose.* Simon and Schuster.

Smith, Don. 1989. *NFL Official Encyclopedia of Football.* Smithmark Publishers.

Smith, Robert. 1963. *Pro Football: The History of the Game and the Great Players.* Doubleday.

———. 1972. *Illustrated History of Professional Football.* Madison Square Press.

Smith, Ron. 1960. *The New York Giants.*

———. 1999. *The Sporting News Selects Football's 100 Greatest Players: A Celebration of the 20th Century's Best.* Sporting News Publishing.

———. 2003. *Heroes of the Hall: Pro Football's Greatest Players.* Sporting News Publishing.

Solomon, George. 1973. *The Team Nobody Wanted.* Henry Regnery Company.

Sporting News. 2002. *Pro Football's Greatest Teams.* Sporting News Publishing.

———. 2005. *Pro Football's Greatest Quarterbacks.* Sporting News Publishing.

———. 2005. *The Complete Pro Football Draft Encyclopedia*. Sporting News Publishing.

St. John, Bob. 1991. *Heart of a Lion*. Taylor Publishing.

———. 2001. *Landry: The Legend and the Legacy*. Thomas Nelson, Inc.

Strock, Don, and Frommer, Harvey. 1991. *Behind the Lines*. Pharos Books.

Sullivan, George. 1968. *Pro Football's All-Time Greats*. Putnam.

———. 2001. *Power Football: The Greatest Running Backs*. Atheneum.

Switzer, Barry. 1990. *Bootlegger's Boy*. William Morrow.

Tarkenton, Fran. 1971. *Broken Patterns: The Education of a Quarterback*. Simon and Schuster.

Tatum, Jack, and Kushner, Bill. 1979. *They Call Me Assassin*. Everest.

Taylor, Lawrence, with Serby, Steve. 2004. *LT: Over the Edge: Tackling Quarterbacks, Drugs, and a World Beyond Football*. Harper Collins.

Telander, Rick. 1976. *Joe Namath and the Other Guys*. Holt, Rinehart, and Winston.

———. 1989. *The Hundred-Yard Lie*. Simon and Schuster.

Theismann, Joe, with Tarcy, Brian. 1997. *The Complete Idiot's Guide to Understanding Football Like a Pro*. Alpha Books.

Thorn, John. 1982. *The Armchair Quarterback (Armchair Library)*. Scribner.

Thorn, John, and Palmer, Pete. 1984. *The Hidden Game of Baseball*. Doubleday.

Tittle, Y. A. 1964. *I Pass*. Watts.

Toperoff, Sam. 1989. *Lost Sundays: A Season in the Life of Pittsburgh and the Steelers*. Random House.

Towle, Mike. 2003. *Johnny Unitas: Mr. Quarterback*. Cumberland House.

Trope, Mike. 1988. *Necessary Roughness*. NTC Publishing Group.

Turney, John. 1999. *All-Pros: The Modern Years*. Professional Football Researchers Association.

Twombly, Wells. 1973. *Blanda: Alive and Kicking*. Avon Books.

Unitas, John, and Fitzgerald, Ed. 1965. *Pro Quarterback: My Own Story*. Simon and Schuster.

Vass, George. 1971. *George Halas and the Chicago Bears*. Regnery.

Vecsey, George. 1974. *The Way it Was: Great Sports Events from the Past*. McGraw Hill.

Vermeil, Dick, et al. 1986. *1986 Pro Football Scouting Report*. Harper Collins.

Walsh, Bill. 1990. *Building a Champion*. St. Martin's Press.

Weiss, Don, and Day, Chuck. 2003. *The Making of the Super Bowl: The Inside Story of the World's Greatest Sporting Event*. McGraw Hill.

Wheeler, Robert. 1975. *Pathway to Glory*. Carlton Press.

Whittingham, Richard. 1981. *The Dallas Cowboys*. Harper Collins.

———. 1984. *What A Game They Played*. Harper Collins.

———. 1987. *Sunday Mayhem: A Celebration of Pro Football in America*. Taylor Publishing.

———. 1989. *Fireside Book of Pro Football*. Fireside.

———. 1991. *The Chicago Bears*. NTC Publishing Group.

———. 1992. *Meat Market: The Inside Story of the NFL Draft*. MacMillan.

———. 2004. *Sunday's Heroes: NFL Legends Talk About the Times of Their Lives*. Triumph Books.

Whittingham, Richard, and Roe, Fred. 1987. *Sunday Mayhem*. Taylor Publishing.

Wiebusch, John. 1997. *Lombardi*. Triumph Books.

Wiggins, David, and Miller, Patrick. 2005. *The Unlevel Playing Field*. University of Illinois Press.

Williams, Doug. 1990. *Quarterblack: Shattering the NFL Myth*. Bonus Books.

Willis, Chris. 2005. *Old Leather: An Oral History of Early Pro Football in Ohio, 1920-1935*. Scarecrow Press.

Wright, Steve. 1975. *I'd Rather Be Wright: Memoirs of an Itinerant Tackle*. Grosset and Dunlap.

Zimmerman, Paul. 1970. *A Thinking Man's Guide to Pro Football*. E.P. Dutton.

———. 1974. *The Last Season of Weeb Ewbank*. Farrar, Strauss and Giroux.

———. 1984. *The New Thinking Man's Guide to Pro Football*. Simon and Schuster.

INDEX

multipurpose stadiums, 31, 37

See also significant moves

FieldTurf system, 60

Filchok, Frankie, 27

Fischer, Pat, **221**, 524

Fisher, Jeff, 87, 272, **287**

Flaherty, Ray, 3, 20, **242–43**, **264**, 532

Flores, Tom, 149, 176, 263, 271, **277**

Flutie, Doug, **110**, 512

Fontes, Wayne, 114, **289**

Foolish Club, 33–34

Ford, Len, 23

Foreman, Chuck, **151**, 515

Fortmann, Dan, 11, 14, **247**, 251

Foster, Barry, 134, 135, 204

Foster, Roy, **188–89**, 520

Fouts, Dan, 38, **102–3**, 140, 279, *314*, 511, 528

Francis, Russ, **179**, 519

Frankford Yellow Jackets, 10, 11

Fraser, Jim, 535

Frazier, Willie, **179**, 518, 533

free substitution, 19, 24, 25

Freeman, Antonio, 531

Friedman, Bennie, 3, 10, **240**

Fritsch, Toni, 533

Fryar, Irving, 158, **168**, 517

Fuller, William, 52, **201**, 521

fumbles, Adjusted Yards and, 65, 67

G

Gabriel, Roman, **90–91**, *315*, 511, 528

Galloway, Joey, **164–65**, *457*, 516

Gannon, Rich, **94–95**, *316*, 511, 528

Garcia, Jeff, 54, **108–9**, *317*, 512, 528

Gardocki, Chris, **231**, 526, 534

Garner, Charlie, 119, **151**, 515

Garrett, Mike, **145–46**, 265, *396*, 514

Garrison, Gary, **167**, *458*, 517

Gastineau, Mark, 44

Gates, Antonio, **179**, 518, 532

Gatski, Frank, 23

George, Bill, 23, **211**, 523

George, Eddie, **131**, 134, 135, *397*, 514

George, Jeff, 49

Gibbs, Joe, 43, 48, 109, 131–32, 162, 172, 205, 258, **261–62**, 263, 270, 279

Gibson, Aaron, 58

Gibson, Claude, 536

Gibson, Denver "Butch," **249**

Gifford, Frank, 28, **146**, 146, *398*, 514

Giles, Jimmie, **179**, 179, 519

Gilliam, John, **165**, *459*, 516, 531

Gillman, Sid, 32, 38, 102, 145, 260, **262**, 279

Gillo, Hank, 531

Gillom, Horace, 18, 535

Ginn, Ted, Jr., 65–66

Givins, Earnest, **168**, 518

Glenn, Howard, 20

Glenn, Terry, **168**, 517

Glover, La'Roi, 58

goal post position, 12, 13, 38

Goebel, Paul, **244**

Goldberg, Marshall, 12, 18, 283

Gonzalez, Tony, 58, **169**, *492*, 518, 532

Gordon, Darrien, **237**

Gordon, Lou, **246**

Gossett, Bruce, 533, 534

Gossett, Jeff, 534

Gould, Robbie, 533

Gradishar, Randy, **213**, 523

Graham, Al, **248–49**

Graham, Otto, 17, **82**, 128, 140, *318*, 510, 529

Grange, Red, 7–8, 138, 140, 214, **241–42**, 244, 250

Granger, Hoyle, **151**, 515, 530

Grant, Bud, 84, **266–67**, 276

Grantham, Larry, 31, **210**, 522

Gray, Mel, **168**, **235**, **237**, 517, 527, 535

Grayson, Dave, 31, **219**, 524

Grbac, Elvis, **110**, 512

Green, Ahman, **136**, *399*, 514

Green, Bobby Joe, 30, **230**, 526, 535

Green, Darrell, 48, **220**, 524

Green, Dennis, 54, 94, 276, **285–86**

Green, Eric, **179**, 519

Green, Roy, **168**, 517, 531

Green, Trent, **102**, *319*, 511

Green Bay Packers, 2, 10, 11, 24, 29, 58, 257–58, 262, 268

Greene, Joe, 37, **192**, 260, 521

Greene, Kevin, 194, 268

Greenwood, L.C., 37, **201**, 521

Gregg, Forrest, 30, **185**, 257, **289**, 519

Grier, Rosey, 191, **201**, 521

Griese, Bob, 76, **98**, 140, *320*, 511

ABOUT THE AUTHOR

Sean Lahman is a football columnist for the *New York Sun* and is a pioneer in the field of sports statistics. He is the author of the annual *Pro Football Prospectus 2002 & 2003* and *Pro Football Forecast 2004* and is a coeditor of the *ESPN Pro Football Encyclopedia*. He has served as an editor for more than a dozen sports reference books, including *Total Baseball* and *Baseball: The Biographical Encyclopedia*. Lahman's Web site, www.seanlahman.com, receives 55,000 visitors per month. He has also constructed the Lahman database, a statistical resource that is famous among baseball statistical gamers. He lives in Rochester, New York.